WAYNE GISSLEN

ADVANCED CULINARY FOUNDATIONS

PHOTOGRAPHY BY J. GERARD SMITH

WILEY

This book was set in 9/12 Meta by Mauna Eichner and Lee Fukui and printed and bound by RR Donnelley & Sons Company. The cover was printed by RR Donnelley & Sons Company.

This book is printed on acid free paper. ♾

Library of Congress Cataloging in Publication Data:

ISBN 978-1-118-67367-6

Printed in the United States of America

10 9 8 7 6 5 4 3 2 1

Contents

Recipe Contents v
Welcome to Le Cordon Bleu x
Preface xi
Acknowledgments xiii

Chapter 1 Understanding Poultry and Game Birds 1

Composition and Structure 2
Inspection and Grading 3
Classification and Market Forms 4
Handling and Storage 8
Doneness 8
Trussing Methods 9
Cutting Up Chicken 10

Chapter 2 Cooking Poultry and Game Birds 15

Roasting and Baking 16
Broiling and Grilling 26
Sautéing, Pan-Frying, and Deep-Frying 31
Simmering and Poaching 38
Braising 42
Dressings and Stuffings 49

Chapter 3 Understanding Fish and Shellfish 53

FIN FISH 54
Composition and Structure 54
Special Problems in Cooking Fish 54
Cutting Fish 54
Varieties and Characteristics 58
Handling and Storage 66

SHELLFISH 68
Mollusks 68
Cephalopods 73
Crustaceans 74
Miscellaneous Seafood 81

Chapter 4 Cooking Fish and Shellfish 83

Baking 83
Broiling and Grilling 86
Sautéing and Pan-Frying 92
Deep-Frying 96
Poaching and Simmering 101
Steaming and Mixed Cooking Techniques 110
Seafood Served Raw 115

Chapter 5 Understanding Meats and Game 121

COMPOSITION, STRUCTURE, AND BASIC QUALITY FACTORS 122
Composition 122
Structure 123
Inspection and Grading 124
Aging 124

UNDERSTANDING THE BASIC CUTS 126
Available Forms: Carcasses, Partial Carcasses, Primals, and Fabricated Cuts 126
Bone Structure 127
Beef, Lamb, Veal, and Pork Cuts 131
Selecting Meats for Your Operation 134
Fabricating Meats 135

COOKING AND HANDLING MEATS 139
Tenderness and Appropriate Cooking Methods 139
Doneness 143
Cooking Variety Meats 146
Game and Specialty Meats 149
Storage of Meats 152

Chapter 6 Cooking Meats and Game 155

Roasting and Baking 156
Broiling, Grilling, and Pan-Broiling 166
Sautéing, Pan-Frying, and Griddling 170
Simmering 177
Braising 182

Chapter 7 Sausages and Cured Foods 193

Curing and Smoking 194
Sausages 199

Chapter 8 Bakeshop Production: Basic Principles and Ingredients 213

BASIC PRINCIPLES OF BAKING 214
Formulas and Measurement 214
Mixing and Gluten Development 217
The Baking Process 218
Staling 219

INGREDIENTS 219
Flours, Meals, and Starches 219
Fats 221
Sugars 222
Liquids 224
Eggs 225
Leavening Agents 226
Salt, Flavorings, and Spices 227

Chapter 9 Yeast Products 231

UNDERSTANDING YEAST PRODUCTS 232
- Yeast Product Types 232
- Mixing Methods 232
- Steps in Yeast Dough Production 233

DOUGH FORMULAS AND TECHNIQUES 238
- Bread and Roll Formulas 238
- Rolled-In Doughs: Danish Pastry and Croissants 242
- Makeup Techniques 243

Chapter 10 Quick Breads 249

- Mixing and Production Methods 250
- Formulas 252

Chapter 11 Cakes and Icings 257

UNDERSTANDING CAKE MAKING 258
- Basic Mixing Methods 258
- Cake Formula Types 261
- Scaling and Panning 262
- Baking and Cooling 264
- Altitude Adjustments 265

CAKE FORMULAS 266
- Creaming Method 266
- Two-Stage Method 268
- Foaming Methods 269

ICINGS: PRODUCTION AND APPLICATION 270
- Producing and Handling Basic Types 270
- Assembling and Icing Cakes 274

Chapter 12 Cookies 279

- Cookie Characteristics and Their Causes 280
- Mixing Methods 281
- Types and Makeup Methods 282
- Panning, Baking, and Cooling 284

Chapter 13 Pies and Pastries 291

PIES 292
- Pie Doughs 292
- Assembly and Baking 296
- Fillings 298

PASTRIES, MERINGUES, AND FRUIT DESSERTS 305
- Puff Pastry 305
- Éclair Paste 309
- Meringues 311
- Fruit Desserts 313

Chapter 14 Creams, Custards, Puddings, Frozen Desserts, and Sauces 315

- Sugar Cooking 316
- Basic Custards and Creams 317
- Puddings 321
- Mousses and Soufflés 323
- Frozen Desserts 325
- Desert Sauces 327

Chapter 15 Cuisines Across Cultures 331

- Italy 332
- Germany 333
- France 335
- Spain 336
- Africa 339
- Middle East 341
- India 347
- Southeast Asia 351
- China 354
- Korea 356
- South America and Caribbean 357
- Mexico 359

Chapter 16 Food Presentation and Garnish 365

- Modern Hot Platter Garnish 366

COLD FOOD PRESENTATION AND BUFFET SERVICE 366
- Buffet Arrangement and Appearance 367
- Cold Platter Presentation 369
- Hot Foods for Buffets 371

Chapter 17 Sandwiches 373

- Breads 374
- Spreads 375
- Fillings 375
- Types of Sandwiches 377
- Making Sandwiches 378

Chapter 18 Hors d'Oeuvres 391

- Serving Hors d'Oeuvres 391
- Canapés 391
- Cocktails 396
- Relishes 396
- Dips 397
- Miscellaneous Hors d'Oeuvres 400

Chapter 19 Dairy and Beverages 417

DAIRY PRODUCTS 418
- Milk and Cream 418
- Butter 420
- Cheese 421

COFFEE AND TEA 430
- Coffee 431
- Tea 433

Chapter 20 Pâtés, Terrines, and Other Cold Foods 437

- The Handling and Service of Cold Dishes 438
- Special Forcemeat Dishes 439
- Terrines Based on Mousselines 448
- Terrines and Other Molds with Gelatin 450
- Foie Gras, Liver Terrines, and Rillettes 453

Chapter 21 Cooking for Vegetarian Diets 459

- Understanding Vegetarian Diets 460
- Menus for Vegetarian Diets 462

Subject Index 476

Recipe Index 479

Recipe Contents

Chapter 2 Cooking Poultry and Game Birds 15

Baked Chicken 17
- Baked Herbed Chicken 17
- Baked Rosemary Chicken 17
- Baked Chicken Parmesan 17

Roast Chicken with Natural Gravy 18
- Roast Herbed Chicken 18
- Roast Chicken with Gravy 18
- Roast Chicken with Cream Gravy 18

Roast Turkey with Giblet Gravy 20
- Roast Capons and Large Chickens 20
- Roast Turkey, Chicken, or Capon with Cream Gravy 20

Roast Duckling à l'Orange 22
- Roast Duckling, Bohemian Style 22
- Roast Goose 22

Stuffed Chicken Legs with Pecan Butter 23

Chicken Poêlé 25

Broiled Chicken 27
- Broiled Chicken, Quantity Method 27
- Broiled Rock Cornish Game Hen 27
- Broiled Tarragon Chicken 27
- Broiled Deviled Chicken (Poulet à la Diable) 27

Chicken Paillard with Grilled Vegetables 28

Grilled Spiced Squab with Couscous and Fig Compote 28
- Grilled Spiced Cornish Hen 28

Grilled Chicken with Garlic and Ginger 29
- Southwestern Grilled Chicken 29
- Grilled Chicken Oriental Style 29
- Spicy Barbecue-Style Grilled Chicken 29
- Grilled Chicken Marinated in Yogurt and Spices 29

Jerk Spice Mixture 30

Jerk Chicken 30

Pan-Fried Chicken 32
- Country-Style Fried Chicken 32

Sautéed Boneless Breast of Chicken with Mushroom Sauce 33

Deep-Fried Chicken 34
- Fried Chicken Maryland 34
- Fried Chicken Breast Strips 34

Tangerine-Marinated Breast of Duck 35

Chicken Teriyaki 36

Chicken Breasts Parmesan 37

Poached Chicken Breast Princesse 39
- Poached Chicken Breast Florentine 39

Chicken or Turkey Pot Pie 40
- Chicken or Turkey Stew 40

Tea-Smoked Duck 41
- Crispy Duck 41

Chicken Fricassée 43
- Chicken Fricassée with Tarragon 43
- Chicken Fricassée à l'Indienne 43
- Fricassée of Turkey Wings 43
- Veal Fricassée 43
- Pork Fricassée 43
- Fricassée à l'Ancienne 43
- Fricassée Brunoise 43
- Fricassée Argenteuil 43

Chicken Chasseur 44
- Chicken Bercy 44
- Chicken Portugaise 44
- Chicken Hongroise 44

Paprika Chicken 45

Coq au Vin 46

Arroz con Pollo (Spanish Rice with Chicken) 47

Duck Confit 48

Basic Bread Dressing 50
- Sausage Dressing 50
- Chestnut Dressing 50
- Mushroom Dressing 50
- Giblet Dressing 50
- Cornbread Dressing 50

Chapter 4 Cooking Fish and Shellfish 83

Baked Cod Fillets Portugaise 85

Broiled Fish Steaks Maître d'Hôtel 87

Grilled Tuna with Balsamic Vinaigrette and Sweet-Sour Baby Onions 88

Grilled Mahi-Mahi with Fruit Salsa 89

Broiled Shrimp, Scampi Style 90
- Shrimp Brochettes 90
- Broiled Scallops 90
- Broiled Fish Fillets or Steaks with Garlic Butter 90

Oysters Casino 91
- Clams Casino 91

Fillets of Sole Meunière 93
- Fillets of Fish Doré 93
- Trout Meunière 93
- Fish Sauté Amandine 93
- Fish Sauté Grenobloise 93
- Sautéed Soft-Shell Crabs 93

Sautéed Scallops with Tomato, Garlic, and Parsley 94
- Sautéed Shrimp 94

Crab Cakes with Roasted Pepper Rémoulade 94
Pan-Fried Catfish with Shrimp Etouffée 95
Fried Breaded Fish Fillets 96
Fried Breaded Scallops 96
Fried Breaded Shrimp 96
Fried Oysters or Clams 96
Fish and Chips 97
Fisherman's Platter 97
Cod Cakes 98
Salmon or Tuna Cakes 98
Deep-Fried Calamari with Spicy Tomato Sauce and Aïoli 99
Shrimp and Vegetable Tempura 100
Ordinary Court Bouillon for Fish 104
Court Bouillon with White Wine 104
Poached Whole Fish 105
Poached Fish Steaks 105
"Boiled" Shellfish (Lobster, Crab, Shrimp) 105
Sole Vin Blanc (Poached Fillets of Sole in White Wine Sauce) 106
Glazed Poached Fish 107
Poached Fish Bonne Femme 107
Poached Fish Dugléré 107
Poached Fish Mornay 107
Poached Fish Florentine 10
Sole Paupiettes with Seafood Mousseline 107
Seafood à la Nage 107
Scallops and Shrimp à la Nage 108
Salmon à la Nage 108
Zuppa di Vongole 109
Zuppa di Cozze 109
Zuppa di Frutti di Mare 109
Zuppa di Pesce 109
Moules Marinière (Steamed Mussels) 112
Steamed Mussels (without wine) 112
Mussels in Cream 112
Mackerel en Papillote 113
Seafood Newburg 114
Seafood Curry 114
Sea Bass Sous Vide with Asian Sweet-and-Sour Sauce 114
Tuna Carpaccio 115
Sushi Rice 116
Nigirizushi (Finger Sushi) 116
Chirashizushi (Scatter Sushi) 116
Tekka-maki (Tuna Roll) 116
Kappa-maki (Cucumber Roll) 116
Tuna Tartare 118
Salmon Tartare 118
Tartare of Salmon and Sea Bass 118
Scallop Seviche 119

Chapter 6 Cooking Meats and Game 155

Roast Rib of Beef au Jus 159
Roast Rib-Eye Roll, Top Round, Sirloin, or Strip Loin 159
Roast Beef with Gravy 159
Roast Beef Gravy 160
Jus Lié 160
Roast Loin of Pork with Sage and Apples 161
Roast Loin or Rack of Veal with Sage and Apples 161
Roast Rack of Lamb 162
Rack of Lamb aux Primeurs (with Spring Vegetables) 162
Rack of Lamb Persillé 162
Persillade 162
Smoke-Roasted Pork Shoulder 163
Smoke-Roasted Shoulder of Boar 163
Spice Rub I 163
Spice Rub II 163
Barbecued Spareribs 164
Glazed Ham with Cider Sauce 164
Ham with Brown Cider Sauce 164
Fruit-Glazed Ham 164
Home-Style Meatloaf 165
Home-Style All-Beef Meatloaf 165
Italian-Style Meatloaf 165
Salisbury Steak 165
Baked Meatballs 165
Roast Loin of Rabbit with Risotto 166
Broiled Strip Loin Steak Maître d'Hôtel 168
Broiled Lamb Chops 168
Grilled Chopped Lamb "Steaks" with Rosemary and Pine Nuts 169
Grilled Chopped Beef "Steaks" with Marjoram 169
Breaded Veal Cutlets 172
Veal Cutlet Sauté Gruyère 172
Schnitzel à la Holstein 172
Veal Cutlet Viennese-Style (Wiener Schnitzel) 172
Veal Parmigiana 172
Veal Cordon Bleu 172
Breaded Pork Cutlets 172
Veal Scaloppine alla Marsala 173
Veal Scaloppine with Sherry 173
Veal Scaloppine à la Crème 173
Veal Scaloppine with Lemon 173
Veal Scaloppine with Mushrooms and Cream 173
Pork Chops Charcutière 174
Pork Chops Robert 174
Pork Chops Piquante 174
Veal Chops 174
Beef Stroganoff 175
Calf's Liver Lyonnaise 176
Sautéed Veal Sweetbreads with Shiitake Mushrooms and Port Wine Sauce 177
New England Boiled Dinner 179
Blanquette of Veal 180
Blanquette of Lamb 180
Blanquette of Pork 180
Irish Lamb Stew 180
Shredded Pork (Carnitas) 181
Picadillo 181
Shortcut Picadillo 181
Beef Short Ribs Sous Vide with Bordelaise Sauce 182
Beef Pot Roast 185
Braised Beef Jardinière 185
Braised Lamb Shoulder 185
Braised Short Ribs 186
Swiss Steak 186
Swiss Steaks in Tomato Sauce 186
Swiss Steaks with Sour Cream 186
Swiss Steaks in Red Wine Sauce 186

Braised Oxtails 186
Braised Lamb Shanks 186
BEEF STEW 187
Beef Stew with Red Wine 187
Boeuf Bourguignon 187
Navarin of Lamb (Brown Lamb Stew) 187
Brown Veal Stew 187
Brown Veal with White Wine 187
Beef Pot Pie 187
CHILE CON CARNE 188
Chile with Beans 188
Game Chile 188
TEXAS RED 188
Texas Short Ribs 188
OSSO BUCO 189
HUNGARIAN GOULASH (VEAL, BEEF, OR PORK) 190
RABBIT WITH MUSTARD 190
SALTIMBOCCA ALLA ROMANA 191

Chapter 7 Sausages and Cured Foods 193

GRAVLAX 197
SMOKED SALMON 198
SMOKED TROUT 198
SMOKED DUCK 199
Smoked Turkey or Chicken 199
QUATRE ÉPICES I 207
QUATRE ÉPICES II 207
PORK SAUSAGE 207
Toulouse Sausage 207
Crêpinettes 207
FRENCH GARLIC SAUSAGE 208
HOT ITALIAN SAUSAGE 208
Mild Italian Sausage 208
Spicy Garlic Sausage 208
VEAL OR BEEF SAUSAGE 208
Venison Sausage 208
FRESH BRATWURST 209
LAMB SAUSAGE 209
Herbed Lamb Sausage 209
DUCK SAUSAGE 209
BOUDIN BLANC (WHITE SAUSAGE) 210

Chapter 9 Yeast Products 231

HARD ROLLS 238
SOFT ROLLS 238
FRENCH BREAD 239
WHITE PAN BREAD 239
Whole Wheat Bread 239
RYE BREAD AND ROLLS 240
FOCACCIA 240
Rosemary Focaccia 240
Olive Focaccia 240
BRIOCHE 241
SWEET ROLL DOUGH 241
Raised Doughnuts 241

Chapter 10 Quick Breads 249

BISCUITS 252
Buttermilk Biscuits 252
Cheese Biscuits 252
Currant Biscuits 252
Herb Biscuits 252
PLAIN MUFFINS 253
Raisin Spice Muffins 253
Date Nut Muffins 253
Blueberry Muffins 253
Whole Wheat Muffins 253
Corn Muffins 253
Bran Muffins 253
Crumb Coffee Cake 253
CORN BREAD, MUFFINS, OR STICKS 254

Chapter 11 Cakes and Icings 257

YELLOW BUTTER CAKE 266
OLD-FASHIONED POUND CAKE 267
Raisin Pound Cake 267
Chocolate Pound Cake 267
Marble Pound Cake 267
WHITE CAKE 268
Yellow Cake 268
DEVIL'S FOOD CAKE 268
SPONGE CAKE (GENOISE) 269
Chocolate Genoise 269
Sponge Roll or Jelly Roll 269
ANGEL FOOD CAKE 269
Chocolate Angel Food Cake 269
SIMPLE BUTTERCREAM 271
Decorator's Buttercream 271
Cream Cheese Icing 271
MERINGUE-TYPE BUTTERCREAM 271
FRENCH BUTTERCREAM 272
Chocolate Buttercream 272
Coffee Buttercream 272
CHOCOLATE GANACHE 273

Chapter 12 Cookies 279

CHOCOLATE CHIP COOKIES 285
Brown Sugar Nut Cookies 285
OATMEAL RAISIN COOKIES 285
SUGAR COOKIES 286
Rolled Brown Sugar Cookies 286
Rolled Chocolate Cookies 286
SHORTBREAD COOKIES 286
PEANUT BUTTER COOKIES 287
BROWNIES 287
Butterscotch Brownies or Blondies 287
ALMOND BISCOTTI 288

Chapter 13 Pies and Pastries 291

FLAKY PIE DOUGH 294
MEALY PIE DOUGH 294
GRAHAM CRACKER CRUST 295
SHORT DOUGH 295
APPLE PIE FILLING (CANNED FRUIT) 300
Dutch Apple Pie Filling 300
Cherry Pie Filling 300
Peach Pie Filling 300
Pineapple Pie Filling 300

BLUEBERRY PIE FILLING (FROZEN FRUIT) 301
Apple Pie Filling 301
Cherry Pie Filling 301
FRESH STRAWBERRY PIE FILLING 301
OLD-FASHIONED APPLE PIE FILLING 302
CUSTARD PIE FILLING 303
Coconut Custard Pie Filling 303
PECAN PIE FILLING 303
PUMPKIN PIE FILLING 304
Sweet Potato Pie Filling 304
Squash Pie Filling 304
PUFF PASTRY 305
BLITZ PUFF PASTRY 307
ÉCLAIR PASTE OR PÂTE À CHOUX 310
MERINGUE 312

Chapter 14 Creams, Custards, Puddings, Frozen Desserts, and Sauces 315

CRÈME ANGLAISE (VANILLA CUSTARD SAUCE) 318
Chocolate Crème Anglaise 318
VANILLA PASTRY CREAM 319
Chocolate Pastry Cream 319
Coffee Pastry Cream 319
Cream Pie Fillings
Vanilla Cream Pie Filling 319
Coconut Cream Pie Filling 319
Banana Cream Pie Filling 319
Chocolate Cream Pie Filling I 319
Chocolate Cream Pie Filling II 319
Butterscotch Cream Pie Filling 319
Lemon Pie Filling 319
Cream Puddings
Vanilla Pudding 319
Coconut Pudding 319
Banana Cream Pudding 319
Chocolate Pudding I and II 319
Butterscotch Pudding 319
BAKED CUSTARD 320
Crème Caramel 320
BLANCMANGE, ENGLISH STYLE 321
RICE PUDDING 322
Raisin Rice Pudding 322
BREAD AND BUTTER PUDDING 322
VANILLA SOUFFLÉ 324
Chocolate Soufflé 324
Lemon Soufflé 324
Liqueur Soufflé 324
Coffee Soufflé 324
CHOCOLATE MOUSSE 325
CHOCOLATE SAUCE 328
CARAMEL SAUCE 328
Hot Caramel Sauce 328
Clear Caramel Sauce 328

Chapter 15 Cuisines Across Cultures 331

ORECHIETTI CON CARCIOFI 332
BRACIOLE CALABRESI 332
FRESH TOMATO SAUCE 333
KARTOFFELSUPPE MIT MIESMUSCHELN UND LACH 333
SCHWEINELENDCHEN IM SCHWARZBRATMANTEL 334
ROTKRAUT UND SPÄTZLE 334
SPÄTZLE 335
POULET SAUTÉ MARENGO 335
LE BLANC DE POISSON BELLE MOUGINOISE 336
CROQUETAS DE JAMÓN 336
BACALAD AL AJO ARRIERO 337
GAMBAS AL AJILLO 337
PAELLA VALENCIANA 338
TAGINE OF CHICKEN, PRESERVED LEMON, AND OLIVES 339
AKARA 339
HARISSA 340
MCHUZI WA BIRINGANI 340
GRILLED TILAPIA 340
AFRICAN HOT SAUCE 341
TABBOULEH 341
QAHWAH 342
KHOBZ 342
FALAFEL 343
TARATOUR BI TAHINI 343
KHUBZ 344
BABA GHANNOUJ 344
MUHAMMARA 345
FATTOUSH 345
SALAD DRESSING 345
GARITHES SAGANAKI 346
SIS KEBAP 346
GARAM MASALA 347
PODINA CHATNI 347
TAMARIND SAUCE 347
BASMATI CHAAVAL 348
KHEERE KA RAITA 348
PORK VINDALOO 349
NAAN 350
CHANA DAL 350
SATAY AYAM 351
SAMBAL KACANG 351
THAI PAPAYA AND MANGO SALAD 352
DUA CHUA 353
PHO BO 353
PUNGENT AND HOT SOUP 354
RED-COOKED DUCK 355
SICHUAN SPICY FIRED BEEF SHREDS 355
TEA LEAF EGGS 356
KIMCHI 356
KALBI-KUI 356
CEVICHE MIXTO 357
JAMAICAN JERK CHICKEN 358
CHIMICHURRI SAUCE 358
MOLE VERDE CON HIERBAS 359
CORN TORTILLAS 359
PAVO CON SALSA DE ACHIOTE A LA YUCATANECA 360
ANCHIOTE PASTE 360
PICO DE GALLO 360
PICKLED RED ONIONS 361
FRIJOLES REFRITOS 361
SALSA DE JITOMATE COCIDA 361

MEXICAN HOT CHOCOLATE 362
BEEF FAJITAS 362
TAMALES DE ESPINACA CON QUESO 363

Chapter 17 Sandwiches 373

CALIFORNIA BURGER 381
California Cheeseburger 381
Cheeseburger (Plain) 381
Cheeseburger with Bacon 381
California Cheeseburger Deluxe 381
SUBMARINE SANDWICH 381
CLUB SANDWICH 382
Bacon, Lettuce, and Tomato Sandwich (BLT) 382
REUBEN SANDWICH 382
GRILLED CHEESE SANDWICH 383
Grilled Ham and Swiss Sandwich 383
Croque Monsieur 383
Grilled Cheese and Bacon Sandwich 383
TURKEY BLT WRAP 384
VEGETARIAN WRAP WITH MIXED BEANS 384
FALAFEL AND ROASTED VEGETABLES IN PITA 385
Traditional Falafel in Pita 385
TAHINI YOGURT DRESSING 385
GRILLED VEGETABLE SANDWICH WITH GOAT CHEESE AND SUN-DRIED TOMATOES 386
GRILLED PORTOBELLO AND BOURSIN SANDWICH 387
Grilled Portobello and Tomato Sandwich 387
PIZZA MARGHERITA 388
Pizza Marinara 388

Chapter 18 Hors d'Oeuvres 391

BLUE CHEESE DIP 397
Cheddar Cheese Dip 397
Garlic Cheese Dip 397
Bacon Cheese Dip 397
Cheese and Chile Dip 397
ROMESCO 397
HUMMUS (CHICKPEA DIP) 398
Babaganouj 398
GUACAMOLE 399
Sour Cream Avocado Dip 399
PARMESAN DIP 399
PROSCIUTTO AND MELON BALLS 402
SPINACH BOREKS 403
RUMAKI 404
CHICKEN SATAY 404
BEEF TERIYAKI SKEWERS 405
DATES STUFFED WITH GORGONZOLA 405
Dates Stuffed with Manchego Cheese 405
Date Rumaki 405
SMOKED TROUT ROLLUPS 406
Smoked Trout Purses 406
CUCUMBER CUPS WITH DILLED SHRIMP SALAD 406
CRÊPES 407
Dessert Crêpes 407
SPICED SHRIMP WITH SMOKED PAPRIKA 408
MUSHROOMS STUFFED WITH TAPENADE 408
DEVILED EGGS 409
MINIATURE GOUGÈRE PUFFS 409
EGG ROLLS OR SPRING ROLLS 410
BRUSCHETTA (BASIC) 412
Bruschetta with Tomato and Basil 412
Bruschetta with Parmesan Cheese 412
Bruschetta with White Beans and Prosciutto 412
SPICY MEAT EMPANADAS 413
Empanadas with Roasted Poblanos and Cheese 413
CAULIFLOWER PAKORAS 414

Chapter 19 Dairy and Beverages 417

WELSH RABBIT 428
CHEESE WAFERS 428
Cheese Straws 428
SWISS FONDUE 429

Chapter 20 Pâtés, Terrines, and Other Cold Foods 437

BASIC PORK FORCEMEAT 441
Veal Forcemeat 441
Chicken Forcemeat I 441
Chicken Forcemeat II 441
Duck, Pheasant, or Game Forcemeat 441
PÂTÉ PASTRY (PÂTE À PÂTÉ) 442
VEAL AND HAM TERRINE 446
Veal and Ham Terrine with Foie Gras 446
Veal and Tongue Terrine 446
Rabbit Terrine 446
Country Terrine 446
Game Terrine 446
Duck Terrine 446
BASIC MOUSSELINE FORCEMEAT 448
Herbed Mousseline 448
TERRINE OF VEGETABLES WITH CHICKEN MOUSSELINE 449
Seafood Terrine with Vegetables 449
TRICOLOR VEGETABLE TERRINE 452
TERRINE OF FOIE GRAS 455
RILLETTES OF PORK 456
Rillettes of Duck, Goose, Rabbit, Turkey, or Chicken 456
RILLETTES OF SALMON, HADDOCK, OR FINNAN HADDIE 457

Chapter 21 Cooking for Vegetarian Diets 459

YELLOW SPLIT PEA AND VEGETABLE CURRY WITH SPICED RICE AND CUCUMBER RAITA 467
Vegan Vegetable and Split Pea Curry 467
NOODLE BOWL WITH STIR-FRIED VEGETABLES, TOFU, AND PEANUTS 468
ZUCCHINI AND EGGPLANT LASAGNE 469
PINTO BEAN ENCHILADAS 470
THREE-BEAN CHILI WITH TOSTADITAS 471
RED RICE, SPINACH WITH TOFU DRESSING, AND EGGPLANT DENGAKU 472
VIETNAMESE VEGETABLE PANCAKES 473
WINTER VEGETABLE GRATIN WITH FETA CHEESE AND BULGUR PILAF 474
FALAFEL 475

Welcome to Le Cordon Bleu!

In support of the Le Cordon Bleu initiative to ensure a quality culinary education, we have customized a book for you that specifically coincides with our curriculum and the teaching methodology of your chefs.

The contents of this book were selected by the curriculum committee and the academic team to support the educational goals of developing and graduating professional cooks and pastry cooks.

Stated more succinctly, learning the core competencies of cookery and pastry as shown in this textbook will focus and assist you in developing efficient skills needed in the kitchen while meeting your educational objectives.

Le Cordon Bleu College for Culinary Arts fosters a unique multi-cultural and educational environment, encouraging you to learn and grow in the lessons you undertake. It is our privilege to be able to help you overcome your toughest challenges and embrace your creative passion.

Working alongside our dedicated professional chefs, we are delighted to provide an environment that prepares and encourages you with unparalleled facilities and a focus on your ability to strive for your best, to follow your passion, and achieve whatever you set out to do.

All areas of your school and the Le Cordon Bleu program, along with your chef instructors, are expected to support the development of your skills as you progress through the program and build your education.

As you take pride going through the Le Cordon Bleu program, always remember to learn, cook, and engage every day with the passion that bought you here to Le Cordon Bleu.

My best and culinary regards,

Chef Edward G. Leonard, CMC
Vice President Culinary Education
Corporate Chef
Le Cordon Bleu North America

Preface

In preparing ***Advanced Culinary Foundations***, I've been struck forcefully by two truths: culinary education has advanced greatly and evolved with the times, and, at the same time, the core curriculum has stayed focused on the essentials, the basic cooking techniques that are the foundation of success in the kitchen.

The changes seen through the years have been in many areas: advances in nutritional understanding; changes in diets, with greater emphasis on vegetables, grains, and other healthful ingredients; stronger sanitation and safety standards; increased understanding and appreciation of ingredients, techniques, and recipes from regional and international cuisines, and the adaptation of these ingredients and techniques to our own cooking; greater understanding of food science and its applications in the kitchen; and revolutionary new directions in cooking practices, such as sous vide techniques and molecular gastronomy.

Advanced Culinary Foundations builds on what you learned in ***Culinary Foundations***, and has incorporated material reflecting these changes while retaining its focus on the center of a chef's training—the comprehensive understanding of ingredients and basic food preparation procedures, and the development of manual skills to apply this knowledge.

What's Important

Readers of ***Advanced Culinary Foundations*** will find a great deal of material reflecting advances in culinary practices and techniques. Among the most important features are those detailed below.

- Hundreds of photographs are included throughout the book, illustrating in even more detail the essential techniques and procedures of a chef's craft as well as finished dishes, key ingredients, and equipment.
- Hundreds of recipes are included, reflecting the increasing diversity of dishes in North American cuisine.
- International cuisines receive increased attention, and in Chapter 15, "Cuisines Across Cultures", you will find recipes organized by country or global region. These recipes, as well as other recipes in the book, are indicated by a globe (see icon at right) in the text. Sidebars throughout the text give background information on these recipes and the cuisines and cultures they come from.

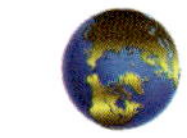

INTERNATIONAL RECIPES

- Core recipes are those specifically designed to illustrate and reinforce basic cooking techniques, and are indicated by a chef's hat (see icon at right). They are placed where appropriate throughout the book.

CORE RECIPES

- Important information devoted to vegetarianism and cooking for the various types of vegetarian diets is included, and is highlighted in Chapter 21, "Cooking for Vegetarian Diets". Recipes suitable for a vegetarian diet are indicated by the symbol shown here.

VEGETARIAN RECIPES

- To aid study and comprehension, "Key Points to Review" are included at strategic points in each chapter.

The Recipes

The recipes in this book are planned and organized to reinforce the basic skills being taught. In each case, specific recipes follow a discussion of theories, guidelines, and general procedures applicable to a defined category of foods and/or cooking methods. Students are encouraged, by means of recipe variations, to see how they can apply these procedures to other ingredients, and to see the similarities and differences among preparations.

Attention to the basics has always been the hallmark of this text. Because the purpose of the book is to teach fundamental cooking techniques, it is important to illustrate them—and to allow the student to experience them—with fundamental, straightforward recipes that reveal the connection between general theory and specific application in the most direct way. Many of the recipes included in this book provide updates and alternatives that will achieve these goals.

Certain recipes, usually those that directly follow an explanation of a procedure, are chosen because they are clear and direct applications of a fundamental technique. These core recipes give the student the opportunity to learn the technique by applying it in the most straightforward way, without the distraction of unusual techniques or unfamiliar ingredients. Of the hundreds of recipes in the book, some are designated as core recipes and are indicated by a special icon, as explained previously. Even if students produce no other recipes, practicing these core recipes, or comparable ones the instructor may wish to substitute, will give a basic foundation in food preparation.

While basic preparations illustrating fundamental principles are the core of the recipe collection, the book builds on these primary techniques to include more advanced styles of preparation. More challenging recipes, including many new to this edition, enable students to refine their techniques and to prepare dishes of increasing sophistication.

What makes a dish feel modern is as much a matter of presentation as it is of ingredients or recipe instructions. How an item, along with its garnish and sauce, is plated can make it look rustic or elegant, simple or elaborate, traditional or modern. Photographs accompanying the recipes illustrate a variety of preparations and plating styles. As the photographs show, a simple item such as a sautéed chicken breast can be as stylish as a complicated dish requiring exotic or expensive ingredients.

While every culinary program has different requirements, the recipes in this book should be adaptable to any purpose. Most major recipes are written for 24 or 25 portions, a quantity that can be converted easily to higher or lower yields if necessary. Those recipes requiring more costly ingredients, those that are generally made to order, and those that are particularly complex are written for smaller yields, such as 8, 10, 12, or 16 portions. In addition, variations often indicate ingredient substitutions so the recipes will fit different budgetary requirements and different local or regional tastes.

Nutritional Information

Cooks and chefs are increasingly aware of the importance of preparing healthful foods. To support this effort, nutritional analyses are included for each main recipe. These analyses were done using the software program Genesis R&D 8.4.0, which calculates nutrients based on ingredients. It is important to realize that the actual nutrients in a prepared dish will vary depending on many factors, just as the taste, texture, and appearance of the dish will vary with the skill of the cook and the quality of the ingredients. The following factors should also be taken into account when reading the nutritional analyses:

- Where a portion size is indicated in the recipe, the analysis is per portion. Where there is no portion size, as for stock and sauce, the analysis is usually per ounce (28.35 g) or per fluid ounce (29.57 mL).

- The following ingredients are not included in the analyses: ingredients listed "to taste" or "as needed"; ingredients in sachets and bouquets garnis; optional ingredients; garnishes such as parsley sprigs.

- If a range is given for an ingredient quantity, the smaller number was used for analysis.

- Adjustments are made for recipes in which the food is degreased or the fat is skimmed off. The amount of fat remaining will vary depending on how thoroughly the item is degreased.

- Fat was calculated for pan-fried and deep-fried foods based on a percentage of the total weight. The amount of fat actually absorbed will vary depending on the temperature of the fat, the cooking time, and the surface area of the food.

- For marinated foods, 10 percent of the marinade is included in the analysis, unless the marinade is used to make a sauce, in which case all the marinade is, of course, included.

- The amount of fat used for sautéing was estimated for the analysis.

- The numbers for each nutrient are rounded off according to FDA rounding rules for food labeling.

- The "(% cal.)" information following the fat content in each analysis refers to percentage of calories from fat. It cannot be used to determine percentage of fat in the total diet.

To help you become more aware of the fat content of prepared foods, those dishes especially low in fat are designated by the heart symbol (see icon at right). *Low in fat* means, according to FDA labeling laws, that the food contains 3 grams of fat or less per reference amount (or serving size indicated in the analysis) if the reference amount is greater than 30 grams (about 1 ounce). This is to prevent making foods sound low in fat just by making the portion size smaller. Main-dish items and meals (weighing at least 6 ounces per serving and containing two or more from the four food groups—bread, cereal, rice and pasta; fruits and vegetables; milk, yogurt and cheese; or meat, poultry, fish, dry beans, eggs, and nuts) must contain 3 grams of fat or less per 100 grams and not more than 30 percent of calories from fat.

LOW IN FAT RECIPES

Goals and Organization of This Book

This book has a dual goal: *understanding*—that is, an understanding of cooking theory, of how to cook—and *performing*—that is, mastery of a set of manual skills and the ability to apply them to a wide range of cooking styles and products.

This book focuses on the development of flexible skills, which are essential for success in a cooking career. Modern food service is evolving rapidly. A tremendous variety of establishments is on the scene today, from executive dining rooms to school cafeterias, from simple short-order coffee shops to the most exclusive restaurants or clubs, from kitchens that make extensive use of convenience foods to those that use only fresh produce. The graduate who understands the workings of foods and the interplay of ingredients, cooking methods, cost factors, and other elements can function successfully in any type of food-service operation.

The Role of the Chef-Instructor

No textbook, of course, can substitute for practical kitchen experience. Furthermore, a book cannot replace an experienced chef-instructor who gives practical demonstrations, supervises students' work, answers questions, and gives advice and assistance as needed. Every instructor has unique experience and has developed special techniques and procedures. Many chefs, in fact, disagree on a number of points. Although this book presents methods and recipes that are widely used and accepted, many instructors will prefer procedures that differ from some explained in this text and may wish to supplement the recipes with their own. Throughout the book, the instructor's input is encouraged. Exposure to a variety of recipes and techniques can only enrich the students' education and deepen their experience.

Features

ILLUSTRATIONS

Hundreds of clear, concise, full-color photographs illustrate basic manual techniques *shown from the point of view of the person performing them.* Additional photographs illustrate ingredients and finished dishes. Numerous line drawings also enhance the text, illustrating hundreds of pieces of equipment you'll encounter in the professional kitchen.

FORMAT

This book is designed to be readable and useful. The format emphasizes and highlights key points in bold type, italics, and numbered sequences, so basic information can be located and reviewed at a glance.

REALISTIC PROCEDURES

Although supported by discussions of cooking theory, procedures given here are based on actual practices in the industry. Attention is given not just to quantity production but also to the special problems of cooking to order. Presentation and service of the finished product are considered in detail, as is pre-preparation, or mise en place—so essential to the organization of a working restaurant. At the same time, the major emphasis is on quality, too often neglected in the quest for convenience.

Even a book as large as this one cannot possibly contain all a cook needs to know. Other information is included if it has a direct bearing on kitchen and bakeshop work. More specialized information, such as stewarding and managerial skills, is necessarily omitted. Finally, although much of what we talk about is strongly influenced by the cooking of other nations, the practices discussed are primarily those of North American food service.

Acknowledgments

Photographer Jim Smith has been my partner in these texts for nearly 30 years. His hundreds of photographs are an indispensable part of this book and valuable teaching tools. I can never thank him enough. Thanks also to Jeremy Grubard, Michael Vasiliauskas, and Vincent Cento for their work in Jim's studio.

During a long and productive session of planning, photography, and recipe testing for this edition, I was fortunate to have the expert assistance of Chef-Instructors Rick Forpahl, David Eisenreich, and Lynn Wolkerstorfer-Isakson of Hennepin Technical College. These chefs have been valuable collaborators on several editions of my books, and their suggestions and critiques have been significant in shaping each revision project. They have put in many long hours. In addition, their students, Zachary Colburn, Daniel Greer, Joe Howe, Michael Schroers, and Anthony E. Snooks, worked hard to help us complete the photography on schedule. Rick Elsenpeter of Lund's market was untiring in his responses to innumerable special requests for meats and seafood. My wife, Meg, assisted our kitchen crew and helped with my research for many of the text revisions. I am grateful to one and all for their help. They were a pleasure to work with. In addition, I would like to thank Hennepin Technical College for the use of their kitchens.

Christin Loudon has again contributed her expertise and culinary understanding to provide nutritional analyses, for which I thank her most warmly. I would also like to thank Drew Appleby, whose expertly written test questions form an important part of the support materials for this text.

Finally, I would like to thank everyone at John Wiley & Sons who worked so hard on this project: Gabrielle Corrado, Michael Olivo, James Metzger, Jenni Lee, Jeff Rucker, Margaret Barrett, Susan Matulewicz, Barbara Russiello, Micheline Frederick, Carole Anson, and Harry Nolan. Thanks to Mauna Eichner and Lee Fukui who have designed and laid out the pages with care and to Madeline Perri who copyedited and coded the manuscript. Thanks to the John Wiley people in Indianapolis who have prepared the files for printing: Kristie Rees, project coordinator; Clint Lahnen, graphics supervisor; Brent Savage, color photos and imaging; Beth Brooks, senior page layout technician; and Cheryl Grubbs, illustrator. Special thanks are due to Julie Kerr, who has worked with me for so long and with such dedication, and to my editor and friend, Mary Cassells.

Reviewers

I would like to acknowledge the faculty and administrators at Le Cordon Bleu schools who have contributed to this book by suggesting revisions and additions and by answering survey questions.

Chapter 1

Chicken Chasseur, page 44.

Understanding Poultry and Game Birds

The versatility, popularity, and relatively low cost of poultry items make them ideal for all kinds of food-service operations, from elegant restaurants to cafeterias and fast-food restaurants. Also, chicken and turkey are popular among diet-conscious people because they are lower in fat and cholesterol than other meats. Game birds, such as pheasant, are also increasing in popularity and availability because they are now raised domestically by many producers. Farm-raised game birds are similar, in many ways, to chicken, so learning techniques for cooking and handling chicken teaches you a great deal about handling these other birds as well.

Learning about poultry is, in some ways, easier than learning about meats like beef and lamb. Because chickens, turkeys, and other poultry are much smaller, they are not cut up in such detail.

However, poultry has its own cooking problems, so it is important to observe both the similarities and the differences between meat and poultry.

After reading this chapter, you should be able to

1. Explain the differences between light meat and dark meat, and describe how these differences affect cooking.
2. Describe four techniques that help keep chicken or turkey breast moist while roasting.
3. Define the following terms used to classify poultry: *kind, class,* and *style.*
4. Identify popular types of farm-raised game birds and the cooking methods appropriate to their preparation.
5. Store poultry items.
6. Determine doneness in cooked poultry, both large roasted birds and smaller birds.
7. Truss poultry for cooking.
8. Cut up chicken into parts.

Composition and Structure

The flesh of poultry and game birds is muscle tissue, as is the flesh of beef, lamb, veal, pork, and game. Its composition and structure are essentially the same as those of meat.

Remember that muscle tissue is composed of

Water (about 75 percent)

Protein (about 20 percent)

Fat (up to 5 percent)

Other elements, including carbohydrate, in small quantities

Remember that muscles consist of *muscle fibers* held together in bundles by *connective tissue*.

Maturity and Tenderness

The tenderness of a piece of meat—or poultry—is related to connective tissue and that connective tissue increases with

- Use or exercise of the muscle.
- Maturity or age of the animal or bird.

1. Use or exercise is of less concern in poultry. Most poultry is so young that it is relatively tender throughout. However, there are differences, discussed in the next section, between ***light meat*** and ***dark meat***.

2. ***Maturity*** is a major consideration when selecting poultry. Young, tender birds are cooked by dry-heat methods, such as broiling, frying, and roasting, as well as by moist-heat methods. Older, tougher birds need slow, moist heat to be made palatable.
   Maturity is the major factor in categorizing each kind of poultry (see p. 4).
   Skin color is determined by diet and is not related to the flavor or tenderness of the poultry.

Free-Range Chickens

Most chickens on the market are produced by large operations that house their poultry indoors in carefully controlled environments and feed them scientifically monitored diets. This process enables the industry to raise healthy chickens quickly and in large numbers to meet the great demand. Many people feel these chickens lack flavor because they are not allowed to move around outdoors. Some farmers, in response, offer ***free-range*** chickens, which are allowed to move around freely and eat outdoors in a more natural environment.

It is important to note that there is no legal definition of *free-range*, and that free-range chickens are considerably more expensive than ordinary chickens. Many people, however, feel free-range chickens are more flavorful and worth the extra cost. Because quality varies from producer to producer, it is necessary to do careful taste-testing to determine whether you want to purchase free-range poultry for your operation.

A term related to free-range is ***organic***, which has recently been defined by the USDA as food produced without using most conventional pesticides, fertilizers made with synthetic ingredients or sewage sludge, bioengineering, or ionizing radiation.

FREE-RANGE VERSUS CAGE-FREE

Some poultry products, especially eggs, are marketed as "cage-free." How does this differ from free-range?

Cage-free simply means the birds aren't kept in cages, but they *are* kept indoors. To be called free-range, they must be allowed outdoors.

Light Meat and Dark Meat

Poultry is not divided into as many small cuts as are meats. Chicken and turkey, however, are usually thought of as consisting of two kinds of parts, depending on the color of the meat. These color differences reflect other differences:

"Light meat"—breast and wings

- Less fat
- Less connective tissue
- Cooks faster

"Dark meat"—legs (drumsticks and thighs)

- More fat
- More connective tissue
- Takes longer to cook

Duck, goose, and squab have all dark meat, but the same differences in connective tissue hold true.

The dark color of dark meat is due to a protein called *myoglobin*. This protein stores oxygen for muscles to use during periods of great activity. The breast muscles of birds are used for flying, and because chickens and turkeys rarely, if ever, fly, these muscles don't need a great deal of myoglobin. In flying birds, such as ducks, the breast muscles have more myoglobin and thus are darker. Active muscles, in addition to being darker, also have more connective tissue.

The cook must observe these differences when preparing poultry.

1. **Cooking whole birds.**
   Everyone has tasted chicken or turkey breast so dry it was difficult to swallow. In fact, light meat is overcooked more often than not because it cooks faster than the legs and is done first. In addition, the breast has less fat than the legs, so it tastes much drier when cooked (or overcooked).

   A major problem in roasting poultry is cooking the legs to doneness without overcooking the breast. Chefs have devised many techniques to help solve this problem. Here are some of them.

   - Roasting breast-down for part of the roasting period. Gravity draws moisture and fat to the breast rather than away from it.
   - Basting with fat only, not with water or stock. Fat protects against drying, but moisture washes away protective fat.
   - Barding, or covering the breast with a thin layer of pork fat. This is usually done with lean game birds.
   - Separating breast from leg sections and roasting each for a different time. This is often done with large turkeys.

2. **Cooking poultry parts.**
   Many recipes have been devised especially for certain poultry parts, such as wings, drumsticks, and boneless chicken breasts. These recipes take into account the different cooking characteristics of each part. For example, flattened boneless chicken breasts can be quickly sautéed and remain juicy and tender. Turkey wings, when braised, release enough gelatin to make a rich sauce.

   Many of these items have especially high customer appeal, especially boneless chicken breast, and are served in the most elegant restaurants.

   Several of the chicken and turkey recipes in Chapter 2 are for specific parts. Those that use cut-up whole chickens can easily be adapted for specific parts. For example, you may want to buy whole chickens, braise the leg sections, and reserve the breasts for other preparations.

Inspection and Grading

Like meat, poultry is subject to federal ***inspection*** and ***grading***. (*Note:* Unlike those for meats, poultry inspection and grading stamps are not stamped on the birds but instead are printed on tags and packing cases.)

Figures 1.1 USDA inspection stamp for poultry

Figures 1.2 USDA grade stamp for poultry

Inspection

1. A guarantee of wholesomeness (fit for human consumption).
2. Indicated by a round stamp (Figure 1.1).
3. Required by U.S. law.

Grading

1. Based on quality.
2. Indicated by a shield stamp and letter grade (Figure 1.2).
3. Not required by U.S. law.

U.S. grades are A, B, and C, A being the best. Grades are based on

Shape of carcass (lack of defects)	Pinfeathers (present or absent)
Amount of flesh	Skin tears, cuts, broken bones
Amount of fat	Blemishes and bruises

Most poultry used in food service is Grade A. Lower grades are used by canners and processors.

Classification and Market Forms

The following terms are used to classify poultry:

Kind—the species, such as chicken, turkey, or duck.

Class—the subdivision of kind, depending on age and sex.

Style—the amount of cleaning and processing.

Live: almost never purchased in food service.

Dressed: killed, bled, and plucked. Also rarely seen in food service.

Ready to cook: dressed and eviscerated, with head and feet removed.

- Whole.
- Cut up, or parts.

State of refrigeration—chilled or frozen.

Table 1.1 describes the kinds and classes of domestic poultry. **Chicken** is the most common kind of poultry in the kitchen. As indicated in the table, age or maturity determines the differences among the classes of chicken. **Rock Cornish game hens** (usually called Cornish hens), **broilers**, and **fryers** are young, tender chickens suitable for sautéing, broiling, or frying, while **roasters** and **capons** are larger chickens that are usually roasted. Older **hens** and (rarely marketed) **roosters** must be simmered or braised to make them tender.

In addition to the common classes of chicken listed in the table, you may also find **poussin** (poo-san) on the market in certain localities. Similar to Rock Cornish game hen but often smaller, a poussin is a young chicken weighing 1 pound (450 g) or less. It commands a fairly high price because of the special techniques required for raising it.

Table 1.1 Domestic Poultry Classes and Characteristics

Kind / Class	Description	Age	Weight range
Chicken			
Rock Cornish game hen	Special breed of young chicken, very tender and delicate.	5 weeks or less	¾–2 lb (0.34–0.9 kg)
Broiler or fryer	Young chicken of either sex. Tender flesh and flexible cartilage. Smooth skin.	6–12 weeks	Broiler: 1½–2½ lb (0.7–1.1 kg) Fryer: 2½–3½ lb (1.1–1.6 kg)
Roaster	Young chicken of either sex. Tender flesh and smooth skin, but less flexible cartilage.	3–5 months	3½–5 lb (1.6–2.3 kg)
Capon	Castrated male chicken. Flesh very tender and well flavored. Large breast. Expensive.	Under 8 months	5–8 lb (2.3–3.6 kg)
Hen or fowl	Mature female. Tough flesh and coarse skin. Hardened breastbone cartilage.	Over 10 months	3½–6 lb (1.6–2.7 kg)
Cock or rooster	Mature male. Coarse skin. Tough, dark meat.	Over 10 months	4–6 lb (1.8–2.7 kg)
Turkey			
Fryer-roaster	Young bird of either sex. Tender flesh, smooth skin, and flexible cartilage.	Under 16 weeks	4–9 lb (1.8–4 kg)
Young turkey (hen or tom)	Young turkeys with tender flesh but firmer cartilage.	5–7 months	8–22 lb (3.6–10 kg)
Yearling turkey	Fully matured turkey that is still reasonably tender.	Under 15 months	10–30 lb (4.5–14 kg)
Mature turkey or old turkey (hen or tom)	Old turkey with tough flesh and coarse skin.	Over 15 months	10–30 lb (4.5–14 kg)
Duck			
Broiler or fryer duckling	Young tender duck with soft bill and windpipe.	Under 8 weeks	2–4 lb (0.9–1.8 kg)
Roaster duckling	Young tender duck with bill and windpipe just starting to harden.	Under 16 weeks	4–6 lb (1.8–2.7 kg)
Mature duck	Old duck with tough flesh and hard bill and windpipe.	Over 6 months	4–6 lb (1.8–2.7 kg)
Goose			
Young goose	Young bird with tender flesh.	Under 6 months	6–10 lb (2.7–4.5 kg)
Mature goose	Tough old bird.	Over 6 months	10–16 lb (4.5–7.3 kg)
Guinea			
Young guinea	Domestic relative of the pheasant. Tender.	3–6 months	¾–1½ lb (0.34–0.7 kg)
Mature guinea	Tough.	Up to 12 months	1–2 lb (0.45–0.9 kg)
Pigeon			
Squab	Very young pigeon with light, tender meat.	3–4 weeks	Under 1 lb (0.45 kg)
Pigeon	Older pigeon with tough, dark meat.	Over 4 weeks	1–2 lb (0.45–0.9 kg)

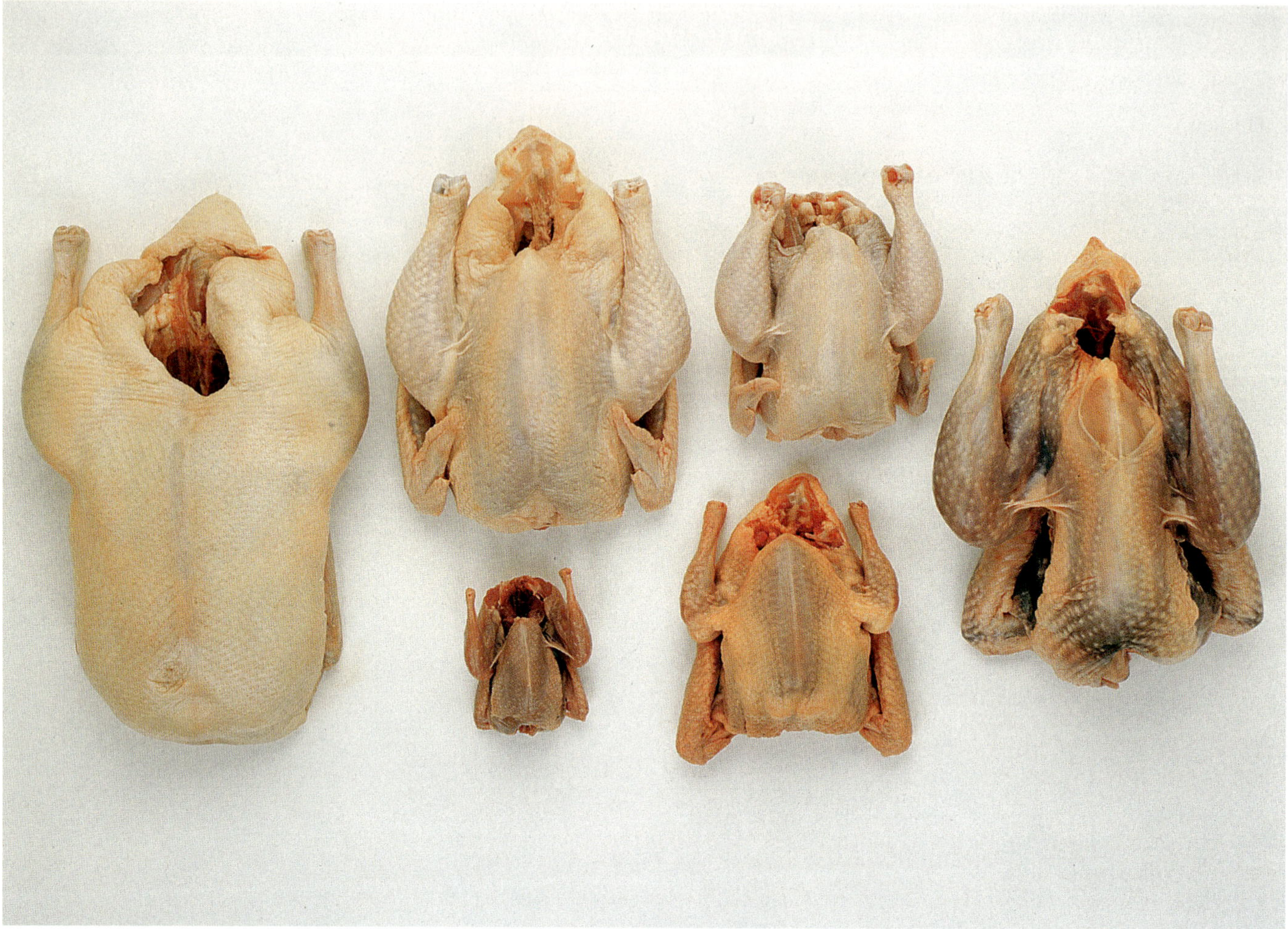

Clockwise from left: duckling, free-range chicken, poussin, guinea fowl, squab, quail

Turkeys are larger birds that are usually roasted, although the cooking of turkey parts is increasingly common. For example, legs may be stewed or braised for special dishes, while breasts are cut into cutlets or scaloppine and sautéed like veal cutlets.

Ducks and **geese** also are usually roasted, although duck parts are sometimes cooked separately. Boneless breast of duck is sautéed or broiled and served rare, sliced into small medallions, and the legs may be braised. Ducks and geese have a thick layer of fat under the skin. Compared with chicken and turkey, they have a low yield. For example, a 4-pound duck yields about 1 pound raw lean meat, and a 4-pound chicken yields about 2 pounds raw lean meat.

Most ducks marketed in North America are a breed called **White Pekin**; this includes the well-known Long Island duck. A specialty item available in some markets is ***magret*** (mah-gray). This is the boneless breast of a breed of duck called **moulard**. It is thicker and meatier than the breast of a regular Pekin.

Guineas are a domestically raised descendant of the pheasant. They taste like a flavorful chicken and are usually cooked and handled like young chickens.

Squabs are young, domestically raised pigeons, usually weighing less than 1 pound (450 g). Their rich, dark meat, which is usually cooked slightly rare to avoid dryness, has a slightly gamy flavor that combines well with flavorful brown sauces.

Game Birds and Specialty Products

In recent years, the availability of such birds as quail and squab has increased dramatically, and they are seen regularly on restaurant menus. The poultry items discussed in this section are classified as game birds, but they are all, in fact, raised domestically. While farm-raised pheasants and partridge lack the full gamy flavor of their wild cousins, they do have a richer, more gamelike taste compared to chicken. With bland, factory-raised chickens dominating the market, cooks and eaters are turning more and more to exotic poultry and are willing to pay the higher price.

Traditionally, true wild game is hung and allowed to age, usually before plucking and dressing. The purpose is essentially the same as for aging beef, namely to allow the natural enzymes in the meat to tenderize it and to develop flavor. Often, game is hung until it becomes high, to the point where spoiled meat is mistaken for aged meat. With today's farm-raised game birds, this procedure is not appropriate. Anyway, most customers prefer a fresh taste to a strong, gamy one.

Quail are small, weighing 4 to 5 ounces (110 to 140 g) each. A normal main-course portion is two birds. They have meaty breasts for their size, but not much meat on the legs. Quail are richly flavored without being gamy. The French name is *caille*.

Partridges are about the size of Rock Cornish game hens, weighing about 1 pound (450 g) each. It is important to look for young, tender birds because mature partridge is likely to be tough. They have excellent flavor, but they are not as delicate as squab or pheasant. The French names are *perdreau* (young partridge) and *perdrix* (mature partridge).

Pheasant is a popular game bird, and farm-raised pheasant is widely available. Most pheasant sold weighs from 2 to 2½ pounds (900 to 1200 g), but young pheasant weighing 1 pound (450 g) or less is also available. This bird has delicate, light-colored meat with subtle flavor similar to that of chicken. Most recipes for chicken are also suitable for pheasant, but the simplest preparations are usually the best, because the flavor stands well on its own and is easily covered by too many spices. Pheasant can be dry if overcooked. The French name is *faisan*.

Many varieties of **wild duck** are eaten, but mallard is the most common. Farm-raised mallards weigh from 1½ to 3 pounds (700 to 1400 g). Unlike domestic duck, wild duck is very lean. It has dark, flavorful flesh.

Handling game birds is easy if you remember that their structure is basically the same as the structure of chickens. All the cutting and trussing techniques you learn for chicken can be applied to these other birds.

Because farm-raised game birds are usually young and tender, they can be roasted, sautéed, grilled, and barbecued. The most important thing to remember about them is they are usually very lean. Therefore, they are best served slightly rare. If cooked to well done, they become dry. This is especially true of wild duck, which is almost inedible if overcooked. Wild duck is usually left rarer than the other birds discussed here. Its meat is then red and juicy.

Pheasant is also very dry if well done. Its light-colored meat is best if still slightly pink at the bone. Quail doesn't become as dry, but it too has the best flavor if still slightly pink at the bone.

Another category of farm-raised birds is the category technically known as ***ratites***. **Ostrich** and **emu** are the most familiar members of this category. Although these meats have lost some popularity in recent years, both are generally available. The meat of both birds is lean and red and resembles venison or very lean beef in appearance, although it is slightly lighter in color than venison.

Because ostrich and emu are so lean, they are best cooked to the medium rare or, at most, medium stage to avoid dryness. Recommended safe internal temperature is 155° to 160°F (68° to 71°C). Grilling, sautéing, and pan-frying are the best cooking methods for small, tender cuts, while larger tender cuts can be roasted. Moist-heat methods, especially braising, are sometimes recommended for less tender cuts, but this often results in excessively dry meat because it is so lean. Take care to avoid overcooking if you braise ostrich or emu. Another option is to grind the less tender cuts. Mixed with seasonings and added moisture, ground emu and ostrich can make excellent burgers, meatballs, and meatloaf.

Ostrich and emu are best cooked like other lean red meats and game. Recipes for venison, in particular, are often excellent when applied to these meats, as are recipes for grilled or sautéed beef. Ostrich producers often recommend cooking their product like veal. This may be slightly misleading because veal is often cooked medium well or well done. Nevertheless, grilled, sautéed, and roast veal recipes can often be used for ostrich and emu as well, as long as the meat is not overcooked. Two recipes developed specifically for ostrich or emu are included in Chapter 2 as a sample.

KEY POINTS TO REVIEW

- How do the differences between light meat and dark meat affect how you cook different poultry parts?
- What are four ways to keep breast meat from becoming too dry when cooking whole poultry?
- What is the significance of *inspection* and *grading* of poultry products?
- What do the terms *kind, class,* and *style* mean with respect to poultry? What are the major kinds and classes of domestic poultry used in food service?
- What are the most important kinds of farm-raised game birds used in food service? Describe each kind.

Handling and Storage

Fresh Poultry

1. Fresh poultry is extremely perishable. It should arrive packed in ice and be kept in ice until used.
2. Ideally, use poultry within 24 hours of receiving. Never hold it for more than 4 days.
3. Poultry often carries salmonella bacteria. Wash all equipment and cutting surfaces after handling poultry to avoid contamination of other foods.

Frozen Poultry

1. Store frozen poultry at 0°F (−18°C) or lower until ready to thaw.
2. Thaw in original wrapper in refrigerator, allowing 1 to 2 days for chickens, 2 to 4 days for larger birds. If pressed for time, thaw in cold, running water in original wrapper.
3. Do not refreeze thawed poultry.

Doneness

Domestic poultry is almost always cooked well done (except squab and sautéed or grilled duck breast). Many cooks, however, cannot tell the difference between well done and overcooked. Chicken and turkey are low in fat, so they quickly become dry and unpalatable when overcooked. Even duck and goose, which are very fatty, taste dry and stringy if cooked too long.

Skilled chefs with years of experience can often tell the doneness of a roast chicken or turkey just by looking at it. Until you gain that much experience, you should rely on other methods.

For Large Roasted Birds

Internal temperature, as tested with a thermometer, is the most accurate guide to doneness. The thermometer should be inserted into the thickest muscle of the inner part of the thigh, away from the bone. The thigh is tested rather than the breast because the thigh is the last part of the bird to become fully cooked.

The recommended safe internal temperature for roast whole poultry is 165°F (74°C). However, the more usual practice is to aim for a final temperature of 180°F (82°C). This higher temperature provides a margin of safety to allow for the difficulty of measuring poultry temperatures accurately. (Most customers do not like to see red or pink at the bone joints of chicken and turkey.) Depending on the size of the bird, removing it from the oven when the thermometer reads between 165° and 175°F (74° and 79°C) should result in a final temperature of 180°F (82°C) after carryover cooking.

For Smaller Birds, Cooked by Any Method

Doneness of smaller birds is determined in the following ways.

1. Looseness of joints. The leg moves freely in its socket.
2. Clear juices. Juices inside the cavity of a roasted bird are clear yellow rather than cloudy and red or pink.
3. Flesh separating from bone. Muscles begin to pull away from bones, especially breastbone and leg bones. Excessively shrunken flesh means it's overcooked and dry.
4. Firmness to touch. Test with finger pressure as you would a steak (see p. 144). This method is especially useful for sautéed boneless chicken breasts.

Not recommended: Do not test by piercing deeply with a fork and twisting the flesh. Too many valuable juices will be lost.

Trussing Methods

Trussing means tying the legs and wings against the body to make a compact, solid unit. It has two main purposes:

1. Even cooking. Extended legs and wings cook too quickly.
2. More attractive appearance, especially when presented or served whole or carved in the dining room.

One of many trussing methods is illustrated in Figure 1.3. Your instructor may wish to show you other methods.

Figure 1.3 Trussing chicken.

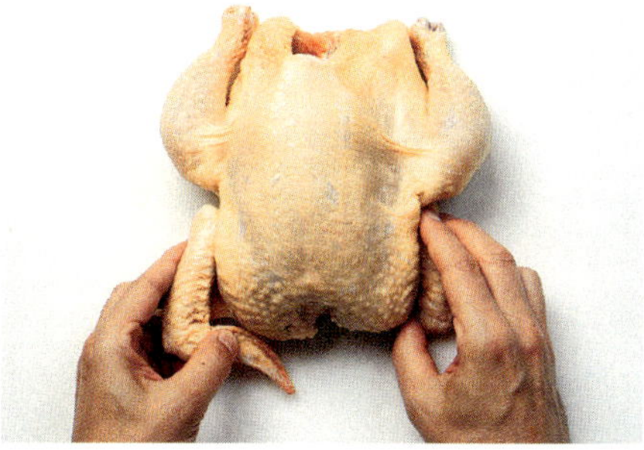

(a) Place the chicken breast up, with the neck end toward you. Tuck the first joint of the wings behind the back.

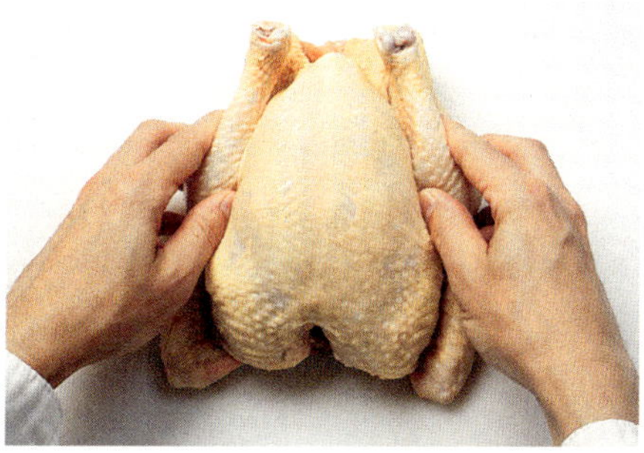

(b) Press the legs forward and down against the body.

(c) Pass the center of a length of twine under the hip bone just ahead of the tail.

(d) Bring the twine up and across the ends of the legs.

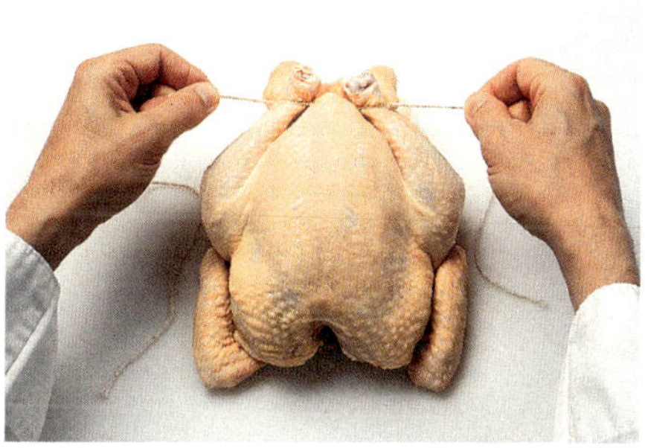

(e) Pass the twine under the ends of the legs as shown and pull tight.

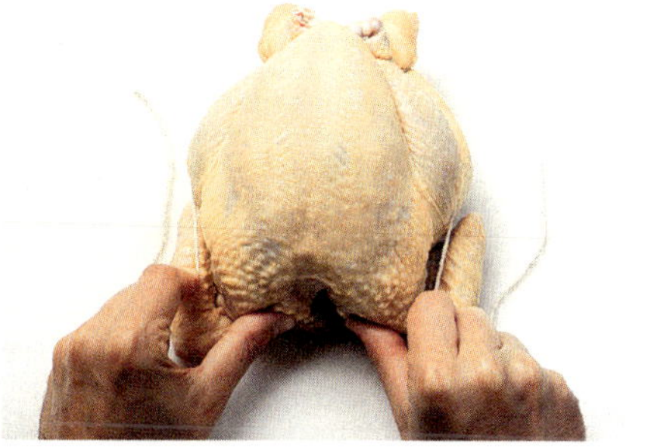

(f) Bring the ends of the twine toward the neck end of the bird. Pull firmly on the twine while pressing on the breast portion with the thumbs as shown.

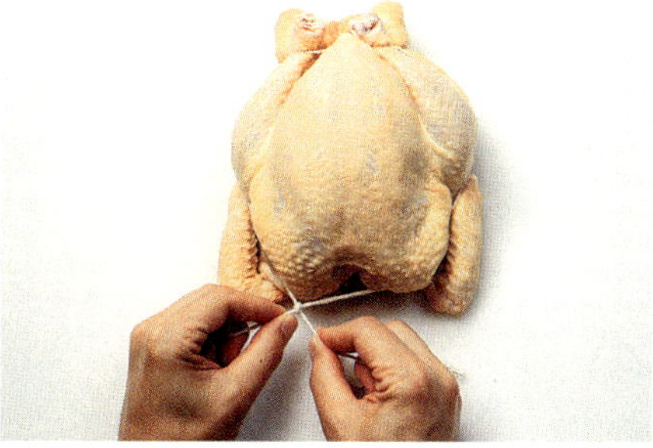

(g) Tie the twine tightly.

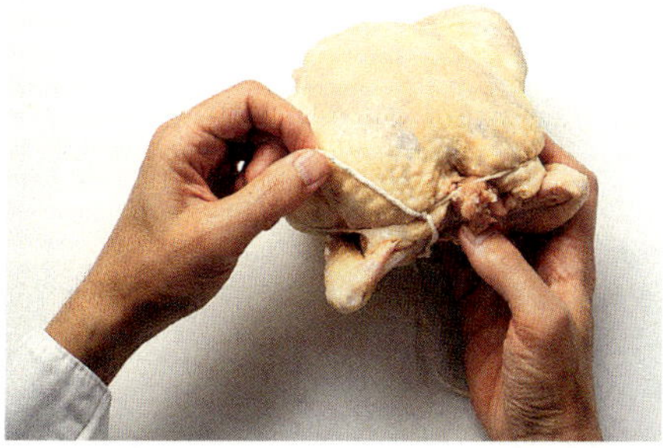

(h) The stub of the neck holds the twine in place, preventing it from slipping behind the back.

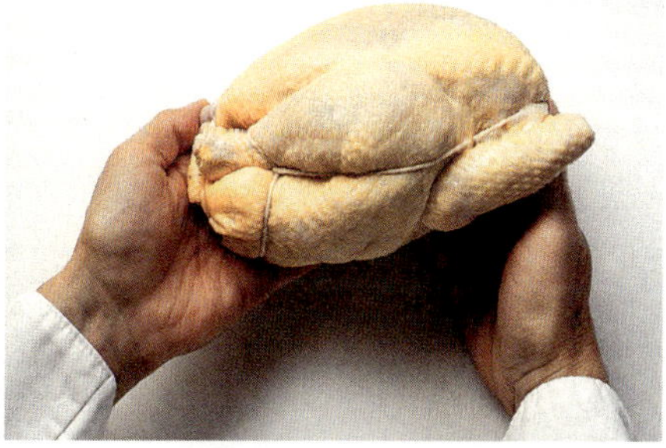

(i) The trussed chicken.

Cutting Up Chicken

There are many ways to cut up chickens. Every chef has his or her preferred methods. Some of these methods are illustrated, step by step, in Figures 1.4, 1.5, and 1.6. These show how to split a chicken for broiling and how to cut whole chickens into quarters and eighths, for both bone-in parts and semi-boneless pieces. Cutting chicken apart at the joints is also known as *disjointing*.

As for meats, it is important to know the bone structure of chicken in order to cut it up. The best way to learn this is to practice cutting chickens.

Figure 1.4 Splitting chicken for broiling.

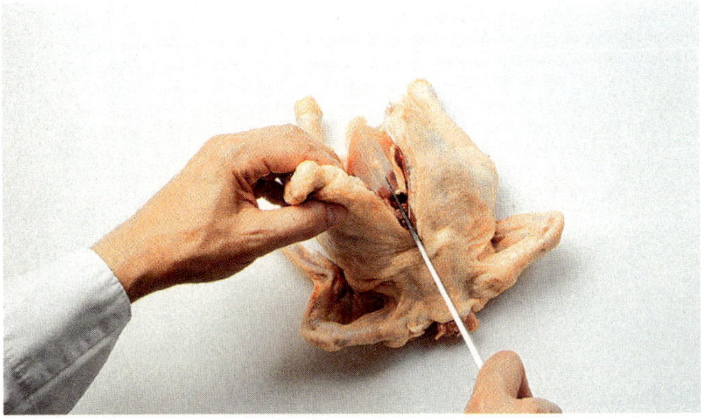

(a) Hold the chicken up by the tail. Cut through the bones to one side of the backbone, all the way to the neck.

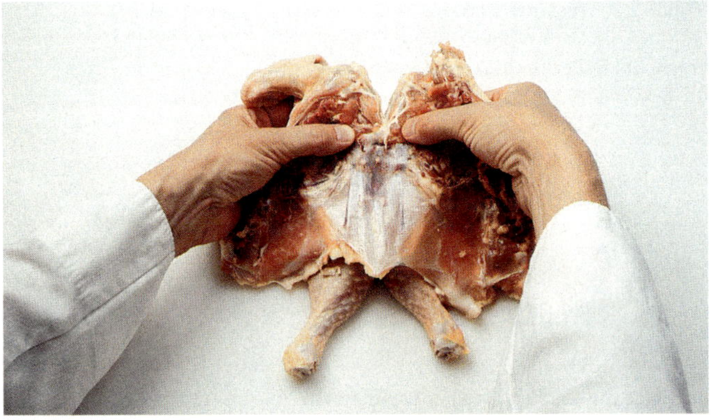

(b) Split the chicken open.

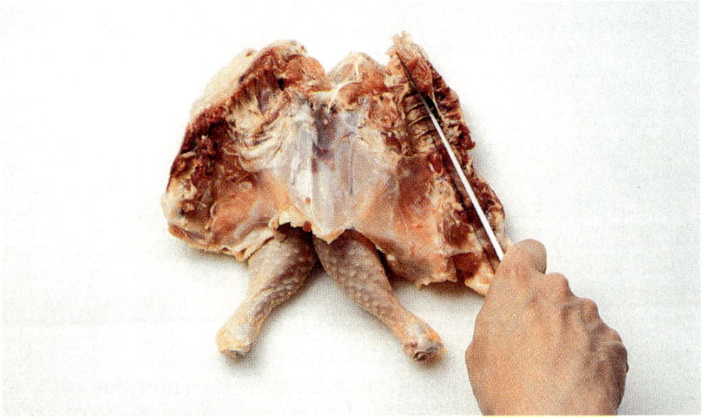

(c) Cut off the backbone as shown.

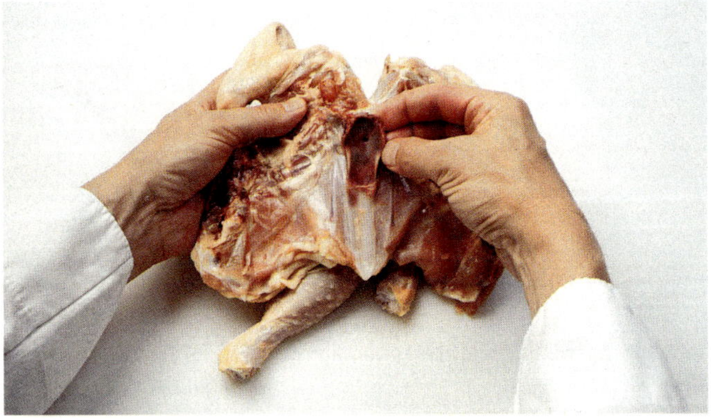

(d) Pull out the breastbone or keel bone. This helps the chicken lie flat and cook evenly.

(e) For a portion size of one-half chicken, cut the chicken in half down the center of the breast. Make a split in the skin below the leg and slip the end of the leg through it as shown to hold the chicken in shape.

(f) Portion-size Cornish game hens are left whole.

Figure 1.5 Cutting chicken into quarters and eighths, bone in.

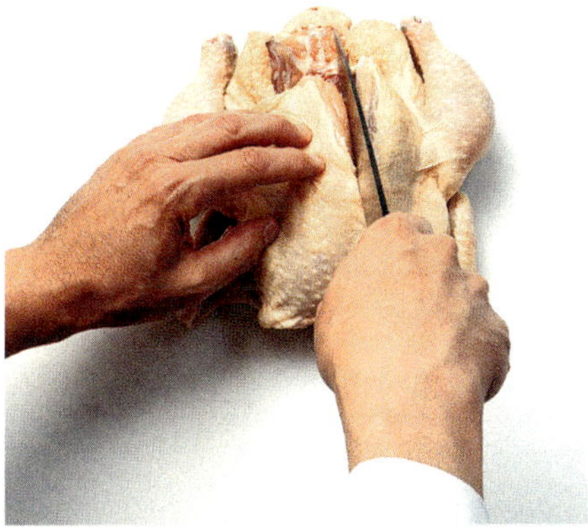

(a) Place the chicken on the cutting board breast up. Split the chicken down the center of the breast with a heavy knife as shown.

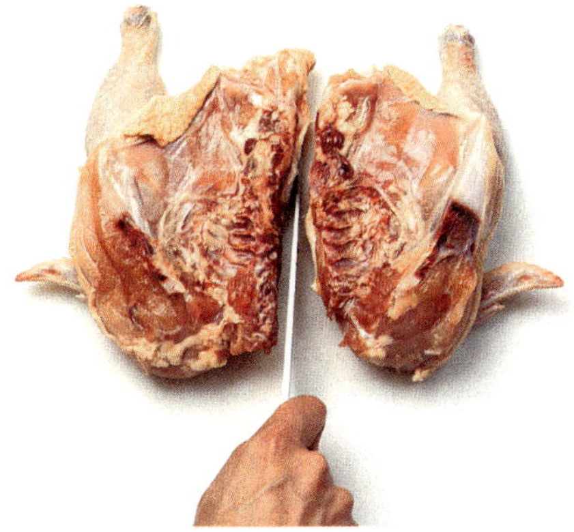

(b) Spread the chicken open and cut through the bones on one side of the backbone.

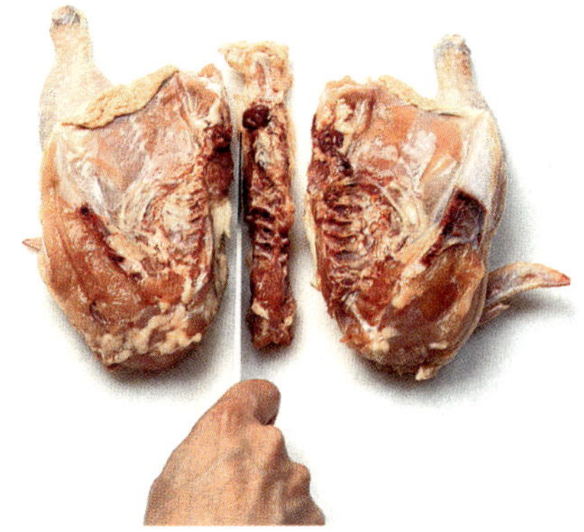

(c) Cut off the backbone completely. Save for stocks.

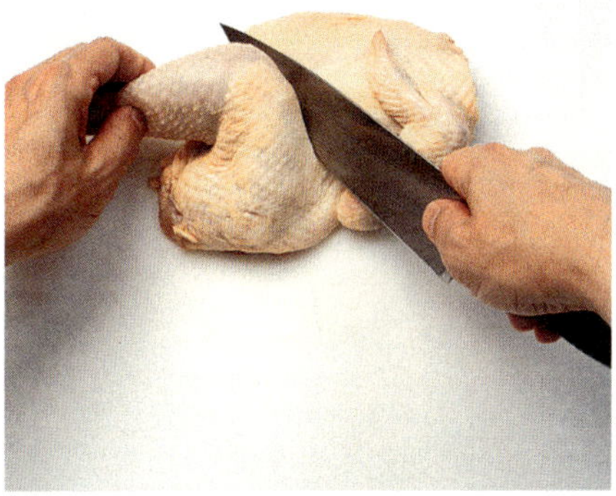

(d) Cut through the skin between the leg and the breast.

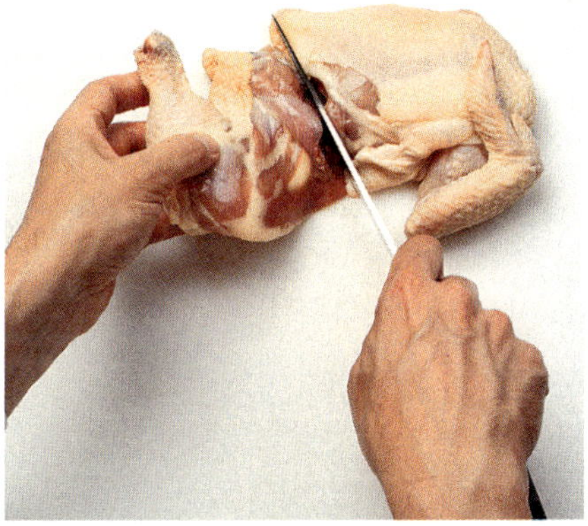

(e) Pull the leg back and cut off the entire leg section. Repeat with the other half. The chicken is now in quarters.

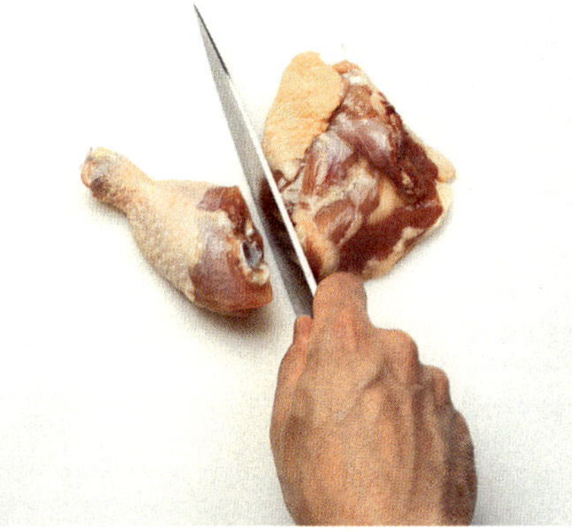

(f) To cut into eighths, cut the drumstick and thigh apart at the joint.

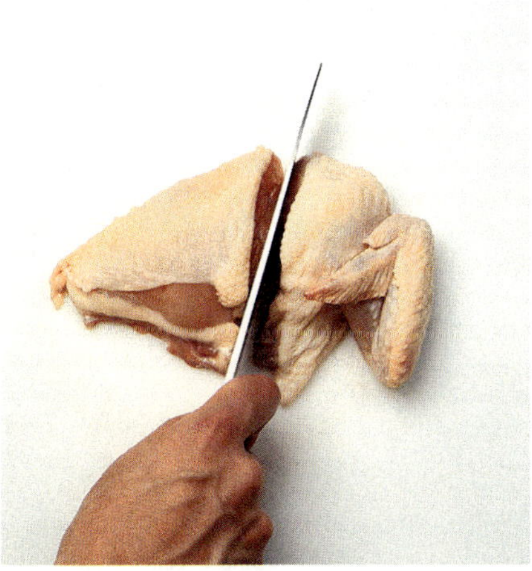

(g) Cut the breast and wing quarter into two equal pieces. (Another method is simply to cut off the wing.)

(h) The chicken cut into eighths. Note that the first joint of each wing has been cut off.

Figure 1.6 Cutting up chickens, semi-boneless.

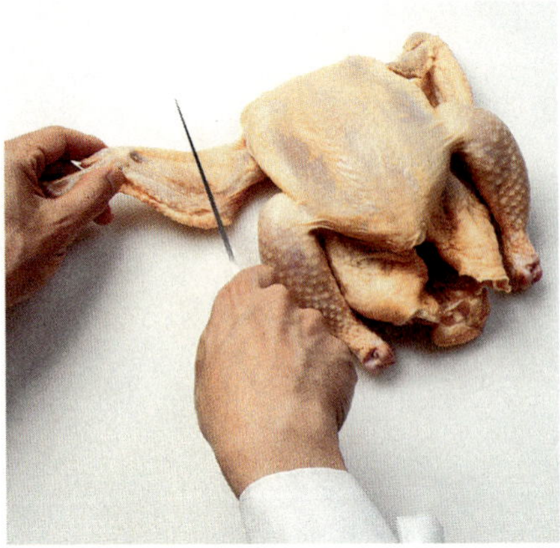

(a) Cut off the wings at the second joint. Save for stocks.

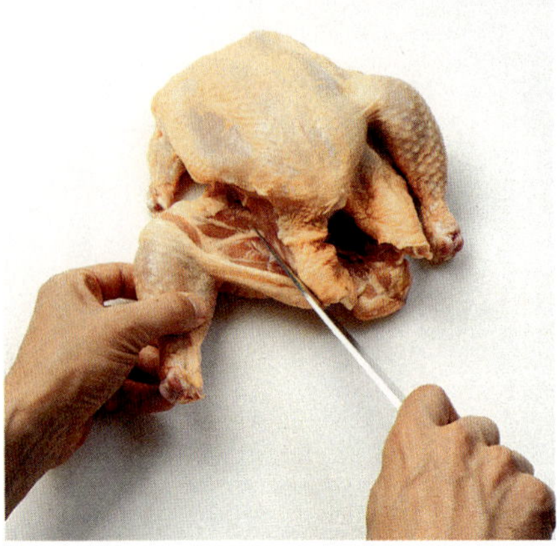

(b) Cut through the skin between the leg and the body.

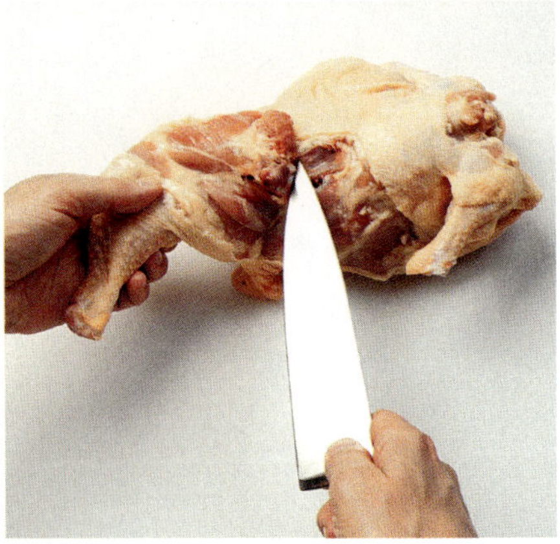

(c) Turn the chicken on its side and pull the leg back. Carefully start to cut the flesh from the bone, being sure to get the "oyster," the little nugget of tender meat in the hollow of the hip bone. Cut through the ligaments at the hip joint.

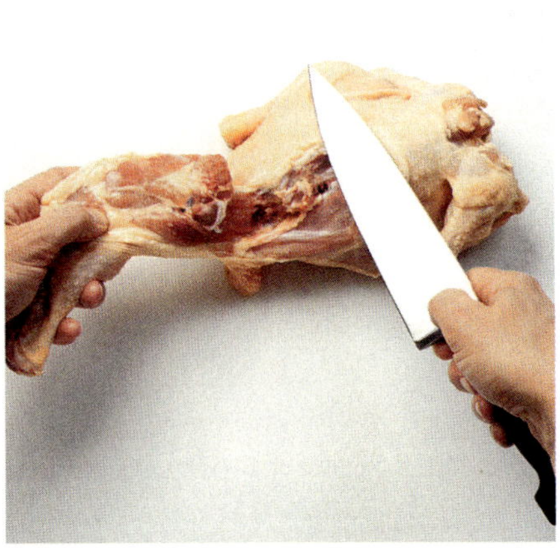

(d) Holding the chicken steady with the knife, pull off the leg. Repeat with the other leg.

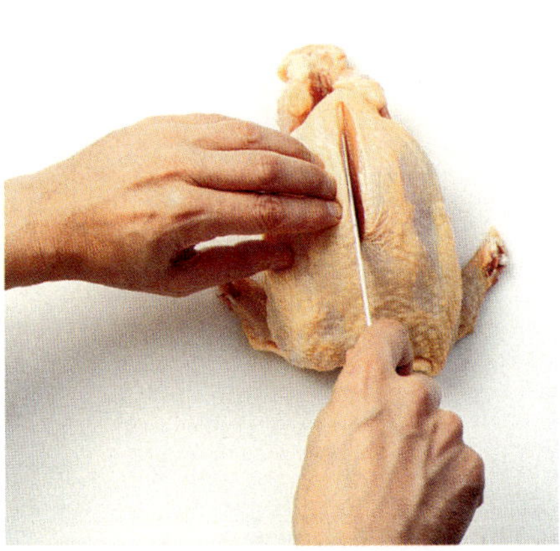

(e) Turn the breast portion upright. Cut down along one side of the ridge of the breastbone to separate the breast meat from the bone.

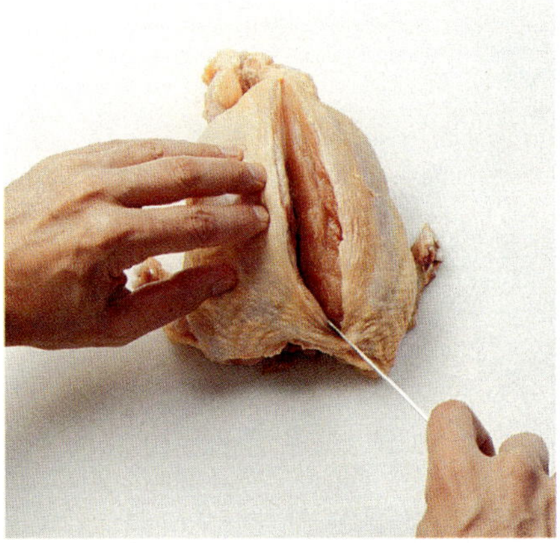

(f) Continue the cut along the wishbone to the wing joint.

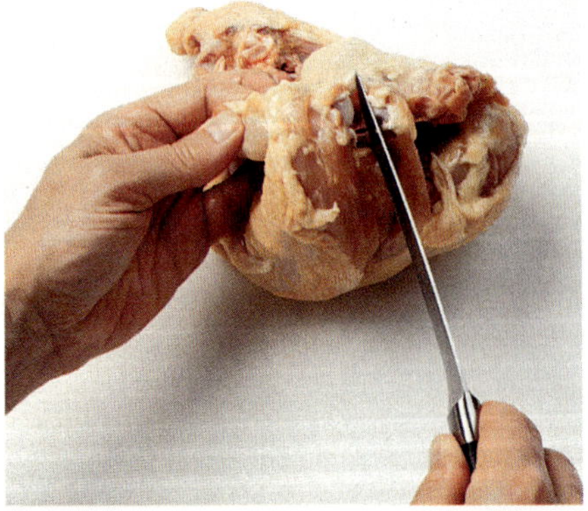

(g) Holding the chicken by the wing, cut through the wing joint.

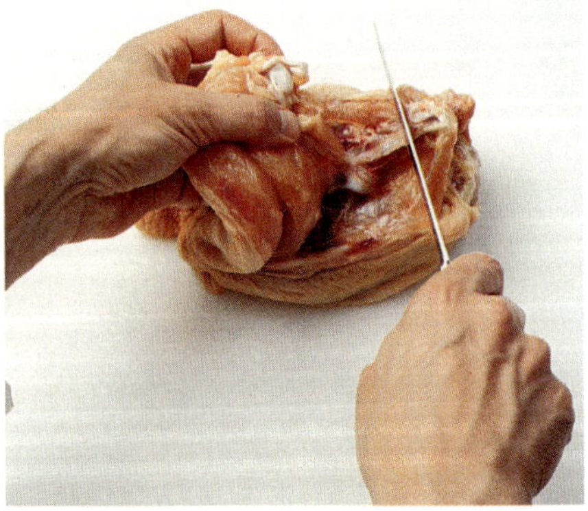

(h) Holding the carcass steady with the knife, pull back on the wing and breast meat.

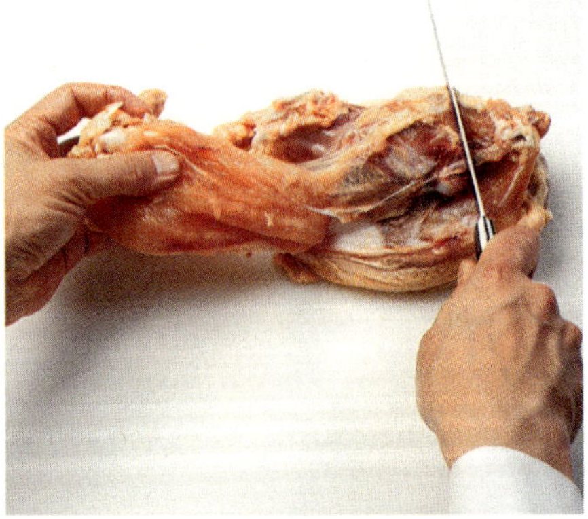

(i) Pull the breast meat completely off the bone. Be sure to hold on to the small "tenderloin" muscle inside the breast so it doesn't separate from the rest of the meat. Repeat with the other side.

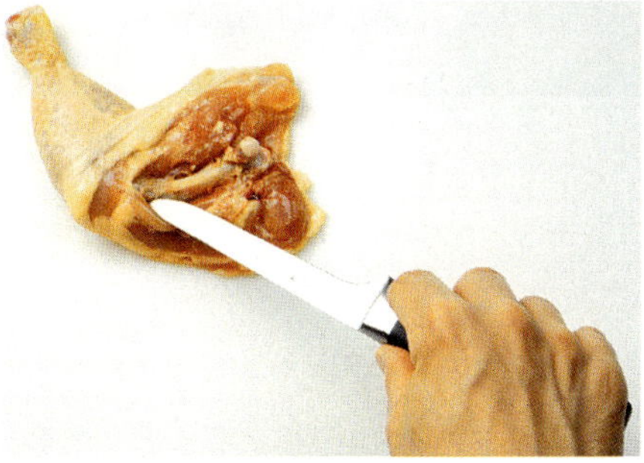

(j) If desired, remove the thigh bone. Cut down along both sides of the bone to separate it from the meat.

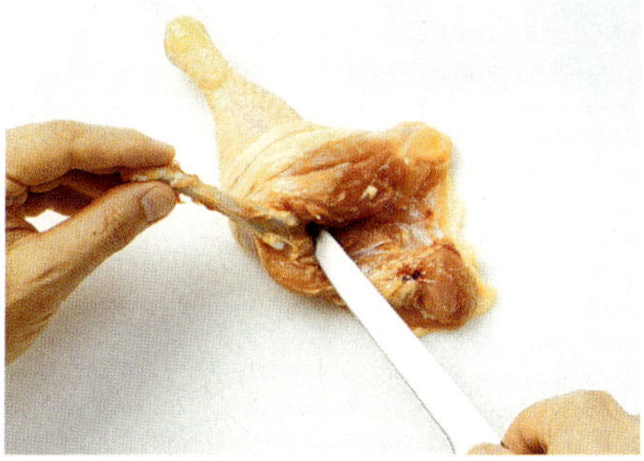

(k) Lift out the bone and cut it off at the joint.

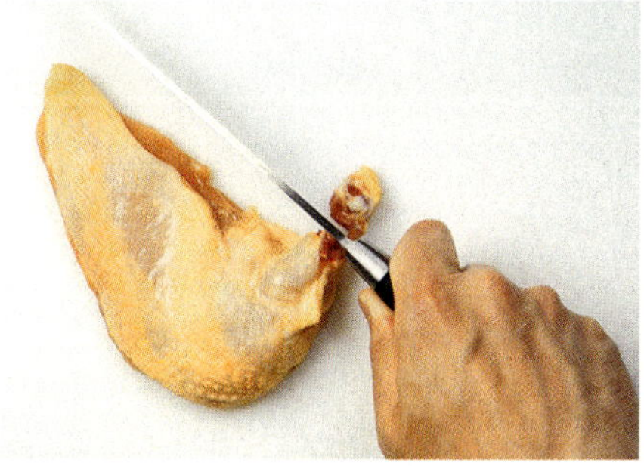

(l) For a neater appearance, chop off the end of the wing bone with the heel of the knife.

(m) A semi-boneless breast with the wing bone left in is known as a *suprême* or an *airline breast*. The wing bone may be left as is or frenched (meat scraped off), as in the illustration.

(n) The cut-up chicken. From left: breast portions without and with wing bone; leg portions without and with thigh bone; wing sections and carcass for stockpot. The drumstick and thigh (bone-in) may be cut apart at the joint, as in Figure 1.5.

KEY POINTS TO REVIEW

- How is fresh poultry properly stored? How is frozen poultry stored and handled?
- How is doneness of poultry determined?
- Why is whole poultry often trussed before cooking?
- What methods are used for cutting up poultry? Describe as thoroughly as possible how to cut chicken into bone-in and semi-boneless parts.

TERMS FOR REVIEW

light meat	free-range	inspection	magret	trussing
dark meat	organic	grading	ratite	suprême
maturity				

QUESTIONS FOR DISCUSSION

1. Why are hens or fowl not roasted in commercial kitchens?
2. Why is the breast section so often dry when whole chickens and turkeys are roasted? Can you suggest ways to remedy this problem?
3. Give a brief description of each of the following classes of poultry. Be sure to mention relative tenderness and approximate size.

Capon	Roaster	Yearling turkey
Roaster duckling	Young tom turkey	Hen or fowl
Broiler/fryer	Rock Cornish hen	

4. How should fresh and frozen poultry be stored?
5. Describe five methods for determining doneness in poultry items.
6. What is the purpose of trussing poultry?
7. Why are most game birds better if not cooked until well done?

Chapter 2

Arroz con Pollo (Spanish Rice with Chicken), page 47.

Cooking Poultry and Game Birds

The muscle tissue of domestic poultry and game birds, as we have said, has basically the same structure as the muscle tissue of meat animals. In particular, the breast meat of chicken and turkey is so similar to veal that they are interchangeable in many recipes.

Imaginative cooks realize that even when two meats are quite different—chicken and beef, for example—interesting new dishes can be made with substitutions that might seem unusual. For example, it is possible to make a delicious chili from chicken or turkey meat, a preparation that has the added advantage of having a lower food cost than beef chili.

Because the basic cooking methods for poultry are the same as for meat, they are not repeated here. But you may want to review them before proceeding with any of the recipes in this chapter. Also, please review the discussion of light and dark meat (pp. 2–3) in the previous chapter, as well as the methods for testing doneness (p. 8).

After reading this chapter, you should be able to

1. Cook poultry by roasting and baking.
2. Cook poultry by broiling and grilling.
3. Cook poultry by sautéing, pan-frying, and deep-frying.
4. Cook poultry by simmering and poaching.
5. Cook poultry by braising.
6. Identify the safety, quality, and practicality concerns associated with preparing dressings and stuffings.
7. List basic ingredients for dressings and stuffings.
8. Prepare dressings and stuffings.

Roasting and Baking

The general procedures for roasting and baking meats also apply to poultry, as illustrated by the following recipes. However, there are some differences in the ways poultry items are handled. The guidelines below should be observed.

Remember that poultry items are almost always cooked well done (except for squab and game birds).

Seasoning and Basting

1. Seasonings and, if desired, a little mirepoix or a bouquet garni should be placed inside the cavity. When roasting whole birds, you need to season the skin only if it is to be served and eaten, as the seasonings will not penetrate the skin.

2. Oil the skin before roasting to help in browning and to protect against drying. The skin may be basted with fat during roasting, but this is unnecessary if the bird is roasted breast down (and turned breast up just at the end of the roasting period to brown).

   Basting is beneficial for large turkeys, which must be subjected to dry heat for several hours. If you baste large poultry during roasting, do it every 20 to 30 minutes. More frequent basting results in the loss of a great deal of heat from the oven because the door is opened so frequently.

3. Basting is unnecessary for duck and goose, which have a great deal of fat under the skin. These birds are usually roasted breast up for that reason.

Temperature

Selection of roasting temperature depends on the product being roasted.

1. *Low-temperature roasting* is best for large items such as turkeys and capons. It results in a tender, juicy product.

   Large turkeys may be roasted at 250° to 325°F (120° to 165°C). For most operations, however, cooking times at the lower end of this range are too long. In addition, if a turkey is stuffed (see pp. 49–50), it is not advisable to roast it at a very low temperature because the interior temperature will take too long to rise, providing a good breeding ground for bacteria.

   Some recipes call for starting large turkeys at a high temperature for 15 to 30 minutes in order to brown them. This is usually not necessary because they will likely brown anyway during the long cooking time.

   Smaller items, such as roasting chickens, are usually roasted at 325° to 375°F (165° to 190°C). Small items roasted at low temperatures may not brown well by the time they are done. In such cases, the heat can be turned up for a few minutes when they are almost done in order to brown them.

2. The *searing* method may be used for chickens under 4 to 5 pounds (2 kg) and for baked chicken parts. Start roasting in the oven at 450°F (230°C) for 15 minutes, then reduce the oven temperature to 250° to 325°F (120° to 160°C). These small items cook so quickly that continuous roasting at a low temperature produces very little browning.

   Ducks and geese also may be started at a high temperature in order to melt off some of the heavy fat layer under the skin and to make the skin brown and crisp.

3. *High-temperature roasting* is used for small items such as squab and game birds, which are often served rare. Cornish hens and other small poultry under 3 pounds (1.35 kg) may also be flash-roasted. Great care is necessary when roasting at high temperatures, however, because the poultry will quickly become overcooked if left in the oven only a few minutes too long. For example, a 2½-pound (1.2-kg) chicken or guinea hen roasted at 450°F (230°C) may be perfectly cooked and nicely browned after 45 minutes but overcooked and dry if left another 10 minutes.

Ducks may also be roasted at a continuously high temperature (400° to 425°F/200° to 220°C) because their fat content protects them from drying. Great care should be used to prevent overcooking, however, because this can happen very quickly at these temperatures. (Goose should not be roasted at a continuously high temperature because of its larger size and the length of time it takes to cook.)

Baked Poultry

Roasting and baking are the same process. Cutting up the chicken doesn't change the cooking method. Baked chicken or turkey parts are treated like roasted poultry.

Chicken parts are sometimes coated with seasoned crumbs or flour and rolled in fat before baking. Such products are sometimes misleadingly called *oven-fried* because of their resemblance to breaded fried chicken.

Poêlés

A *poêlé* (pwah lay) is a classical preparation for white meats and poultry in which the item is cooked with a matignon (see sidebar on page 25) in a covered container and basted with butter before and during cooking. Because the container is covered, the procedure is not a dry-heat method and, therefore, is not a genuine roasting procedure. Nevertheless, poêléing is usually translated as "butter-roasting" and is traditionally discussed along with other roasting procedures. (Escoffier also refers to a poêlé as a roast.) In this book, we follow this tradition and include the method here rather than with moist-heat procedures.

The recipe on page 25 illustrates the classical procedure for a poêlé, following Escoffier's method. Several alternatives to this procedure are indicated in the recipe notes and in the sidebar on page 25.

THE POÊLE

The term *poêlé* is derived from the word for a type of cooking utensil, the *poêle* (pwahl). At one time, this term was used for the kind of covered casserole used to cook meats and poultry by the method described in the text. In French kitchens today, however, the *poêle* is a type of sauté pan or frying pan. Consequently, in modern French, the verb *poêler* usually means "to sauté or pan-fry."

In this text, as in most English-speaking kitchens, we use the word *poêlé* to refer to the classical procedure described in the text. To avoid confusion, however, it is helpful to be aware of how the word is used in modern French. In fact, many familiar cooking terms have slightly different meanings in French. For example, *casserole*, a term used in the preceding paragraph, refers in French to what we would call a saucepan.

Baked Chicken

PORTIONS: 24 PORTION SIZE: ¼ CHICKEN

U.S.	METRIC	INGREDIENTS
8 oz	250 g	Flour
5 tsp	25 mL	Salt
½ tsp	2 mL	White pepper
2 tsp	10 mL	Paprika
½ tsp	2 mL	Dried thyme
15 lb	7 kg	Fryer chicken parts or quarters (see Note)
1 lb	500 g	Melted butter, oil, or a mixture of butter and oil

PROCEDURE

1. Combine the flour and seasonings in a pan.
2. Dry the chicken pieces with paper towels if they are wet. Dredge in the seasoned flour.
3. Dip the chicken in the fat so that all sides are coated. Let excess drip off.
4. Arrange the chicken pieces on a sheet pan or in baking pans, skin side up. If using both dark and light meat parts, place them on separate pans.
5. Bake the chicken at 350°F (175°C) until done, about 1 hour.

Per serving: Calories, 450; Protein, 38 g; Fat, 30 g (61% cal.); Cholesterol, 150 mg; Carbohydrates, 6 g; Fiber, 0 g; Sodium, 590 mg.

Note: If you are starting with whole chickens, cut them into quarters or eighths, as shown in **Figure 2.5**. Any chicken parts may be used for this recipe. For example, you might bake just the legs and use the breasts and wings for other preparations.

VARIATIONS

Baked Herbed Chicken

Add 1 tbsp (15 mL) dried tarragon, 1 tsp (5 mL) dried marjoram, 2 tbsp (30 mL) fresh chives, and 2 tbsp (30 mL) dried parsley to the flour mixture. Omit paprika.

Baked Rosemary Chicken

Prepare as in basic recipe. After placing chicken parts in baking pans, sprinkle with dried rosemary, about 4 tsp (20 mL) for 24 portions. Fifteen minutes before chicken is done, sprinkle with 3–4 fl oz (90–125 mL) lemon juice.

Baked Chicken Parmesan

Instead of flour for dredging, use 1 cup (100 g) parmesan cheese mixed with 1½ cups (150 g) fine dry bread crumbs. Season as in basic recipe.

Roast Chicken with Natural Gravy

PORTIONS: 24 PORTION SIZE: ¼ CHICKEN PLUS 2 FL OZ (60 ML) JUS

U.S.	METRIC	INGREDIENTS
6	6	Chickens, 3–3½ lb (1.4–1.6 kg) each
to taste	to taste	Salt
to taste	to taste	Pepper
as needed	as needed	Oil or butter
		Mirepoix:
6 oz	175 g	Onion, medium dice
3 oz	90 g	Carrots, medium dice
3 oz	90 g	Celery, medium dice
3 qt	3 L	Strong chicken stock
2 oz	60 g	Cornstarch or arrowroot
2 fl oz	60 mL	Water or stock, cold
to taste	to taste	Salt
to taste	to taste	Pepper

PROCEDURE

1. Remove giblets from chickens. Check inside cavities to make sure they are well cleaned. Reserve giblets for other use.
2. Season the insides of the chickens with salt and pepper.
3. Truss the chickens.
4. Rub the outside of the chickens with oil or butter (butter promotes faster browning). Season the skin with salt and pepper, as it will be served with the meat.
5. Place the mirepoix in a roasting pan. Place a rack over the mirepoix, and place the chickens breast down on the rack.
6. Place the chickens in an oven preheated to 450°F (230°C). After 15 minutes (not longer), turn the heat down to 325°F (165°C).
7. When the chickens have been in the oven 45–60 minutes, turn them breast side up. Baste with the fat in the roasting pan and finish roasting. Total cooking time is about 1½ hours.
8. Remove the chickens from the roasting pan and hold them in a warm place for service.
9. Set the roasting pan on the range over high heat and brown the mirepoix well, but do not let it burn. Pour off the fat.
10. Add the strong stock to deglaze the pan. Boil until the gravy is reduced by about one-third. Degrease carefully. See **Figure 2.1**.
11. Stir the starch with the cold water or stock. Stir it into the gravy. Bring to a boil and simmer until thickened.
12. Strain into a bain-marie, using a china cap lined with cheesecloth. Season carefully with salt and pepper.
13. Quarter the chickens, or carve them as shown in **Figure 2.2**. Serve a quarter-chicken with 2 oz (60 mL) gravy.

Per serving: Calories, 350; Protein, 45 g; Fat, 17 g (45% cal.); Cholesterol, 105 mg; Carbohydrates, 2 g; Fiber, 0 g; Sodium, 140 mg.

VARIATIONS

Roast Herbed Chicken

Place 3–4 parsley stems and a pinch each of tarragon and marjoram in the cavity of each bird.

After turning the chicken breast-up in the roasting pan, rub the skin with chopped parsley, tarragon, and marjoram.

Roast Chicken with Gravy

Save 4 oz (125 g) of the fat skimmed from the juices and make a blond roux with the fat and 4 oz (125 g) bread flour. Beat the roux into the juices and simmer until thickened.

Roast Chicken with Cream Gravy

Prepare as in basic recipe, but use only 1½ qt (1.5 L) chicken stock. Boil until reduced to 1 qt (1 L) and strain (step 9). Add 1 qt (1 L) hot milk and thicken with 8 oz (250 g) blond roux. Finish with 4 fl oz (125 mL) heavy cream.

Roast Chicken with Natural Gravy, Whipped Potatoes, Glazed Root Vegetables, Roasted Garlic, Peas

Figure 2.1 Preparing pan gravy.

(a) Remove the rack of cooked poultry from the roasting pan.

(b) If the mirepoix is not already browned, set it over a burner to brown it. Degrease the pan.

(c) Deglaze the pan with stock.

(d) Bring to a simmer and cook until reduced by about one-third. Stir in a starch slurry or a roux to thicken. Simmer until the desired texture is reached.

(e) Strain the gravy.

Figure 2.2 Carving roast chicken.

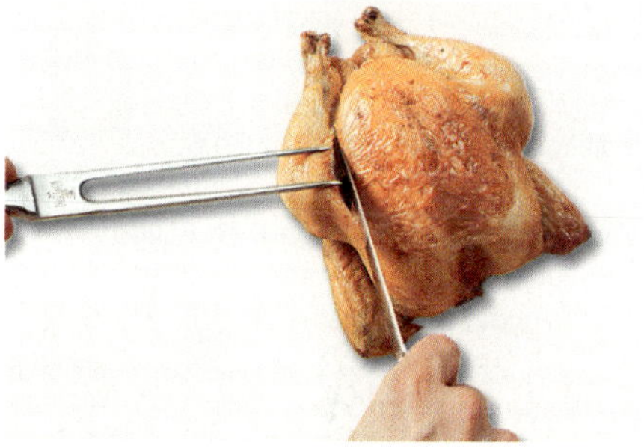

(a) Place the chicken on a clean, sanitary cutting board. Cut through the skin between the leg and the breast sections.

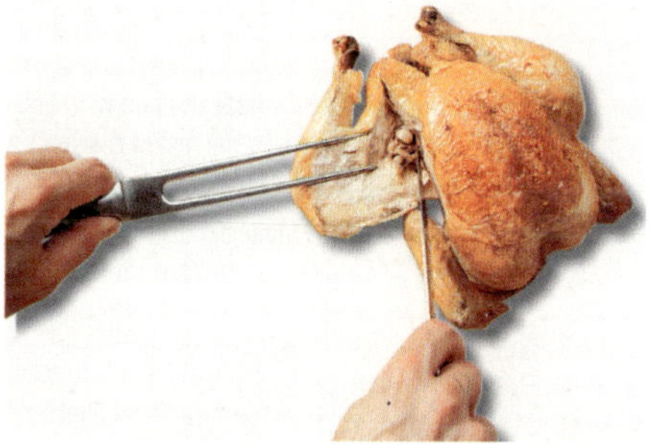

(b) Pull the leg away from the body of the chicken with the fork. Using the knife, cut between the thigh bone and the hip to separate the leg completely.

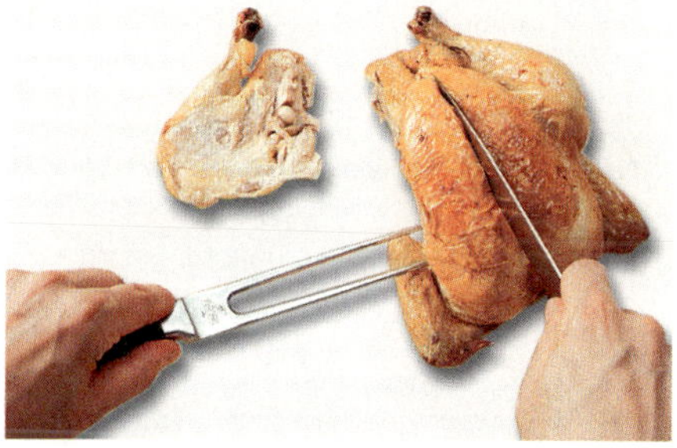

(c) Hold the chicken steady by bracing the backbone with the fork. Cut through the breast between the two halves, just to one side of the keel bone.

(d) Pull the breast section away from the bone. With the knife, cut through the joint where the wing bone is attached to the body. Separate the breast and wing section completely from the carcass. Repeat steps (a) through (d) on the other side of the chicken.

(e) Cut the wings from the breast portions and cut the drumsticks apart from the thighs.

Roast Turkey with Giblet Gravy

YIELD: ABOUT 7 LB (3.5 KG) SLICEABLE MEAT	PORTIONS:	PORTION SIZE:
	22	5 OZ (150 G)
	28	4 OZ (125 G)
	36	3 OZ (100 G)

U.S.	METRIC	INGREDIENTS	PROCEDURE
1	1	Turkey, dressed, 20 lb (10 kg)	1. Remove the giblets from the cavity of the turkey. Check inside the turkey to make sure it is well cleaned. Lock the wings in place by twisting the wing tips behind the back of the turkey.
to taste	to taste	Salt	2. Season the inside of the turkey with salt and pepper. Rub the skin thoroughly with oil.
to taste	to taste	Pepper	3. Place the turkey on one side in a roasting pan, on a rack if possible (see Note).
as needed	as needed	Oil	4. Place in an oven preheated to 325°F (165°C). (Lower temperatures are preferable if production schedule permits. See p. 16 for explanation.)
			5. Roast 1½ hours. Turn the turkey on the other side. Roast another 1½ hours. Baste turkey with drippings (fat only) every 30 minutes.
			6. While turkey is roasting, place turkey heart, gizzard, and neck in a saucepan. (Reserve the liver for another use, or add it to bread dressing.) Cover the giblets with water and simmer until very tender, 2–3 hours. Reserve the broth and the giblets for gravy.
		Mirepoix:	7. Turn the turkey breast-up. Place the mirepoix in the pan.
8 oz	250 g	Onions, chopped medium	8. Return the turkey to the oven and continue to roast. Baste occasionally by spooning the fat in the pan over the turkey.
4 oz	125 g	Carrots, chopped medium	9. The turkey is done when a thermometer inserted into the thickest part of the inside of the thigh reads 180°F (82°C). Total roasting time is about 5 hours. (See Chapter 1 for a discussion of how to determine doneness.)
4 oz	125 g	Celery, chopped medium	10. Remove the turkey from the roasting pan and let stand in a warm place at least 15 minutes before carving.
3 qt	3 L	Chicken stock, hot	11. Drain off and save the fat from the roasting pan.
6 oz	175 g	Bread flour	12. Set the roasting pan with the mirepoix and drippings on the range to reduce the moisture and brown the mirepoix. Brown lightly if a light gravy is desired. Brown heavily if a dark gravy is desired.
to taste	to taste	Salt	13. Deglaze the pan with about 1 qt (1 L) of the chicken stock. Pour into a saucepan with the rest of the stock and the giblet broth (from step 6). Bring to a simmer. Degrease well.
to taste	to taste	Pepper	14. Make a blond roux with the flour and 6 oz (175 g) of the fat from the roasting pan. Beat the roux into the gravy to thicken it.
			15. Simmer at least 15 minutes, or until the gravy is smooth and no raw flour taste remains. Strain and season.
			16. Chop or dice the giblets very fine and add to the gravy.
			17. Slice the turkey and serve desired portion with 2 fl oz (60 mL) gravy. See **Figure 2.3** for slicing techniques. For quantity service, see procedures demonstrated in **Figure 2.4**.

Per 5 ounces (141.75 g): Calories, 460; Protein, 68 g; Fat, 16 g (33% cal.); Cholesterol, 135 mg; Carbohydrates, 6 g; Fiber, 0 g; Sodium, 170 mg.

Note: Because of the difficulty of handling large turkeys, many chefs do not use a rack. Also, large turkeys are easier to turn if they are placed first on one side, then on the other, rather than breast-down.

For more even cooking, separate leg and thigh sections from breast section. Roast dark and light meat on separate pans, if many turkeys are being prepared. Remove each part from oven when done.

VARIATIONS

Roast Capons and Large Chickens

Prepare like roast turkey. Reduce roasting time, depending on size of bird. A 6-lb (2.7-kg) bird requires about 3 hours at 325°F (165°C).

Roast Turkey, Chicken, or Capon with Cream Gravy

Prepare as in basic recipe, but use half stock and half milk for the gravy instead of all stock. When gravy is finished, add 8 oz (250 mL) heavy cream.

Figure 2.3 Carving roast turkey.

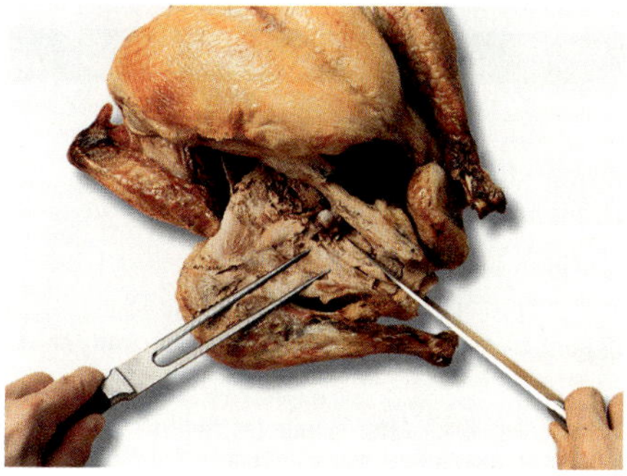

(a) Place the turkey on a clean, sanitary cutting board. Cut through the skin between the leg and the body. Pull the leg outward with a fork. The leg should pull off easily, but use the knife as necessary to separate the thigh from the hip.

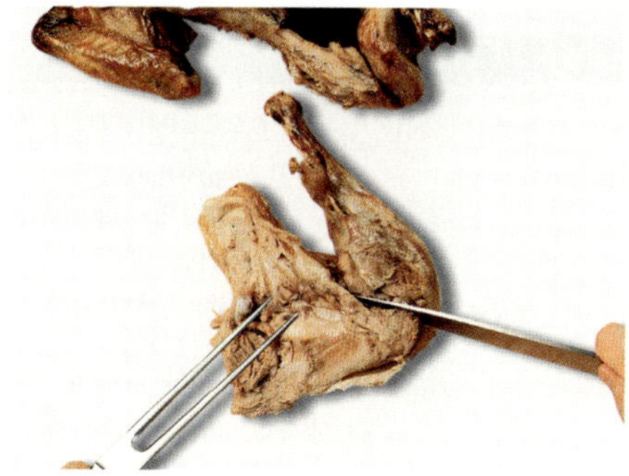

(b) Cut the drumstick and thigh apart at the joint. Repeat with the other leg.

(c) Cut the meat from the drumstick and thigh in thin slices.

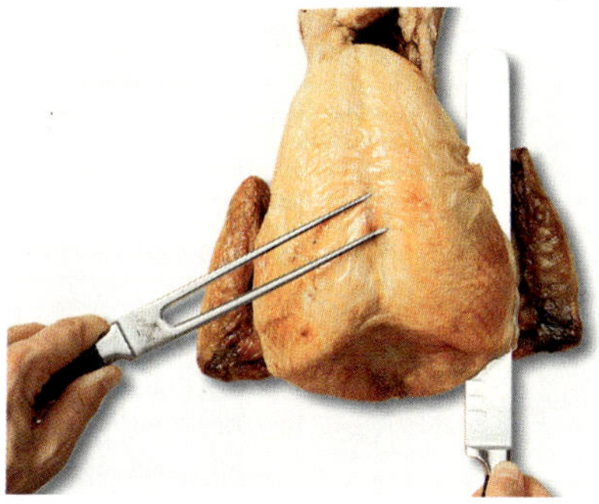

(d) Make a horizontal cut just above the wing, cutting all the way through to the bones of the body cavity. This cut helps the breast slices separate evenly.

(e) With long, smooth strokes, cut the breast into thin slices.

(f) When the slices become too large, change the angle of the knife slightly as shown. Continue until both sides of the breast are completely sliced.

(g) An alternative method is to cut off an entire half-breast in one piece. This piece can then be sliced as shown. Cut across the grain, holding the knife at an angle to get broader slices.

Figure 2.4 Quantity service of roast turkey and dressing.

(a) Using a scoop, place measured portions of baked dressing in hotel pans, as shown, or on sheet pans.

(b) Place measured portions of dark meat slices on top of the mounds of dressing.

(c) Place light meat slices on last, using the best-looking slices for the tops. Cover the pans. Refrigerate if they are to be held for later service. To serve, ladle a small amount of stock over the portions to keep them moist, and reheat, covered, in a moderate oven. Ladle 2 fl oz (60 mL) gravy over the portions when served.

Roast Duckling à l'Orange

PORTIONS: 8 PORTION SIZE: ¼ DUCKLING

U.S.	METRIC	INGREDIENTS
2	2	Ducklings, about 5 lb (2.3 kg) each
to taste	to taste	Salt
to taste	to taste	Pepper
1½ pt	720 mL	Demi-glace
3	3	Oranges
1½ fl oz	45 mL	Lemon juice
3 oz	90 g	Sugar
2 fl oz	60 mL	Wine vinegar, red or white
2 fl oz	60 mL	Orange liqueur, such as Curaçao (optional)
4 fl oz	120 mL	Chicken stock or white wine
		Garnish:
as desired	as desired	peeled orange sections (optional)

PROCEDURE

1. Make sure the ducklings are well cleaned. Use the neck, gizzard, and heart in preparing the sauce (step 5); save the liver for another use.
2. Season the cavities with salt and pepper.
3. Place the ducks breast-up on a rack in a roasting pan. (*Caution:* Do not use baking sheets or shallow pans. The pans must be deep enough to hold the large quantity of fat from the ducks.)
4. Place the pan in an oven heated to 450°F (230°C). After 15 minutes, reduce heat to 375°F (190°C) and continue roasting until the ducks are done, about 1½ hours in all. (See discussion of roasting temperatures on pp. 16–17.)
5. While the duck is roasting, prepare the sauce. Add the duck neck and giblets (except liver) to the demi-glace and simmer slowly about 1 hour, or until reduced to 1 pt (500 mL). Strain. Keep the sauce hot.
6. Peel the zest from the oranges in long strips. Cut them into julienne (or use a zester). Blanch the zests in boiling water 5 minutes. Drain and cool in ice water. Drain again and reserve the zest.
7. Squeeze enough juice from the oranges to measure 4 fl oz (120 mL). Add to the lemon juice and set aside.
8. Make a gastrique: Heat the sugar in a small saucepan over low heat until it melts. As soon as it turns a golden caramel color, remove from the heat, cool briefly, and add the vinegar and fruit juices. Simmer until the caramel is dissolved and the liquid is reduced by half.
9. Add the demi-glace and bring to a simmer.
10. If the sauce is too thin, adjust the consistency by adding a little more demi-glace and reducing. The sauce should be just thick enough to coat lightly. It should not be heavy.
11. If desired, add the liqueur and simmer a few minutes.
12. When the ducklings are done, remove them from the pan. (Check to be sure they are done by pouring the juices in the cavity into a pan. There should be no trace of pink in the juices.)
13. Drain off all the fat from the roasting pan.
14. Deglaze the pan with the stock or wine, stirring to dissolve all the brown drippings.
15. Reduce the liquid by half. Degrease and strain into the sauce.
16. Cut the ducklings into 8 pieces each.
17. To serve, place 1 breast piece and 1 leg piece on each plate, garnish the top with some of the blanched orange peels, and ladle on 2 fl oz (60 mL) sauce. Garnish the plate with orange sections, if desired.

Per serving: Calories, 900; Protein, 46 g; Fat, 71 g (71% cal.); Cholesterol, 215 mg; Carbohydrates, 20 g; Fiber, 1 g; Sodium, 200 mg.

VARIATIONS

Ducklings may be roasted following steps 1–4 of the basic recipe and served without a sauce, with a pre-prepared Bigarade Sauce, or simply with applesauce. Special seasonings create different products, such as the following recipe:

Roast Duckling, Bohemian Style

Season the cavity of each duckling with salt, pepper, and about ½ tsp (2 mL) caraway seeds. Place on rack in roasting pan and season the breast with salt, pepper, and another ½ tsp (2 mL) caraway. Roast as in the basic recipe. Serve without sauce, but Braised Red Cabbage and Potato Dumplings or Spaetzle.

Roast Goose

Roast goose at a continuous low temperature of 350°F (175°C). Because goose is much larger than duckling, the roasting time is long enough for the skin to crisp and brown at a low roasting temperature. Plan 20–25 minutes per pound for roasting time, but determine doneness by minimum internal cooking temperature of 165°F (74°C).

Stuffed Chicken Legs with Pecan Butter

PORTIONS: 6 PORTION SIZE: 1 CHICKEN LEG

U.S.	METRIC	INGREDIENTS	PROCEDURE
1 oz	30 g	Shallots, chopped fine	1. Sweat the shallots and garlic in the butter. Do not let them brown. Cool thoroughly.
1 small clove	1 small clove	Garlic, chopped fine	
¼ oz	7 g	Butter	
2 oz	60 g	Pecans, chopped fine	2. Combine the cooled shallot mixture, pecans, soft butter, bread crumbs, salt, and pepper in a bowl. Mix together.
2 oz	60 g	Butter, soft	
1 tbsp	15 ml	Parsley, chopped	
½ oz	15 g	Dry bread crumbs, preferably panko (see Note)	
to taste	to taste	Salt	
to taste	to taste	Pepper	
6	6	Large chicken legs (drumstick and thigh in one piece)	3. Partially bone the chicken legs as shown in **Figure 2.5**, removing the thigh bone but leaving in the drumstick bone. 4. Stuff the legs with the pecan mixture as shown in the illustration. 5. Arrange the legs, skin side up, in a pan (such as a baking pan or sauté pan) just large enough to hold them. It is not necessary to tie them if baked this way; they should retain their shape and hold the stuffing. 6. Bake at 400°F (200°C) until their internal temperature reaches 165°F (74°C). 7. If the chicken needs more color, brown under a salamander or broiler. 8. Remove the chicken from the pan and keep warm while you prepare the pan juices.
to taste	to taste	Salt	
to taste	to taste	Pepper	
8 fl oz	240 mL	Chicken stock	9. Degrease the pan in which the chicken was cooked. Deglaze with the stock. Reduce by half. 10. Add the demi-glace. Reduce by one-third. Strain and season to taste. 11. Plate the chicken legs. If desired, cut them in half and arrange to display the stuffing. 12. Moisten each portion with about 1 fl oz (30 mL) of the pan juices.
8 fl oz	240 mL	Demi-glace	
to taste	to taste	Salt	
to taste	to taste	Pepper	

Per serving: Calories, 570; Protein, 47 g; Fat, 40 g (64% cal.); Cholesterol, 185 mg; Carbohydrates, 4 g; Fiber, 1 g; Sodium, 230 mg.

Note: Coarse, panko-style bread crumbs should be used to create a light texture for the stuffing. Each chicken leg will hold about 1 oz (30 g) stuffing made with panko. If finer crumbs are used, the amount of stuffing may need to be increased, as the stuffing will be denser.

VARIATIONS

Chicken breasts can be used instead of legs. Flatten the breasts with a meat mallet, stuff, and roll up starting from a long side.

Many mixtures can be used for stuffing in place of the pecan butter. The following are a few suggestions:

Mushroom duxelles

Mixture of dried fruits, such as prunes and apricots, soaked and simmered until soft, mixed with browned almond slices and sautéed minced shallot

Lightly steamed mixed vegetables julienne or brunoise, seasoned with fresh herbs and mixed with grated parmesan cheese.

Stuffed Chicken Legs with Pecan Butter

Figure 2.5 Boning and stuffing a chicken leg.

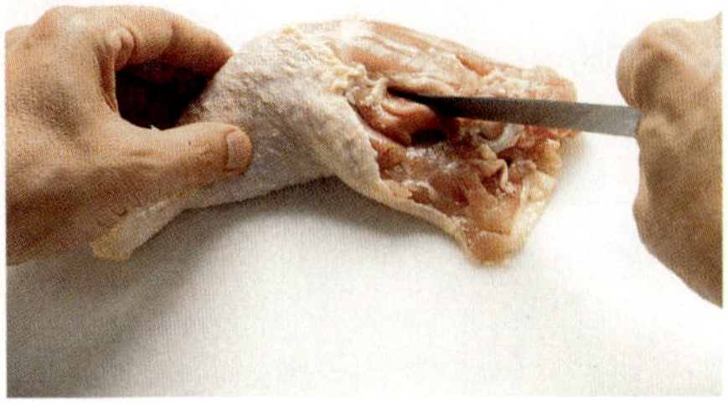

(a) Make a shallow cut along the thigh bone.

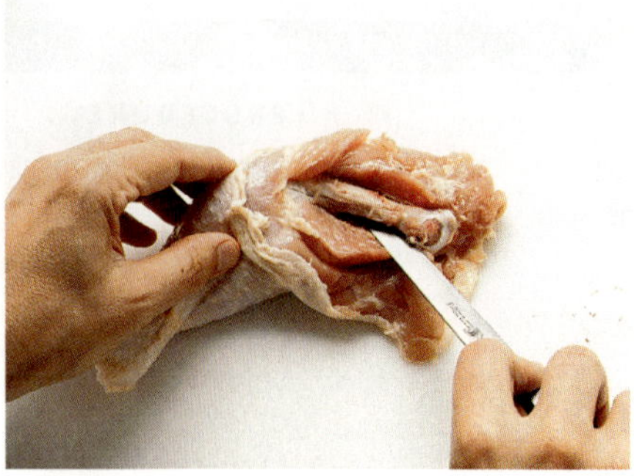

(b) Continue to cut along the bone to free it from the meat.

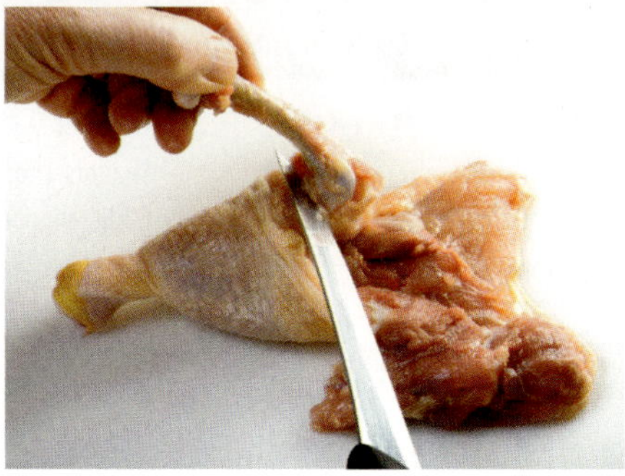

(c) The thigh bone is completely freed from the meat.

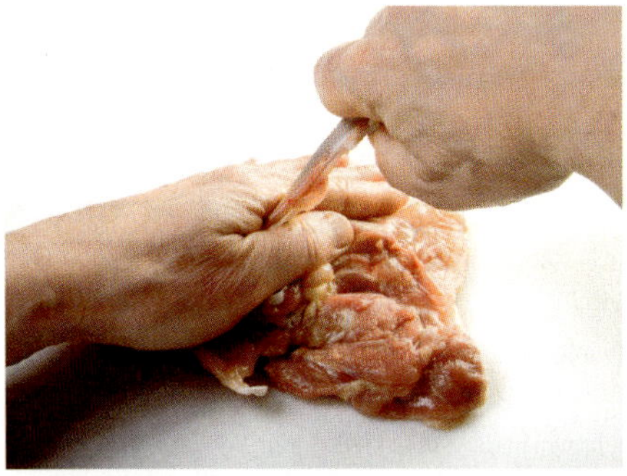

(d) Grasp the end of the thigh bone with one hand and wrap the fingers of the other hand around the bone near the joint. Pulling on the bone as shown separates some of the drumstick meat from the bone, making more room for stuffing.

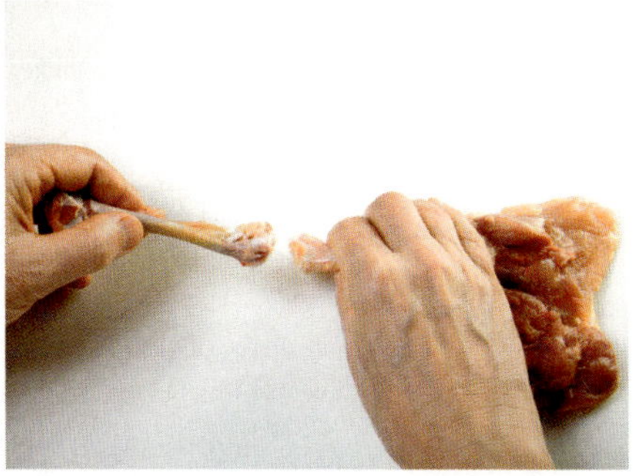

(e) Cut the thigh bone from the drumstick bone at the joint. The bones are shown here as separated.

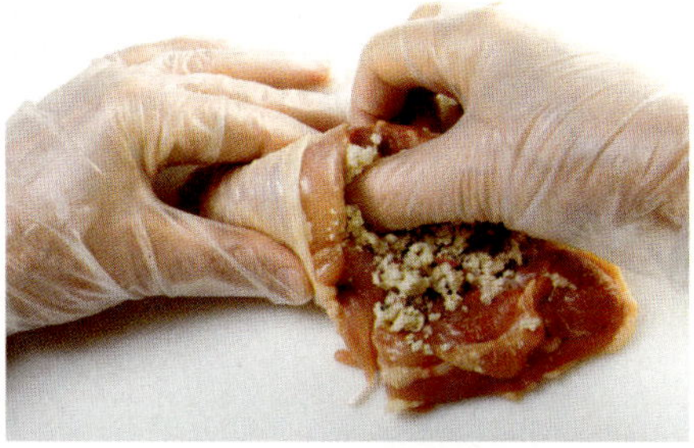

(f) For some of the stuffing into the space in the drumstick created in step d.

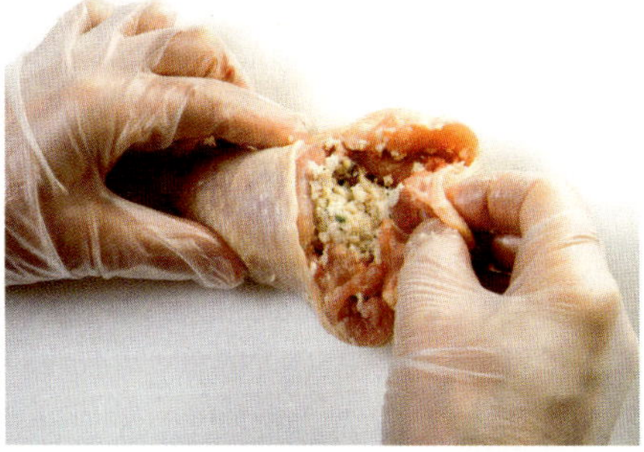

(g) Wrap the thigh meat around the stuffing.

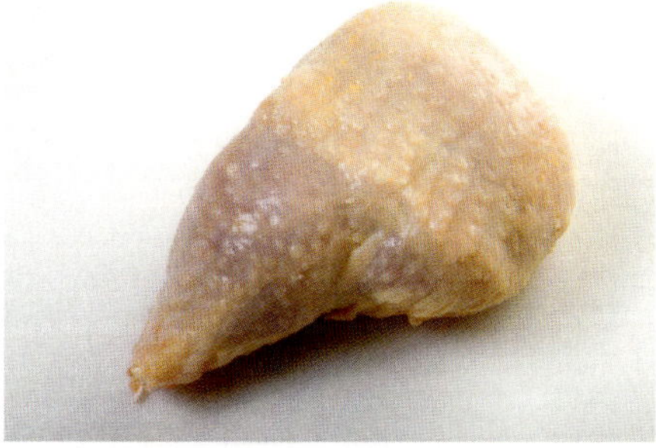

(h) Legs stuffed in this manner, if carefully handled, can be baked without tying and will retain their shape. Note that the end of the drumstick bone has also been cut off for a neater, more compact appearance.

Chicken Poêlé

PORTIONS: 4 PORTION SIZE: ¼ CHICKEN, 2 FL OZ (60 ML) SAUCE

U.S.	METRIC	INGREDIENTS	PROCEDURE
1	1	Whole chicken, about 4 lb (2 kg)	1. Season the cavity of the chicken with salt and pepper. Stuff the herbs into the cavity.
to taste	to taste	Salt	2. Truss the chicken. Season the skin with additional salt and pepper.
to taste	to taste	Pepper	
3 large sprigs	3 large sprigs	Parsley	
1 sprig	1 sprig	Fresh thyme	
2 sprigs	2 sprigs	Fresh tarragon	
		Raw matignon:	3. Place the matignon in the bottom of a brazier or casserole just large enough to hold the chicken.
4 oz	120 g	Onion, brunoise	4. Place the chicken, breast up, on the matignon and baste generously with butter.
2 oz	60 g	Carrot, brunoise	5. Cover the brazier or casserole and place in an oven preheated to 350°F (175°C). Let cook 1 hour. Two or three times during this period, uncover and brush the chicken with the butter and fat at the bottom of the pan.
2 oz	60 g	Celery, brunoise	6. After 1 hour of cooking, uncover the pan so the chicken will brown slightly. Continue to cook until the chicken is done, about 30 minutes more.
1 oz	30 g	Lean ham, cut paysanne	
2 oz, or more as needed	60 g, or more as needed	Butter, melted	
1 fl oz	30 mL	Madeira	7. Remove the chicken to a platter or another pan, cover, and keep warm while preparing the sauce.
1 pt	500 mL	Brown stock	8. Add the Madeira to the matignon and juices in the pan and simmer until the liquid is reduced slightly.
to taste	to taste	Salt	9. Add the brown stock. Bring to a boil and reduce by half.
to taste	to taste	Pepper	10. Strain the liquid through a china cap lined with several layers of cheesecloth (see Note).
			11. Degrease the liquid (see Note). Season to taste with salt and pepper.
			12. Carve the chicken. Plate as desired. Serve the juices in a sauceboat on the side.

Per serving: Calories, 750; Protein, 71 g; Fat, 46 g (56% cal.); Cholesterol, 250 mg; Carbohydrates, 8 g; Fiber, 1 g; Sodium, 540 mg.

Note: The liquid should not be degreased earlier than this step. The fat absorbs some of the flavors of the matignon and chicken during cooking, and some of these flavors are transferred back to the stock when it is reduced, resulting in a more flavorful sauce.

Escoffier directs that the sauce be strained before being degreased, so this recipe follows the classical procedure. Many chefs prefer to leave the vegetables in the sauce. If they were cut carefully, this is an attractive and flavorful variation.

If desired, the sauce may be thickened lightly with a slurry of arrowroot or cornstarch.

Chicken Poêlé

MATIGNON

A classical matignon is a mixture of aromatic ingredients used to add flavor to a meat or other product. It is similar to a mirepoix, but with several important differences. First, a pork product, usually ham, is added to the vegetables. Second, in most cases the mixture is sweat in butter and deglazed with Madeira or another wine.

Although a matignon is usually cooked in butter before use, Escoffier specifically directs that a raw matignon be used for the poêlé procedure, so we follow those instructions in the basic recipe included here. The matignon cooks fully during the poêléing process and contributes its flavor to the poultry and juices. Nevertheless, when preparing this dish, some chefs prefer to sweat the matignon in butter before adding it to the pan.

Broiling and Grilling

Tender, young poultry items may be cooked on the grill or broiler using the same procedure as for steaks and chops.

Use lower temperatures than for meats. The outside can be burned easily before the inside is cooked through. Poultry skin, in particular, browns and then burns very easily. For quantity production, broiled chicken is sometimes finished in the oven on sheet pans, preferably on racks.

Start poultry pieces skin side down. This helps keep flavorful juices from dripping out. Brush generously with melted butter or other fat before and during broiling.

Because the skin of broiled chicken is often eaten, it may be seasoned before cooking.

- Large or thick poultry items are not well suited to broiling and grilling because it takes so long for the heat to penetrate to the center and cook them through. For example, turkey thighs could be broiled if you kept the heat low enough, but, in practice, this is rarely done. On the other hand, if you boned them out and flattened them lightly with a cutlet mallet, you would make them more suitable for broiling and grilling.
- Grilled meat and poultry items are fairly simple, straightforward dishes, without the variety of ingredients and components you find in, for example, stews. However, there are several ways you can give variety to grilled poultry:

1. **Marinate the poultry or rub it with seasonings before cooking.**
   Keep in mind that marinade ingredients such as sugar and tomato burn easily, so use these with care. Also, herbs on the surface of the poultry burn easily. Charred rosemary can give a pleasant aroma to the food, but herbs such as parsley, if used in large quantity and allowed to burn, may taste like burned leaves.
2. **Baste with seasoned butter, marinade, or other flavorings during broiling.**
   Again, be careful with ingredients that burn easily. Use them only toward the end of cooking.
3. **Serve with an appropriate sauce or seasoned butter.**
   Flavored butters can be placed on top of grilled poultry, but sauces should be underneath or on the side so they don't detract from the crisp, browned skin.
4. **Select vegetable garnishes for variety and interest.**
   Well-chosen and carefully plated garnishes should be thought of as part of the whole presentation, not just something served on the side.

KEY POINTS TO REVIEW

- What techniques are used for seasoning and basting roast poultry?
- What are the factors to consider when determining the temperature at which to roast poultry?
- What poultry items are best suited to broiling and grilling?
- What are four ways to give flavor variety to broiled and grilled poultry?

Broiled Chicken

PORTIONS: 10 PORTION SIZE: ½ CHICKEN

U.S.	METRIC	INGREDIENTS
5	5	Broiler chickens, about 2 lb (900 g) each
4 fl oz	125 mL	Melted butter or oil
to taste	to taste	Salt
to taste	to taste	Pepper

Per serving: Calories, 600; Protein, 59 g; Fat, 39 g (60% cal.); Cholesterol, 215 mg; Carbohydrates, 0 g; Fiber, 0 g; Sodium, 270 mg.

PROCEDURE

1. Split the chickens in half and prepare for broiling, as shown in **Figure 1.4** (if chickens are large, cut into quarters).
2. Brush the chickens on both sides with melted butter. Season with salt and pepper.
3. Place the chickens skin side down on broiler rack (or on grill). Broil at moderately low heat until the chicken is half cooked and well browned on one side.
4. Turn the chickens over. (Use tongs or fork, but do not pierce the flesh with the fork.) Continue to broil until the chicken is done (no pink near thigh bone) and well browned on second side. (See first variation below for oven method.)
5. Remove from broiler. To serve, place half a chicken on dinner plate, skin side up.

VARIATIONS

Broiled Chicken, Quantity Method

For large quantities, or for bigger chickens (quartered instead of halved), use slightly higher heat (set the broiler rack higher), and broil until browned on both sides, as in basic recipe. Remove from broiler and place in baking pans or on sheet pans. Finish cooking in the oven at 325°–350°F (165°–175°C).

Broiled Rock Cornish Game Hen

Remove backbones from hens and prepare for broiling (see **Figure 1.4**). Broil as in the basic recipe for any of the variations. Serve 1 hen per portion.

Broiled Tarragon Chicken

Before brushing with melted butter, rub each chicken half with ¼ tsp (1 mL) dried tarragon and 1–2 tsp (5–10 mL) chopped fresh parsley.
Broil as in basic recipe.

Broiled Deviled Chicken (Poulet à la Diable)

When the chicken is almost completely cooked, brush the tops (skin side) lightly with about 1 tbsp (15 mL) mustard per portion and sprinkle with 1 oz (30 g) bread crumbs per portion. Return to the broiler to brown the crumbs. Serve with 2 fl oz (60 mL) Sauce Diable per portion.

Broiled Deviled Chicken

Chicken Paillard with Grilled Vegetables

PORTIONS: 12 PORTION SIZE: 1 CHICKEN BREAST, ABOUT 6 OZ (175 G)

U.S.	METRIC	INGREDIENTS
12	12	Boneless, skinless chicken breasts, about 6 oz (175 g) each
3	3	Garlic cloves, chopped
1 tbsp	15 mL	Fresh rosemary, chopped
1½ tsp	7 mL	Salt
½ tsp	2 mL	Pepper
3 fl oz	90 mL	Lemon juice
3 fl oz	90 mL	Olive oil
as desired	as desired	Grilled Vegetable Medley
12	12	Fresh rosemary sprigs

Per serving: Calories, 250; Protein, 34 g; Fat, 11 g (41% cal.); Cholesterol, 95 mg; Carbohydrates, 1 g; Fiber, 0 g; Sodium, 370 mg.

PROCEDURE

1. Place each chicken breast between sheets of plastic film. With a meat mallet, carefully pound to a uniform thickness of about ¼ in. (6 mm).
2. Combine the garlic, rosemary, salt, and pepper. Lightly rub the flattened chicken breasts on both sides with the mixture. Sprinkle both sides with the lemon juice, then with the olive oil. Let marinate 2–4 hours in the refrigerator.
3. Preheat a grill or broiler to very hot. Place the chicken breasts on the grill, skin side (that is, the side that had the skin on) down, and grill until about one-fourth done. Rotate on the grill, to mark. Continue to cook until about half done. Turn over and continue to grill until just cooked through.
4. Plate and serve at once with an assortment of grilled vegetables. Garnish each portion with a sprig of rosemary.

Paillard with Grilled Vegetables

Grilled Spiced Squab with Couscous and Fig Compote

PORTIONS: 12 PORTION SIZE: 1 SQUAB, PLUS GARNISH

U.S.	METRIC	INGREDIENTS
12	12	Whole squab
1 tbsp	15 mL	Salt
1 tbsp	15 mL	Quatre Épices
¾ tsp	3 mL	Dried thyme
¾ tsp	3 mL	Black pepper
as needed	as needed	Olive oil
3 pt	750 mL	Water
1½ tsp	7 mL	Salt
12 oz	375 g	Instant couscous (uncooked)
1 lb	500 g	Tender, young salad greens, such as mesclun
6 fl oz	175 mL	Basic Vinaigrette made with red wine vinegar and olive oil
36	36	Cherry tomatoes, cut in half
12 oz	360 g	Fig Compote

Per serving: Calories, 1300; Protein, 69 g; Fat, 94 g (68% cal.); Cholesterol, 325 mg; Carbohydrates, 42 g; Fiber, 5 g; Sodium, 1180 mg.

PROCEDURE

1. Split the squab for broiling, as shown in **Figure 1.4**, leaving the birds in one piece.
2. Combine the salt, spices, thyme, and pepper. Rub the squab with the spice mixture. Refrigerate several hours.
3. Brush the squab lightly with olive oil. Place on the grill or broiler, starting skin side down. Grill or broil, turning as necessary, until the breast portion is medium rare.
4. Combine the water and salt in a saucepan and bring to a boil. Stir in the couscous. Cover and let stand 5 minutes. Remove the cover and fluff with a kitchen fork.
5. Wash and drain the salad greens. Toss with the vinaigrette. Place a small mound of greens at the top of each dinner plate. Top with halved cherry tomatoes.
6. At the bottom center of each plate, place a small mound of couscous. In the center of the plate, above the couscous, place 1 oz (30 g) fig compote.
7. Split the squab in half. Place 1 half-squab on each side of the couscous.

VARIATION

Grilled Spiced Cornish Hen

Prepare and grill Cornish hens using the same procedure as in the basic recipe, but make sure the chicken is more thoroughly cooked.

Grilled Chicken with Garlic and Ginger

PORTIONS: 8 PORTION SIZE: APPROXIMATELY 12 OZ (375 G), BONE IN

U.S.	METRIC	INGREDIENTS	PROCEDURE
6–8 lb	2.8–3.6 kg	Chicken parts or halves, or whole Cornish hens	1. Cut the chickens into parts or halves for broiling. If using Cornish hens, split down the back and flatten, or cut into halves.
6 fl oz	180 mL	Lemon or lime juice	2. Combine the lemon or lime juice, oil, ginger, garlic, salt, and pepper to make a marinade.
2 fl oz	60 mL	Vegetable oil	3. Marinate the chicken 3–4 hours.
1 oz	30 g	Fresh ginger root, grated	
2 tsp	10 mL	Garlic, chopped fine	
to taste	to taste	Salt	
to taste	to taste	Pepper	
as needed	as needed	Melted butter	4. Remove the chicken from the marinade. Broil or grill the chicken until done. Baste with the marinade several times during cooking.
to taste	to taste	Ginger Oil (optional)	5. Shortly before the chicken is done, brush the pieces once or twice with melted butter.
			6. If desired, drizzle a few drops of ginger oil around the chicken after plating.

Per serving: Calories, 430; Protein, 42 g; Fat, 27 g (59% cal.); Cholesterol, 140 mg; Carbohydrates, 1 g; Fiber, 0 g; Sodium, 150 mg.

VARIATIONS

Substitute any of the following for the chicken parts in the above recipe or in any of the following variations:

Chicken or turkey brochettes (cubes of boneless meat on skewers)

Turkey paillards (broad slices of turkey breast pounded thin)

Boneless chicken breast

Chicken or turkey thighs, boned out and lightly pounded

Turkey cutlets (thick slices of turkey breast)

Southwestern Grilled Chicken

Substitute the following ingredients for the marinade in the basic recipe:

4 oz	120 g	Tomato, puréed
4 tsp	20 mL	Very finely chopped jalapeño
4 tbsp	60 mL	Chopped cilantro
3 fl oz	90 mL	Red wine vinegar

Grilled Chicken Oriental Style

Substitute the following ingredients for the marinade in the basic recipe. Brush the chicken with the marinade frequently during grilling.

8 fl oz	250 mL	Soy sauce
2 fl oz	60 mL	Rice wine or sherry
2 fl oz	60 mL	Chicken stock or water
1 fl oz	30 mL	Lemon juice
2 tsp	10 mL	Sugar
4 tsp	20 mL	Ginger root, grated

Spicy Barbecue-Style Grilled Chicken

Substitute the following ingredients for the marinade in the basic recipe. Toss the chicken pieces by hand so they are well coated.

2 fl oz	60 mL	Worcestershire sauce
1 fl oz	30 mL	Red wine vinegar
4 tsp	20 mL	Paprika
2 tsp	10 mL	Chili powder
1 tsp	5 mL	Dry mustard
1 tsp	5 mL	Crushed garlic
½ tsp	2 mL	Black pepper
1 tsp	5 mL	Salt

Grilled Chicken Marinated in Yogurt and Spices

Substitute the following ingredients for the marinade in the basic recipe. Marinate the chicken overnight.

8 oz	250 g	Unflavored yogurt
2 oz	60 g	Onion, grated
½ tsp	2 mL	Crushed garlic
½ tsp	2 mL	Grated ginger root
1 tsp	5 mL	Ground cumin
½ tsp	2 mL	Ground cardamom
pinch	pinch	Mace
½ tsp	2 mL	Cayenne
½ tsp	2 mL	Black pepper
1 tsp	5 mL	Salt

TANDOORI CHICKEN

The *tandoor* is a clay oven widely used in northern India. With wood or coal as a fuel, it cooks foods quickly at a high temperature. Tandoori chicken is especially popular in Indian restaurants in North America and Europe. In the original version, whole chickens are marinated in yogurt and spices, usually strongly colored with a red food coloring, then impaled on skewers and lowered into the tandoor. Western kitchens approximate this dish by cooking the chicken on a grill or in a very hot oven.

The marinade for Grilled Chicken Marinated in Yogurt and Spices (above) is similar to typical marinades for tandoori chicken, but without the red coloring.

Jerk Spice Mixture

YIELD: 1 CUP (240 ML)

U.S.	METRIC	INGREDIENTS
4 tbsp	60 mL	Ground allspice
4 tbsp	60 mL	Dried thyme
3 tbsp	45 mL	Black pepper
1 tbsp	15 mL	Nutmeg
1 tbsp	15 mL	Cinnamon
2 oz	60 g	Salt

PROCEDURE

1. Combine all ingredients and mix well.
2. Store in an airtight container until needed.

Per serving: Calories, 45; Protein, 1 g; Fat, 1 g (16% cal.); Cholesterol, 0 mg; Carbohydrates, 11 g; Fiber, 5 g; Sodium, 4930 mg.

Note: Traditional Jamaican jerk relies on fresh Scotch bonnet chiles rather than dried chiles for its heat. Therefore, this formula doesn't include cayenne or other chile spices. If you wish a spice blend that can be used to give a jerk flavor to foods without a complete marination, add 1½ tsp (7 mL) cayenne, or to taste, to the spice mix. In addition, 2 tbsp (30 mL) each garlic powder and onion powder may be added to the mix if fresh garlic and onion will not be used in cooking.

JAMAICAN JERK

Jerk is a traditional Jamaican cooking style in which meats are marinated in a mixture that includes allspice and Scotch bonnet peppers, as well as a variety of other spices, before barbecuing or grilling over a smoking fire. Pork, goat, and chicken are the most popular foods cooked by this method, but beef, fish, and sausage are also flavored and grilled this way.

Jerk Chicken

PORTIONS: 8 PORTION SIZE: 10 OZ (300 G)

U.S.	METRIC	INGREDIENTS
1 cup	240 mL	Jerk Spice Mix (above)
4–8	4–8	Scotch bonnet chiles, stemmed, seeded, and chopped (see Note)
8	8	Garlic cloves, chopped
8	8	Scallions, sliced
6 oz	180 g	Onion, chopped
1 oz	30 g	Brown sugar
4 fl oz	120 mL	Lime juice
3 fl oz	90 mL	Vegetable oil
2 fl oz	60 mL	Soy sauce
5 lb	2.4 kg	Chicken parts

PROCEDURE

1. Combine the spice mix, chiles, garlic, scallions, sugar, lime juice, oil, and soy sauce in a blender. Blend to a paste. (Do half of the ingredients at a time if you have a small blender, and combine the two batches.)
2. Place the chicken in a nonreactive container. Add the spice mixture and stir so all pieces of chicken are coated.
3. Marinate, refrigerated, at least 1 hour but up to 48 hours.
4. Before cooking, remove from the marinade and let stand at room temperature 20–30 minutes.
5. Grill over low heat until done. Alternatively, cook in a smoker oven at 300°F (150°C).

Per serving: Calories, 360; Protein, 39 g; Fat, 21 g (54% cal.); Cholesterol, 125 mg; Carbohydrates, 2 g; Fiber, 0 g; Sodium, 170 mg.

Note: Wear gloves when handling the chiles. They are extremely hot and can burn the skin. Reduce or increase the quantity of chiles according to taste and tolerance for spicy-hot foods.

Jerk Chicken with Grilled Pineapple

Sautéing, Pan-Frying, and Deep-Frying

Because chicken and turkey are lean, tender meats, cooking in fat is an appropriate and popular way to prepare them. The procedures for sautéing and pan-frying meats apply to chicken as well. Also, please note the following guidelines that apply particularly to poultry and game bird items.

Tender game birds and specialty poultry items may also be cooked by sautéing or pan-frying. For most game birds, only the breasts are usually cooked by these methods. The legs are small and have more connective tissue, so they require longer cooking. They are often braised or roasted until tender and served as garnish for the breast, either bone-in or as boneless meat.

For lean items, such as squab, partridge, and quail, the breasts are best if not cooked well done but rather kept somewhat pink inside, or even rare, to preserve moisture. Breast of pheasant and guinea may also be served with a little pink in the interior, although because this meat is so similar to the white meat of chicken, many customers may prefer it well done.

Dark red poultry, such as ostrich and emu steaks and breast of duck, are also lean and most often served medium to medium rare. Remember, however, that the minimum safe temperature for ostrich and emu is 155°F (68°C). Duck breasts present a special case for pan-frying because of the heavy layer of fat between the skin and the meat. Pan-fried duck breasts are started skin side down and cooked until much of the fat is rendered and the skin is crisp. This takes several minutes, or most of the cooking time. To finish, they are turned over and cooked skin side up for just a few moments, until they reach the desired doneness.

Sautéing

1. Boneless chicken breasts, thin slices of turkey breast, and other quick-cooking items are ideal for sautéing.

2. Larger items, such as bone-in chicken cut into eighths, are harder to cook to doneness by sautéing because they need longer cooking times. Such items are often browned by sautéing and then finished by another method, such as baking or braising. Breasts of game birds, on the other hand, may be cooked rare or medium and can thus be easily cooked from start to finish on the stovetop.

3. Classical cuisine features preparations for chicken called *sautés*, many of which are actually made by braising. The basic procedure for sautéing meats is used, except the chicken is only partially cooked by sautéing. It is then finished by simmering briefly in the sauce made by deglazing the pan. Recipes for this kind of preparation are included under "Braising," page 42.

Pan-Frying

1. Pan-fried chicken is usually breaded or floured before cooking for even browning and crispness.

2. About ¼ inch (½ cm) or more of fat is needed in the pan to pan-fry chicken.

3. The side that will face up on the plate should be browned first for best appearance. This is called the *presentation side*. For chicken pieces, it is usually the skin side.

4. After browning on all sides over moderately high heat, lower the heat so the chicken cooks to doneness without overbrowning. Pan-fried chicken takes 30 to 45 minutes to cook.

Deep-Frying

1. The procedure for deep-frying is like that for pan-frying, except the item doesn't have to be turned because it is submerged in the hot fat.
2. Pieces from small chickens (under 2½ lb/l kg) are best for deep-frying. Larger pieces require such a long cooking time that the surface may brown too much. If necessary, fried items may be finished in the oven.
3. Fry chicken at 325° to 350°F (160° to 175°C) for even cooking.

Pan-Fried Chicken

PORTIONS: 24 PORTION SIZE: ½ CHICKEN
48 ¼ CHICKEN

U.S.	METRIC	INGREDIENTS
12	12	Chickens, 2½ lb (1.1 kg) each
1 lb	450 g	Flour
5 tsp	25 mL	Salt
1 tsp	5 mL	White pepper
as needed	as needed	Oil

Per ½ chicken: Calories, 820; Protein, 75 g; Fat, 51 g (57% cal.); Cholesterol, 235 mg; Carbohydrates, 11 g; Fiber, 0 g; Sodium, 580 mg.

PROCEDURE

1. Cut chickens into 8 pieces, as shown in **Figure 1.5**.
2. Place the flour in a small hotel pan and season with salt and pepper.
3. Pour about ¼ in. (0.5 cm) oil into enough heavy iron skillets to hold all the chicken pieces in a single layer. Heat over moderately high heat.
4. Dredge the chicken pieces in the seasoned flour and shake off excess.
5. Place the pieces skin side down in the hot oil. Let the pieces fall away from you to avoid splashing hot oil on yourself.
6. Fry the chicken until golden brown on the bottom. Turn the pieces with tongs and brown the other side.
7. Lower the heat slightly to avoid overbrowning. Continue to cook the chickens, turning once or twice more, until cooked through. Breast meat cooks faster than leg meat—remove it when it is done. Total cooking time will be 20–40 minutes, depending on the size of the chickens and the temperature of the fat.
8. Remove the chicken from the pan and drain well. Place on hot dinner plates or hold for service in counter pans. Do not cover pans or hold too long, or chicken will lose its crispness.

VARIATIONS

For slightly crustier, browner chicken, dip in milk before dredging in flour.

Alternative Method, Quantity Service: Brown chickens in hot oil as in basic recipe. Place on sheet pans or in baking pans skin side up, and finish cooking in a 350°F (175°C) oven.

Country-Style Fried Chicken

Fry chickens as in basic recipe. For 24 portions: Pour all but 4 oz (125 g) fat from the pans. Add 4 oz (125 g) flour and make a blond roux. Stir in 2½ qt (2.5 L) milk and bring to a boil. Stir constantly as the gravy thickens. Simmer a few minutes to eliminate all raw starch taste, and season with salt and white pepper. Adjust the consistency with stock, water, or additional milk if necessary. Strain. Serve the chicken with gravy and mashed potatoes.

Sautéed Boneless Breast of Chicken with Mushroom Sauce

PORTIONS: 10 PORTION SIZE: 1 CHICKEN BREAST, ABOUT 4 OZ (125 G), 2 FL OZ (60 ML) SAUCE

U.S.	METRIC	INGREDIENTS
2 oz	60 g	Clarified butter
10	10	Boneless, skinless chicken breasts from 5 chickens, 3½ lb (1.6 kg) each
to taste	to taste	Salt
to taste	to taste	White pepper
2 oz	60 g	Flour for dredging
to taste		
to taste		

PROCEDURE

1. Add enough clarified butter to a sauté pan to just cover the bottom with a thin film. Place on the range over moderate heat.
2. While the pan is heating, season the chicken breasts and dredge in flour. Shake off excess flour.
3. Place the breasts in the hot pan, presentation side (that is, the side that had the skin) down.
4. Sauté over moderate heat until lightly browned and about half cooked. The heat must be regulated so the chicken doesn't brown too fast.
5. Turn the chicken over and complete the cooking.
6. Remove the chicken from the pan and place on hot dinner plates for service. Keep warm.

U.S.	METRIC	INGREDIENTS
10 oz	300 g	White mushrooms, sliced
1 fl oz	30 mL	Lemon juice
2½ cups	600 mL	Suprême Sauce, hot

7. Add the mushrooms to the pan and sauté briefly. After a few seconds, before the mushrooms start to darken, add the lemon juice. Toss the mushrooms in the pan as they sauté.
8. Add the suprême sauce to the pan and simmer a few minutes, or until reduced to the proper consistency. (The juices from the mushrooms will dilute the sauce.)
9. Ladle 2 fl oz (60 mL) sauce over each portion and serve immediately.

Per serving: Calories, 360; Protein, 36 g; Fat, 20 g (51% cal.); Cholesterol, 145 mg; Carbohydrates, 8 g; Fiber, 1 g; Sodium, 200 mg.

VARIATIONS

Alternative (Quick) Method: Sauté the chicken as in basic recipe. Plate and ladle 2 fl oz (60 mL) prepared Mushroom Sauce (made with suprême sauce as a base) over each portion.

Other sauces based on chicken stock may be used in place of mushroom sauce to serve with sautéed chicken breasts, including suprême, aurora, Hungarian, and ivory.

Sautéed Chicken Breast with Ivory Sauce, Broccoli, Parisienne Potatoes

Deep-Fried Chicken

PORTIONS: 24 PORTION SIZE: ½ CHICKEN

U.S.	METRIC	INGREDIENTS
12	12	Chickens, about 2 lb (900 g) each
		Standard Breading Procedure (see Note):
8 oz	250 g	Flour
2 tsp	10 mL	Salt
1 tsp	5 mL	White pepper
2	2	Eggs
2½ cups	600 mL	Milk
1½ lb	750 g	Dry bread crumbs

Per serving: Calories, 880; Protein, 63 g; Fat, 58 g (61% cal.); Cholesterol, 205 mg; Carbohydrates, 22 g; Fiber, 1 g; Sodium, 520 mg.

Note: Quantities given for breading materials are only guidelines. You may need more or less depending on the shapes of the chicken pieces, the care used in breading, and other factors. In any case, you need enough so even the last piece to be breaded can be coated easily and completely.

PROCEDURE

1. Cut chickens into 8 pieces.
2. Set up breading station: seasoned flour, egg wash, and crumbs.
3. Pass the chicken through the Standard Breading Procedure.
4. Heat the fat in a deep fryer to 325°–350°F (165°–175°C).
5. Fry the chicken until golden brown and cooked through. Fry light meat and dark meat pieces in separate baskets, as the light meat cooks faster.
6. Remove from the fat, drain well, and serve immediately.

VARIATIONS

Alternative Method: For larger chickens or for quantity service, brown the chicken in the deep fryer. Drain, place on sheet pans, and finish in the oven at 350°F (175°C).

Fried Chicken Maryland

Fry the chicken as in basic recipe. Serve each portion with the following sauce and garnish:

2 fl oz (60 mL) cream sauce, suprême sauce, or horseradish sauce made with béchamel, placed on the plate under the chicken

2 strips crisp bacon, placed in a cross on top of the chicken

2 Corn Fritters

2 banana quarters, breaded and fried

Fried Chicken Breast Strips

Cut boneless, skinless chicken breasts into strips about ¾ in. (2 cm) wide.
Bread and fry as in basic recipe. Serve with desired dipping sauce, such as barbecue sauce or blue cheese dressing.

Tangerine-Marinated Breast of Duck

PORTIONS: 12 PORTION SIZE: 6 OZ (180 G)

U.S.	METRIC	INGREDIENTS
12	12	Boneless duck breast halves, skin on, about 6 oz (180 g) each
1½ oz	45 mL	Shallots, chopped fine
1 fl oz	30 mL	Soy sauce
4 fl oz	120 mL	Tangerine juice
½ tsp	2 mL	Grated tangerine zest
¼ tsp	1 mL	Cinnamon
¼ tsp	1 mL	Crushed star anise

PROCEDURE

1. With a sharp knife, score the duck skin in a diamond pattern. Cut through the skin and into the layer of fat but not into the meat. (This is easiest to do if the duck is chilled.)
2. In a nonreactive container, combine the shallots, soy sauce, tangerine juice and zest, cinnamon, and star anise and mix together.
3. Add the duck breasts, turning them to coat on both sides. Refrigerate 2–4 hours.
4. Remove the breasts from the marinade. Pat them dry with clean towels. Discard the marinade and any pieces of star anise clinging to the meat.
5. Pan-fry the breasts skin side down in a sauté pan over moderately high heat about 6 minutes, or until the skin is well browned and crisp and much of the fat has rendered. Turn over and pan-fry another 4 minutes. The breasts should still be rare.
6. Remove from the pans and let rest 5 minutes in a warm place.

U.S.	METRIC	INGREDIENTS
1 lb 8 oz	720 g	Wheatberries with Pecans (prepared without poblanos)
as needed	as needed	Tangerine suprêmes)
12 fl oz	360 mL	Oriental Vinaigrette (optional)

7. Place 2 oz (60 g) wheatberries on each plate.
8. Cut each duck breast diagonally into thin slices. Fan the slices out, leaning them against the mound of wheatberries.
9. Top the wheatberries with a few tangerine suprêmes.
10. If desired, drizzle a little vinaigrette onto the plate around the duck breast.

Per serving: Calories, 340; Protein, 32 g; Fat, 16 g (43% cal.); Cholesterol, 165 mg; Carbohydrates 16 g; Fiber, 3 g; Sodium, 510 mg.

Tangerine-Marinated Breast of Duck

Chicken Teriyaki

PORTIONS: 16 PORTION SIZE: 1 CHICKEN BREAST OR THIGH

U.S.	METRIC	INGREDIENTS
		Teriyaki sauce:
3 fl oz	75 mL	Sake
7 fl oz	175 mL	Soy sauce
6 fl oz	150 mL	Mirin (sweet rice wine)
2 tbsp	25 mL	Sugar
as needed	as needed	Vegetable oil
16	16	Boneless chicken breasts or thighs, skin on or off as desired

Per serving: Calories, 280; Protein, 31 g; Fat, 11 g (38% cal.); Cholesterol, 85 mg; Carbohydrates, 6 g; Fiber, 0 g; Sodium, 780 mg.

PROCEDURE

1. Combine the sake, soy sauce, mirin, and sugar. Heat to a simmer to dissolve the sugar. Cool.
2. Heat a thin film of oil in a skillet. Put in the chicken pieces, skin side down. Cook until browned and half done. Turn and cook the other side.
3. Remove the chicken and degrease the pan.
4. Deglaze the pan with the teriyaki sauce and bring the sauce to a boil.
5. Return the chicken to the pan. Turn it in the pan until it is lightly glazed.
6. Remove the chicken from the pan and reserve the sauce. Cut each piece of chicken crosswise, on the diagonal, into strips ½ in. (1 cm) wide.
7. Plate the chicken, keeping each piece assembled in its original form. Spoon a little of the sauce on top.

VARIATIONS

Other items, such as small beefsteaks, fish fillets, and scallops, can be cooked this way. In the case of fish fillets, keep the skin on, if possible, and use the skin side as the presentation side.

TERIYAKI

The Japanese word *yaki* is often translated as "grilled," although it is less specific in Japanese and is also used to mean "pan-broiled" or "griddled." ***Teriyaki*** can be translated as "glaze-grilled." In the West, the term usually refers to a meat or fish that is marinated in a soy sauce mixture before being cooked, and sometimes the meat is even simmered in the sauce. In Japan, however, the item is usually not marinated, and the teriyaki sauce is applied only at the end of cooking to give the food an attractive and flavorful glaze.

Japanese food is, in general, delicately seasoned. Western palates, however, usually demand more seasoning. For example, few Japanese would douse a bowl of plain rice with soy sauce, as Westerners tend to do in Asian restaurants.

For a more Western-style teriyaki, you may marinate the chicken in the accompanying recipe in the teriyaki sauce for several hours or overnight before pan-frying it. The result, however, will not be as authentic.

Chicken Breasts Parmesan

PORTIONS: 10 PORTION SIZE: 1 CHICKEN BREAST, ABOUT 4 OZ (125 G)

U.S.	METRIC	INGREDIENTS	PROCEDURE
3 oz	90 g	Flour	1. Place the flour in a small counter pan and season with salt and white pepper.
1 tsp	5 mL	Salt	2. Beat the eggs in a bowl and mix in the parmesan cheese and milk. Place the bowl next to the seasoned flour when ready for service.
½ tsp	2 mL	White pepper	
4	4	Eggs	
3 oz	90 g	Parmesan cheese, grated	
1 fl oz	30 mL	Milk	
10	10	Boneless, skinless chicken breasts from 5 chickens, 3½ lb (1.6 kg) each	3. Flatten the chicken breasts lightly with a meat mallet.
4 oz	125 mL	Clarified butter	4. If cooking to order, select a sauté pan just large enough to hold in a single layer the number of portions being cooked. If cooking all the chicken breasts at once, use a very large skillet or enough sauté pans to hold all the breasts in a single layer.
			5. Place the pan (or pans) over moderate heat and add enough clarified butter to just cover the bottom.
			6. Dip the chicken breasts in the flour and shake off excess. Dip in the cheese batter, turning the pieces to coat both sides.
			7. Cook over moderate heat until the bottom is golden. Turn the pieces over. Reduce the heat to low and continue to cook until the chicken is cooked through. It should feel somewhat firm when done.
20	20	Lemon slices	8. Place each portion on a hot plate and top with 2 lemon slices. Serve immediately.

Per serving: Calories, 350; Protein, 40 g; Fat, 18 g (47% cal.); Cholesterol, 190 mg; Carbohydrates, 5 g; Fiber, 0 g; Sodium, 510 mg.

VARIATION

Alternative Method: As soon as the first side is browned, turn the pieces over, cover the pans, and place in an oven at 350°F (175°C) for 8–10 minutes. This procedure requires less attention from the cook, an advantage in busy kitchens.

Simmering and Poaching

Simmering and poaching are both methods of cooking in a liquid. The major difference is the temperature. In simmering, the liquid is a little below the boiling point and bubbling very gently. In poaching, the temperature is even lower, and the liquid is not really bubbling. Also, less liquid is usually used for poaching.

Simmering

1. The simmering method is used to cook fowl and other tough items that require long cooking in moist heat to be made tender. Cooking time is about 2½ hours.
2. The cooking liquid is usually water seasoned with salt and, most often, mirepoix and herbs as well.
3. Simmered fowl yields a rich, flavorful broth. The meat can be used for soups, creamed dishes, casseroles, salads, and similar preparations.
4. Start the fowl in cold water if a flavorful soup is your main objective. Start with hot water to retain more flavor in the meat.

Poaching

1. The poaching method is used to gently cook tender poultry in order to retain moisture and to develop a light, subtle flavor. Cooking time is usually short because the product is naturally tender.
2. The cooking liquid is usually stock, sometimes with the addition of wine and other flavorings and seasonings. Cold liquid is added to the poultry product in the pan to cover partway, and the pan must be covered to retain steam. Covering also helps prevent drying and discoloration.
3. After cooking, the liquid may be used to make a sauce, such as suprême sauce, to serve with the cooked product.
4. It is important to drain the poultry well after cooking, because any remaining liquid may spoil the appearance of the sauce on the plate.
5. Poaching may be done on the rangetop or in the oven. Oven poaching provides more even heat.

Poached Chicken Breast Princesse

PORTIONS: 24 PORTION SIZE: ½ CHICKEN BREAST, 2 FL OZ (60 ML) SAUCE, PLUS GARNISH

U.S.	METRIC	INGREDIENTS	PROCEDURE
24	24	Boneless, skinless half-breasts from12 chickens, 3 lb (1.2 kg) each	1. Select a baking pan just large enough to hold the chicken breasts in a single layer. Butter the inside of the pan.
as needed	as needed	Butter	2. Season the chicken breasts with salt and pepper. Place them in the pan, presentation side (that is, the side that had the skin on) up.
as needed	as needed	Salt	3. Sprinkle with the lemon juice and add enough chicken stock to barely cover the chicken.
as needed	as needed	White pepper	4. Cover the chicken with a buttered piece of parchment or waxed paper.
¼ cup	60 mL	Lemon juice	5. Bring to a simmer on top of the stove. Finish poaching in a 325°F (165°C) oven or over low heat on the stove. Cooking time will be 5–10 minutes.
1½ qt (approximately)	1.5 L (approximately)	Chicken stock, cold	6. Remove the chicken breasts from the liquid. Place them in a hotel pan, cover, and keep them warm.
		Beurre manié:	7. Reduce the poaching liquid over high heat to about 2½ pt (1.1 L).
3 oz	90 g	Butter, softened	8. Knead the butter and flour together to make a beurre manié.
3 oz	90 g	Flour	9. With a wire whip, beat the beurre manié into the simmering stock to thicken it. Simmer a minute to cook out any starchy taste.
2½ cups	600 mL	Heavy cream, hot	10. Add the hot cream to the sauce. Season to taste.
to taste	to taste	Salt	
72	72	Asparagus tips, cooked, hot	11. Place each chicken breast, well drained, on a plate, and coat with 2 fl oz (60 mL) sauce. Garnish with 3 asparagus tips. Serve immediately.

Per serving: Calories, 330; Protein, 37 g; Fat, 17 g (47% cal.); Cholesterol, 140 mg; Carbohydrates, 6 g; Fiber,1 g; Sodium, 140 mg.

VARIATIONS

Alternative Method: Poach the chicken as in the basic recipe. Plate immediately and coat with prepared suprême sauce. Save poaching liquid for next day's sauce.

Other sauces may be used to coat poached chicken breasts, including:

Allemande	Aurora	Hungarian
Ivory	Mushroom	

Poached Chicken Breast Florentine

Poach the chicken as in the basic recipe. Place each portion on a bed of buttered spinach, well drained. Coat with Mornay sauce.

Optional: Sprinkle with parmesan cheese and brown under the broiler.

Chicken or Turkey Pot Pie

PORTIONS: 25 PORTION SIZE: 3 OZ (90 G) MEAT, 2 OZ (60 G) VEGETABLES, 4 FL OZ (125 ML) SAUCE

U.S.	METRIC	INGREDIENTS
5 lb	2.3 kg	Cooked chicken or turkey meat (light and dark meat)
12 oz	350 g	Potatoes, medium dice
12 oz	350 g	Carrots, medium dice
12 oz	350 g	Tiny white onions, peeled
12 oz	350 g	Peas
3 qt	3 L	Chicken velouté
to taste	to taste	Salt
to taste	to taste	Pepper
2 tsp	10 mL	Dried tarragon
25	25	Flaky pie pastry covers

Per serving: Calories, 520; Protein, 25 g; Fat, 32 g (55% cal.); Cholesterol, 80 mg; Carbohydrates, 34 g; Fiber, 5 g; Sodium, 430 mg.

PROCEDURE

1. Cut the chicken or turkey into ¾-in. (1-cm) dice.
2. Cook the vegetables separately in boiling salted water. Drain and cool.
3. Season the velouté to taste with salt and pepper. Add the tarragon.
4. Prepare the pastry and cut out circles to cover the tops of casserole serving dishes. You will need about 2 oz (60 g) pastry per portion.
5. Divide the light and dark meat evenly among individual serving casseroles (3 oz/ 90 g per portion).
6. Divide the vegetables evenly among the casseroles (about ½ oz/15 g per portion of each vegetable).
7. Ladle about 4 fl oz (125 mL) velouté into each casserole.
8. Top the dishes with the pastry. Cut holes in the centers to allow steam to escape.
9. Place the dishes on a sheet pan. Bake at 400°F (200°C) until the crust is well browned.

VARIATIONS

Vegetable ingredients may be varied as desired. Other vegetables that may be used include celery, mushroom caps, and lima beans.

Chicken or Turkey Stew

Prepare the meat, vegetables, and velouté as in the basic recipe. Omit pastry. Combine the ingredients in a saucepot and bring to a simmer. Hold for service.

Tea-Smoked Duck

YIELD: 1 DUCK

U.S.	METRIC	INGREDIENTS	PROCEDURE
3 tbsp	45 mL	Coarse salt	1. Toast the salt and peppercorns in a dry skillet over moderate heat, until peppercorns are fragrant.
1 tbsp	15 mL	Sichuan peppercorns	2. Cool the mixture, then crush with a rolling pin.
1	1	Duck, about 5 lb (2.3 kg)	3. Clean the duck well, removing excess fat. Flatten the duck slightly by pressing down on the breastbone to break it. 4. Rub the duck inside and out with the salt and peppercorn mixture. 5. Put the duck in a hotel pan, weight it, and refrigerate 1–2 days.
6	6	Scallions, trimmed	6. Rinse the duck.
4 slices	4 slices	Ginger root	7. Put the scallions and ginger slices in the cavity. 8. Steam the duck 1–1½ hours, or until tender.
3 oz	90 g	Raw rice	9. Line a large wok or other heavy pan with aluminum foil.
½ cup	125 mL	Brown or black tea leaves	10. Mix together the rice, tea leaves, and sugar. Put the mixture in the bottom of the wok.
2 oz	60 g	Sugar	11. Put the duck on a rack over the tea mixture and cover the pan tightly. 12. Set the pan over high heat 5 minutes, then over moderate heat 20 minutes. Turn the heat off and let stand another 20 minutes without uncovering. 13. Cool the duck. Chop it into pieces measuring 1–2 in. (3–5 cm), bones and all. Alternatively, bone it out and cut the meat into strips 1 in. (2.5 cm) wide. This dish is normally served at room temperature.

Per ⅙ recipe: Calories, 520; Protein, 30 g; Fat, 43 g (75% cal.); Cholesterol, 130 mg; Carbohydrates, 2 g; Fiber, 1 g; Sodium, 2969 mg.

VARIATIONS

For spicier duck, add 1 tsp (5 mL) five-spice powder to the dry marinade after toasting.

Crispy Duck

This variation may be made with smoked duck or with steamed but unsmoked duck (step 8). When the duck is cool, cut it into quarters. You may bone it if desired, but try to keep it in its original shape. Deep-fry until the skin is crisp. Drain, cut up, and serve at once.
(Optional step: Rub cornstarch into the skin before deep-frying.)

Braising

A moist-heat cooking method, braising may be used to tenderize tough poultry products. Also, as for veal and pork, it can be used to provide moistness and flavor to tender poultry items. Coq au vin, the well-known braised chicken in red wine, was originally made with a tough old rooster (coq), but today the same recipe is applied to tender young chicken.

Poultry products are braised using the same procedures as for meats, except that mirepoix is frequently omitted. Other flavoring ingredients may be used instead, depending on the recipe. Methods 1 and 2 (p. 184) are used when the chicken is to be browned. Method 3 (p. 184) is used for fricassées, white stews in which the chicken is sautéed without browning.

Braised "Sautés"

If you review the procedure for sautéing meats (p. 171), you will see that if the product is not completely cooked when browned in step 5 and then finished by simmering it in the sauce in step 10, the result is a braised item. This procedure may be used for classical "sautés," which are often braised items. (An alternative method is to finish cooking the chicken or meat in a covered pan in the oven while you are making the sauce. This is also braising because the cover holds in moisture.)

KEY POINTS TO REVIEW

- What poultry items are best for sautéing?
- What is the difference between sautéing and pan-frying, when applied to poultry?
- What poultry items are best for deep-frying? At what temperature should they be fried?
- What are the differences between simmering and poaching? Describe each procedure as it is applied to poultry items.
- What is a classical sauté, and why does it sometimes become a braised item rather than a sautéed one? How would cook the item if you wanted it to be a true sauté rather than a braise?

Chicken Fricassée

PORTIONS: 24 PORTION SIZE: ¼ CHICKEN, 3 FL OZ (90 ML) SAUCE

U.S.	METRIC	INGREDIENTS
6	6	Chickens, 2½–3 lb (1.1–1.4 kg) each
to taste	to taste	Salt
to taste	to taste	White pepper
6 oz	175 g	Butter
12 oz	350 g	Onion, cut brunoise
6 oz	175 g	Flour
3 qt (approximately)	3 L (approximately)	Chicken stock
		Sachet:
1	1	Bay leaf
1	1	Small piece of celery
4	4	Parsley stems
¼ tsp	1 mL	Thyme
		Liaison:
5	5	Egg yolks, beaten
1 pt	500 mL	Heavy cream
2 tbsp	30 mL	Lemon juice
to taste	to taste	Salt
to taste	to taste	White pepper
to taste	to taste	Nutmeg

Per serving: Calories, 440; Protein, 39 g; Fat, 27 g (56% cal.); Cholesterol, 175 mg; Carbohydrates, 8 g; Fiber, 0 g; Sodium, 180 mg.

PROCEDURE

1. Cut the chickens into 8 pieces each. Season with salt and white pepper.
2. Melt the butter in a brazier over moderate heat.
3. Add chicken and onion. Sauté very lightly so the chicken is seared on all sides, but do not brown.
4. Add the flour and stir so it combines with the fat to make a roux. Cook another 2 minutes, without browning.
5. Gradually stir in enough stock to cover the chicken. Bring to a simmer, stirring, until the sauce thickens.
6. Add the sachet.
7. Cover and place in a slow oven (300°F/150°C) or over very low heat on the range. Cook until tender, 30–45 minutes.
8. Remove the chicken from the sauce and keep it warm in a covered pan.
9. Degrease the sauce. Reduce it over high heat to proper thickness. You should have about 2 qt (2 L) sauce. Strain through cheesecloth.
10. Combine the egg yolks and cream. Temper with a little hot sauce, and add the liaison to the sauce. Bring to just below the simmer. Do not boil.
11. Season to taste with lemon juice, salt, white pepper, and nutmeg. Pour the sauce over the chicken.

VARIATIONS

Chicken Fricassée with Tarragon

Add 1 tbsp (15 mL) dried tarragon to the sachet.

Chicken Fricassée à l'Indienne

Add 4 tbsp (60 mL) curry powder when making the roux.

Fricassée of Turkey Wings

Prepare as in the basic recipe, using 1 or 2 turkey wings per portion, depending on size. Cut large turkey wings into 2 pieces.

Veal Fricassée

Prepare as in the basic recipe, using 10 lb (4.5 kg) boneless veal shoulder, cut into large dice. Use white veal stock.

Pork Fricassée

Use 10 lb (4.5 kg) boneless, diced pork and pork, veal, or chicken stock.

Fricassée à l'Ancienne

Fricassée Brunoise

Fricassée Argenteuil

Chicken Chasseur

PORTIONS: 10 PORTION SIZE: ½ CHICKEN, 3 FL OZ (90 ML) SAUCE

U.S.	METRIC	INGREDIENTS
5	5	Chickens, 2–2¼ lb (0.9–1 kg) each (see Note)
to taste	to taste	Salt
to taste	to taste	Pepper
2 fl oz	60 mL	Oil
2 oz	60 g	Shallots or onions, cut brunoise
8 oz	250 g	Mushrooms, sliced
8 fl oz	250 mL	White wine
1½ pt	750 mL	Demi-glace
8 oz	250 g	Tomato concassé, fresh
		or
4 oz	125 g	Drained, chopped canned tomatoes
to taste	to taste	Salt
to taste	to taste	Pepper
2 tbsp	30 mL	Chopped parsley

PROCEDURE

1. Cut the chickens into 8 pieces. Season with salt and pepper.
2. Heat the oil in a brazier or large sauté pan. Brown the chicken well on all sides.
3. Remove the chicken pieces from the pan. Cover and keep them hot.
4. Add the shallots and mushrooms to the pan and sauté lightly without browning.
5. Add the white wine and reduce by three-fourths over high heat.
6. Add the demi-glace and tomatoes and bring to a boil. Reduce slightly. Season with salt and pepper.
7. Place the chicken in the sauce. Cover and simmer slowly on the stove or in the oven at 325°F (165°C), 20–30 minutes, or until done.
8. When the chicken is done, remove it from the pan and reduce the sauce slightly over high heat. Add the chopped parsley and check the seasonings.
9. Serve ½ chicken (2 pieces dark meat and 2 pieces light meat) per portion. Cover with 3 fl oz (90 mL) sauce.

Per serving: Calories, 780; Protein, 76 g; Fat, 47 g (55% cal.); Cholesterol, 250 mg; Carbohydrates,72 g; Fiber, 1 g; Sodium, 290 mg.

Note: Large chickens may be used, if desired. For 3½-lb (1.6-kg) chickens, use ¼ chicken per portion (1 piece dark meat and 1 piece light meat).

VARIATIONS

Alternative Method: Brown chickens as in the basic recipe. Drain excess fat. Ad 1 qt (1 L) prepared chasseur sauce and finish cooking the chickens as in the basic method.

Chicken Bercy

Method 1: Prepare as in the basic recipe, but omit the mushrooms and tomato.

Method 2: Brown chickens as in the basic recipe. Add 1 qt (1 L) prepared Bercy sauce and simmer the chickens until done.

Chicken Portugaise

Method 1: Prepare as in the basic recipe, but omit the mushrooms and wine. Use 4 oz (125 g) onions, cut brunoise, and add 1 tsp (5 mL) chopped garlic. Substitute tomato sauce for the demi-glace.

Method 2: Brown chicken as in the basic recipe. Add 1 qt (1 L) portugaise sauce and simmer the chicken until done.

Chicken Hongroise

Prepare as in the basic recipe, but sauté chicken only lightly. Do not brown. Omit mushrooms and wine. Use Hungarian (hongroise) sauce instead of demi-glace. When the chicken is cooked, add 4–6 fl oz (125–175 mL) heavy cream (tempered or heated) to the sauce. Omit parsley garnish. Serve with rice pilaf.

Chicken Chasseur

Paprika Chicken

PORTIONS: 24 PORTION SIZE: 1/4 CHICKEN, 3 FL OZ (90 ML) SAUCE

U.S.	METRIC	INGREDIENTS
4 fl oz	125 mL	Oil
6	6	Chickens, disjointed, 3–3½ lb (1.4–1.6 kg) each
1½ lb	700 g	Onions, chopped fine
1 lb	450 g	Green bell pepper, small dice
2 oz	60 g	Flour
6 tbsp	90 mL	Hungarian paprika
1 pt	500 mL	Chicken stock
1 lb	450 g	Canned tomatoes, crushed
2 tsp	10 mL	Salt
1 pt	500 mL	Sour cream

PROCEDURE

1. Heat the oil in a skillet and brown the chicken lightly on all sides.
2. Remove the chicken from the pan and place in a brazier.
3. Add the onion and green pepper to the fat in the pan. Sauté until soft but not browned.
4. Add the flour and stir to make a roux. Cook the flour slowly a few minutes.
5. Add the paprika and stir to blend in.
6. Stir in the chicken stock, tomatoes, and salt. Bring to a boil. The sauce will be very thick at this point.
7. Pour the sauce over the chicken. Cover and simmer over very low heat or in a 325°F (165°C) oven until the chicken is tender, 30–40 minutes.
8. When the chicken is tender, remove it from the sauce and place in a hotel pan.
9. Degrease the sauce. Stir in the sour cream. Simmer 1 minute, but do not boil. Adjust the seasonings.
10. Pour the sauce over the chicken in the hotel pan.
11. Serve with egg noodles, spaetzle, or rice.

Per serving: Calories, 440; Protein, 46 g; Fat, 24 g (50% cal.); Cholesterol, 120 mg; Carbohydrates, 8 g; Fiber, 1 g; Sodium, 370 mg.

Coq au Vin

PORTIONS: 12 PORTION SIZE: ¼ CHICKEN, 2½ FL OZ (75 ML) SAUCE

U.S.	METRIC	INGREDIENTS	PROCEDURE
12 oz	350 g	Salt pork or slab bacon	1. Cut the salt pork or bacon into bâtonnet shapes, 1 × ¼ × ¼ in. (2 × ½ × ½ cm).
1 fl oz	30 mL	Oil	2. Place the bacon pieces in a saucepan. Cover with cold water. Bring to a boil and drain.
			3. Add the oil to a large sauté pan and place over moderate heat. When hot, add the blanched bacon. Sauté until lightly browned. Remove with a slotted spoon and set aside.
3	3	Chickens, 3½ lb (1.6 kg) each, cut into 8 pieces	4. Increase the heat to high. Add the chickens to the fat remaining in the pan and brown well on all sides. Remove the chicken from the pan.
24	24	Tiny white onions, peeled and parboiled	5. Add the onions and mushrooms to the pan and sauté until browned. Remove with a slotted spoon and set aside with the bacon pieces. Pour off the fat from the pan.
1½ lb	700 g	Small mushroom caps	
1 qt	1 L	Dry red wine	6. Add the wine and stock to the pan and bring to a boil.
1 pt	500 mL	Chicken stock	7. Add the sachet.
		Sachet:	8. Return the chicken to the pan. Bring the liquid back to a boil. Cover and cook in a 300°F (150°C) oven or over very low heat on top of the stove until chicken is done, 30–40 minutes.
½ tsp	2 mL	Dried thyme	
1	1	Bay leaf	
4	4	Large garlic cloves, crushed	
		Beurre manié:	9. Remove the chicken from the cooking liquid and place in a heated pan or on a serving platter. Garnish with the mushrooms, onions, and bacon pieces.
2 oz	60 g	Butter, softened	10. Degrease the cooking liquid carefully.
2 oz	60 g	Flour	11. Place over high heat and boil until the liquid is reduced to about 1 qt (1 L).
to taste	to taste	Salt	12. Mix the butter and flour to make beurre manié. Beat in the beurre manié a little at time, just enough to thicken the sauce lightly.
as needed	as needed	Chopped parsley	13. Add salt to taste.
			14. Strain the sauce over the chicken and garnish.
			15. At service time, sprinkle each portion with a little chopped parsley.

Per serving: Calories, 690; Protein, 50 g; Fat, 41 g (54% cal.); Cholesterol, 165 mg; Carbohydrates, 10 g; Fiber, 2 g; Sodium, 480 mg.

Coq au Vin

Arroz con Pollo (Spanish Rice with Chicken)

PORTIONS: 24 PORTION SIZE: ¼ CHICKEN, 5 OZ (150 G) RICE

U.S.	METRIC	INGREDIENTS	PROCEDURE
6	6	Chickens, 3 lb (1.4 kg) each	1. Cut the chickens into 8 pieces each.
3 fl oz	90 mL	Olive oil	2. Heat the olive oil in a large sauté pan. Brown the chicken pieces on all sides. Transfer to a brazier as they are browned. Drain off and discard about one-third of the fat in the pan.
1 lb	500 g	Onion, small dice	3. Place the onion, green pepper, and garlic in the sauté pan in which the chicken was browned. Sauté over medium heat until the vegetables are almost tender.
1 lb	500 g	Green bell peppers, medium dice	4. Add the paprika and rice and stir until the grains are coated with fat.
4 tsp	20 mL	Garlic, chopped fine	5. Add the stock and tomatoes. Bring to a boil. Season the liquid to taste with salt and pepper.
2 tsp	10 mL	Paprika	6. Pour the contents of the pan over the chicken in the brazier. Cover and place in a 325°F (165°C) oven until the rice and chicken are cooked, about 20–30 minutes.
1 qt	1 L	Long-grain rice, raw	
3 pt	1.5 L	Chicken stock	
2 lb	900 g	Fresh tomatoes, 1-in. (2.5-cm) dice *or*	
1½ lb	700 g	Canned tomatoes, diced	
to taste	to taste	Salt	
to taste	to taste	Pepper	
1¼ lb	600 g	Frozen peas, thawed	7. At service time, stir in the peas and garnish the top with pimiento strips.
4 oz	125 g	Pimientos, cut into thin strips	

Per serving: Calories, 580; Protein, 49 g; Fat, 26 g (41% cal.); Cholesterol, 145 mg; Carbohydrates, 35 g; Fiber, 3 g; Sodium, 160 mg.

Arroz con Pollo (Spanish Rice with Chicken)

Duck Confit

PORTIONS: 8 (SEE NOTE)

U.S.	METRIC	INGREDIENTS
8 lb	3.6 kg	Duck parts, preferably legs
1 oz	30 g	Salt
1 tsp	5 mL	White pepper
½ tsp	2 mL	Nutmeg
½ tsp	2 mL	Powdered bay leaf
pinch	pinch	Ground cloves
as needed	as needed	Extra duck fat

Per serving: Calories, 620; Protein, 35 g; Fat, 52 g (77% cal.); Cholesterol, 155 mg; Carbohydrates, 0 g; Fiber, 0 g; Sodium, 1480 mg.

Note: The exact weight of the finished confit can vary considerably.

PROCEDURE

1. Trim off excess fat from the duck and reserve.
2. If you are using duck legs (the ideal part for this preparation), leave the thigh attached to the drumstick.
3. Rub the duck pieces with the salt and spices. Refrigerate overnight.
4. Render the trimmed fat plus as much extra fat as needed. You will need enough rendered fat to completely cover the duck pieces.
5. Put the duck and the rendered fat in a brazier, large saucepan, or casserole. Simmer gently in the fat over low heat or in a 300°F (150°C) oven until very tender, 1½–2 hours.
6. Remove the cooked duck from the fat and pack into a clean crock or other container. Pour the melted fat over the meat so it is completely covered, but be careful not to pour in any of the juices. Refrigerate. (The degreased juices may be used for another purpose, such as cooking beans.)
7. Remove duck pieces and use as needed. For best storage, remaining pieces must be kept covered by the fat. For serving, the confit is usually browned in a little of the fat until it is heated through and the skin is crisp. Serve with such accompaniments as braised cabbage, cooked white beans, or sautéed potatoes with garlic, or on a bed of salad greens.

CONFIT OF DUCK AND GOOSE

Confit means "preserved." Confit of duck and goose originated as a byproduct of the production of foie gras, as a way to make use of and preserve the meat of birds raised and fed for their enlarged, fattened livers. After the parts are cooked by the procedure in the recipe on this page, they are packed in crocks and enough fat is poured over them to seal them from the air, thus preserving them for a time.

Today, of course, refrigeration makes this method of preserving unnecessary. But confit is more popular than ever because of the tenderness and flavor the cooking method yields. In the case of ducks, the legs are usually made into confit, while the boneless breasts are reserved for pan-frying and serving rare. A special breed of duck called *moulard*, with a large, meaty breast, is used for foie gras production. It is this duck whose legs are traditionally made into confit. However, the legs of any domestic duck can be used in this recipe.

Duck Confit with Walnut Mesclun Salad

Dressings and Stuffings

Stuffing chickens and turkeys is usually not practical in production kitchens. Baking the stuffing separately gives better results, for these reasons:

1. **Safety.**
   Stuffing inside a bird is an ideal breeding ground for bacteria that cause food poisoning.
2. **Quality.**
   Additional roasting time is needed to heat the stuffing through. The result is often overcooked poultry.
3. **Efficiency**
   Filling poultry with stuffing and removing it after roasting is impractical, time consuming, and messy.

Stuffing that is baked separately is usually called *dressing*.

Is poultry ever stuffed? Yes. Small birds served whole as one or two portions can be stuffed and often are. Stuffed Cornish hens or small game birds such as quail are popular items.

Basic Ingredients of Dressings

1. Starch base, such as bread or rice.
2. Aromatic vegetables, generally onions and celery.
3. Fat, such as butter or chicken fat, for sautéing the vegetables and for providing richness.
   Dressings for chicken and turkey, which are lean, may require more fat than dressings for duck and goose, which are fatty.
4. Liquid, usually stock, to provide moisture.
5. Seasonings, herbs, and spices.
6. Eggs, sometimes added as a binder but not always necessary.
7. Other ingredients for flavor, character, and bulk, such as:

Sausage	Chestnuts
Oysters	Fruits
Giblets	Nuts

Guidelines for Making Dressings

1. All ingredients that require cooking must be completely cooked before combining with other dressing ingredients. They will cook very little more during baking or roasting.
2. Cool all ingredients before combining to avoid growth of dangerous bacteria.
3. Never let baked or unbaked dressing stay in the Food Danger Zone longer than 1 hour.
   - Refrigerate unbaked dressing if it is not to be baked immediately.
   - Hold baked dressing above 135°F (57°C) for service, or chill as rapidly as possible.
   - Reheat baked dressing rapidly in oven or steamer to an internal temperature of 180°F (82°C).
4. Bake dressing in shallow pans (2 in./5 cm deep) for rapid cooking, to get it above the Danger Zone quickly.
5. Do not overmix bread dressings, or they will become pasty. Toss ingredients together lightly.
6. For light texture, do not pack dressings into baking pans; instead, spoon loosely.
7. If you stuff poultry instead of baking the dressing separately, fill the birds loosely. Do not pack. Stuffings expand during cooking.

KEY POINTS TO REVIEW

- What are three reasons that "stuffing" is best baked in a separate pan rather than inside a bird?
- What are the basic ingredients of a basic poultry dressing or stuffing?
- What precautions should you take to ensure that poultry dressings or stuffings are safe to eat?

Basic Bread Dressing

YIELD: ABOUT 4 LB (2 KG)

U.S.	METRIC	INGREDIENTS
1 lb	500 g	Onion, small dice
½ lb	250 g	Celery, small dice
½ lb	250 g	Fat such as butter, chicken fat, or bacon fat
2 lb	1 kg	White bread, 2 days old
1 oz	30 g	Chopped fresh parsley
1 tsp	5 mL	Sage
½ tsp	2 mL	Dried thyme
½ tsp	2 mL	Dried marjoram
½ tsp	2 mL	White pepper
2 tsp	10 mL	Salt
1–2 pt	0.5–1 L	Chicken stock, cold

Per 1 ounce: Calories, 70; Protein, 1 g; Fat, 3.5 g (47% cal.); Cholesterol, 10 mg; Carbohydrates, 8 g; Fiber, 0 g; Sodium, 175 mg.

PROCEDURE

1. Sauté the onion and celery lightly in the fat until tender but not browned. Cool thoroughly.
2. Cut the bread into small cubes. If desired, crusts may be trimmed first.
3. Combine the bread and cooked vegetables in a large stainless-steel bowl. Add the herbs and seasonings and toss gently until all ingredients are well mixed.
4. Add the stock a little at a time, and mix the dressing lightly after each addition. Add just enough to make the dressing slightly moist, neither dry nor soggy. Adjust the seasonings.
5. Place in a greased baking pan and bake at 375°F (190°C), until hot at the center, about 1 hour.

VARIATIONS

Sausage Dressing

Cook 1 lb (500 g) crumbled pork sausage meat, drain, and cool. Use some of the drained fat to cook the vegetables for the dressing. Add the cooked sausage to the dressing before adding the stock.

Chestnut Dressing

Reduce the bread to 1½ lb (750 g). Add 1 lb (500 g) cooked, coarsely chopped chestnuts to the dressing before adding the stock.

Mushroom Dressing

Cook 2 lb (1 kg) sliced mushrooms with the onion and celery. Proceed as in the basic recipe.

Giblet Dressing

Add ½ lb (250 g) cooked, chopped chicken or turkey gizzards and hearts to the dressing before adding the stock.

Cornbread Dressing

Substitute cornbread for all or part of the white bread in Basic Bread Dressing or Sausage Dressing.

QUESTIONS FOR DISCUSSION

1. Describe the three roasting methods discussed in this chapter: low-temperature roasting, searing, and high-temperature roasting. When is each used?
2. True or false: Chicken should be broiled at a lower temperature than steaks. Explain your answer.
3. What is meant by the term *presentation side*?
4. Why is it difficult to cook large chicken pieces by deep-frying? How can this problem be solved?
5. What are the differences between simmering and poaching as applied to poultry?
6. Give three reasons for baking dressing in a separate pan rather than stuffing it into roast poultry.

Chapter 3

Grilled Tuna with Balsamic Vinaigrette and Sweet-Sour Baby Onions, page 88.

Understanding Fish and Shellfish

At one time, fresh fish was enjoyed only in limited areas—along the seacoast and, to a lesser extent, around lakes and rivers. Today, thanks to modern refrigeration and freezing technology, fish products are enjoyed much more widely.

For the cook, the difficulties of understanding fish and shellfish are, in some ways, the reverse of those for meat. With meat, we are presented with only a few animals but a bewildering array of cuts from each. With fish, we see only a few cuts but hundreds of species, each with its own characteristics and cooking requirements.

For this reason, it is especially important that students learn the basic principles of structure, handling, and cooking so they can utilize the many varieties of seafood in a systematic way.

Fish products are divided into two categories: ***fin fish***, or fish with fins and internal skeletons, and ***shellfish***, or fish with external shells but no internal bone structure. Because these two categories have many differences, it is helpful to look at them separately, as we do in this chapter.

After reading this chapter, you should be able to

1. Explain how the cooking qualities of fish are affected by its lack of connective tissue.
2. Determine doneness in cooked fish.
3. Demonstrate the appropriate cooking methods for fat and lean fish.
4. List seven basic market forms of fish.
5. Dress and fillet round fish and flatfish.
6. List and describe common varieties of saltwater and freshwater fin fish used in North American food service.
7. Identify the characteristics of fresh fish, and contrast them with characteristics of not-so-fresh fish.
8. Store fish and fish products.
9. Understand the popular varieties of shellfish, and discuss their characteristics.
10. Outline the special safe handling and cooking procedures for shellfish.
11. Open clams and oysters, split lobsters, and peel and devein shrimp.

Fin Fish

Composition and Structure

The edible flesh of fish, like that of meat and poultry, consists of water, proteins, fats, and small amounts of minerals, vitamins, and other substances. The differences, however, are perhaps more important than the similarities.

Fish has very little connective tissue. This is one of the most important differences between fish and meat. It means that

1. *Fish cooks very quickly*, even at low heat (just enough heat to coagulate the proteins).
2. *Fish is naturally tender*. Toughness is the result not of connective tissue but of the toughening of the protein by high heat.
3. *Moist-heat cooking methods* are used not to create tenderness but to preserve moistness and provide variety.
4. *Cooked fish must be handled very carefully* or it will fall apart.

Special Problems in Cooking Fish

Doneness and Flaking

When fish is cooked, the flesh breaks apart into its natural separations. This is called ***flaking***. Most books, somewhat misleadingly, say that fish is done when it flakes easily. Unfortunately, some cooks interpret this as "nearly falling apart." Because fish continues to cook in its retained heat even when removed from the fire, it is often dreadfully overcooked by the time it reaches the customer. *Fish is very delicate and is easily overcooked.*

Observe these tests for doneness:

1. The fish just *separates into flakes*—that is, it is beginning to flake but does not yet fall apart easily.
2. If bone is present, the flesh separates from the bone, and the bone is no longer pink.
3. The flesh has turned from translucent to opaque (usually white, depending on the kind of fish).

Remember, the major flaw in fish preparation is *overcooking*.

Cooking Fat Fish and Lean Fish

The fat content of fish ranges from 0.5 percent to 20 percent.

Lean fish are those that are low in fat. Examples: flounder, sole, cod, red snapper, bass, perch, halibut, pike.

Fat fish are those that are high in fat. Examples: salmon, tuna, trout, butterfish, mackerel.

COOKING LEAN FISH

Because lean fish has almost no fat, it can easily become dry, especially if overcooked. It is often served with sauces to enhance moistness and give richness.

Moist-heat methods. Lean fish is especially well suited to poaching. This method preserves moistness.

Dry-heat methods. Lean fish, if it is broiled or baked, should be basted with butter or oil. Take special care not to overcook it, or the fish will be dry.

Dry-heat methods with fat. Lean fish may be fried or sautéed. The fish gains palatability from the added fat.

COOKING FAT FISH

The fat in these fish enables them to tolerate more heat without becoming dry.

Moist-heat methods. Fat fish, like lean fish, can be cooked by moist heat. Poached salmon and trout are very popular.

Dry-heat methods. Fat fish are well suited to broiling and baking. The dry heat helps eliminate excessive oiliness.

Dry-heat methods with fat. Large fat fish, like salmon, and stronger-flavored fish, like bluefish and mackerel, may be cooked in fat, but care should be taken to avoid excessive greasiness. Smaller ones, like trout, are often pan-fried. Drain the fish well before serving.

Cutting Fish

Market Forms

Fish are available in several forms, as illustrated in Figure 3.1. Or they may be cut by the cook into these forms, depending on how they are to be cooked.

Buying Processed Fish Versus Cutting Them Yourself

Most food-service establishments purchase fish in the forms in which they intend to cook them. They find it less expensive to pay the purveyor to do the cutting than to hire and train the personnel and to allocate the storage and workspace to do it in-house.

Some restaurants still buy whole fish. Here are a few reasons why they do:

1. Their clientele demands it. Some high-priced luxury restaurants stake their reputations on using only the freshest, most unprocessed ingredients. They are able to charge enough to cover their high labor costs.
2. They are located in the heart of a fresh fish market, where fresh whole fish, delivered daily, are economical. They can best take advantage of seasonal bargains.
3. They are high-volume specialty restaurants and find it more economical to clean the fish themselves and watch the market for the best prices every day.
4. They make fish stocks and use the bones.
5. They serve the whole fish. Examples: sautéed or poached trout presented whole; whole cold poached fish as a buffet display.

Your purchasing decisions will depend on what you plan to do with the fish and what forms are most economical for those purposes.

Figure 3.1 Market forms of fish.

(a) Whole or round: completely intact, as caught

(b) Drawn: viscera removed

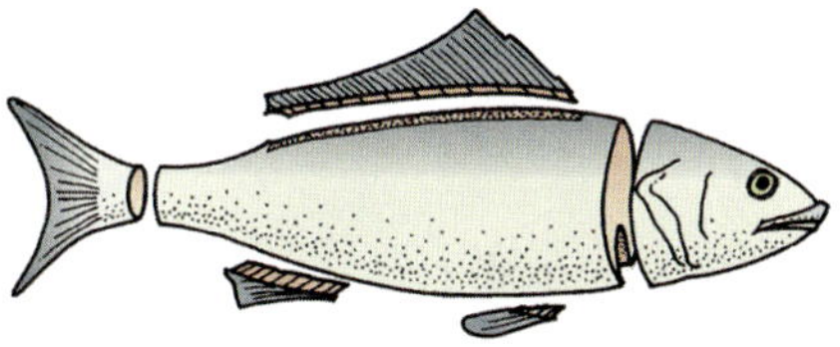

(c) Dressed: viscera, scales, head, tail, and fins removed

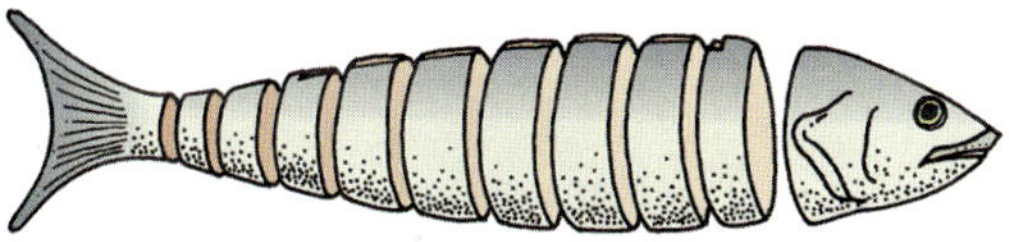

(d) Steaks: cross-section slices, each containing a section of backbone

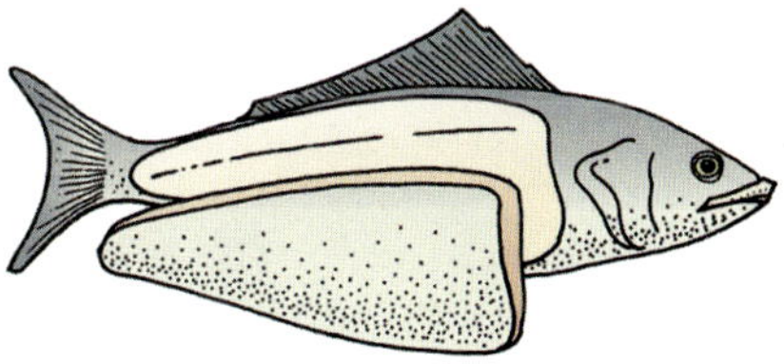

(e) Fillets: boneless sides of fish, with skin on or off

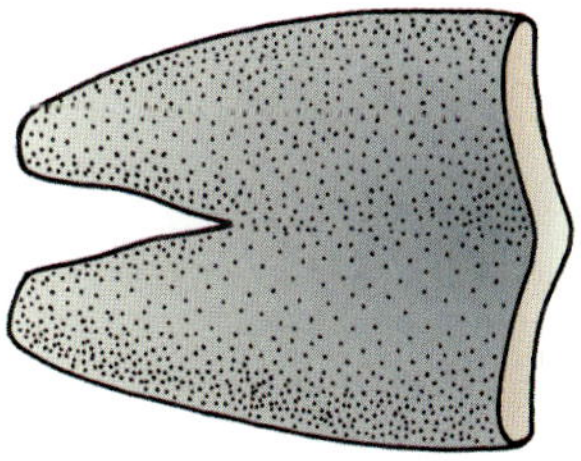

(f) Butterflied fillets: both sides of a fish still joined, but with bones removed

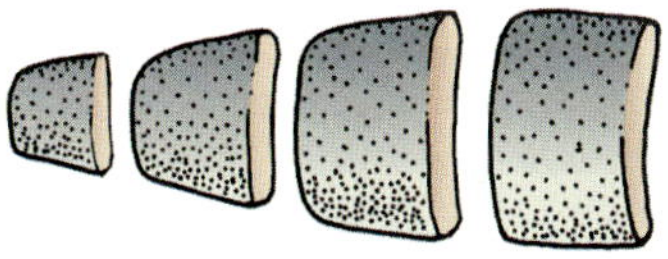

(g) Sticks or tranches: cross-section slices of fillets

Dressing and Filleting

Although most of you will work with ready-to-cook fish products, you should know how to clean and fillet whole fish.

1. **Dressing.**
   Figure 3.2 illustrates how to dress a whole fish.

2. **Filleting.**
   There are two basic shapes of fish: ***flatfish*** (like flounder and sole) and ***round fish*** (like cod and trout). They are filleted differently. Flatfish have four fillets; round fish have two. Figures 3.3 and 3.4 show the two methods for filleting these fish.

   After a large fish, such as salmon, is filleted, it may be necessary for some recipes to cut the fillets into thinner slices, or escalopes. Figure 3.5 shows this procedure.

Figure 3.2 Dressing a fish.

(a) Scale the fish. Lay the fish flat on the work surface. Rub a scaling tool or the back of a knife against the scales from tail to head. Repeat until all the scales are removed. Rinse. (Exceptions: Trout, with very tiny scales, and scaleless fish, like catfish, are not scaled.)

(b) Eviscerate. Slit the belly and pull out the viscera. Rinse the cavity.

(c) Cut off the tail and fins. Scissors are easiest to use.

(d) Remove the head. Cut through the flesh just behind gills. Cut or break the backbone at the cut and pull off the head.

(e) The fish is *dressed*.

Figure 3.3 Filleting flatfish.

(a) Use a thin-bladed, flexible knife. Cut off the head, just behind the gills. (This step is optional.)

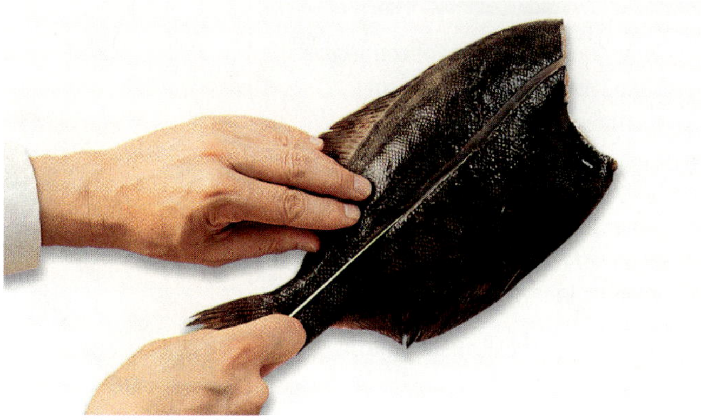

(b) Make a cut from head to tail just to one side of the center line, down to the backbone.

(c) Turn the knife so it is almost parallel to the table. Making long, smooth cuts, cut horizontally against the backbone toward the outer edge of the fish. Gently separate the fillet from the bone.

(d) Remove the fillet completely. Repeat to remove the three remaining fillets.

(e) To skin, place the fillet skin side down on the work surface with the tail pointing toward you. Holding the skin at the tail end, slide the knife between the skin and flesh, scraping against the skin to avoid cutting into the fillet. ***Note:*** Dover or English sole is skinned before filleting. Cut through the skin at the tail. Holding the tail with one hand, peel off the skin toward the head. ***Caution:*** Do not do this with flounder. You will tear the flesh.

Figure 3.4 Filleting round fish.

(a) Cut into the top of the fish along one side of the backbone from head to tail. Cut against the bone with smooth strokes of the knife to separate the flesh from the bone.

(b) Cut under the flesh toward the tail; detach it.

(c) Cut along the curved rib bones and finish detaching the fillet at the head end. Turn the fish over and repeat to remove the second fillet. Lightly run your finger along the flesh side of the fillets to see if any bones remain in them. Using a needlenose pliers, pull out any you find. Skin the fillets as for flatfish.

KEY POINTS TO REVIEW

- How does the amount of connective tissue in fish affect its cooking qualities?
- How is fish tested for doneness?
- What are some examples of fat fish and lean fish? What are appropriate cooking methods for each type?
- What are the basic market forms of fish?
- How is filleting flatfish different from filleting round fish?

Figure 3.5 Cutting escalopes of salmon.

(a) Holding the knife at a sharp angle, cut a thin slice of the fillet, slicing toward the tail or thin end.

(b) The cut slice. Weigh the slice to check for accuracy of cutting, then continue making slices.

Varieties and Characteristics

Hundreds of varieties of fish are eaten around the world. However, relatively few species account for the majority of the fish used in food service in the United States and Canada. Below are the most common varieties that are used fresh. Some are illustrated in the following photographs.

There is a significant difference in flavor between freshwater fish and saltwater fish, because saltwater fish, as might be expected, have more salt in their flesh. The following survey of fish varieties divides them into these two basic categories. However, some fish may spend part of their lives in the ocean and part in fresh water. Salmon, for example, lives in the ocean but migrates up rivers to lay eggs, or *spawn*. Fish that live in salt water but spawn in fresh water are called ***anadromous***. Shad and arctic char are two other examples of anadromous fish. On the other hand, fish that live in fresh water but swim downstream to spawn in the ocean are called ***catadromous***. Eel is a catadromous fish.

In the following listing, fish are categorized by where they spend most of their adult lives. Thus, anadromous fish such as salmon are listed with saltwater fish, while the catadromous fish such as eel are listed with freshwater fish.

Saltwater Fish—Flatfish

These are all popular in commercial kitchens. Flatfish have lean, white flesh and a mild, delicate flavor. They are all very flat, oval in shape, with both eyes on one side of the head.

You should note that, in North American waters, there are no true sole. All fish marketed as sole, such as lemon sole, gray sole, and Pacific Dover sole, are actually flounder. True Dover sole, from Atlantic waters off Europe, is the only actual sole in this list. Also, be aware that both true Dover sole and the flounder called Pacific Dover sole are both sometimes called English sole.

FLOUNDER

Flounder

Type: Lean.

Varieties: Winter flounder, lemon sole, gray sole, Pacific Dover sole, sand dab.

Characteristics: White flesh; fine flakes; mild, sweet flavor.

Weight: ½ to 5 lb (0.2 to 2.3 kg).

SOLE (DOVER SOLE OR ENGLISH SOLE)

Type: Lean.

Characteristics: Narrower, more elongated than flounder. Flesh similar to flounder, but firmer in texture. One of the most prized of all fish. Expensive.

Weight: 1 to 2 lb (0.5 to 1 kg).

Dover sole

HALIBUT

Type: Lean.

Characteristics: Looks like a giant flounder, with thicker flesh, delicate flavor. Cut into steaks and fillets.

Weight: 4 to 100 lb or more (2 to 45 kg).

Halibut
Courtesy of Alaska Seafood Marketing Institute

TURBOT

Type: Lean.

Characteristics: Large, broad flatfish. White, firm, delicate flesh.

Weight: 1 to 25 lb (0.5 to 11 kg).

Turbot

Saltwater Fish—Round Fish

ARCTIC CHAR

Type: Fat. Anadromous.

Characteristics: Similar to both salmon and trout, to which it is related. Flesh is similar to salmon but with less fat, although with more fat than trout.

Weight: Usually around 4 lb (1.8 kg), but can be as large as 25 lb (11 kg).

BLACK SEA BASS

Type: Lean.

Characteristics: Small, black-skinned fish with firm, delicate, sweet white flesh.

Weight: Up to 3 lb (1.5 kg).

Black sea bass

BLUEFISH

Type: Fat.

Characteristics: Flavorful, oily flesh that is bluish when raw, grayish when cooked. Abundant and inexpensive.

Weight: 1 to 10 lb (0.5 to 4.5 kg).

Bluefish

CHILEAN SEA BASS

Type: Fat.

Varieties: This fish is not a bass; the name is a marketing term for the Patagonian toothfish. Because, due to its popularity, it has been seriously overfished, numbers have declined dramatically. Fishing is highly regulated, and imports to North America must be labeled as legally caught, although there is much illegal fish on the market. Many chefs have agreed to stop serving this fish in order to slow or halt the illegal fishing that threatens its survival.

Characteristics: White, oily flesh with large flakes, firm texture, and mild flavor.

Weight: Usually around 20 lb (9 kg), although it can be much larger.

Cod

COD

Type: Lean.

Varieties: Small, young cod is called *scrod*.

Characteristics: Lean, white, delicately flavored flesh with large flakes. One of the most widely used food fish in North America. Most fish sticks and similar items are made from cod.

Weights: Scrod: 1 to 2½ lb (0.5 to 1 kg). Cod: 2½ to 25 lb and up (1 to 11 kg).

ESCOLAR

Type: Fat.

Characteristics: A firm, white, oily fish containing a fat that is not metabolized by the human body. Because of this fat, some people become ill when eating this fish. The fat seems to act like a laxative. In the United States, the Food and Drug Administration banned escolar in 1990, but its sale is once again legal. Food-service operators who serve escolar should advise customers of its potential dangers.

Weight: 65 to 110 lb (30 to 35 kg).

Grouper

GROUPER

Type: Lean.

Characteristics: Many varieties with varying shape and skin color. Firm white fish, similar in texture and flavor to red snapper. Tough skin.

Weight: Up to 700 lb (300 kg), but most groupers on the market weigh 5 to 15 lb (2.3 to 7 kg).

HADDOCK

Type: Lean.

Varieties: Finnan haddie is smoked haddock, not a separate kind of fish.

Characteristics: Similar to cod, but generally smaller.

Weight: 1 to 5 lb (0.5 to 2.3 kg).

Herring

HERRING

Type: Fat.

Characteristics: Small, full-flavored, oily fish. Most herring sold to food-service and retail establishments is pickled or smoked rather than fresh, but fresh herring is sometimes available. Smoked herring are sometimes called *kippers*. Fresh herring are excellent butterflied or left whole and grilled. Because of their high fat content, they do not keep well, so they should be checked carefully for freshness when purchased.

Weight: Up to 8 oz (240 g).

Blue runner, a type of jack

Jack

JACK

Type: Fat.

Varieties: Members of the jack family include kingfish, blue runner, yellowtail, amberjack, and golden thread. The best-known jack is the pompano, listed separately.

Characteristics: Smooth, shiny skin; firm, oily flesh; strong flavor. Some varieties are much stronger in flavor than others.

Weight: Varies greatly depending on variety.

JOHN DORY

Also known as *St. Peter's fish*, *St Pierre*.

Type: Lean.

Characteristics: Identified by the characteristic black spot ("St. Peter's thumbprint") on each side of the body behind the head. Firm, sweet, white flesh with fine flakes; broad, thin fillets.

Weight: About 2 lb (900 g) average.

Boston mackerel

MACKEREL

Type: Fat.

Varieties: Spanish and Boston mackerel are the most common small varieties. King mackerel is larger, usually cut into steaks.

Characteristics: Fat, firm flesh with rich flavor and slightly dark color.

Weight: ½ to 5 lb (0.2 to 2.3 kg).

Spanish mackerel

MAHI-MAHI

Also known as *dorado* and *dolphinfish* (not related to the mammal called dolphin).

Type: Lean.

Characteristics: Firm, fine-textured, pinkish flesh with rich, sweet taste. Becomes very dry when overcooked, so best cooked with moist heat or with fat or served with a sauce.

Weight: 5 to 40 lb (2.3 to 18 kg).

Mahi-mahi

MONKFISH

Also known as *lotte*, *anglerfish*, *bellyfish*.

Type: Lean.

Characteristics: Large, ugly fish, but only tail is used. White, very firm flesh with fine texture, somewhat like lobster. Rich flavor. Holds up well in soups and stews, but dries out easily if cooked dry without fat.

Weight: 5 to 50 lb (2.3 to 23 kg).

Monkfish

OCEAN PERCH

Type: Lean.

Varieties: Many. Red-skinned varieties (redfish) are especially popular and more expensive.

Characteristics: Mild, somewhat bony.

Weight: Depends on variety, but typically about 1 lb (0.5 kg).

ORANGE ROUGHY

Type: Lean.

Characteristics: A South Pacific fish increasingly available in some markets. Texture and flavor similar to red snapper.

Weight: ¾ to 2 lb (0.3 to 1 kg).

Pompano

POMPANO

Type: Fat.

Characteristics: Small fish with rich, sweet-flavored flesh. Expensive. A variety of jack (see entry above).

Weight: ¾ to 2 lb (0.3 to 1 kg).

Porgy

PORGY

Type: Lean.

Characteristics: Small, oval fish. Sweet and mild, but quite bony.

Weight: Up to 2 lb (1 kg).

RED MULLET

Red mullet

Also known as *rouget barbet* (roo-zhay bar-bay), *rouget*.

Type: Lean.

Varieties: A member of the goatfish family. In addition to the Mediterranean variety discussed here, similar varieties are found in North American waters.

Characteristics: Mediterranean fish resembling a small red snapper. Rich flavor, with a slight taste of shrimp or lobster. Always cooked with skin on, because much of the desired flavor comes from the skin.

Weight: Usually 12 oz (350 g) or less.

Red snapper

RED SNAPPER

Type: Lean.

Characteristics: Firm, delicate, sweet white flesh with large flakes. Large, coarse bones. Skin is red. Highly prized, and popular in restaurants.

Weight: 1 to 15 lb (0.5 to 7 kg).

Salmon

SALMON

Type: Fat. Anadromous.

Varieties: Atlantic, chinook, sockeye, coho, chum, humpback.

Characteristics: Rich pink to red flesh, with somewhat meaty texture and flavor. One of the most prized of all fish. Much is canned or smoked.

Weight: 4 to 25 lb (2 to 11 kg).

SARDINE

See Herring. True sardines are closely related to herring, but are scarce. Most fish sold as sardines are actually small herring. Usually sold canned.

Sardine

SHAD

Type: Fat. Anadromous.

Characteristics: Oily, rich flavor and many bones in several rows in each fillet. Its roe (egg sacs) is especially prized. Fresh shad is highly seasonal (February to June).

Weight: 1½ to 5 lb (0.7 to 2.3 kg).

SHARK

Type: Fat.

Varieties: Mako shark is the variety usually used.

Characteristics: Firm texture, similar to swordfish, but softer and a little moister and with finer grain; less expensive. Has cartilage skeleton, no bones. Usually cut into steaks.

Weight: 25 to 40 lb (11 to 18 kg).

SKATE

Also known as *ray*.

Type: Lean.

Characteristics: May be sold whole, but often only the triangular wings are marketed. Skeleton is cartilage, not bone; tough skin, gray on top, white on bottom. Flesh consists of sweet, white, gelatinous strips of meat extending the width of the wings; two fillets per wing, one above and one below the cartilage.

Weight: Some varieties weigh up to a ton, but most sold for food weigh 1 to 4 lb (0.5 to 2 kg) per wing.

Skate wings, top view (left) and bottom view (right)

STRIPED BASS

Type: Lean.

Varieties: Wild striped bass is highly prized but available in only small numbers in recent years. Farmed striped bass, developed in response to demand, is a cross between white bass and wild striped bass.

Characteristics: Firm, white, delicately flavored fish with large flakes.

Weight: 1 to 10 lb (0.5 to 4.5 kg).

Striped bass

SWORDFISH

Type: Fat.

Characteristics: Very large, fat fish with dense, meaty, not flaky, texture. High yield. Sold mostly as steaks. Expensive.

Weight: Up to 1,000 lb (450 kg).

TILEFISH

Type: Lean.

Characteristics: Firm, sweet, mild white flesh, pinkish when raw. Used mostly for steaks, but smaller ones can be filleted or poached whole.

Weight: 4 to 8 lb (1.8 to 3.6 kg).

Tilefish

TRIGGERFISH

Type: Lean.

Characteristics: Tough-skinned fish with firm, meaty, white to gray-white flesh. Low yield because of large head.

Weight: About 2 lb (900 g) average.

Triggerfish

TUNA

Type: Fat.

Varieties: Yellowfin and bluefin have red flesh, gray when cooked. Albacore (more often canned than used fresh) has pink flesh, off-white when cooked. Some other varieties are also available.

Characteristics: Meaty texture and appearance. Belly cuts much fattier than back ("loin"). Red-fleshed varieties often served raw as sashimi or sushi. When cooked, usually cut into steaks and grilled. Should not be cooked well done, or will be very dry.

Weight: Depends on variety. May be several hundred pounds (100 kg and up).

WAHOO OR ONO

Type: Fat.

Characteristics: Firm flesh similar in texture to mackerel and tuna, to which it is related. Pale pink flesh turns white when cooked. The biology of this fish is not well known, and there are concerns about overfishing. It is a popular sport fish.

Weight: 11 to 80 lb (5 to 35 kg), but can be much larger.

Weakfish

WEAKFISH

Also called *sea trout*, but unrelated to trout.

Type: Lean.

Characteristics: Mild, light-gray flesh with soft texture.

Weight: Up to 10 lb (4.5 kg).

Whiting

WHITING

Type: Lean.

Characteristics: Fragile, white flesh with mild flavor. Fillets must be handled carefully or they will break up.

Weight: ¼ to 3 lb (0.1 to 1.4 kg).

Catfish

Freshwater Fish

CATFISH

Type: Fat to somewhat lean, depending on origin.

Varieties: Bullhead is similar, but it is not the same species.

Characteristics: Firm flesh with abundant flavor. Layer of fat directly under skin. Catfish has no scales and is usually skinned before frying or pan-frying. Farmed catfish is milder and usually leaner than wild catfish.

Weight: 1 to 8 lb (0.5 to 3.6 kg).

EEL

Type: Fat.

Characteristics: A long, slender, snakelike fish with a slippery skin. Flesh is firm, mild, and oily. Must be alive until shortly before cooking or flesh will be mushy. Skin before cooking and fillet or cut into 1½-in. (4-cm) lengths. Popular in Japanese restaurants (where it is called *unagi*), served filleted and grilled, basted with a soy-based glaze.

Weight: Typically 2 to 4 lb (900 g to 1.8 kg), but can be much smaller or larger.

Eel

PERCH

Type: Lean.

Varieties: Yellow perch is the most common. Walleyed pike is actually a perch, not a pike. Zander (French: *sandre*) is a popular European perch sometimes mislabeled in North America as European walleye, although it is different from, and usually less expensive than, true walleye.

Characteristics: Mild-flavored, flaky white flesh with firm texture and fine grain.

Weight: ½ to 5 lb (0.2 to 2.3 kg).

Perch

PIKE

Type: Lean.

Varieties: Northern pike is most common in North America. Walleyed pike or walleye is not a pike but a perch.

Characteristics: Firm white flesh similar to perch but not as thick, and with many small bones.

Weight: 2 to 12 lb (1 to 5.4 kg).

TILAPIA

Type: Lean.

Characteristics: Nearly always from aquafarms, because wild tilapia often taste muddy. Firm, mild white flesh.

Weight: Up to 3 lb (1.4 kg); usually about 1½ lb (700 g).

Tilapia

TROUT

Type: Fat.

Varieties: Lake trout, river trout, brook trout, rainbow trout, steelhead trout, many local varieties.

Characteristics: Soft, fine-textured flesh with rich, delicate flavor. Color of flesh may be white, pink, or reddish.

Weight: Lake trout: 4 to 10 lb (2 to 4.5 kg). Others: ½ to 3 lb (0.2 to 1.4 kg).

Trout

WHITEFISH

Type: Fat.

Characteristics: Flaky, white flesh with somewhat sweet flavor.

Weight: 1½ to 6 lb (0.7 to 2.7 kg).

Whitefish

ZANDER (SEE PERCH)

Handling and Storage

Fish and shellfish are among the most perishable foods you will handle. It is especially important to store them carefully and use them quickly. The fishy taste that turns many people away from fish is actually a sign of decomposition. Fresh fish tastes and smells sweet and fresh.

Guidelines for checking fish quality are summarized in Table 3.1.

Table 3.1 Checklist for Fish Freshness

Characteristics	Fresh Fish	Not-So-Fresh Fish
Overall appearance	Good appearance, clear slime, moist and pliable fins	Dry or cloudy appearance, dried fins, bruises or cuts in flesh
Odor (see Note)	Fresh and mild, no off-odors	Strong fishy odor
Eyes	Clear, shiny, bulging	Cloudy, sunken
Gills	Red or pink	Gray or brown
Texture of flesh	Firm, elastic	Soft, dents easily
Scales	Shiny, tight on skin	Loose, not shiny
Belly cavity	No belly burn; natural-colored flesh, pink or red along backbone (see Note)	Belly burn: browned, decomposed flesh along ribs and backbone

Note: Because most fish is not purchased whole or dressed but as fillets, steaks, or other portions, odor must be your primary check for freshness.
Belly burn results when the intestines are left in the cavity too long, resulting in spoilage.

Storing Fresh Fish

OBJECTIVES

1. To maintain temperature of 29° to 32°F (−2° to 0°C).
2. To keep the fish moist.
3. To prevent fish odors and flavors from transferring to other foods.
4. To protect the delicate flesh from being bruised or crushed.

METHODS

1. On crushed ice—the preferred method. Use drip pans to allow for drainage of melted ice. Change ice daily. Cover container or store in separate box away from other foods. Whole fish should be ***drawn***—that is, viscera removed (see Figure 3.1)—as soon as possible because the entrails deteriorate quickly. Whole or drawn fish are not wrapped. Cut fish (fillets, steaks, portions) should be wrapped or left in original moistureproof wrap.

2. In refrigerated box at 29° to 32°F (−2° to 0°C) if crushed ice storage is not available or practical. Wrap all fish or leave in original moistureproof wrap.

STORAGE TIME

Fresh fish may be stored 1 or 2 days. If it must be kept longer, you may (1) wrap and freeze it immediately, or (2) cook and then refrigerate it for later use in recipes calling for cooked fish.

Check stored fish for freshness just before you use it. Even if it was fresh when received, it may not be fresh after a few days in storage.

Frozen, Canned, and Other Processed Fish

FEDERAL INSPECTION

In the United States, the National Oceanic and Atmospheric Administration (NOAA) and the Department of Commerce conduct voluntary seafood inspection programs to promote the safety of processed fish and shellfish. Processors who wish to take part in the programs must pay for the service, but they may then use official seals or marks on their product packaging and in advertising, including the PUFI seal (Processed Under Federal Inspection, Figure 3.6) and the U.S. Grade A shield (Figure 3.7).The PUFI seal indicates the product is packed under federal inspection and is safe and wholesome, of good quality, and properly labeled. In addition, companies that operate with a written HACCP quality management program may take advantage of the Department of Commerce's HACCP-based inspection program.

Figure 3.6 Seafood PUFI seal (U.S.)

Figure 3.7 Seafood grade shield (U.S.)

FROZEN FISH

Frozen seafood products account for more of the fish served today than do fresh. If it were not for the wide availability of frozen seafood products, commercial kitchens would serve much less fish than they do.

CHECKING QUALITY

1. Frozen products should be frozen, not thawed, when received.
2. Look for fresh, sweet odor or none at all. Strong, fishy odor means poor handling.
3. Items should be well wrapped, with no freezer burn.
4. Some frozen fish is glazed with a thin layer of ice to prevent drying. Check for shiny surface to make sure glaze has not melted off or evaporated.

STORAGE

1. Store at 0°F (−18°C) or colder.
2. Keep well wrapped to prevent freezer burn.
3. Maximum storage time:

    Fat fish: 2 months.

    Lean fish: 6 months.

4. Rotate stock—first in, first out.

THAWING AND HANDLING

1. Frozen raw fish.
    - Thaw in refrigerator, never at room temperature. Allow 18 to 36 hours, depending on size. Alternative method, if pressed for time: Keep in original moistureproof wrapper and thaw under cold running water.
    - Small pieces (fillets, steaks, portions) up to 8 oz (250 g) can be cooked from frozen state to make handling easier and to prevent excessive drip loss. Large fish should be thawed for more even cooking from surface to interior.
    - Fillets or other portions to be breaded or prepared in some other way before cooking may be partially thawed (for example, for a few seconds in a microwave) and then prepped and cooked. They will be easier to handle than if fully thawed.
    - Handle thawed fish as you would fresh fish.
    - Do not refreeze.
2. Breaded and battered fish, fully prepared entrées, and other frozen, prepared fish items.
    - Read and follow package directions.
    - Most of these items are cooked from the frozen state, usually in the deep fryer, oven, microwave, or steamer.

CANNED FISH

1. Check cans for signs of damage. Discard swollen cans (or return to the supplier).
2. Store, like other canned goods, in a cool, dry place.
3. Opened canned fish should be placed in covered containers, labeled with the contents and date, and refrigerated. It will keep for 2 or 3 days.

KEY POINTS TO REVIEW

- What are the four main kinds of saltwater flatfish used in food service? List examples of saltwater round fish and freshwater fish and briefly describe each.
- What are the key signs of freshness in fish?
- How should fresh fish be stored? How should frozen fish be stored and thawed?

SHELLFISH

Shellfish are distinguished from fin fish by their hard outer shells and their lack of backbone or internal skeleton.

There are two classifications of shellfish:

1. ***Mollusks*** are soft sea animals that fall into three main categories:
   - ***Bivalves***, which have a pair of hinged shells (such as clams and oysters).
   - ***Univalves***, which have a single shell (such as abalone and conch).
   - ***Cephalopods*** (such as octopus, squid, and cuttlefish).

   From the scientist's point of view, there are other mollusks as well, but they do not concern us here.
2. ***Crustaceans*** are animals with segmented shells and jointed legs.

Mollusks

The most important mollusks in commercial kitchens are oysters, clams, mussels, scallops, squid, and octopus.

Oysters

CHARACTERISTICS

St. James River oysters

Pine Island oysters

1. Oysters have rough, irregular shells. The bottom shell is slightly bowl-shaped. The top shell is flat.
2. The flesh of the oyster is extremely soft and delicate and contains a high percentage of water.
3. Oysters are available all year, even in months without an *R* in their names, but they are at their best in the fall, winter, and spring.
4. There are four main varieties in the United States and Canada, depending on their origin. Note in particular that the dozens of varieties of Eastern oysters are all the same species; their flavors differ, however, depending on the environment in which they grew.

   Eastern: Known by many local names, depending on their place of origin, such as Bluepoint (Long Island), Box Oyster (Long Island), Chesapeake Bay, Chincoteague (Virginia), Cotuit (Nantucket), Kent Island (Maryland), Malpeque (Prince Edward Island, Canada), Patuxent (Maryland), Apalachicola (Florida), Breton Sound (Louisiana), Wellfleet (Massachusetts).

   Olympia: Very small, from the Pacific coast.

   Belon: European oyster now grown in North America. Shells are flatter than those of Eastern oysters. More properly called *European flat oysters*, reserving the term *Belon* for those flat oysters grown near the mouth of the Loire River in France. Prized for their intense, briny flavor.

   Japanese or Pacific: Usually large oysters from the Pacific coast. The much smaller kumamoto oyster is of the same species.

MARKET FORMS

1. Live, in the shell.
2. Shucked—fresh or frozen. Shucked oysters are graded by size as follows.

Grade	Number per Gallon (3.8 liters)
Extra Large or Counts	160 or fewer
Large or Extra Selects	161 to 210
Medium or Selects	211 to 300
Small or Standards	301 to 500
Very Small	Over 500

3. Canned—rarely used in food service.

CHECKING FRESHNESS

1. Oysters in the shell must be alive to be good to eat. Tightly closed shells, or shells that close when jostled, indicate live oysters. Discard dead ones.
2. Live or shucked oysters should have a very mild, sweet smell. Strong odors indicate spoilage.

OPENING OYSTERS

1. Scrub shells thoroughly before opening.
2. Oysters to be served raw must be opened in a way that leaves the bottom shell intact and the tender oyster undamaged. The technique illustrated in Figure 3.8 is one common way of opening oysters. Your instructor may wish to show you another method.
3. Oysters to be cooked may be opened by spreading them on a sheet pan and placing them in a hot oven just until the shells open. Remove from shells and cook immediately. Discard any that do not open.

STORAGE

1. Keep live oysters in a cold, wet place in the cartons or sacks in which they arrived. They should keep at least 1 week.
2. Store fresh shucked oysters in their original container in the refrigerator at 30° to 34°F (−1° to 1°C). They will keep up to 1 week.
3. Keep frozen oysters in the freezer at 0°F (−18°C) or colder, until ready for use. Thaw in refrigerator 24 hours or more, depending on size of container.

COOKING OYSTERS

1. Cook just enough to heat through to keep oysters juicy and plump. Overcooking makes them shrunken and dry.
2. Cooking methods: Poaching, deep-frying, baking on the half-shell with toppings, in soups and stews.

Clams

CHARACTERISTICS

There are two major kinds of clams from the east coast of North America: hard shell and soft shell. The West Coast also has some local varieties.

1. *Hard-shell clams* or *quahogs*. These go by different names, depending on size.

   Littlenecks are the smallest. They are the most tender for eating raw or for steaming.

   Cherrystones are medium-sized, and perhaps the most common. They can be eaten raw and are good for steaming, though tougher than littlenecks.

   Chowders, the largest, are also called *quahogs* in the Northeast. Rather tough, they are chopped for cooking in chowders or cut into strips for frying.

Figure 3.8 Opening oysters.

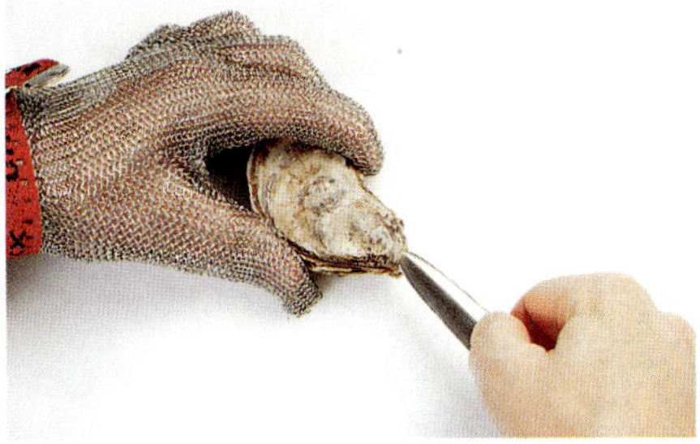

(a) Examine the shell to see that it is tightly closed, indicating a live oyster. Rinse the shell under cold running water. Hold oyster in left hand, as shown. (Left-handers will hold oyster in right hand.) Hold the oyster knife near the tip as shown. Insert the knife between the shells near the hinge.

(b) Twist the knife to break the hinge.

(c) Slide the knife under the top shell and cut through the adductor muscle (which closes the shells) near the top shell. Try not to cut the flesh of the oyster, or it will lose plumpness. Remove the top shell.

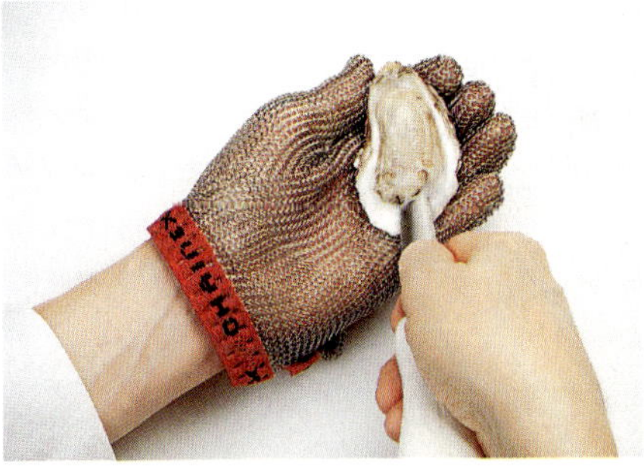

(d) Carefully cut the lower end of the muscle from the bottom shell to loosen oyster. Remove any particles of shell from the oyster before serving.

Clams, clockwise from top left: steamers, littlenecks, cherrystones, chowder clams.

Cockles

2. *Soft-shell clams*. These are sometimes called *longnecks* because of the long tube that protrudes from between the shells. They have very thin shells that do not close completely. They are also called *steamers* because the usual way to serve them is to steam them and serve them with their own broth and with melted butter for dipping.

3. *Cockles*. These are not actually clams. They are from a different family, even though they look like tiny clams that are usually no more than 1 in. (2.5 cm) across. They can be cooked like clams and are almost always served in the shell.

MARKET FORMS (HARD-SHELL CLAMS)

1. Live, in the shell.
2. Shucked, fresh or frozen.
3. Canned, whole or chopped.

CHECKING FRESHNESS

Same as for oysters. Clams in the shell must be alive. Live and shucked clams should smell fresh.

OPENING CLAMS

1. Scrub shells thoroughly before opening.
2. Hard-shell clams are sometimes sandy inside, and soft-shell clams nearly always are. They can be flushed as follows:
   - Make a salt brine, using ⅓ cup salt per gallon of water (20 mL salt per liter).
   - Soak the clams in the brine 20 minutes.
   - Drain and repeat until the clams are free of sand.
   - Some chefs put cornmeal in the water and refrigerate the clams in it for a day. The clams eat the cornmeal and expel the sand.
   - Rinse in fresh water before using.
3. Opening hard-shell clams is different from opening oysters. This technique is illustrated in Figure 3.9.
4. Like oysters, clams to be cooked may be opened by spreading on sheet pans and placing in a hot oven just until the shells open. Discard any that do not open because they were likely dead before cooking.

STORAGE

Same as for oysters.

COOKING CLAMS

1. Clams become tough and rubbery if overcooked. Cook just enough to heat through.
2. When steaming clams in the shell, steam just until shells open.
3. Cooking methods: Steaming, poaching, deep-frying, baking on the half-shell with toppings, simmering in soups and chowders.

Mussels

CHARACTERISTICS

The most common mussels resemble small black or dark-blue clams. Their shells are not as heavy as clamshells. Their flesh is yellow to orange in color and firm but tender when cooked. Mussels are harvested worldwide and are also extensively farmed.

Figure 3.9 Opening clams.

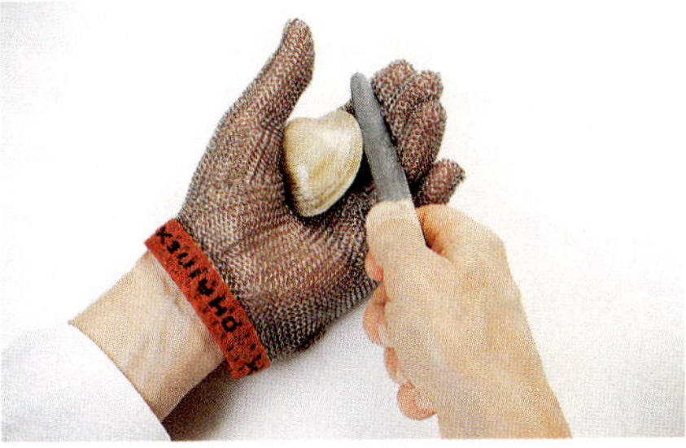

(a) Examine the shell to see that it is tightly closed, indicating a live clam. Rinse the shell under cold running water. Avoid jostling the clam too much, or it will "clam up" tighter. Hold clam in left hand as shown (or in right hand if you are left-handed). Place the sharp edge of the clam knife against the crack between the shells.

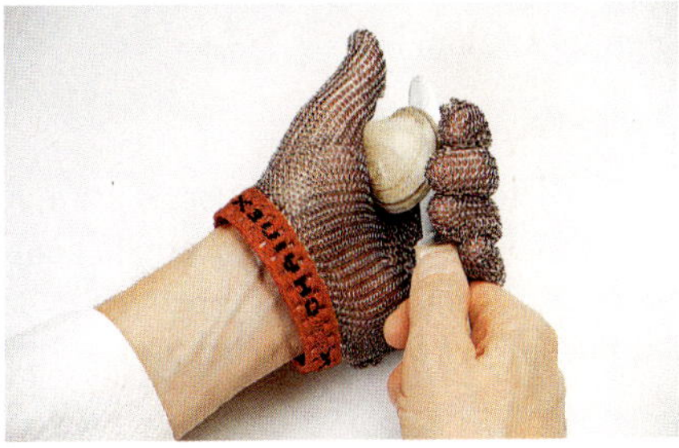

(b) Squeeze with the fingers of the left hand, forcing the knife between the shells.

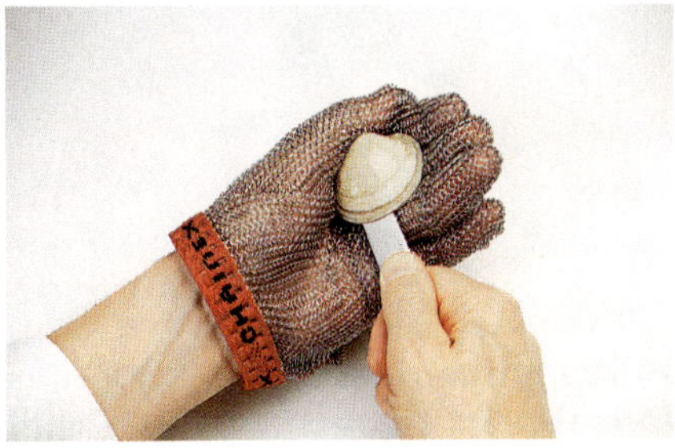

(c) Change the angle of the blade as shown in the illustration and slide the knife against the top shell to cut the adductor muscles (clams have two; oysters have only one). Be careful not to cut or pierce the soft clam.

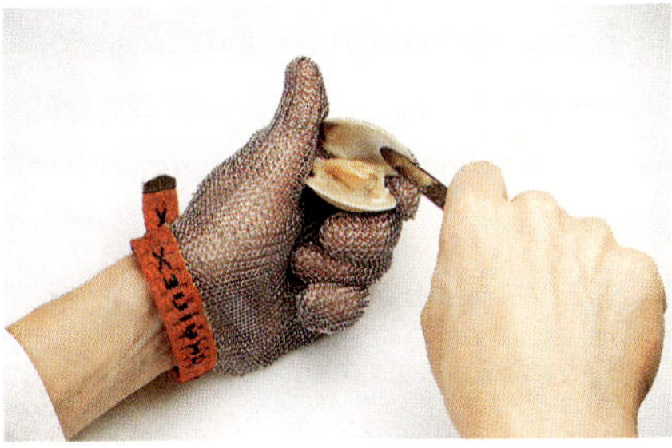

(d) Open the clam and finish detaching the meat from the upper shell.

(e) Cut the muscles against the lower shell to loosen the clam completely. Discard the top shell. Remove any particles of shell from the clam before serving.

Green mussels, from New Zealand and Southeast Asia, are larger and have a lighter-colored gray or tan shell with a green edge. Green mussels often command premium prices.

MARKET FORMS

Most mussels are sold alive in the shell. Many are also sold shucked and packed in brine.

Mussels, left to right: green, blue (wild), blue (farm-raised)

CHECKING FRESHNESS

1. Like oysters and clams, mussels must be alive to be good to eat. Check for tightly closed shells or shells that just close when jostled.
2. Discard any mussels that are very light in weight or seem to be hollow. Also, discard any that are much too heavy—they are probably full of sand.

CLEANING

1. Clean shells thoroughly:
    - Scrub well under cold running water.
    - Scrape off barnacles, if any, with a clam knife.
    - Remove the beard, a fibrous appendage protruding from between the shells (see Figure 3.10). Do not do this until just before cooking, because it may kill the shellfish.
2. Mussels may be sandy inside if not commercially grown. They may be soaked in brine and flour or cornmeal like clams (see previous section) to rid them of sand.

New Zealand green lips

Figure 3.10 When cleaning mussels, pull off the fibrous beard that extends from between the shells.

STORAGE
Keep refrigerated at 32° to 35°F (0° to 2°C) and protect from light. Store in original sack and keep sack damp.

COOKING
Unlike oysters and clams, mussels are almost never served raw. They are usually steamed and served in their cooking broth, in soups, or chilled and served with mayonnaise-type sauces. Cook only until shells open and mussels are heated through. Do not overcook. Discard any that are not open after cooking.

Scallops

CHARACTERISTICS

1. Scallops are almost always sold shucked. The only part we usually eat is the *adductor muscle*, which closes the shell. If live scallops in the shell are available, leave the orange, crescent-shaped coral attached to the adductor muscle when shucking.
2. There are two main kinds of scallop:

   Bay scallops: Small, with delicate flavor and texture; expensive; 32 to 40 per lb (70 to 88 per kg) on average.

   Sea scallops: Larger, not as delicate as bay scallops, but still tender unless overcooked; 10 to 15 per lb (22 to 33 per kg) on average.
3. Scallops are creamy white in color and have a sweet flavor.
4. They are available all year.

MARKET FORMS

1. Fresh, shucked. Sold by volume or weight.
2. Frozen.
   - IQF (individually quick frozen).
   - In 5-lb (2.3-kg) blocks.

Scallops with roe or coral

CHECKING FRESHNESS
A sweet, clean smell is a sign of freshness. Strong fishy odor or a brownish color is a sign of age or spoilage.

HANDLING

1. Shucked scallops can be cooked without further preparation. They are improved, however, if you pull off the small, tough tendon or sinew on the side of each, as shown in Figure 3.11.
2. Large sea scallops are sometimes cut into smaller pieces before cooking.

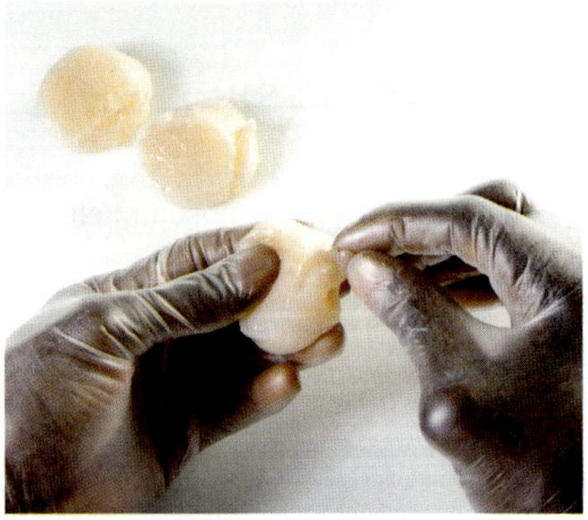
Figure 3.11 Removing the tendon from the side of a scallop

STORAGE
Keep scallops covered and refrigerated at 30° to 34°F (–1° to 1°C). Do not let them rest directly on ice, or they will lose flavor and become watery.

COOKING SCALLOPS
Scallops are cooked in almost every way that fish are cooked. The most popular methods are sautéing, deep-frying, broiling, and poaching.

Cephalopods

Cephalopods are classified as mollusks, even though they have no external shell. The term *cephalopod* means "head-foot," referring to the fact that these animals have tentacles, or "legs," attached to the head and surrounding the mouth. The most important cephalopods in the North American kitchen are squid and octopus. A third type, cuttlefish, is similar to squid but is usually seen only in limited markets.

Squid

Squid are usually referred to on menus by their Italian name, *calamari*. They are soft-bodied animals somewhat resembling octopus, but they have 10 tentacles, 2 of them longer than the others.

Squid must be skinned and eviscerated. The head, beak, and the internal plastic-like quill are discarded. The hollow body and tentacles are eaten. Figure 3.12 illustrates how to clean squid.

Somewhat chewy, squid are cut up and either fried quickly or simmered about 45 minutes in a seasoned liquid or sauce.

Note: The similar *cuttlefish* has a shorter, thicker body than does squid. Instead of a thin, transparent interior quill, it has a hard, chalky cuttlebone.

Octopus

Octopus (the name means "eight feet") range in size from less than an ounce to many pounds. All sizes are firm-textured, even chewy, but the larger sizes are usually considered too tough to eat. Because of its texture, octopus requires either mechanical tenderization (such as pounding with a mallet) or long, slow cooking in a court bouillon.

Like squid, octopus is cleaned by cutting off the tentacles, discarding the head and beak, and eviscerating the body cavity. Pull the skin off the body pouch and tentacles; it may be necessary to parboil the octopus a few minutes to loosen the skin. The skin is reddish gray, turning purple-red when cooked.

Figure 3.12 Cleaning squid.

(a) Pull off the head. The interior organs will come out with it.

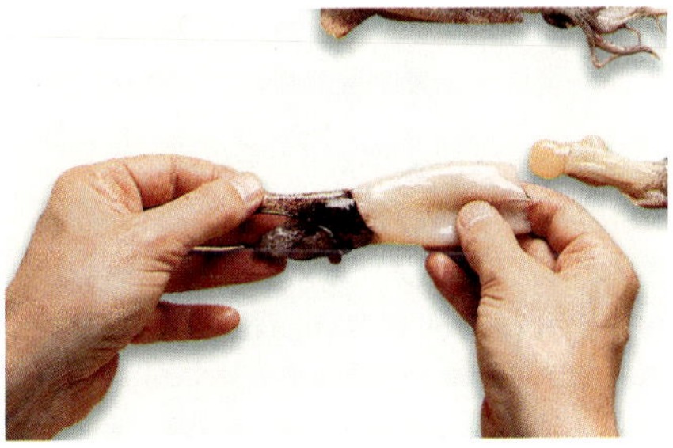

(b) Pull off the skin.

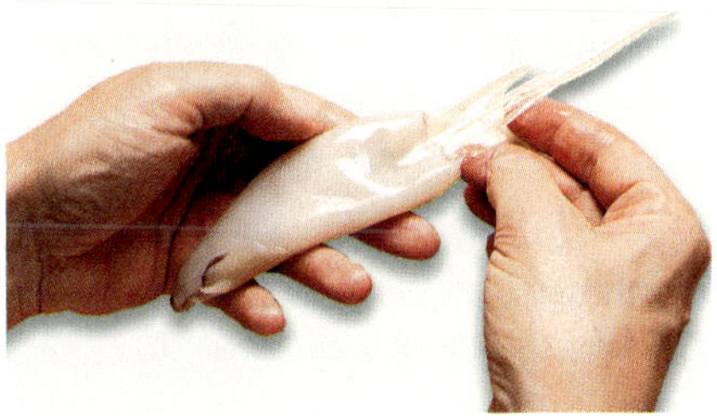

(c) Pull out the plastic-like quill from the body sac. Rinse out the sac to clean it well.

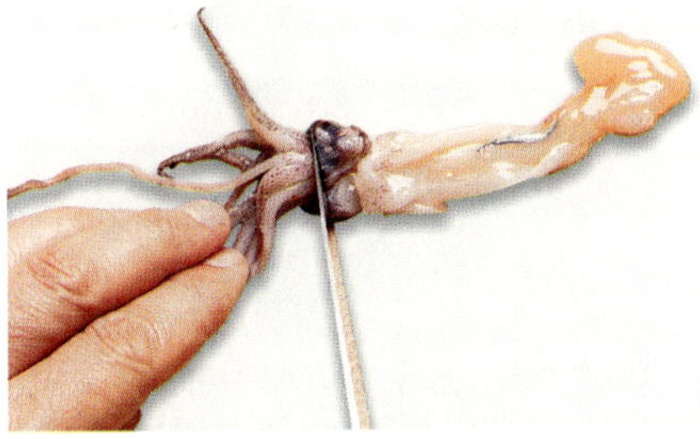

(d) Cut off the tentacles just above the eyes. Discard the head and organs.

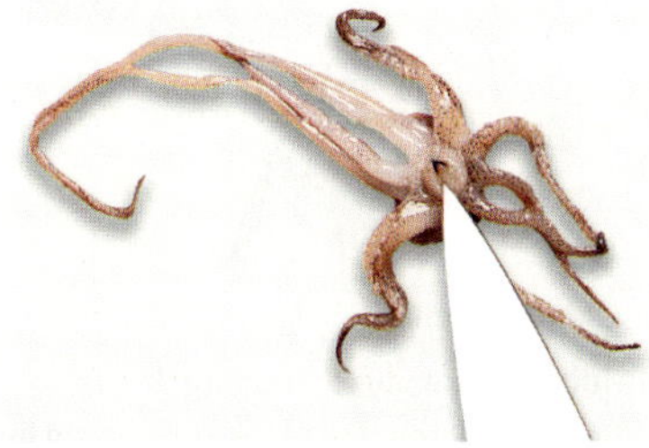

(e) Be sure to remove the hard beak, which is found at the center of the tentacle cluster, as shown by the tip of the knife in this picture.

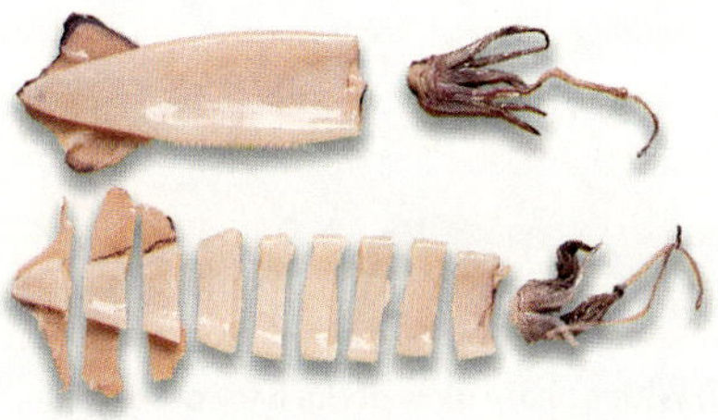

(f) The body sac may be left whole for stuffing or cut into rings for frying, sautéing, or stewing.

Crustaceans

The most important crustaceans in commercial kitchens are lobsters, rock lobsters or langoustes, shrimp, and crabs.

Lobsters

CHARACTERISTICS

1. The northern lobster is perhaps the most prized of all shellfish. It has a large, flexible tail, four pairs of legs, and two large claws. Its shell is dark green or bluish green but turns red when cooked.
2. Meat from the tail, claws, and legs is eaten. It is white and sweet, with a distinctive taste. Claw meat is considered especially good. The *coral* (roe or eggs), which is dark green when raw and red when cooked, and the green *tomalley* (liver) in the thorax or body portion are also eaten.
3. Lobsters are classified by weight.

Chicken	1 lb (450 g)
Quarters	1¼ lb (575 g)
Selects	1½ to 2¼ lb (675 to 1025 g)
Jumbos	over 2½ lb (1130 g)

4. Lobsters weighing over 20 lb (9 kg) have been caught, but they are rare.

Figure 3.13 Splitting a lobster for broiling

(a) Place the lobster on its back on a cutting board. With a firm thrust of a French knife, pierce the head.

(b) Bring the knife down firmly through the center of the lobster to split it in half.

(c) With the hands, crack the back of the shell by spreading the lobster open.

(d) Pull out and discard stomach, a sac just behind the eyes.

(e) If desired, remove the tomalley for use in the crumb stuffing.

(f) With a sharp blow of the back of the knife, crack the claws.

(g) The lobster is ready for broiling. If it is broiled as shown, the end of the tail should be weighted to keep it from curling.

(h) You may also split the tail all the way through and curl up the two sides as shown. In this position, weighting the tail is not necessary. Note the claws have been broken off and placed beside the lobster.

Figure 3.14 Cutting a lobster for sautés and stews.

(a) Place the lobster on the cutting board. Pierce the head with a firm thrust of the knife point to kill the lobster quickly.

(b) Cut off the legs and claws.

(c) Remove the tail section from the thorax, either by breaking it off or by inserting the knife behind the thorax as shown and cutting through the flesh.

(d) Cut the thorax in half lengthwise.

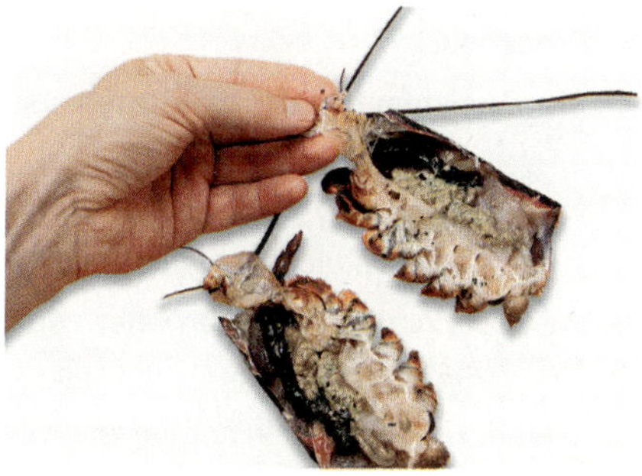

(e) Remove and discard the stomach, a sac just behind the eyes.

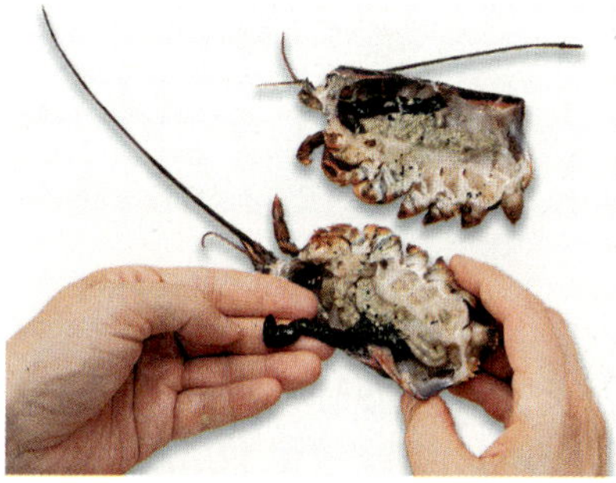

(f) Remove the tomalley and coral for use in the sauce to accompany the lobster.

5. Yield: A 1-lb lobster yields about ¼ lb cooked meat, or a 500-g lobster yields about 125 g cooked meat.
6. Sometimes customers request female lobsters in order to get the coral, so you should be able to tell females from males. Look at the pairs of tiny legs (called *swimmerets*) under the tail. If the pair closest to the front is soft and flexible, the lobster is female. If it is hard, the lobster is male.

(g) Cut the tail into pieces where the segments join. This is a small lobster. Large tails should be cut into more pieces (at least four or five) so each piece is not too large.

MARKET FORMS

1. Live.
2. Cooked meat, fresh or frozen.

CHECKING FRESHNESS

1. Live lobster must be alive when cooked. This is indicated by movement of the legs and claws and by a tightly curled tail.
2. If the lobster is dead when cooked, the meat will fall apart. If it is alive, the meat will be firm and the tail will spring back when straightened.
3. Sleepers (dying lobsters) should be cooked immediately so the meat will still be usable.
4. Cooked lobster meat (fresh or thawed) should smell fresh and sweet.

(h) The cut-up lobster, ready to cook.

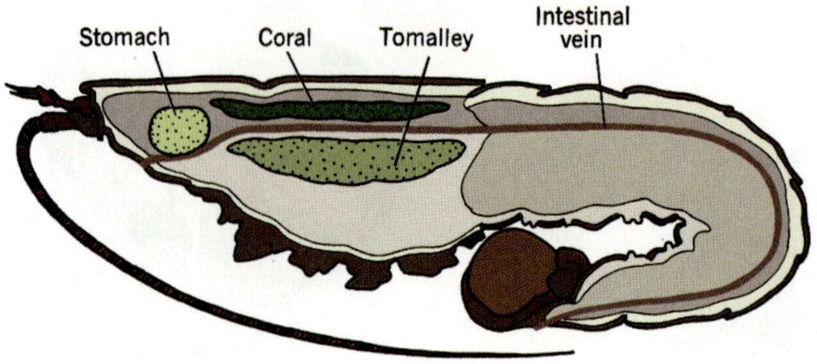

Figure 3.15 Cross-section of a female lobster showing the location of the stomach, tomalley, coral, and vein.

HANDLING

1. Live lobsters are either cooked live or cut up before cooking (as for broiling or sautéing). Live lobsters are plunged headfirst into boiling water to kill them instantly. They are then simmered 5 to 6 minutes per lb (500 g). If served hot, they are drained well and split in half, and the claws are cracked.
2. Splitting and cutting up live lobsters is necessary for certain preparations. Figure 3.13 shows splitting a lobster for broiling. Figure 3.14 shows cutting up a lobster for sautés and stews. Note that the methods are somewhat different.
3. The thorax section contains three parts you should recognize. Figure 3.15 shows their location.
   - The stomach, or sac, located just behind the eyes, is often sandy and should be discarded.
   - The tomalley, or liver, is pale green. It is eaten plain or removed, mashed, and added to sauces that accompany the lobster.
   - The coral, or roe, is red when cooked and dark green when raw. It is present only in females. Like the tomalley, it is considered a delicacy.
   - The intestinal vein may be removed from the split lobster if it contains dark material, but is often left in if it is clear.

STORAGE

1. Live lobsters can be kept in two ways:
   - Packed in moist seaweed or in moist, heavy paper, kept in a cool place.
   - In saltwater. Special lobster tanks are used in restaurants for display and so customers can select their own lobster. Air must be bubbled through the water to keep the lobsters alive.
2. Cooked lobster meat must be covered and refrigerated at 30° to 34°F (–1° to 1°C). It is very perishable and should be used in 1 or 2 days.

COOKING LOBSTERS

1. Lobster meat becomes tough if cooked at too high a temperature or for too long. Boiling too long will also make the meat dry. Whole lobster is usually cooked by dropping into boiling water and then simmering 5 to 6 minutes per lb (500 g). For jumbo lobsters, reduce the cooking time slightly.
2. Whole or cut-up lobster can be cooked by simmering in water or court bouillon, simmering in sauce or soup, sautéing, baking, or broiling.

Rock Lobsters

CHARACTERISTICS

1. Rock lobsters are also known as *spiny lobsters* or *langoustes*. They are warm-water relatives of northern lobsters but have no claws. Only the tails are marketed, sold as lobster tails.

2. The flesh of the rock lobster tail is similar to that of the northern or Maine lobster, but it is drier and coarser, with less flavor.
3. Rock lobster tails weigh 2 to 12 oz (60 to 340 g).
4. ***Langoustines***, or ***langostinos***, are smaller relatives of the rock lobster. These small shellfish are often marketed as ***rock shrimp***. When out of the shell, they look like shrimp, but their flavor is milder and sweeter than shrimp. ***Scampi*** (plural form of *scampo*) refers not to shrimp but to a variety of langoustine from Italian waters. The name *scampi* is often used, incorrectly, for large shrimp broiled with butter and garlic.

MARKET FORMS

Nearly all rock lobster tails are sold IQF (individually quick frozen).

HANDLING AND COOKING

1. Rock lobsters are handled and cooked much like northern lobsters. The most common cooking methods are steaming, simmering, and broiling.
2. Tails to be broiled will be moister if poached 5 minutes before splitting and broiling.
3. Tails steamed or simmered whole should have the shells split before serving as a convenience to the customer.

Shrimp

CHARACTERISTICS

1. Shrimp are small crustaceans that look somewhat like tiny, clawless lobsters. Only the tail is marketed and eaten, as a rule.
2. Shrimp come in many varieties, depending on where they are caught, but the particular variety is usually of little importance to the cook.
3. Shrimp are classified by count per pound—the higher the count, the smaller the shrimp. (For example, 16/20 means 16 to 20 per pound.) Classification systems differ by market—that is, in different markets a given size shrimp may have different names.
4. Large shrimp are more expensive per pound but require less work to peel and devein.
5. Yield: 1 lb raw shrimp (tails) in the shell yield about ½ lb peeled, cooked shrimp (500 g raw yields 250 g peeled, cooked).
6. The term ***prawn*** is sometimes used for large shrimp, sometimes for langoustines (see above). Use of the term varies from region to region.

MARKET FORMS

1. *Green shrimp* are raw shrimp in the shell.

    Fresh: Not widely available, except near source of supply.

    Frozen: In 5-lb (2.3-kg) blocks.
2. P/D (peeled, deveined): Usually IQF (individually quick frozen).
3. PDC (peeled, deveined, and cooked): Usually IQF.

    Note: IQF shrimp are usually glazed (see p. 67).

CHECKING FRESHNESS

1. Frozen shrimp should be solidly frozen when received.
2. Glazed shrimp should be shiny, with no freezer burn.
3. All shrimp should smell fresh and sweet. A strong fishy or iodine smell indicates age or spoilage.

Figure 3.16 Peeling and deveining shrimp.

(a) Pull off the legs with your forefinger.

(b) Peel back the shell as shown and remove.

(c) For deep-fried and broiled shrimp, leave on the tail section of the shell for appearance. This also gives you something to hold when dipping the shrimp in batter.

(d) For most other preparations, remove the tail section of the shell.

(e) With a paring knife, make a shallow cut down the back of the shrimp and pull out the intestinal vein, which is just below the surface.

(f) To butterfly shrimp, make the cut in step (e) deeper so the shrimp can be spread open as shown.

STORING

1. Like other frozen fish, shrimp should be kept frozen at 0°F (−18°C) or lower until ready for use.
2. Thaw in refrigerator, allowing sufficient slack time.
3. Fresh or thawed shrimp in the shell are stored on crushed ice, like whole fish.
4. Peeled shrimp lose soluble nutrients and flavor when stored unwrapped on ice. They should be wrapped before placing on ice or covered and simply refrigerated.

HANDLING

1. Shrimp served hot must normally be peeled and deveined before cooking. Figure 3.16 shows how.
2. Shrimp to be served cold may be peeled after cooking to preserve flavor.
3. Large shrimp are sometimes butterflied, as shown in Figure 3.16f. This is done for appearance (makes shrimp seem larger, with more surface area for breading) and to speed cooking by reducing thickness.

COOKING SHRIMP

Like most shellfish, shrimp become tough and rubbery when cooked at too high a heat. Shrimp can be cooked by simmering, deep-frying, sautéing, broiling, and baking.

Crabs

Six kinds of crab are important in commercial kitchens.

1. **Alaskan king crab.**
   Largest of the crabs, weighing 6 to 20 lb (2.7 to 9 kg). The meat can be removed in large chunks, making it especially attractive to serve in restaurants. It is expensive.
2. **Alaskan snow crab.**
   Smaller than the king crab. Often used as a less expensive substitute.
3. **Dungeness crab.**
   Another West Coast crab, weighing 1½ to 4 lb (0.7 to 1.8 kg). The meat is very sweet.
4. **Blue crab.**
   Small crab from the East Coast, weighing about 5 oz (150 g). Most frozen crabmeat is from blue crabs.
5. **Soft-shell crab.**
   Actually a molting blue crab, harvested before the new shell has hardened. It is sautéed or fried and eaten shell and all; only the gills and head are removed.

   Soft-shell crabs must be cleaned before being cooked. The procedure is shown in Figure 3.17.

Figure 3.17 Cleaning soft-shell crabs.

(a) Soft-shell crabs, seen from the bottom and top.

(b) Cut off the head just behind the eyes.

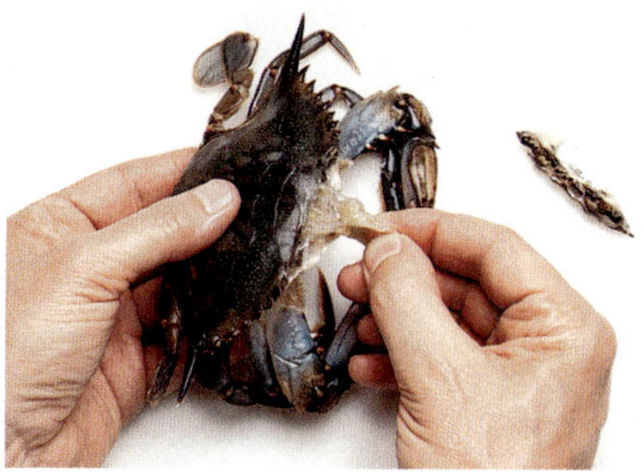

(c) Pull out the stomach sac.

(d) Pull back one side of the soft top shell to reveal the feathery gills.

(e) Pull off the gills. Repeat on the other side.

(f) Cut off the apron on the underside. The wide apron indicates this is a female crab. Males have a much narrower apron.

6. **Stone crab.**
   Popular in the Southeast. Only the claws are eaten.

MARKET FORMS

1. Live. Crabs taste best when fresh, but very few (except soft-shell crabs) are purchased live because of the labor required to pick the meat. An average blue crab yields less than 1 oz (30 g) meat.
2. Cooked, frozen, in the shell.

   King crab legs, whole and split.

   Snow and stone crab claws.

   Soft-shell crabs, whole.
3. Cooked, frozen meat. All varieties.

FRESHNESS AND STORAGE

1. Live crabs should be kept alive until cooked. They are packed in damp seaweed and kept cool.
2. Frozen crabmeat should be treated like any other frozen fish. It is very perishable when thawed.

HANDLING AND COOKING

1. Hard-shell crabs are picked of their meat after cooking.
   - Simmer 10 to 15 minutes in salted water (½ cup salt/gal or 30 mL/L). Cool rapidly in ice water.

Blue crab

Dungeness crab

Alaskan king crab legs

Alaskan snow crab legs

- Break off the pointed shell on the underside (called the *apron*) and remove the top shell.
- Remove and discard the spongy gills and the stomach, which is just behind the eyes.
- Pick out the body meat.
- Crack the legs and claws with a mallet or the back of a heavy knife and pick out the meat.

2. Soft-shell crabs.
   - With a knife or shears, cut off the head section, just behind the eyes.
   - Lift the pointed, outside corners of the top shell and pull out the spongy gills.
   - Cut off the apron, the small flap on the underside.
   - Dredge the crab in flour for sautéing, or bread or batter it for deep-frying.
3. Frozen crabmeat.
   - Crabmeat is usually watery. You may need to squeeze out excess moisture before cooking. Whenever possible, save the liquid for use in sauces and soups.
   - Frozen crabmeat is already cooked. It needs only to be heated through to be prepared for serving.

Crayfish

Crayfish or *crawfish* (the preferred term in the southern United States) are freshwater relatives of the lobster. Not long ago, they were used almost exclusively in Southern regional cuisine and in French restaurants. With the spreading popularity of Southern cuisines, including Creole and Cajun, they have become more widely available.

Crayfish are marketed live and frozen (peeled tail meat or whole).

Miscellaneous Seafood

Several other seafood items play a role in food-service kitchens. They are classified with fish, even though some of them spend part or all of their lives on land, like frogs and snails.

Snails or escargots are popular hors d'oeuvres when baked in their shells with a highly seasoned butter. Fresh snails require long, slow cooking before being baked with escargot butter, but canned snails are fully cooked and ready to prepare. Canned snails can be improved, however, by first simmering them in white wine and seasonings.

Frogs' legs are often compared to chicken in taste and texture (but then, so are a lot of things). Only the hind legs are used, and they are sold in pairs. They may be sautéed, deep-fried, or poached and served with a sauce.

Surimi is a processed seafood product made by grinding lean, inexpensive white fish, combining it with flavorings, and forming it into various shapes. The most popular shapes are shredded crab and crab leg segments, but other items, such as lobster claws, are also available. Coloring is added for a realistic appearance. Originally from Japan, surimi has found growing acceptance in North America because of the reasonably good quality of the product and the high cost of crab and lobster.

KEY POINTS TO REVIEW

- What are the four most important kinds of shelled mollusk in food service? Describe the characteristics and handling of each kind.
- What are the two most important kinds of cephalopod in food service? Describe the characteristics and handling of each kind.
- What are five kinds of crustacean used in food service? Describe the characteristics and handling of each kind.

TERMS FOR REVIEW

fin fish	dressed	cephalopod	rock shrimp
shellfish	anadromous	crustacean	scampi
flaking	catadromous	cockle	prawn
lean fish	drawn	calamari	crayfish
fat fish	mollusk	coral	surimi
flatfish	bivalve	tomalley	
round fish	univalve	langoustine/langostino	

QUESTIONS FOR DISCUSSION

1. Fish has very little connective tissue. How does this affect the ways in which you handle it and cook it?
2. Based on what you learned about fat and lean fish and about individual species of fish, suggest at least one cooking method for each of the following.

Mackerel	Salmon
Cod	Perch
Flounder	Swordfish
Trout	Whitefish
Red snapper	Halibut

3. List and describe the major market forms of fresh fish.
4. What are the differences between filleting flatfish and round fish? Describe or demonstrate.
5. You have just received delivery of fresh whole red snapper and fresh cod fillets. What should you check before accepting the shipment? After accepting the fish, what do you do with them?
6. You are making a casserole of shrimp with a prepared Newburg sauce and frozen, glazed cooked shrimp. When you add the frozen shrimp to the sauce, it thins out so much it is no longer usable. Why did this happen, and how could you have prevented it?
7. What is the most important indication of freshness in fresh oysters, clams, lobsters, and crabs? Describe how you would preserve this freshness.
8. How does opening oysters differ from opening clams, and how is it similar?
9. What happens to most kinds of shellfish when they are overcooked?

Chapter 4

Scallop Seviche, page 119.

Cooking Fish and Shellfish

Because most fish and shellfish have little connective tissue, the procedures for cooking them are somewhat different from those for cooking meats and poultry. When we cook meats, we are often concerned with tenderizing the product. Fish is naturally tender, however, and cooking—especially overcooking—is more likely to toughen the product and dry it out.

In this chapter, we apply basic cooking principles to the preparation of fish dishes. Our goals are to cook the product just to doneness, to preserve moisture and texture, and to preserve and enhance natural flavors.

Of course, your study of these procedures depends on your understanding of the basic information on fish in the previous chapter. In particular, you may want to review the sections on testing for doneness and on fat and lean fish and their appropriate cooking methods.

After reading this chapter, you should be able to

1. Cook fish and shellfish by baking.
2. Cook fish and shellfish by broiling.
3. Cook fish and shellfish by sautéing and pan-frying.
4. Cook fish and shellfish by deep-frying.
5. Cook fish and shellfish by poaching in court bouillon.
6. Cook fish and shellfish by poaching in fumet and wine.
7. Cook fish and shellfish by mixed cooking techniques.
8. Prepare dishes made of raw seafood.

Baking

Whole fish and fish portions may be cooked by baking in an oven. Although large whole fish may be baked, this is usually not practical in volume food service. The method is more often used with steaks and fillets and with small fish. Baking is also a popular method for preparing shellfish such as stuffed clams or oysters.

Baking is often combined with other cooking methods. For example, partially broiled fish can be finished by baking. Baked fish casseroles are usually made with cooked fish.

Whole fish or portions of fish baked in the oven may also be referred to as roasted, as is currently the fashion. The term *roasting* may be applied both to basic baking and to moist baking, discussed below.

Guidelines for Baking Fish

1. Fat fish are better for baking because they are less likely to dry out.
2. Lean fish may be baked successfully if great care is taken not to overcook them. Basting with butter or oil helps prevent drying.
3. In most cases, baking temperatures are from 350° to 400°F (175° to 200°C). Large fish are best baked at the lower end of this range so they bake more evenly.

   It is also possible to bake thin fillets or slices of fillets (cut like scaloppine) at very high temperatures. Great care must be used in this case because the fish may cook in a minute or less, and a few seconds too long might ruin it. The effect of the high heat is almost like broiling, and the normal guidelines for broiling thin fish fillets should be followed, as explained in the next section.
4. It is not possible to give specific baking times because fish vary so much in shape and composition. Different ingredients and types of baking pans also affect the baking time. The following guideline is helpful, however: Measure the thickness of the fish at the thickest point. At 400°F (200°C), baking time is about 10 minutes per inch (2.5 cm) of thickness.
5. Serving baked fish with a sauce or seasoned butter enhances its moistness and improves palatability. Serving with lemon also enhances the fish.
6. If fish is baked with a moist topping or sauce, strictly speaking, it is no longer being cooked by a dry-heat method. However, because the basic procedure is the same, the fish is treated as if it were.

Procedure for Baking Fish

1. Collect all equipment and food supplies.
2. Prepare and season fish (whole, steaks, fillets) as directed in the recipe.
3. Place the fish on oiled or buttered baking sheets. Brush tops with oil or butter.
   Alternative method: Dip fish in oil or melted butter to coat both sides. Place on baking sheets.
4. Apply toppings, if desired. Examples: seasoned bread crumbs, lemon slices, mushrooms or other vegetable garnish, and sauces.
5. Bake at 350° to 400°F (175° to 200°C) until done. If the fish is lean and has no moist topping, baste with oil or butter during baking.

Moist Baking or Braising

As we noted above, if fish is baked with moist ingredients or with liquids, strictly speaking, the method is no longer a dry-heat method, although such preparations are included in this section. In French cooking, baking fish—usually whole fish or large pieces—with vegetables and liquid is called *braising*. To avoid confusion with the braising method as applied to meats, however, we avoid that term and refer to such dishes as *baked*.

This procedure is the same as the basic procedure for baking fish described above, with the following special features:

1. The baking pan should be just large enough to hold the fish, so you will not need too much liquid.
2. The bottom of the pan is buttered or oiled, then covered with a layer of sliced or chopped vegetables, such as carrots, onions, shallots, and mushrooms. The vegetables may be raw or first sautéed gently in butter or oil. The fish is then placed on top of the vegetables.

3. Frequently, a small amount of liquid, such as equal parts wine and fish stock, is added. Just enough liquid is used to cover the fish about halfway or less. During baking, the fish is basted with this liquid.

4. The fish may be baked uncovered or covered only lightly. It should not be covered tightly, however, because the liquid must be able to reduce somewhat so it will become more concentrated and more flavorful. Remember also that liquid will be released from the fish, diluting the cooking liquid.

5. For service, the fish is removed from the dish. The liquid is strained, degreased, reduced, and finished in various ways, such as by adding butter, cream, or velouté sauce.

You can see that this is a sort of combination technique. Because it often uses wine and other liquids, the method is, in some ways, similar to poaching in wine, as explained on page 102.

Baked Cod Fillets Portugaise

PORTIONS: 24 PORTION SIZE: 5 OZ (150 G) FISH, 2 FL OZ (60 ML) SAUCE

U.S.	METRIC	INGREDIENTS	PROCEDURE
24	24	Cod fillets, 5-oz (150-g) portions	1. Place cod fillets on a well-oiled baking sheet or baking pan, flesh side up (that is, skin side down).
⅓ cup	75 mL	Lemon juice	2. Brush the fish lightly with lemon juice. Then brush generously with the butter or oil and season lightly with salt and pepper.
8 fl oz	250 mL	Melted butter or oil	3. Place the pan in a preheated 350°F (175°C) oven until done, about 10–15 minutes.
to taste	to taste	Salt	4. Halfway through the cooking time, check the fish and, if the tops appear to be drying out, brush with more butter or oil.
to taste	to taste	White pepper	
1½ qt	1.5 L	Portuguaise Sauce	5. Serve each portion with 2 fl oz (60 mL) sauce. Nap the sauce across the center of the portion. Do not cover the entire fillet.

Per serving: Calories, 170; Protein, 16 g; Fat, 10 g (53% cal.); Cholesterol, 60 mg; Carbohydrates, 4 g; Fiber, 1 g; Sodium, 250 mg.

VARIATIONS

Many other fish may be baked according to the basic recipe, such as

Haddock (fillets or steaks)	Pike (fillets)	Halibut (steaks or fillets)	Salmon (fillets or steaks)
Snapper (fillets)	Perch (fillets)	Bluefish (fillets)	Swordfish (steaks)
Bass (fillets)	Flounder (fillets)	Mackerel (fillets)	Whitefish (fillets)

Other appropriate sauces may be used, such as

Melted butter	Tomato and tomato-based sauces such as Creole (not for salmon or for very delicate fish like flounder)
Beurre noisette	Mustard (for strong-flavored fish only, such as mackerel or bluefish)
Maître d'hôtel butter	Curry (not for salmon or other fat fish)

Broiling and Grilling

Broiled and grilled seafood items, like grilled meats, are increasingly popular. Customers perceive them as simpler and more healthful and, because they are prepared quickly, as fitting the faster pace of modern life.

Grilled dishes are, in their purest form, simple and straightforward, but they lend themselves to many variations in presentation. By varying sauces, vegetable accompaniments, and garnishes, you can offer a great assortment of grilled fish on the menu. And, because the sauces and accompaniments are generally prepared ahead of time, these dishes are still quick to prepare, even if the presentation is elaborate.

A slightly crisped, browned, or grill-marked surface is important to the appeal of grilled or broiled fish. Do not cover the item with sauce, and do not serve too much sauce. A small piece of seasoned butter or a drizzle of a flavorful condiment or sauce can be used to decorate the top of the item. In most other cases, it is better to place sauces on the side. Appropriate healthful sauces include vegetable coulis and salsas. For richer dishes, beurre blanc is a good accompaniment, especially for lean fish like halibut.

Another popular approach is to serve the fish without a sauce, except perhaps for a small dab of a condiment such as a relish or chutney, and to complement the fish with an attractive variety of vegetables.

Guidelines for Broiling or Grilling Fish

1. Because of the intense heat of the broiler, great care is needed to avoid overcooking the fish.
2. Select appropriate fish for broiling or grilling. Small slices and thin fillets are usually too delicate to be placed directly on the grid of a broiler or grill. Arrange them on oiled sheet pans, broiler platters, or other baking dishes or pans, and cook under a broiler. Whole fish or thick slices of firm fish such as salmon, shark, and swordfish can be placed directly on the grill if care is taken to avoid breaking them up. Be sure the grid is clean and oiled to prevent sticking.
3. Fat fish is best for broiling because it doesn't get as dry as lean fish. However, all fish, fat or lean, should be coated with a fat before broiling to reduce drying.
4. Lean fish may be dredged in flour before dipping in oil or melted butter. The flour helps form a flavorful browned crust.
5. Instead of being dredged with flour, fish may be coated with fat and then with bread crumbs or cornmeal. Use caution, however, as bread crumbs burn very easily. Use this technique only with items that cook quickly.
6. If the fish has an attractive skin (such as red snapper and black sea bass), the skin may be left on and used as the presentation side. This enhances appearance and also helps hold the delicate flesh together. Make sure the fish is thoroughly scaled. To prevent splitting during cooking, score the skin with a sharp knife, making a series of parallel cuts across the fish or cutting in a diamond pattern for larger fish. For small fillets, scoring may not be necessary.
7. Broil fish to order and serve immediately.
8. Broiled fish may be garnished lightly with paprika if more color is desired, but don't overdo it. A common fault in broiling or baking fish is coating them with a heavy layer of paprika, which ruins their delicate flavor.
9. Thick cuts should be turned once during broiling in order to cook evenly. Thin pieces may be arranged on an oiled pan and broiled on one side only. Lobster is also broiled without turning.

Procedure for Broiling or Grilling Fish

1. Collect all equipment and food supplies.
2. Prepare the fish as required: Season and coat with oil or butter, with flour and then fat, or with fat and then bread crumbs or cornmeal.
3. Preheat the broiler or grill.
4. With a wire brush, remove burned or charred particles of food from the broiler grate or grill. Brush the grate with an oiled cloth to coat it lightly with oil.
5. Broil thick cuts on both sides, turning once. Broil thin pieces on one side only.
6. Serve immediately, with appropriate sauce and garnish.

KEY POINTS TO REVIEW

- What are the steps in the basic procedure for baking fish? Describe guidelines for success in baking fish.
- What is braising of fish, and how does it compare to baking?
- What are the steps in the basic procedure for broiling or grilling fish? Describe guidelines for success in broiling and grilling fish.

Broiled Fish Steaks Maître d'Hôtel

PORTIONS: AS NEEDED PORTION SIZE: 5–6 OZ (150–175 G)

U.S.	METRIC	INGREDIENTS
as needed	as needed	Fish steaks, 5–6 oz (150–175 g) each (see Note)
to taste	to taste	Salt
to taste	to taste	White pepper
as needed	as needed	Oil or melted butter

PROCEDURE

1. Season the steaks with salt and pepper.
2. Place the oil or melted butter in a small pan. Dip both sides of the steaks in it to coat completely.
3. Place on the rack of a preheated broiler. Broil under medium heat until half cooked. Turn over with a spatula. At this point, it may be necessary to brush the tops of the steaks with more oil or butter if they are becoming dry.
4. Complete the cooking on the second side.

U.S.	METRIC	INGREDIENTS
as needed	as needed	Maître d'Hôtel Butter
as needed	as needed	Lemon wedges

5. Plate the fish. Place a slice of seasoned butter on top of each steak. Garnish the plate with a lemon wedge. Serve immediately.

Per serving: Calories, 320; Protein, 27 g; Fat, 22 g (63% cal.); Cholesterol, 105 mg; Carbohydrates, 2 g; Fiber, 1 g; Sodium, 2460 mg.

Note: Salmon, tuna, and swordfish steaks are ideal for broiling, but they are also expensive. Other fish steaks that may be broiled include cod, haddock, halibut, king mackerel, and large bluefish.

Fillets may also be broiled using this recipe if they are thick or firm enough to avoid breaking up on the grill.

VARIATIONS

For lean white fish (halibut, cod, etc.), dredge in flour and shake off excess before dipping in the melted butter or oil. Broil as in basic recipe.

Other compound butters may be used in place of maître d'hôtel butter.

For fat fish, omit the butter and serve the fish with a small quantity of flavorful vinaigrette.

Grilled Tuna with Balsamic Vinaigrette and Sweet-Sour Baby Onions

PORTIONS: 4 PORTION SIZE: 5–6 OZ (150–180 G) TUNA

U.S.	METRIC	INGREDIENTS	PROCEDURE
1 fl oz	30 mL	Balsamic vinegar	1. Make a vinaigrette with the vinegar, water, herbs, salt, pepper, and olive oil.
½ oz	15 mL	Water	2. Mix in the diced red pepper.
¼ tsp	1 mL	Parsley, chopped	
¼ tsp	1 mL	Chives, chopped	
to taste	to taste	Salt	
to taste	to taste	White pepper	
2½ fl oz	75 mL	Olive oil	
1 oz	30 g	Roasted red pepper, small dice	
4	4	Tuna steaks, 5–6 oz (150–180 g) each	3. Season the tuna steaks with a little salt and brush with a little of the vinaigrette.
to taste	to taste	Salt	4. Grill the steaks until rare or medium rare.
8 oz	240 g	Cipolline in Agrodolce	5. For each portion, arrange the onions in the center of the plate.
			6. Cut the steak in half to display the interior. Arrange the two halves on top of the onions.
			7. Spoon a little vinaigrette around the tuna.

Per serving: Calories, 450; Protein, 36 g; Fat, 26 g (54% cal.); Cholesterol, 65 mg; Carbohydrates, 14 g; Fiber, 1 g; Sodium, 220 mg.

Grilled Tuna with Balsamic Vinaigrette and Sweet-Sour Baby Onions

Grilled Mahi-Mahi with Fruit Salsa

PORTIONS: 12 PORTION SIZE: 6 OZ (180 G)

U.S.	METRIC	INGREDIENTS	PROCEDURE
3 fl oz	90 mL	Lemon juice	1. In a nonreactive container, mix together the lemon juice, salt, white pepper, and cayenne.
1 tsp	5 mL	Salt	2. Place the fish fillets in the mixture, turning them to coat all sides. Let stand 15 minutes.
¼ tsp	1 mL	White pepper	3. Remove the fish from the marinade. Dip the fillets in the oil and remove, letting the excess oil drip off.
⅛ tsp	0.5 mL	Cayenne	4. Grill the fillets on a preheated, seasoned grill or broiler. Grill until just done. Do not overcook, or the fish will be dry.
12	12	Mahi-mahi fillets, 6 oz (180 g) each	
4 fl oz, or as needed	125 mL, or as needed	Vegetable oil	
1 lb 2 oz	600 g	Fruit Salsa	5. Plate the fillets. Next to each fillet, place 1½ oz (50 g) fruit salsa.

Per serving: Calories, 210; Protein, 32 g; Fat, 6 g (27% cal.); Cholesterol, 125 mg; Carbohydrates, 5 g; Fiber, 1 g; Sodium, 170 mg.

Broiled Shrimp, Scampi Style

PORTIONS: 10 PORTION SIZE: 4½ OZ (125 G)

U.S.	METRIC	INGREDIENTS
50	50	Shrimp, size 16/20
6 oz	175 g	Butter
½ cup	125 mL	Oil, preferably olive oil (see Note)
1 tbsp	15 mL	Garlic, very finely chopped
1 fl oz	30 mL	Lemon juice
2 tbsp	30 mL	Chopped parsley
to taste	to taste	Salt
to taste	to taste	Pepper

PROCEDURE

1. Peel, devein, and butterfly the shrimp as shown in **Figure 3.16**. Leave tails on.
2. Place shrimp in individual service casserole dishes or in a shallow baking pan, tails up and cut side down. (Shrimp will curl more when cooked, so tails stand up as shrimp are broiled.)
3. Keep refrigerated until needed.
4. Heat butter and oil in a saucepan until the butter is melted.
5. Add the garlic, lemon juice, parsley, salt, and pepper.
6. Pour the butter sauce over the shrimp.
7. Place under the broiler at medium heat. Broil until the tops are lightly browned. (Don't worry if the tips of the tails burn a little; this is normal.)
8. Transfer the shrimp to the oven above the broiler for a few minutes to finish cooking.

Per serving: Calories, 250; Protein, 7 g; Fat, 25 g (88% cal.); Cholesterol, 95 mg; Carbohydrates, 1 g; Fiber, 0 g; Sodium, 210 mg.

Note: All butter may be used, instead of a mixture of butter and oil. Or, if you are using a good-quality olive oil, use more oil and less butter or all olive oil.

Serve this dish with rice or with plenty of bread to soak up the flavorful butter.

VARIATIONS

The shrimp can be marinated 1–2 hours in the oil, chopped garlic, lemon juice, and seasonings. Add the butter at cooking time. Or omit the butter when cooking, and serve small cups of garlic butter on the side.

Shrimp Brochettes

Marinate the shrimp as indicated above. Put the shrimp on skewers and broil, basting several times with the marinade and melted butter.

Broiled Scallops

Place the scallops in individual service casseroles (5–6 oz/150–175 g per portion). Top each portion with 1 tbsp (15 mL) dry bread crumbs. Pour the butter sauce over the scallops and broil as in basic recipe.

Broiled Fish Fillets or Steaks with Garlic Butter

Use fillets or steaks of any lean, white fish. Place fish on sheet pans and prepare according to procedure for Broiled Scallops, using the bread crumbs.

Oysters Casino

PORTIONS: 12 PORTION: 3 OYSTERS (APPETIZER PORTION)

U.S.	METRIC	INGREDIENTS	PROCEDURE
36	36	Oysters	1. Open oysters as shown in **Figure 3.8**. Discard top shell. 2. Place oysters on a sheet pan or in a shallow baking pan (see Note).
½ lb	225 g	Butter	3. Place the butter in the bowl of a mixer and beat with the paddle attachment until soft and smooth.
2 oz	60 g	Green bell pepper, chopped fine	4. Add the green pepper, pimiento, shallots, parsley, and lemon juice. Mix until evenly combined. Season to taste with salt and pepper. (Casino butter can be rolled in parchment, refrigerated or frozen, and sliced to order.)
1 oz	30 g	Pimiento, chopped fine	
1 oz	30 g	Shallots, chopped fine	
¼ cup	60 mL	Chopped parsley	
1 fl oz	30 mL	Lemon juice	
to taste	to taste	Salt	
to taste	to taste	White pepper	
9 strips	9 strips	Bacon	5. Cook the bacon in the oven or on the griddle until about half cooked. Drain. 6. Cut each strip into 4 pieces.
			7. Place about 2 tsp (10 mL) butter mixture on top of each oyster. 8. Top each oyster with a piece of bacon. 9. Run the oysters under the broiler until the bacon is brown and the oysters are hot. Do not overcook.

Per serving: Calories, 610; Protein, 26 g; Fat, 51 g (75% cal.); Cholesterol, 230 mg; Carbohydrates, 12 g; Fiber, 0 g; Sodium, 860 mg.

Note: Broiled or baked oysters and clams are often placed on beds of rock salt to hold them steady.

VARIATIONS

Clams Casino

Prepare as in basic recipe, using cherrystone or littleneck clams.

Oysters Casino

Sautéing and Pan-Frying

As in meat cookery, the exact distinction between sautéing and pan-frying fish is impossible to draw. For many purposes, the two terms are used interchangeably.

A classic method for sautéing fish is called ***à la meunière*** (mun yair). In this preparation, the product is dredged in flour and sautéed in clarified butter or oil. It is then plated and sprinkled with lemon juice and chopped parsley, and freshly prepared hot brown butter (beurre noisette) is poured over it. When the hot butter hits the lemon juice, it creates a froth. The fish should then be served at once.

Other sautéed fish preparations may call for Standard Breading Procedure or for dredging the fish with a product other than flour, such as cornmeal. Also, a variety of garnishes may be used.

The procedures and variations just described apply to most popular sautéed and pan-fried fish recipes. In general, because most types of fin fish are so delicate, especially if filleted, they do not lend themselves to a great many sautéing variations. Rather, variety is created with accompaniments, sauces, and garnishes. On the other hand, firm shellfish, like shrimp and scallops, are easy to sauté, and there is a greater variety of recipes for them.

Guidelines for Sautéing and Pan-Frying Fish and Shellfish

1. Lean fish are especially well suited to sautéing because the cooking method supplies fat the fish lack. Fat fish may also be sautéed, as long as you take care not to get it too greasy.
2. Sautéed fish is usually given a coating of flour, breading, or other starchy product before sautéing. This forms a crust that browns attractively, enhances the flavor, and helps hold the fish together and prevent sticking.
3. Fish may be soaked in milk briefly before dredging in flour. This helps the flour form a good crust.
4. Clarified butter and oil are the preferred fats for sautéing and pan-frying. Whole butter is likely to burn, unless the fish items are very small.
5. Use a minimum of fat. About ⅛ inch (3 mm), or enough to cover the bottom of the pan, is enough.
6. Observe the guidelines for the basic sautéing procedure (p. 171). In particular, be sure the pan is hot before adding the fish to it. After the item has begun to cook, adjust the heat as necessary. Small items, such as shrimp and scallops, are sautéed over high heat. Larger items, such as whole fish or thick steaks, require lower heat to cook evenly.
7. Very large fish may be browned in fat and then finished in the oven, uncovered.
8. Brown the most attractive side—the presentation side—first. For fillets, this is usually the flesh side or the side against the bone, not the skin side.
9. Handle fish carefully during and after cooking to avoid breaking the fish or the crisp crust.
10. Sauté or fry to order and serve immediately.

Procedure for Cooking Fish à la Meunière

1. Collect all equipment and food supplies.
2. Heat a small amount of clarified butter in a sauté pan.
3. Season the fish and dredge in flour. Shake off excess.
4. Place the fish in the pan, presentation side down.
5. Sauté the fish, turning once with a spatula, until both sides are brown and the fish is just cooked through.
6. Remove the fish from the pan with a spatula and place on a serving plate, presentation side up.
7. Sprinkle the fish with lemon juice and chopped parsley.
8. Heat some raw butter in the sauté pan until it turns light brown. Pour it over the fish immediately.
9. Serve at once.

Fillets of Sole Meunière

PORTIONS: 10 PORTION SIZE: 4 OZ (125 G)

U.S.	METRIC	INGREDIENTS
20	20	Sole fillets, 2 oz (60 g) each
to taste	to taste	Salt
to taste	to taste	White pepper
3 oz	90 g	Flour
6 oz	175 g	Clarified butter or oil, or a mixture of butter and oil
1 fl oz	30 mL	Lemon juice
¼ cup	60 mL	Chopped parsley
5 oz	150 g	Butter
20	20	Slices of peeled lemon

PROCEDURE

1. Have all ingredients ready, but do not season and flour the fish until immediately before cooking.
2. Unless you are cooking to order, use as many sauté pans as necessary to hold all the fillets, or cook them in several batches. Place the sauté pans over medium heat so they will be ready as soon as the fish is floured.
3. Season the fillets with salt and pepper. Place the clarified butter in the hot pans to heat. Dredge the fish in flour and shake off excess. Place the fish in the pans flesh side (presentation side) down.
4. Sauté until lightly browned. Turn over with a spatula and brown the other side. Be careful not to break the fillets when turning.
5. Remove the fillets from the pan with a spatula, being careful not to break them. Plate the fish on hot dinner plates.
6. Sprinkle the fish with lemon juice and chopped parsley.
7. Heat the butter in small saucepan or sauté pan until it turns light brown (beurre noisette).
8. Pour the hot butter over the fish.
9. Quickly place a lemon slice on top of each fillet and serve immediately.

Per serving: Calories, 370; Protein, 20 g; Fat, 29 g (71% cal.); Cholesterol, 130 mg; Carbohydrates, 7 g; Fiber, 0 g; Sodium, 370 mg.

VARIATIONS

Other white fish fillets, as well as shellfish such as scallops and shrimp, may be cooked by the same procedure.

Placing the fish in milk before dredging in flour helps form an attractive, well-browned crust. However, the fish must be drained well before flouring, or the flour coating may be heavy and pasty.

Fillets of Fish Doré

Sauté the fish as in the basic recipe, but serve without the lemon juice, chopped parsley, and beurre noisette. Garnish the plate with lemon and parsley sprig. (*Doré* means "golden.")

Trout Meunière

Prepare whole, drawn trout as in the basic recipe. Dip the fish in milk before dredging in flour to form a better crust.

Fish Sauté Amandine

Prepare as in the basic recipe. Brown sliced almonds in the butter used for garnishing. Omit garnish of lemon slices, and garnish plate with lemon wedges.

Fish Sauté Grenobloise

Prepare as in the basic recipe. Garnish the fish with capers and diced, peeled lemon sections in addition to the chopped parsley before pouring on the brown butter.

Sautéed Soft-Shell Crabs

Prepare as in the basic recipe. Serve 2 per portion. Chopped parsley and lemon slices may be omitted.

Scallops Meunière

Sautéed Scallops with Tomato, Garlic, and Parsley

PORTIONS: 10 PORTION SIZE: 4 OZ (125 G)

U.S.	METRIC	INGREDIENTS
2½ lb	1.25 kg	Bay or sea scallops
2 fl oz	60 mL	Olive oil
2 fl oz	60 mL	Clarified butter
2 tsp	10 mL	Finely chopped garlic
4 oz	125 g	Drained, chopped canned or fresh tomato
¼ cup	60 mL	Chopped parsley
to taste	to taste	Salt

Per serving: Calories, 160; Protein, 9 g; Fat, 13 g (73% cal.); Cholesterol, 35 mg; Carbohydrates, 2 g; Fiber, 0 g; Sodium, 310 mg.

PROCEDURE

1. If you are using sea scallops and they are very large, cut them in halves or quarters. Dry the scallops with paper towels.
2. Heat the oil and butter in a large sauté pan until it is very hot.
3. Place the scallops in the sauté pan and sauté quickly. Shake the pan often to keep the scallops from sticking.
4. When the scallops are about half cooked, add the garlic. Continue to sauté until the scallops are lightly browned.
5. Add the tomato and parsley and sauté a few seconds, just enough to heat the tomato.
6. Add salt to taste and serve immediately.

VARIATIONS

Omitting the tomato makes a slightly different but equally good dish.

Sautéed Shrimp

Use peeled, deveined shrimp. Sauté as in basic recipe.

Crab Cakes with Roasted Pepper Rémoulade

PORTIONS: 16 PORTION SIZE: 4 OZ (125 G)

U.S.	METRIC	INGREDIENTS
3 lb	1.4 kg	Crabmeat
4 oz	125 g	Fresh bread crumbs
6 oz	175 g	Mayonnaise
4	4	Eggs, beaten
2 tsp	10 mL	Prepared mustard
2 tsp	10 mL	Worcestershire sauce
2 tsp	10 mL	Salt
½ tsp	2 mL	White pepper
3 tbsp	45 mL	Chopped parsley
8	8	Scallions, chopped fine
as needed	as needed	Clarified butter, for cooking
3 oz	90 g	Roasted red bell peppers, peeled, cored, and seeded
1 pt	500 mL	Rémoulade Sauce
16	16	Lemon wedges

Per serving: Calories, 440; Protein, 21 g; Fat, 36 g (72% cal.); Cholesterol, 145 mg; Carbohydrates, 7 g; Fiber, 0 g; Sodium, 1070 mg.

Note: This mixture has very little bread filler, so it may be somewhat difficult to handle. If desired, add more bread crumbs to make a firmer mixture that will pack more easily into cakes. The texture of the crabmeat may also affect the texture of the cakes and the quantity of bread crumbs needed.

PROCEDURE

1. Pick over the crabmeat to remove any bits of shell.
2. Mix together the bread crumbs, mayonnaise, eggs, mustard, Worcestershire sauce, salt, pepper, parsley, and scallions. Fold in the crabmeat.
3. Form by hand into round cakes. For each portion, allow 1 large cake, about 4 oz (125 g), or 2 small cakes, about 2 oz (60 g) each (see Note).
4. Pan-fry the cakes in butter until browned on both sides and cooked through.
5. Cut the roasted peppers into brunoise. Mix into the rémoulade.
6. Serve each crab cake with 1 fl oz (30 mL) sauce and 1 lemon wedge.

Pan-Fried Catfish with Shrimp Etouffée

PORTIONS: 12 PORTION SIZE: 4 OZ (125 G) CATFISH, 3½ OZ (100 G) ETOUFFÉE

U.S.	METRIC	INGREDIENTS
3 oz	90 g	Butter
1½ lb	750 g	Shrimp, small, peeled, and deveined
6 oz	180 g	Onion, chopped
3 oz	90 g	Green bell pepper, chopped
3 oz	90 g	Celery, chopped
2 oz	60 g	Scallion, sliced thin
2	2	Garlic cloves, chopped
3 tbsp	45 mL	Flour
12 fl oz	375 mL	Water or fish stock
¼ tsp	1 mL	Dried thyme
½ tsp	2 mL	Paprika
¼ tsp	1 mL	Cayenne
¼ tsp	1 mL	Black pepper
1 tbsp	15 mL	Worcestershire sauce
4 tbsp	60 mL	Chopped parsley
to taste	to taste	Salt

PROCEDURE

1. Heat the butter in a sauté pan over moderate heat.
2. Add the shrimp. Sauté just until they turn pink.
3. Remove the shrimp from the pan with a slotted spoon, leaving the butter in the pan.
4. Add the onion, green pepper, celery, scallions, and garlic to the pan. Sauté until soft.
5. Stir in the flour to make a roux. Continue to cook until the roux is brown.
6. Stir in the water or stock. Bring to a simmer, stirring constantly, and simmer until thickened and no longer tasting of raw flour.
7. Add the shrimp, thyme, paprika, cayenne, pepper, and Worcestershire sauce. Simmer 3–4 minutes, or until the shrimp are cooked.
8. Stir in the parsley.
9. Add salt to taste.

U.S.	METRIC	INGREDIENTS
1½ tsp	7 mL	Salt
1½ tsp	7 mL	Paprika
¼ tsp	1 mL	Cayenne
½ tsp	2 mL	Dried thyme
¼ tsp	1 mL	Black pepper
¼ tsp	1 mL	White pepper
3 lb	1.4 kg	Catfish fillets
as needed	as needed	Clarified butter

10. Mix together the salt and spices.
11. Cut the catfish fillets into 4-oz (125-g) portions.
12. Sprinkle the fillets with the spice mixture to coat both sides lightly.
13. Sauté the catfish in clarified butter until lightly browned on both sides and cooked through.
14. To serve, portion the shrimp etouffée on hot dinner plates. Top with the catfish fillets.
15. Serve with rice.

Per serving: Calories, 270; Protein, 32 g; Fat, 13 g (44% cal.); Cholesterol, 165 mg; Carbohydrates, 5 g; Fiber, 1 g; Sodium, 560 mg.

Pan-Fried Catfish with Shrimp Etouffée

Deep-Frying

KEY POINTS TO REVIEW

- What are the steps in the basic procedure for sautéing fish à la meunière?
- What are the guidelines for success in sautéing and pan-frying fish?
- What kinds of fish and seafood items are most appropriate for deep-frying?
- Why is fish usually breaded or battered before being deep-fried?

Deep-frying is perhaps the most popular method of preparing fish in North America. While fried fish may not be the most subtle or refined preparation, it can be of very high quality if the fish is fresh and not overcooked, the frying fat is of good quality, and the item is served without delay after cooking.

Lean fish—either small whole fish or small portions such as fillets or sticks—and shellfish such as shrimp, clams, oysters, and scallops are best for deep-frying.

Fish to be fried is breaded or battered to protect it from the frying fat and to protect the frying fat from it. Also, the breading or batter provides a crisp, flavorful, and attractive coating.

Frozen breaded fish portions are widely used. They should be fried without thawing.

Fried fish is usually served with lemon and/or a cold sauce such as tartar, rémoulade, or cocktail sauce on the side.

Fried Breaded Fish Fillets

PORTIONS: 25 PORTION SIZE: 4 OZ (125 G)

U.S.	METRIC	INGREDIENTS	PROCEDURE
		Standard Breading Procedure (see Note):	1. Set up a breading station: Place the flour in one pan, the eggs beaten with milk in a shallow bowl, and the bread crumbs in another pan.
4 oz	125 g	Flour	
4	4	Whole eggs, beaten	
1 cup	250 mL	Milk	
1¼ lb	625 g	Dry bread crumbs	
25	25	4-oz (125-g) fillets of lean, white fish, such as haddock, perch, pike, bass, sole, or flounder	2. Season the fish lightly with salt and white pepper. 3. Bread the fish fillets by passing them through the flour, egg wash, and crumbs. Press the crumbs on firmly. 4. Fry the fillets until golden brown in deep fat heated to 350°F (175°C).
to taste	to taste	Salt	
to taste	to taste	White pepper	
25	25	Parsley sprigs	5. Drain and serve immediately. Garnish each portion with a parsley sprig and lemon wedge. Serve with 1 fl oz (25 mL) tartar sauce.
25	25	Lemon wedges	
25 fl oz	750 mL	Tartar sauce	

Per serving: Calories, 490; Protein, 25 g; Fat 36 g (66% cal.); Cholesterol, 115 mg; Carbohydrates, 16 g; Fiber, 1 g; Sodium, 430 mg.

Note: Quantities given for breading materials are only guidelines. You may need more or less, depending on the shapes of the fish pieces, the care used in breading, and other factors. In any case, you will need enough so even the last piece to be breaded can be coated easily and completely.

VARIATIONS

Breaded fish fillets may also be pan-fried in butter or oil (see previous section).

Fried Breaded Scallops

Prepare as in the basic recipe. Use wire baskets in the breading station to simplify the procedure.

Fried Breaded Shrimp

Peel, devein, and butterfly shrimp, as shown in **Figure 3.16**. Leave tails on. Bread and fry as in the basic recipe.

Fried Oysters or Clams

Prepare like scallops.

Fish and Chips

PORTIONS: 12 PORTION SIZE: 8 OZ (240 G) FISH, 6 OZ (180 G) FRENCH FRIES

U.S.	METRIC	INGREDIENTS
		Batter (see Note):
7½ oz	225 g	Flour
½ tsp	2 mL	Salt
¼ tsp	1 mL	White pepper
12 fl oz	360 mL	Beer
12	12	Cod fillets, 8 oz (240 g) each
as needed	as needed	Flour for dredging
4½ lb	2.2 kg	French Fries
24 fl oz	7200 mL	Rémoulade Sauce or Tartar Sauce

PROCEDURE

1. Mix together the flour, salt, and pepper in a bowl.
2. Gradually beat in the beer to make a smooth batter. This step must be done just before cooking, or the batter will lose its carbonation. The carbonation from the beer provides leavening.
3. Dredge the fillets in flour. Shake off excess.
4. One at a time, dip the fillets in the batter and then drop into a deep fryer heated to 350°F (175°C). Fry until golden.
5. Drain on absorbent paper.
6. Serve with French fries on plates or in paper-lined baskets. Serve each portion with 2 fl oz (60 mL) rémoulade or tartar sauce in a cup.

Per serving: Calories, 1040; Protein, 46 g; Fat 72 g (62% cal.); Cholesterol, 130 mg; Carbohydrates, 50 g; Fiber, 3 g; Sodium, 970 mg.

Note: The quantity of batter needed varies greatly, depending on the fish. Thin fillets need more batter per unit of weight of fish because there is more surface area per unit of weight.

VARIATIONS

Substitute club soda for the beer in the batter.

Instead of the cod, use another lean, white fish, such as haddock, flounder, halibut, sole, or snapper.

Fisherman's Platter

Instead of using only one type of fish, use a variety of fish and seafood. For example: two kinds of fish fillets plus squid rings and shrimp.

Fish and Chips

Cod Cakes

PORTIONS: 25 PORTION SIZE: 2 CAKES, 2½ OZ (75 G) EACH

U.S.	METRIC	INGREDIENTS	PROCEDURE
4 lb	1.8 kg	Cooked cod	1. Flake the fish until it is well shredded.
4 lb	1.8 kg	Potato purée	2. Combine with the potato, egg, and egg yolk. Mix well.
3	3	Whole eggs	3. Season to taste with salt, pepper, and a little ground ginger.
2	2	Egg yolks	4. Scale the mixture into 2½-oz (75-g) portions. Shape into round, slightly flattened cakes.
to taste	to taste	Salt	5. Pass the cakes through the Standard Breading Procedure.
to taste	to taste	White pepper	6. Deep-fry at 350°F (175°C) until golden brown.
pinch	pinch	Ground ginger	
		Standard Breading Procedure:	
as needed	as needed	Flour	
as needed	as needed	Egg wash	
as needed	as needed	Bread crumbs	
as desired	as desired	Tomato sauce *or* tartar sauce	7. Serve 2 cakes per portion. Accompany with tomato sauce or tartar sauce.

Per serving: Calories, 280; Protein, 23 g; Fat, 6 g (19% cal.); Cholesterol, 110 mg; Carbohydrates, 33 g; Fiber, 2 g; Sodium, 360 mg.

VARIATION

Salmon or Tuna Cakes

Prepare as in the basic recipe, using well-drained canned salmon or tuna.

If you have duchesse potato mixture on hand, simply combine equal parts fish and duchesse mixture. No additional eggs are needed, as the potatoes already contain eggs.

Salmon Cakes with Mixed Greens

Deep-Fried Calamari with Spicy Tomato Sauce and Aïoli

PORTIONS: 12 PORTIONS SIZE: 6 OZ (175 G) SQUID, 2 FL OZ (60 ML) EACH SAUCE

U.S.	METRIC	INGREDIENTS
4½ lb	2.25 kg	Small cleaned squid (see **Figure 3.12**)
4 fl oz	125 mL	Lemon juice
1 lb	500 g	Flour
3 tbsp	45 mL	Salt
1½ pt	750 mL	Italian Tomato Sauce for Pasta
to taste	to taste	Hot red pepper sauce
1½ pt	750 mL	Aïoli I or Aïoli II
as desired	as desired	Optional garnish: deep-fried parsley leaves

PROCEDURE

1. Slice the body sacs of the squid crosswise into rings. Leave the tentacle sections whole, or cut them in half if they are large.
2. Combine the squid with the lemon juice and marinate, refrigerated, 2–3 hours.
3. Mix the flour and salt.
4. Drain the squid and dry on clean towels. Immediately before cooking, toss the squid with the flour, then shake in a large strainer to remove excess flour.
5. Deep-fry at 350°F (175°C) just until lightly golden. Remove from the fryer and drain.
6. Heat the tomato sauce and season to taste with the hot pepper sauce.
7. Heap the fried squid in the center of the serving plates, accompanied by 2 fl oz (60 mL) of each of the sauces in small cups. If desired, top with a little deep-fried parsley.

Per serving: Calories, 700; Protein, 30 g; Fat, 50 g (64% cal.); Cholesterol, 395 mg; Carbohydrates, 33 g; Fiber, 2 g; Sodium, 1710 mg.

VARIATION

For other versions of deep-fried calamari, bread the squid or dip in batter.

Deep-Fried Calamari with Spicy Tomato Sauce and Aïoli

Shrimp and Vegetable Tempura

PORTIONS: 16 PORTION SIZE: 3 SHRIMP, PLUS VEGETABLES

U.S.	METRIC	INGREDIENTS	PROCEDURE
48	48	Large shrimp	1. Peel the shrimp, leaving the tails attached. Devein and butterfly them.
4	4	Green bell peppers	2. Core and seed the peppers. Cut each one lengthwise in 8 wedges or strips.
1 lb 4 oz	600 g	Sweet potatoes	3. Peel the sweet potatoes. Cut into slices about ⅙ in. (4 mm) thick.
32	32	Small mushrooms (or halves or quarters of large mushrooms)	4. Clean the mushrooms and trim the bottoms of the stems.
1½ lb	750 g	Cake flour or other low-gluten flour	5. Sift the flour into a mixing bowl.
1½ pt	750 mL	Water, ice cold	6. Mix together the water and egg yolks.
6	6	Egg yolks	7. Mix the liquid into the flour until just combined. Do not worry about a few lumps. The batter should be somewhat thinner than pancake batter.
1½ pt	750 mL	Dashi	8. Make a dipping sauce by combining the dashi, soy sauce, and mirin.
5 fl oz	150 mL	Soy sauce	
3 fl oz	100 mL	Mirin (sweet rice wine)	
as needed	as needed	Flour for dredging	9. Divide the shrimp and vegetables equally into 16 portions. Fry the vegetables first, then the shrimp, by dredging with flour, shaking off the excess, then dipping in the batter and dropping into clean frying fat at 350°F (175°C). Fry just until lightly golden.
8 oz	250 g	Daikon (large white Japanese radish), grated	10. Drain and serve at once. Tempura is traditionally served on a bamboo tray covered with a clean piece of absorbent paper. Accompany with about 2 fl oz (60 mL) dipping sauce in a shallow bowl. Put a small mound each of grated daikon and grated ginger on each serving tray. The diner mixes these to taste into the dipping sauce.
3 tbsp	45 mL	Grated fresh ginger root	

Per serving: Calories, 380; Protein, 11 g; Fat 12 g (28% cal.); Cholesterol, 115 mg; Carbohydrates, 56 g; Fiber, 3 g; Sodium, 560 mg.

TEMPURA

Tempura (TEM-poo-rah) is not a native Japanese dish but rather originated with the deep-fried dishes Portuguese traders and missionaries introduced to Japan in the sixteenth century. Japanese cooks transformed the dish by perfecting a particularly light, lacy batter and by serving the tempura with a dipping broth based on dashi and soy sauce and flavored with grated ginger and daikon radish.

Poaching and Simmering

Poaching is cooking in a liquid at very low heat. Fillets and other small portions are sometimes cooked in a small amount of liquid, usually fish fumet and/or wine, and served with a sauce made of the poaching liquid. This procedure is called ***shallow poaching***, because the item is only partially submerged in the liquid. Whole fish and thick steaks may be cooked completely submerged in a seasoned liquid called *court bouillon*. The liquid is not used to make a sauce, and the fish may be served hot or cold. This procedure is called the ***submersion method***. Because these are two distinct procedures, we discuss them separately.

The two methods are illustrated in their most basic form in the recipes on pages 105 and 106. In addition, this section contains recipes using a variety of techniques for preparing fish dishes by cooking in flavorful liquids.

The Submersion Method: Poaching and Simmering in Court Bouillon

Court bouillon (koor bwee yohn) may be defined as water containing seasonings, herbs, and usually an acid, used for cooking fish. The name means "short broth" in French, so called because it is made quickly, unlike stocks.

In quantity food service, this method is perhaps used most often for cooking large whole fish to be decorated and served cold on a buffet. Slightly higher simmering temperatures are used for cooking crustaceans, such as lobster, crab, and shrimp.

The famous preparation called ***truite au bleu*** (blue trout) is made by poaching trout that are alive until cooking time. The fish must be alive and must not be washed in order for the fish to turn blue. Live fish have a protective slippery coating on the skin, and the blue color results from the vinegar in the court bouillon reacting with this coating.

Guidelines for Poaching Fish in Court Bouillon

1. Both fat and lean fish may be cooked by this method.
2. Seasoned liquid for cooking fish may be as simple as salted water. More often, however, it contains flavoring ingredients such as spices, herbs, and mirepoix, and acid ingredients such as lemon juice, vinegar, and white wine.
3. Cook flavoring ingredients in court bouillon to extract the flavors before cooking the fish.
4. Cooking temperature is 160° to 180°F (70° to 80°C), well below boiling. A temperature of 160°F (70°C) is sufficient to cook fish, and it reduces the likelihood of overcooking. Higher temperatures are harmful to the delicate texture and flavor of fish.

   Lobsters, crabs, and shrimp may be cooked at a simmer because their textures are less fragile. The terms *boiled lobster* and *boiled fish* are often used but inaccurate. Lobster and fish should never be boiled.
5. Start shellfish, small fish, and portion cuts in hot liquid to preserve flavors. Start large fish in cold liquid to cook more evenly and to avoid sudden contractions that would split the skin and spoil the appearance.
6. Special fish poachers with racks are best for poaching. They allow the fish to be removed from the liquid without damage. If these utensils are not available, wrap the fish in cheesecloth so it can be lifted out easily, or tie the fish loosely to a board.
7. Serve poached fish with an appropriate sauce, such as hollandaise for hot fish and a mayonnaise-based sauce for cold fish. Mild vinaigrettes go well with both hot and cold poached fish.

Procedure for Poaching Fish in Court Bouillon

1. Collect all equipment and food supplies.
2. Prepare court bouillon.
3. Place the fish in a suitable pan with liquid to cover.
   Start small fish and portions in simmering liquid.
   Start shellfish in boiling liquid.
   Start large fish in cold liquid.
4. Cook fish at below the simmer, 160° to 180°F (70° to 80°C). Lobsters, crabs, and shrimp may be cooked at a gentle simmer.
5. If fish is to be served hot, remove from liquid and serve immediately.
6. If fish is to be served cold, stop the cooking by adding ice to the liquid, and cool the fish in the court bouillon to retain moisture.

Shallow Poaching

The procedure of shallow-poaching fish is based on one of the great dishes of classical cuisine: sole or other white fish poached in fumet and white wine. If well prepared, it can be one of the most exquisite dishes on the menu.

This method of preparation is best for lean, delicate white fish, such as sole, halibut, turbot, haddock, cod, pike, and perch. It is also used for salmon and trout. The fish is always served with a sauce made from the ***cuisson***—that is, the poaching liquid.

The procedure and recipe given here are for fillets of sole au vin blanc (in white wine). This is the basic preparation, and most other classical poached fish recipes are variations on it. Many of the variations involve only different garnishes.

Because of the delicacy of flavors, this preparation requires good-quality fish and well-made stock, and the wine should have a good flavor. A cheap, bad-tasting wine will spoil the dish.

The basic classical procedure is detailed in this section. Using this procedure as a pattern, the technique of shallow poaching can also be used for other fish preparations, substituting other cooking liquids for the fumet, wine, velouté, and cream.

CUISSON

The basic meaning of the French word *cuisson* is "cooking." If you order a steak in a restaurant in Paris and are asked how you would like the cuisson, you are being asked whether you would like the meat cooked rare, medium, or well done.

In the context of poaching or simmering foods, *cuisson* refers to the cooking liquid, which may be used as the base of a sauce. This term is commonly used in restaurant kitchens on both sides of the Atlantic.

Procedure for Poaching Fish in Fumet and Wine

1. Collect all equipment and food supplies. Select a pan just large enough to hold the fish portions in a single layer. This will enable you to use a minimum amount of poaching liquid. Also, use a pan with low, sloping sides. This makes it easier to remove the fragile cooked fish from the pan.
2. Butter the bottom of the pan and sprinkle with chopped shallots.
3. Arrange the fish portions in the pan in a single layer. Season them lightly.
4. Add enough fish fumet and white wine to almost cover the fish. Use no more liquid than necessary so the flavor will be more concentrated and less reduction will be required later.
5. Cover the fish with a piece of buttered parchment or other paper and cover the pan with a lid. The paper holds in the steam to cook the top of the fish. It is sometimes omitted if the pan has a tight lid, but it does help the fish cook more evenly. (Some chefs like to cut a vent hole in the center of the parchment, but this is not necessary, because the steam can easily vent from around the edges.)
6. Bring the liquid just to a simmer and finish poaching in the oven at moderate heat. Thin fillets will cook in just a few minutes. Fish may be poached on top of the range, but the oven provides more even, gentle heat from both top and bottom.
7. Drain the liquid into a wide pan and keep the fish warm. After a few minutes of standing, more liquid will drain from the fish. Add this to the rest.
8. Reduce the cuisson over high heat to about one-fourth its volume.
9. Add fish velouté and heavy cream and bring to a boil. Adjust seasoning with salt, white pepper, and lemon juice.
10. Strain the sauce.
11. Arrange the fish on plates for service, coat with the sauce, and serve immediately.

Variations in Sauce Production

Using a prepared velouté, as in the standard method just given, makes the sauce production very quick, and the procedure can easily be used for cooking to order.

An alternative method may be used if no velouté is available or if a large quantity of fish is being poached for banquet service:

1. Use a larger quantity of fumet and wine for cooking the fish and reduce it by only about half, depending on the amount of sauce needed.
2. Thicken the liquid with roux or beurre manié and simmer until no raw starch taste remains.
3. Finish the preparation as in the basic method.

Another popular method uses no starch thickener. Instead, the reduced poaching liquid is lightly bound with heavy cream or raw butter.

- To bind the sauce with cream, add about 2 oz (60 mL) heavy cream per portion to the reduced cooking liquid and continue to reduce until the sauce is lightly thickened.
- To bind with butter, whip raw butter into the reduced cooking liquid as for monter au beurre. Use about ½ oz (15 g) butter or more per portion.

A further variation is known as ***à la nage***, which means "swimming." To serve poached seafood à la nage, reduce the cooking liquid only slightly, season, and strain it carefully. If desired, enrich the liquid with a very small quantity of butter. Serve the seafood with the liquid in a soup plate or other plate deep enough to hold the juices.

The procedure of shallow poaching in wine and fumet can be adapted to other preparations. In place of the fumet and wine in step 4, substitute other liquids as directed in the recipe. To finish the sauce, reduce the cuisson and, instead of finishing the sauce with velouté and cream, finish it as directed in the individual recipe.

Glazing

Poached fish is sometimes glazed before serving. This is done as follows:

1. According to the particular recipe, combine the finished sauce with egg yolk, hollandaise sauce, and/or lightly whipped cream. Alternatively, combine the reduction of the cooking liquid with Mornay sauce instead of fish velouté.
2. Coat the fish with the sauce and run the plate or platter under the salamander or broiler for a few seconds, or until the sauce is golden brown.

   Note: It's a good idea to test a little of the sauce under the salamander before coating the fish to make sure it will brown.

Ordinary Court Bouillon for Fish

YIELD: 1 GAL (4 L)

U.S.	METRIC	INGREDIENTS
1 gal	4 L	Water
8 fl oz	250 mL	White vinegar, wine vinegar, or lemon juice
8 oz	250 g	Onions, sliced
4 oz	125 g	Celery, sliced
4 oz	125 g	Carrots, sliced
2 oz	60 g	Salt
¼ tsp	2 mL	Peppercorns, crushed
1	1	Bay leaf
½ tsp	1 mL	Dried thyme
10–12	10–12	Parsley stems

Per 1 fl oz (29.57 mL): Calories, 0; Protein, 0 g; Fat, 0 g (0% cal.); Cholesterol, 0 mg; Carbohydrates, 0 g; Fiber, 0 g; Sodium, 170 mg.

PROCEDURE

1. Combine all ingredients (**Figure 4.1**) in a stockpot or saucepot and bring to boil.
2. Reduce heat and simmer 30 minutes.
3. Strain and cool.

Figure 4.1 Court bouillon ingredients

Court Bouillon with White Wine

YIELD: 1 GAL (4 L)

U.S.	METRIC	INGREDIENTS
2 qt	2 L	Water
2 qt	2 L	White wine
4 oz	125 g	Onions, sliced
4 oz	125 g	Celery, coarsely chopped
4 oz	125 g	Leeks, coarsely chopped
1	1	Bay leaf
½ tsp	2 mL	Peppercorns, crushed
½ tsp	2 mL	Dried thyme
10–12	10–12	Parsley stems
2	2	Whole cloves
1 oz	30 g	Salt

Per 1 ounce: Calories, 40; Protein, 0 g; Fat, 0 g (0% cal.); Cholesterol, 0 mg; Carbohydrates, 2 g; Fiber, 0 g; Sodium, 274 mg.

PROCEDURE

1. Combine all ingredients in a stock pot and bring to a boil.
2. Reduce heat and simmer about 20 minutes.
3. Strain and cool.

Poached Whole Fish

PORTIONS: 10 PORTION SIZE: 4 OZ (125 G)

U.S.	METRIC	INGREDIENTS
5 lb	2.5 kg	Drawn fish *or*
4 lb	2 kg	Dressed fish (1 large or 2 or more smaller fish; see Note)
3 qt or as needed	3 L or as needed	Court bouillon, cold
		Suggested sauces: Hollandaise Mousseline Beurre noisette Herb vinaigrette

PROCEDURE

1. Place the clean dressed or drawn fish on the lightly oiled rack of a fish poacher. If a rack is unavailable, wrap the fish in cheesecloth or tie it loosely on a board so it can be lifted out when cooked.
2. Place the fish in the poaching pan and pour in enough court bouillon to cover the fish completely.
3. Set the pan over moderately low heat and slowly bring barely to a simmer.
4. Reduce heat to very low and cook the fish at below the simmering point until done. The fish will feel firm, not mushy, at its thickest part, and the backbone, as seen inside the cavity, will no longer be pink. Total cooking time will vary from 5 to 20 minutes, depending on the size of the fish and the exact cooking temperature. In general, plan on about 8–10 minutes for every inch of thickness at the thickest point.
5. For serving hot: Remove fish from liquid, drain well, and serve immediately with choice of sauce.

   For serving cold: Add ice to the court bouillon to stop the cooking. Cool the fish rapidly in the liquid and refrigerate. Drain when chilled.

Per serving: Calories, 220; Protein, 47 g; Fat, 2 g (9% cal.); Cholesterol, 140 mg; Carbohydrates, 0 g; Fiber, 0 g; Sodium, 320 mg.

Note: For attractive presentations, such as for buffet work, fish is often poached with the head on. Suggested fish for poaching whole:

Haddock	Red snapper	Striped bass
Cod	Salmon	Trout

VARIATION

Poached Fish Steaks

Prepare as in basic recipe, except start with boiling court bouillon. Drain the cooked fish, remove skin and center bone, and serve immediately with selected sauce. Suggested fish steaks: cod, haddock, halibut, turbot, salmon.

"Boiled" Shellfish (Lobster, Crab, Shrimp)

Prepare as for fish steaks using salted water, court bouillon, or acidulated water (4 oz lemon juice and ½ oz salt per quart of water/125 mL lemon juice and 15 g salt per liter). Water may simmer when cooking shellfish.

Sole Vin Blanc (Poached Fillets of Sole in White Wine Sauce)

PORTIONS: 8 PORTION SIZE: 4 OZ (125 G) FISH, 2 FL OZ (60 ML) SAUCE

U.S.	METRIC	INGREDIENTS
16	16	Sole fillets, 2 oz (60 g) each
1 oz	30 g	Butter
1 oz	30 g	Shallots, fine dice
3½ fl oz	100 mL	White wine
7 fl oz or as needed	200 mL or as needed	Fish stock

PROCEDURE

1. Fold the fillets in half or roll them up, starting with the large end (see **Figure 4.2**). Be sure the skin side of the fillet is on the inside of the fold or the roll (called *paupiette*).
2. Butter the inside of a shallow pan or pans just large enough to hold the fish in a single layer. Sprinkle with the shallots. Lay the fillets on top of the shallots in a single layer.
3. Pour the wine into the pan and add enough stock to almost cover the fish.
4. Butter a piece of parchment or waxed paper cut the same size as the pan. Cover the fish closely with it, buttered side down (**Figure 4.3**). Cover the pan.
5. Set the pan on the range and bring just barely to a simmer. Do not boil.
6. Place the pan in a hot oven (400°F/200°C) and cook the fish until it is just barely done, about 5 minutes.
7. Drain the poaching liquid into a broad sauté pan. Keep the fish covered in a warm, not hot, place. If more liquid collects under the fish as it stands, add this to the rest.

U.S.	METRIC	INGREDIENTS
1 pt	500 mL	Fish Velouté
1	1	Egg yolks
2½ fl oz	75 mL	Heavy cream
4 tsp	20 g	Butter
to taste	to taste	Salt
to taste	to taste	White pepper
as needed	as needed	Lemon juice

8. Reduce the poaching liquid over high heat to about one-fourth its volume.
9. Add the velouté and bring to a simmer. Reduce to about 10 fl oz (300 mL).
10. Beat the egg yolk, then mix in the cream to make a liaison.
11. Whip in a little of the hot velouté to temper the liaison. Stir the tempered liaison into the sauce.
12. Swirl in the raw butter (monter au beurre). Season to taste with salt, pepper, and a few drops of lemon juice if necessary.
13. To serve, place 2 fillets on a dinner plate and coat with 2 fl oz (60 mL) sauce.

Per serving: Calories, 260; Protein, 25 g, Fat, 14 g (51% cal.); Cholesterol, 125 mg; Carbohydrates, 4 g; Fiber 0 g; Sodium, 190 mg.

Paupiettes of Sole Dugléré; Buttered Spinach; Steamed Potatoes

VARIATIONS

Any lean white fish may be poached using this recipe or any of the variations below. For example:

Halibut	Cod	Perch	Haddock
Turbot	Pike	Scallops	

For a sauce that is lower in fat, omit the liaison and the final monter au beurre. Finish the sauce with the desired amount of heavy cream, 6–12 fl oz (175–350 mL).

À la Carte Service, Fast Method: Poach fish as in the basic recipe. Plate the fish as soon as it is cooked. Coat it with a pre-prepared white wine sauce. The poaching liquid may be reused throughout the service period and then used to make velouté for the next day's sauce. Other sauces based on fish velouté or béchamel may be used instead of white sauce:

Bercy	Normandy	Nantua
Herb	Mushroom	Mornay

Glazed Poached Fish

Prepare as in the basic recipe. Immediately before serving, fold 1 pt (500 mL) hollandaise and 8 fl oz (250 mL) heavy cream, whipped, into the sauce. Coat the fish and brown it quickly under the salamander.

Poached Fish Bonne Femme

Add 1½ lb (700 g) sliced mushrooms to the shallots in the poaching pan. Poach as in the basic recipe. Omit egg yolks. Do not strain the sauce.

Poached Fish Dugléré

Add 1½ lb (400 g) tomato concassé and 4 tbsp (60 mL) chopped parsley to the pan when poaching the fish. Poach as in the basic recipe. Omit liaison, but stir 5 oz (150 g) raw butter into the sauce before serving. Do not strain.

Poached Fish Mornay

Strain the reduced poaching liquid (after step 8) and add a little of it to a thick Mornay Sauce for Glazing, just enough to thin it to the desired consistency. Coat the fish with the sauce and brown under the salamander or broiler.

Note: Scallops are often prepared à la Mornay and served in scallop shells with a duchesse potato border. The dish is called *Coquille St Jacques Mornay*. (*St Jacques* is the French term for "scallop," and *coquille* means "shell.")

Poached Fish Florentine

Prepare like Poached Fish Mornay, but place the cooked fish on beds of cooked, buttered spinach before coating with sauce.

Sole Paupiettes with Seafood Mousseline

Before rolling, spread the fillets with a thin layer of seafood mousseline.

Seafood à la Nage

Double the quantity of fish stock. Omit the velouté, liaison, and final butter. After poaching, reduce the cooking liquid only slightly. Season carefully and strain. Serve the seafood with the broth.

Figure 4.2 Rolling and folding sole fillets.

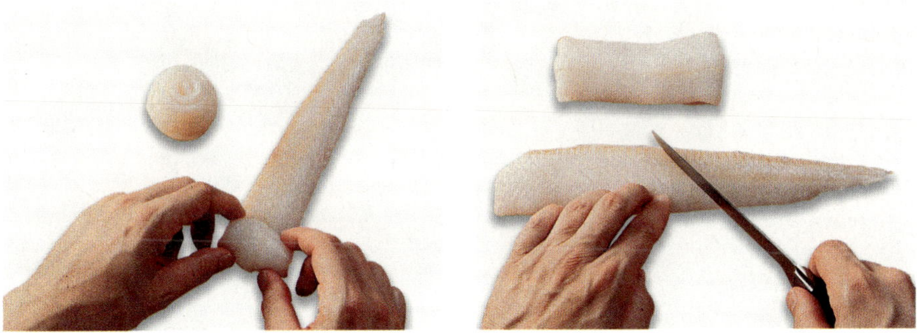

(a) To make paupiettes, or rolled fillets of sole, lay the fillets on the work surface skin side up. Starting at the large end, roll tightly. As the fish cooks, the connective tissues on the skin side shrink and keep the roll tight. If you roll the fillet skin side out, it unrolls as it cooks.

(b) If the fillets are to be poached flat or folded, first make a series of very shallow cuts in the skin side as shown. This helps keep the tissues from shrinking and deforming the fillet. Fold so the flesh side is out (skin side on the inside).

Figure 4.3 When shallow-poaching fish, cover the fish with a piece of buttered parchment. (Parchment has been folded back to show the fish.)

Scallops and Shrimp à la Nage

PORTIONS: 12   PORTION SIZE: 8 OZ (240 G)

U.S.	METRIC	INGREDIENTS	PROCEDURE
9 oz	270 g	Carrots, trimmed and peeled	1. Cut the carrots, leeks, and celery into julienne.
9 oz	270 g	Leeks, trimmed and cleaned	2. Sweat the vegetables in butter for a few minutes.
6 oz	180 g	Celery, trimmed	3. Add the court bouillon and simmer until the vegetables are cooked but still slightly crisp. Remove them from the court bouillon with a slotted spoon.
1½ oz	45 g	Butter	
3 pt	1.5 L	Court Bouillon with White Wine (p. 104), strained	
1 lb 8 oz	720 g	Shrimp, peeled and deveined	4. Return the court bouillon to a simmer. Add the shrimp and scallops. Poach them gently until they are just cooked, about 5 minutes.
1 lb 8 oz	720 g	Scallops	5. Remove the seafood from the court bouillon with a slotted spoon and keep warm.
to taste	to taste	Salt	6. Bring the court bouillon to a boil and reduce by one-third.
			7. Season and strain through cheesecloth or a fine chinois.
2 tbsp	30 mL	Chives, chopped	8. Divide the shrimp, scallops, and vegetables among broad soup plates or other appropriate dishes for service.
			9. Pour the hot court bouillon (reheated if necessary) over them. Sprinkle with chives and serve immediately.

Per serving: Calories, 220; Protein, 20 g; Fat, 4 g (16% cal.); Cholesterol, 115 mg; Carbohydrates, 11 g; Fiber, 1 g; Sodium, 740 mg.

VARIATIONS

A small amount of crème fraîche or herb butter may be stirred into the broth after it is reduced in step 6.

Salmon à la Nage

Omit the shrimp and scallops. For each portion, use one boneless, skinless salmon fillet, 4–5 oz (125–150 g).

Scallops and Shrimp à la Nage

Zuppa di Vongole

PORTIONS: 16

U.S.	METRIC	INGREDIENTS	PROCEDURE
15 lb	7 kg	Small clams, such as littlenecks	1. Scrub the clams under cold water to remove sand and grit from the shells.
1 pt	500 mL	Water	2. Put the clams and water in a heavy covered pot and heat gently, just until the clams open. Set the clams aside. Strain and reserve the liquid.
			3. Depending on how you wish to serve them, you can leave the clams in the shell or shell all but 4–6 of them per portion to use as garnish.
6 fl oz	175 mL	Olive oil	4. Heat the olive oil in a large pot. Sauté the onion until soft but not brown.
5 oz	150 g	Onion, small dice	5. Add the garlic and cook another minute.
3–5	3–5	Garlic cloves, chopped	6. Add the parsley and the wine and boil for 1 minute.
6 tbsp	90 mL	Chopped parsley	7. Add the tomatoes and the reserved clam juice. Simmer 5 minutes.
12 fl oz	350 mL	White wine	8. Taste for seasoning and adjust if necessary.
1½ lb	700 g	Canned plum tomatoes, with juice, coarsely chopped	9. Add the clams and reheat them gently. Do not overcook, or the clams will be tough.
			10. Serve with plenty of crusty bread for dipping in the broth.

Per serving: Calories, 680; Protein, 93 g; Fat, 18 g (25% cal.); Cholesterol, 240 mg; Carbohydrates, 22 g; Fiber, 1 g; Sodium, 470 mg.

VARIATIONS

Zuppa di Cozze

Substitute mussels for the clams.

Zuppa di Frutti di Mare

Use a mixture of clams, mussels, squid (cut up), and shrimp (shelled). Keep all the items separate. Cook the clams and mussels as in the basic recipe. Add the squid at the same time as the tomatoes and broth. Simmer slowly, covered, until tender. Add the shrimp and cook just 1 minute before adding the clams and mussels.

Zuppa di Pesce

Use a mixture of shellfish and fin fish, as desired. Add each type of fish just long enough before the end of cooking so it cooks through without overcooking.

Zuppa di Vongole

Steaming and Mixed Cooking Techniques

The recipes in this section are placed here because they are difficult to classify as one of the basic cooking methods, although they are all based on moist-heat methods. Most of the recipes share two characteristics:

1. The item cooks in its own juices and, usually, a small amount of added liquid.

2. The item is served with its flavorful cooking liquid.

In some cases, enough liquid is added to barely cover, and the item simmers. In other cases, little liquid is added and the item cooks in the steam trapped by the pot lid.

The French term ***étuver*** (ay too vay) is used for this kind of procedure, in which the item cooks slowly in very little liquid. The word is usually translated as "stew," but this may be misleading. More precisely, it means "to cook or steam in its own juices" or "to sweat."

Note that all the procedure variations in this section are moist-heat cooking methods, but that the items are not submerged in liquid but rather steamed in an enclosed container. For this reason, simple steaming procedures are also discussed here.

In addition, this section includes two traditional recipes for dishes made with cooked seafood.

Variations

Note the following three variations represented by the recipes in this section.

1. The product is cooked for a few minutes in fat over low heat, along with mirepoix or onion, to begin extracting juices. A little liquid is then added, the pot is covered, and the item is cooked.

2. The product is sautéed over high heat. Then other ingredients and liquids are added and the item is cooked, covered, over low heat.

3. The product is simply placed in a pot with liquids and flavoring ingredients. The pot is covered, and the item is steamed or simmered. Example: Moules Marinière (p. 112).

Cooking en Papillote

An unusual version of the third variation above is called cooking ***en papillote*** (on poppy-yote), or in paper. The fish item, plus flavoring ingredients and sauce, is tightly enclosed in a piece of parchment so steam cannot escape. When the paper package is heated, the item steams in its own moisture. All the juices, flavors, and aromas are held inside the paper, which is not opened until it is placed before the customer.

Sometimes a starch-thickened sauce is used in cooking fish en papillote. In this case, the fish is usually precooked (poached) so it will not exude juices that would dilute and spoil the sauce. The problem with this method is that the fish is often overcooked by the time it reaches the customer.

Stovetop Steaming

The simplest method of steaming is to place the item on a rack above simmering liquid, cover the pan, and steam until done. Because it does not come in contact with seasoned liquid or fat during cooking, steamed seafood is usually delicate in flavor, even more so than submersion-poached seafood. For this reason, this method is usually used when the cook wants to emphasize the pure, natural taste of the best-quality seafood.

Three methods are available to season and flavor steamed seafood:

1. Apply salt and other seasonings directly to the item.
2. Season the steaming liquid with aromatic herbs and other ingredients. The steam rising from the liquid carries a little of the aroma to the fish. This method gives only the subtlest and most delicate flavors to fish and is most effectively used with mild-tasting seafood.
3. Serve the seafood with an appropriate sauce. Accompaniments as simple as melted butter and lemon wedges are classic accompaniments to steamed seafood.

Compartment Steaming

Several precautions should be observed if you cook fish and shellfish in a compartment steamer.

1. Watch the cooking time carefully. Fish cooks quickly, especially in the high heat of a steamer, and is easily overcooked.
2. Avoid pressure-steaming fish and shellfish, if possible. The high temperatures toughen fish protein very quickly. Lobster tails and similar items can become rubbery.

Procedure for Steaming Seafood

1. Collect all equipment and food supplies. Select a pan large enough to hold the seafood and a rack that will hold the seafood above the simmering liquid.
2. Prepare the fish or seafood items for cooking. Trim and portion as necessary. Season as desired.
3. Pour water or other cooking liquid into the pan. There should be enough to last the entire cooking period without going dry, but not so much that it comes in contact with the seafood. Add aromatics and seasonings as desired. Bring to a boil.
4. Place the seafood on the rack and set above the liquid. Cover the pan and steam until done.
5. Remove the seafood from the rack. Serve with desired sauce and/or accompaniments.

KEY POINTS TO REVIEW

- What are the steps in the basic procedure for poaching fish in court bouillon (submersion poaching)? Describe guidelines for success in poaching fish in court bouillon.
- What are the steps in the basic procedure for shallow-poaching fish in wine and fumet? Describe guidelines for success in shallow-poaching fish.
- What are some common variations in sauce production for shallow-poached fish?
- What tools and procedures are used for steaming fish? How is fish cooked en papillote?

Moules Marinière (Steamed Mussels)

PORTIONS: 10 PORTION SIZE: APPROX. 12 OZ (360 G)

U.S.	METRIC	INGREDIENTS
7 lb	3.2 kg	Mussels, in shells
3 oz	90 g	Shallots or onions, chopped fine
6	6	Parsley stems
¼ tsp	1 mL	Pepper
1 cup	250 mL	White wine
¼ cup	60 mL	Chopped parsley
3 oz	90 g	Butter
to taste	to taste	Salt
to taste	to taste	Lemon juice

PROCEDURE

1. Scrub the mussels well with a stiff brush and remove the beards. Clean them well by soaking them according to the procedure given in Chapter 3.
2. Place the mussels in a stockpot or large saucepot. Add the shallots or onions, parsley stems, pepper, and wine.
3. Cover the pot and set it over moderately high heat. Cook until the mussels open, about 5 minutes.
4. Drain the mussels and strain the liquid through cheesecloth into a broad saucepan. Bring to a boil.
5. Add the parsley and butter. Swirl the liquid in the pan until the butter is melted. Season to taste with salt and a few drops of lemon juice.
6. For service, remove the top shells of the mussels (or leave them on, if desired). Place the mussels in broad soup plates and pour the sauce over them.

Per serving: Calories, 220; Protein, 20 g; Fat, 11 g (44% cal.); Cholesterol, 65 mg; Carbohydrates, 8 g; Fiber, 0 g; Sodium, 540 mg.

VARIATION

Steamed Mussels (without wine)

Substitute water for the wine and add 2 fl oz (60 mL) lemon juice. Increase the onion or shallot to 6 oz (175 g) and add 3 oz (90 g) sliced celery.

Mussels in Cream

Prepare the basic recipe. Reduce the cooking liquid by half and add 1 cup (250 mL) heavy cream or a liaison of 2 egg yolks and 1 cup (250 mL) heavy cream.

Moules Marinière

Mackerel en Papillote

PORTIONS: 1 PORTION SIZE: 4 OZ (125 G)

U.S.	METRIC	INGREDIENTS
1	1	Mackerel fillet, 4 oz (125 g) (see Note)
2 tsp	10 mL	Melted butter
to taste	to taste	Salt
to taste	to taste	White pepper
2 tsp	10 mL	Chopped parsley
pinch	pinch	Dried marjoram
1 tsp	5 mL	Very finely chopped shallots
2	2	Thin lemon slices

Per serving: Calories, 290; Protein, 20 g; Fat, 23 g (71% cal.); Cholesterol, 85 mg; Carbohydrates, 1 g; Fiber, 0 g; Sodium, 150 mg.

Note: Pompano or bluefish may be used.

PROCEDURE

1. Cut out a piece of parchment in a heart shape, as shown in **Figure 4.4**. (Foil may be used instead of parchment.) The piece must be big enough to hold the fish and still have room for crimping the edges. Oil the parchment and place on the workbench oiled side down. (If using foil, place it oiled side up.)
2. Place the fillet on one side of the heart. Brush with melted butter and sprinkle with salt, pepper, parsley, marjoram, and chopped shallot. Lay the lemon slices on top.
3. Fold and crimp the parchment, as shown in the illustration, to enclose the fish tightly.
4. Place the folded package in a sauté pan or, if several orders are being done at once, on a sheet pan. Set on the range to start the cooking.
5. As soon as the paper begins to puff, place the pan in a hot oven (450°F/230°C). Bake until the parchment is puffed and browned, 5–8 minutes. (If the paper doesn't brown, you may run it under the broiler for a second.)
6. Serve immediately. The parchment should be cut open in front of the customer.

VARIATION

Instead of the parsley, shallots, and lemon slices, top fillets with a thin layer of Duxelles.

Figure 4.4 Preparing foods en papillote.

(a) Cut out a heart-shaped piece of parchment by folding a parchment sheet in half and cutting half a heart from the folded side. Oil or butter the parchment and place on the work surface, oiled side down.

(b) Place the fish fillet or other item plus any sauce, topping, or seasoning, on one side of the heart.

(c) Fold over the other half of the heart. Starting at the top of the fold, make a small crimp in the edges as shown.

(d) Continue crimping around the edge. Each crimp holds the previous one in place.

(e) When you reach the bottom of the heart, fold the point under to hold it in place. The papillote is now ready for cooking.

Seafood Newburg

PORTIONS: 25 PORTION SIZE: 7 OZ (200 G)

U.S.	METRIC	INGREDIENTS
2½ lb	1.2 kg	Cooked sea scallops
2½ lb	1.2 kg	Cooked crabmeat
1¼ lb	600 g	Cooked, peeled shrimp
4 oz	125 g	Butter
2½ tsp	12 mL	Paprika
8 fl oz	250 mL	Sherry
2½ qt	2.5 mL	Cream sauce, hot
to taste	to taste	Salt
to taste	to taste	White pepper

PROCEDURE

1. If the sea scallops are large, cut them in halves or quarters.
2. Pick over the crabmeat to make sure it contains no pieces of shell. If the pieces of meat are large, cut them into ½-in. (1-cm) dice.
3. Cut the shrimp in half lengthwise.
4. Heat the butter in a large saucepan or sauté pan. Add the paprika and the seafood. Sauté over moderate heat until heated through and coated lightly with butter.
5. Add the sherry and simmer for a minute.
6. Add the cream sauce and bring to a simmer. Season to taste with salt and white pepper.
7. Serve with rice or in patty shells.

Per serving: Calories, 330; Protein, 26 g; Fat, 19 g (53% cal.); Cholesterol, 145 mg; Carbohydrates, 11 g; Fiber, 0 g; Sodium, 550 mg.

VARIATION

Different proportions of seafood may be used. Lobster meat may also be included.

Seafood Curry

Omit paprika and sherry. Substitute curry sauce (made with fish velouté) for the cream sauce. Garnish with toasted, sliced almonds, if desired.

Sea Bass Sous Vide with Asian Sweet-and-Sour Sauce

PORTIONS: 4 PORTION SIZE: 1 FISH FILLET, 6 OZ (180 G)

U.S.	METRIC	INGREDIENTS
1 oz	30 g	Fresh ginger root
as needed	as needed	Water
4	4	Sea bass fillets, skin on, 6 oz each
to taste	to taste	Salt

PROCEDURE

1. Review the guidelines for safe sous vide cooking.
2. Peel and grate the fresh ginger. Gather the grated ginger in a small square of cheesecloth and squeeze out the juice into a small ramekin. Discard the solids. Dilute the juice with approximately 3 times its volume of water.
3. Brush the skin side of the fillets lightly with the ginger juice.
4. Sprinkle both sides of the fillets lightly with salt.
5. Vacuum-pack each fillet in a plastic bag.
6. Cook at 140°F (60°C) for 12 minutes in a thermal bath.

U.S.	METRIC	INGREDIENTS
2 fl oz	60 mL	Oil
6 fl oz	180 mL	Asian Sweet-and-Sour Sauce
1 fl oz	30 mL	Basil Oil, if possible made with Thai basil
as needed	as needed	Thai basil or cilantro leaves

7. Remove the fillets from their bags. Heat the oil in a sauté pan over high heat. Carefully place the fillets in the pan, skin side down, and cook just until the skin is lightly browned, about 1 minute.
8. For each portion, spoon a pool of 1½ fl oz (45 mL) sauce in the center of each plate. Spread the sauce a little with the back of a spoon. Place a fillet on the sauce, skin side up. Drizzle a little basil oil around the outside of the sauce.
9. Garnish the top of the fish with a few leaves of Thai basil or cilantro. If desired, deep-fry the herb garnish.

Per serving: Calories, 480; Protein, 33 g; Fat, 28 g (53% cal.); Cholesterol, 75 mg; Carbohydrates, 22 g; Fiber, 2 g; Sodium, 125 mg.

Seafood Served Raw

Raw oysters and clams have long been enjoyed in North American restaurants as well as in homes. Smoked salmon, too, has always been a popular raw seafood item, although many people don't think of it as raw fish because it has been processed.

More recently, with the popularity of Japanese sushi and sashimi, many more people enjoy eating items made with raw fish, and chefs are experimenting with new ways to serve raw seafood items. Because of the danger of contamination from polluted fishing waters, however, many health officials advise against serving raw seafood. Nevertheless, these items remain popular. If you choose to serve raw seafood, observe the following guidelines:

1. Use only the freshest fish.
2. Buy the fish from a reliable purveyor.
3. Use only saltwater seafood from clean waters. Do not use freshwater fish, which is more likely than saltwater fish to contain parasites. To destroy possible parasites in saltwater fish, freeze it, and then thaw it before use.
4. Observe the strictest sanitation procedures.
5. Keep the fish cold. Handle it as little as possible.

Four kinds of raw fish recipes are included in this section. ***Fish tartare*** is a mixture of chopped raw fish mixed with various condiments and seasonings. ***Fish carpaccio*** is a dish consisting of very thin slices of firm, meaty fish such as tuna, served with various garnishes and usually with a piquant sauce such as a vinaigrette. *Carpaccio* (karpachio) is the Italian word for a dish of thin slices of raw beef, served the same way. ***Seviche,*** or *ceviche*, (seh vee chay, or, in Spanish, seh bee chay) is a preparation, native to Latin America, of raw seafood marinated in an acid mixture. The acid coagulates the protein so the texture of the raw fish resembles that of cooked fish. It is common to say the acid "cooks" the fish. However, because the food is not subjected to heat, it is important to still think of the item as raw, for sanitation reasons. ***Sushi*** is seasoned Japanese short-grain rice garnished with one or more foods, usually, but not always, raw fish.

Sushi has become especially popular in Western countries, but there is much confusion about it. Sushi is often equated with raw fish, but in fact the term refers to cooked rice lightly flavored with seasoned vinegar. The rice is served with various garnishes, which include not only raw fish (the most popular garnish) but also cooked seafood and many kinds of vegetables and pickles.

KEY POINTS TO REVIEW

- What are five safety guidelines for serving raw fish items?
- What is seviche? How is it made?
- What is the basic meaning of the term *sushi*? How is sushi rice made?
- What is seafood tartare, and how is it made?
- What is tuna carpaccio, and how is it made?

Tuna Carpaccio

PORTIONS: 8 PORTION SIZE: 2½ OZ (75 G)

U.S.	METRIC	INGREDIENTS	PROCEDURE
1 lb 4 oz	600 g	Yellowfin tuna or other red-fleshed tuna	1. On a slicing machine, or with a very sharp knife, cut the tuna into slices weighing 2½ oz (75 g) each. 2. Place each slice between two sheets of plastic film. Carefully pound each slice until it is paper thin, being careful to keep it of even thickness. 3. If the carpaccio is not to be served immediately, keep it between the layers of plastic film and refrigerate.
8–12 oz 8–12 fl oz	240–360 g 240–360 mL	Micro greens or baby arugula Mustard Vinaigrette	4. Lay each portion of tuna flat in the center of a cold plate. 5. Toss the greens with just enough of the vinaigrette to coat them lightly. 6. Arrange the greens in a mound in the center of the sheet of tuna. 7. Drizzle the remaining vinaigrette over the tuna.

Per serving: Calories, 270; Protein, 18 g; Fat, 22 g (72% cal.); Cholesterol, 35 mg; Carbohydrates, 1 g; Fiber, 1 g; Sodium, 280 mg.

Sushi Rice

YIELD: ABOUT 2½ LB (1.1 KG)

U.S.	METRIC	INGREDIENTS
3 cups	750 mL	Japanese short-grain rice (see Note)
3½ cups	875 mL	Water, cold
3–4 fl oz	100–125 mL	Sushi vinegar (see Note)

PROCEDURE

1. Wash the rice in several changes of cold water. Drain well.
2. Put the drained rice in a heavy saucepan and add the measured water. Cover tightly and let stand at least 30 minutes.
3. With the cover in place, set the pan over high heat and bring to a boil. When the water boils, reduce the heat to medium and let cook until all the water is absorbed. Do not remove the cover to check, but listen to the sounds. The bubbling will stop, and there will be a faint hissing sound.
4. Reduce the heat to very low and cook another 5 minutes. Then remove from heat and let stand at least 15 minutes before removing the cover. You now have the basic white rice that is eaten with Japanese meals.
5. In Japan, mixing in the vinegar is done in special wooden tub used only for this purpose (to avoid off flavors). The advantage of wood is that it absorbs excess moisture. If you use a nonabsorbent mixing bowl, transfer the rice to a clean bowl whenever the mixing bowl becomes coated with moisture. Using a wooden paddle or plastic spatula, break up the hot rice to get rid of all lumps. At the same time, fan the rice to cool it.
6. When the rice is slightly warm to the touch, begin adding the sushi vinegar. Add a little at a time while mixing gently. The rice is ready when it has a glossy appearance and a very mild taste of the vinegar. The vinegared rice is best if used within 2–3 hours, and it must not be refrigerated.

Per 1 ounce: Calories, 40; Protein, 1 g; Fat, 0g (0% cal.); Cholesterol, 0 mg; Carbohydrates, 9 g; Fiber, 0 g; Sodium, 105 mg.

Note: Do not confuse Japanese short-grain rice with glutinous rice, which is an entirely different product.

Sushi vinegar is commercially available, but it can also be madein the kitchen. Combine 1 pint (500 mL) Japanese rice vinegar, 8 oz (250 g) sugar, and 4 oz (125 g) salt. Heat and stir until the sugar and salt are dissolved, then cool.

VARIATIONS

Nigirizushi (Finger Sushi)

1. Prepare *wasabi* (green horseradish) by mixing wasabi powder with a little water to form a thick paste. Let stand, covered, a few minutes to allow flavor to develop.
2. Prepare sushi toppings by cutting very fresh fish fillets (use saltwater fish or smoked salmon) into slices about 1½ × 2½ in. (4 × 6 cm). Tuna, the most popular fish for sushi, is tender and is usually cut about ¼ in. (6 mm) thick. Other fish are cut thinner.
3. Wet your hands with cold water to keep the rice from sticking to them, then pick up about 2 tbsp (30 mL) sushi rice. Shape it into firm oval about 1½ in. (4 cm) long (see **Figure 4.5**). Pick up a slice of fish in one hand. Dip a finger of the other hand in the wasabi and spread a very small amount on the underside of the fish slice. Drape the fish over the rice, with the wasabi underneath next to the rice, and press it gently but firmly in place. Serve with soy sauce for dipping.

Chirashizushi (Scatter Sushi)

Fill a serving bowl half full of sushi rice. Carefully and attractively arrange an assortment of raw fish, cooked shrimp, crabmeat, and neatly cut vegetables such as snow peas, cucumbers, carrots, mushrooms, and pickled ginger on top of the rice.

Tekka-maki (Tuna Roll)

Make kappa-maki, but instead of cucumber, use raw tuna cut into bâtonnet strips.

Kappa-maki (Cucumber Roll)

To make rolled sushi, you will need a special bamboo mat called a *sudare* (see **Figure 4.5**). You could also use a sheet of parchment, but the roll will be harder to make.

1. Peel a cucumber. Cut it in half and scrape out the seeds. Cut lengthwise into julienne.
2. Cut a sheet of *nori* (a type of seaweed for rolled sushi) in half crosswise. Toast it by passing it briefly above a burner flame, being careful not to burn it.
3. Put the bamboo mat on the table in front of you with the bamboo strips horizontal. Put the half-sheet of nori on the mat, smooth side down.
4. Cover the two-thirds of the nori closest to you with a layer of sushi rice about ¼ in. (6 mm) thick.
5. Spread a light streak of wasabi from right to left across the middle of the rice.
6. Lay strips of cucumber evenly on top of the strip of wasabi.
7. Lift the edge of the mat closest to you and roll up firmly. This is best done by lifting the mat with the thumbs while holding the cucumber in place with the fingers. Press the roll in the mat gently but firmly to make it tight.
8. Wipe the blade of a very sharp knife, then cut the roll in half crosswise. Do not saw the roll but cut it cleanly with a single stroke. Wiping the blade on a damp cloth after every cut, cut each half-roll into 3 or 4 pieces.

Figure 4.5 Making sushi.

(a) For nigirizushi, wet your hands with cold water to keep the rice from sticking to them. Form a bit of rice into a small oval in one hand.

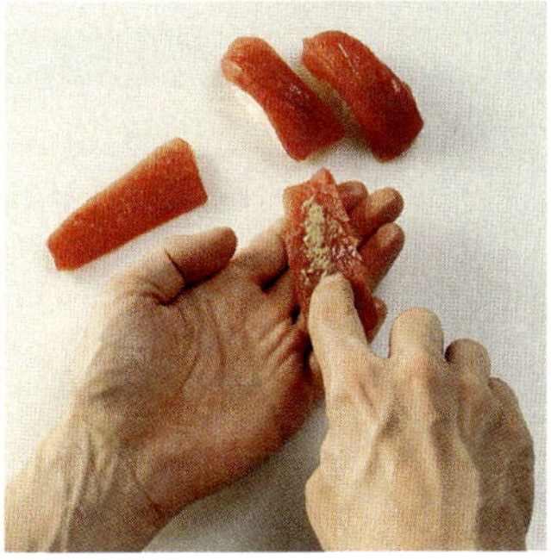

(b) In the other hand, pick up a slice of fish and smear a dab of wasabi on the bottom of it.

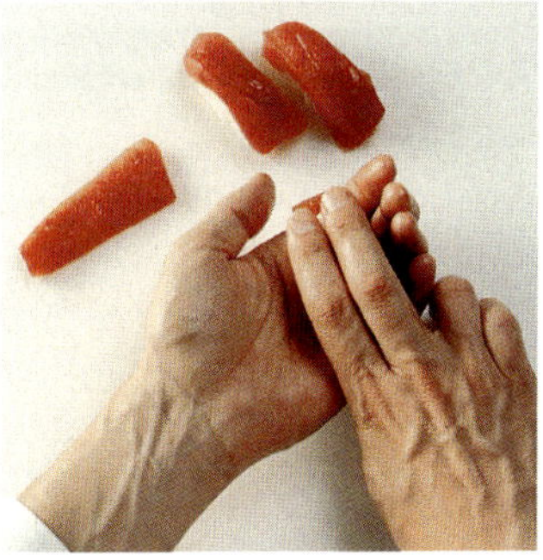

(c) Top the rice with the fish, wasabi side against the rice, and press in place in the palm of one hand with two fingers of the other.

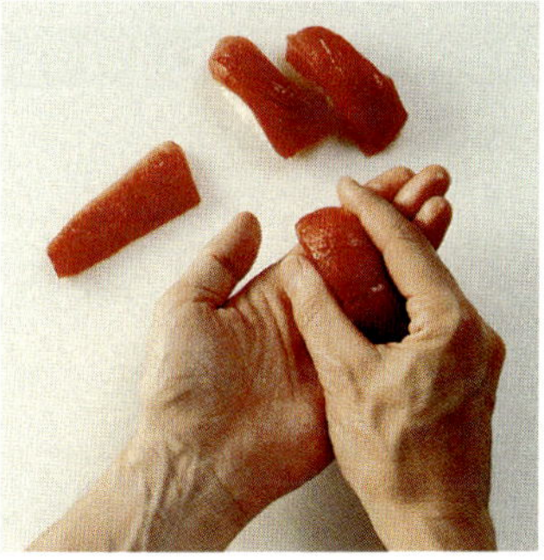

(d) Turn it over and press the same way. Then press the sides with the thumb and forefinger to finish shaping it.

(e) For rolled sushi, put a half-piece of nori on the sudare (bamboo mat). Wetting your hands with cold water to keep the rice from sticking to them, spread a layer of sushi rice over the bottom two-thirds of the nori.

(f) Lay strips of the filling across the middle of the rice.

(g) Holding the filling in place with the fingers, lift the corner of the mat with the thumbs and roll up.

(h) Press the mat firmly and evenly to make a tight roll.

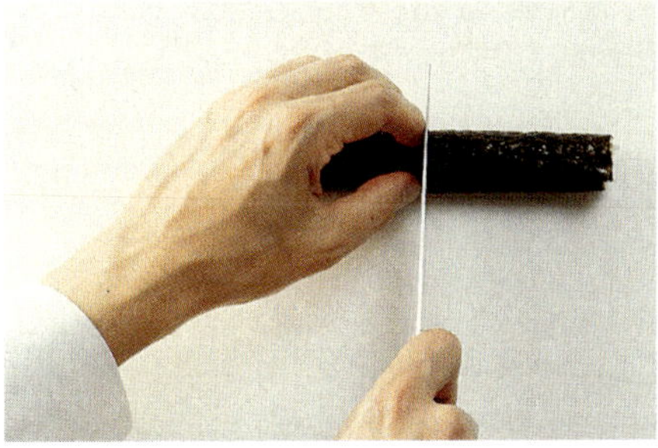

(i) Using a dampened knife, cut the roll in half with a single forward stroke.

(j) Wipe the blade between cuts, and cut each half-roll into three or four pieces.

SUSHI: A JAPANESE CLASSIC

Fish and rice dominate the cuisine of the island nation of Japan, and these two staples are combined in sushi, a classic Japanese preparation that is especially popular in the West. Sushi originated many years ago as a way of preserving fish by salting it and packing it with vinegared rice. When the fish was eaten, the rice was discarded.

In Japan, it takes many years of apprenticeship to become a sushi master, or *itamae* (ee-tah-mah-eh). A master is skilled in preparing rice properly, making rice fingers of just the right size and compactness for nigirizushi, and especially in selecting, judging, and cutting the many varieties of fresh seafood used as toppings.

When one is eating nigirizushi, it is considered improper to dip the rice ball into soy sauce. The large amount of soy sauce absorbed by the rice masks the fresh flavor of the toppings and makes the rice ball break up. Instead, turn the sushi over and dip the seafood topping lightly in the sauce.

Incidentally, in Japanese, an initial *S* sound, as in the word *sushi*, may change to a *Z* sound when it is in the middle of a compound word, as in *nigirizushi*.

Tuna Tartare

YIELD: APPROX. 1 LB 12 OZ (850 G) PORTIONS 8 PORTION SIZE: 3½ OZ (105 G)

U.S.	METRIC	INGREDIENTS
1 lb 8 oz	720 g	Sashimi-quality tuna, well trimmed
1 oz	30 g	Shallots, minced
2 tbsp	30 mL	Parsley, chopped
2 tbsp	30 mL	Fresh tarragon, chopped
2 tbsp	30 mL	Lime juice
1 fl oz	30 mL	Dijon-style mustard
2 fl oz	60 mL	Olive oil
to taste	to taste	Salt
to taste	to taste	White pepper

Per serving: Calories, 200; Protein, 21 g; Fat, 12 g (54% cal.); Cholesterol, 35 mg; Carbohydrates, 2 g; Fiber, 0 g; Sodium, 130 mg.

PROCEDURE

1. Mince the tuna with a knife. The most effective way to do this is to cut it into thin slices, cut the slices into thin strips, and cut the strips into very small dice. (The fish may also be chopped with a food processor, although the result is not as good as hand cutting. Pulse the machine, and be careful not to process the fish to a paste.) Do not pass the fish through a grinder, as this produces an undesirable texture.
2. Mixed the chopped tuna with the remaining ingredients shortly before serving, seasoning to taste with salt and pepper. Do not mix too long in advance, as the acidity of the lime juice coagulates the protein as for seviche (p. 115).
3. Tuna tartare may be served very simply mounded on a small plate or in more elaborate ways (see variations).

Tuna Tartare

VARIATIONS

Omit the shallots, parsley, tarragon, lime juice, and mustard. Add some chopped chives and a dash of hot pepper sauce.

Place a round biscuit cutter in the center of a plate. Fill it with the tartare and smooth the top. Remove the cutter (see **Figure 4.6**). Garnish and decorate as desired. For example, place a fresh herb leaf or dab of caviar on top, and place spoonfuls of caviar around the disk of tartare. With a squeeze bottle or spoon, place a ring of vinaigrette on the plate around the tartare.

Salmon Tartare

Substitute salmon for the tuna. Be sure all bones, skin, and sinews are removed from the salmon. In addition, cut away the dark, fatty tissue that runs down the centerline of the fillet on the skin side.

Tartare of Salmon and Sea Bass

In place of the tuna, use 12 oz (340 g) sea bass and 12 oz (340 g) salmon.

Figure 4.6 Shaping food with a ring mold.

(a) Position a ring mold on the plate. Fill with the food and level the top with a palette knife or spatula.

(b) Carefully lift off the mold.

Scallop Seviche

PORTIONS: 12 PORTION SIZE: 4 OZ (125 G)

U.S.	METRIC	INGREDIENTS	PROCEDURE
2 lb	1 kg	Sea scallops (see Note)	1. Cut the scallops into quarters vertically, then slice crosswise ¼ in. (6 mm) thick.
8 fl oz	250 mL	Lime juice	2. In a nonreactive container, mix together the scallops, lime juice, and onion.
4 oz	125 g	Red onion, chopped fine	3. Refrigerate about 12 hours, or until the scallops have the texture of cooked scallops.
1	1	Jalapeño, seeded and chopped fine	4. Drain the scallops and onions, discarding the lime juice.
6 tbsp	90 mL	Chopped cilantro	5. Gently toss the scallops with the jalapeño, cilantro, avocado, and tomato.
2	2	Avocados, medium dice	6. Add salt to taste.
8 oz	250 g	Tomato, peeled and seeded, small dice	7. Mix in the olive oil
to taste	to taste	Salt	
4 fl oz	125 mL	Olive oil	
as needed	as needed	Lettuce leaves	8. To serve, line small bowls or cups with lettuce leaves and spoon in the seviche.

Per serving: Calories, 220; Protein, 14 g; Fat, 15 g (61% cal.); Cholesterol, 25 mg; Carbohydrates, 8 g; Fiber, 2 g; Sodium, 130 mg.

Note: As an alternative to sea scallops, use bay scallops and leave them whole.

Scallop Seviche

TERMS FOR REVIEW

à la meunière
shallow poaching
submersion method
court bouillon
truite au bleu
cuisson
à la nage
étuver
en papillote
fish tartare
fish carpaccio
seviche
sushi

QUESTIONS FOR DISCUSSION

1. What major precaution must be taken when baking or broiling lean fish?
2. Describe the procedure for cooking fish à la meunière.
3. Which side of a fish fillet is the presentation side?
4. What techniques can you use for lifting whole poached fish out of court bouillon without breaking it or damaging its appearance?
5. What temperatures are best for poaching fish?
6. What is one advantage of using the oven to poach fish fillets?
7. Describe two methods for making a finished sauce out of the cooking liquid (fumet and wine) used for poaching fish fillets.
8. Discuss the precautions a cook should take to ensure raw fish is safe to eat.

Chapter 5

Roast Rack of Lamb; White Beans Bretonne; Steamed Brussels Sprout Leaves, page 162.

Understanding Meats and Game

Meat is muscle tissue. It is the flesh of domestic animals (cattle, hogs, and lambs) and of wild game animals (such as deer). As a cook, chef, or food-service operator, you will spend more of your time and money on meats than on any other food.

It is important, then, to understand meats thoroughly in order to cook them well and profitably. Why are some meats tender and some tough? How can you tell one cut from another when there are so many? How do you determine the best way to cook each cut?

In order to answer questions like these, it is helpful to start at the most basic level of composition and structure. We then proceed to discuss grading and inspection, basic cuts, and appropriate cooking and storage methods. In addition, we discuss the characteristics of variety meats and of popular game meats. Only then can we best approach the individual cooking methods and recipes presented in the following chapters.

After reading this chapter, you should be able to

1. Describe the composition and structure of meat, and explain how they relate to meat selection and cooking methods.
2. Explain the use of the federal meat inspection and grading system in selecting and purchasing meats.
3. Explain the effect of aging on meat, and identify the two primary aging methods.
4. Identify the primal cuts of beef, lamb, veal, and pork, and list the major fabricated cuts obtained from each of them.
5. Select appropriate cooking methods for the most important meat cuts, based on the meat's tenderness and other characteristics.
6. Prepare variety meats.
7. Identify the characteristics of game meats, and select the appropriate cooking methods for them.
8. Determine doneness in cooked meat.
9. Store fresh meat and frozen meat to gain the maximum shelf life.

Composition, Structure, and Basic Quality Factors

Composition

Muscle tissue consists of three major components: water, protein, and fat.

Water

Water is about 75 percent of muscle tissue. With such a high percentage of water, you can see why *shrinkage* can be a big problem in cooking meat. Too much moisture loss means dry meat, loss of weight, and loss of profit.

Protein

Protein is an important nutrient and the most abundant solid material in meat. About 20 percent of muscle tissue is protein.

Protein *coagulates* when it is heated. This means it becomes firmer and loses moisture. ***Coagulation*** is related to doneness. When protein has coagulated to the desired degree, the meat is said to be "done." Doneness is discussed later in this chapter.

After protein has coagulated, applying higher heat toughens it.

Fat

Fat accounts for up to 5 percent of muscle tissue. Of course, more fat may surround the muscles. A beef carcass can be as much as 30 percent fat.

Because of health and dietary concerns, many meat animals are being bred and raised with a lower fat content than in past years. Nevertheless, a certain amount of fat is desirable for three reasons:

1. **Juiciness.**
   Marbling is fat deposited within the muscle tissue. The juiciness we enjoy in well-marbled beef is due more to fat than to moisture.
   Surface fat protects the meat—especially roasts—from drying out during cooking as well as in storage. Adding surface fats where they are lacking is called *barding*.

2. **Tenderness.**
   Marbling separates muscle fibers, making them easier to chew.

3. **Flavor.**
   Fat is perhaps the main source of flavor in meat. A well-marbled Prime (top grade) steak tastes "beefier" than the same cut of a lower grade.

Carbohydrate

Meat contains a very small amount of carbohydrate. From the standpoint of nutrition, its quantity is so small that it is insignificant. It is important, however, because it plays a neces-sary part in the complex reaction, called the *Maillard reaction*, that takes place when meats are browned by roasting, broiling, or sautéing. Without these carbohydrates, the desirable flavor and appearance of browned meats would not be achieved.

Structure

Muscle Fibers

Lean meat is composed of long, thin muscle fibers bound together in bundles. These determine the *texture* or *grain* of a piece of meat. Fine-grained meat is composed of small fibers bound in small bundles. Coarse-textured meat has large fibers.

Feel the cut surface of a tenderloin steak, and compare its smooth texture to the rough cut surface of brisket or bottom round.

Connective Tissue

Muscle fibers are bound together in a network of proteins called ***connective tissue***. Each muscle fiber also is covered in a sheath of connective tissue.

It is important for the cook to understand connective tissue for one basic reason: *Connective tissue is tough.* To cook meats successfully, you should know

- Which meats are high in connective tissue and which are low.
- What are the best ways to make tough meats tender.

1. **Meats are highest in connective tissue if**
   - They come from muscles that are more exercised. Muscles in the legs, for example, have more connective tissue than muscles in the back.
   - They come from older animals. Veal is more tender than meat from a young steer, which, in turn, is more tender than meat from an old bull or cow. (Young animals have connective tissue, too, but it becomes harder to break down as the animal ages.)

2. **Meats high in connective tissue can be made more tender by using proper cooking techniques.**
   There are two kinds of connective tissue: collagen, which is white in color, and elastin, which is yellow.

   - ***Collagen.***
     Long, slow cooking in the presence of moisture breaks down or dissolves collagen by turning it into gelatin and water. Of course, muscle tissue is about 75 percent water, so moisture is always present when meats are cooked. Except for very large roasts, however, long cooking by a dry-heat method has the danger of evaporating too much moisture and drying out the meat. Therefore, *moist-heat cooking methods at low temperatures are most effective for turning a meat high in connective tissue into a tender, juicy finished product.*

     Other factors also help tenderize collagen:

     Acid helps dissolve collagen. Marinating meat in an acid mixture, or adding an acid such as tomato or wine to the cooking liquid, helps tenderize it.

     Enzymes are naturally present in meats. They break down some connective tissue and other proteins as meat ages (see "Aging," pp. 124–125). These enzymes are inactive at freezing temperatures, slow-acting under refrigeration, active at room temperature, and destroyed by heat above 140°F (60°C).

     Tenderizers are enzymes such as papain (extracted from papaya) that are added to meats by the cook or injected into the animal before slaughter. Exercise care when using enzyme tenderizers. Too long an exposure at room temperature can make the meat undesirably mushy.

- *Elastin.*
  Older animals have a higher proportion of elastin than younger animals.
  Elastin is not broken down in cooking. Tenderizing can be accomplished only by *removing the elastin* (cutting away any tendons) and by mechanically breaking up the fibers, as in

  Pounding and cubing (cubed steaks)

  Grinding (hamburger)

  Slicing the cooked meat very thin against the grain (as in London broil)

Inspection and Grading

Cooks and food-service operators in the United States are assisted in their evaluation of meats by a federal inspection and grading system.

Figure 5.1
USDA inspection stamp for meat

Inspection

1. *Inspection* is a *guarantee of wholesomeness*, not of quality or tenderness. It means the animal was not diseased and the meat is clean and fit for human consumption.
2. That the meat passed inspection is indicated by a round stamp (Figure 5.1).
3. Inspection is required by U.S. federal law. All meat must be inspected.

Quality Grading

Figure 5.2
USDA grade stamp for meat

1. *Grading* is a *quality* designation.
2. The grade is indicated by a shield stamp (Figure 5.2).
3. Grading is not required by U.S. law. (Some packers use a private grading system and give different brand names to different grades. Reliability of private grades depends on the integrity of the packer.)

Quality grading is based on the texture, firmness, and color of the lean meat, the age or maturity of the animal, and the marbling (the fat within the lean).

All these factors must be considered together. For example, old, tough meat can still have marbling, but it would rate a low grade because of the other factors. Table 5.1 summarizes USDA meat grades.

Yield Grading

In addition to quality grading, beef and lamb are graded according to how much usable meat in proportion to fat they have. This is called ***yield grading***. The meatiest grade is Yield Grade 1. Poorest yield (much exterior fat) is Yield Grade 5.

Pork is yield-graded from 1 to 4, but most pork is sold already cut and trimmed.

Veal, which has little fat, is not yield-graded.

Aging

Green Meat

Soon after slaughter, an animal's muscles stiffen due to chemical changes in the flesh. This stiffness, called *rigor mortis*, gradually disappears. Softening takes three to four days for beef, less time for smaller carcasses like veal, lamb, and pork. This softening is caused by enzymes in the flesh.

Table 5.1 **USDA Meat Grades**

Characteristics	Beef	Veal	Lamb	Pork
Highest quality, highest price, limited supply.	Prime	Prime	Prime	Pork used in food service is consistent in quality and is not quality-graded. It is inspected for wholesomeness and graded for yield.
High in quality, generally tender and juicy. Abundant supply. Widely used in food service as well as in retail.	Choice	Choice	Choice	
Lean meat, not as fine or tender. Economical. Can be tender and flavorful if cooked carefully. Used in many institutional food-service operations.	Select	Good	Good	
Least frequently used in food service. Highest of these grades are sometimes used in institutional food service. Lowest of these grades are used by canners and processors.	Standard Commercial Utility Cutter Canner	Standard Utility Cull	Utility Cull	

Note: Quality varies within grades. For example, the best Choice beef is close to Prime, while the lowest Choice beef is close to Select.

Green meat is meat that has not had enough time to soften. It is tough and relatively flavorless. Because it takes several days for meats to reach the kitchen from the slaughterhouse, green meat is seldom a problem with commercially available meats, except when meat is frozen while still green. The problem is sometimes encountered with game killed for home consumption, if the hunter cuts and freezes the meat when it is too fresh.

Aged Meat

Enzyme action continues in muscle tissue even after meat is no longer green. This tenderizes the flesh even more and develops more flavor. Holding meats in coolers under controlled conditions to provide time for this natural tenderizing is called ***aging***.

Beef and lamb can be aged because high-quality carcasses have enough fat cover to protect them from bacteria and from drying. Veal has no fat cover, so it is not aged. Pork does not require aging.

Aging does not mean just storing meat in the refrigerator. *There is a difference between aged meat and old meat.* Conditions must be carefully controlled so the meat becomes naturally tender without spoiling. There are two primary methods used for aging.

1. **Wet aging.**
   Today, most wholesale meat carcasses are broken down into smaller cuts and enclosed in plastic vacuum packs. These packs are usually known by the trade name ***Cryovac®***. The air- and moistureproof packaging protects the meat from bacteria and mold, and it prevents weight loss due to drying. (However, Cryovac-aged meats often lose more weight in cooking than do dry-aged meats.) Vacuum-pack meats must be refrigerated.

KEY POINTS TO REVIEW

- What are the three main components of meat?
- What is connective tissue? How does it affect our choice of cooking techniques for meat?
- What is the difference between inspection and grading?
- What are the best two grades of beef? of lamb? of pork? of veal?
- What are the two types of aging? What effect does aging have on meat?

2. **Dry aging.**

   Dry aging is the process of storing meats, usually large cuts, under carefully controlled conditions. The meat is not packaged or wrapped, and it is exposed to air on all sides. Temperature, humidity, and air circulation are precisely controlled to prevent spoilage. Ultraviolet lights are sometimes used in aging coolers to kill bacteria.

   Dry-aged meat can lose up to 20 percent of its weight through moisture loss, depending on the size of the cut and how long it is aged. Consequently, dry aging is a more expensive process than wet aging. Dry-aged meats are usually available from specialty purveyors only, and at a higher price than wet-aged meats. Many customers are willing to pay a premium for fine dry-aged steaks because they are considered the best for flavor and texture.

   Aging increases tenderness and flavor. An off taste is not characteristic of aged meat. *If a meat smells or tastes spoiled, it probably is.* Sometimes meats in vacuum packs have a musty aroma when first opened, but this disappears quickly.

   Aging costs money. Storage costs, weight loss due to drying, and heavier trimming due to dried and discolored surfaces all add to the price of aged meat (although wet aging costs less than dry aging). As a meat purchaser, you must decide how much quality is worth how much cost for your particular establishment.

UNDERSTANDING THE BASIC CUTS

The following discussion of meat cuts focuses on the four primary meat categories in the wholesale and retail markets: beef, lamb, veal, and pork. Keep in mind, however, that game animals, discussed later in the chapter, have the same bone and muscle structure and are generally divided into the same or similar cuts as nongame animals.

Meat cuts are based on two factors:

1. The muscle and bone structure of the meat.
2. Uses of and appropriate cooking methods for various parts of the animal.

Food-service suppliers in the United States may follow a set of specifications called *Institution Meat Purchase Specifications* (IMPS). (IMPS, including numbers and names of cuts, are the same as the North American Meat Processors Association, or NAMP, specifications.) All cuts are described in detail and listed by number. This simplifies purchasing, as you can order by number exactly the cut you want.

IMPS/NAMP CLASSIFICATIONS

The IMPS/NAMP system assigns a series of numbers to each major category of meat, as detailed in Table 5.2. Beef, for example, is the 100 series. This means all large beef cuts, from whole carcass to primals and prepared roasts, are assigned a three-digit number from 100 to 199. Portion-size and smaller cuts of beef, such as steaks and stew meat, are assigned a four-digit number, also beginning with 1. For example, a whole beef rib, roast-ready, has the number 109; a beef rib steak, bone in, is 1103.

Note that variety meats and processed meat products, such as cured and smoked meats and sausages, are also categorized (see Table 5.2).

Available Forms: Carcasses, Partial Carcasses, Primals, and Fabricated Cuts

Beef, lamb, veal, and pork may be purchased in some or all of these forms. Mutton and goat are also given NAMP classification numbers, as indicated in Table 5.2, but they have minimal importance in North American food service and are not covered here.

Carcasses

The carcass is the whole animal, minus the entrails, head, feet, and hide (except pork, from which only the entrails and head are removed). Whole carcasses are rarely purchased by food-service operators because of the skill and labor required in cutting and because of the problem of total utilization.

Sides, Quarters, Foresaddles, Hindsaddles

These represent the first step in breaking down a carcass.

Again, these larger cuts are no longer frequently used in food service. Fewer establishments cut their own meats.

1. Beef is split first through the backbone into sides. Sides are divided between the 12th and 13th ribs into forequarter and hindquarter.
2. Veal and lamb are not split into sides but are divided in half into foresaddle and hindsaddle. For veal, the cut is made between the 11th and 12th ribs. Lamb, on the other hand, is split either between the 12th and 13th rib or after the 13th rib, depending on the cutting style. For more information, see the charts on pages 132–133.
3. Pork carcasses are not divided in this way. They are cut directly into primal cuts (see below).

Primal or Wholesale Cuts

These are the primary divisions of quarters, foresaddles, hindsaddles, and carcasses. These cuts, called ***primal cuts***, are still used, to some extent, in food service, because they

1. Are small enough to be manageable in many food-service kitchens.
2. Are still large enough to allow a variety of cuts for different uses or needs.
3. Are easier to utilize completely than quarters or halves.

Each primal may be ***fabricated***, or cut up and trimmed, in several ways. Primal cuts are always the starting point for smaller cuts. For this reason, it will benefit you to be able to identify each one. Study the charts and photos in Figures 5.3 through 5.6. (Please note the lamb chart in Figure 5.5 shows the traditional cuts, not the alternative cuts mentioned in the preceding section.) Learn the names of the primals, their location on the carcass, and the most important cuts that come from each. Then, whenever you work with a piece of meat, try to identify it exactly and match it with its primal cut.

Table 5.2
IMPS/NAMPS Meat Categories

Series Number	Series Name
100	Fresh Beef
200	Fresh Lamb and Mutton
300	Fresh Veal and Calf
400	Fresh Pork
500	Cured, Cure and Smoked, and Cooked Pork Products
600	Cured, Dried, and Smoked Beef Products
700	Variety Meats and Edible Byproducts
800	Sausage Products
11	Fresh Goat

Fabricated Cuts

Primal cuts are fabricated into smaller cuts for roasts, steaks, chops, cutlets, stewing meat, ground meat, and so forth, according to individual customer requirements and, if applicable, IMPS/NAMP specifications.

The amount of trim and exact specifications can have many variations. For example, a beef primal rib can be trimmed and prepared for roasting at least nine ways.

Portion-controlled cuts are ready-to-cook meats cut according to customer's specifications. Steaks and chops are ordered either by weight per steak or by thickness. Portion-controlled cuts require the least work for the cook of all meat cuts. They are also the most expensive per pound of all categories of cuts.

Bone Structure

Knowing the bone structure of meat animals is essential for:

1. **Identifying meat cuts.**
   The distinctive shapes of the bones are often the best clue to the identification of a cut. Note how the shapes of the bones in the photographs in Figures 5.3 through 5.6 help your recognition.
2. **Boning and cutting meats.**
   Bones are often surrounded by flesh. You need to know where they are even if you can't see them.
3. **Carving cooked meats.**
   Same reason as number 2.

Figure 5.3 Beef.

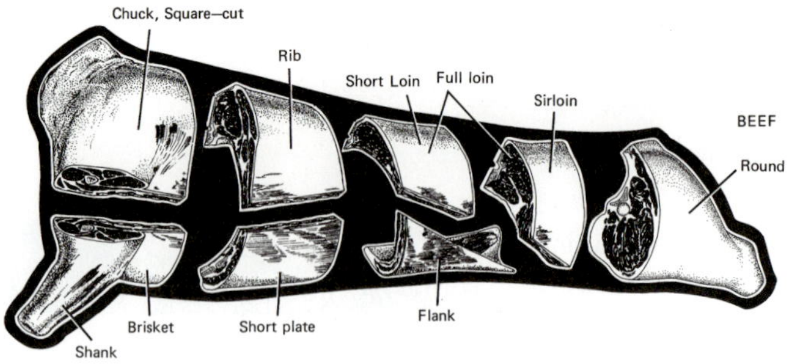

(a) Primal (wholesale) beef meat cuts
Courtesy National Livestock and Meat Board

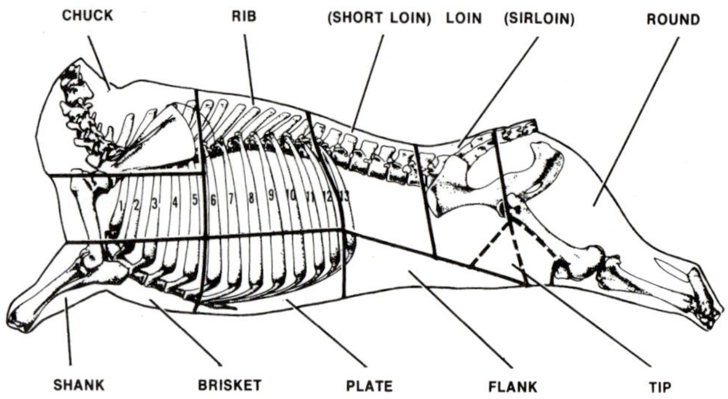

(b) Primal (wholesale) beef cuts and their bone structure
Courtesy National Livestock and Meat Board

Beef chuck, boneless, separated into blade, clod, and arm (IMPS/NAMPS 115)

Beef rib, roast ready
(IMPS/NAMPS 109)
(Reprinted with permission of John Wiley & Sons, Inc.)

Beef rib steak
(IMPS/NAMPS 1103)

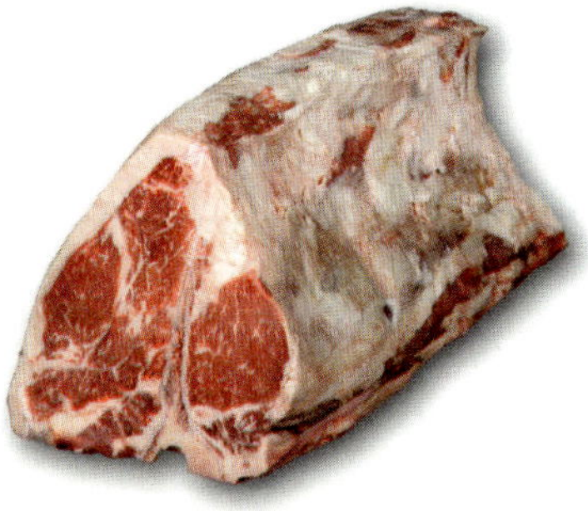

Beef short loin
(IMPS/NAMPS 174)
(Reprinted with permission of John Wiley & Sons, Inc.)

Beef porterhouse steak
(IMPS/NAMPS 1173)

Beef loin
(IMPS/NAMPS 172)
(Reprinted with permission of John Wiley & Sons, Inc.)

Beef T-bone steak
(IMPS/NAMPS 1174)

Beef tenderloin, trimmed
(IMPS/NAMPS 189A)

Beef strip loin
(IMPS/NAMPS 175)
(Reprinted with permission of John Wiley & Sons, Inc.)

Beef outside (bottom) round
(IMPS/NAMPS 170)

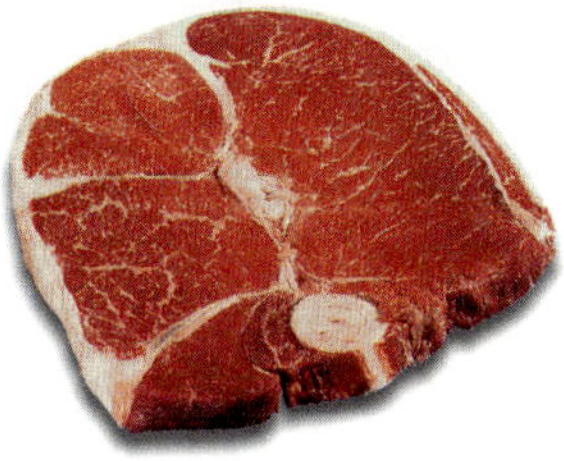

Beef round steak
(IMPS/NAMPS 1170)

Beef inside (top) round
(IMPS/NAMPS 168)

Beef knuckle, untrimmed
(IMPS/NAMPS 167)
(Reprinted with permission of John Wiley & Sons, Inc.)

Beef shank, cross-cuts
(IMPS/NAMPS 117)

Beef flank steak
(IMPS/NAMPS 193)

Figure 5.4 Veal

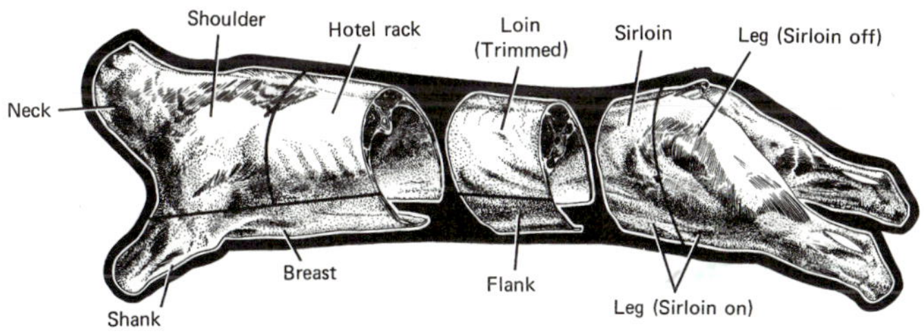

(a) Primal (wholesale) veal meat cuts
Courtesy National Livestock and Meat Board

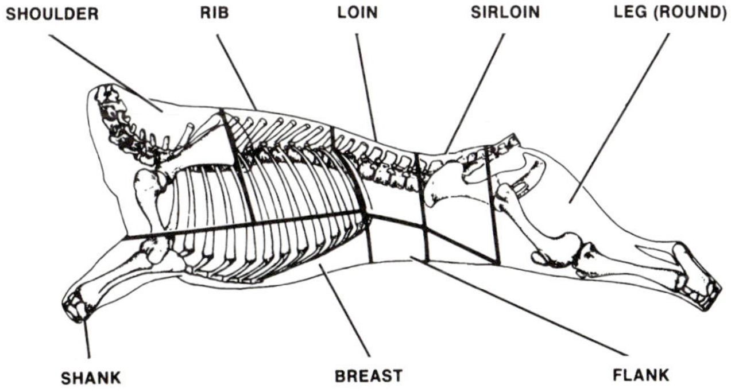

(b) Primal (wholesale) veal cuts and their bone structure
Courtesy National Livestock and Meat Board

Veal rib roast
(IMPS/NAMPS 306)

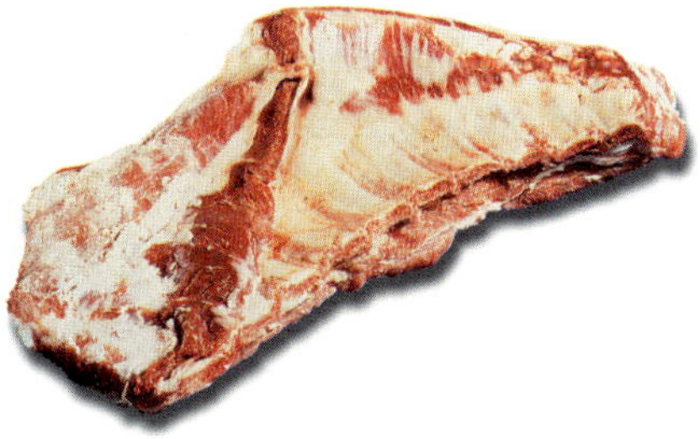

Veal breast
(IMPS/NAMPS 313)

Figure 5.5 Lamb.

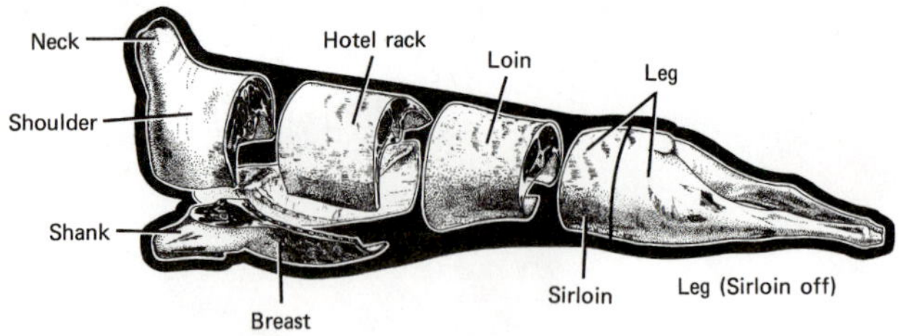

(a) Primal (wholesale) lamb meat cuts
Courtesy National Livestock and Meat Board

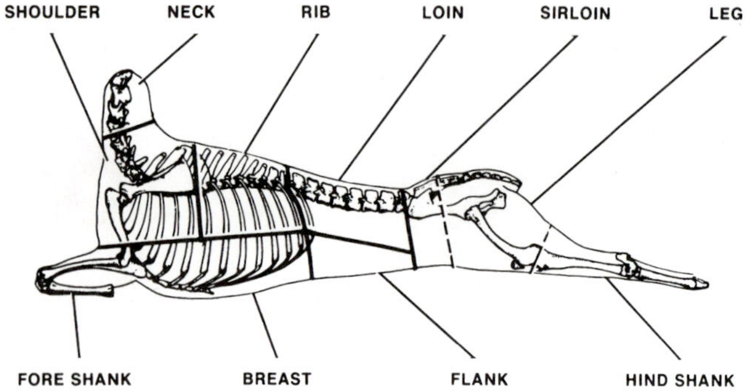

(b) Primal (wholesale) lamb cuts and their bone structure
Courtesy National Livestock and Meat Board

Lamb loin roast
(IMPS/NAMPS 232A)

Lamb arm chop
(IMPS/NAMPS 1207)

Lamb shoulder blade chop
(IMPS/NAMPS 1207)

Lamb rib chop
(IMPS/NAMPS 1204)

Lamb loin chop
(IMPS/NAMPS 1232A)

Lamb, square-cut shoulder, whole
(IMPS/NAMPS 207)

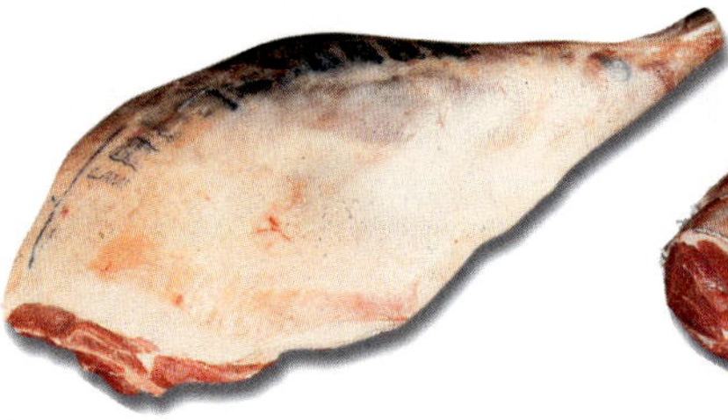

Lamb, whole leg
(IMPS/NAMPS 233)

Lamb, boneless shoulder, rolled and tied
(IMPS/NAMPS 208)

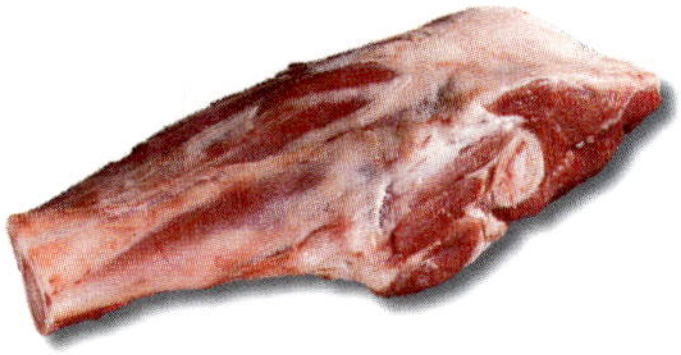

Lamb foreshank
(IMPS/NAMPS 210)

Figure 5.6 Pork.

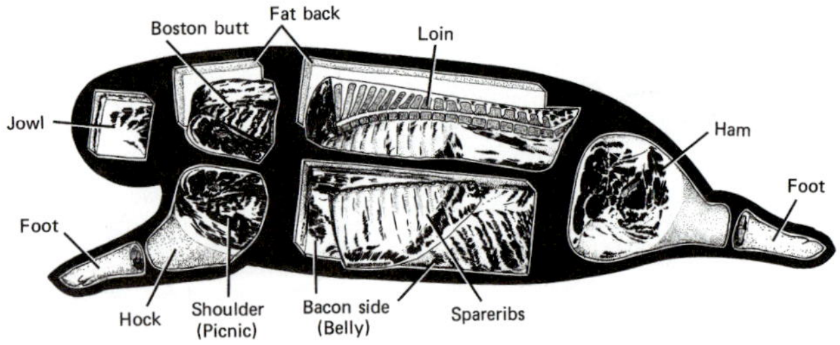

(a) Primal (wholesale) pork meat cuts
Courtesy National Livestock and Meat Board

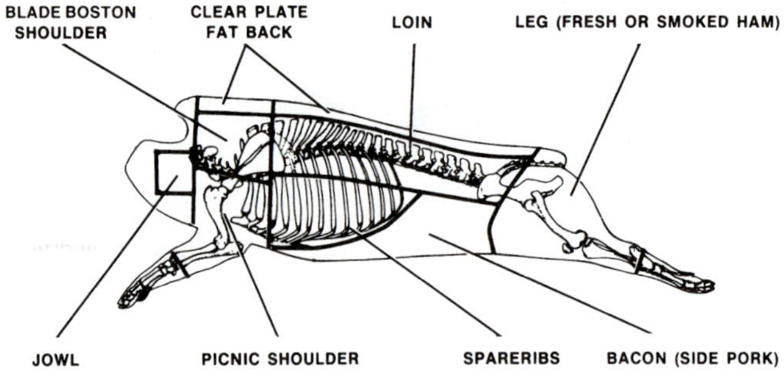

(b) Primal (wholesale) pork cuts and their bone structure
Courtesy National Livestock and Meat Board

Pork tenderloin
(IMPS/NAMPS 415)

Pork shoulder butt
(IMPS/NAMPS 406)

Full pork loin (includes ribs)
(IMPS/NAMPS 410)

Pork loin chops
(IMPS/NAMPS 1410)

Pork rib half and loin half roasts
(IMPS/NAMPS 410)

Study the chart of the beef skeleton in Figure 5.7 and learn the names of the major bones. Then compare the charts in Figures 5.3 through 5.6. You will see the bone structures for all the animals are identical (except for pork, which has more than 13 ribs). Even the names are the same.

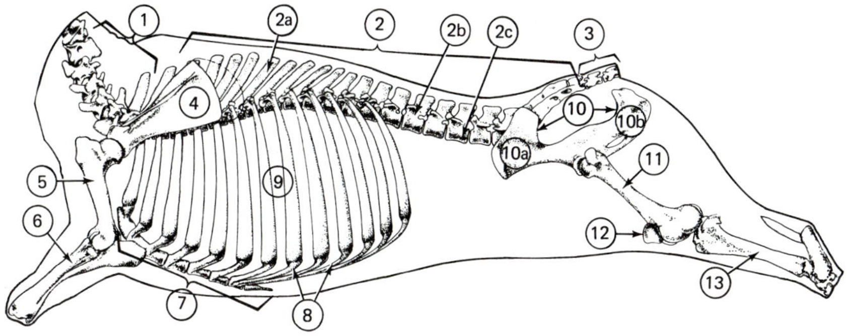

Figure 5.7 Beef bone structure

1. Neck bone
2. Backbone
2a. Feather bone
2b. Finger bone
2c. Chine bone
3. Tailbone
4. Blade bone
5. Arm bone
6. Foreshank bone
7. Breastbone
8. Rib cartilage
9. Ribs
10. Pelvis
10a. Hip bone
10b. Rump or aitch bone
11. Leg or round bone
12. Kneecap
13. Hindshank bone

The photographs in Figures 5.3 through 5.6 depict typical primal and fabricated cuts of beef, lamb, veal, and pork (courtesy National Livestock and Meat Board and National Pork Producers Council).

MEAT-CUTTING TERMINOLOGY

Although the public refers to retail meat cutters as *butchers*, the meat industry uses this term another way. To *butcher* means to kill and dress a meat animal. To *fabricate* means to cut raw meat into smaller pieces.

A third term, *carve*, also means to cut meat, but this always refers to cooked meat.

Beef, Lamb, Veal, and Pork Cuts

Beef Primal Cuts and Fabricated Cuts

Primal	Major Bones	Common Fabricated Cuts	Primary Cooking Methods
Forequarter			
Chuck (square cut)	Ribs 1–5 Blade bone Backbone (including chine and feather bones) Neck bones Arm bone	Shoulder clod Triangle Boneless inside chuck Chuck tender Chuck short ribs Cubed steaks Stew meat Ground chuck	Moist heat
Brisket	Rib bones Rib cartilage Breastbone	Boneless brisket and corned beef brisket Ground beef	Moist heat
Shank	Shankbone	Stew meat Ground beef	Moist heat
Note: Square-cut chuck, brisket, and shank, in one piece, are called *cross-cut chuck.*			
Rib	Ribs 6–12 Backbone (chine and feather bones)	Rib roasts (prime rib) Rib steaks Short ribs	Dry heat Moist heat
Short plate	Rib bones Tip of breastbone Rib cartilage	Short ribs Stew meat Ground beef	Moist heat

Beef Primal Cuts and Fabricated Cuts *(continued)*

Primal	Major Bones	Common Fabricated Cuts	Primary Cooking Methods
Hindquarter			
(Full loin)		Full tenderloin (to have tenderloin in one piece, it must be stripped out of loin before loin is split into short loin and sirloin)	Dry heat
Short loin	Rib 13 Backbone (chine, feather bones, finger bones; see Note 1)	Club steaks T-bone steaks Porterhouse steaks Strip loin Strip loin steaks Short tenderloin	Dry heat
Sirloin	Backbone Hip bone (part of pelvis)	Top sirloin butt Bottom sirloin butt Butt tenderloin	Dry heat
Flank	Tip of rib 13	Flank steak Ground beef	Moist heat (exception: flank steak cooked as London broil)
Round	Round (leg) bone Aitch bone (part of pelvis) Shankbone Tailbone	Knuckle (sirloin tip) Inside (top) round Outside (bottom) round Eye of round (part of outside round) Rump Hind shank	Moist heat and dry heat

Note 1: Finger bones are the short horizontal bones attached to those chine bones that have no ribs attached. They are stems of the *Ts* in T-bones.

Lamb Primal Cuts and Fabricated Cuts

Primal	Major Bones	Common Fabricated Cuts	Primary Cooking Methods
Foresaddle			
Shoulder	Ribs 1–4 or 1–5 (see Note 2) Arm Blade Backbone (chine and feather bones) Neck bones	Shoulder roasts Shoulder chops Stew meat Ground lamb	Moist heat and dry heat
Breast and shank	Rib bones Rib cartilage Breastbone Shankbone	Riblets Breast Stew meat Ground lamb	Moist heat
Hotel rack	Ribs 5–12 or 6–13 (see Note 2) Backbone	Rib roasts (rack) Crown roast Ribs, chops	Dry heat
Note: Hotel rack plus connecting portions of breast is called a *bracelet*.			
Hindsaddle			
Loin (with or without flank)	Rib 13 (optional; see Note 2) Backbone (chine, feather bones, finger bones)	Loin roast Loin chops	Dry heat
Leg	Backbone Tailbone Pelvis Round bone Hindshank	Leg roast Leg chops Sirloin chops Shank	Dry heat Moist heat
Note: Hotel rack and loin attached are called *lamb back*; used mostly for chops.			

Note 2: There are two cutting styles for lamb carcasses. In style A, the carcass is divided between the 4th and 5th ribs and again between the 12th and 13th ribs. In style B, the cuts are made between the 5th and 6th ribs and again behind the 13th rib. Both styles yield 8-rib racks. Style B produces a rack with a more uniform eye muscle through the length of the rack.

Veal Primal Cuts and Fabricated Cuts

Primal	Major Bones	Common Fabricated Cuts	Primary Cooking Methods
Foresaddle			
Shoulder (square cut)	Ribs 1–4 or 1–5 (see Note 3) Blade bone Backbone (chine and feather bones) Neck bones Arm bone	Shoulder roasts Shoulder chops Shoulder clod steaks Cubed steaks Stew meat Ground veal	Moist heat and dry heat
Breast	Rib bones Rib cartilage Breastbone	Boneless breast Cubed steaks Ground veal	Moist heat
Shank	Shankbone	Shank cross-cut (osso buco)	Moist heat
Hotel rack	Ribs 5–11 or 6–11 (see Note 3) Backbone (chine and feather bones)	Rib roast Rib chops	Dry heat and moist heat
Note: Hotel rack plus connecting portions of breast is called a *bracelet*.			
Hindsaddle			
Loin (with or without flank)	Ribs 12 and 13 Backbone (chine, feather bones, finger bones)	Saddle (loin roast) Loin chops	Dry heat and moist heat
Leg	Backbone Tailbone Pelvis (hip bone, aitch bone) Round bone Hindshank	Leg roast Scaloppine or cutlets Shank cross-cut (osso buco)	Dry heat Moist heat
Note: Hotel rack and loin attached are called *veal back*; used mostly for chops.			

Note 3: The shoulder may be separated from the rack between the 4th and 5th ribs to yield a 7-rib rack, or between the 5th and 6th ribs to yield a 6-rib rack.

Pork Primal Cuts and Fabricated Cuts

Primal	Major Bones	Common Fabricated Cuts	Primary Cooking Methods
Shoulder picnic	Shoulder (arm) bone Shankbone	Fresh and smoked picnic Hocks Ground pork Sausage meat	Moist heat
Boston butt	Blade bone (rib bones, back and neck bones are removed)	Butt steaks Shoulder roasts Daisy (smoked) Ground pork Sausage meat	Dry heat and moist heat
Loin	Rib bones (see Note 4) Backbone (chine, feather bones, finger bones) Hip bone	Loin roast Loin and rib chops Boneless loin Country-style ribs Canadian-style bacon (smoked)	Dry heat and moist heat
Ham	Aitch bone Leg bone Hindshank bone	Fresh ham Smoked ham Ham steaks	Dry heat and moist heat
Belly	None	Bacon	Dry heat and moist heat
Spare ribs	Rib bones Breastbone	Spareribs	Moist heat
Fatback and clear plate	None	Fresh and salt fatback Salt pork Lard	(Used as cooking fats)
Jowl	None	Jowl bacon	Moist heat
Feet	Foot bones		Moist heat

Note 4: Pork has more than 13 ribs (unlike beef, lamb, and veal) due to special breeding to develop long loins.

Selecting Meats for Your Operation

Deciding Which Forms to Purchase

Whether you buy whole carcasses, fabricated cuts, or anything in between depends on four factors:

1. How much meat-cutting skill you or your staff has.
2. How much work and storage space you have.
3. Whether or not you can use all cuts and lean trim on your menu.
4. Which form gives you the best cost per portion after figuring in labor costs.

Meat purveyors can usually cut meat more economically than food-service operators can because they deal in large volume. Carcasses or primal cuts cost less per pound than fabricated cuts, but they have more waste (fat and bone) and require more labor (which costs money). However, some operators still do some of their own cutting, depending on how they answer the four questions above. They feel cutting their own meat gives them greater control over quality.

Some compromises are available. If you want the quality of freshly cut steaks, for example, you might buy boneless strip loins and cut your own steaks to order. You need not buy primal loins.

Specifications

When buying meat, you must indicate the following specifications:

1. **Item name.**
   Include IMPS/NAMPS number, if applicable.
   Example: 173 Beef Short Loin, Regular

2. **Grade.**
   Example: U.S. Choice
   (You may also want to specify division of grade, such as the upper half or lower half of U.S. Choice.)

3. **Weight range for roasts and large cuts.**
   Portion weight or thickness (not both) for steaks and chops.

4. **State of refrigeration.**
   Chilled or frozen.

5. **Fat limitations, or average thickness of surface fat.**
   Example: ¾ inch average, 1 inch maximum.
   (This does not apply to veal.)

Meat purchasers may also have to choose whether or not to purchase irradiated meat. ***Irradiation*** is the process of exposing foods to radiation in order to kill bacteria, parasites, and other potentially harmful organisms. Irradiation does not harm the meat, make it radioactive, or change its structure, flavor, or nutritional value. Foods treated with radiation must be labeled as such. In the United States, for example, the Food and Drug Administration (FDA) requires that irradiated foods include labeling with either the statement "treated with radiation" or "treated by irradiation" and the international symbol for irradiation, the radura (Figure 5.8).

Figure 5.8
The radura is the international symbol for irradiation.

Some operators refuse to purchase irradiated foods because they or their customers have concerns about their health effects. The procedure has generated much controversy for other reasons as well. For example, some see the availability of the process as an excuse to avoid normal sanitation procedures. Nevertheless, there is so far no evidence that these foods are harmful for human beings to eat.

Fabricating Meat

Even though few operations today purchase large cuts, such as primals, and break them down in-house, you still need to know a number of trimming and fabricating techniques to finish or modify the fabricated cuts you purchase. The illustrations in this section demonstrate important procedures. These procedures are used for recipes in Chapter 6.

One term you will encounter often when trimming meat is ***silverskin***, a thin layer or membrane of connective tissue that often covers the surface of a muscle. For braised meats, it is not always necessary to remove silverskin, unless it is very heavy, because slow cooking breaks down the collagen of the tissue. However, for roasts, sautés, and grills of tender meats, it should be removed for two reasons: (1) It is tough and would be unpleasantly chewy in the cooked product; (2) It usually shrinks when cooked, making the meat deform or curl.

To remove silverskin:

1. Hold the blade of the knife parallel to the silverskin and perpendicular to the grain of the meat.
2. Insert the tip of the blade just under the silverskin.
3. Hold the knife so the edge of the blade angles slightly upward. Carefully slip the blade under the silverskin in the direction of the grain of the meat while holding the meat steady with your other hand. (Angling the blade upward keeps it from digging into the meat.)
4. Repeat until all silverskin is removed.

This technique is illustrated in Figures 5.9, 5.15, and 5.16.

Figure 5.9 Preparing beef tenderloin.

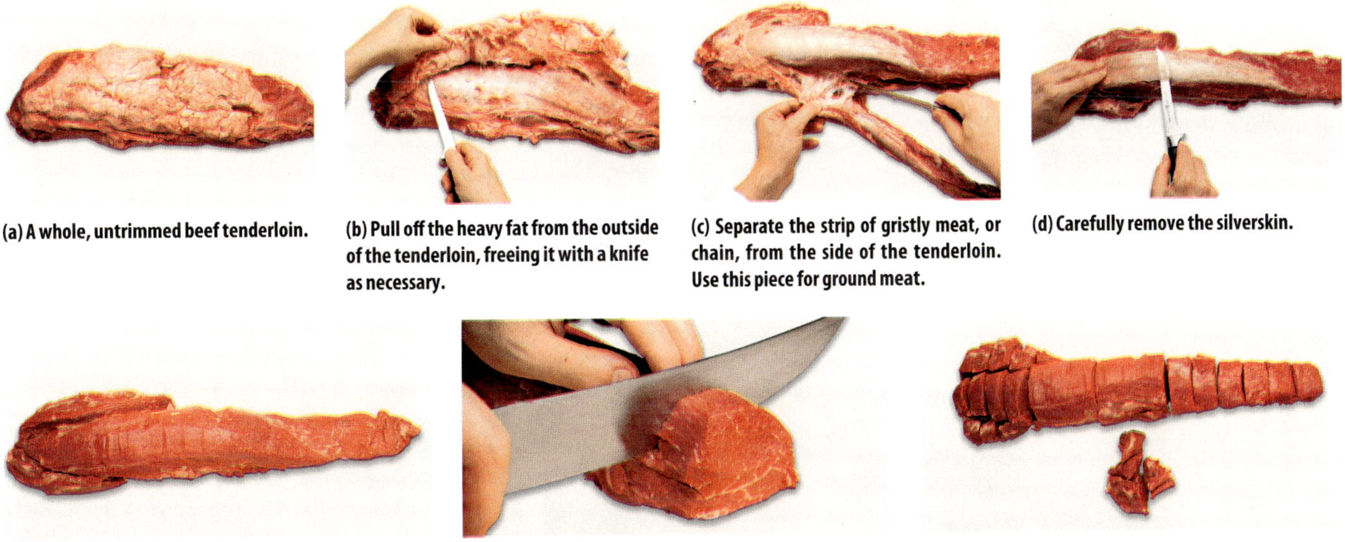

(a) A whole, untrimmed beef tenderloin.

(b) Pull off the heavy fat from the outside of the tenderloin, freeing it with a knife as necessary.

(c) Separate the strip of gristly meat, or chain, from the side of the tenderloin. Use this piece for ground meat.

(d) Carefully remove the silverskin.

(e) The fully trimmed tenderloin before cutting.

(f) Cut into steaks of the desired size.

(g) This tenderloin has been cut into a variety of steaks as a demonstration. From left to right: four fillet steaks, two large pieces for Châteaubriand, two tournedos, four fillets mignons. In front: trimmings from both ends.

Figure 5.10 Shaping medallions.

Figure 5.11 Preparing a leg of lamb for roasting.

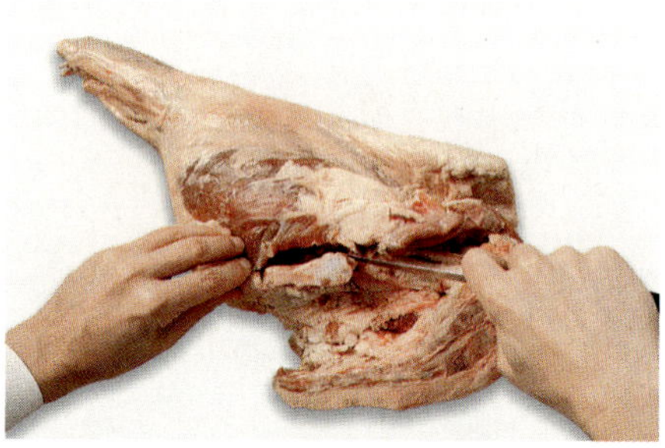

(a) Begin by removing the hip and tail bones.

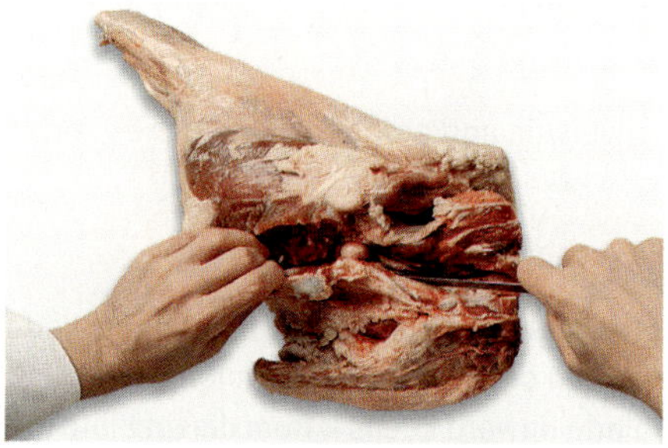

(b) With a sharp-pointed boning knife, cut along the hip bone to separate bone from meat. Always cut against the bone.

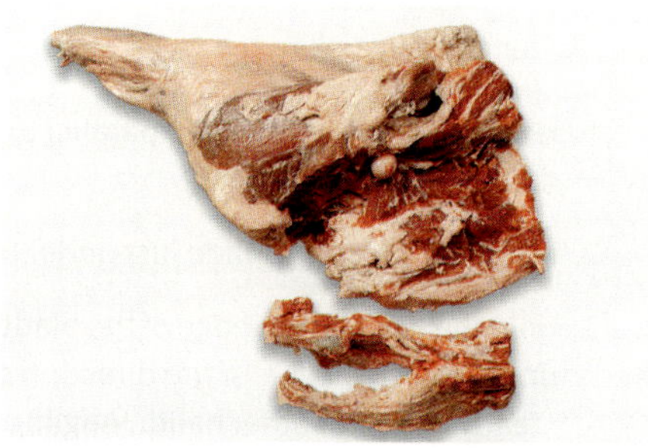

(c) Continue until the hip bone and tailbone are completely removed. Note the round ball joint at the end of the leg bone in the center of the meat.

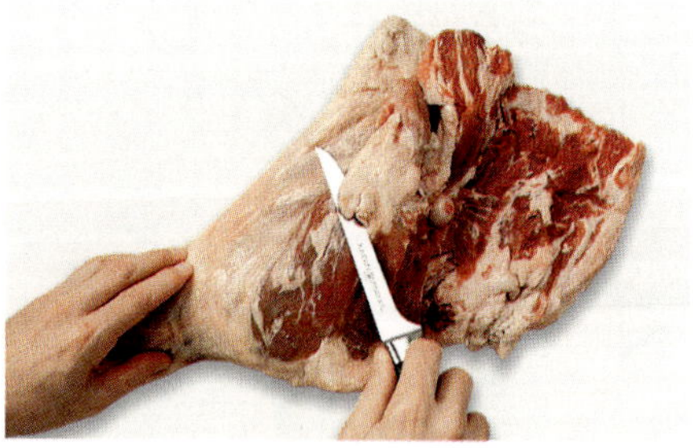

(d) Trim off excess external fat, leaving a thin covering.

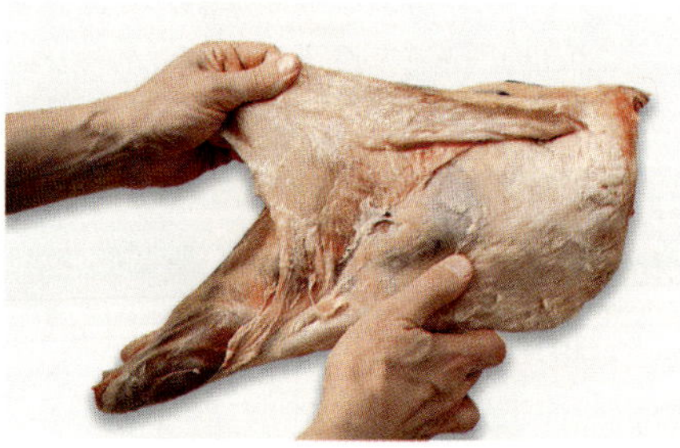

(e) Pull off the skin or fell on the outside of the leg.

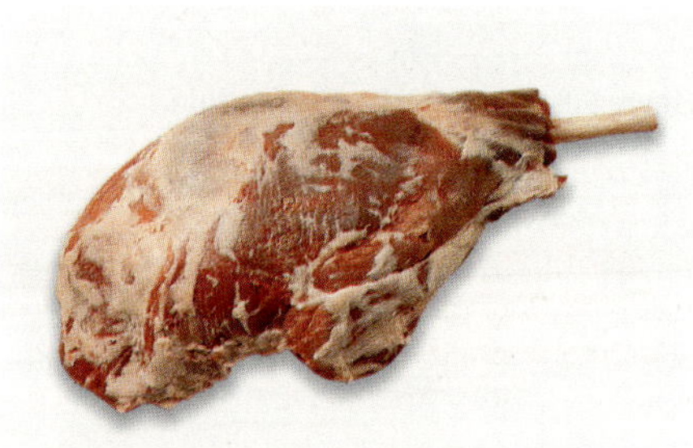

(f) Full leg of lamb, ready for roasting. The end of the shankbone and part of the shank meat have been removed.

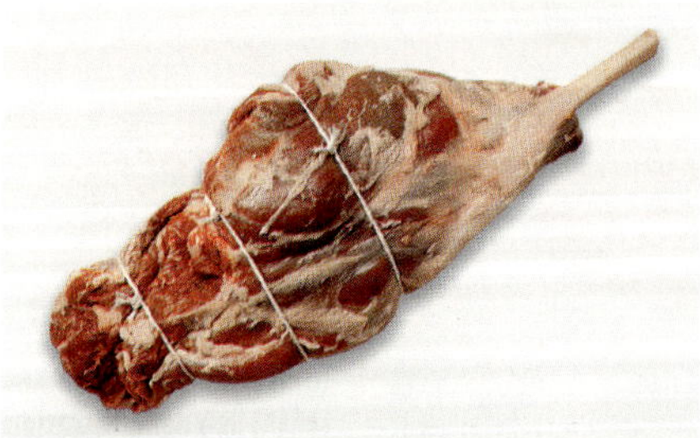

(g) The leg may be tied into a more compact shape.

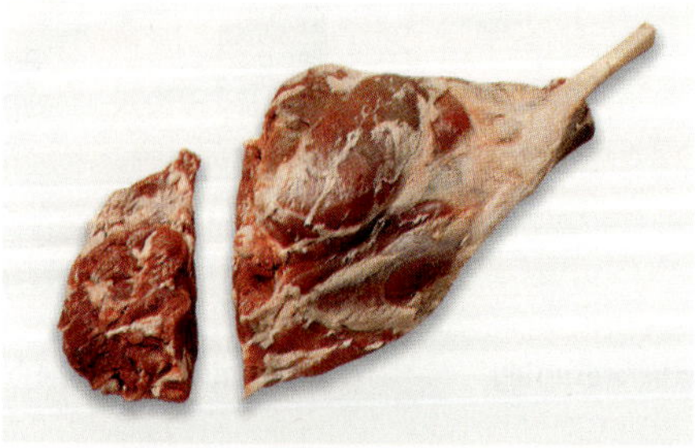

(h) The sirloin portion may be cut off and used for another purpose, such as shish kebabs.

Figure 5.12 Preparing a rack of lamb for roasting.

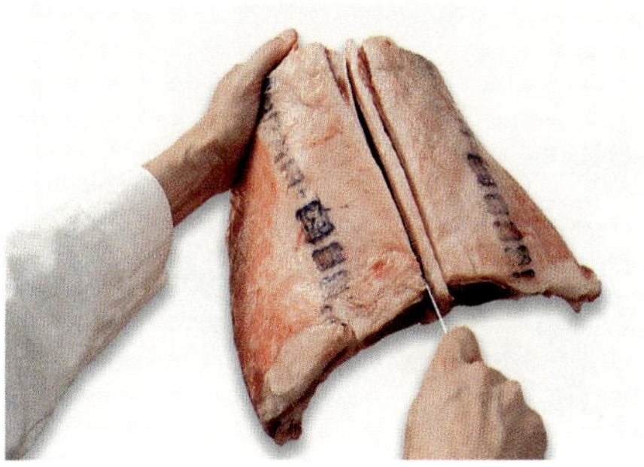

(a) Begin by cutting down on both sides of the feather bones all the way to the chine bone.

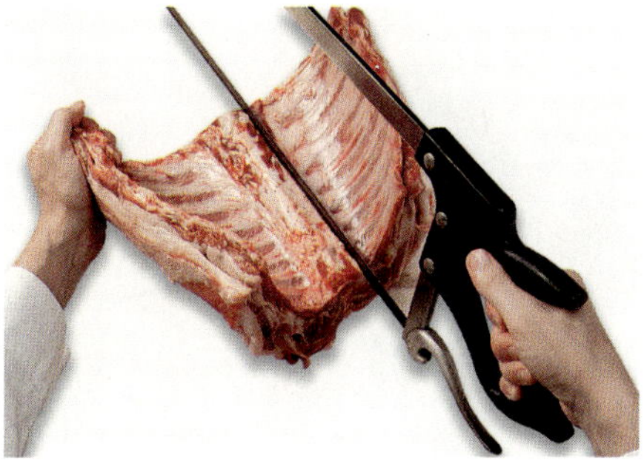

(b) If a meat saw is available, turn the rack over and cut through the rib bones where they attach to the chine bone.

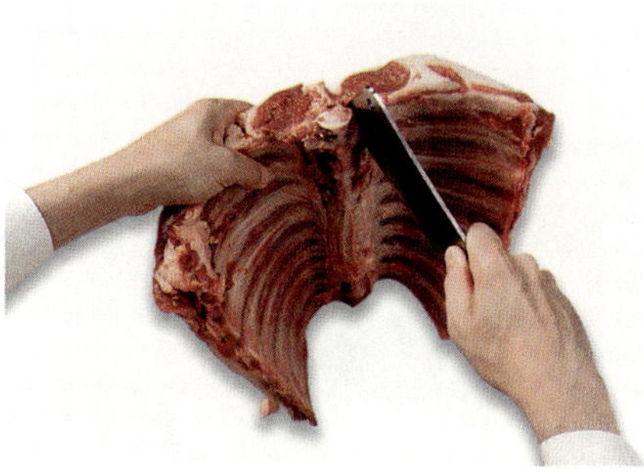

(c) If a meat saw is not available, use a cleaver. Stand the roast on end and cut through the rib bones where they join the chine bone. This separates one rack.

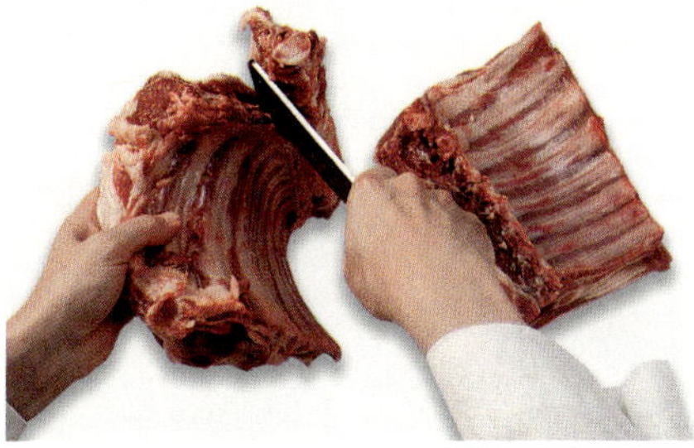

(d) Repeat the procedure on the other side of the chine.

(e) The two halves are separated from the chine.

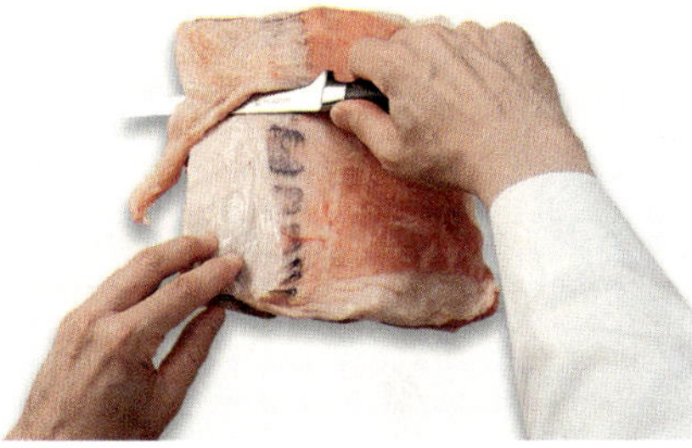

(f) Trim excess fat from the top of the meat, leaving a thin protective covering. During this step, you should also remove the shoulder blade cartilage, which is embedded in the layers of fat.

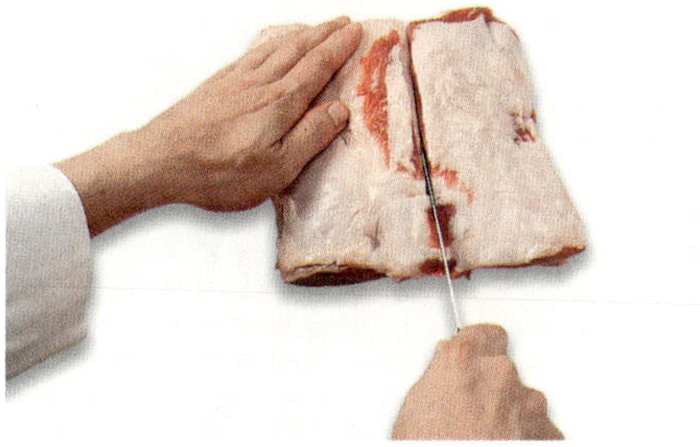

(g) To trim the fat and meat from the ends of the bones (called *frenching* the bones), first cut through the fat in a straight line down to the bone, keeping the cut about 1 in. (2.5 cm) from the tip of the eye muscle.

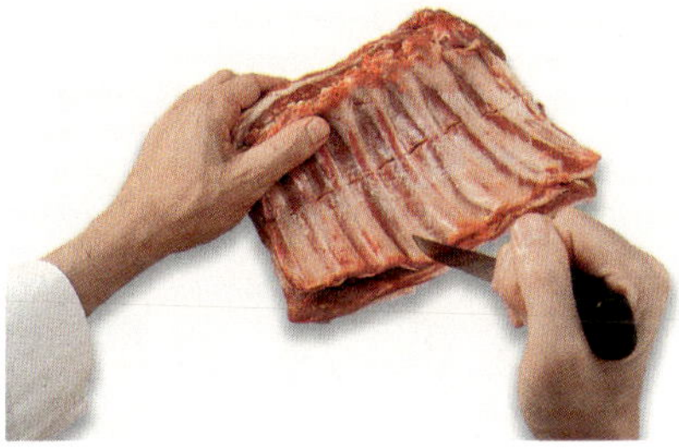

(h) Score the membrane covering the rib bones. Pull and cut the layer of fat from the bones.

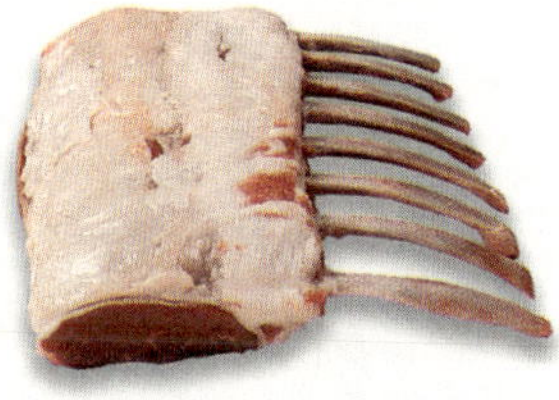

(i) The roast is trimmed and ready to cook.

Figure 5.13 Butterflying and stuffing a pork loin.

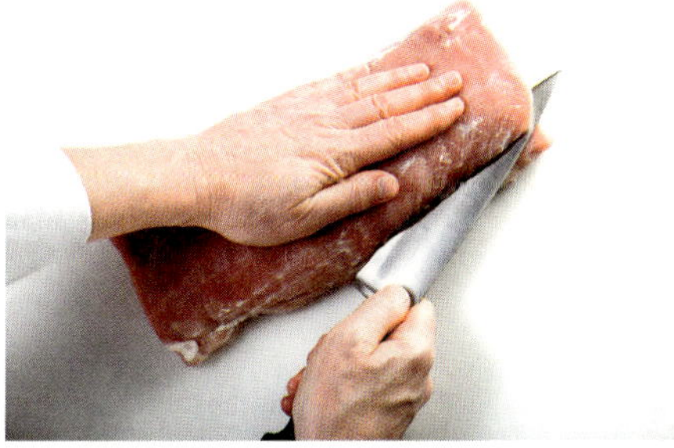

(a) To butterfly, hold the knife blade parallel to the table and cut through the center of the loin as shown. Do not cut all the way through, but leave the meat attached at one edge.

(b) Open the cut meat and spread the filling on the bottom half.

(c) Fold the top half over the filling to reform the loin.

Figure 5.14 Tying a roast.

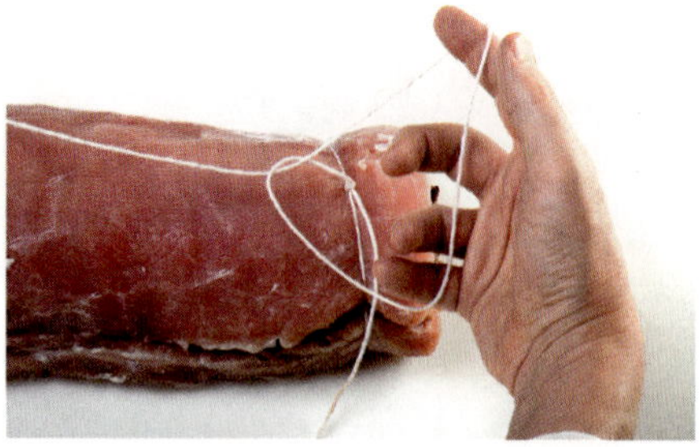

(a) Tie a length of butcher's twine tightly around one end of the roast. After tying the knot securely, twist the length of twine into a loop as shown.

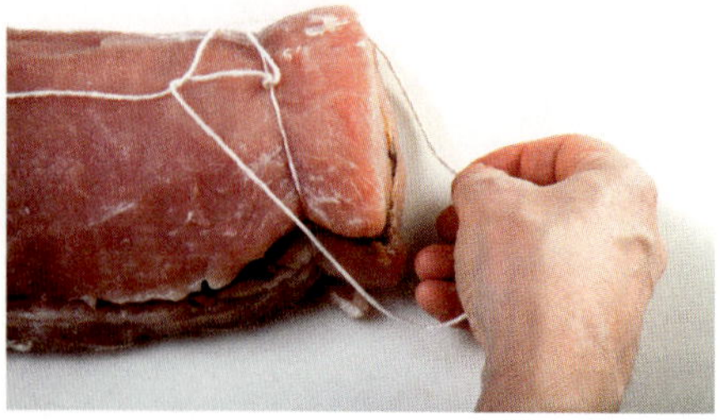

(b) Pass the loop over the end of the roast.

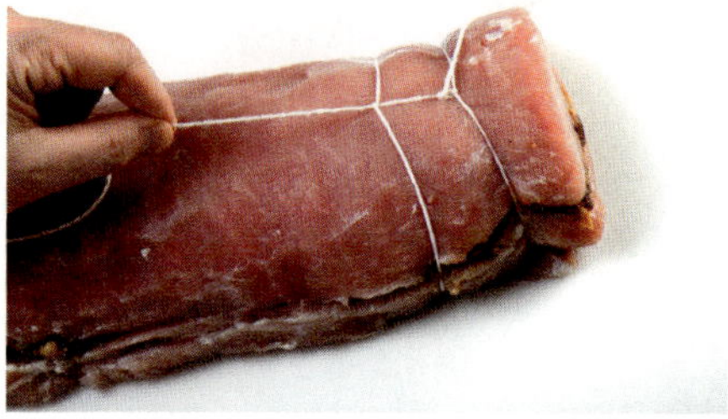

(c) Position the loop an inch or two (2.5-5 cm) from the first loop and pull the loose end to tighten.

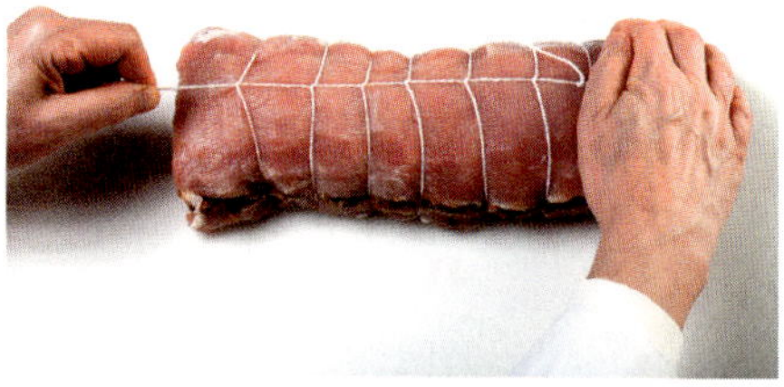

(d) Continue making loops and tightening them until the whole length of meat is tied.

(e) Turn the meat upside down. Pass the loose end of the twine under the last loop and wind it once around as shown.

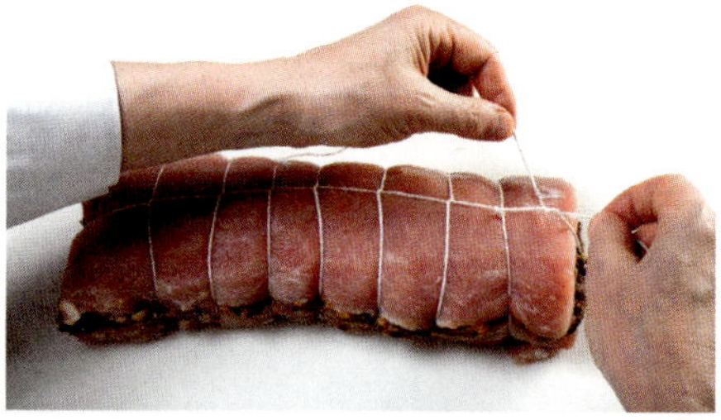

(f) Repeat step e with each of the loops. When you reach the end of the roast, tie it off securely to the short length of twine from the knot made in the first step.

Figure 5.15 Trimming, cutting, and pounding veal for scaloppine.

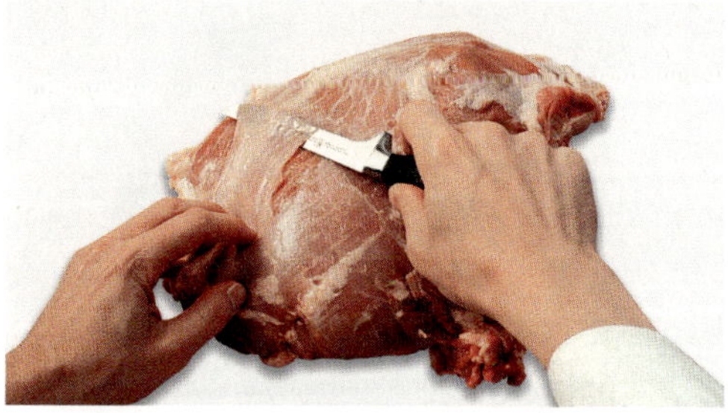

(a) Remove all tendons and connective tissue (silverskin) from the veal. Slip the point of a thin boning knife under the skin. Angle the edge of the blade upward against the skin and cut it away carefully without cutting through the meat.

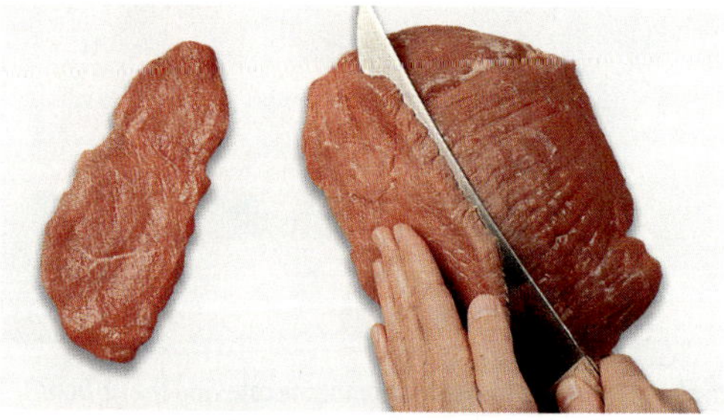

(b) Holding the blade of the knife at an angle if necessary to get a broader slice, cut *across* the grain of the meat as shown to make thin slices.

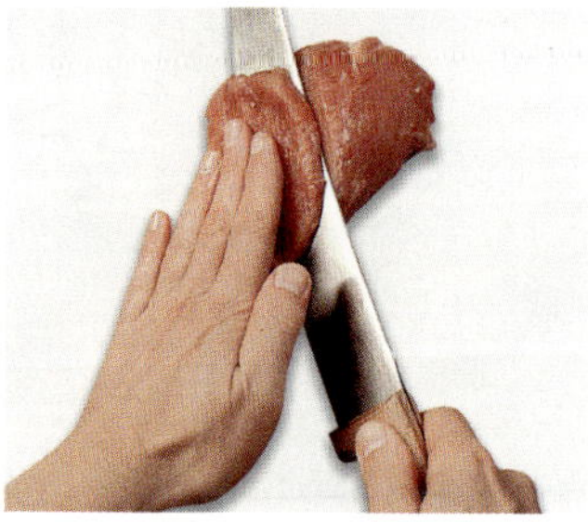

(c) Broader slices can be cut from narrower pieces of meat by butterflying. Cut the slice almost through the meat but . . .

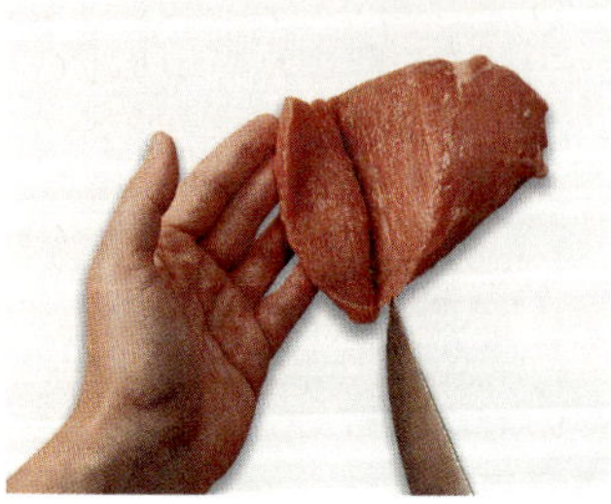

(d) . . . leave it attached.

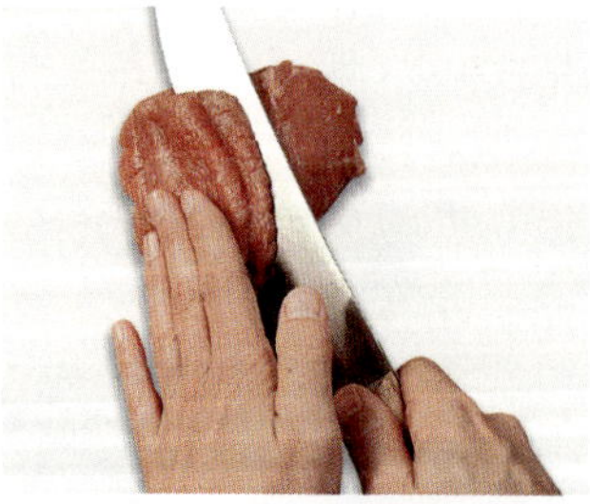

(e) Then cut a second slice the same way, but cut all the way through.

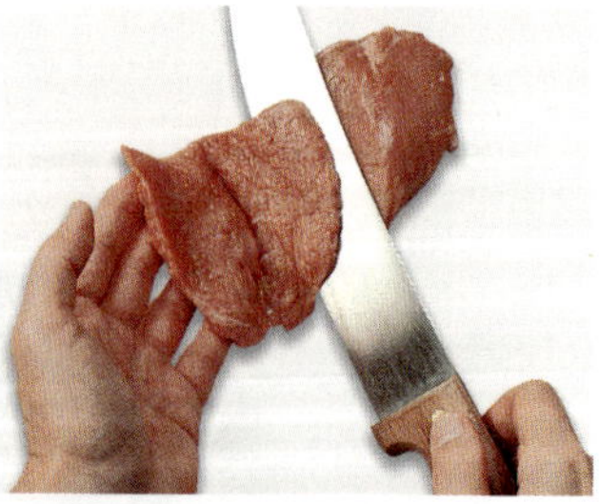

(f) A butterflied scaloppine is twice as large as a single slice. Unfortunately, it has a seam in the center that often detracts from the appearance of the finished dish, unless the veal is breaded or covered with a topping.

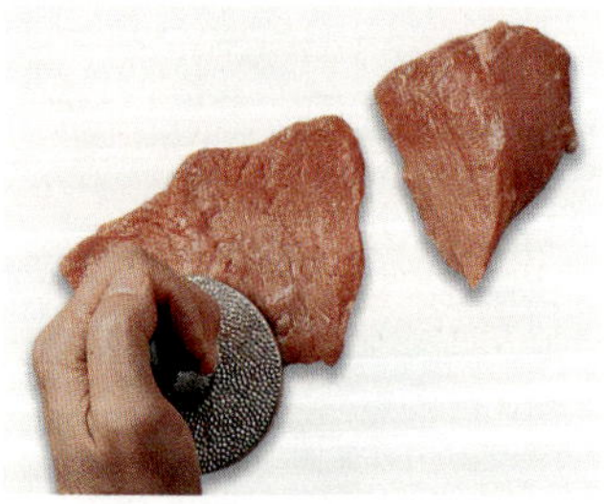

(g) If desired, pound the cutlet to an even thickness with a cutlet mallet. This helps disguise the seam in a butterflied cutlet.

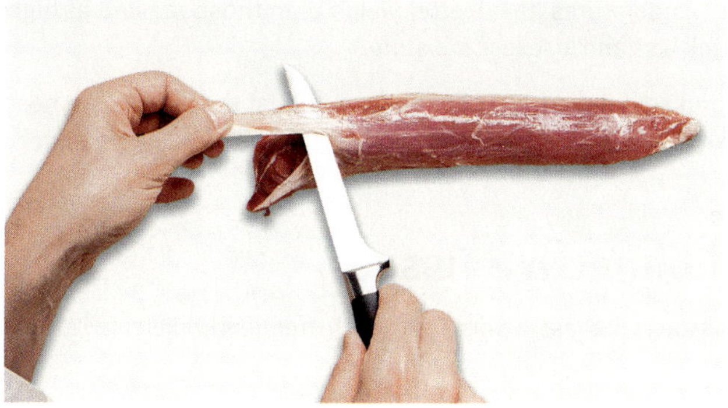

Figure 5.16 Trimming a pork tenderloin.

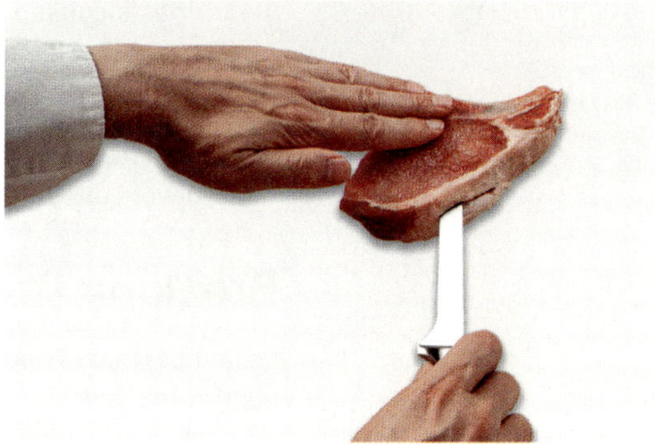

Figure 5.17 For stuffed pork chops, cut a pocket in the chops as shown.

Figure 5.18 Larding meat using a larding needle.

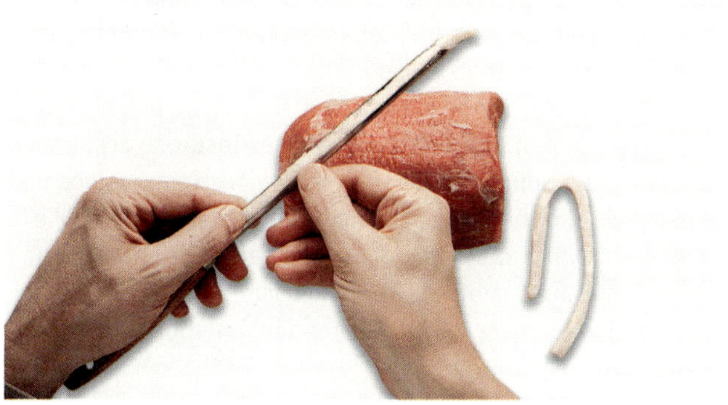

(a) Cut a strip of fatback to fit inside the needle.

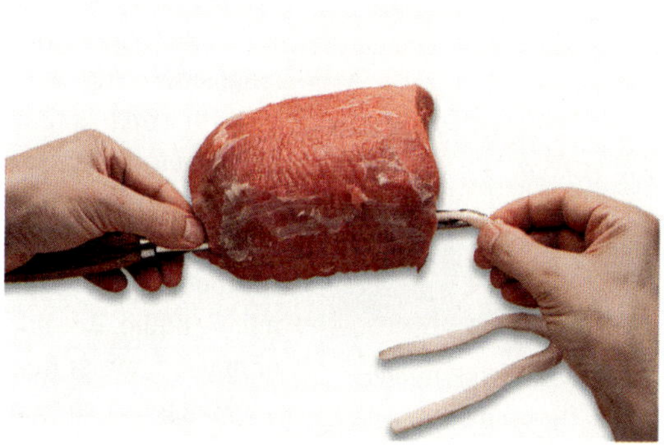

(b) Insert the needle through the meat. Pull out the needle, holding the strip of fat so it stays inside the meat.

Cooking and Handling Meats

Tenderness and Appropriate Cooking Methods

The heat of cooking affects tenderness in two ways:

1. It tenderizes connective tissue if moisture is present and cooking is slow.
2. It toughens protein. Even meats low in connective tissue can be tough and dry if cooked at excessively high heats for too long.

The Principles of Low-Heat Cooking

1. High heat toughens and shrinks protein and results in excessive moisture loss. Therefore, low-heat cooking should be the general practice for most meat cooking methods.
2. Broiling seems to be a contradiction to this rule. The reason carefully broiled meat stays tender is that it is done quickly. It takes time for the heat to be conducted to the interior of the meat, so the inside never gets very hot. Meat broiled to the point of being well done, however, is likely to be dry.

3. Roasts cooked at low temperatures have better yields than those roasted at high heat—that is, they shrink less and lose less moisture.

4. Because both liquid and steam are better conductors of heat than air, moist heat penetrates meat quickly. Therefore, to avoid overcooking, meat should be simmered, never boiled.

Breaking Down Connective Tissue

Remember that connective tissue is highest in muscles that are frequently exercised and in mature animals.

Look again at the primary cooking methods (column 4) in the table of meat cuts (p. 131). You should detect a pattern of tender cuts, cooked primarily by dry heat; slightly less tender cuts, cooked sometimes by dry and sometimes by moist heat; and least tender cuts, cooked almost always by moist heat.

The concept of moist-heat cooking needs further explanation as it applies to breaking down connective tissue in meat. The usual explanation of the effect of moist heat on connective tissue is that heat breaks down collagen in the presence of moisture. But meat is about 75 percent water, so *moisture is always present.* Collagen breaks down because of long, slow cooking, no matter what cooking method is used.

The catch is that, for small cuts of meat, dry-heat cooking methods are usually short, quick methods. Cooking must be short, in part because too long an exposure to dry heat results in excessive moisture loss from the product. The terms *moist-heat cooking method* and *dry-heat cooking method* refer to the way in which heat is transferred from the heat source to the food, whether by dry means, like hot air or radiation, or moist means, like steam or simmering liquid. Because the product is surrounded by moisture when it is simmered, steamed, or braised, moist-heat cooking methods promote moisture retention, not moisture loss, so cooking time can be as long as desired.

A tough steak on the grill or in the oven doesn't have enough time to become tender before it is dried out. On the other hand, large cuts of less tender meat can be roasted successfully because they are too large to dry out during a long roasting time. A 40-pound (18-kg) roast steamship round of beef can be tender because it takes hours to cook even to the rare stage. A grilled steak cut from the same round, however, is likely to be tough.

To summarize: Long, slow cooking tenderizes collagen. Moist-heat methods are most suitable for long, slow cooking. Dry-heat methods usually are short, quick cooking methods, suitable only for tender cuts, except when larger items are roasted for a relatively long time. The following list summarizes the cooking characteristics of the major cuts.

1. **Rib and loin cuts.**

   Always the most tender cuts, used mostly for roasts, steaks, and chops.

   Beef and lamb. Because these meats are often eaten rare or medium done, the rib and loin are used almost exclusively for roasting, broiling, and grilling.

   Veal and pork. Pork is generally eaten well done, and veal is most often eaten well done, although many people prefer it slightly pink in the center. Therefore, these meats are occasionally braised, not to develop tenderness but to help preserve juices. Veal chops, which are very low in fat, may be broiled if great care is taken not to overcook them and dry them out. A safer approach is to use a method with fat, such as sautéing or pan-frying, or to use moist heat.

2. **Leg or round.**

   Beef. The cuts of the round are less tender and are used mostly for braising.

   Top grades, such as U.S. Prime, U.S. Choice, Canada Prime, and Canada AAA, can also be roasted. The roasts are so large that, roasted at low temperatures for a long time, the beef's own moisture helps dissolve collagen. Inside round (top round) is favored for roasts because of its size and relative tenderness.

   Beef round is very lean. It is best roasted rare. Lack of fat makes well-done round taste dry.

MILK-FED, GRAIN-FED, OR GRASS-FED

The properties of meats are determined, in part, by the diet of the animals. Most of the beef on the market in North America is grain-fed, even though grass, not grain, is the natural diet of cattle. Feeding cattle grain enables producers to raise and fatten them for market more quickly than letting them browse on grass does. Grain-fed beef is tender and has more marbling than grass-fed beef, and it is preferred by most North American consumers. Grass-fed or pastured beef is usually perceived as less tender and less juicy, although it is lower in saturated fat and may have more health benefits. Its flavor is often described as "beefier" than that of grain-fed beef. Grass-fed beef is common in some other countries, such as the beef-eating and beef-producing nation of Argentina. In North America, producers of pastured beef are campaigning for more consumer recognition.

(continues next page)

Veal, lamb, and pork. These meats are from young animals and therefore tender enough to roast.

Legs make excellent roasts because large muscles with few seams and uniform grain allow easy slicing and attractive portions.

Figure 5.19 shows the muscle structure of the round in cross section. A center-cut steak from a whole round of beef, lamb, veal, or pork has this same basic structure.

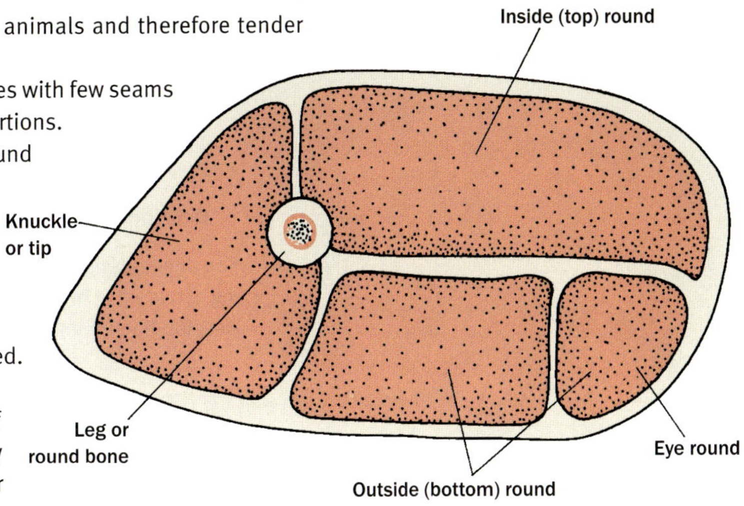

Figure 5.19 Location of the muscles in a whole center-cut round steak of beef, veal, lamb, or pork.

3. **Chuck or shoulder.**

Beef. Beef chuck is a tougher cut that is usually braised. Although chuck is not the ideal choice for braising if uniform slices are desired, it makes braised dishes of excellent eating quality. Its connective tissue is easily broken down by moist cooking, yielding moist, tender meat with abundant gelatin content.

Veal, lamb, and pork. These are most often braised but are young enough to be roasted or cut into chops for broiling. Shoulder roasts are not the most desirable because they consist of many small muscles running in several directions. Therefore, they do not produce attractive, solid slices.

4. **Shanks, breast, brisket, and flank.**

These are the least tender cuts, even on young animals, and are almost always cooked by moist heat.

Shanks are desirable for braising and simmering because their high collagen content is converted into gelatin that gives body to braising liquids and good eating quality to the meat.

Beef flank steaks can be broiled (as London broil) if they are cooked rare and cut across the grain into thin slices. This cuts the connective tissue into chewable pieces (see mechanical tenderization, p. 124).

5. **Ground meat, cubed steaks, and stew meat.**

These can come from any primal cut. They are usually made from trimmings, although whole chucks are sometimes ground into chopped meat. Ground meat and cubed steaks can be cooked by dry or moist heat because they are mechanically tenderized. Stew meat is, of course, cooked by moist heat.

The effect of diet can be seen in other meat animals. Traditionally, the highest-quality veal is considered to be so-called milk-fed veal, more properly called *formula-fed.* The meat is light pink in color and mild and delicate in flavor. Calves fed solid food or allowed into a pasture have darker, more reddish meat with a somewhat beefier flavor. Ethical objections exist about the raising of formula-fed veal because the animals are penned and not allowed much movement. As for the flavor of milk-fed versus pastured veal, this is a matter of personal preference.

The youngest lamb is called *spring lamb.* It is slaughtered before it begins a diet of solid food, and its meat is light in color and delicate in flavor. Older lamb is darker in color and has a more pronounced flavor. After the age of one year, this meat is no longer called lamb but *mutton,* and it has a still darker color and stronger flavor. Little mutton is sold in North America. (In some markets the name *mutton* may also be used for goat meat, although this is not traditional English usage.)

Other Factors Influencing Choice of Cooking Methods

1. **Fat content.**

Meats high in fat, such as Prime beef or lamb, are generally cooked without added fat, such as by roasting or broiling.

Meats low in fat, such as veal, are often cooked with added fat to prevent dryness. Sautéing, pan-frying, or braising is generally preferable to broiling for veal chops that are cooked well done.

Fat can be added to lean meats in two ways:

- *Barding.* Tying slices of fat, such as pork fatback, over meats with no natural fat cover to protect them while roasting.
- *Larding.* Inserting strips of fat with a larding needle into meats low in marbling.

These two techniques were developed in Europe when meats were much leaner and not as tender. They are not often used with today's tender, grain-fed meats. These techniques are useful, however, when cooking lean game, such as venison.

2. **Developing tenderness is not the only goal of cooking.**

   Other goals are

   - Developing flavor.
   - Preventing excessive shrinkage and nutrient loss.
   - Developing appearance.

   You must often compromise to get a balanced result. For example, preliminary browning of a roast at high heat increases shrinkage but may be desirable for some roasts to develop flavor and appearance.

Searing and "Sealing"

SEARING

Searing meats at high heat creates desirable flavor and color by browning the surfaces. It was long believed that searing the surface of meat "seals the pores," keeping in juices.

This does not actually happen. Meat does not have pores but rather an open network of fibers. Think of the surface of a steak as resembling the cut end of a thick rope. There are no pores to seal. It is true that heavy browning creates a kind of crust on the surface of the meat, but this crust is no more waterproof than an unbrowned surface.

You can easily demonstrate this. Place a steak or chop on a hot griddle or grill and sear it well. Turn it over and continue cooking. As it cooks, you will see meat juices driven up through the seared top surface. You will continue to hear a sizzling sound, which is the sound of moisture escaping from the meat and quickly vaporizing. Remove the finished steak from the grill and let it set on a plate for a few minutes, and you will see a small pool of juices collect. Everyone who has cooked a steak has seen this demonstration that searing doesn't seal.

Roasts cooked from the start at a low temperature retain more juices than roasts that are seared at high heat first.

Steaks, chops, and cutlets cooked quickly at high heat retain more moisture at first because the intense heat instantly evaporates the juices from the surface of the meat and forces internal juices further into the meat. This permits browning, because moisture creates steam and inhibits browning. However, overcooked steaks are dry whether or not they were seared.

BLANCHING AND "SEALING"

Dropping meat into boiling water doesn't seal the pores either. What actually happens is this: Many proteins dissolve in cold water. When heated, these proteins coagulate and become froth or scum on the surface of the water. When meat is placed into boiling water, some of the protein coagulates inside that meat, and not as much is carried out of the meat with the lost moisture. Prolonged cooking shrinks meat as much if started in boiling water as if started in cold water.

Cooking Frozen Meats

Some sources recommend cooking some meats from the frozen state, without thawing, in order to eliminate drip loss that occurs during defrosting. However, it is usually better to thaw before cooking because of the following reasons:

1. Frozen meats lose no moisture from defrosting but lose more during cooking. The total loss is about the same as for thawed meats. Besides, the perception of juiciness depends as much or more on fat content than on moisture content.
2. Cooking frozen meats complicates the cooking process and requires adjustments in procedure. It is possible for roasts to be cooked on the outside but still frozen in the center. Frozen steaks, too, are more difficult to cook evenly than thawed steaks. Thawed meats, on the other hand, are handled like fresh meats.
3. Cooking frozen meats requires extra energy, and energy is expensive. A hard-frozen roast may take 3 times as long to cook as a thawed roast.

Doneness

Definitions

The meaning of the term ***doneness*** depends on whether the cooking method uses dry heat or moist heat.

1. **Dry heat.**
   Meat is "done" when the proteins have reached the desired degree of coagulation, as indicated by internal temperature.

2. **Moist heat.**
   Meat is "done" when connective tissues have broken down enough for the meat to be palatable. With a few exceptions, meat cooked by moist heat is always well done.

Dry-Heat Cooking

The object of dry-heat cooking is to achieve the desired degree of doneness (protein coagulation) while preserving natural tenderness and juiciness.

DEGREE OF DONENESS

As meat cooks, its pigments change color. These color changes indicate degrees of doneness.

Red meat (beef and lamb) changes from red to pink to gray or gray-brown.

- Rare: browned surface; thin layer of cooked (gray) meat; red interior
- Medium: thicker layer of gray; pink interior
- Well done: gray throughout

(Of course, there are stages in between.)

White meat (veal and pork) changes from pink or gray-pink to white or off-white. It is generally cooked well done, although many cuts of veal may be considered done when still slightly pink in the center.

Trichinosis is a disease caused by a parasite that lives in the muscle tissue of hogs and some wild animals. In countries in which this disease is a problem, pork must be cooked long enough to eliminate this danger. This parasite is killed at 137°F (58°C), but, to be safe, pork should be cooked to at least 150° to 155°F (66° to 68°C). At this stage, pork is only medium to medium-well done. Some people are happy to eat pork that is still pink in the center, but most people prefer it to be cooked slightly more than this. On the other hand, it is not necessary to cook pork to 185°F (85°C), as older guidelines said. At this temperature, pork is overcooked and dry. For diners who avoid any trace of pink in pork, perhaps the best doneness range is 160° to 170°F (71° to 77°C).

TESTING DONENESS

Determining doneness is one of the most difficult and critical aspects of meat cooking. Anyone can put a steak on the grill or a roast in the oven. But it takes experience and skill to take it off the fire at the right time.

Color change cannot be used to test doneness because it would be necessary to cut the meat. Piercing the meat and examining the color of the juices is not a reliable method.

INTERNAL TEMPERATURE

Testing the interior of meat with a meat thermometer is the most accurate method of testing doneness. Thermometers are of two types: *standard*, which are inserted before roasting and left in the roast; and *instant-read*, which are inserted at any time, read as soon as the needle stops moving, and pulled out. Whatever thermometer you use, make sure it is *clean and sanitary* before inserting it in the meat.

The tip of the thermometer should be inserted into the center of the thickest part of the flesh, not touching fat or bone. Table 5.3 gives internal temperatures of meats at various degrees of doneness.

In general, regional traditions of eating well-done or overcooked meats are decreasing, and more people are eating meat cooked rare. For decades, meats cooked to an internal temperature of 140°F (60°C) were called *rare*, but by today's standards, this is more like medium. Current preferences are reflected in the temperatures given in Table 5.3.

It should be stated that the USDA and other agencies caution that meats may contain harmful bacteria and parasites. Although studies are still being done, these agencies suggest meats be cooked to at least 145°F (63°C) in order to be completely safe. The USDA requires that beef precooked for foodservice sale (such as precooked roast beef for sandwiches) be heated to an internal temperature of at least 145°F (63°C) when it is processed.

Table 5.3 Interior Temperatures of Cooked Meats

Meat	Rare	Medium	Well Done
Beef	130°F (54°C)	140°–145°F (60°–63°C)	160°F (71°C)
Lamb	130°F (54°C)	145°F (63°C)	160°F (71°C)
Veal	—	145°–150°F (63°–66°C)	160°F (71°C)
Pork	—	145°–150°F (63°–66°C)	160°–170°F (71°–77°C)

CARRYOVER COOKING

Internal temperature continues to rise even after the meat is removed from the oven. This is because the outside of roasting meat is hotter than the inside. This heat continues to be conducted into the meat until the heat is equalized throughout the roast.

Carryover cooking can raise internal temperatures from 5°F (3°C) for small cuts to as much as 25°F (14°C) for very large roasts, such as a steamship round. The usual range is 10° to 15°F (6° to 8°C) for average roasts. Exact temperature change depends on the size of the cut and on the oven temperature.

Remove roasts from the oven when internal temperature is 10° to 15°F (6° to 8°C) below the desired reading. Let the roast stand 15 to 30 minutes before slicing. For example, a beef rib roast cooked rare should be removed from the oven when the thermometer reads 115° to 120°F (46° to 49°C). Carryover cooking will bring the temperature to 130°F (54°C) after the roast has stood for 30 minutes.

TOUCH

The small size of steaks and chops makes using a thermometer impractical. The cook must depend on his or her sense of touch.

Meat gets firmer as it cooks. Pressing it lightly with the finger indicates its doneness. Press the center of the lean part, not the fat.

Rare. Feels soft, gives to pressure, though not as soft and jellylike as raw meat.

Medium. Feels moderately firm and resilient, springs back readily when pressed.

Well done. Feels firm, does not give to pressure.

TIME-WEIGHT RATIO

Many charts give roasting times per pound of meat. However, these can be approximate only and should be used in estimating and planning cooking times, not in determining doneness.

Many factors other than weight and oven temperature determine cooking time:

1. Temperature of the meat before roasting.
2. Amount of fat cover (fat acts as an insulator).
3. Bones (bones conduct heat faster than flesh, so boneless roasts cook more slowly than bone-in roasts of the same weight).

4. Size, type, and contents of the oven.

5. Number of times the oven door is opened.

6. Shape of the cut (a flat or a long, thin cut cooks more quickly per pound than a round, compact cut).

You can see why roasting requires experience and judgment. To be really accurate and useful, a complete roasting chart that took all variables into consideration, including all meat cuts, sizes, oven temperatures, and so on, would be the size of a small book.

Point 6 above is a key point. It is the *thickness* of a cut, not its *weight*, that determines cooking time—the time needed for the heat to penetrate to the center. Half a pork loin roasts in about the same time as a whole pork loin, even though it weighs half as much. The thickness is the same.

Perhaps the most useful roasting time charts are those you make yourself. When you regularly roast the same cuts in the same way with the same equipment and find they always take the same length of time, you may use those times as indicators of doneness. Many foodservice operators have developed charts based on their own practices, and the correct times are indicated on their individual recipe cards.

Moist-Heat Cooking

Meat cooked by moist heat is cooked well done and actually beyond well done. Doneness is indicated by tenderness, not by temperature.

Piercing with a meat fork is the usual test for doneness. When the prongs of the fork go in and slide out easily, the meat is done.

Low temperatures—no higher than simmering—are essential to avoid toughening protein in moist-cooked meats. Oven temperatures of 250° to 300°F (120° to 150°C) are usually sufficient to maintain a simmer.

Juiciness

Three main factors determine the juiciness—or, more accurately, the perception of juiciness—in cooked meat. Despite the myths about basting with stock and about searing meat to "seal in the juices," the following are the only factors that have any significant effect on juiciness.

1. **Internal fat.**
   Fat makes meat taste juicy. This is why well-marbled meats taste juicier than lean meats. We understand the health effects of too much fat in the diet, but there is no getting around the fact that high fat content makes meat taste juicier. When lean meats are cooked, other measures (such as using sauces and, especially, avoiding overcooking) are used to increase palatability.

2. **Gelatin.**
   This factor is most important in braised meats. Gelatin, converted from connective tissue, helps bind water molecules and hold them in the meat. Also, the texture of the gelatin improves the texture of the meat in the mouth. This is why braised beef shank tastes so much juicier than braised outside round.

3. **Protein coagulation.**
   As you know, as protein coagulates or is cooked, it breaks down and begins to lose water. The more it is cooked, the more it contracts and forces out moisture. No matter how much you try to sear to "seal in the juices," this moisture will be lost. The only way to minimize the loss is to avoid overcooking.

KEY POINTS TO REVIEW

- What are the primal cuts of beef? of lamb? of veal? of pork? What are the main fabricated cuts from each of these primal cuts?
- How do you determine the most appropriate cooking methods for the various fabricated cuts of meat?
- How can you tell when meat is done?

Cooking Variety Meats

Variety meats, also known as *offal*, include the organs, glands, and other meats that don't form a part of the dressed carcass of the animal.

For cooking purposes, we can divide the most popular variety meats into two groups:

Glandular Meats	**Muscle Meats**
Liver	Heart
Kidneys	Tongue
Sweetbreads	Tripe
Brains	Oxtails

Glandular meats do not consist of muscle tissue like regular meats but instead are internal organs or glands. This fact is important for two reasons.

First, because they do not consist of bundles of muscle fibers, the texture of glandular meats is unlike that of regular meats. Because they are not muscle tissue, they are naturally tender and do not need long, slow cooking like muscular variety meats do. If organ meats are dry and tough, it is usually because they have been overcooked.

Second, glandular meats are much more perishable than muscle meats. While some muscle meats, especially beef, benefit from aging, organ meats must be very fresh to be of the best quality. Liver, sweetbreads, and brains must be used within a day or two after purchase. If brains or sweetbreads must be kept longer, they should be blanched as described below so they will keep another day or two.

Heart, tongue, oxtails, and tripe are made of muscle tissue, just like other meats from the carcass. They are all tough, however, and must be cooked for a long time by simmering or braising in order to be made tender.

Liver

Calf's liver is the most prized because it is tender and delicate in flavor. It is easily recognized by its pale, pinkish color. Most calf's liver is served pan-fried, sautéed, or broiled.

Beef liver is darker in color (see accompanying photo), stronger in flavor, and tougher than calf's liver. It is also pan-fried or broiled, and it is frequently braised.

Pork liver is also available, but it is used mostly in pâtés and sausages.

Top: calf's-liver slice. Bottom: beef-liver slice.

PREPARATION

- Remove outer skin.
- Slice on the bias about 1/4 inch (0.5 cm) thick. Slicing is easier if the liver is partially frozen.
- Remove tough membranes.

COOKING

Cook to order. Do not cook ahead.

- To broil: Brush with (or dip in) oil or melted butter. Broil according to basic procedure for meats.
- To pan-fry, griddle, or sauté: Dredge in seasoned flour. Cook in desired fat over moderately high heat.
- *Do not overcook*, unless customer requests well done. To be moist, liver must be slightly pink inside. Liver cooked well done is very dry.
- Serve with bacon, French-fried or smothered onions, or seasoned butter.

Kidneys

Veal and lamb kidneys are the most popular, especially in the more upscale restaurants. They are usually prepared by sautéing and broiling. Beef kidneys are tougher and more strongly flavored. They are often cooked by braising and served in specialty items, like steak and kidney pie. Pork livers are not often used.

Veal kidneys weigh 8 to 12 oz (225 to 350 g) each. Lamb kidneys are very small, 1½ to 3 oz (40 to 85 g) each. If you purchase whole lamb or veal carcasses, you will find a pair of kidneys inside the cavity, attached to the small of the back in the region of the tenderloin and surrounded by a heavy layer of fat or suet.

PREPARATION

If the kidney is encased in fat, pull the fat away with your hands and use a knife to cut it away from the core area where the ducts emerge from inside the kidney.

Lamb kidneys are usually broiled and served two or three per portion, or as part of a mixed grill. Butterfly them by splitting them almost in half, starting at the curved or convex side. Spread them open and skewer them to hold them open during cooking.

Veal kidneys can be broiled like lamb kidneys, but they are most often cut up, sautéed, and served in a sauce. To prepare them for sautéing, first split them in half. Remove the white ducts from the center. Then cut into large dice or thick slices.

Left: lamb kidney. Right: veal kidney.

COOKING

There are two main pitfalls to cooking kidneys. First, they become tough and rubbery if overcooked. Properly cooked, they are pink in the middle and still tender and juicy. Cooking time is very short.

Second, they have a high moisture content, which can interfere with proper sautéing. Make sure the pan is very hot before adding the kidneys, and do not overcrowd the pan. Failure to do this results in kidneys that are boiled in their juices rather than sautéed.

To avoid overcooking when sautéing over high heat, do not try to brown the kidneys too heavily. Brown them only lightly and remove them from the pan when they are still somewhat rare. Set them aside while you deglaze the pan and prepare the sauce. During this time, some juices will be released from the kidneys. Drain this juice and add it to the sauce if desired, or discard it if you feel the flavor is too strong. Finally, add the kidneys to the sauce and warm them gently. Do not let them simmer long. Serve at once.

Sweetbreads

Sweetbreads are the thymus glands of calves and young beef animals. (The gland gradually disappears as the animal matures.) They are considered a delicacy and are often expensive. Sweetbreads are mild in flavor and delicate in texture. They are usually braised or breaded and sautéed in butter.

Before cooking, sweetbreads should be prepared according to the following procedure (see Figure 5.20):

1. Soak in several changes of cold water for several hours or overnight. This removes blood, which would darken the meat when cooked.
2. Blanch in simmering salted water for 10 minutes. Some chefs like to add a little lemon juice or vinegar to the water to preserve whiteness and make the meat firmer.
3. Refresh under cold water and peel off membranes and connective tissue.
4. Press between two trays, with a light weight on top, and refrigerate for several hours. If desired, wrap in cheesecloth before pressing, as shown in Figure 5.20.
5. Prepare for cooking:
   - For braising, leave whole or cut into large dice.
   - For breading and sautéing, split in half horizontally. Pass through Standard Breading Procedure or dredge in flour.

Brains

Brains are not a popular item, but they are delicate in both flavor and texture. Calf's brains are the most frequently used.

Figure 5.20 Preparing sweetbreads.

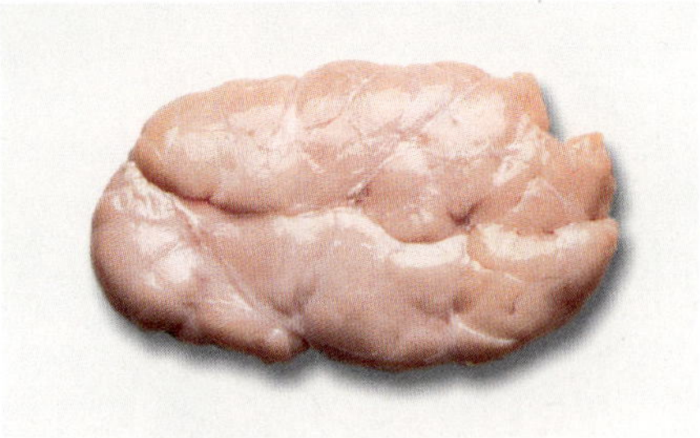

(a) Raw sweetbreads.

(b) After the sweetbread has been blanched, peel off the membrane.

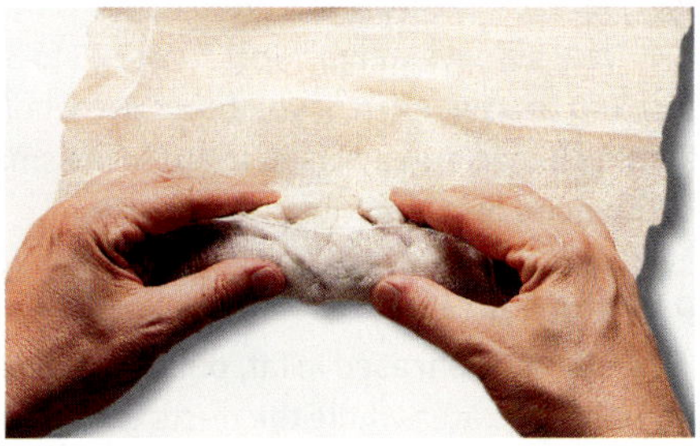

(c) Wrap the sweetbreads in clean cheesecloth.

(d) Tie the ends securely.

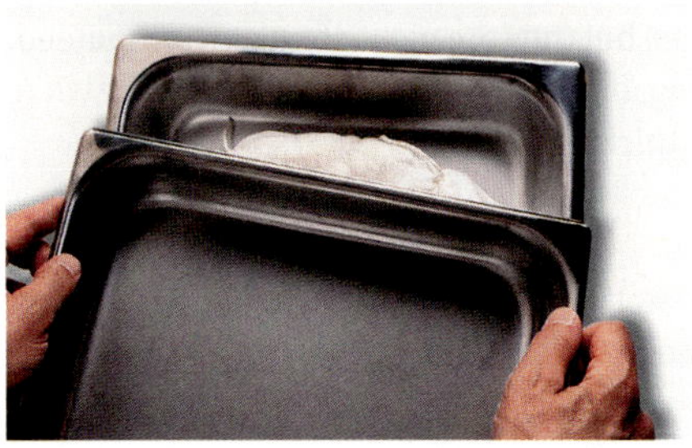

(e) Place in a hotel pan or other flat pan and top with another pan.

(f) Place weights in the top pan and refrigerate for several hours.

Brains are very perishable and should be cooked as soon as possible. They are also fragile and must be handled carefully.

Brains must be pre-prepared according to the following procedure. They may then be served hot with black butter or cooled and then dipped in batter, deep-fried, and served with tomato sauce.

1. Soak in fresh water, as for sweetbreads.
2. Peel off outer membrane (this may be done before or after poaching).
3. Poach 20 minutes in court bouillon made of 1 oz (25 mL) lemon juice or vinegar per pint (500 mL) of salted water, plus a bouquet garni.
4. Drain and serve immediately, or cool in fresh, cold water.

Heart

Heart, usually from veal or beef, is very tough and lean. It can be braised or simmered, or it may be ground and added to chopped meat for casserole dishes and meatloaf.

Before cooking, trim coarse fibers and veins inside and at top.

Tongue

Cooked beef tongue is popular as a cold, sliced meat for sandwiches. It may be fresh, cured, or smoked. Veal and lamb tongues are also available.

Tongue is almost always cooked by simmering. After simmering, remove the skin and trim the gristle at the base of the tongue before slicing.

Oxtails

Oxtails contain flavorful meat and a rich gelatin content, making them highly desirable for soups and stews.

To disjoint oxtails, cut into sections at the joints with a French knife or butcher knife. Do not use a cleaver, or you may splinter the bones.

Tripe

Tripe is the muscular stomach lining of meat animals. Although lamb and pork tripe are sometimes available, beef tripe is by far the most widely used. Because cattle have four stomachs, there are four kinds of beef tripe. Honeycomb tripe, from the second stomach, is the kind most widely available. Other kinds, however, can be substituted in recipes that call for honeycomb tripe. In France, another type of beef tripe, known as *gras-double*, is popular; it is smooth rather than honeycombed.

Most tripe that comes from the market has been partially cooked, but it still requires several hours of simmering to be made tender. Undercooked tripe is chewy and somewhat rubbery, but tripe that has simmered long enough is tender, with a pleasant gelatinous texture.

To prepare, first remove any lumps of fat by pulling or cutting them off. Next, blanch the tripe, if desired. Although it is already partially cooked when purchased, blanching freshens it. Place it in a pot with cold, salted water. Bring to a boil, simmer 5 to 10 minutes, drain, and rinse under cold water.

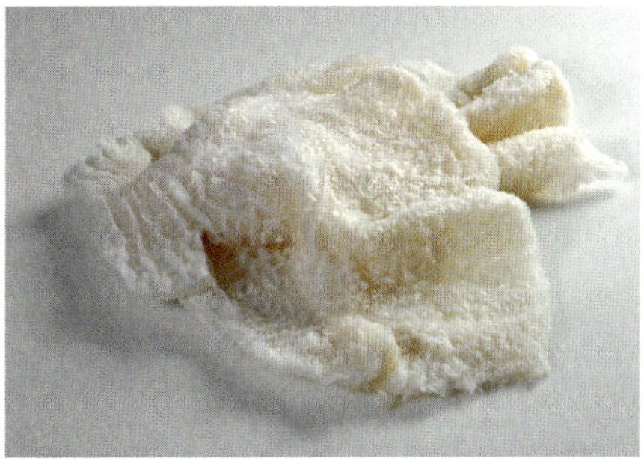

Tripe

Other Variety Meats

INTESTINES

The most common use for intestines is to make sausage casings.

Chitterlings are pork intestines that are treated like tripe. They are blanched or simmered, and then braised or fried. Chitterlings are generally available in 10-pound (4.5-kg) pails. Because they shrink a great deal when simmered, this quantity yields only 3 pounds (1.3 kg) or less of finished product.

CAUL

Pig's *caul* is a fatty membrane covering the animal's stomach. It looks somewhat like a delicate piece of lace. Its main uses are to line terrines and to wrap forcemeats and other foods so they hold their shape during cooking and do not dry out. Sausage patties wrapped in caul are called *crépinettes*. The advantage of using caul instead of fatback to line terrines is that the caul is so thin it melts away almost completely during cooking.

FEET

Feet are exceptionally rich in gelatin. For this reason, they are added to soups, stews, and stocks to add richness and body. Indeed, some stews made with feet, such as Tripes à la Mode de Caen, may be so rich in gelatin that not only do they solidify when cold but they can even be unmolded and sliced like cold cuts.

Pig's feet are readily available in most markets. Calf's feet and ox's feet are also available, but often only on the wholesale market. The feet from older animals have less gelatin. If a recipe calls for a calf's foot but none is available, in most cases you can substitute two pig's feet.

KEY POINTS TO REVIEW

- What is the difference between glandular variety meats and muscular variety meats? List the most important types of each.
- Muscular variety meats are nearly always cooked by what cooking methods? Why?
- What are the most appropriate cooking methods for liver?
- How are sweetbreads prepared for cooking?

Game and Specialty Meats

The term *game* is used to refer to poultry and meat animals normally found in the wild. However, most of the "wild" game that has become so popular on restaurant menus is actually from farm-raised animals. Venison farms, in particular, have become numerous and productive, supplying a growing demand.

Although a great variety of game, large and small, can be found on hunters' tables, the supply of game for the restaurant and retail markets is more limited. Venison, the most popular game item, is the main subject of this section. Other products, such as boar and hare, are occasionally available as well. In addition, domestic rabbit is considered here, although its meat has little in common with true game.

Note that the term *venison* is sometimes used in a broader sense to mean meat from deer, elk, moose, caribou, antelope, and pronghorn. However, when any of these meats is offered for sale, the name of the animal must appear on the packaging.

The French terms for game meats are often used on menus and in cooking manuals and references. To clarify these terms, a list of those most commonly used follows:

Chevreuil: often translated as "venison" but refers specifically to the roe deer, the most prized European variety
Cerf: red deer; often farm raised
Daim: fallow deer; often farm raised
Marcassin: young boar, especially under six months of age
Sanglier: boar
Lapin: rabbit
Lapereau: young rabbit
Lièvre: hare
Levraut: young hare
Venaison: usually translated as "venison," the term in fact refers to the meat of any game animal

BONE STRUCTURE OF GAME

The bone and muscle structure of furred game such as venison and elk is the same as that of familiar meats such as beef and lamb. The carcasses are also broken down and fabricated in the same ways. After you have become familiar with the charts and diagrams on pages 128–131, you can apply the same cuts to venison and other large game.

Unlike those larger game animals, however, rabbit is cut differently, so separate illustrations are provided in this section beginning on page 152.

Venison

Several varieties of deer are raised on farms for use as meat, including the red deer and the smaller fallow deer. Deer meat is typically called **venison**. An important advantage of farm-raised venison, besides its year-round availability, is that the cook can be assured it is from young, tender animals. In the wild, young animals less than two years old are likely to have tender meat, but the meat rapidly becomes tough as the animal matures and ages. The tradition of marinating game for several days in strong wine marinades originates, in large part, from efforts to tenderize hunted game enough to make it palatable.

MARINATION, FLAVOR, AND TENDERNESS

The first thing to be said about farm-raised venison is that it is milder in flavor than venison hunted in the wild. It has little, if any, of the strong, gamy flavor usually associated with wild game. In fact, a farm-raised venison steak tastes rather like an especially flavorful lean cut of beef. Those who enjoy strong, gamy flavors may even find farmed venison a little bland. Although it does have some tenderizing effect, marination is not necessary for commercially raised venison because the meat is already tender. Nevertheless, marinating is widely used as a flavoring technique. Much of the flavor traditionally associated with venison, in fact, is due less to its gaminess than to the red wine marinades that were invariably used.

To retain more of the natural flavor of the meat, cook it without marination, or let it marinate for only a short period (30 minutes to 3 or 4 hours) with the desired seasonings and flavoring ingredients. Modern quick marinades are often simple and may contain only a few ingredients.

FAT CONTENT

Venison, like other game, is very low in fat. This makes it especially popular with health-conscious diners. The meat is likely to become dry unless the cook takes great care.

The loin and leg, being tender, are best cooked by dry-heat methods and served rare or medium done. If cooked longer, they will dry out. Roast these cuts whole, either bone-in or deboned, or cut them into steaks, cutlets, and medallions, and sauté, pan-fry, or broil them, taking care not to overcook.

Whole leg of venison, completely boned, seamed, and vacuum packed, is available. Weights range from 5 to 10 pounds (2 to 4.5 kg). Whole bone-in saddle weighs 5 to 20 pounds (2.3 to 9 kg), while the loin muscle weighs about half that after boning and trimming.

Tougher cuts, chiefly the shoulder, neck, and breast, are braised, stewed, or made into ground meat or sausage. These cuts are also lean, but because they are higher in connective tissue and gelatin, they take more readily to stewing and braising.

To generalize, farm-raised venison can be treated like very lean beef. Take care not to cook it to the point of dryness.

Boar

Boar is a type of wild pig. Its meat is somewhat similar to pork, except it is leaner and its flavor fuller and richer. Boar is now raised commercially on a few farms and is available in limited quantities.

Boar is somewhat more difficult to cook than venison and other game because, like pork, it must be cooked until well done. At the same time, it is leaner and less tender than domestic pork, so it tends to be somewhat dry and chewy. Special care must be taken to cook it adequately without overcooking. Because boar is usually tougher than farm-raised venison, its legs or hams are better suited for braising or slow roasting, while the loins can be used for roasts or cut into medallions and sautéed.

Traditionally, boar is handled much like venison, and typical recipes call for red wine marinades. Although marinating a white meat in red wine may seem strange at first, this treatment actually works very well with boar. The red wine accentuates the more pronounced flavor of boar (as compared to pork) and makes it taste more like game.

Other Large Game

Other meats are sometimes found in food service kitchens. *Elk, caribou, moose,* and *antelope* are all similar to venison and are handled in much the same way. The first three of these, especially moose, are larger than deer, so it may be necessary to allow for longer cooking times when using venison recipes for them.

Buffalo, or *American bison,* is raised on ranches in the western United States and Canada and handled like beef. Flavor and cooking characteristics are similar to those of beef, but the meat is somewhat richer in flavor and has less fat and cholesterol than beef.

Rabbit

Domestic rabbit is a versatile meat that can be cooked in most of the same ways as chicken. In fact, in some countries it is classified as poultry. Some typical recipes for rabbit are included in Chapter 6, but nearly any chicken recipe can be used for domestic rabbit as well. In addition, many recipes for veal or pork are adaptable to rabbit.

Rabbit's light, delicate meat is often compared to chicken, but there are differences. It is somewhat more flavorful than chicken, with a mild but distinctive taste that is not exactly like that of other poultry or meat. Also, it is very lean (more like chicken or turkey breast than legs) and can become dry if overcooked.

Rabbit takes well to marination; it can also be cooked without prior marination. Either way, it can be cooked by long, slow simmering, braising, or stewing, or it can be quickly cooked by sautéing, grilling, or roasting.

The structure of rabbit, of course, is like that of other land mammals rather than like that of poultry. Cutting methods divide the meaty hind legs, the bonier forelegs, and the choice saddle or back section (*râble* in French). The whole carcass, cut up, is used for stews and sautés, while the saddle alone is often roasted. It may be boned or bone-in. (See Figure 5.21.)

Small rabbits, 3 pounds (1.5 kg) or less, are the best for cooking. Mature rabbits, weighing 4 to 5 pounds (about 2 kg), tend to be tougher and drier.

Hare

Hare is a wild cousin of the rabbit. (Please note that rabbits and hares are different animals. The American jackrabbit, for example, is actually a hare, not a rabbit.) Unlike domestic rabbit, with its light-colored, delicate meat, hare has flesh that is dark reddish-brown and gamy.

Hares 7 to 8 months old and weighing about 6 pounds (2.7 kg) make the best eating. Larger ones, over 8 pounds (3.6 kg), are likely to be tough and stringy.

Because its structure is the same, hare is cut the same way as rabbit.

ROAST SADDLE OF HARE

Like other game, hare is very lean and therefore becomes dry if overcooked. If roasted, it should be removed from the oven while rare or at least still pink. Rare roast hare has an attractive, deep red color. A typical classic preparation of saddle of hare is as follows. Note that this is also the classic treatment for roast venison.

1. Marinate the saddle of hare in a red wine marinade.

HANGING GAME

Much of the strong flavor associated with game comes from the practice of hanging. Hunters, processing game for their own use, often allow a dressed carcass to hang much longer than necessary to soften the meat (see "green meat," p. 125), or long enough for it to become high, or actually near spoilage.

The farm-raised game discussed here and used in commercial kitchens is not hung. Thus, its flavor is milder.

INSPECTION OF GAME

In the United States, wild game that can be hunted legally under federal or state authority may not be sold. Farm-raised game species, if raised under the appropriate regulations, may be sold. Some animals are inspected by the USDA and others by the FDA. Imported game must meet the same standards of wholesomeness as domestically produced game.

In Canada, the Canadian Food Inspection Agency (CFIA) oversees inspection of game offered for sale. Just as for domesticated meats, federal and provincial inspection of farm-raised game for wholesomeness is mandatory. Game may be imported only from countries that have approved inspection systems. As in the United States, hunted game may not be sold.

Figure 5.21 Cutting rabbit for stews and sautés.

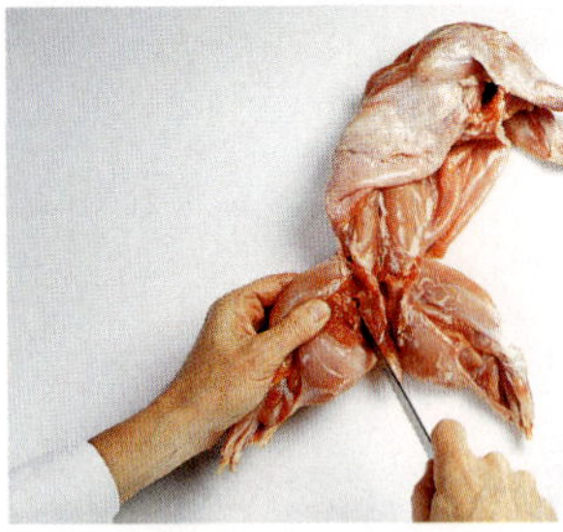

(a) Cut off the hind legs, separating them at the hip joint.

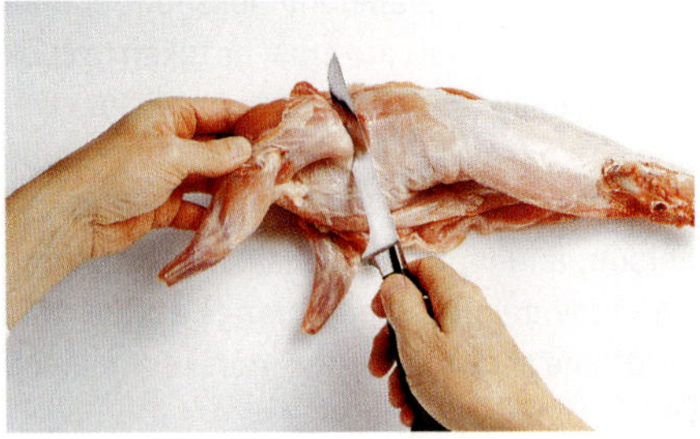

(b) Cut off the forelegs by cutting under the shoulder blade.

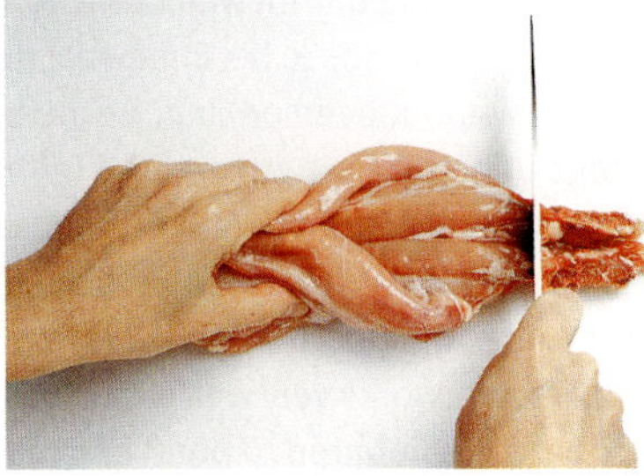

(c) Cut off the hip bone.

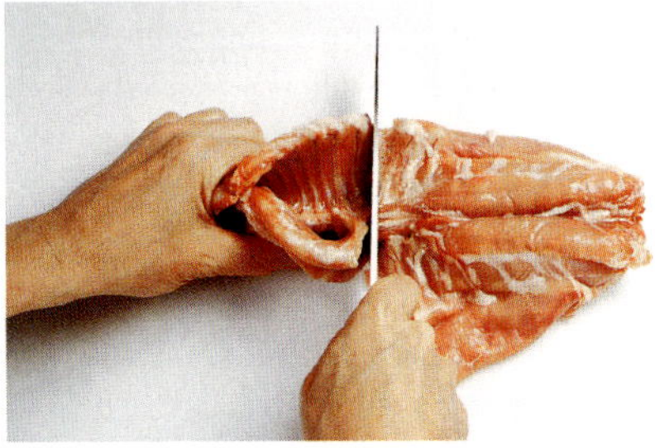

(d) Cut through the backbone to separate the bony rib section from the meaty loin or saddle.

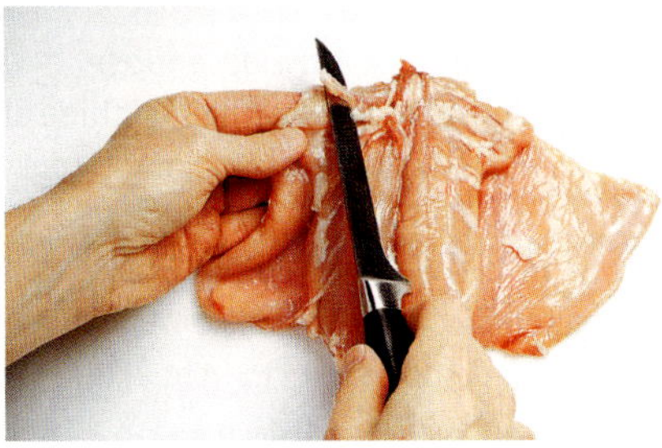

(e) Carefully separate the remaining rib bones from the loin and remove them. The saddle can then be cut crosswise through the backbone into pieces if desired.

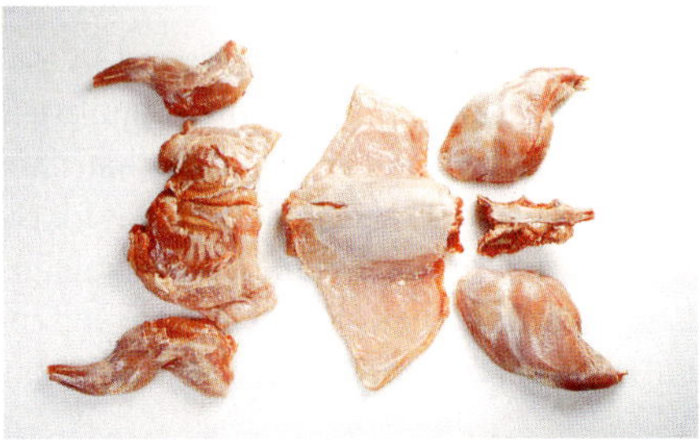

(f) This is the cut-up rabbit, with the forelegs and rib section on the left, the saddle in the center, and the hind legs and hip bone on the right.

2. Brown it on top of the stove and roast it rare or medium done, about 15 minutes at 425°F (220°C).
3. Remove the loin muscles from the bone and cut lengthwise into thin slices. Remove the tenderloins from the underside of the saddle and leave whole or slice as desired.
4. Serve with a poîvrade sauce.

Storage of Meats

The quality of a finished meat product depends not only on proper selection and cooking of the meat but also on its proper storage. Fresh meat is highly perishable. The high cost of meat makes it essential to avoid spoilage.

Fresh Meats

1. Check purchases on arrival to ensure the purchased meat is of good quality.
2. Do not wrap tightly. Bacteria and mold thrive in moist, stagnant places. Air circulation inhibits their growth. Store meat loosely arranged on pans or racks to allow air circulation between pieces, but cover cut surfaces to prevent excessive drying.
3. Do not open vacuum-packed meats until ready to use.
4. Store at 32° to 36°F (0° to 2°C). Meat does not freeze until about 28°F (−2°C).
5. Keep meats separated in the cooler (or, even better, in separate coolers) and on the worktable to avoid cross-contamination.
6. Use as soon as possible. Fresh meats keep well only two to four days. Ground meats keep even less well because so much surface area is exposed to bacteria. Cured and smoked products may keep up to one week. For these reasons, frequent deliveries are better than long storage.

7. Do not try to rescue meats that are going bad by freezing them. Freezing will not improve the quality of spoiling meat.
8. Keep coolers clean.

FROZEN MEATS

1. Wrap frozen meats well to prevent freezer burn.
2. Store at 0°F (−18°C) or colder.
3. Rotate stock—first in, first out. Frozen meats do not keep indefinitely. Recommended shelf life at 0°F (−18°C) for beef, veal, and lamb: 6 months; for pork: 4 months (pork fat turns rancid easily in the freezer).
4. Defrost carefully. Tempering in the refrigerator is best. Defrosting at room temperature encourages bacterial growth.
5. Do not refreeze thawed meats. Refreezing increases loss of quality.
6. Keep freezers clean.

KEY POINTS TO REVIEW

- What are the most important kinds of game used in food service?
- How does the fat content of game meats affect its cooking qualities?
- What are the proper ways to store fresh meats? frozen meats?

TERMS FOR REVIEW

coagulation	aging	irradiation	gras-double
marbling	Cryovac	silverskin	caul
connective tissue	dry aging	barding	game
collagen	primal cuts	larding	venison
elastin	fabricated (cuts)	doneness	boar
inspection	portion-controlled cuts	carryover cooking	hare
grading	butcher	variety meats	
yield grade	fabricate	sweetbreads	
green meat	carve	tripe	

QUESTIONS FOR DISCUSSION

1. Many people assume that the leaner a meat is, the better it is. Do you agree? Explain.
2. What is connective tissue? Why is it important for the cook to understand connective tissue?
3. Flank steak (beef) is high in connective tissue, yet it is often broiled and served in thin slices as London broil. How is this possible?
4. Why are portion-controlled meats so widely used in food service, even though their per-pound cost is higher?
5. Can you explain why veal loin, a tender cut, is sometimes braised, while veal shoulder, a less tender cut, is sometimes roasted?
6. Which of the following cuts are you more likely to braise? Which might you roast?

Beef chuck	Ground pork	Beef rib
Corned beef brisket	Veal rib	Lamb leg
Lamb shanks	Beef strip loin	Pork shoulder

7. You wish to cook a roast rib of beef to a final internal temperature of 145°F (63°C). Why, then, would you remove the roast from the oven when the temperature on the meat thermometer reads 130°F (54°C)?
8. Why are weight-time roasting charts inadequate for determining the doneness of roast meats?
9. Describe the fat content of game meats such as venison, boar, and elk. Explain how the fat content affects how these meats are handled and cooked.
10. How does farm-raised venison differ from wild venison?

Chapter 6

Roast Loin of Rabbit with Risotto, page 166.

Cooking Meats and Game

This chapter presents basic cooking methods as they apply to beef, lamb, veal, pork, and game such as venison. It is important that you have read and understood the basic material in Chapter 5, especially the sections on matching particular cuts to appropriate cooking methods and on testing for doneness. If necessary, please review those sections as well as the discussion of basic cooking methods.

The procedures given here are general. Be aware they may be modified slightly in specific recipes. Nevertheless, the basic principles still hold. In addition, your instructors may wish to show you variations or methods that differ from those presented here.

The recipes that follow each of the procedures—for roasting, sautéing, braising, and so on—are intended to illustrate the basic techniques. Each time you prepare one of these recipes, you should be thinking not just about the product you are making but also about the techniques you are using and how they can be applied to other products. It is helpful to compare the recipes in each section, how they are alike and how they are different. This way you will be learning to cook, not just to follow recipes.

After reading this chapter, you should be able to

1. Cook meats by roasting and baking.
2. Cook meats by broiling, grilling, and pan-broiling.
3. Cook meats by sautéing, pan-frying, and griddling.
4. Cook meats by simmering.
5. Cook meats by braising.
6. Cook variety meats.

Roasting and Baking

Remember the definitions of *roast* and *bake*: to cook foods by surrounding them with hot, dry air, usually in an oven. Roasting is a dry-heat method. No water is used, and the meat is not covered, so steam can escape. There is no real distinction between the terms *roast* and *bake*. Both terms are used for the same procedure, but the word *bake* is more likely to be used for small cuts of meat, vegetables, fish, breads, and pastries.

In principle, roasting meats is a simple procedure. The prepared cut of meat is placed in an oven at a selected temperature, and it is removed when done. What could be easier?

However, there are many variables, and chefs often disagree about proper roasting procedures, especially when it comes to the fine points. In this section, you will learn a roasting procedure you can apply to most meats. But first we discuss in more detail several of the points of disagreement and some of the possible variations.

Seasoning

Salt added to the surface of meat just before roasting penetrates the meat only a fraction of an inch during cooking. The same is true of the flavors of herbs, spices, and aromatics. In the case of smaller cuts of meat, such as beef tenderloin and rack of lamb, the seasoned, browned crust that forms during roasting is an important part of the flavor of the finished dish. Although opinions vary, many chefs advocate seasoning such roasts immediately before roasting so the salt doesn't have time to draw moisture to the surface, which inhibits browning.

In the case of large roasts, such as beef ribs and steamship rounds, there is so little crust in proportion to meat that seasoning before roasting has little effect. Also, if the surface of the roast is mostly fat covering or bone, the seasoned fat and bones may not even be served, so the seasoning has little effect.

With roasts of any size, two alternatives to seasoning just before roasting are often used:

- Marinate the meat or apply seasonings in advance, to give the time for flavors to penetrate. Brining is most suitable for pork. It is not often used for red meats.
- Serve the meat with a flavorful sauce, gravy, or jus. The sauce serves as a seasoning and flavoring for the meat.

Another way to add flavor to roasted meats is to smoke-roast them. Commercial smoker ovens roast meats in the same way as conventional ovens, except they also have a smoke-generating unit that passes smoke through the oven chamber, flavoring foods as they cook. The flavor of wood smoke in cooked meats is so popular that some restaurants have even installed wood-burning hearth ovens to bake and roast meats, pizza, and other items.

Temperature

LOW-TEMPERATURE ROASTING

As we discussed on page 142, it was once thought that starting the roast at a high temperature "seals the pores" by searing the surface, thus keeping in more juices.

We now know this is not the case. Repeated tests have shown that *continuous roasting at a low temperature* gives a superior product with

1. Less shrinkage.
2. More flavor, juiciness, and tenderness.
3. More even doneness from outside to inside.
4. Greater ease in carving.

Low roasting temperatures generally range from 250° to 325°F (120° to 160°C), depending on

1. *The size of the cut.* The larger the cut, the lower the temperature. This ensures the outer portion is not overcooked before the inside is done.

2. *The operation's production schedule.* Lower temperatures require longer roasting times, which may or may not be convenient for a particular operation.

SEARING

If a well-browned, crusted surface is desired for appearance, as when the roast is to be carved in the dining room, a roast may be started at high temperature (400°–450°F/200°–230°C) until it is browned. The temperature should then be lowered to the desired roasting temperature and the meat roasted until done, as for low-temperature roasting.

HIGH-TEMPERATURE ROASTING

Very small pieces of meat that are to be roasted rare may be cooked at a high temperature, from 375° to 450°F (190° to 230°C). The effect is similar to that of broiling: a well-browned, crusted exterior and a rare interior. The meat is in the oven for so short a time that shrinkage is minor. Examples of cuts that may be roasted at a high temperature are rack of lamb and beef tenderloin.

CONVECTION OVENS

If a convection oven is used for roasting, the temperature should be reduced about 50°F (25°C). Many chefs prefer not to use convection ovens for large roasts because the drying effect of the forced air seems to cause greater shrinkage. On the other hand, convection ovens are effective in browning and are good for high-temperature roasting.

Fat Side Up or Fat Side Down

Roasting meats fat side up provides continuous basting as the fat melts and runs down the sides. This method is preferred by perhaps the majority of chefs, although there is not complete agreement.

In this book, we use the fat-side-up method. In the classroom, you should be guided by the advice of your instructor.

Basting

Basting is unnecessary if the meat has a natural fat covering and is roasted fat side up. For lean meats, barding has the same effect. *Barding* is covering the surface of the meat with a thin layer of fat, such as sliced pork fatback or bacon.

If a roast is basted by spooning pan drippings over it, use only the fat. Fat protects the roast from drying, while moisture washes away protective fat and allows drying. Juices used in basting will not soak into the meat.

Basting with drippings or juices may be used to increase the appetite appeal of the roast because it enhances browning. Gelatin and other solids dissolved in the juices are deposited on the surface of the meat, helping form a flavorful brown crust. This does not increase juiciness, however. Some cookbooks claim basting forms a waterproof coating that seals in juices, but this is not the case.

Basting sometimes produces more tender roasts for an unexpected reason: Frequent basting interrupts and slows the cooking. Every time the oven door is opened, the temperature in the oven drops considerably, so the roasting time is longer and more connective tissue breaks down. Thus, it is not the basting but the lower temperature that increases tenderness.

Use of Mirepoix

Mirepoix is often added during the last part of the roasting time to flavor the roast and to add extra flavor to the pan juices.

Many chefs feel, however, that mirepoix adds little flavor, if any, to the roast and that it is actually harmful because the moisture of the vegetables creates steam around the roast. Mirepoix can be more easily added when the gravy is being made. If no gravy or juice is to be served, mirepoix may not be needed at all.

The use of mirepoix is more important for white meats—veal and pork—which, because they are usually cooked well done, lose more juices and need a good gravy or jus to give them moistness and flavor.

Gravy and Jus

The procedure for making jus, given here in the recipe for roast prime rib of beef au jus, is the same as the procedure for making pan gravy, except no roux or other thickening agents are used. In other words, use the methods for making pan gravy.

Basic Procedure for Roasting Meats

1. Collect all equipment and food supplies. Select roasting pans that have low sides (so moisture vapor does not collect around the roast) and that are just large enough to hold the roast. If pans are too large, drippings will spread out too thin and burn.
2. Prepare or trim the meat for roasting. Heavy fat coverings should be trimmed to about ½ inch (1 cm) thick.
3. If desired, season the meat several hours ahead or the day before.
4. Place the meat fat side up on a rack in the roasting pan. The rack holds the roast out of the drippings. Bones may be used if no rack is available. Bone-in rib roasts need no rack because the bones act as a natural rack.
5. Insert a meat thermometer (clean and sanitary) so the bulb is in the center of the meat, not touching bone or fat. (Omit this step if you are using an instant-read thermometer.)
6. Do not cover or add water to the pan. Roasting is a dry-heat cooking method.
7. Place the meat in a preheated oven.
8. Roast to desired doneness, allowing for carryover cooking.
9. If desired, add mirepoix to the pan during the last half of the cooking period.
10. Remove the roast from the oven and let stand in a warm place 15 to 30 minutes. This allows the juices to be reabsorbed through the meat so less juice is lost when the meat is sliced. Also, resting the meat makes slicing easier.
11. If the meat must be held, place it in an oven or warmer set no higher than the desired internal temperature of the roast.
12. While the roast is resting, prepare jus or pan gravy from the drippings. Mirepoix may be added to the drippings now if it was not added in step 8.
13. Slice the roast as close as possible to serving time. In almost all cases, slice the meat against the grain for tenderness.

Roast Rib of Beef au Jus

YIELD: 10 LB (4.5 KG) BONELESS, TRIMMED MEAT
PORTIONS: 25 — **PORTION SIZE: 6½ OZ (175 G), 1½ OZ (50 ML) JUS**
20 — **8 OZ (225 G), 1½ OZ (50 ML) JUS**

U.S.	METRIC	INGREDIENTS	PROCEDURE
20 lb	9 kg	Beef rib, roast ready, bone in (one average-size rib roast)	1. Place the meat fat side up in a roasting pan. 2. Insert a meat thermometer so the bulb is in the center of the meat, not touching bone or fat. 3. Place meat in a preheated 300°F (150°C) oven. Roast until rare or medium done, as desired, allowing for carryover cooking. Thermometer readings: Rare: 120°F (49°C) Medium 130°F (54°C) (Outer slices will be cooked more than center.) Roasting time will be at least 3–4 hours. 4. Remove the meat from the pan and let stand in a warm place 30 minutes before carving.
		Mirepoix:	5. Drain off all but 3–4 oz (100 g) of the fat from the roasting pan. Be careful to retain any juices in the pan. Add the mirepoix to the pan (see **Figure 6.1**). 6. Set the pan over high heat and cook until mirepoix is brown and moisture has evaporated, leaving only fat, mirepoix, and browned drippings. 7. Pour off any excess fat.
8 oz	250 g	Onion	
4 oz	125 g	Carrot	
4 oz	125 g	Celery	
2 qt	2 L	Brown stock	8. Pour about 1 pt (500 mL) stock into the roasting pan to deglaze it. Stir over heat until brown drippings are dissolved. 9. Pour the deglazing liquid and mirepoix into a saucepot with the remaining stock. Simmer until mirepoix is soft and liquid is reduced by about one-third. 10. Strain through a china cap lined with cheesecloth into a bain-marie. Skim fat carefully. Season to taste with salt and pepper. 11. For service, stand the roast on its widest end. Cut down beside the bones to free the meat, and slice the meat across the grain. 12. Serve each portion with 1½ oz (50 mL) jus.
to taste	to taste	Salt	
to taste	to taste	Pepper	

Per serving: Calories, 810; Protein, 52 g; Fat, 65 g (74% cal.); Cholesterol, 180 mg; Carbohydrates, 0 g; Fiber, 0 g; Sodium, 150 mg.

VARIATIONS

Roast Rib-Eye Roll, Top Round, Sirloin, or Strip Loin

These cuts may be roasted by the same procedure; roast them on a rack.

Roast Beef with Gravy

Roast the desired cut of beef according to the basic recipe. Prepare gravy according to the following recipe.

Figure 6.1 Preparing pan jus.

(a) After removing the cooked meat from the roasting pan, degrease the pan. Add mirepoix to the pan and brown on the stovetop or in the oven.

(b) Deglaze with brown stock.

(c) Pour the mirepoix and deglazing liquid into a saucepan. Simmer for the desired time.

(d) Strain through a fine chinois or a china cap lined with cheesecloth.

Roast Beef Gravy

YIELD: ABOUT 1½ QT (1.5 L) PORTIONS: 25 PORTION SIZE: 2 FL OZ (60 ML)

U.S.	METRIC	INGREDIENTS	PROCEDURE
as needed	as needed	Pan drippings from roast beef (previous recipe)	1. After removing the roast, add the mirepoix to the drippings in the roasting pan.
		Mirepoix:	2. Set the pan over high heat and cook until mirepoix is brown and moisture has evaporated, leaving only fat, mirepoix, and browned drippings (see **Figure 6.1**).
8 oz	250 g	Onion	3. Pour off and save the fat.
4 oz	125 g	Carrot	
4 oz	125 g	Celery	
2 qt	2 L	Brown stock	4. Deglaze the pan with some of the stock. Pour the deglazing liquid and mirepoix into a saucepot with the remaining stock. Add the tomato purée. Bring to a boil and reduce heat to a simmer.
4 oz	125 g	Tomato purée	
4 oz	125 g	Flour	5. Make a brown roux with the flour and 4 oz (125 g) of the reserved fat. Cool the roux slightly and beat it into the simmering stock to thicken it.
to taste	to taste	Salt	6. Simmer 15–20 minutes, or until all raw flour taste is cooked out and the liquid is reduced slightly.
to taste	to taste	Pepper	7. Strain through a china cap into a bain-marie.
to taste	to taste	Worcestershire sauce	8. Season to taste with salt, pepper, and Worcestershire sauce.

Per serving: Calories, 35; Protein, 1 g; Fat, 1.5 g (40% cal.); Cholesterol, 5 mg; Carbohydrates, 4 g; Fiber, 0 g; Sodium, 10 mg.

VARIATION

Jus Lié

Omit tomato purée and roux. Thicken liquid with 1½ oz (50 g) cornstarch or arrowroot blended with ½ cup (100 mL) cold water or stock.

Roast Loin of Pork with Sage and Apples

PORTIONS: 25 PORTION SIZE: 1 CHOP, ABOUT 6 OZ (175 G) WITH BONE, 2 FL OZ (60 ML) GRAVY

U.S.	METRIC	INGREDIENTS
14½ lb	6.6 kg	Pork loins, center cut, bone in
1 tsp	5 mL	Salt
½ tsp	2 mL	Pepper
1 tbsp	15 mL	Dried sage
		Mirepoix:
8 oz	250 g	Onion
4 oz	125 g	Carrot
4 oz	125 g	Celery
8 oz	250 g	Apples, peeled, cored, and diced

PROCEDURE

1. With a meat saw, cut off the chine bones so the loins can be carved into chops after roasting.
2. Rub the pork with salt, pepper, and sage.
3. Place the chine bones in a roasting pan. Place the pork loins fat side up on top of the bones. Insert a meat thermometer into the thickest part of the muscle.
4. Place in oven at 325°F (165°C) and roast for 1 hour.
5. Place the mirepoix and the apples in the bottom of the pan and continue to roast until the thermometer reads 160°F (71°C). Total cooking time is 2–2½ hours.
6. Remove the roast from the pan and hold in a warm place.

U.S.	METRIC	INGREDIENTS
2½ qt	2.5 L	Chicken stock, veal stock, or pork stock
5 oz	150 g	Flour
to taste	to taste	Salt
to taste	to taste	Pepper
8	8	Tart apples
2 oz	60 g	Butter
1 tbsp	15 mL	Sugar

7. Set the roasting pan over moderate heat and cook until moisture has evaporated and mirepoix is well browned. Drain off and reserve the fat.
8. Deglaze the pan with the stock and pour the contents into a saucepot. Skim well.
9. Make a brown roux with the flour and 5 oz (150 g) of the pork fat. Thicken the gravy with the roux and simmer 15 minutes, or until thickened and slightly reduced.
10. While the gravy is simmering, core the apples. They may be peeled or not, as desired. Cut the apples crosswise into slices about ⅜ in. (1 cm) thick. Sauté the slices in a little butter over moderately high heat. Sprinkle them with sugar as they cook. Continue to sauté on both sides until browned and caramelized.
11. Strain the gravy and adjust the seasonings.
12. Cut the roast into chops between the rib bones. Serve each portion with 2 oz (60 mL) gravy. Garnish with caramelized apple slices.

Per serving: Calories, 420; Protein, 40 g; Fat, 22 g (48% cal.); Cholesterol, 105 mg; Carbohydrates, 13 g; Fiber, 2 g; Sodium, 210 mg.

VARIATIONS

Other pork cuts may be roasted as in the basic recipe: full loin, loin ends, boneless loin, fresh ham, shoulder.

Roast Loin or Rack of Veal with Sage and Apples

Substitute loin or rack of veal for pork in the basic recipe. Use brown stock instead of white stock.

Roast Rack of Lamb

PORTIONS: 8 PORTION SIZE: 2 CHOPS, 1 FL OZ (30 ML) JUS

U.S.	METRIC	INGREDIENTS	PROCEDURE
2	2	Racks of lamb, 8 ribs each	1. Prepare lamb for roasting.
to taste	to taste	Salt	2. Place any trimmed-off bones in the bottom of a roasting pan. Place the meat fat side up on top of the bones. Season with salt, pepper, and thyme.
to taste	to taste	Pepper	3. Place in a hot oven (450°F/230°C) and roast to desired doneness. Rack of lamb is usually roasted rare or medium. Test doneness with a meat thermometer or by the touch method, as for steaks. Total time is about 30 minutes.
to taste	to taste	Dried thyme	4. Remove the lamb from the roasting pan and hold in a warm place. Leave the bones in the pan.
			5. Set the roasting pan over moderate heat to caramelize the juices and clarify the fat. Pour off the fat.
2	2	Garlic cloves, chopped	6. Add the garlic to the pan and cook 1 minute.
1 pt	500 mL	White or brown veal stock	7. Deglaze the pan with the stock and reduce by half. Strain, degrease, and season to taste.
			8. Cut the meat between the ribs into chops. Serve 2 chops per portion with 1 oz (30 mL) jus.

Per serving: Calories, 280; Protein, 19 g; Fat, 22 g (72% cal.); Cholesterol, 75 mg; Carbohydrates, 0 g; Fiber 0 g; Sodium, 70 mg.

VARIATIONS

Rack of Lamb aux Primeurs (with Spring Vegetables)

Place the racks on one or two heated serving platters. Garnish the platters with an assortment of spring vegetables, cooked separately: tournéed carrots, tournéed turnips, buttered peas, green beans, rissolé potatoes. Pour the jus into a warm gooseneck or sauceboat. Carve and serve the meat, vegetables, and jus in the dining room.

Rack of Lamb Persillé

Prepare as in basic recipe. Combine the ingredients for Persillade, listed below. Before carving and serving, spread the top (fat side) of each rack with 1 tbsp (15 g) soft butter. Pack the persillade onto the top of the racks and brown under the salamander.

Persillade

4 cloves garlic, minced

2 oz (60 g) fresh bread crumbs (about 1 cup)

⅓ cup (80 mL) chopped parsley

Roast Rack of Lamb; White Beans Bretonne; Steamed Brussels Sprout Leaves

Smoke-Roasted Pork Shoulder

YIELD: APPROX. 4 LB (2 KG) TRIMMED, BONELESS MEAT

U.S.	METRIC	INGREDIENTS
8 lb	4 kg	Pork shoulder or butt
2 oz, or as needed	60 g, or as needed	Spice Rub I (below)

Per serving: Calories, 60; Protein, 7 g; Fat, 3 g (49% cal.); Cholesterol, 25 mg; Carbohydrates, 0 g; Fiber, 0 g; Sodium, 140 mg.

PROCEDURE

1. Trim excess external fat from the meat.
2. Rub the meat with the spice rub so it is completely coated with a thin layer.
3. Refrigerate the meat overnight.
4. Cook the meat on racks in a smoke roaster at 250°–275°F (120°–135°C) until very tender, about 6 hours. When done, the meat should be tender enough to pull apart with a fork.
5. The pork may be cut from the bones and sliced or cut into chunks and served with a barbecue sauce on the side, or it may be shredded, mixed with a little barbecue sauce, and used as a sandwich filling.

VARIATION

Smoke-Roasted Shoulder of Boar

Substitute shoulder of boar for the pork shoulder.

Spice Rub I

YIELD: APPROX. 6 OZ (180 G)

U.S.	METRIC	INGREDIENTS
1½ oz	45 g	Paprika
1 oz	30 g	New Mexico chili powder
2 tbsp	30 mL	Dried oregano
2 tbsp	20 mL	Dried thyme
4 tsp	20 mL	Ground coriander
4 tsp	20 mL	Ground cumin
2 oz	60 g	Salt
2 tbsp	30 mL	Black pepper

Per serving: Calories, 60; Protein, 7 g; Fat, 3 g (49% cal.); Cholesterol, 25 mg; Carbohydrates, 0 g; Fiber, 0 g; Sodium, 140 mg.

PROCEDURE

1. Combine all ingredients and mix well.
2. Store in a tightly sealed container in a dark place.

Spice Rub II

YIELD: APPROX. 7 OZ (200 G)

U.S.	METRIC	INGREDIENTS
1½ oz	45 g	Paprika
1½ oz	45 g	Chili powder
2 tsp	10 mL	Dry mustard
2 tbsp	30 mL	Onion powder
1 tsp	5 mL	Celery seed
2 tsp	10 mL	Dried thyme
1 oz	30 g	Sugar
2 oz	60 g	Salt
2 tbsp	30 mL	Black pepper

Per serving: Calories, 60; Protein, 7 g; Fat, 3 g (49% cal.); Cholesterol, 25 mg; Carbohydrates, 0 g; Fiber, 0 g; Sodium, 140 mg.

PROCEDURE

1. Combine all ingredients and mix well.
2. Store in a tightly sealed container in a dark place.

Barbecued Spareribs

PORTIONS: 24 PORTION SIZE: 10 OZ (300 G)

U.S.	METRIC	INGREDIENTS
18 lb	8.5 kg	Fresh pork spareribs
6 oz, or as needed	180 g, or as needed	Spice Rub I or II
2½ qt	2.5 L	Barbecue Sauce or Chili Barbecue Sauce

Per serving: Calories, 730; Protein, 47 g; Fat, 54 g (68% cal.); Cholesterol, 190 mg; Carbohydrates, 11 g; Fiber, 2 g; Sodium, 1010 mg.

PROCEDURE

1. Weigh the spareribs and cut them into 12-oz (350 g) portions.
2. Rub the ribs with the spice rub so they are completely coated with a thin layer.
3. Refrigerate overnight.
4. Place the ribs in a roasting pan with the inside of the ribs down.
5. Place the ribs in a smoker oven or a conventional oven at 300°F (150°C). Bake 1 hour.
6. Drain the fat from the pans.
7. Spoon about 1 pt (500 mL) barbecue sauce over the ribs to coat them with a thin layer. Turn them over and coat with more sauce.
8. Bake 45 minutes. Turn and coat the ribs with the remaining sauce.
9. Bake until tender, 30–60 minutes more.
10. Serve the portions whole, or cut into separate ribs for easier eating.

Barbecued Spareribs

Glazed Ham with Cider Sauce

PORTIONS: 25 PORTION SIZE: 5 OZ (150 G) HAM, 2 FL OZ (60 ML) SAUCE

U.S.	METRIC	INGREDIENTS
15 lb	7 kg	Smoked ham
3–4 tbsp	45–60 mL	Prepared mustard
6 oz	175 g	Brown sugar
¼ tsp	1 mL	Ground cloves
1½ qt	1.5 L	Apple cider
8 oz	250 g	Raisins, seedless (optional)
3 oz	100 g	Brown sugar
⅓ tsp	2 mL	Nutmeg
1 tsp	5 mL	Grated lemon rind
6 tbsp	50 g	Cornstarch
to taste	to taste	Salt

PROCEDURE

1. Place the ham(s) in a stockpot with enough water to cover. Bring to a boil and reduce heat to a simmer. Simmer 1 hour. Drain.
2. Cut off skin and excess fat. Leave fat covering about ½ in. (1 cm) thick. Score the fat with a knife.
3. Place the ham fat side up in a roasting or baking pan. Spread with a thin layer of prepared mustard. Mix the sugar and cloves and sprinkle over the ham.
4. Bake at 350°F (175°C) about 1 hour. (Caution: Sugar burns easily, so check ham after 30–45 minutes.)
5. Place cider, raisins, sugar, nutmeg, and lemon rind in a saucepan and simmer 5 minutes.
6. Mix cornstarch with a little cold water or cold cider and stir into the sauce. Simmer until thickened.
7. Add salt to taste.
8. Slice ham. Serve 5-oz (150-g) portion with 2 oz (60 mL) sauce on the side.

Per serving: Calories, 300; Protein, 32 g; Fat, 7 g (21% cal.); Cholesterol, 70 mg; Carbohydrates, 25 g; Fiber, 1 g; Sodium, 1680 mg.

Note: The amount of cooking required depends on the type of ham. Aged country hams must be soaked 24 hours in cold water, scrubbed, and simmered about 20 minutes per pound (500 g). Hams labeled *tenderized* or *ready to cook* may be baked without simmering (starting with step 2) or just blanched before baking (place in cold water, bring to a boil, and drain).

VARIATIONS

Ham with Brown Cider Sauce

When ham is baked, drain fat from pan and deglaze with 1½ pt (750 mL) cider. Add 1½ qt (1.5 L) demi-glace or espagnole and simmer until reduced and thickened. Flavor to taste with mustard and a little sugar.

Fruit-Glazed Ham

Omit mustard-sugar glaze. During last half of baking, spoon fruit preserves (apricot, pineapple, or peach) over ham to glaze.

Home-Style Meatloaf

PORTIONS: 25 PORTION SIZE: 4 OZ (125 G)

U.S.	METRIC	INGREDIENTS
1 lb	500 g	Onions, fine dice
8 oz	250 g	Celery, fine dice
2 oz	60 mL	Oil
12 oz	375 g	Soft bread crumbs
12 fl oz	375 mL	Tomato juice, stock, or milk
2½ lb	1.25 kg	Ground beef
2½ lb	1.25 kg	Ground pork
2½ lb	1.25 kg	Ground veal
5	5	Eggs, beaten slightly
1 tbsp	15 mL	Salt
½ tsp	2 mL	Black pepper
3 pt	1.5 L	Tomato sauce, Spanish sauce, Creole sauce, or sour cream sauce

PROCEDURE

1. Sauté the onions and celery in oil until tender. Remove from pan and cool thoroughly.
2. In a large bowl, soak the bread crumbs in the juice, stock, or milk.
3. Add the sautéed vegetables and the meat, eggs, salt, and pepper. Mix gently until evenly combined. Do not overmix.
4. Form the mixture into 2 or 3 loaves in a baking pan, or fill loaf pans with the mixture.
5. Bake at 350°F (175°C) 1–1½ hours, or until done. Test with a meat thermometer for an internal temperature of 165°F (74°C).
6. For service, cut the loaves into 4-oz (125 g) slices. Serve with 2 oz (60 mL) sauce per portion.

Per serving: Calories, 360; Protein, 27 g; Fat, 21 g (53% cal.); Cholesterol, 135 mg; Carbohydrates, 16 g; Fiber, 2 g; Sodium, 680 mg.

VARIATIONS

Home-Style All-Beef Meatloaf

In place of the mixture of beef, pork, and veal, use 7½ lb (3.75 kg) ground beef.

Italian-Style Meatloaf

Add the following ingredients to the basic mix:

4 tsp (20 mL) chopped garlic, sautéed with the onion

1 oz (30 g) parmesan cheese

⅔ cup (150 mL) chopped parsley

1½ tsp (7 mL) basil

1 tsp (5 mL) oregano

Salisbury Steak

Divide meat mixture for all-beef meatloaf into 6-oz (175 g) portions. Form into thick, oval patties and place on a sheet pan. Bake at 350°F (175°C) about 30 minutes.

Baked Meatballs

Divide basic meat mixture or Italian-Style Meatloaf mixture into 2½-oz (75 g) portions using a No. 16 scoop. Form into balls and place on sheet pans. Bake at 350°F (175°C). May be served with tomato sauce over pasta.

Roast Loin of Rabbit with Risotto

PORTIONS: 8 PORTION SIZE: 5–6 OZ (140–160 G) RABBIT, 4 OZ (125 G) RISOTTO, SAUCE AND GARNISH

U.S.	METRIC	INGREDIENTS	PROCEDURE
2½–3 lb	1–1.3 kg	Boneless saddles of rabbit	1. Trim the meat as necessary, leaving the meat in whole pieces.
as needed	as needed	Oil	2. Heat the oil in a sauté pan. Add the rabbit meat and brown it on all sides.
			3. Transfer to an oven heated to 450°F (230°C) and roast 5–10 minutes, or until medium done (slightly pink in center). Remove the meat from the pan and keep warm.
2 oz	60 g	Shallot, chopped fine	4. Add the shallots, carrots, mushrooms, and garlic. Brown lightly.
2 oz	60 g	Carrot, chopped fine	5. Add the vermouth or wine and reduce by half.
4 oz	125 g	Mushroom, chopped fine	6. Add the stock and reduce by half.
1	1	Garlic clove, chopped fine	7. Strain. Season to taste with salt.
4 fl oz	125 g	Dry white vermouth or white wine	
1 pt	500 mL	Rabbit stock or chicken stock, rich and concentrated	
to taste	to taste	Salt	
2 lb	1 kg	Risotto alla Parmigiana	8. Place a mound of risotto in the center of each plate.
as desired	as desired	Carrot, small dice, cooked, hot	9. Cut the rabbit meat into thick slices and arrange over the risotto.
as desired	as desired	Zucchini, small dice, cooked, hot	10. Place a few pieces of diced carrot and zucchini on the plate.
			11. Spoon the sauce onto the plate around the meat.

Per serving: Calories, 490; Protein, 35 g; Fat, 22 g (27% cal.); Cholesterol, 100 mg; Carbohydrates, 32 g; Fiber, 3 g; Sodium, 224 mg.

Roast Loin of Rabbit with Risotto

Broiling, Grilling, and Pan-Broiling

Broiling and grilling are dry-heat cooking methods, which use very high heat to cook meat quickly. Properly broiled meats have a well-browned, flavorful crust on the outside, and the inside is cooked to the desired doneness and still juicy.

It may be helpful to think of broiling and grilling as browning techniques rather than cooking techniques. This is because the best, juiciest broiled meats are those cooked to the rare or medium-done stage. Because of the intense heat, it is difficult to broil meats to the well-done stage and still keep them juicy. Pork and veal, which are usually eaten well done, are generally better griddled, sautéed, or braised than broiled or grilled. (Veal can be broiled successfully if the customer prefers it a little pink inside.)

For best results, only high-quality, tender cuts with a good fat content should be broiled.

Temperature Control

The object of broiling is not just to cook the meat to the desired doneness but also to form a brown, flavorful, crusty surface.

The goal of the broiler cook is to create the right amount of browning—not too much or too little—by the time the inside is cooked to the desired doneness. To do this, he or she must broil the item at the right temperature.

In general, the shorter the cooking time, the higher the temperature, or else the meat won't have time to brown. The longer the cooking time, the lower the temperature, or the meat will brown too much before the inside is done.

Cooking time depends on two factors:

1. The desired doneness.
2. The thickness of the cut.

In other words, a well-done steak should be cooked at a lower heat than a rare one. A thin steak cooked rare must be broiled at a higher temperature than a thick one cooked rare.

To control the cooking temperature of a broiler, raise or lower the rack. On a grill, set different areas for different temperatures and grill meats in the appropriate area.

Seasoning

As with roasting, chefs disagree on when to season. Some feel that meats should not be seasoned before broiling. This is because salt draws moisture to the surface and retards browning.

Procedure for Broiling or Grilling Meats

In a broiler, the heat source is above the food. In a grill, the heat is below the food. Except for this difference, the basic procedure is the same for both. Make sure you understand how to test broiled meats for doneness (p. 143) before starting.

1. Collect and prepare all equipment and food supplies. Trim excess fat from meats to avoid flare-ups that can char the meat too much and coat it with smoky residue. If necessary, score the fatty edges of meats to prevent curling.
2. Preheat the broiler or grill.
3. If necessary, brush the grill with a wire brush to clean off any charred food particles.
4. Brush the meat with oil, or dip it in oil and let the excess drip off. Place the item on the broiler or grill. The oil helps prevent sticking and keeps the product moist. This step may be unnecessary for meats high in fat. Using too much oil can cause grease fires. Alternatively, wipe the grill with an oiled towel before placing the meat on it.
5. When one side is brown and the meat is cooked halfway, turn it over with a fork (piercing only the fat, never the meat, or juices will be lost) or with tongs. Figure 6.2 illustrates the technique for grill-marking steaks and other meats.
6. Cook the second side until the meat is cooked to the desired doneness. If the meat is to be brushed with a glaze or sauce, such as a barbecue sauce, it is usually best to wait until the product is partially cooked on each side before applying the first coat. Many glazes or sauces burn if cooked too long. After the item has cooked on both sides and is one-half to three-fourths done, brush the top with a light coat of the sauce. Turn over and repeat as necessary.
7. Remove from the broiler or grill and serve immediately.

Figure 6.2 Grill-marking steaks.

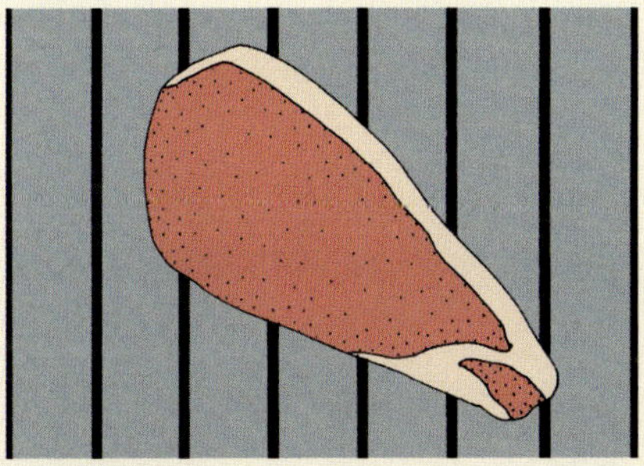

(a) Place the meat on a preheated grill at an angle as shown.

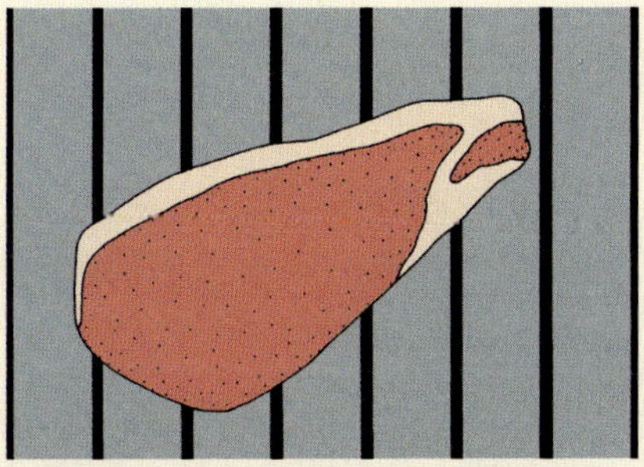

(b) When the meat is about one-fourth done, turn the meat 60–90 degrees, as shown. Do not turn it over.

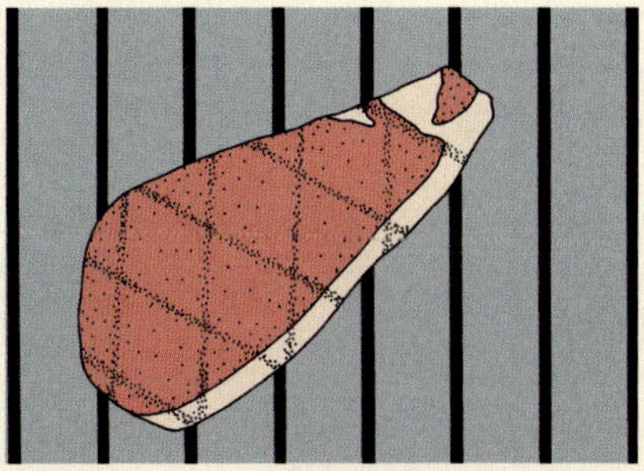

(c) When the steak is about half done, turn it over. The grill marks will appear as shown.

Others feel that seasoning before broiling improves the taste of the meat because the seasonings become part of the brown crust rather than something sprinkled on afterward.

Generally, if you have a professional broiler that has been properly preheated, it is not difficult to brown meat that has been salted. Low-powered broilers such as those found in home kitchens, on the other hand, do not get as hot. In such cases, it is better to salt after broiling, not before.

One way around this problem is to serve the meat with a seasoned butter. Another option is to marinate the meat in seasoned oil 30 minutes or more before broiling. Be sure to dry marinated meats well before placing them on the broiler.

KEY POINTS TO REVIEW

- What are the steps in the basic procedure for roasting meats?
- What are the factors to consider when determining at what temperature to roast meats?
- What are the steps in the basic procedure for broiling and grilling meats?
- What are the steps in the basic procedure for pan-broiling meats?

Sauces and Accompaniments for Grilled and Broiled Meats

Many kinds of sauces and accompaniments are appropriate for grilled meats, including compound butters; butter sauces such as béarnaise; brown sauce variations such as Bercy, mushroom, and bordelaise; tomato sauce variations; and salsas and relishes. For other examples, see the recipes in this section. Note that, unlike pan sauces made by deglazing sauté pans, all these sauces are prepared in advance because broiling or grilling does not give you the opportunity to deglaze a pan.

Part of the appeal of broiled and grilled meats is their brown, crisp surface. For this reason, it is best not to cover the item with the sauce. Also, less sauce is usually served with grilled items than with sautéed items. Serve the sauce on the side or around the meat or, at most, in a thin ribbon across only part of the meat.

Similarly, vegetables and accompaniments for broiled and grilled meats should, in most cases, not be heavily sauced. Grilled vegetables are often good choices as accompaniments.

Procedure for Pan-Broiling Meats

1. Preheat an iron skillet over a high flame until it is very hot. Do not add fat. (The pan should, of course, be well seasoned.)
2. Proceed as for grilling. Pour off any fat that accumulates during cooking, if necessary.

Pan-Broiling

Broiling very thin steaks (minute steaks) to the rare stage is difficult because the heat is not high enough to form a good brown crust without overcooking the inside.

Pan-broiling in a heavy iron skillet is an answer to this problem.

Broiled Strip Loin Steak Maître d'Hôtel

YIELD: 10 PORTIONS

U.S.	METRIC	INGREDIENTS	PROCEDURE
10	10	Strip loin steaks, boneless, 10–12 oz (300–350 g) each	1. Trim steaks as necessary, leaving a thin layer of fat on the edge.
to taste	to taste	Salt	2. Season the steaks to taste with salt and pepper. Brush lightly with oil.
to taste	to taste	Black pepper	3. Place the steaks on a preheated grill or broiler.
as needed	as needed	Vegetable oil	4. When the steak is about one-fourth done, turn it 60–90 degrees to grill-mark it (see **Figure 6.2**). 5. When the steak is half done, turn it over and complete the cooking to the desired doneness. If turning with a fork, pierce the fat, not the meat, or juices will be lost.
5 oz	150 g	Maître d'Hôtel Butter	6. Remove the steaks from the broiler and immediately place on a hot plate. Top each steak with a ½-oz (15-g) slice of seasoned butter.

Per 8 ounces: Calories, 550; Protein, 60 g; Fat, 33 g (55% cal.); Cholesterol, 185 mg; Carbohydrates, 0 g; Fiber, 0 g; Sodium, 250 mg.

VARIATIONS

Other steaks may be cooked by the same method, including *rib steak, rib-eye steak, tenderloin, club steak, porterhouse, T-bone, and sirloin. Chopped beef patties* may also be prepared using this recipe.

Other seasoned butters and sauces make good accompaniments to broiled steaks, including:

Garlic Butter	Chasseur Sauce	Mushroom Sauce (brown)	Béarnaise Sauce	Anchovy Butter	Madeira Sauce	Bercy Sauce (brown)
Foyot Sauce	Bordelaise Sauce	Périgueux Sauce	Lyonnaise Sauce	Choron Sauce	Marchand de Vin Sauce	

Broiled Lamb Chops

Prepare as for broiled steaks, using rib, loin, or shoulder chops.

Grilled Chopped Lamb "Steaks" with Rosemary and Pine Nuts

PORTIONS: 25 PORTION SIZE: 5 OZ (150 G)

U.S.	METRIC	INGREDIENTS
6 oz	175 g	Onion, chopped fine
2 fl oz	60 g	Salad oil
6½ lb	3.25 kg	Ground lamb
8 oz	250 g	Soft, fresh bread crumbs
8 oz	250 g	Toasted pine nuts
10 fl oz	300 mL	Milk
½ cup	30 g	Chopped parsley
2 tsp	10 mL	Rosemary
2½ tsp	12 mL	Salt
1 tsp	5 mL	White pepper
25 strips	25 strips	Bacon

Per serving: Calories, 460; Protein, 25 g; Fat, 37 g (72% cal.); Cholesterol, 95 mg; Carbohydrates, 7 g; Fiber, 1 g; Sodium, 520 mg.

Note: The patties may be browned under the broiler, arranged on a sheet pan, and finished in the oven at 375°F (190°C).

PROCEDURE

1. Sauté the onion in oil until tender. Do not brown. Cool thoroughly.
2. Combine all ingredients except bacon in a bowl. Mix gently until evenly combined. Do not overmix.
3. Scale the meat into 5-oz (150-g) portions. Form the portions into thick patties, about ¾ in. (2 cm) thick.
4. Wrap a strip of bacon around each patty and fasten with picks.
5. Grill or broil the patties under moderate heat until done, turning once (see Note).
6. Remove the picks before serving.

VARIATIONS

Ground beef or veal may be used instead of the lamb.

Grilled Chopped Beef "Steaks" with Marjoram

Substitute ground beef for the ground lamb. Substitute marjoram for the rosemary. Omit the pine nuts.

Sautéing, Pan-Frying, and Griddling

If you review the general definitions of sautéing, pan-frying, and griddling, you will see the differences among these methods are largely a matter of degree. Sautéing uses high heat and a small amount of fat and is usually used for small pieces of food. Pan-frying uses moderate heat, a moderate amount of fat, and is usually employed for larger items, such as chops. But at what point does moderate heat become high heat and a small amount of fat become a moderate amount of fat? It is impossible to draw an exact dividing line between sautéing and pan-frying.

Each time you cook a piece of meat, you must judge how much heat and how much fat to use to do the job best. This depends on the kind of food and the size of the pieces. Following are guidelines to help you make the right judgments.

Guidelines for Sautéing, Pan-Frying, and Griddling

1. Use only tender cuts for sautéing.
2. Smaller or thinner pieces of meat require higher heat. The object is to brown or sear the meat in the time it takes to cook it to the desired doneness. Very small or thin pieces cook in just a few moments.
3. If large or thick items are browned over high heat, it may be necessary to finish them at lower heat to avoid burning them.
4. The amount of fat needed is the amount required to conduct the heat to all surfaces so the item cooks evenly. Flat items need much less fat than irregularly shaped items like chicken pieces. Sautéing small pieces of meat requires little fat because the items are tossed or flipped so all sides come in contact with the hot pan.
5. When sautéing small pieces of food, do not overload the pan, and do not flip or toss the food more than necessary. This will cause the temperature to drop too much, and the meat will simmer in its juices rather than sauté.
6. Use clarified butter or oil or a mixture of the two for sautéing. Whole butter burns easily.
7. Dredging meats in flour promotes even browning and helps prevent sticking. Flour meats immediately before cooking, not in advance, or the flour will get pasty. Also, shake off excess flour before adding meat to the pan.
8. Meats to be pan-fried are often breaded.
9. When pan-frying several batches, strain or skim the fat between batches. Otherwise, burned food particles from previous batches may mar the appearance of the meat.
10. Griddling and pan-frying are preferable to broiling and grilling for cooking pork and veal chops because the lower temperatures keep these meats moister when cooked well done. Hamburgers cooked well done are also moister if cooked on a griddle.

Deglazing the Pan

A sauce made by deglazing the pan often accompanies sautéed meats. To **deglaze** means to swirl a liquid in a sauté or other pan to dissolve cooked particles of food remaining on the bottom. The deglazing liquid can be used to flavor a sauce in one of two ways:

1. *Add the reduced deglazing liquid to a prepared sauce.* The deglazing liquid adds flavor and color to the sauce.
2. *Use the deglazing liquid to make a freshly prepared sauce.* Add stock or other liquids and other flavoring and thickening ingredients and finish the sauce as indicated in the recipe.

Stir-Frying

The Chinese technique of stir-frying is very much like sautéing, except that in sautéing, the food items are usually tossed by flipping the pan, while in stir-frying, the pan is left stationary and the foods are tossed with spatulas or other tools. Although true Chinese stir-frying is done in a round-bottomed pan, called a *wok*, set over a special burner, you can use the same technique with a standard sauté pan.

General Procedures for Sautéing and Pan-Frying Meats

The following procedures are presented together so you can compare them. Keep in mind that these are the two extremes and that many recipes require a procedure that falls somewhere between the two.

The procedure for pan-frying applies to griddling as well, although only a small amount of fat can be used on a griddle.

Sautéing

1. Collect all equipment and food supplies.
2. Prepare meats as required. This may include dredging with flour.
3. Heat a small amount of fat in a sauté pan until very hot.
4. Add the meat to the pan. Do not overcrowd the pan.
5. Brown the meat on all sides, flipping or tossing it in the pan as necessary so it cooks evenly.
6. Remove the meat from the pan. Drain excess fat, if any.
7. Add any sauce ingredients to be sautéed, such as shallots or mushrooms, as indicated in the recipe. Sauté them as necessary.
8. Add liquid for deglazing, such as wine or stock. Simmer while swirling and scraping the pan to release food particles on the bottom so they can dissolve in the liquid. Reduce the liquid.
9. Add a prepared sauce or other sauce ingredients, and finish the sauce as indicated in the recipe.
10. Serve the meat with the sauce, or return the meat to the sauce in the pan to reheat briefly and coat it with the sauce. Do not let the meat cook in the sauce. Serve.

Pan-Frying

1. Collect all equipment and food supplies.
2. Prepare meats as required. This may include breading or dredging with flour.
3. Heat a moderate amount of fat in a sauté pan or skillet until hot.
4. Add the meat to the pan.
5. Brown the meat on one side. Turn it with a spatula and brown the other side. Larger pieces may need to be finished at reduced heat after browning. If required, they may finish cooking, uncovered, in the oven.
6. Serve immediately.

Basic Procedure for Stir-Frying

1. Heat a wok or sauté pan over high heat until very hot.
2. Add a small quantity of oil and let it heat.
3. Add seasonings for flavoring the oil—one or more of the following: salt, garlic, ginger root, scallions.
4. If meat, poultry, or seafood items are part of the dish, add them at this point. As when sautéing, do not overload the pan. Leave the food pieces untouched for a few moments so they begin to brown properly. Then stir and toss them with a spatula so they sear and cook evenly.
5. If any liquid seasoning for the meat, such as soy sauce, is used, add it now, but only in small quantities, so the meat continues to fry and does not start to simmer or stew.
6. Remove the meat from the pan or leave it in, depending on the recipe. If a small quantity of quick-cooking vegetables is used, the meat can sometimes be left in the pan and the vegetables cooked with it. Otherwise, remove the meat when it is almost done and keep it on the side while cooking the vegetables.
7. Repeat steps 2 and 3 if necessary.
8. Add the vegetables to the pan and stir-fry. If more than one vegetable is used, add the longer-cooking ones first and the quicker-cooking ones last.
9. Some dishes are dry-fried, meaning prepared without liquid or sauce. In this case, simply return the meat item, if any, to the pan to reheat with the vegetables, then serve. Otherwise, proceed to the next step.
10. Add liquid ingredients, such as stock or water, and continue to cook and stir until the vegetables are almost cooked.
11. Add the meat item, which was removed in step 6, to the pan to reheat.
12. Optional but widely used step: Add a mixture of cornstarch and water to the pan and cook until lightly thickened.
13. Serve at once.

KEY POINTS TO REVIEW

- When sautéing meats, what are the factors to consider when deciding on how much heat to use?
- What are the steps in the basic procedure for sautéing meats?
- What are the steps in the basic procedure for pan-frying meats?
- What are the steps in the basic procedure for stir-frying meats?

Breaded Veal Cutlets

PORTIONS: 24 PORTION SIZE: 4 OZ (125 G)

U.S.	METRIC	INGREDIENTS
6 lb	3 kg	Veal cutlets (scaloppine): 24 pieces, 4 oz (125 g) each (See **Figure5.15** for preparation of veal)
to taste	to taste	Salt
to taste	to taste	Pepper
		Standard Breading Procedure (see Note):
4 oz	125 g	Flour
4	4	Eggs
1 cup	250 mL	Milk
1½ lb	750 g	Bread crumbs, dry or fresh
8 oz	250 mL	Oil or clarified butter, or a mixture of oil and butter

PROCEDURE

1. Lightly flatten each piece of veal with a meat mallet. Do not pound too hard, or you may tear the meat.
2. Season the meat with salt and pepper and pass through Standard Breading Procedure.
3. Heat about ¼ in. (5 mm) oil or butter in a large sauté pan. Place the cutlets in the pan and pan-fry until golden brown. Turn and brown the other side. Remove from the pan and place on hot plates.

U.S.	METRIC	INGREDIENTS
12 oz	375 g	Butter

4. Heat the butter in a small saucepan or sauté pan until lightly browned. Pour ½ oz (15 g) brown butter over each portion.

Per serving: Calories, 550; Protein, 31 g; Fat, 38 g (63% cal.); Cholesterol, 165 mg; Carbohydrates, 19 g; Fiber, 1 g; Sodium, 380 mg.

Note: Quantities given for breading materials are only guidelines. You may need more or less, depending on the shapes of the meat pieces, the care used in breading, and other factors. In any case, you will need enough so even the last piece to be breaded can be coated easily and completely.

Veal Cutlet, Viennese-Style

VARIATIONS

Veal Cutlet Sauté Gruyère

Top each cooked cutlet with 1 or 2 thin slices of tomato and 1 slice of Gruyère cheese. Pass under a broiler to melt cheese. Serve with tomato sauce placed under the cutlet or in a ribbon (cordon) around the cutlet.

Schnitzel à la Holstein

Top each portion with a fried egg and 4 anchovy fillets placed around the edge of the egg.

Veal Cutlet Viennese-Style (Wiener Schnitzel)

Top each cutlet with 1 peeled lemon slice and 1 anchovy fillet rolled around a caper. Garnish the plate with chopped hard-cooked egg white, sieved egg yolk, and chopped parsley.

Veal Parmigiana

Top each cutlet with 2 fl oz (60 mL) tomato sauce, 1 slice of mozzarella cheese, and 2 tbsp (30 mL) parmesan cheese. Pass under a broiler to melt cheese.

Veal Cordon Bleu

Use 2 thin 2-oz (60-g) cutlets per portion. Sandwich 1 thin slice ham and 1 thin slice of Swiss cheese between 2 cutlets. Pound edges lightly to seal. Bread and fry as in basic recipe.

Breaded Pork Cutlets

Cutlets from pork leg or loin may be breaded and pan-fried like veal. They must be cooked well done.

Veal Scaloppine alla Marsala

PORTIONS: 10 PORTION SIZE: 4 OZ (125 G)

U.S.	METRIC	INGREDIENTS
2½ lb	1.25 kg	Small veal scaloppine: 20 pieces, 2 oz (60 g) each (See **Figure 5.15** for preparation of veal)
to taste	to taste	Salt
to taste	to taste	White pepper
for dredging	for dredging	Flour
2 fl oz	60 mL	Oil

PROCEDURE

1. Lightly flatten each piece of veal with a meat mallet. Do not pound hard, or you may tear the meat.
2. Dry the meat, season it with salt and pepper, and dredge it in flour. Shake off excess. (Do not do this step until immediately before cooking.)
3. Heat the oil in a large sauté pan until very hot. Add the veal and sauté over high heat just until lightly browned on both sides. (If necessary, sauté the meat in several batches.)
4. Remove the meat from the pan and drain the excess oil.

U.S.	METRIC	INGREDIENTS
4 fl oz	125 mL	Marsala wine
8 fl oz	250 mL	Strong white stock, veal or chicken (see Note)
2 oz	60 g	Butter, cut in pieces
2 tbsp	30 mL	Chopped parsley

5. Add the Marsala to the pan and deglaze.
6. Add the stock and reduce over high heat by about half.
7. Add the pieces of butter and swirl the pan until they are melted and blended with the sauce.
8. Add the veal to the pan and bring just to the simmer. Turn the meat to coat it with the sauce.
9. Serve immediately, 2 pieces per portion, sprinkled with chopped parsley.

Per serving: Calories, 360; Protein, 27 g; Fat, 26 g (65% cal.); Cholesterol, 115 mg; Carbohydrates, 2 g; Fiber, 0 g; Sodium, 120 mg.

Note: Brown sauce may be used instead of white stock. However, the white stock makes a more delicate product without masking the flavor of the veal.

VARIATIONS

Veal Scaloppine with Sherry

Substitute sherry for the Marsala.

Veal Scaloppine à la Crème

Prepare as in basic recipe, but omit the wine. Deglaze the pan with the stock. Add 1 cup (250 mL) heavy cream and reduce until thickened. Omit the butter. Season the sauce with a few drops of lemon juice. Taste carefully for salt.

Veal Scaloppine with Lemon

Substitute 3 fl oz (90 mL) lemon juice for the 4 fl oz (125 mL) wine. After plating, top each piece of veal with 1 lemon slice and sprinkle with chopped parsley.

Veal Scaloppine with Mushrooms and Cream

Prepare as for Veal Scaloppine à la Crème, but sauté ½ lb (250 g) sliced mushrooms in butter in the sauté pan before deglazing.

Pork Chops Charcutière

PORTIONS: 24 PORTION SIZE: 6 OZ (175 G) CHOP, 2 FL OZ (60 ML) SAUCE

U.S.	METRIC	INGREDIENTS	PROCEDURE
24	24	Pork chops, 6 oz (170 g) each	1. Trim excess fat from chops if necessary.
as needed	as needed	Oil	2. Add enough oil to a skillet, sauté pan, or griddle to make a thin film. Heat over moderate heat. 3. Place the chops in the hot pan or on the griddle and cook until browned and about half done. Turn over and cook until well done and browned on the second side.
1½ qt	1.5 L	Charcutière Sauce	4. Place the chops on hot dinner plates for service (or place them in a hotel pan if they must be held). 5. Spoon a ribbon of sauce (2 oz/60 mL) around each plated chop.

Per serving: Calories, 260; Protein, 28 g; Fat, 13 g (46% cal.); Cholesterol, 90 mg; Carbohydrates, 4 g; Fiber, 0 g; Sodium, 180 mg.

Sautéed Veal Chop; Zucchini with Tomatoes

VARIATIONS

Pork Chops Robert

Use Robert Sauce instead of charcutière sauce.

Pork Chops Piquante

Use Piquante Sauce instead of charcutière sauce.

Veal Chops

These may be cooked by the same basic procedure and served with an appropriate sauce, such as a well-seasoned demi-glace or a mixture of demi-glace and cream. Other suggestions; Ivory Sauce, Hungarian Sauce, Mushroom Sauce (white), Aurora Sauce.

Beef Stroganoff

PORTIONS: 10 PORTION SIZE: 6 OZ (180 G)

U.S.	METRIC	INGREDIENTS	PROCEDURE
2 oz	60 g	Clarified butter	1. Heat the butter in a sauté pan and sauté the onion and mushrooms briefly without letting them brown.
4 oz	120 g	Onion, brunoise	2. Add the white wine. Reduce by half over high heat.
8 oz	240 g	Mushrooms, sliced	3. Stir in the tomato paste and mustard, and then add the demi-glace. Reduce over high heat until lightly thickened.
2 fl oz	60 mL	White wine	4. Stir in the sour cream. Season to taste with salt and pepper.
1 oz	30 g	Tomato paste	5. Keep the sauce hot in a bain-marie.
2 tsp	10 mL	Prepared mustard	
1½ pt	720 mL	Demi-glace	
10 fl oz	300 mL	Sour cream	
to taste	to taste	Salt	
to taste	to taste	Pepper	
2 fl oz	60 mL	Vegetable oil	6. Heat the oil in a sauté pan over high heat until almost to the smoke point. Sauté the beef quickly, until well browned but not overcooked. It should still be slightly pink inside. If necessary, sauté in several batches or in more than one pan to avoid overcrowding the pan.
2½ lb	1.2 kg	Beef tenderloin, trimmed of all fat, cut into thin strips about 1½ × 1 in. (4 × 2.5 cm) (see Note)	7. Remove the meat from the pan and discard excess fat.
			8. Add the sour cream sauce to the pan and bring to a simmer. Stir in the meat and adjust the seasonings.
			9. Serve immediately with noodles or spaetzle.

Per serving: Calories, 410; Protein, 28 g; Fat, 29 g (7% cal.); Cholesterol, 120 mg; Carbohydrates, 7 g; Fiber, 1 g; Sodium, 160 mg.

Note: Trimmings and ends left after cutting steaks from the center portion of the tenderloin are usually used for this dish. Less tender cuts of beef may be used if the meat is simmered in the sauce until tender. The item will then be braised rather than sautéed.

Beef Stroganoff

Calf's Liver Lyonnaise

PORTIONS: 10 PORTION SIZE: 1 SLICE LIVER, 1½ OZ (50 G) ONION GARNISH

U.S.	METRIC	INGREDIENTS	PROCEDURE
2 lb	1 kg	Onions	1. Peel and slice the onions.
3 oz	90 g	Butter	2. Heat the butter in a sauté pan and add the onions. Sauté them over medium heat until tender and golden brown.
1 cup	250 mL	Demi-glace or strong brown stock	3. Add the demi-glace or stock and cook a few minutes, until the onions are nicely glazed. Season to taste.
to taste	to taste	Salt	4. Place in a bain-marie and keep warm for service.
to taste	to taste	Pepper	
10 slices	10 slices	Calf's liver, ½ in. (6 mm) thick, about 4 oz (125 g) each	5. Season the liver and dredge in flour. Shake off excess flour.
as needed	as needed	Salt	6. Pan-fry the liver in butter or oil over moderate heat until browned on both sides and slightly firm to the touch. Do not overcook or use high heat.
as needed	as needed	Pepper	7. Serve each portion with 1½ oz (45 g) onion mixture.
as needed	as needed	Flour	
as needed	as needed	Clarified butter or oil	

Per serving: Calories, 310; Protein, 24 g; Fat, 19 g (54% cal); Cholesterol, 445 mg; Carbohydrates, 13 g; Fiber, 1 g; Sodium, 250 mg.

Calf's Liver Lyonnaise

Sautéed Veal Sweetbreads with Shiitake Mushrooms and Port Wine Sauce

PORTIONS: 10 PORTION SIZE: 4 OZ (125 G) SWEETBREADS, PLUS SAUCE AND GARNISH

U.S.	METRIC	INGREDIENTS
2½ lb	1.25 kg	Sweetbreads, blanched, trimmed, and pressed according to the procedure on p. 147
to taste	to taste	Salt
to taste	to taste	Pepper
as needed	as needed	Flour
as needed	as needed	Clarified butter

PROCEDURE

1. Slice the sweetbreads in half horizontally.
2. Season the sweetbreads with salt and pepper. Dredge them with flour and shake off the excess.
3. Heat butter in a sauté pan over moderately high heat. Sauté the sweetbreads until golden brown on both sides. Place on hot dinner plates.

U.S.	METRIC	INGREDIENTS
as needed	as needed	Clarified butter
1¼ lb	625 g	Shiitake mushrooms, caps only, cut into strips
to taste	to taste	Salt
to taste	to taste	Pepper
1 pt	500 mL	Port Wine Sauce

4. Heat additional butter in the sauté pan and quickly sauté the mushrooms over high heat just until tender, about 1 minute. Add salt and pepper to taste.
5. Spoon the sauce around (not over) the sweetbreads. Distribute the mushrooms around the sweetbreads.
6. Serving suggestion: A green vegetable, such as small green beans, makes a good complement to the plate.

Per serving: Calories, 330; Protein, 23 g; Fat, 16 g (43% cal.); Cholesterol, 340 mg; Carbohydrates, 17 g; Fiber, 1 g; Sodium, 270 mg.

VARIATION

Instead of dredging the sweetbreads in flour, bread them using the Standard Breading Procedure. Omit the port wine sauce and top each portion with a little beurre noisette.

Sautéed Veal Sweetbreads with Shiitake Mushrooms and Port Wine Sauce

Simmering

Meats are not often simmered. Part of the reason simmered meats are not as popular as meats cooked in other ways may be that they lack the kind of flavor produced by browning with dry heat.

However, simmering is used effectively for less tender cuts for which browning is not desired or not appropriate. Popular examples of simmered meats are cured products such as ham and corned beef, fresh or cured tongue, fresh beef brisket, and white stews such as veal blanquette.

The term ***stewing*** means cooking small pieces of meat by simmering or braising (a composite method that includes both browning and simmering). Stews cooked by braising are covered in the next section. See also the discussion of stewing and braising on pages 182–183.

One difference between stews and many other simmered meats is that stews are served in a sauce or gravy made of the cooking liquid.

This section also contains a recipe for short ribs cooked sous vide. Although this is not a standard simmering method, it is included here because no dry heat is used except for finishing, and the meat cooks in its own moisture.

Liquids and Flavoring Ingredients for Simmered Meats

The kind of meat to be cooked determines the kind and amount of cooking liquid to use as well as the flavorings and seasonings to use.

- *For fresh meats,* use enough liquid to cover the meat completely, but don't use too much, as flavors will be diluted. Water is the main cooking liquid, but other liquids, such as wine, can be added to flavor the meat. Use herbs, spices, and a generous amount of mirepoix to give a good flavor to the meat.
- *For cured meats,* especially those that are heavily salted or smoked, use a generous amount of water to help draw excess salt or smoky flavor from the meat. In some cases, such as country hams, the water may even have to be changed during cooking to remove salt from the meat. Heavily seasoned cured meats, such as corned beef, are often simmered in pure, unseasoned water, but milder cured meats may be simmered with mirepoix and herbs. Do not add salt, however, because cured meats already contain a great deal of salt.

Basic Procedure for Simmering Meats

1. Collect all equipment and food supplies.
2. Prepare meat for cooking. This may include cutting, trimming, tying, or blanching.
3. Prepare the cooking liquid:
   - For fresh meats, start with boiling liquid, usually seasoned.
   - For cured and smoked meats, start with cold, unsalted liquid to help draw out some of the salt from the meats.
   - For both kinds of meats, use enough liquid to cover the meat completely.
   - Add mirepoix and seasonings as desired. (See the discussion of seasonings and flavorings above.)
4. Place the meat in the cooking liquid and return (or bring) to a boil.
5. Reduce heat to a simmer and skim the surface. Meat must never boil for any length of time. Simmering yields a more tender, juicier product than boiling.
6. Simmer until the meat is tender, skimming as necessary. To test for doneness, insert a kitchen fork into the meat. The meat is tender if the fork slides out easily. This is called *fork tender.*
7. If the meat is to be served cold, cool it in its cooking liquid to retain moistness. Cool rapidly in a cold-water bath, as for stocks.

New England Boiled Dinner

PORTIONS: 16 PORTION SIZE: 3 OZ (90 G) MEAT, PLUS ASSORTED VEGETABLES

U.S.	METRIC	INGREDIENTS	PROCEDURE
5½ lb	2.75 kg	Corned beef brisket	1. Trim excess fat from corned beef if necessary. 2. Place the beef in a stockpot or steam kettle. Cover with cold water. 3. Bring to a boil and reduce heat to a simmer. Simmer until the meat feels tender when pierced with a fork. Cooking time will be 2–3 hours. 4. To hold and serve hot, place the cooked meat in a steam-table pan and add some of the cooking liquid to keep it moist.
2 heads	2 heads	Green cabbage	5. Prepare the vegetables: Cut each cabbage into 8 wedges; pare the turnips and carrots and cut them into serving-size pieces; peel the onions; scrub the beets and potatoes.
2 lb	1 kg	Turnips	6. Cook the cabbage, turnips, carrots, onions, and potatoes separately in a little of the beef cooking liquid.
2 lb	1 kg	Carrots	7. Steam the beets, then peel them.
48	48	Pearl onions	
32	32	Baby beets	
32	32	Small red-skinned potatoes	
as needed	as needed	Horseradish Sauce or prepared horseradish	8. To serve, cut the meat across the grain into slices, holding the knife at an angle to get broader slices. Serve with horseradish sauce or prepared horseradish.

Per serving: Calories, 700; Protein, 35 g; Fat, 26 g (46% cal.); Cholesterol, 75 mg; Carbohydrates, 81 g; Fiber, 17 g; Sodium, 2240 mg.

VARIATION

To serve the corned beef cold, cool the beef in some of its cooking liquid, to keep it moist, in a cold-water bath. When cool, remove from the liquid and refrigerate, covered. Cold corned beef may be reheated in its cooking liquid.

New England Boiled Dinner

Blanquette of Veal

PORTIONS: 25 PORTION SIZE: 5 OZ (150 G)

U.S.	METRIC	INGREDIENTS
10 lb	5 kg	Boneless, trimmed veal breast, shoulder, or shank
1	1	Medium onion stuck with 2 cloves
1	1	Bouquet garni
4 tsp	20 mL	Salt
2½ qt (approximately)	2.5 L (approximately)	White veal stock
		Roux:
4 oz	125 g	Butter, clarified
4 oz	125 g	Flour
		Liaison:
5	5	Egg yolks
1 pt	500 mL	Heavy cream
to taste	to taste	Lemon juice
pinch	pinch	Nutmeg
pinch	pinch	White pepper

PROCEDURE

1. Cut the veal into 1-in. (2.5- cm) dice.
2. Blanch the meat: Place in a saucepot and cover with cold water. Bring to a boil, drain, and rinse the meat under cold water (see Note).
3. Return the meat to the pot and add the onion stuck with cloves, bouquet garni, and salt.
4. Add enough stock to just cover the meat.
5. Bring to a boil, skim, cover, and lower heat to a slow simmer.
6. Simmer until meat is tender, about 1½ hours. Skim when necessary.
7. Strain the stock into another pan. Reserve the meat and discard the onion and bouquet garni.
8. Reduce the stock to about 2⅔ pt (1.25 L).
9. Meanwhile, prepare a white roux with the butter and flour. Beat into the stock to make a velouté sauce and simmer until thickened and no raw flour taste remains.
10. Remove the sauce from the heat. Beat the egg yolks and cream together, temper with a little of the hot sauce, and stir into the sauce.
11. Combine the sauce and meat. Heat gently; do not boil.
12. Season to taste with a few drops of lemon juice, a pinch of nutmeg and white pepper, and more salt if needed.

Per serving: Calories, 350; Protein, 35 g; Fat, 21 g (55% cal.); Cholesterol, 230 mg; Carbohydrates, 4 g; Fiber, 0 g; Sodium, 550 mg.

Note: Blanching eliminates impurities that discolor the sauce. This step can be omitted, but the product will have a less attractive appearance.

VARIATIONS

Blanquette of Lamb

Prepare as in basic recipe, using lamb shoulder or shank. If desired, use white lamb stock.

Blanquette of Pork

Prepare as in basic recipe, using pork shoulder or butt. If desired, use white pork stock.

Irish Lamb Stew

PORTIONS: 16 PORTION SIZE: 8 OZ (250 G) MEAT, VEGETABLES, AND BROTH

U.S.	METRIC	INGREDIENTS
3½ lb	1.75 kg	Lean, boneless lamb shoulder or shanks
3 pt (approximately)	1.5 L (approximately)	Water or white lamb stock
1	1	Small onion stuck with 2 cloves
		Sachet:
1	1	Bay leaf
1 clove	1 clove	Garlic
4	4	Whole peppercorns
6	6	Parsley stems
¼ tsp	1 mL	Dried thyme
to taste	to taste	Salt
1 lb	500 g	Onions, sliced thin
8 oz	250 g	Leeks (white part), sliced
2 lb	1 kg	Potatoes, peeled and sliced thin
as needed	as needed	Chopped parsley

PROCEDURE

1. Cut meat into 1-in. (2½ -cm) cubes.
2. Bring the water to a boil in a large, heavy saucepot. Add the lamb. There should be just enough liquid to cover the meat; add more liquid if necessary.
3. Return to a boil, reduce heat to a simmer, and skim the scum carefully.
4. Add the onion stuck with cloves, the sachet ingredients tied in a piece of cheesecloth, and salt to taste. Simmer 1 hour.
5. Add the onions, leeks, and potatoes. Continue to simmer until the meat is tender and the vegetables are cooked. The potatoes should break down somewhat and thicken the stew.
6. Remove and discard the sachet and the onion stuck with cloves. Correct the seasoning.
7. Garnish each portion with chopped parsley.

Per serving: Calories, 200; Protein, 18 g; Fat, 7 g (33% cal.); Cholesterol, 60 mg; Carbohydrates, 14 g; Fiber, 2 g; Sodium, 55 mg.

VARIATION

Carrots and white turnips may be cooked with the stew or cooked separately and added as a garnish.

Shredded Pork (Carnitas)

YIELD: ABOUT 3½ LB (1.6 KG)

U.S.	METRIC	INGREDIENTS
6 lb	2.8 kg	Pork butt or shoulder, boned
1	1	Onion, medium, cut in half
1	1	Garlic clove, chopped
1 tbsp	15 mL	Salt
¼ tsp	1 mL	Pepper
1 tsp	5 mL	Dried oregano
1 tsp	5 mL	Cumin seeds

Per ounces: Calories, 390; Protein, 31 g; Fat, 28 g (67% cal.); Cholesterol, 120 mg; Carbohydrates, 0 g; Fiber, 0 g; Sodium 590 mg.

PROCEDURE

1. Remove most of the large chunks of fat from the pork, leaving a little of it on. Cut the meat into strips measuring 1 × 2 in. (2.5 × 5 cm).
2. Put the pork in a large pot with the rest of the ingredients. Add water to barely cover the meat.
3. Bring to a boil, reduce heat, and simmer slowly, uncovered, until all the liquid has evaporated. By this time, the meat should be tender. If it is not, add more water and continue to cook until it is.
4. Remove the onion and discard it.
5. Lower the heat and let the meat cook in the rendered fat, stirring from time to time, until browned and very tender. Shred the meat slightly.
6. Serve as a snack, an appetizer, or a filling for tortillas, either as it is or moistened with any of the sauces in this section or with guacamole.

VARIATIONS

Picadillo

Add a little extra water to the basic recipe so some liquid is left when the meat is tender. Drain and degrease the liquid and use it to make Tomato Broth for Chiles Rellenos. Heat 3 oz (90 g) oil or lard and sauté 6 oz (175 g) onion, medium dice, and 4 cloves garlic, chopped. Add the meat and a sachet containing 10 peppercorns, 1 small cinnamon stick, and 6 cloves, and brown slowly. Add 4 oz (125 g) raisins, 4 oz (125 g) slivered almonds, and 2 lb (900 g) peeled, seeded, chopped tomatoes. Cook slowly until almost dry. Serve as is or as a stuffing for Chiles Rellenos.

Shortcut Picadillo

Instead of preparing Shredded Pork, use 5 lb (2.3 kg) raw ground pork. Sauté it with the onion and garlic in the picadillo recipe, then proceed as directed with the rest of the recipe.

Beef Short Ribs Sous Vide with Bordelaise Sauce

PORTIONS: 1 PORTION SIZE: 5 OZ (150 G)

U.S.	METRIC	INGREDIENTS	PROCEDURE
5 oz to taste to taste	150 g to taste to taste	Beef short ribs, boneless, in one piece Salt Pepper	1. Review the guidelines for safe sous vide cooking. 2. Season the meat with salt and pepper. Place the meat in a plastic bag appropriate for sous vide cooking and seal it under vacuum. 3. Place the sealed meat in a hot bain-marie set at 158°F (70°C) and cook 20 hours. At the end of cooking time, the interior of the meat should be 158°F (70°C). 4. If the meat is not to be finished and served immediately, chill it as quickly as possible in an ice bain-marie or blast cooler. The interior of the meat must reach 37°F (3°C) or colder in less than 90 minutes.
as needed 1 fl oz	as needed 30 mL	Oil Bordelaise Sauce; omit the marrow garnish)	5. For finishing and serving, rewarm the meat, still sealed in its plastic bag, in a warm bain-marie at 140°F (60°C). 6. Open the bag and remove the meat. 7. Heat a thin film of oil in a sauté pan. Brown the meat lightly on top and bottom. 8. Serve the meat with the sauce around it.

Per serving: Calories, 290; Protein, 21 g; Fat, 22 g (3% cal.); Cholesterol, 70 mg; Carbohydrates, 2 g; Fiber, 0 g; Sodium, 60 mg.

Beef Short Ribs Sous Vide with Bordelaise Sauce

Braising

Braising is a combination of dry-heat and moist-heat cooking methods. Meats are first browned or seared in fat or in a hot oven, then simmered in a flavorful liquid until tender.

The popularity of properly braised items is due to the flavor imparted by the browning and by the sauce made from the braising liquid. Clearly, the quality of a braised meat depends greatly on the quality of the stock the meat is cooked in. Other liquids used in braising include wine, marinades, tomato products, and, occasionally, water.

Popular Types of Braised Meat Dishes

1. **Large cuts.**
   Large cuts of meat braised whole, sliced, and served with a sauce or gravy are sometimes called ***pot roasts***.

2. **Individual portion cuts.**
   Meats may be cut into portion sizes before braising instead of afterward. When portion cuts of beef round are braised in a brown sauce, the process is sometimes called *swissing*, and the product is called ***Swiss steak***.

   Other braised portion-cut meats include short ribs, lamb shanks, and pork chops.

3. **Stews.**

Stews are made of meats cut into small pieces or cubes. Most stews are made by braising, but some are cooked by simmering only, without first browning or searing the meat.

Stews are usually made with enough liquid or gravy to cover the meat completely while cooking. However, so-called dry stews are braised in their own juices or in a very little added liquid.

Brown stews are made by browning the meat thoroughly before simmering. A ***fricassée*** (free kah say) is a white stew made by cooking white meat in fat over low heat without letting it brown, then adding liquid. Compare this to a ***blanquette*** (blawn ket), which is a white stew made by simmering the meat in stock without first cooking it in fat. The cooking method for blanquettes, therefore, is simmering rather than braising.

Note: This use of the term *fricassée* is its traditional or classical usage. Today the word is used for many kinds of stews.

Many other dishes can be classified as braised stews, even if we don't normally think of them that way. Chili, for example, is a braised dish made of finely cut or ground beef or pork. Even meat sauce for spaghetti is actually a braised meat or a stew.

Many chefs prefer to use the term *braising* only for large cuts of meat, and they use the term *stewing* for small cuts. However, the basic cooking method—using first dry heat, then moist heat—is the same for both large and small cuts. (Review the discussion of stews on pages 177–178.)

Guidelines for Braising Meats

The basic principle of braising is a combination of searing or browning and then simmering. This process accomplishes two things: *it cooks the meat*, and *it produces a sauce*. (You will use some of your sauce-making techniques when you braise meats.)

Before giving basic procedures that apply to most popular braised meats, we discuss factors that affect the quality of the finished product.

1. **Seasoning.**

The meat may be seasoned before browning, or it may receive its seasonings from the cooking liquid while braising. But remember that salt on the surface of meat retards browning. Also, herbs may burn in the high heat necessary for browning.

Marinating the meat for several hours or even several days before browning is an effective way to season meat because the seasonings have time to penetrate it. The marinade is often included as part of the braising liquid.

2. **Browning.**

Dry the meat thoroughly before browning. Small pieces for stew may be dredged in flour for better browning. In general, red meats are well browned; white meats are browned less heavily, usually until they are golden.

3. **Amount of braising liquid.**

The amount of liquid to be added depends on the type of preparation and on the amount of sauce required for serving. Do not use more liquid than necessary, or the flavors will be less rich and less concentrated.

Pot roasts usually require about 2 oz (60 mL) sauce per portion, and this determines the amount of liquid needed. The size of the braising pot used should allow the liquid to cover the meat by one-third to two-thirds.

Stews usually require enough liquid to cover the meat.

Some items are braised with no added liquid. They are browned, then covered, and the item cooks in its own moisture, which is trapped by the pan lid. Pork chops are frequently cooked in this way. If roasted, sautéed, or pan-fried items are covered during cooking, they become, in effect, braised items.

4. **Vegetable garnish.**

Vegetables to be served with the meat may be cooked along with the meat or cooked separately and added before service.

If the first method is used, the vegetables should be added just long enough before the end of cooking for them to be cooked through but not overcooked.

5. **Adjusting the sauce.**

Braising liquids may be thickened by a roux either before cooking (Method 2) or after cooking (Method 1). In some preparations, the liquid is left unthickened or is naturally thick, such as tomato sauce.

In any case, the sauce may require further adjustment of its consistency by

- Reducing.
- Thickening with roux, beurre manié, or other thickening agent.
- The addition of a prepared sauce, such as demi-glace or velouté.

Basic Procedures for Braising Meats

Method 1: Braising in Unthickened Liquid

1. Collect all equipment and food supplies.
2. Cut or trim the meat as required. Dry it thoroughly. For stews, the meat may be dredged with flour.
3. Brown the meat thoroughly on all sides in a heavy pan with a small amount of fat, or in an oven.
4. Remove the meat from the pan and brown mirepoix in the fat left in the pan.
5. Return the meat to the pan and add the required amount of liquid.
6. Add a sachet or other seasonings and flavorings.
7. Bring the liquid to a simmer, cover the pot tightly, and simmer in the oven or on top of the range until the meat is tender.

   Oven braising provides more uniform heat. Temperatures of 250° to 300°F (120° to 150°C) are sufficient to maintain a simmer. Do not let boil.
8. Remove the meat from the pan and keep it warm.
9. Prepare a sauce or gravy from the braising liquid. This usually includes the following:
   - Skim fat.
   - Prepare a brown roux with this fat or with another fat if desired.
   - Thicken the braising liquid with the roux. Simmer until the roux is cooked thoroughly.
   - Strain and adjust seasonings.
10. Combine the meat (sliced or whole) with the sauce.

Method 2: Braising in Thickened Liquid

1. Collect all equipment and food supplies.
2. Prepare the meat for cooking, as required.
3. Brown the meat thoroughly in a heavy pan with fat or in a hot oven.
4. Remove the meat from the pan (if required) and brown mirepoix in remaining fat.
5. Add flour to make a roux. Brown the roux.
6. Add stock to make a thickened sauce. Add seasonings and flavorings.
7. Return the meat to the pan. Cover and simmer in the oven or on the range until the meat is tender.
8. Adjust the sauce as necessary (strain, season, reduce, dilute, etc.).

Method 3: Classic Fricassées

1. Follow Method 2, *except:*
   - Do not brown the meat. Cook it gently in the fat without browning.
   - Add flour to the meat in the pan and make a blond roux.
2. Finish the sauce with a liaison of egg yolks and cream.

Figure 6.3 Preparing braised meats.

(a) Brown the meat well in a heavy pan.

(b) Remove the meat from the pan. Add the mirepoix to the pan and brown well.

(c) Add flour to the mirepoix. Stir to combine the flour with the fat and brown the roux.

(d) Add stock to the pan and whip to combine with the roux. Add seasonings and flavorings and return the meat to the pan. For portion cuts, there should be just enough liquid to cover the meat.

KEY POINTS TO REVIEW

- What are the steps in the basic procedure for simmering meats?
- What are the three basic procedures for braising meats? How are they alike, and how are they different?

Beef Pot Roast

PORTIONS: 25 PORTION SIZE: 4 OZ (125 G) MEAT, 2 FL OZ (60 ML) SAUCE

U.S.	METRIC	INGREDIENTS
10 lb	5 kg	Beef bottom round, well trimmed (see Note)
4 fl oz	125 mL	Oil
		Mirepoix:
8 oz	250 g	Onion, medium dice
4 oz	125 g	Celery, medium dice
4 oz	125 g	Carrot, medium dice
6 oz	175 g	Tomato purée
		or
12 oz	375 g	Tomatoes, canned
2½ qt	2.5 L	Brown stock
		Sachet:
1	1	Bay leaf
pinch	pinch	Dried thyme
6	6	Peppercorns
1	1	Garlic clove
4 oz	125 g	Flour

PROCEDURE

1. Dry the meat so it will brown more easily. Heat the oil in a brazier over high heat and brown the meat well on all sides. Remove from pan. (*Alternative method:* Brown meat in a very hot oven.)
2. Add the mirepoix to the brazier and brown it.
3. Add the tomato product, the stock, and the sachet. Bring to a boil, cover, and place in an oven preheated to 300°F (150°C), or just hot enough to maintain a simmer.
4. Braise the meat until tender, 2–3 hours.
5. Remove meat from pan and keep warm for service in a covered pan. Discard sachet. (See alternative method of service given below.)
6. Skim the fat from the braising liquid and reserve 4 oz (125 g) of it.
7. Make a brown roux with the flour and the reserved fat. Cool the roux slightly.
8. Bring the braising liquid to a simmer and beat in the roux. Simmer the sauce at least 15–20 minutes, or until thickened and reduced slightly.
9. Strain the sauce and adjust the seasonings.
10. Slice the meat across the grain. The slices should not be too thick. Serve each 4-oz (125-g) portion with 2 fl oz (60 mL) sauce.

Per serving: Calories, 320; Protein, 38 g; Fat, 15 g (45% cal.); Cholesterol, 90 mg; Carbohydrates, 4 g; Fiber, 0 g; Sodium, 70 mg.

Note: Other cuts of beef from the round, or from the chuck or brisket, may be used instead of bottom round. Braised round makes the best slices, but it tends to be dry. Chuck and brisket are moister when braised because they have a higher fat content.

For quicker, more uniform cooking and easier handling, cut meats for braising into 5–7 lb (2–3 kg) pieces.

VARIATIONS

Alternative Method of Service: Cool beef as soon as it is cooked. For service, slice cold meat on an electric slicer and arrange in hotel pans. Add sauce, cover pans, and reheat in oven or steamer. Individual portions may also be reheated to order in the sauce.

Braised Beef Jardinière

Garnish the finished product with 1 lb (500 g) each carrots, celery, and turnips, all cut bâtonnet and boiled separately, and 1 lb (500 g) pearl onions, boiled and sautéed until brown.

Braised Lamb Shoulder

Prepare boned, rolled shoulder of lamb according to the basic recipe. Use either regular brown stock or brown lamb stock.

Braised Short Ribs

PORTIONS: 25 PORTION SIZE: 10 OZ (300 G) MEAT WITH BONE, 2 FL OZ (60 ML) SAUCE

U.S.	METRIC	INGREDIENTS
25	25	Short rib sections, 10 oz (300 g) each
8 oz	250 mL	Oil
10 oz	300 g	Onion, medium dice
5 oz	150 g	Celery, medium dice
5 oz	150 g	Carrot, medium dice
5 oz	150 g	Bread flour
2½ qt	2.5 L	Brown stock
5 oz	150 mL	Tomato purée
2	2	Bay leaves
to taste	to taste	Salt
to taste	to taste	Pepper

Per serving: Calories, 299; Protein, 29 g; Fat, 17 g (52% cal.); Cholesterol, 55 mg; Carbohydrates, 6 g; Fiber, 0 g; Sodium, 70 mg.

PROCEDURE

1. Dry the meat so it will brown more easily.
2. Heat the oil in a heavy brazier until very hot. Brown the meat well on both sides. Remove it and set aside.
3. Add the onion, celery, and carrot to the fat in the pan and sauté until browned.
4. Stir in the bread flour to make a roux. Cook until the roux is browned.
5. Stir in the stock and tomato purée and simmer until the sauce thickens. Add the bay leaves and season to taste with salt and pepper.
6. Return the short ribs to the pan. Cover and braise in the oven at 300°F (150°C) until tender, about 2 hours.
7. Transfer the short ribs to a hotel pan for service.
8. Strain the sauce (optional). Degrease. Adjust the seasoning and consistency and pour over the short ribs.

VARIATIONS

Short ribs and the variations that follow may be braised in a prepared brown sauce or espagnole instead of a specially made sauce. Omit steps 4, 5, and 6.

If desired, use 1 lb (500 g) chopped canned tomatoes instead of the purée. Alternatively, use 2 oz (55 g) tomato paste; add the paste to the browned mirepoix and continue to brown until the paste turns a rusty brown color.

Swiss Steak

Instead of the short ribs, use beef round steaks, about 5 oz (150 g) per portion. Omit celery and carrot if desired.

Swiss Steaks in Tomato Sauce

Reduce flour to 2½ oz (75 g). For braising liquid, use 2½ pt (1.25 L) brown stock, 2½ lb (1.25 kg) chopped canned tomatoes with their juice, and 1¼ lb (625 g) tomato purée. Season with bay leaf, oregano, and basil. After removing cooked steaks, reduce sauce to desired consistency. Do not strain. Garnish each portion with chopped parsley.

Swiss Steaks with Sour Cream

Prepare as in the basic Swiss Steak recipe, above. When steaks are cooked, finish the sauce with 1 pt (500 mL) sour cream, 2½ fl oz (75 mL) Worcestershire sauce, and 2 tbsp (30 g) prepared mustard.

Swiss Steaks in Red Wine Sauce

Prepare as in the basic Swiss Steak recipe, above, but add 1 pt (500 mL) dry red wine to the braising liquid.

Braised Oxtails

Allow 1 lb (500 g) oxtails per portion. Cut into sections at joints.

Braised Lamb Shanks

Allow 1 lamb shank per portion. Add chopped garlic to mirepoix if desired.

Braised Short Ribs with Steamed Broccoli and Mashed Potatoes

Beef Stew

PORTIONS: 25 PORTION SIZE: 8 OZ (250 G)

U.S.	METRIC	INGREDIENTS
6 lb	3 kg	Beef chuck, boneless and well trimmed of fat
4 fl oz	125 mL	Oil
1 lb	500 g	Onion, fine dice
2 tsp	10 mL	Chopped garlic
4 oz	125 g	Flour
8 oz	250 g	Tomato purée
2 qt	2 L	Brown stock
		Sachet:
1	1	Bay leaf
pinch	pinch	Thyme
small sprig	small sprig	Celery leaves
1 lb	500 g	Celery, EP
1½ lb	750 g	Carrots, EP
1 lb	500 g	Small pearl onions, EP
8 oz	250 g	Tomatoes, canned, drained, and coarsely chopped
8 oz	250 g	Peas, frozen, thawed
to taste	to taste	Salt
to taste	to taste	Pepper

PROCEDURE

1. Cut the meat into 1-in. (2.5-cm) cubes.
2. Heat the oil in a brazier until very hot. Add the meat and brown well, stirring occasionally to brown all sides. If necessary, brown the meat in several small batches to avoid overcrowding the pan.
3. Add the onion and garlic to the pan and continue to cook until onion is lightly browned.
4. Add the flour to the meat and stir to make a roux. Continue to cook over high heat until the roux is slightly browned.
5. Stir in the tomato purée and stock and bring to a boil. Stir with a kitchen spoon as the sauce thickens.
6. Add the sachet. Cover the pot and place in an oven at 325°F (165°C). Braise until the meat is tender, 1½–2 hours.
7. Cut the celery and carrots into large dice.
8. Cook the celery, carrots, and onions separately in boiling salted water until just tender.
9. When meat is tender, remove the sachet and adjust seasoning. Degrease the sauce.
10. Add celery, carrots, onions, and tomatoes to the stew.
11. Immediately before service, add the peas. Alternatively, garnish the top of each portion with peas. Season with salt and pepper.

Per serving: Calories, 240; Protein, 27 g; Fat, 9 g (34% cal.); Cholesterol, 60 mg; Carbohydrates, 13 g; Fiber, 2 g; Sodium, 150 mg.

Note: For more elegant service, remove the cooked meat from the sauce before adding the vegetables. Strain the sauce and pour it back over the meat.

VARIATIONS

Vegetables for garniture may be varied as desired.

Beef Stew with Red Wine

Prepare as in basic recipe, but use 2½ pt (1.25 L) dry red wine and 1½ pt (750 mL) brown stock instead of 2 qt (2 L) brown stock.

Boeuf Bourguignon

Prepare Beef Stew with Red Wine, using rendered salt pork or bacon fat instead of oil. (Cut the pork into bâtonnet shapes, sauté until crisp, and save the cooked pork for garnish.) Increase garlic to 2 tbsp (30 mL). Omit vegetable garnish (celery, carrots, pearl onions, tomatoes, and peas) indicated in basic recipe, and substitute lardons (cooked salt pork or bacon pieces), small mushroom caps browned in butter, and boiled pearl onions browned in butter. Serve with egg noodles.

Navarin of Lamb (Brown Lamb Stew)

Prepare as in basic recipe, using lamb shoulder instead of beef chuck. Increase garlic to 2 tbsp (30 mL).

Brown Veal Stew

Prepare as in basic recipe, using veal shoulder or shank.

Brown Veal with White Wine

Prepare Brown Veal Stew, replacing 1 pt (500 mL) stock with white wine.

Beef Pot Pie

Fill individual casserole dishes with stew and vegetable garnish. Top with pie pastry. Bake in a hot oven (400°–450°F/200°–225°C) until the crust is brown.

Chile con Carne

PORTIONS: 24 PORTION SIZE: 8 OZ (250 G)

U.S.	METRIC	INGREDIENTS
2½ lb	1.25 kg	Onion, small dice
1¼ lb	625 g	Green bell pepper, small dice
1 oz	30 g	Garlic, chopped
4 fl oz	125 g	Oil
5 lb	2.5 kg	Ground beef
1 No. 10 can	1 No. 10 can	Tomatoes
10 oz	300 g	Tomato paste
2½ pt	1.25 L	Brown stock
3 oz	90 g	Chili powder
to taste	to taste	Salt
to taste	to taste	Pepper

Per serving: Calories, 310; Protein, 20 g; Fat, 19 g (54% cal.); Cholesterol, 55 mg; Carbohydrates, 16 g; Fiber, 4 g; Sodium, 380 mg.

PROCEDURE

1. Sauté the onion, pepper, and garlic in oil in a heavy saucepot until tender but not browned. Remove from the pot.
2. Add the meat to the pot and brown over high heat, breaking it up with a spoon as it browns. Drain off the fat.
3. Return the vegetables to the pot and add the remaining ingredients.
4. Simmer uncovered until the chili is reduced to the desired thickness, 45–60 minutes. Stir occasionally during the cooking period.

VARIATION

Chile with Beans

Add 4 lb (2 kg) (drained weight) cooked or canned and drained kidney beans or pinto beans about 15 minutes before the end of cooking.

Game Chile

In place of the ground beef, use ground bison, venison, elk, caribou, or boar.

Texas Red

YIELD: 6 LB 12 OZ (3 KG) PORTIONS: 12 PORTION SIZE: 9 OZ (250 G)

U.S.	METRIC	INGREDIENTS
6 lb	2.75 kg	Lean beef, preferably chuck or shank, well trimmed
2 fl oz	60 mL	Vegetable oil
1 oz	30 g	Garlic, chopped fine
5 oz	140 g	Chili powder
1½ tbsp	22 mL	Ground cumin
1½ tbsp	22 mL	Dried oregano
1–2 tsp	5–10 mL	Cayenne
2 qt	2 L	Brown stock or beef broth
2 oz	60 g	Cornmeal or masa harina
4 fl oz	120 mL	Cold water
to taste	to taste	Salt

Per serving: Calories, 380; Protein, 46 g; Fat, 16 g (38% cal.); Cholesterol, 90 mg; Carbohydrates, 12 g; Fiber, 5 g; Sodium, 200 mg.

PROCEDURE

1. Cut the beef into 1-in. (2.5-cm) cubes.
2. In a brazier, brown the beef in the vegetable oil over high heat. Brown a little at a time so as not to overcrowd the pan.
3. Add the garlic, chili powder, cumin, oregano, and cayenne to the beef over moderate heat. Stir and cook a few minutes, until the spices are aromatic.
4. Add the stock. Bring to a boil, cover, and place in an oven at 325°F (165°C) for 1½–2 hours, or until the beef is tender.
5. Degrease the cooking liquid carefully.
6. Mix the cornmeal or masa harina with the cold water to make a smooth paste.
7. Stir the cornmeal mixture into the beef mixture.
8. Simmer 30 minutes to thicken the cooking liquid.
9. Season to taste with salt.

VARIATION

Texas Short Ribs

In place of the lean beef, use 7 lb 8 oz (3.4 kg) beef short ribs. After the ribs are tender, remove them from the braising liquid and carefully degrease the liquid. Add just enough cornmeal or masa harina to lightly thicken the liquid, about half the amount in the basic recipe.

Texas Red

Osso Buco

PORTIONS: 12 PORTION SIZE: 1 PIECE, APPROXIMATELY 8 OZ (240 G) COOKED WEIGHT, PLUS 1½ FL OZ (45 ML) SAUCE

U.S.	METRIC	INGREDIENTS	PROCEDURE
12 pieces	12 pieces	Veal shank, cut crosswise into thick slices, about 11 oz (320–350 g) each	1. Tie each piece of veal shank tightly around the circumference to hold the meat to the bone.
to taste	to taste	Salt	2. Lightly season the meat with salt and pepper.
to taste	to taste	Pepper	3. Heat the oil in a brazier just large enough to hold the pieces of veal shank in a single layer.
2 fl oz	60 mL	Vegetable oil	4. Dredge each piece of meat in flour to coat completely, then shake off the excess.
as needed	as needed	Flour	5. Brown the meat on all sides in the oil.
1½ oz	45 g	Clarified butter	6. Remove the meat from the pan and set it aside.
		Mirepoix:	7. Drain off excess oil from the pan, then add the clarified butter.
8 oz	250 g	Onion, small dice	8. Add the mirepoix and garlic. Brown lightly.
4 oz	125 g	Carrot, small dice	
4 oz	125 g	Celery, small dice	
¼ oz	7 g	Garlic, chopped	
8 fl oz	250 ml	Dry white wine	9. Return the meat to the pan and add the white wine. Simmer about 10 minutes.
1 lb	500 g	Canned plum tomatoes, coarsely chopped, with their juice	10. Add the tomatoes, lemon zest, stock, and sachet. Bring to a simmer, cover, and place in an oven at 325°F (160°C). Braise until the meat is very tender, 1½–2 hours.
2–3 strips	2–3 strips	Lemon zest, in wide strips	11. Remove the meat from the pan with a slotted spoon and set aside in a warm place.
1 pt	500 mL	Brown stock	12. Strain and degrease the sauce. Reduce the sauce, if necessary, to about 1½ fl oz (45 mL) per portion. The flour on the meat should have been enough to thicken the sauce to a very light consistency.
		Sachet:	
8	8	Parsley stems	
¼ tsp	1 mL	Dried thyme	
1	1	Bay leaf	
		Gremolada (optional):	13. The traditional but optional seasoning finish for osso buco is called gremolada. Mix together the lemon zest, parsley, garlic, and anchovy. Just before serving, sprinkle the gremolada over the osso buco and turn the meat so it gets an even coating of the mixture.
1½ tsp	7 mL	Grated lemon zest	14. Serve 1 piece of veal shank per portion, along with 1½ fl oz (45 mL) sauce. Osso buco is traditionally served with Risotto Milanese as well.
1½ tbsp	22 mL	Chopped parsley	
½ tsp	2 ml	Garlic, chopped fine	
2	2	Anchovy filets, chopped fine (optional)	

Per serving: Calories, 360; Protein, 42 g; Fat, 14 g (11% cal.); Cholesterol, 170 mg; Carbohydrates, 10 g; Fiber, 2 g; Sodium, 260 mg.

Osso Buco

Hungarian Goulash (Veal, Beef, or Pork)

PORTIONS: 25 PORTION SIZE: 8 OZ (250 G)

U.S.	METRIC	INGREDIENTS	PROCEDURE
7½ lb	3.75 kg	Boneless, lean meat: Veal (shoulder, shank, or breast), beef (chuck), or pork (shoulder or butt)	1. Cut the meat into 1-in. (2.5-cm) cubes. 2. Heat the fat in a brazier and sauté the meat until lightly seared on all sides. 3. Add the onions and sweat over moderate heat. Continue to cook until most of the liquid that forms is reduced. 4. Add the paprika, garlic, and caraway seeds and stir.
5 fl oz	150 mL	Oil, lard, or rendered beef suet	
2½ lb	1.25 kg	Onions, fine dice	
5 tbsp	75 mL	Hungarian paprika	
2 tsp	10 mL	Garlic, crushed	
½ tsp	2 mL	Caraway seeds	
10 oz	300 g	Chopped, drained canned tomatoes or tomato purée	5. Add the tomatoes and stock, cover, and simmer until the meat is almost tender, about 1 hour in the oven (325°F/165°C) or on the range.
2½ qt	2.5 L	White stock	
2½ lb	1.25 kg	Potatoes, medium dice	6. Add the potatoes and continue to cook until the meat and potatoes are tender. 7. The potatoes will thicken the sauce slightly but, if necessary, reduce the sauce a little. Degrease and season to taste. 8. Serve with spaetzle or noodles.
to taste	to taste	Salt	

Per serving: Calories, 250; Protein, 27 g; Fat, 10 g (35% cal.); Cholesterol, 35 mg; Carbohydrates, 14 g; Fiber, 2 g; Sodium, 120 mg.

Rabbit with Mustard

PORTIONS: 8 PORTION SIZE: APPROXIMATELY 8 OZ (250 G), INCLUDING SAUCE

U.S.	METRIC	INGREDIENTS	PROCEDURE
4–5 lb	2 kg	Rabbit	1. Clean and cut up the rabbit for stewing. 2. Brown the rabbit in oil in a heavy pan. 3. Remove the rabbit pieces from the pan and keep them warm. Degrease the pan.
as needed	as needed	Oil	
½ oz	15 g	Butter	4. Add the butter to the pan. Sweat the shallot in the butter, but do not brown. 5. Add the mustard, salt, pepper, thyme, wine, and stock to the pan and return the browned rabbit to the pan. Cover and braise slowly over low heat or in a low oven until the meat is cooked. 6. Remove the rabbit from the liquid and set aside.
1 oz	30 g	Shallot, chopped	
2 oz	60 g	Prepared mustard, Dijon-style or grainy	
to taste	to taste	Salt	
to taste	to taste	Pepper	
¼ tsp	1 mL	Dried thyme	
8 fl oz	250 mL	White wine	
8 fl oz	250 mL	Chicken stock	
8 fl oz	250 mL	Heavy cream	7. Reduce the cooking liquid by about one-third. Skim any excess fat from the top. 8. Temper the heavy cream and add it to the reduced liquid. Simmer and reduce until the sauce is lightly thickened. Adjust the seasonings. Return the rabbit pieces to the sauce.

Per serving: Calories, 450; Protein, 30 g; Fat, 28 g (58% cal.); Cholesterol, 150 mg; Carbohydrates, 2 g; Fiber, 0 g; Sodium, 260 mg.

Saltimbocca alla Romana

PORTIONS: 16 PORTION SIZE: 2 PIECES

U.S.	METRIC	INGREDIENTS
32	32	Veal scaloppine, 1½–2 oz (45–60 g) each
to taste	to taste	Salt
to taste	to taste	White pepper
32	32	Thin slices of prosciutto, about the same diameter as the scaloppine
32	32	Fresh sage leaves
4 oz	125 g	Butter
12 fl oz	350 mL	White wine

Per serving: Calories, 320; Protein, 28 g; Fat, 21 g (60% cal.); Cholesterol, 115 mg; Carbohydrates, 0 g; Fiber, 0 g; Sodium, 800 mg.

PROCEDURE

1. Pound the scaloppine with a cutlet pounder. Season with salt and white pepper. Put 1 slice of prosciutto and 1 sage leaf on top of each and fasten with a toothpick.
2. Sauté briefly in butter on both sides.
3. Add the wine and continue to cook until the meat is done and the wine is partly reduced, no more than 5 minutes.
4. Remove the meat from the pan and serve, ham side up, with a spoonful of the pan juices over each.

TERMS FOR REVIEW

deglaze
stewing
pot roast
Swiss steak
fricassée
blanquette

QUESTIONS FOR DISCUSSION

1. List four advantages of roasting at a low temperature.
2. When might you use high temperatures for roasting?
3. What is the purpose of basting?
4. In the recipe for Home-Style Meatloaf (p. 165), why are the sautéed vegetables cooled after cooking in step 1?
5. Which steaks require the highest broiler heat, thick ones or thin ones? steaks to be cooked rare or steaks to be cooked well done?
6. Why is it important not to overload the pan when sautéing meats?
7. Why is the menu term *boiled beef* inaccurate?

Chapter 7

Slicing gravlax and smoked salmon, page 197.

Sausages and Cured Foods

Sausages have been popular since ancient times. They were first made to utilize and preserve trimmings and less desirable cuts from a meat carcass. Most people have heard the expression about using "every part of the hog except the squeal." The preparation of sausages is an important part of this process.

The French term ***charcutier*** (shar koo tyay; the feminine form is *charcutière* [shar koo tyair]) means "one who prepares and sells pork products." The art of the charcutier is called ***charcuterie*** (shar koo tree). We use this term more generally to refer to the production of sausages, pâtés, smoked ham, and other cured and smoked products.

The main part of this chapter is devoted to the production of fresh sausages, which are easily prepared in any kitchen with relatively simple equipment. We also introduce the subject of cured and smoked sausages with an overview of curing and smoking. Preparing smoked hams and cured, air-dried meat products is an advanced subject beyond the scope of this book. However, reading the first section of this chapter will enable you to understand how these items are produced. A small sampling of recipes gives you some experience with curing and smoking before you proceed to the main section on sausages.

After reading this chapter, you should be able to

1. Prepare simple dry-cured and brine-cured foods.
2. Prepare simple smoked foods.
3. Prepare fresh, cured, and smoked sausages.

Curing and Smoking

Curing and smoking have been important methods for preserving foods, especially protein foods, since prehistoric times. Before the days of modern preservation techniques such as canning, freezing, and refrigeration, curing and smoking, as well as drying, enabled people to store food in times of abundance for use in times of scarcity. Today we use these techniques for their contribution to flavor perhaps even more than for their preservative qualities. We smoke foods because we like the taste, not because we must in order to preserve them.

Nevertheless, it is important to understand how curing works to preserve foods so we can avoid spoilage and food-borne disease that can result from improper curing or improper handling of cured foods.

Ingredients for Curing Foods

Ingredients used in cures fill two main functions: preserving the food, and changing its flavor and texture. The following discussion of cure ingredients and processes is somewhat simplified, but it introduces the most important principles.

Clockwise from top: table salt, curing salt, kosher salt

SALT

Salt has been one of the most important food preservatives throughout most of human history. When a food comes in direct contact with salt, a two-way process takes place in an effort to make the salt concentrations inside and outside the food more nearly equal. Moisture from inside the cell walls of the food is drawn out and dilutes the salt used for the cure. At the same time, dissolved salt is absorbed into the cells to increase the salt concentration there. The result is foods that have less moisture and are saltier. Both the moisture reduction and the increased salt content make the food less hospitable to bacteria that cause spoilage and disease.

Of course, the reduced moisture and the increased salt content also change the flavor and texture of the food.

NITRITES AND NITRATES

Some foods, especially meats, are susceptible to contamination by the bacteria that cause botulism. Nitrites and nitrates are added to the cures for these foods to make them safe from botulism infection. ***Sodium nitrite*** ($NaNO_2$) is the most important of these chemicals. Even in the very small quantities in which it is used, sodium nitrite has strong preservative powers. In addition, it keeps meats red or pink, which is why products like cured ham, corned beef, and certain sausages have their characteristic color.

Nitrites gradually break down inside the cured foods, but by the time they lose their effectiveness, the curing and, in some cases, smoking procedures are finished, the food is cooked or refrigerated, and the food remains safe. On the other hand, when the food is raw and air-dried, as in the case of prosciutto and various salamis, a stronger chemical, ***sodium nitrate*** ($NaNO_3$) is used. Nitrates break down more slowly than nitrites and therefore are effective for a longer time. (Potassium nitrate, or saltpeter, is sometimes used in cures, but it is not as safe and is strongly regulated. It should be avoided.)

Nitrates and nitrites are the subject of controversy regarding their safety. Substances called ***nitrosamines*** form when foods containing nitrates or nitrites are subjected to very high heat, such as when bacon is fried. Nitrosamines are known to cause cancer. Using only nitrites to cure foods usually avoids this problem because the nitrites break down quickly and are not usually a factor when the food is cooked. Nitrates, on the other hand, because they remain in meats longer, should not be used for curing bacon for this reason.

Some people feel that all use of nitrites and nitrates should be avoided because of the nitrosamine factor. However, if only nitrites and not nitrates are used in foods that will be exposed to extreme heat, the risk is low—much lower than the risk of botulism. So far, we know of no adequate substitute for these chemicals in curing pork and other meats.

Two special mixtures are employed that make it easy to add nitrites and nitrates in very low but sufficient concentration:

1. ***Prague Powder #1***, or curing salt, is a blend of 6 percent sodium nitrite and 94 percent sodium chloride, or regular table salt. It is colored pink so it will not be confused with regular salt, and thus it is often called ***tinted curing mix (TCM)***. It is also sold under various trade names, such as InstaCure I.

2. ***Prague Powder #2*** is similar to Prague Powder #1 except that it contains nitrates in addition to nitrites. It is used in curing products that have a long curing and drying period, as explained above. Prague Powder #2 is not used in any of the recipes in this chapter.

Fish and seafood are usually cured without the use of nitrites. Fish is almost always cured under refrigeration, and the salt cure is sufficient to protect it, even when it is cold smoked (p. 196).

The quantity of nitrite to be added to meats depends on several factors, including the type of meat, the type of cure, and the length of curing time. For cooked sausage, the USDA recommends 156 parts nitrite per million parts meat. This is equivalent to 1 ounce (30 g) nitrite per 400 pounds (192 kg) meat. To translate this to quantities similar to those used in this chapter, 10 pounds (4.5 kg) cooked sausage requires about 0.025 ounces (0.7 g) nitrite. This is the amount of nitrite contained in 0.4 ounces or 2 teaspoons (11 g or 10 mL) Prague Powder #1.

Keep in mind, however, that not all the nitrite specified in a recipe may be absorbed into the meat. In the case of the basic dry cures and brine cures (described below), part of the curing medium is discarded after the cure is complete. Therefore, enough nitrite must be used so the portion that is absorbed is adequate for the cure. The only exception is the case of sausages, in which all of the curing medium is mixed directly with the meat. The recipes in this book contain appropriate quantities of nitrite to cure the product.

SUGARS

Ordinary white sugar (sucrose) and other forms of sugar, including corn syrup, honey, and maple syrup, are used in some cures. Sugars modify the flavor of the food and counteract some of the harsh flavor of the highly concentrated salt in the cure. Also, because salt extracts so much moisture, sugar adds to the perception of moistness in the cured product. Using less sweet forms of sugar, such as corn syrup and dextrose, provides the advantages of sugar without adding too much sweetness.

HERBS, SPICES, AND OTHER FLAVORINGS

Nearly any spice or flavoring that can be used in cooking can be used in curing. Traditional recipes, of course, use traditional seasonings. Most of our most familiar cured sausages, for example, are of European origin and use such seasonings as garlic, pepper, coriander, caraway, nutmeg, and dry mustard. Many chefs today are experimenting with unusual ingredients to give a modern accent to cured meats, poultry, fish, and sausages.

Curing Methods

The two basic types of cure are ***dry cures*** and ***brine cures***. With both of these methods, the food item remains in contact with the curing mixture, which contains salt plus any of the other ingredients discussed above, until the curing medium has penetrated the food uniformly. The difference between the methods is that in brines, the salt is dissolved in water, whereas in dry cures, it is not.

DRY CURES

In a dry cure, the cure ingredients (salt, plus seasonings and, in many cases, sugar and Prague Powder) are mixed together and packed or rubbed over the food product to coat it completely. The length of time required to dry-cure meats depends on their thickness. Lean meat 1 inch (2.5 cm) thick requires 3 to 8 hours, while a whole ham needs about 45 days. During a long cure, the food is repeatedly turned and rubbed with the cure mixture in order to maintain uniform contact. It is important that the entire surface area be coated.

The curing procedure for sausages could be considered a dry cure. However, in this case, the cure is mixed directly with the meat. Because no time is required for the cure to penetrate to the center of the meat, the curing process takes place quickly, although the products may be air-dried or smoked for a longer period before being consumed.

BRINE CURES

A brine is a solution of salt and other curing ingredients in water. The simplest way to use a brine is to immerse the meat in the brine and let it soak until the cure is complete. Compared with dry cures, brines are especially useful for poultry items, which are difficult to coat evenly with a dry cure because of their shape. Items that float, such as poultry, must be held down with a weight so they are completely submerged in the brine.

Simple brine soaking is used for small meat items, but because the brine takes time to penetrate to the center of large items such as hams, another method is used to speed the process. Brine is pumped or injected into the meat to make sure it penetrates evenly. After injection, the meat may be soaked in brine as well. Commercial operations use a variety of high-speed equipment for injecting brine. In addition, small pumps are available for brining by hand.

The length of time required for brining depends on the size and thickness of the item. Of course, meats injected with brine need less time in the brine soak.

Fresh brine should be made for each batch of cured meats. Do not reuse brines because they are diluted and contaminated with juices from the first batch of meats.

Smoking

Smoking has been used as a way of drying and preserving foods since prehistoric times. Smoking does have some preservative effects but, for modern cooking, it is more important for the flavors it gives to meats, poultry, and seafood. Even smoked cheeses and vegetables are enjoyed for their special flavors.

The first rule of smoking foods is *do not smoke meats, poultry, and fish that have not been cured.* The reason is a matter of food safety. During smoking, foods spend time in the Food Danger Zone—that is, at a temperature favorable for the growth of bacteria. Without the preservative effects of curing, smoking could be unsafe. (This rule does not apply to *smoke roasting* and *barbecuing*, which are more properly considered cooking methods rather than smoking methods because they take place at higher temperatures.)

After meats, poultry, and fish are cured, they should be allowed to dry slightly before being smoked. So air can circulate all around the foods, place them on racks or hang them from hooks under refrigeration until the surface is dry to the touch. This preliminary drying allows the smoke to penetrate the foods more effectively.

The two basic types of smoking are ***cold smoking*** and ***hot smoking***. In cold smoking, the temperature inside the smokehouse is kept at or below 85°F (30°C). At these temperatures, the foods take on the flavor of the smoke but are not cooked.

In hot smoking, the temperature inside the smokehouse may be as high as 165°F (74°C) for sausage and meats, and as high as 200°F (93°F) for fish and poultry. These temperatures are high enough to cook the foods being smoked. Higher temperatures are usually avoided because they result in excessive shrinkage. Foods may be hot smoked until they reach an internal temperature of 150° to 165°F (65° to 74°C) to ensure they are fully cooked. Alternatively, they may be hot smoked for a shorter period and then poached until they reach this internal temperature. This second method is used when a less intense smoke flavor is desired. No matter which method is used, hot-smoked foods are always sold fully cooked.

A typical smoker consists of the following elements:

- An enclosed chamber for holding the foods to be smoked
- A source of smoke
- A means to circulate the smoke around the food and then to exhaust it
- A way of controlling the temperature inside the chamber

The smoke source consists of a receptacle for wood chips or sawdust plus a heating element, usually electric. If the smoker is to be used for cold smoking, the smoke generator should be outside the main chamber that holds the food. If the smoke generator is inside the food chamber, as in some less expensive smokers, the temperature will rise too high for cold smoking. This type of smoker is used only for hot smoking. Foods to be smoked are arranged on racks or hung from hangers with enough space between them so the smoke circulates freely around all surfaces. Commercially made smokers are safest to use, as improperly built smokers may present a fire hazard. If a smoker is used indoors, it is essential to provide for ventilation of the exhausted smoke to the outdoors.

Hickory is perhaps the most popular wood for smoking, but other hardwoods that may be used include oak, mesquite, and fruitwoods such as apple and cherry. Soft woods, like pine, are not used because they release bitter, tarry components when burned. It is important to use woods from a reliable source. Pressure-treated woods should never be used, as they contain toxic chemicals such as arsenic.

To summarize, the smoking process consists of the following steps:

1. Curing (dry cure or brine cure)
2. Air-drying
3. Smoking (hot smoking or cold smoking)

KEY POINTS TO REVIEW

- What are the main ingredients used in curing? What is the purpose of each of them?
- What are the two main types of cures?
- Should foods be cured before being smoked? Why or why not?
- What are the two basic kinds of smoking processes? Describe them.

Gravlax

U.S.	METRIC	INGREDIENTS
2½ lb	1.2 kg	Salmon fillet, skin on
4 oz	125 g	Coarse salt
4 oz	125 g	Sugar
¼ tsp	1 mL	White pepper
2 oz	60 g	Fresh dill sprigs

Per 1 ounce (28.35 g): Calories, 70; Protein, 8 g; Fat, 4 g (50% cal.); Cholesterol, 20 mg; Carbohydrates, 1 g; Fiber, 0 g; Sodium, 240 mg.

PROCEDURE

1. Pass your fingertips over the surface of the salmon fillet to locate any bones. Pull them out with needlenose pliers.
2. Mix the salt, sugar, and pepper.
3. Select a stainless-steel, glass, ceramic, or other nonreactive pan to hold the salmon for curing. Sprinkle a little of the salt mixture on the bottom of the pan and lay the salmon on it skin side down. Cover the flesh side of the fillet completely with a layer of the salt mixture. Then top with the dill, again covering the fillet completely.
4. If you are doubling this recipe and curing 2 fillets, salt the second fillet in the same manner and invert it on top of the first so the dill is sandwiched between the fillets and the skin side of each fillet is toward the outside.
5. Cover the pan well and refrigerate 1 day. Turn the fillet or fillets over and refrigerate another day (for a total of 2 days). *Note:* Some instructions say to place a weight on the fish during the cure. This is optional. Weighting the fish produces a slightly drier, firmer finished product.
6. After 2 days, drain off any liquid that accumulated in the pan. Carefully scrape all the dill and curing mixture from the fish.
7. To serve, cut on a sharp diagonal—that is, with the knife almost parallel to the table—into broad, paper-thin slices (**Figure 7.1**).

Figure 7.1 Slice gravlax and smoked salmon on the diagonal into paper-thin slices. Cut toward the tail end.

Smoked Salmon

YIELD: 1 LB 14 OZ (850 G) WITHOUT SKIN

U.S.	METRIC	INGREDIENTS
2½ lb	1.2 kg	Salmon fillet, skin on
6 oz	180 g	Coarse salt
3 oz	90 g	Sugar
2 tsp	10 mL	Coarse black pepper
1 tsp	5 mL	Dry mustard
½ tsp	2 mL	Ground allspice
¼ tsp	1 mL	Cayenne
2 oz	60 g	Onion, chopped fine

Per 1 ounce (28.35 g): Calories, 70; Protein, 8 g; Fat, 4 g (53% cal.); Cholesterol, 25 mg; Carbohydrates, 0 g; Fiber, 0 g; Sodium, 240 mg.

PROCEDURE

1. Pass your fingertips over the surface of the salmon fillet to locate any bones. Pull them out with needlenose pliers.
2. Mix the salt, sugar, pepper, dry mustard, allspice, and cayenne.
3. Select a stainless-steel, glass, ceramic, or other nonreactive pan to hold the salmon for curing. Sprinkle a little of the salt mixture on the bottom of the pan and lay the salmon on it skin side down. Cover the flesh side of the fillet completely with a layer of the salt mixture. Then top with the chopped onion, distributing it evenly over the fillet.
4. If you are doubling this recipe and curing 2 fillets, salt the second fillet in the same manner and invert it on top of the first so the onion is sandwiched between the fillets and the skin side of each fillet is toward the outside.
5. Cover the pan well and refrigerate 12–24 hours.
6. Remove the fillet from the pan and rinse off all the salt mixture and onion. Place on a rack set on a sheet pan, skin side down, and allow to dry, uncovered, in the refrigerator until a thin, dry skin (called a *pellicle*) has formed on the surface of the flesh.
7. Cold smoke at 86°F (30°C).
8. To serve, cut on a sharp diagonal—that is, with the knife almost parallel to the table—into broad, paper-thin slices.

Smoked Trout

YIELD: 10 FILLETS, 6–7 OZ (180–200 G) EACH

U.S.	METRIC	INGREDIENTS
2 qt	2 L	Water
8 oz	250 g	Salt
2 oz	60 g	Light brown sugar
4	4	Bay leaves
2 tsp	10 mL	Black peppercorns
1 tsp	5 mL	Coriander seed
½ tsp	2 mL	Whole allspice
½ tsp	2 mL	Dry mustard

PROCEDURE

1. Prepare the brine: Combine the water, salt, sugar, bay leaves, peppercorns, coriander, allspice, and mustard in a pot. Bring to a simmer, stirring until the salt and sugar are dissolved.
2. Cool, then chill the brine.

U.S.	METRIC	INGREDIENTS
10	10	Trout fillets, about 8 oz (250 g) each

Per fillet: Calories, 320; Protein, 47 g; Fat, 12 g (36% cal.); Cholesterol, 135 mg; Carbohydrates, 2 g; Fiber, 0 g; Sodium, 3420 mg.

3. Place the trout fillets in a stainless-steel, plastic, or other nonreactive pan in a single layer. Add enough cold brine to completely cover the fillets. Place a light weight on top of the fish to keep them submerged.
4. Refrigerate 6–8 hours.
5. Remove from the brine and rinse in cold water. Blot dry.
6. Arrange on racks and allow to dry several hours in the refrigerator.
7. Hot smoke at 185°F (85°C) until the internal temperature of the fish reaches 145°F (63°C), about 1–1½ hours. Cool, then refrigerate.

Smoked Duck

YIELD: 2 SMOKED DUCKS

U.S.	METRIC	INGREDIENTS	PROCEDURE
1½ gal	6 L	Water	1. Prepare the brine: Heat the water in a pot until it is warm. Add the salt, sugar, and Prague Powder and stir until they are dissolved. Add the bay leaves and onion powder.
12 oz	360 g	Salt	2. Cool, then chill the brine.
6 oz	180 g	Sugar	
3 oz	90 g	Prague Powder #1	
3	3	Bay leaves	
2 tsp	10 mL	Onion powder	
2	2	Small ducks, about 4 lb (1.8 kg) each	3. Place the ducks in a stainless-steel, plastic, or other nonreactive container. Pour enough brine over them to cover them completely. Weight them to keep them submerged.

4. Allow to cure in the refrigerator 2 days. (*Note:* Large ducks take 3–4 days to cure.)
5. Remove the ducks from the brine and rinse well.
6. Place on a rack and let dry in the refrigerator at least 8 hours.
7. Hot smoke at 185° (85°C) until the internal temperature of the duck reaches 165°F (74°F).

Per 1 duck, without skin: Calories, 510; Protein, 79 g; Fat, 17 g (32% cal.); Cholesterol, 305 mg; Carbohydrates, 4 g; Fiber, 0 g; Sodium, 4330 mg.

VARIATIONS

Smoked Turkey or Chicken

Brine turkey or chicken as in the basic recipe. Turkey requires 4–6 days to cure in the brine, depending on the size. Chickensrequire 2–4 days, depending on their size.

Sausages

A ***sausage*** is a mixture of ground meat, usually pork, and seasonings stuffed into a casing. The term *sausage* may also be used for the meat mixture itself, without the casing. Reduced to its simplest form, sausage meat may be nothing more than ground pork seasoned with salt.

Although there are hundreds or even thousands of kinds of sausages, the majority are based on the same few basic principles. These principles are simple enough that we can make a wide variety of sausages in the kitchen and not have to rely entirely on commercial products. Furthermore, it is not necessary to restrict ourselves to traditional sausage recipes. Many chefs are experimenting with ingredients and seasonings to add variety to the menu.

Categories of Sausages

Sausages can be classified into three basic groups:

Fresh sausages

Cured sausages

Smoked sausages

A ***fresh sausage***, by USDA definition, is one that contains no nitrates or nitrites. It is basically a mixture of ground meat, seasonings, and flavorings. Although they are often raw, fresh sausages may contain cooked ingredients, or they may even be fully cooked before being sold. Any fresh raw sausage containing pork, of course, must be fully cooked before being served and eaten.

A ***cured sausage*** is one that contains nitrites or nitrates of sodium. These chemicals help prevent spoilage and food-borne disease, as explained in the first part of this chapter. Incidentally, they also keep the meat red or pink, even when cooked. Cured sausages may be sold raw or cooked, soft and moist like fresh sausages, semidried and firm, or dried and hard like salami. Pork salamis, which are Italian in origin, and similar cured, dried sausages are raw, but the curing, aging, and drying process renders them safe to eat. As explained on page 194, air-dried sausages meant to be eaten raw are made with nitrates in addition to nitrites for a longer lasting cure.

Smoked sausages may be hot smoked and, therefore, cooked, or cold smoked. Smoking may be light or heavy, depending on the sausage. Sausages, like other smoked meats, are cured before being smoked. The cure mixture is mixed directly with the sausage meat.

Basic Sausage Ingredients

The basic ingredients of sausage meat are the following:

Lean pork

Pork fat, preferably hard fatback, ground with the meat

Salt

Spices, herbs, and other seasonings and flavorings

In the case of cured sausage, curing mixes containing nitrites or nitrates are added to the above list.

THE MEAT

Pork is the most commonly used meat in sausage making, but other meats or mixtures of meat may be used. Beef, veal, lamb, chicken, turkey, duck, liver, rabbit, and venison all find their way into sausages. Mixtures of pork plus one or more of these meats are often used. More exotic sausages may include such ingredients as sweetbreads and brains.

Certified pork—that is, pork certified to be free of trichinosis—is used for sausages meant to be air-dried and eaten uncooked.

THE FAT

Pork fat or other fat, such as the beef fat used in all-beef sausages, is an important ingredient. Because our impression of juiciness in any cooked meat is largely due to the meat's fat content, some fat is included in sausage mixtures. Without it, the texture of the cooked sausage would be very dry.

In most traditional sausages, fat makes up 25 to 50 percent of the total weight, with 33 percent fat being the norm. In other words, proportions of fat to lean range from 3 parts lean plus 1 part fat (the leanest sausages) to 1 part lean plus 1 part fat (rich, fatty sausages). Varying the proportions changes the character of the sausage.

Hard fatback is preferred over other fats for pork sausage. Softer fats are more likely to melt out of the sausage during cooking. A quick and easy way to make pork sausages without worrying about the ratio of fat to lean is to use whole pork butt. The ratio of fat to lean in this cut is very good for sausages.

In today's diet-conscious atmosphere, it may make sense to try to create low-fat sausages. But be advised that extra care is required when making sausages with less than 25 percent fat. Lean sausages should never be overcooked, as overcooking makes them dry. Keep the meat mixture cold to avoid damage to the texture of the meat and fat. With care, it is possible to make tasty sausages with a fat content as low as 10 or 15 percent. One should not expect, however, that the eating qualities of lean sausages will be the same as those of fattier sausages.

Cereal ingredients and fillers (rice, barley, bread crumbs, and so on) can be used to help reduce fat content. Because these starches absorb and retain moisture, they enhance the total moisture content of low-fat sausages.

SEASONINGS

Herbs, spices, and other flavorings account for the primary differences among sausages. Many, if not most, of the world's fresh sausages are made of nothing more than ground pork and seasonings. It is the seasonings that give them their characteristic flavor. A glance at the recipes in this section will confirm this.

Some of the major spices and herbs used in sausage making are:

Allspice	Cumin	Paprika
Caraway seeds	Fennel seed	Parsley
Cayenne or hot red pepper	Ginger	Pepper, black and white
Cinnamon	Mace	Sage
Cloves	Marjoram	Tarragon
Coriander	Mustard	Thyme
	Nutmeg	

Other important ingredients include:

Garlic	Chives	Vinegar
Onion	Wine, white and red	Eggs
Shallots		

Standardized spice mixtures are often used to season sausages, pâtés, and similar items. One of the most common is ***quatre épices*** (French for "four spices"), a mixture that exists in many versions. It can usually be obtained commercially, or it can be homemade.

CURE MIXES

Sausages to be air-dried are cured with both nitrate and nitrite, as explained on page 194. For other cured sausages, only nitrite, usually in the form of Prague Powder #1, is used. Other ingredients, such as dextrose and additional salt, may be combined with the Prague Powder to make the cure mix. The cure mix may be incorporated into the sausage in one of two ways:

1. It may be mixed with the meat after it is diced. The diced meat is then chilled thoroughly before being ground.

2. It may be combined with the remaining spices and seasonings and mixed into the ground meat.

Refer to individual recipes for more detailed instructions on making and incorporating cure mixes.

OTHER INGREDIENTS

A number of sausages are characterized by unusual or exotic ingredients. Some of these are traditional and time-honored, such as the black truffles included in some regional French sausages and the chestnuts or raisins in other specialty sausages.

Other unusual sausages are modern innovations by creative chefs. It is no longer uncommon, when reading today's restaurant menus, to come across sausages with such ingredients as sun-dried tomatoes or fresh vegetables like sweet bell peppers and spinach. In theory, there is no limit to what can be stuffed into sausage casings. The main requirement is that the ingredients complement or enhance one another, just as the meat, seasonings, and vegetable garnish on a dinner plate should complement one another.

Casings

Natural casings are made from the intestines of meat animals. *Sheep casings* are the smallest, ranging from ¾ inch (18 mm) to more than 1 inch (25 mm) in diameter. They are used for breakfast links, frankfurters, and similar sausages. *Hog casings* are medium-sized, about 1 to 1½ inches (3 to 4 cm) in diameter, depending on what part of the intestines they are taken from. They are used for many popular fresh sausages, such as Italian sausages and fresh bratwurst. *Beef casings* range in size from the so-called *beef round*, about 1¾ inches (45 mm) in diameter, through *beef middles*, 2½ inches (63 mm), to the large *beef bung*, more than 4 inches (100 mm) in diameter.

Natural casings are often sold packed in salt. Because of the preservative effect of the salt, the casings keep indefinitely as long as they are refrigerated. Natural casings are easy to use if they are handled correctly. Before being stuffed, they must be untangled, rinsed, and flushed, and examined for holes according to the following procedure.

Procedure for Preparing Natural Casings

1. Carefully remove the casings, one at a time, from the salt pack, and unravel them. Because a single casing may be 12 feet (4 m) long, it is easiest to do this on a large workbench. Separate the individual lengths and keep them separate in their own little stacks on the bench. When unraveling them, do not pull hard, because this may cause knotting.

   Unravel slightly more casing than you think you will need. It is easier to return unused casings to the salt pack than it is to separate and flush additional casings when you run out before you have stuffed your whole batch of meat.

2. Partially fill a large bowl with clean water and set it in a sink under the faucet. Take hold of the end of one casing and drop the rest of it into the bowl of water. Open the end of the casing and run cold water into it, enough to fill about 12 inches (30 cm) of it. Holding the casing at both ends of this "water sausage," allow the water to flush through the casing from one end to the other.

   This accomplishes two purposes. It rinses out the inside of the casing, and it identifies any holes that might be present. Pinpoint-size holes are no problem, but if a large hole is found, simply cut the casing in two at that point. Short pieces may be discarded for the sake of efficiency.

3. If you are making a small quantity of sausages and stuffing them immediately, each casing can be put on the stuffing horn as it is rinsed. If this is not the case, the casing must be stored for later use. Select a container with a cover and fill it about three-fourths full of cold water. Drop in the casing and let one end hang over the edge.

   Repeat with remaining casings. Fill the container to the top with cold water, cover, and refrigerate until needed. By letting the ends of the casings hang over the edge, you can remove one at a time from the container without tangling them. If the end of the casing dries out, simply cut it off.

Because the supply of natural casings is not nearly large enough to accommodate all the sausages produced, other types of casings have come into wide use. ***Collagen casings*** are molded from animal materials and are completely edible, like natural casings. Unlike natural casings, they are uniform in size, making portion control easier. Various types are manufactured for different uses. Some are used only for fresh sausages, as they are not strong enough to hold the weight of the sausages if they are hung for smoking. Other types are stronger and intended to be used for smoked sausages. Most collagen casings must be refrigerated to keep them from becoming dry and brittle. To use, dip them in water for a few seconds to soften them if they are dry, then put them on the sausage stuffing nozzle.

Synthetic fibrous casings are made from a plastic material and are not edible. They are widely used for salamis and luncheon meats, and the casing is peeled off before or after slicing. These casings are nonperishable and need no refrigeration. They must be soaked in water before using to make them flexible. Soaking time varies, and the manufacturer should specify the recommended time.

Equipment

Most fresh sausages can be made with no special equipment other than a meat grinder and a device for getting the meat into the casings.

The working parts of a meat grinder are a rotating blade and a selection of dies in various sizes. The size of the die determines the fineness of the grind. A screw forces the meat from the feed tube to the blade, and the blade chops the meat as it is forced through the holes of the die.

Before grinding meat, it is important to be sure of the following two points:

1. The equipment must be clean and sanitary. Make sure there is no trace of food from previous jobs hiding in the many nooks and crannies of the grinder, blades, and dies.

2. The equipment must be cold in order to avoid warming the meat. Refrigerate the grinder parts or set them in ice water before use.

The sausage stuffer is the second piece of equipment necessary for making sausages. The simplest stuffer resembles a funnel. The casings are pushed over the narrow end and the meat is pushed through the wide end by hand or with a wooden plunger. These are adequate for making a few pounds of sausage but are not suitable for larger batches.

Larger stuffers have detachable nozzles or horns for different casing sizes. The nozzle is attached to a cylindrical reservoir that holds the meat, which is pushed through by a piston. On smaller machines, the piston is simply pushed through by hand. These machines are suitable for small-scale production such as might be done in a small to medium-size restaurant. For large-scale commercial production, larger machines are used. The piston in a large machine is operated by means of a crank and a sequence of gears.

The Grind

The grind of the meat determines the texture of the sausage. We can divide sausage meat into two categories based on grind. Most common sausages are made simply of meat and fat ground to varying degrees of fineness or coarseness, mixed with seasonings, and stuffed into casings. We refer to these as ***basic grind*** sausages. Some sausages, on the other hand, including familiar ones like frankfurters, mortadella, and bologna, are made with meat and fat ground to a smooth purée and blended with a little liquid, such as water or milk. We refer to these as ***emulsified*** or ***emulsion grind*** sausages because of the added liquid content and the emulsion of the fat with the meat and liquid.

BASIC GRIND

The fineness or coarseness of the grind is an important characteristic of any sausage. For example, one identifying feature of Toulouse Sausages (p. 207) is their coarse texture. The meat is chopped by hand rather than ground. On the other hand, typical breakfast sausages have a fairly fine grind.

To grind meat, cut it into pieces small enough to fit easily into the feed tube of the grinder, then chill it well. For the best texture, start with the largest die, no matter what final grind is needed. Then grind with the next smaller die, until the desired texture is achieved. This process is called ***progressive grinding***. Control the coarseness of the grind by selecting the proper die for the final grind, as indicated in the recipe. As indicated in the procedure below, the meat, fat, and seasonings are mixed until uniformly blended after the meat is ground.

The meat mixture must be kept cold during grinding. When the mixture gets too warm, the fat becomes soft and begins to lose its structure. As a result, it may melt out too readily when the sausage is cooked, resulting in excessive shrinkage, poor texture, and dryness. If the kitchen is warm, return the meat to the refrigerator to chill it thoroughly after cutting it up and before grinding it. If it must be ground more than once, return it to the refrigerator between grindings.

Additional textural variation in basic grind sausages can be created by mixing chunks or dice of meat or other ingredients into a more finely ground forcemeat, as is often done in pâtés.

When following any sausage recipe, adhere closely to the grinding and processing directions in order to achieve the proper texture and character.

Procedure for Making Fresh and Cured Basic Grind Sausages

1. Weigh the meats and fat. Cut them into chunks small enough to fit into the grinder.
2. If the sausages are to be cured, toss the cure mix with the diced meat at this point. Alternatively, combine the cure mix with the salt and spices in step 4.
3. Chill the meat well before proceeding.
4. Measure the salt and spices.
5. Grind the meat and fat, following the directions in the recipe to achieve the proper fineness or coarseness of grind.
6. Chill the meat well. Ideally, the meat should be chilled to 32° to 35°F (0° to 2°C) before mixing and stuffing. Best practice is to grind the meat directly into a bowl set in an ice bath.
7. Combine the meat, salt, and spices and mix thoroughly. This is best done by hand in a large tub or other container. It can also be done with a mixing machine using the paddle attachment.

   If the recipe calls for cold water or other liquid, mix the salt and spices with the water first, then mix this combination with the meat. This facilitates a better distribution of the spices than mixing them dry with the meat.

   Many recipes say to refrigerate the meat overnight after it is mixed to allow it to absorb the seasonings and the flavors to blend. However, it is easier to stuff the sausages immediately after mixing. If the salted meat mixture is allowed to stand, it becomes firmer and thus harder to force through the stuffer. Stuffing immediately allows the casings to be filled more uniformly and with fewer air bubbles. Besides, the meat can absorb the seasonings just as well in the casings as in the meat tub.
8. Test for seasonings. Do not taste the raw meat. Rather, make a small ball or patty and cook it in a small sauté pan or poach it in water. Then cool the meat slightly and taste. If more salt or other seasoning is needed, add it to the sausage mixture.
9. Place the meat in the stuffer, one handful at a time. Pack each handful firmly into the stuffer to eliminate air bubbles.
10. Slide the casings onto the nozzle. To help the casings slide on easily, moisten both them and the stuffer nozzle with water.
11. Stuff the sausages, following the directions for your equipment (see Figure 7.2). The sausages will pull the casings off the nozzle as the meat flows through it, but it is best to hold your hand at the end of the nozzle to help control the rate at which the casing is pulled from the nozzle. From time to time, as the casing is filled, it is necessary to push the bunched-up, unfilled casing toward the end of the nozzle so it will slide off more easily. Do not stuff the casings too tightly. If the meat is packed too tightly, it will be difficult to twist the sausage into links.
12. After all the meat is stuffed into casings, remove any air bubbles by pricking the casing and pressing the surface to expel the air.
13. Twist the sausage into links of uniform size.

Figure 7.2 Stuffing sausages.

(a) A small sausage stuffer fitted with a medium nozzle. This stuffer holds 5 lb (2.3 kg) meat at a time.

(b) Flush out the casings with fresh, cold water, while looking for holes.

(c) Slide the casings onto the proper size nozzle.

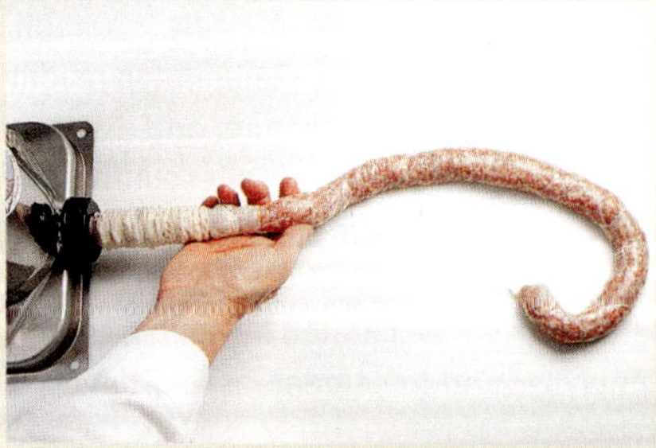

(d) When stuffing the casings, use one hand to guide the casing as it slides off the nozzle.

(e) Pinch and twist the sausage into links of the desired size.

EMULSIFIED GRIND

In the finest-textured sausages, the meat is actually puréed to a smooth paste. Puréed raw meat is capable of absorbing a good deal of moisture, and water or milk is usually added to improve the texture. Because of the addition of liquid to the meat purée, the resulting grind is called an *emulsified grind*. For sausages that include milk, a recipe may indicate either liquid milk or water plus dried milk solids. The dried milk is added at the same time as the spice mixture.

Because grinding meat to a smooth paste generates heat, water is added in the form of ice to keep the temperature low. If liquid milk is called for, freeze it into chunks.

Because a meat grinder is not capable of grinding sausage to this texture, the grinding procedure is done in two stages. First, grind the meat and fat separately using the fine die on the meat grinder. Keep the two separate and chill them after this grinding. Second, grind the meat to a smooth paste with a food chopper (buffalo chopper) or food processor. Place the lean meat in the bowl of the chopper and run it a few seconds. Then add the ice and continue to grind until smooth. Monitor the temperature carefully. Do not allow it to rise above 50°F (10°C). Add the fat and continue to grind to blend it in. Continue to monitor the temperature. Do not allow it to rise above 58°F (14°C).

Emulsified sausages are usually cooked in water after stuffing, then chilled in cold water. If they are to be smoked, they are smoked first and then cooked.

Procedure for Making Fresh and Cured Emulsified Sausages

1. Keeping the meat and fat separate, grind them with the fine die of a meat grinder, following steps 1 through 6 of the basic sausage-making procedure above. Chill well.
2. If indicated in the recipe, mix the seasonings with the lean meat. (Alternatively, add the seasonings at the same time as the ice in step 3.)
3. Place the lean meat in the bowl of a food chopper or food processor. Run the chopper a few turns, then add the ice. Continue to chop to a fine paste. Do not allow the temperature to rise above 50°F (10°C).
4. Add the fat and continue to grind to blend it in. Continue to monitor the temperature. Do not allow it to rise above 58°F (14°C).
5. Follow steps 8 through 12 in the procedure on page 204 to test the seasonings and stuff the casings.

Smoking Sausages

The procedure for smoking sausages is the same as for smoking other meats (see Figure 7.3). Refer to page 196 for basic information on smoking and follow the instructions in individual recipes. Note in particular the following points:

1. Only cured sausages should be smoked.
2. The sausages should be dried briefly before being smoked, like other smoked foods (see p. 196). Hang them so that air can circulate around them and allow to dry about 1½ hours or as indicated in the recipe.
3. Hot smoke or cold smoke as indicated in the recipe. Air-dried sausages to be eaten raw are cold smoked. Sausages that are sold cooked are generally hot smoked. After smoking, they are usually poached to an internal temperature of 160° to 165°F (71° to 74°C), then cooled quickly in ice water and blotted dry.

Figure 7.3 Finished sausages before removing from the smoker

Cooking Sausages

Although sausages are sometimes ingredients or components of more elaborate dishes, they are also popular as standalone menu items like other meats. Preparation of sausages before cooking is minimal. In most cases, sausages may be considered ready to cook—or, in the case of fully cooked sausages, ready to heat. Fresh raw sausages containing pork must be fully cooked before serving, like other fresh pork products. If a fresh sausage contains no pork, such as the lamb sausage on page 209, it may be served somewhat less done. Removing it from the heat when still pink inside helps retain juices.

Fully cooked sausages need only be heated through before serving. Cooking times, however, are nearly the same as for raw sausages. In other words, the time it takes for the heat to penetrate to the center is about the same.

The following cooking methods are most often used for sausages.

SIMMERING

Place sausages in a pan with enough salted water to cover. Bring to a simmer and simmer until completely cooked. Do not let the water boil. This is likely to make the sausages burst or shrink excessively.

Time depends on the thickness of the sausage. Sausages in hog casings take about 20 minutes to cook; smaller ones may take as little as 10 minutes, larger ones 30 minutes or more.

Raw sausages may be simmered until cooked through, then finished by one of the following methods.

SAUTÉING AND PAN-FRYING

Sausages are sautéed or pan-fried using the same techniques as for other meats. For many kinds of sausage, the browning that results makes them more appetizing than simmered ones.

If the sausages are not raw, it is necessary only to cook them until they are lightly browned and heated through. If they are raw, lower heat is necessary so they have time to become completely cooked by the time they are browned.

Sautéing and pan-frying are used not only for sausages in casings but also for patties and *crêpinettes*, which are sausage patties wrapped in caul fat (see p. 207). Do not press on the patties with the spatula while cooking. This forces out juices and makes them dry.

BRAISING

Because fresh raw sausages may require long cooking times, braising is often the preferred cooking method. The sausages are browned by sautéing them over moderate heat for up to 5 minutes, then finished using a moist-heat cooking method. Cooking with moisture may take any of several forms, including the four methods listed below. These methods are suitable not only for fresh sausages but also for fully cooked and smoked sausages that are served hot.

- Covering the pan to hold in steam.
- Adding a small amount of liquid (water, stock, wine, and so on), covering the pan, and cooking until done.
- Glazing—that is, adding a small amount of stock and continuing to cook. The pan may be covered or left uncovered at the beginning, but the last part of cooking takes place with the cover off. The sausages are basted with the stock as it reduces, giving them a glaze. Any stock remaining in the pan after the sausages are cooked will be reduced and thickened, and it may be served with the sausages as a sauce. This cooking method is especially suitable for patties and crêpinettes.
- Cooking the sausages in a casserole or stew after they are browned. Sauerkraut, bean dishes, and gumbos are examples.

BROILING AND GRILLING

Brush the sausages with oil to prevent sticking, and broil or grill as for other meats. Moderate heat is usually best. High heat may brown the sausages too much before they are fully cooked, and it is more likely to cause splitting.

About the Sausage Recipes

Before proceeding to the sausage recipes that follow, please take note of the following points.

1. Refer to the general procedures for making sausages on pages 204–205. Some of these points are not repeated in each recipe.
2. Ratios of fat to lean are not specified in most of the recipes. Refer to the explanation of fat-lean ratios on page 200 and adjust the amount of fat in the recipes as desired.

KEY POINTS TO REVIEW

- What are the three basic categories of sausages?
- What are the main ingredients of sausages?
- What are the steps in the procedure for preparing natural sausage casings?
- What are the steps in the procedure for making basic grind sausages?
- What are the steps in the procedure for making emulsified sausages?

Quatre Épices I

YIELD: 1¼ OZ (37 G)

U.S.	METRIC	INGREDIENTS
4 tbsp	25 g	Ground white or black pepper
2 tsp	4 g (10 mL)	Nutmeg
2 tsp	4 g (10 mL)	Ground cloves
2 tsp	4 g (10 mL)	Cinnamon

Per 1 ounce (28.35 g): Calories, 90; Protein, 3 g; Fat, 2 g (13% cal.); Cholesterol, 0 mg; Carbohydrates, 19 g; Fiber, 8 g; Sodium, 10 mg.

PROCEDURE

1. Combine the ingredients and mix well.
2. Store in a tightly sealed container.

Quatre Épices II

YIELD: 1¼ OZ (34 G)

U.S.	METRIC	INGREDIENTS
10 tsp	20 g	Ground white pepper
3 tsp	6 g (15 mL)	Nutmeg
3 tsp	6 g (15 mL)	Ground ginger
1 tsp	2 g (5 mL)	Ground cloves

Per 1 ounce (28.35 g): Calories, 100; Protein, 3 g; Fat, 3 g (21% cal.); Cholesterol, 0 mg; Carbohydrates, 18 g; Fiber, 7 g; Sodium, 5 mg.

PROCEDURE

1. Combine the ingredients and mix well.
2. Store in a tightly sealed container.

Pork Sausage

YIELD: 6 LB (3 KG)

U.S.	METRIC	INGREDIENTS
6 lb	3 kg	Pork and pork fat
2 tbsp	30 g	Salt
2 tsp	4 g (10 mL)	Quatre épices
6 fl oz	200 mL	Water, cold

Per 1 ounce (28.35 g): Calories, 70; Protein, 5 g; Fat, 5 g (69% cal.); Cholesterol, 20 mg; Carbohydrates, 0 g; Fiber, 0 g; Sodium, 160 mg.

PROCEDURE

1. Cut the meat and fat into cubes small enough to fit into the grinder. Chill thoroughly.
2. Grind the meat once with the large die and again with the small die. If necessary, chill the meat between grindings.
3. Mix the salt and spices with the water. Add to the ground meat and mix thoroughly by hand.
4. Stuff into hog casings or sheep casings.

VARIATIONS

Toulouse Sausage

Use the ingredients specified in the recipe, but grind the meat coarsely. This can be done in three ways, with slightly different results for each method:

1. Chop the meat coarsely with a knife.
2. Grind only once, using the large die of the grinder.
3. Grind briefly in a food processor, just until achieving a coarse texture.

Stuff into hog casings.

Toulouse sausages should have a fat content of at least 33 percent—that is, 1 part fat to 2 parts lean.

Crêpinettes

Weigh out 3½-oz (100-g) portions of sausage meat. Shape them into oval patties. Cut squares of caul fat (p. 149) and wrap the sausage portions in the squares. Cook by pan-frying, glazing (see p. 206), or grilling.

Other ingredients are often mixed with the sausage meat. Classic additions include blanched, peeled pistachios (2–3 oz per lb sausage meat/125–175 g per kg); chopped, cooked chestnuts (4 oz per lb/250 g per kg); or fresh, diced truffle (whatever quantity the budget allows).

Other sausage mixtures, such as those in the other recipes in this section, may be used to make crêpinettes.

French Garlic Sausage

YIELD: 7 LB (3.5 KG)

U.S.	METRIC	INGREDIENTS
6 lb	3 kg	Pork and pork fat
1 lb	500 g	Pork rind (skin)
2 tbsp	30 g	Salt
1½ tsp	3 g (7 mL)	Black pepper
2 tsp	8 g	Crushed garlic
½ tsp	2 mL	Ground sage
½ tsp	2 mL	Dried marjoram
½ tsp	2 mL	Dried thyme
4 fl oz	125 mL	Dry white wine

Per 1 ounce (28.35 g): Calories, 70; Protein, 5 g; Fat, 5 g (69% cal.); Cholesterol, 20 mg; Carbohydrates, 0 g; Fiber, 0 g; Sodium, 150 mg.

PROCEDURE

1. Cut the meat and fat into cubes small enough to fit into the grinder. Chill thoroughly.
2. Simmer the pork rind in salted water at least 2 hours, or until very tender. Chill thoroughly.
3. Grind the meat once with the large die and again with the medium die. If necessary, chill the meat between grindings.
4. Repeat this grinding procedure with the pork rind. Mix the ground pork rind with the ground meat.
5. Mix the salt and spices with the wine. Add to the ground meat and mix thoroughly by hand.
6. Stuff into hog casings.

Hot Italian Sausage

YIELD: 6 LB (3 KG)

U.S.	METRIC	INGREDIENTS
6 lb	3 kg	Pork and pork fat
2 tbsp	30 g	Salt
2 tsp	10 mL	Black pepper
2 tsp	10 mL	Fennel seeds
4 tsp	20 mL	Paprika
2 tsp	10 mL	Crushed red pepper
1 tsp	5 mL	Ground coriander
2 tsp	10 mL	Sugar
6 fl oz	200 mL	Water, cold

Per 1 ounce (28.35 g): Calories, 70; Protein, 5 g; Fat, 5 g (69% cal.); Cholesterol, 20 mg; Carbohydrates, 0 g; Fiber, 0 g; Sodium, 160 mg.

PROCEDURE

1. Cut the meat into cubes small enough to fit into the grinder. Chill the meat thoroughly.
2. Grind once with the medium die.
3. Mix the salt and spices with the cold water. Add to the ground meat and mix thoroughly by hand.
4. Stuff into hog casings.

VARIATIONS

Mild Italian Sausage

Omit the paprika, crushed red pepper, and coriander.

Spicy Garlic Sausage

Omit the fennel and coriander. Add 2 tsp (10 mL) dried oregano and 1–2 tsp (5–10 mL) chopped garlic.

Veal or Beef Sausage

YIELD: 6 LB (3 KG)

U.S.	METRIC	INGREDIENTS
4 lb	2 kg	Pork and pork fat
2 lb	1 kg	Veal or beef, lean
2 tbsp	30 g	Salt
2 tsp	4 g (10 mL)	Quatre épices
6 fl oz	200 mL	Water, cold

Per 1 ounce (28.35 g): Calories, 60; Protein, 5 g; Fat, 4 g (64% cal.); Cholesterol, 20 mg; Carbohydrates, 0 g; Fiber, 0 g; Sodium, 170 mg.

PROCEDURE

1. Cut the meat into cubes small enough to fit into the grinder. Chill the meat thoroughly.
2. Grind the meat once with the large or medium die for coarse sausage. For a finer texture, grind once more with the small die. If necessary, chill the meat between grindings.
3. Mix the salt and spices with the water. Add to the ground meat and mix thoroughly by hand.
4. Stuff into hog casings.

VARIATIONS

Instead of the meat ratios given in the main recipe, use 3 lb (1.5 kg) pork and pork fat and 3 lb (1.5 kg) veal or beef. These proportions make a somewhat leaner sausage with more of the flavor of the veal or beef.

Venison Sausage

Prepare as in the basic recipe or the first variation, substituting venison for the veal or beef. Add 4 juniper berries, crushed to a powder, to the spice mixture. Substitute chilled red wine for the cold water.

Fresh Bratwurst

YIELD: 6 LB (3 KG)

U.S.	METRIC	INGREDIENTS
6 lb	3 kg	Pork and pork fat
2 tbsp	30 g	Salt
3 tsp	15 mL	White pepper
¼ tsp	1 mL	Mace
1 tsp	5 mL	Ground coriander
½ tsp	2 mL	Ground ginger
6 fl oz	200 mL	Water, cold

Per 1 ounce (28.35 g): Calories, 70; Protein, 5 g; Fat, 5 g (69% cal.); Cholesterol, 20 mg; Carbohydrates, 0 g; Fiber, 0 g; Sodium, 160 mg.

PROCEDURE

1. Cut the meat and fat into cubes small enough to fit into the grinder. Chill thoroughly.
2. Grind the meat once with the large die and again with the small die. If necessary, chill the meat between grindings.
3. Mix the salt and spices with the water. Add to the ground meat and mix thoroughly by hand.
4. Stuff into hog casings.

VARIATION

Following the procedure on page 205, make an emulsified grind instead of a basic grind. Omit the water indicated in the recipe and add 12 oz (400 g) ice as indicated in the procedure.

Lamb Sausage

YIELD: 6 LB (3 KG)

U.S.	METRIC	INGREDIENTS
6 lb	3 kg	Lamb shoulder (see Note)
2 tbsp	30 g	Salt
4 tsp	20 mL	Chopped garlic
2 tbsp	30 mL	Paprika
1 tsp	5 mL	Cayenne
1 tsp	5 mL	Black pepper
2 tbsp	30 mL	Ground cumin
2 tsp	10 mL	Dried oregano
1 tsp	5 mL	Cinnamon
4 tbsp	60 mL	Chopped cilantro
6 fl oz	200 mL	Water, cold

Per 1 ounce (28.35 g): Calories, 80; Protein, 5 g; Fat, 6 g (73% cal.); Cholesterol, 20 mg; Carbohydrates, 0 g; Fiber, 0 g; Sodium, 160 mg.

Note: Include some fat with the lean or, if desired, include some pork fat. If pork fat is used, the finished sausage must be cooked to the well-done stage. If all lamb is used, the sausage may be served slightly rare.

PROCEDURE

1. Cut the meat and fat into cubes small enough to fit into the grinder. Chill thoroughly.
2. Grind the meat once with the medium die.
3. Mix the salt and spices with the water. Add to the ground meat and mix thoroughly by hand.
4. Stuff into hog casings.

VARIATIONS

For a simpler, more straightforward flavor, omit the oregano, cinnamon, and cilantro.

Herbed Lamb Sausage

The flavor of the sausages made by the main recipe is characteristic of the Middle East and parts of North Africa. For a lamb sausage of a more European or North American character, omit the paprika, cumin, oregano, cinnamon, and cilantro. Add 2 tsp (10 mL) dried thyme, 2 tsp (10 mL) dried rosemary, and 1 oz (30 g) chopped shallot.

Duck Sausage

YIELD: 6 LB (3 KG)

U.S.	METRIC	INGREDIENTS
6 lb	3 kg	Boneless duck meat and fat
2 tbsp	30 g	Salt
2 tsp	10 mL	Quatre épices
6 oz	185 g	Pine nuts, toasted, or pistachios, blanched and peeled
6 oz	185 g	Marinated sun-dried tomatoes, drained and chopped
½ tsp	2 mL	Dried thyme

Per 1 ounce (28.35 g): Calories, 160; Protein, 3 g; Fat, 17 g (91% cal.); Cholesterol, 25 mg; Carbohydrates, 1 g; Fiber, 0 g; Sodium, 160 mg.

PROCEDURE

1. Cut the meat and fat into cubes small enough to fit into the grinder. Chill thoroughly.
2. Grind the meat once with the medium die.
3. Mix the salt, spices, nuts, and sun-dried tomatoes. Add to the ground meat and mix thoroughly by hand.
4. Stuff into small hog casings.

Boudin Blanc (White Sausage)

YIELD: 7 LB (3.6 KG)

U.S.	METRIC	INGREDIENTS	PROCEDURE
1 lb 8 oz	750 g	Chicken breast, boneless and skinless	1. Cut the chicken, pork, and fat into cubes small enough to fit into the grinder. Combine the chicken with the lean pork, but keep the pork fat separate.
2 lb	1 kg	Lean white pork	2. Grind the meat once with the large die, then once with the small die. Chill.
1 lb 8 oz	750 g	Pork fat	3. Grind the fat once with the large die, then once with the small die. Chill.
12 oz	375 g	Onion, chopped	4. Simmer the onions in the milk until they are tender. Pour this mixture over the bread crumbs in a bowl. Cool, then set in the freezer until partly frozen.
1 pt	500 mL	Milk	5. Place the ground meat in the bowl of a food chopper or food processor. Chop a few seconds, then add the partially frozen milk mixture. Grind until the mixture is uniformly blended.
8 oz	250 g	Fresh bread crumbs	
4	4	Eggs	6. Beat together the eggs, salt, pepper, mace, and parsley (if used). Add to the meat in the grinder and continue to grind to a smooth paste. Check the temperature to make sure it does not rise above 50°F (10°C). If necessary, chill before continuing.
3 tbsp	45 mL	Salt	7. Add the fat to the grinder and continue to grind until the mixture is smooth and uniform. Do not let the temperature rise above 58°F (14°C).
2 tsp	10 mL	White pepper	8. Stuff into hog casings.
½ tsp	2 mL	Mace	9. Poach the sausages by simmering them slowly in water until cooked through, about 20 minutes. Drain and plunge into ice water to cool. Drain again and refrigerate.
1 oz	30 g	Parsley, chopped (optional)	

Per 1 ounce (28.35 g): Calories, 90; Protein, 4 g; Fat, 7 g (72% cal.); Cholesterol, 25 mg; Carbohydrates, 2 g; Fiber, 0 g; Sodium, 210 mg.

VARIATIONS

Other white meats, such as veal or rabbit, can be used instead of chicken.

TERMS FOR REVIEW

charcutier
charcuterie
sodium nitrite
sodium nitrate
nitrosamine
Prague Powder #1
tinted curing mix (TCM)
Prague Powder #2
dry cure
brine cure
cold smoking
hot smoking
sausage
fresh sausage
cured sausage
smoked sausage
certified pork
quatre épices
natural casing
collagen casing
basic grind
emulsified grind
emulsion grind
progressive grinding

QUESTIONS FOR DISCUSSION

1. Explain how salt helps preserve meats.
2. Nitrites and nitrites are both used to cure meats. Explain how their use differs. Against which food-borne disease are they important in protecting cured foods?
3. Explain why smoked meats are cured before smoking.
4. Describe the basic differences between fresh, cured, and smoked sausages.
5. What are the four basic kinds of ingredients in sausage meat? List ways this basic formula can be changed to create different types of sausages.
6. Why should sausage meat be kept cold when it is being ground and processed?
7. Describe the procedure for preparing natural sausage casings for stuffing.

Chapter 8

Piping choux paste for cream puffs.

Bakeshop Production: Basic Principles and Ingredients

At one time, it was common for food-service establishments to produce their own breads, desserts, and other baked goods. Today, many operations find it more economical to buy these products from commercial bakeries. However, many other owners and chefs have discovered that offering fresh, "home-baked" breads, cakes, and pastries attracts customers and increases profits. With little more than an oven and a mixer, many cooks turn out attractive baked items that set their operations apart from competitors.

For this reason, it is important for you to learn the fundamentals of baking, even if you intend to become a cook rather than a baker. These chapters will not make a professional baker out of you. A baker requires far more technical and specialized information than can be presented in this short space. But you will learn the basic methods for producing a wide variety of breads, desserts, and pastries with only the simplest of resources.

In this chapter, we introduce bakeshop production with a discussion of the basic processes and ingredients common to nearly all baked goods. This will give you the understanding necessary to proceed to actual production in the succeeding chapters.

After reading this chapter, you should be able to

1. Explain why it is important to weigh baking ingredients.
2. Use a baker's balance scale.
3. Calculate formulas based on baker's percentages.
4. Explain the factors that control the development of gluten in baked products.
5. Explain the changes that take place in a dough or batter as it bakes.
6. Prevent or retard the staling of baked items.
7. Describe the major ingredients of baked goods and their functions and characteristics.

Basic Principles of Baking

If you consider that most bakery products are made of the same few ingredients—flour, shortening, sugar, eggs, water or milk, and leavening—you should have no difficulty understanding the importance of accuracy in the bakeshop, where slight differences in proportions or procedures can mean great differences in the final product.

If you have begun your food-service studies in a kitchen production laboratory, you surely have been told many times of the importance of measurement, not only for portion control and cost control but also for consistency in the quality of the final product. However, you have, no doubt, also learned there is a great deal of margin for error and that it is possible (if not desirable) to cook many foods without measuring anything. Coming into the bakeshop, where measurement is absolutely essential, may be a bit of a shock to you after your kitchen experiences, but it should reinforce the habits of accuracy you may have let slip.

If, on the other hand, you are beginning your practical studies in the bakeshop, then you will do well to pay particular attention to the principles of measurement presented here. They will be valuable to you throughout your career.

Formulas and Measurement

Bakers generally talk about *formulas* rather than *recipes*. If this sounds more like the chemistry lab than the kitchen, it is with good reason. The bakeshop is much like a chemistry laboratory both in the scientific accuracy of all the procedures and in the complex reactions that take place during mixing and baking.

Measurement

All ingredients must be weighed. Accuracy of measurement, as we have already said many times, is critical in the bakeshop. Measurement is by weight rather than by volume because weight is much more accurate. Unlike in recipes for the home baker, you will not see a professional baker's formula calling for 6 cups flour.

To demonstrate to yourself the importance of weighing rather than measuring by volume, measure 1 cup flour in two ways. (1) Sift some flour and lightly spoon it into a dry measure. Level the top and weigh the flour. (2) Scoop some unsifted flour into the same measure and pack it lightly. Level the top and weigh the flour. Note the difference. No wonder home recipes can be so inconsistent!

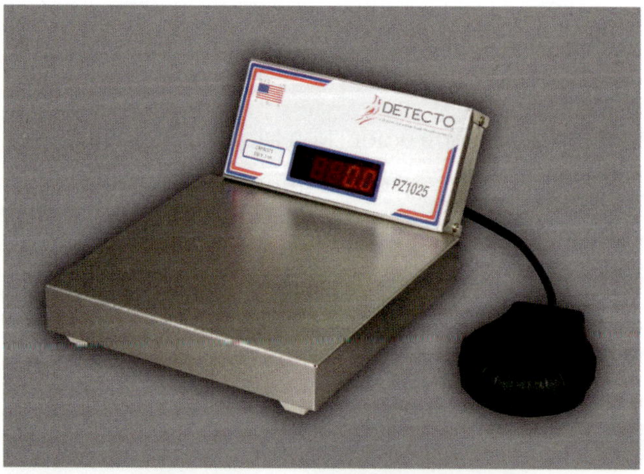

Digital professional scale
Courtesy of Cardinal Detecto

Procedure for Using a Baker's Balance Scale

The principle of using a baker's scale is simple: The scale must balance before setting the weights, and it must balance again after scaling. The example cited illustrates using a scale with U.S. units. The same procedure is used for metric scales.

1. Set the scale scoop or other container on the left side of the scale.
2. Balance the scale by placing counterweights on the right side and/or adjusting the ounce weight on the horizontal bar.
3. Set the scale for the desired weight by placing weights on the right side and/or by moving the ounce weight. For example, to set the scale for 1 pound 8 ounces, place a 1-pound weight on the right side and move the ounce weight to the right 8 ounces. If the ounce weight is already over 8 ounces, so that you cannot move it another 8, add 2 pounds to the right side of the scale and subtract 8 ounces by moving the ounce weight 8 places to the left. The result is still 1 pound 8 ounces.
4. Add the ingredient being scaled to the left side until the scale balances.

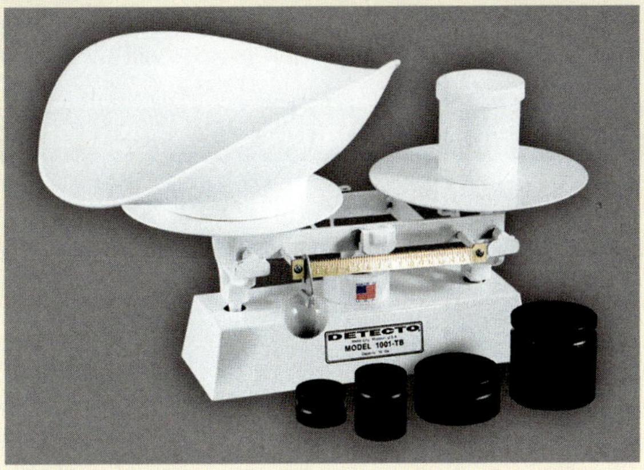

Balance scale
Courtesy of Cardinal Detecto

The baker's term for weighing out ingredients is *scaling*.

The following ingredients may be measured by *volume* because they weigh *1 pound per pint or 1 kilogram per liter*:

Water Milk Eggs

Thus, if a formula calls for 2 pounds eggs, you may measure 2 pints (1 quart). (Liquid flavoring ingredients, such as vanilla extract, normally measured in very small quantities, may also be measured by volume; 1 tablespoon equals ½ ounce.) In the metric system, 1 milliliter water weighs 1 gram; 1 liter weighs 1 kilogram. All other liquid ingredients (such as corn syrup and molasses) and all dry ingredients are normally weighed.

Baker's Percentages

Bakers use a simple but versatile system of percentages for expressing their formulas. Bakers' percentages express the amount of each ingredient used as a percentage of the amount of flour used.

To put it differently, the percentage of each ingredient is its total weight divided by the weight of the flour and multiplied by 100 percent, or

$$\frac{\text{weight of ingredient}}{\text{weight of flour}} \times 100\% = \%\text{ of ingredient}$$

Thus, flour is always 100 percent. (If two kinds of flour are used, their total is 100 percent.) Any ingredient that weighs the same as the flour is also given as 100 percent. The following ingredients from a cake formula illustrate how these percentages are used. Both U.S. and metric examples are given. (Note that numbers may be rounded off for practical measuring.) Check the figures with the above equation to make sure you understand them.

Ingredient	Weight		Percentage
Cake flour	5 lb		100 %
Sugar	5 lb		100 %
Baking powder		4 oz	5 %
Salt		2 oz	2.5 %
Emulsified shortening	2 lb	8 oz	50 %
Skim milk	3 lb		60 %
Egg whites	3 lb		60 %
	18 lb	14 oz	377.5 %

Ingredient	Weight	Percentage
Cake flour	2500 g	100 %
Sugar	2500 g	100 %
Baking powder	125 g	5 %
Salt	60 g	2.5 %
Emulsified shortening	1250 g	50 %
Skim milk	1500 g	60 %
Egg whites	1500 g	60 %
	9435 g	377.5 %

The advantage of using baker's percentages is that the formula is easily adapted for any yield, and single ingredients may be varied without changing the whole formulation. Please remember that these numbers do not refer to the percentage of the total yield. They are simply a way of expressing *ingredient proportions*. The total of these percentage numbers will always be greater than 100 percent.

Procedure for Calculating the Weight of an Ingredient If the Weight of Flour Is Known

1. Change the ingredient percentage to decimal form by moving the decimal point two places to the left.
2. Multiply the weight of the flour by this decimal to get the weight of the ingredient.

Example (U.S.): A formula calls for 20 percent sugar and you are using 10 pounds flour. How much sugar do you need?

20% = 0.20

10 lb × 0.20 = 2 lb sugar

Note: In the U.S. system, weights must normally be expressed all in one unit, either ounces or pounds, in order for the calculation to work.

Example (Metric): A formula calls for 20 percent sugar and you are using 5000 grams (5 kg) flour. How much sugar do you need?

20% = 0.20

5000 g × 0.20 = 1000 g sugar

Procedure for Converting a Formula to a New Yield

1. Change the total percentage to decimal form by moving the decimal point two places to the left.
2. Divide the desired yield by this decimal figure to get the weight of flour.
3. If necessary, round off this number to the next highest figure. This will allow for losses in mixing, makeup, and panning, and it will make calculations easier.
4. Use the weight of flour and remaining ingredient percentages to calculate the weights of the other ingredients, as in the previous procedure.

Example: In the previous sample cake formula, how much flour is needed if you require 6 pounds (3000 g) cake batter?

6 lb = 96 oz

377.5% = 3.775

96 oz ÷ 3.775 = 25.43 oz

or, rounded off, 26 oz (1 lb 10 oz)

3000 g ÷ 3.775 = 794.7 g

or, rounded off, 800 g

Clearly, the percentage system we have been discussing is used only when flour is a major ingredient, as in breads, cakes, and cookies. For these formulas, we use a written format different from our regular recipe format in this book.

In these formulas, the indicated yield is the total weight of the ingredients. This figure indicates the weight of the batter or dough. It is the figure we need to know for the purpose of scaling the dough or batter into loaves or pans. The finished weight of the baked goods will be less because moisture is lost during baking.

Also, please note that all yields, including percentage totals, are rounded off to the next lower whole number. This eliminates unimportant fractions and makes reading and calculating easier.

Selection of Ingredients

In addition to measuring, there is another basic rule of accuracy in the bakeshop: *Use the exact ingredients specified.*

As you will learn in this chapter, different flours, shortenings, and other ingredients do not function alike. Bakers' formulas are balanced for specific ingredients. Do not substitute bread flour for pastry flour or regular shortening for emulsified shortening, for example. They won't work the same way.

Occasionally, a substitution may be made, such as active dry yeast for compressed yeast (see p. 226), but not without adjusting the quantities or rebalancing the formula.

KEY POINTS TO REVIEW

- What is the proper way to measure bakeshop ingredients? Why?
- What is the procedure for weighing ingredients using a baker's balance scale?
- How do you use baker's percentages to calculate the weight of ingredients in a baking formula?

Mixing and Gluten Development

What Is Gluten?

Gluten is a substance made up of proteins present in wheat flour; it gives structure and strength to baked goods.

In order for gluten to be developed, the proteins must first absorb water. Then, as the dough or batter is mixed or kneaded, the gluten forms long, elastic strands. As the dough or batter is leavened, these strands capture the gases in tiny pockets or cells, and we say the product rises. When the product is baked, the gluten, like all proteins, coagulates or solidifies and gives structure to the product.

How Does the Baker Control Gluten?

Flour is mostly starch, but its protein or gluten content, not its starch, concerns the baker most. Without gluten proteins to give structure, baked goods would not hold together.

The baker must be able to control the gluten, however. For example, we want French bread to be firm and chewy, which requires much gluten. On the other hand, we want cakes to be tender, which means we want very little gluten development.

Ingredient proportions and mixing methods are determined, in part, by how they affect the development of gluten. The baker has several methods for adjusting gluten development.

1. **Selection of flours.**

   Wheat flours are classified as *strong* or *weak*, depending on their protein content.

   Strong flours come from *hard wheat* and have a high protein content.

   Weak flours come from *soft wheat* and have a low protein content.

   Thus, we use strong flours for breads and weak flours for cakes.

   Only wheat flour develops gluten. To make bread from rye and other grains, the formula must be balanced with some high-gluten wheat flour, or the bread will be heavy.

2. **Shortening.**

   Any fat used in baking is called a ***shortening*** because it shortens gluten strands. It does this by surrounding the particles and lubricating them so they do not stick together. Thus, *fats are tenderizers*. A cookie or pastry that is very crumbly due to high fat content is said to be short.

   You can see why French bread has little or no fat, while cakes contain a great deal.

3. **Liquid.**

   Because gluten proteins must absorb water before they can be developed, the amount of water in a formula can affect toughness or tenderness. To keep them tender, pie crusts and crisp cookies are made with very little liquid.

4. **Mixing methods.**
   In general, the more a dough or batter is mixed, the more the gluten develops. Thus, bread doughs are mixed or kneaded for a long time to develop the gluten. Cakes, pie crusts, muffins, and other products that must be tender are mixed for a short time.
   It is possible to overmix bread dough, however. Gluten strands stretch only so far. They break if the dough is overmixed.

The Baking Process

The changes undergone by a dough or batter as it bakes are basically the same for all baked products, from breads to cookies and cakes. You should know what these changes are so you can learn how to control them.

The stages in the baking process take place as follows. Be aware that many of these steps occur at the same time, not one after the other. For example, escape of water vapor and other gases begins almost at once, but it is more rapid later in the baking process.

1. **Melting of fats.**
   Different fats melt—and release trapped gases—at different temperatures, so the proper shortening should be selected for each product. Most fats used in baking melt between 90°and 130°F (32° and 55°C).
   As the fats melt, they surround the air cells and make the product more tender.

2. **Formation and expansion of gases.**
   Some gases are already present in the dough, as in proofed bread dough and in sponge cake batters. As they are heated, the gases expand and leaven the product.
   Some gases are not formed until heat is applied. Yeast and baking powder form gases rapidly when first placed in the oven. Steam is also formed as the moisture of the dough is heated.
   As the product rises, the cell walls become thinner as they are stretched by the expanding gases. This tenderizes the product.
   Leavening and leavening agents are discussed in more detail beginning on page 226.

3. **Killing of yeast and other microorganisms.**
   In addition to yeast, doughs may contain other microorganisms, including bacteria and molds. Most of these, including yeast, die when the item reaches about 140°F (60°C). When yeast dies, fermentation stops and no more gas is released.

4. **Coagulation of proteins.**
   Like all proteins, gluten and egg proteins coagulate or solidify when they reach high enough temperatures. This is the process that gives structure to baked goods.
   Correct baking temperature is important. If the temperature is too high, coagulation will start too soon, before the expansion of gases has reached its peak. The product will have poor volume or a split crust. If the temperature is too low, the proteins will not coagulate soon enough, and the product may collapse.

5. **Gelatinization of starches.**
   The starches absorb moisture, expand, and become firmer.

6. **Escape of water and other gases.**
   This takes place throughout the baking process, but it is fastest during the later stages of baking. Water evaporation decreases the weight of the product and also enables crust formation.

7. **Crust formation and browning.**
   Browning occurs when sugars caramelize and starches and proteins undergo Maillard browning. This contributes to flavor. Milk, sugar, and egg increase browning.
   A crust is formed as water evaporates from the surface and leaves it dry.

Staling

Staling is the change in texture and aroma of baked goods due to the change in structure and the loss of moisture by the starch granules. Stale baked goods have lost their fresh-baked aroma and are firmer, drier, and more crumbly than fresh products.

Prevention of staling is a major concern of the baker because most baked goods lose quality rapidly.

Staling can be slowed by these techniques:

1. **Protecting the product from air.**
   Wrapping bread in plastic and covering cakes with icing are two examples.
   Unfortunately, hard-crusted breads, which stale rapidly, should not be wrapped, or the crusts will become soft. These bread products should always be served fresh.

2. **Adding moisture retainers to the formula.**
   Fats and sugars are good moisture retainers, and products high in these ingredients keep best.
   Some of the best French bread has no fat at all, and if it is not served within hours of baking, it will begin to stale. For longer keeping, bakers often add a very small amount of fat and/or sugar to the formula.

3. **Freezing.**
   Baked goods frozen *before* they become stale maintain quality for longer periods. They should be served very soon after thawing. Frozen breads may be reheated with excellent results if they are served immediately.
   Refrigerating actually seems to speed staling rather than slowing it. Only baked goods that could develop health hazards, such as those with cream fillings, are refrigerated.

Loss of crispness is caused by absorption of moisture, so it is, in a sense, the opposite of staling. This is a problem with low-moisture products such as cookies and pie crusts. The problem is usually solved by proper storage in airtight wraps or containers to protect the products from moisture in the air. Prebaked pie shells should be filled as close to service time as possible.

KEY POINTS TO REVIEW

- What is gluten? What are four ways to control gluten development in doughs and batters?
- What are seven changes that take place in doughs and batters as they are baked?
- How can you slow the rate at which baked goods become stale?

INGREDIENTS

The following introduction to baking ingredients is necessarily simplified. If you decide to pursue a career as a baker, you will need to learn a great deal of technical information. However, the basic information presented here is enough to enable you to produce a full range of baked items in a small bakeshop or restaurant kitchen.

Flours, Meals, and Starches

White Wheat Flour

White wheat flour is milled from wheat kernels after the outer covering, called *bran*, and the germ are removed. Wheat flour contains 63 to 73 percent starch and 7 to 15 percent protein. The rest is moisture, fat, sugar, and minerals.

Wheat flour is the source of the protein called *gluten*, which you remember is one of the essential elements in baking. Bakers select flour on the basis of its gluten content. Flours high in protein are called *strong*, and those low in protein are called *weak*. (*Note:* Rye, barley, oats, and some other grains also contain gluten proteins, but these proteins do not develop into a gluten structure as do the proteins in wheat flour. Thus, for the baker, these other grains in effect do not contain gluten, but people with gluten intolerance may still have to avoid them in their diets.)

For our purposes, in the small bakeshop, we need to know about three kinds of wheat flour.

1. ***Bread flour*** is a strong flour used for making breads, hard rolls, and any product that requires high gluten. The best bread flours are called *patents*. *Straight* flours are also strong flours.
2. ***Cake flour*** is a weak or low-gluten flour made from soft wheat. It has a soft, smooth texture and a pure white color. Cake flour is used for cakes and other delicate baked goods that require low gluten content.
3. ***Pastry flour*** is lower in gluten than bread flour but higher than cake flour. It has the same creamy white color as bread flour, not the pure white of cake flour. Pastry flour is used for cookies, pie pastry, some sweet yeast doughs, biscuits, and muffins.

Being able to identify these three flours by sight and touch is an important skill because, sooner or later, someone will dump a bag of flour into the wrong bin, and you will need to recognize the problem.

Bread flour feels slightly coarse when rubbed between the fingers. If squeezed into a lump, it falls apart as soon as the hand is opened. Its color is creamy white.

Cake flour feels smooth and fine. It stays in a lump when squeezed in the palm of the hand. Its color is pure white.

Pastry flour feels like cake flour but has the creamy color of bread flour.

All-purpose flour, seen in retail markets, is not often found in bakeshops. This flour is formulated to be slightly weaker than bread flour so it can be used for pastries as well. A professional baker, however, prefers to use flours formulated for specific purposes because these give the best results.

Whole Wheat Flour

Whole wheat flour is made by grinding the entire wheat kernel, including the bran and germ. The germ, which is the embryo of a new wheat plant, is high in fat, which can become rancid. This is why whole wheat flour does not keep as well as white flour.

Because it is made from wheat, whole wheat flour contains gluten, so it can be used alone in bread making. However, a bread made with 100 percent whole wheat will be heavy because the gluten strands are cut by the sharp edges of the bran flakes. Also, the fat from the wheat germ contributes slightly to the shortening action. This is why most whole wheat breads are strengthened with white bread flour.

Bran flour is flour to which bran flakes have been added. The bran may be coarse or fine, depending on specifications.

Rye Flour

Next to white and whole wheat, rye is the most popular flour in bread making. Because rye flour does not develop much gluten, breads made with it are heavy unless some hard wheat flour is added.

Rye flour is available in three shades, *light, medium,* and *dark. Rye meal* or ***pumpernickel*** is a coarse meal made from the whole rye grain.

Rye blend is a mixture of rye flour and hard wheat flour.

Other Flours

Products milled from other grains are occasionally used to add variety to baked goods. These include cornmeal, buckwheat flour, soy flour, potato flour, oat flour, and barley flour. The term *meal* is used for products that are not as finely ground as flour.

All these products must normally be used in combination with wheat flour because they do not form gluten.

Starches

In addition to flours, other starch products are also used in the bakeshop. Unlike flour, they are used primarily to thicken puddings, pie fillings, and similar products.

The most important starches in dessert production are as follows:

1. *Cornstarch* has a special property that makes it valuable for certain purposes. Products thickened with cornstarch set up almost like gelatin when cooled. For this reason, it is used to thicken cream pies and other products that must hold their shape.
2. *Waxy maize* and other *modified starches* also have valuable properties. They do not break down when frozen, so are used for products that are to be frozen. Also, they are clear when cooked, and give a brilliant, clear appearance to fruit pie fillings.

   Waxy maize does not set up firm like cornstarch but rather makes a soft paste, which has the same consistency hot and cold. Thus, it is not suitable for cream pie fillings.
3. *Instant starches* are precooked or pregelatinized, so they thicken cold liquids without further cooking. They are useful when heat will damage the flavor of the product, as in fresh fruit glazes (such as strawberry).

Fats

We have said that one of the main functions of fats in baking is to shorten gluten strands and tenderize the product. We can summarize the reasons for using fats in baked items as follows:

- To tenderize the product and soften the texture.
- To add moistness and richness.
- To increase keeping quality.
- To add flavor.
- To assist in leavening when used as creaming agents or when used to give flakiness to puff pastry, pie dough, and similar products.

Shortenings

Any fat acts as a shortening in baking because it shortens gluten strands and tenderizes the product. However, we usually use the word *shortening* to mean any of a group of solid fats, usually white and tasteless, that are specially formulated for baking.

Because shortenings are used for many purposes, manufacturers have formulated different kinds of fats with different properties. Following are the three main types of shortening.

REGULAR SHORTENINGS

These shortenings have a tough, waxy texture, and small particles of the fat tend to hold their shape in a dough or batter. This type of shortening does not melt until a high temperature is reached.

Regular shortening has good creaming ability. This means that a large quantity of air can be mixed into it to give a batter lightness and leavening power. Therefore, it is used in products mixed by the creaming method, such as certain cookies.

Because of its texture, this type of shortening is used for flaky products such as pie crusts and biscuits. It is also used in breads and many pastries. Unless another shortening is specified, regular shortening is generally used.

EMULSIFIED SHORTENINGS

These are soft shortenings that spread easily throughout a batter and quickly coat the particles of sugar and flour. Because of their easy spreading, they give a smoother and finer texture to cakes and make them moister.

Emulsified shortening is often used whenever the weight of sugar in a cake batter is greater than the weight of flour. Because this shortening spreads so well, a simpler mixing method can be used. Such cakes are referred to as *high-ratio* cakes, so emulsified shortening is sometimes called *high-ratio shortening*.

In addition, emulsified shortening is used in certain icings because it can hold more sugar and liquid without curdling.

PUFF PASTRY SHORTENINGS

Puff pastry shortenings are firm like regular shortening. They are especially formulated for puff pastry and other doughs that form layers, such as Danish pastry.

Butter and Margarine

Shortenings are manufactured to have certain textures and hardness. Butter, on the other hand, is a natural product that doesn't have these advantages. It is hard and brittle when cold and soft at room temperature, and it melts easily. Consequently, doughs made with butter are hard to handle. Margarine is a little easier to handle, but it has many of the same disadvantages.

On the other hand, butter and margarine have two major advantages.

1. **Flavor.**
   Shortenings are intentionally flavorless, but butter has a highly desirable flavor.

2. **Melting qualities.**
   Butter melts in the mouth. Shortenings do not. After eating pastries or icings made with shortening, one can be left with an unpleasant film of shortening coating the mouth.

For these reasons, many bakers and pastry chefs feel the advantages of butter outweigh its disadvantages for some purposes.

Oils

Oils are liquid fats. They are not often used as shortening in baking because they spread through a batter or dough too thoroughly and shorten too much. Their usefulness in the bakeshop is limited primarily to greasing pans and proofing bowls, to deep-frying doughnuts, and to serving as a wash for some kinds of rolls. A few quick breads and cakes use oil as a shortening.

Lard

Lard is the rendered fat of hogs. Because of its plastic quality, it was once highly valued for making flaky pie crusts. Since the development of modern shortenings, it is not often used in the bakeshop.

Sugars

Sugars or sweetening agents are used for the following purposes in baking:

- To add sweetness and flavor.
- To create tenderness and fineness of texture by weakening the gluten structure.
- To give crust color.

- To increase keeping qualities by retaining moisture.
- To act as creaming agents with fats.

We customarily use the term *sugar* for regular refined sugars derived from sugar cane or beets. The chemical name for these sugars is ***sucrose***. However, other sugars of different chemical structure are also used in the bakeshop. The following are the more important sugars.

Regular Refined Sugars, or Sucrose

Refined sugars are classified by the size of grains.

1. **Granulated sugar.**

   Regular granulated, also called *fine granulated* or *table sugar,* is the most familiar and the most commonly used.

   Very fine and *ultrafine* sugars are finer than regular granulated. They are prized for making cakes and cookies because they make a more uniform batter and can support higher quantities of fat.

   Sanding sugars are coarser and are used for coating doughnuts, cakes, and other products.

2. **Confectioners' or powdered sugars.**
   Confectioners' sugars are ground to a fine powder and mixed with a small amount of starch to prevent caking. They are classified by coarseness or fineness.

   10X is the finest sugar. It gives the smoothest texture in icings.

   6X is the standard confectioners' sugar. It is used in icings, toppings, and cream fillings.

   Coarser types (*4X* and *XX*) are used for dusting or for any purposes for which 6X and 10X are too fine.

Molasses and Brown Sugar

Molasses is concentrated sugar cane juice. *Sulfured molasses* is a byproduct of sugar refining. It is the product that remains after most of the sugar has been extracted from cane juice. *Unsulfured molasses* is not a byproduct but a specially manufactured sugar product. Its taste is less bitter than that of sulfured molasses.

Molasses contains large amounts of sucrose, plus other sugars, acids, and impurities.

Brown sugar is mostly sucrose, but it also contains varying amounts of molasses and other impurities. The darker grades contain more molasses.

Because molasses and brown sugar contain *acids*, they can be used with baking soda to provide leavening (see p. 226).

Molasses retains moisture in baked goods and so prolongs freshness. However, crisp cookies made with molasses quickly become soft for the same reason.

Corn Syrup

Corn syrup is a liquid sweetener consisting mainly of a sugar called *glucose*. It is made by converting cornstarch into simpler sugar compounds by the use of enzymes.

Corn syrup aids in retaining moisture and is used in some icings and in candy making.

Glucose Syrup

While corn syrup contains other sugars in addition to glucose, pure glucose syrup is also available. It resembles corn syrup but is colorless and nearly tasteless. If a recipe calls for glucose syrup and none is available, substitute light corn syrup.

Honey

Honey is a natural sugar syrup consisting largely of glucose and fructose, plus other compounds that give it flavor. Honeys vary considerably in flavor and color, depending on their source. Flavor is the major reason for using honey, especially because it can be expensive.

Honey contains invert sugar, which means it stays smooth and resists crystallizing. Like molasses, it contains *acid*, which enables it to be used with baking soda as a leavening.

Malt Syrup

Malt syrup is used primarily in yeast breads. It serves as food for the yeast and adds flavor and crust color to the breads.

KEY POINTS TO REVIEW

- What three main types of white wheat flour are used in the bakeshop? Describe them.
- What five functions do fats have in baked goods?
- What is the difference between regular and emulsified shortening? When compared with shortening, what are two advantages and one disadvantage of using butter in baked goods?
- What five functions do sugars have in baked goods? What is the difference between regular granulated sugar and confectioners' sugar?

Liquids

Gluten cannot be developed without moisture, so liquids are essential to the baking process.

Pie crusts provide a good illustration of how liquids function in baking. If too much water is incorporated in a pie dough, a lot of gluten develops and the crust is tough. If no water at all is used, no gluten develops and the crust does not hold together.

Some of the moisture in doughs and batters changes to steam during baking. This contributes to leavening.

Water

Water is the basic liquid in baking, especially in breads.

Tap water is normally suitable for most baking purposes. However, in some localities, the water may be *hard*, meaning it contains many dissolved minerals. These minerals interfere with proper gluten development. In these areas, the water may have to be treated for use in baking.

Milk and Cream

Milk products, as described in Chapter 9, are important in baking. These products include liquid whole and skim milk, buttermilk, and dry milk solids.

Milk contributes to the texture, flavor, nutritional value, keeping quality, and crust color of baked goods.

1. Whole milk contains fat, which must be calculated as part of the shortening in a dough. For this reason, whole and skim milk are not interchangeable in a formula unless adjustments are made for the fat.
2. Buttermilk, which is slightly acid, is often used in conjunction with baking soda as a leavening agent in quick breads.

3. Cream is not often used as a liquid in doughs and batters, except in a few specialty products. In these instances, it is used as a shortening as well as a liquid because of its fat content.

   Cream is more important in the production of fillings and toppings.

4. Dry milk is often used because of its convenience and low cost. In some formulas, it is not necessary to reconstitute it. The milk powder is included with the dry ingredients, and water is used as the liquid.

Other Sources of Liquid

Eggs, honey, molasses, and even butter (about 15 percent water) contribute moisture to a dough or batter. In many cookies, for example, eggs are the only liquid in the formula.

Eggs

Forms

Eggs are purchased in the following forms:

1. Whole shell eggs.
2. Frozen: whites, yolks, whole, and whole with extra yolks.
3. Dried: whole, whites, yolks.

Functions

Eggs perform the following functions in baking:

1. **Structure.**
   Like gluten protein, egg protein coagulates to give structure to baked products. This is especially important in high-ratio cakes, where the high sugar and fat content weakens the gluten.

   If used in large quantities, eggs make baked products tough or chewy unless balanced by high fat and sugar, which are tenderizers.

2. **Emulsification of fats.**
   Egg yolks contain natural emulsifiers, which help produce smooth batters. This contributes to both volume and texture.

3. **Leavening.**
   Beaten eggs incorporate air in tiny cells or bubbles. In a batter, this trapped air expands when heated and aids in leavening.

4. **Shortening action.**
   The fat in egg yolks acts as a shortening. This is an important function in products that are low in other fats.

5. **Moisture.**
   Whole eggs are about 70 percent water, egg whites about 86 percent water, and egg yolks about 49 percent water. This moisture must be calculated as part of the total liquid in a formula.

6. **Flavor.**

7. **Nutritional value.**

8. **Color.**
   Yolks impart a yellow color to doughs and batters. Also, eggs brown easily and contribute to crust color.

Leavening Agents

Leavening is the production or incorporation of gases in a baked product to increase volume and to produce shape and texture. These gases must be retained in the product until the structure is set enough (by the coagulation of gluten and egg protein) to hold its shape.

Exact measurement of leavening agents is important because small changes can produce major defects in baked products.

Yeast

Fermentation is the process by which yeast acts on carbohydrates and changes them into carbon dioxide gas and alcohol. This release of gas produces the leavening action in yeast products. The alcohol evaporates completely during and immediately after baking.

Yeast is a microscopic plant. As a living organism, it is sensitive to temperatures.

34°F (1°C)	Inactive; storage temperature.
60° to 70°F (15° to 20°C)	Slow action.
70° to 90°F (20° to 32°C)	Best growth; proofing temperature for bread doughs.
Above 100°F (38°C)	Reaction slows.
140°F (60°C)	Yeast is killed.

Yeast is available in three forms:

1. *Fresh yeast*, also called *compressed yeast*, is moist and perishable and is preferred by professional bakers. It is usually purchased in 1-lb (450-g) cakes.

2. *Active dry yeast* is a dry, granular form of yeast. Active dry yeast must be rehydrated in 4 times its weight of warm water—about 110°F (43°C)—before use. When using active dry yeast in a bread formula, use part of the water in the formula to dissolve the yeast. Do not add more water.

3. *Instant dry yeast* is also a dry granular form of yeast, but it does not have to be dissolved in water before use. It can be added in its dry form because it absorbs water much more quickly than regular dry yeast. It also produces more gas than regular dry yeast, so less of it is needed. Instant dry yeast is sometimes called *rapid-rise* or *quick-rise* yeast.

In this book, when yeast is required in a formula, fresh yeast is specified. To substitute dry yeast, use the following guidelines.

To convert fresh yeast to regular active dry yeast, multiply the quantity by 0.5. For example, if the formula calls for 1½ ounces fresh yeast, multiply by 0.5 to get ¾ ounce active dry yeast.

To convert fresh yeast to instant dry yeast, multiply the quantity by 0.35. For example, if the formula calls for 40 g fresh yeast, multiply by 0.35 to get 14 g instant yeast.

Yeast contributes flavor in addition to leavening action.

Chemical Leaveners

Chemical leaveners are those that release gases produced by chemical reactions.

BAKING SODA

Baking soda is the chemical sodium bicarbonate. If *moisture* and an *acid* are present, soda releases carbon dioxide gas, which leavens the product.

Heat is not necessary for the reaction (although the gas is released faster at higher temperatures). For this reason, products leavened with soda must be baked at once, or the gases will escape and leavening power will be lost.

Acids that react with soda in a batter include honey, molasses, buttermilk, fruits, cocoa, and chocolate. Sometimes cream of tartar is used for the acid. The amount of soda used in a formula is generally the amount needed to balance the acid. If more leavening power is needed, baking powder, not more soda, is used.

BAKING POWDER

Baking powders are mixtures of baking soda plus an acid to react with it.

Because baking powders do not depend on acid ingredients for their leavening power in a formula, they are more versatile.

Single-acting baking powders require only moisture to be able to release gas. Like baking soda, they can be used only if the product is to be baked immediately after mixing.

Double-acting baking powders release some gas when cold, but they require heat for complete reaction. Thus, cake batters made with these can incorporate the leavening agent early in the mixing period and can stand for some time before being baked.

Do not include more baking powder than necessary in a formula because undesirable flavors may be created.

BAKING AMMONIA

Baking ammonia is the chemical ammonium carbonate. It decomposes during baking to form carbon dioxide gas and ammonia gas. Only heat and moisture are necessary for it to work. No acids are needed.

Because it decomposes completely, it leaves no residue that can affect flavor. However, it can be used only in small products, like cookies, which allow the ammonia gas to be completely driven off.

Baking ammonia releases gases quickly, so it is sometimes used in products like cream puffs where rapid leavening is desired.

Air

Air is incorporated into a batter primarily by two methods, creaming and foaming. This air expands during baking and leavens the product.

1. *Creaming* is the process of beating fat and sugar together to incorporate air. It is an important technique in cake and cookie making. Some pound cakes and cookies are leavened almost entirely by this method.
2. *Foaming* is the process of beating eggs, with or without sugar, to incorporate air. Foams made with whole eggs are used to leaven sponge cakes, while angel food cakes, meringues, and soufflés are leavened with egg white foams.

Steam

When water turns to steam, it expands to 1,600 times its original volume. Because all baked products contain some moisture, steam is an important leavening agent.

Puff pastry, cream puffs, popovers, and pie crusts use steam as their major or only leavening agent.

If the starting baking temperature for these products is high, steam is produced rapidly and leavening is greatest.

Salt, Flavorings, and Spices

Salt

Salt plays an important role in baking. It is more than just a seasoning or flavor enhancer. It also has these functions:

1. Salt strengthens gluten structure and makes it more stretchable. Thus, it improves the texture of breads.

2. Salt inhibits yeast growth. It is, therefore, important for controlling fermentation in bread doughs and in preventing the growth of undesirable wild yeasts.

For these reasons, the quantity of salt in a formula must be carefully controlled.

Chocolate and Cocoa

Chocolate and cocoa are derived from cocoa or cacao beans. When the beans are roasted and ground, the resulting product is called *chocolate liquor*, which contains a white or yellowish fat called *cocoa butter*.

Cocoa is the dry powder that remains after part of the cocoa butter is removed from chocolate liquor.

Dutch process cocoa is processed with an alkali. It is slightly darker, smoother in flavor, and more easily dissolved in liquids than regular cocoa.

Bitter or *unsweetened chocolate* is straight chocolate liquor. In some less expensive brands, some of the cocoa butter may be replaced by another fat.

Sweet chocolate is bitter chocolate with the addition of sugar in varying amounts. If the percentage of sugar is low, it is sometimes called *semisweet* or *bittersweet*.

Milk chocolate is sweet chocolate with the addition of milk solids. It is used primarily in candy making. (None of the recipes in this book call for milk chocolate.)

Cocoa and chocolate are high in starch. When cocoa is added to a cake formula, it is sometimes considered part of the flour proportion for this reason.

Spices

The most important spices in the bakeshop are cinnamon, nutmeg, mace, cloves, ginger, caraway, cardamom, allspice, anise, and poppy seed.

Because spices are used in small quantities, it is not much more expensive to use the best quality, and the results are superior.

Spices should be measured by weight unless the quantity is so small that measuring spoons are necessary.

Extracts and Emulsions

Extracts are flavorful oils and other substances dissolved in alcohol. These include vanilla, lemon, and bitter almond.

Emulsions are flavorful oils mixed with water with the aid of emulsifiers such as vegetable gums. Lemon and orange are the most frequently used emulsions.

The flavorings of extracts and emulsions may be natural or artificial. Natural flavorings give the best results, but they are often expensive. Artificial flavorings must be used in moderation to avoid creating strong or undesirable flavors in baked items.

KEY POINTS TO REVIEW

- What are the two main liquids used to make doughs and batters? How do liquids affect gluten development?
- What eight functions do eggs have in baked goods?
- What three types of yeast are used in the bakeshop? How does yeast make bread rise?
- What is the difference between baking soda and baking powder?

TERMS FOR REVIEW

gluten
strong flour
weak flour
shortening
staling
bread flour
cake flour
pastry flour
whole wheat flour
pumpernickel
rye blend
regular shortening
emulsified shortening
sucrose
confectioners' sugar
leavening
fermentation
fresh yeast
active dry yeast
instant dry yeast
chemical leavener
single- and double-acting baking powders
creaming
foaming
extract
emulsion

QUESTIONS FOR DISCUSSION

1. Below are ingredients for a white cake. The weight of the flour is given, and the proportions of other ingredients are indicated by percentages. Calculate the weights required for each.

Cake flour	3 lb or 1500 g (100%)
Baking powder	4%
Shortening	50%
Sugar	100%
Salt	1%
Milk	75%
Egg whites	33%
Vanilla	2%

2. Discuss four factors that affect the development of gluten in doughs and batters.
3. Why do some cakes fall if they are removed from the oven too soon?
4. Which kind of cake would you expect to have better keeping qualities—a sponge cake, which is low in fat, or a high-ratio cake?
5. Why is white wheat flour used in rye breads? in whole wheat breads? Some bakeries in Europe produce a kind of pumpernickel bread with 100 percent rye flour. What would you expect its texture to be like?
6. Describe how to distinguish among bread, pastry, and cake flours by touch and sight.
7. What is the difference between regular and emulsified shortenings?
8. Shortbread is a type of cookie made with flour, butter, and sugar, but no liquid. What would you expect its texture to be like? Why?

Chapter 9

Assorted yeast breads.

Yeast Products

After reading this chapter, you should be able to

1. Prepare breads and dinner rolls.
2. Prepare sweet dough products.
3. Prepare Danish pastry and croissants.

In its simplest form, bread is nothing more than a dough of flour and water, leavened by yeast and baked. In fact, some hard-crusted French breads contain *only* these ingredients, plus salt. Other kinds of bread contain additional ingredients, including sugar, shortening, milk, eggs, and flavorings. But flour, water, and yeast are still the basic building blocks of all breads.

Yet for something that seems so simple, bread can be one of the most exacting and complex products to make. Success in bread making depends largely on your understanding of two basic principles: gluten development, which we discussed in the previous chapter, and yeast fermentation, which we have touched on and which we study in greater detail here.

This chapter focuses on the production of many kinds of yeast products, including breads, dinner rolls, sweet rolls, Danish pastry, and croissants.

UNDERSTANDING YEAST PRODUCTS

Yeast Product Types

Although all yeast doughs are essentially made according to the same basic principles, it is useful to divide yeast products into categories such as the following.

Regular Yeast Dough Products

LEAN DOUGH PRODUCTS

A ***lean dough*** is one that is low in fat and sugar.

- Hard-crusted breads and rolls, including French and Italian breads, kaiser rolls and other hard rolls, and pizza. These are the leanest of all bread products.
- Other white breads and dinner rolls. These have a higher fat and sugar content and, sometimes, also contain eggs and milk solids. Because they are slightly richer, they generally have soft crusts.
- Whole-grain breads. Whole wheat and rye breads are the most common. Many varieties of rye bread are produced with light or dark flours or with pumpernickel flour and various flavorings, especially molasses and caraway seeds.

RICH DOUGH PRODUCTS

There is no exact dividing line between rich and lean doughs but, in general, rich doughs contain higher proportions of fat, sugar, and, sometimes, eggs.

- Nonsweet breads and rolls, including rich dinner rolls and brioche. These have a high fat content but low enough sugar to be served as dinner breads. Brioche dough is especially rich, made with a high proportion of butter and eggs.
- Sweet rolls, including coffee cakes and many breakfast and tea rolls. These have high fat and sugar and, often, eggs. They are usually made with a sweet filling or topping.

Rolled-In Yeast Dough Products

Rolled-in doughs, also called ***laminated doughs***, are those in which a fat is incorporated into the dough in many layers by means of a rolling and folding procedure. The alternating layers of fat and dough give the baked product a flaky texture.

- Nonsweet rolled-in doughs: croissants.
- Sweet rolled-in doughs: Danish pastry.

Mixing Methods

Mixing yeast doughs has three main purposes:

1. To combine all ingredients into a uniform, smooth dough.
2. To distribute the yeast evenly throughout the dough.
3. To develop gluten.

Three principal mixing methods are used for yeast doughs: the ***straight dough method***, the ***modified straight dough method***, and the ***sponge method***.

Straight Dough Method

There is only one step in this method, as practiced by many bakers.

Some bakers dissolve the compressed yeast in some of the water before adding the remaining ingredients. Others omit this step. Active dry yeast, on the other hand, must be rehydrated before mixing.

The advantage of softening the yeast in water is that it helps ensure that the yeast is evenly distributed in the dough.

Procedure: Straight Dough Mixing Method

If desired, rehydrate yeast in all or part of the water. Combine all ingredients in the mixing bowl and mix.

Modified Straight Dough Method for Rich Doughs

For rich sweet doughs, the method is modified to ensure even distribution of the fat and sugar.

Procedure: Modified Straight Dough Method

1. Soften the yeast in part of the water.
2. Combine the fat, sugar, salt, milk solids, and flavorings. Mix until well combined, but do not whip until light.
3. Add the eggs gradually, as fast as they are absorbed.
4. Add the liquid and mix briefly.
5. Add the flour and yeast. Mix into a smooth dough.

Sponge Method

Sponge doughs are prepared in two stages.

Procedure: Sponge Method

1. Combine the liquid (or part of the liquid), the yeast, and part of the flour (and, sometimes, part of the sugar). Mix into a thick batter or soft dough. Let ferment until double in bulk.
2. Punch down and add the rest of the flour and remaining ingredients. Mix to a uniform, smooth dough.

KEY POINTS TO REVIEW

- What are the steps in the straight dough method?
- What are the steps in the modified straight dough method?
- What are the steps in the sponge method?

Steps in Yeast Dough Production

The production of yeast breads involves 12 basic steps. These steps are applied to yeast products in general, with variations depending on the particular product.

1. Scaling ingredients
2. Mixing
3. Bulk fermentation
4. Folding or punching
5. Scaling or portioning of dough
6. Rounding
7. Benching
8. Makeup and panning
9. Proofing
10. Baking
11. Cooling
12. Storing

As you can see, mixing of ingredients into a dough is only one part of a complex procedure.

Scaling Ingredients

All ingredients must be weighed accurately. The only items that may be measured by volume are water, milk, and eggs, which may be scaled at 1 pint per pound (1 L per kg).

Mixing

Use the *dough arm* attachment when using a vertical mixer. Mix for the specified time.

The first two purposes of mixing—combining the ingredients into a dough and distributing the yeast—are accomplished during the first part of mixing. The remaining time is necessary to develop the gluten. Overmixed and undermixed doughs have poor volume and texture.

It is necessary for you to learn to tell by sight and feel when a dough is thoroughly mixed. This can be done only through experience and with the guidance of your instructor. A properly developed dough feels smooth and elastic. A lean dough should not be sticky.

Sometimes it is necessary to add a little more flour if the dough hasn't lost its stickiness after most of the mixing time has passed.

Rich doughs are generally undermixed slightly because greater tenderness is desired for these products.

Note: Mixing speeds and times given in bread formulas in this book are guidelines only. Small mixers might be damaged if they are run at too high a speed with a stiff dough. In such cases, use a lower speed and extend the mixing time as necessary. Depending on the mixer, developing a dough at first or slow speed requires about twice as much mixing time as at second speed. Follow the manufacturer's recommendations.

Bulk Fermentation

Fermentation is the process by which yeast acts on the sugars and starches in the dough to produce carbon dioxide gas and alcohol.

Gluten becomes smoother and more elastic during fermentation. An underfermented dough does not develop proper volume, and the texture will be coarse. A dough that ferments too long or at too high a temperature becomes sticky, hard to work, and slightly sour.

An underfermented dough is called a ***young dough***. An overfermented dough is called an ***old dough***.

Doughs with weak gluten, such as rye doughs and rich doughs, are usually underfermented or "taken to the bench young."

Procedure for Fermenting Yeast Doughs

1. Place the dough in a lightly oiled container and oil the surface to prevent a crust from forming. (This may not be necessary if humidity is high—about 75 percent.)
2. Cover the container lightly and let the dough rise at a temperature of about 80°F (27°C).
3. Fermentation is complete when the dough has doubled in volume. If fermentation is complete, a dent will remain after the hand is pressed into the top of the dough.

Folding or Punching

Punching is *not* hitting the dough with your fist. It is a method of deflating the dough that *expels carbon dioxide, redistributes the yeast* for further growth, *relaxes the gluten*, and *equalizes the temperature* throughout the dough.

A second fermentation and punching may or may not take place, depending on the product.

Procedure for Punching Yeast Doughs

Pull up the dough on all sides, fold over the center, and press down. Then turn the dough upside down in the bowl.

Scaling or Portioning of Dough

Using a baker's scale, divide the dough into pieces of uniform weight, according to the product being made.

During scaling, allowance is made for weight loss due to evaporation of moisture in the oven. This weight loss is 10 to 13 percent of the weight of the dough. Allow an extra 1½ to 2 ounces of dough for each 1 pound of baked bread, or 50 to 65 grams per 500 grams baked bread.

Rounding

After scaling, the pieces of dough are shaped into smooth, round balls. This procedure forms a kind of skin by stretching the gluten on the outside of the dough into a smooth layer. Rounding simplifies later shaping of the dough and also helps retain gases produced by the yeast.

Your instructor will demonstrate rounding techniques. Machines are also available that divide and round portions of dough automatically. Figure 9.1 illustrates a piece of dough being rounded by hand.

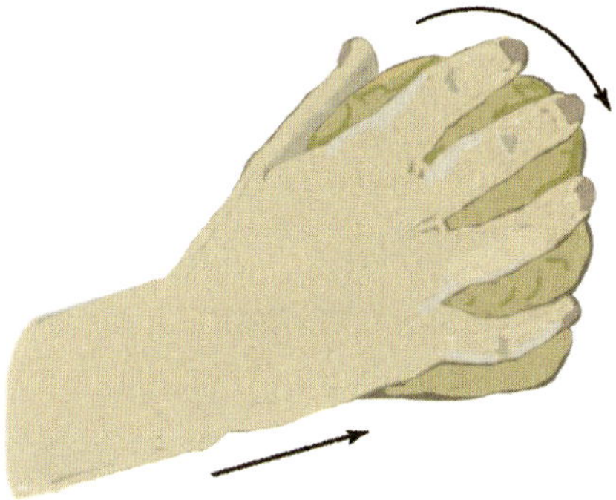

Figure 9.1 To round a piece of dough, roll it on the bench with the palm of your hand. As you rotate the dough, use the edge of your hand to pinch the dough against the bench. This movement stretches the surface of the dough so it is completely smooth except for a seam at the bottom where it was pinched together.

Benching

Rounded portions of dough are allowed to rest on the bench 10 to 15 minutes. This relaxes the gluten to make shaping the dough easier. Also, fermentation continues during this time.

Makeup and Panning

The dough is shaped into loaves or rolls and placed in pans or on baking sheets. For all loaves and rolls, the seam must be centered on the bottom to avoid splitting during baking.

Breads and rolls take a great many forms. A variety of shapes and techniques is presented in the next section.

Proofing

Proofing is a continuation of the process of yeast fermentation, which increases the volume of the shaped dough. Bakers use different terms to distinguish between fermentation of the mixed dough and proofing of the made-up product before baking. Proofing temperatures are generally higher than fermentation temperatures.

If a proof box is not available, come as close to these conditions as you can by covering the products to retain moisture and setting them in a warm place.

Underproofing results in poor volume and dense texture. Overproofing results in coarse texture and some loss of flavor.

Rich doughs are slightly underproofed because their weaker gluten structure will not withstand much stretching.

Procedure for Proofing Yeast Dough Products

Place the panned products in a proof box at 80° to 85°F (27° to 30°C) and 70 to 80 percent humidity, as indicated in the formula. Proof until double in bulk.

Baking

As you recall from the previous chapter, many changes take place in a dough during baking. The most important changes are these:

1. *Oven spring*, which is the rapid rising in the oven due to production and expansion of trapped gases as a result of the oven heat. The yeast is very active at first but is killed when the temperature inside the dough reaches 140°F (60°C).

2. Coagulation of proteins and gelatinization of starches. In other words, the product becomes firm and holds its shape.

3. Formation and browning of the crust.

Load the ovens carefully, as proofed doughs are fragile until they become set by baking.

Oven temperatures must be adjusted for the product being baked. Rolls spaced apart are baked at a higher temperature than large loaves so they become browned in the short time it takes to bake them. In general, lean breads such as those popular in North America are baked at 400° to 425°F (200° to 220°C), while some French breads and rolls are baked at 425° to 475°F (220° to 245°C). Rich doughs and sweet doughs are baked at a lower temperature, 350° to 400°F (175° to 200°C), because their fat, sugar, and milk content makes the crust brown faster.

Hard-crusted breads are baked with steam injected into the oven during the first part of the baking period. This aids the formation of a thin, crisp crust.

Rye breads also benefit from baking with steam for the first 10 minutes.

A break on the side of the loaf is caused by continued rising after the crust is formed. To allow for this final expansion, hard-crusted breads are cut or scored before baking by making shallow slashes on the top of the loaf with a sharp knife or razor.

Small rolls bake completely without a break, so they are usually not scored.

Baking times vary considerably, depending on the product. A golden-brown crust color is the normal indication of doneness. Loaves that are done sound hollow when thumped.

Cooling

After baking, bread must be removed from pans and cooled rapidly on racks to allow the escape of excess moisture and alcohol created during fermentation.

Rolls baked apart from each other on sheets may be left on them because they will get adequate air circulation.

If soft crusts are desired, breads may be brushed with melted shortening before cooling.

Do not cool in a draft, or crusts may crack.

Storing

Breads to be served within 8 hours may be left on racks. For longer storage, wrap cooled breads in moistureproof bags to retard staling. Bread must be thoroughly cooled before wrapping, or moisture will collect inside the bags.

Wrapping and freezing maintains quality for longer periods. Refrigeration, on the other hand, increases staling.

Hard-crusted breads should not be wrapped (unless frozen), or the crusts will soften.

Because of the complexity of bread production, many things can go wrong. To remedy common bread faults, check Table 9.1 for possible causes and correct your procedures.

Table 9.1 Bread Faults and Their Causes

Fault	Causes
Shape	
Poor volume	Too much salt Too little yeast Weak flour Under- or overmixing Improper fermentation or proofing Oven too hot
Too much volume	Too little salt Too much yeast Too much dough scaled Overproofing

FAULT	CAUSES
Shape *(continued)*	
Poor shape	Too much liquid Improper molding or makeup Improper proofing Too much steam in oven
Split or burst crust	Overmixing Underfermentation Improper molding—seam not on bottom Oven too hot Not enough steam in oven
Texture and crumb	
Too dense or close-grained	Too little yeast Underproofing Too much salt Too little liquid
Too coarse or open	Too much yeast Too much liquid Incorrect mixing time Improper fermentation Overproofing Pan too large
Streaked crumb	Improper mixing procedure Poor molding or makeup techniques Too much flour used for dusting
Poor texture or crumbly	Fermentation time too long or too short Overproofing Baking temperature too low Flour too weak Too little salt
Gray crumb	Fermentation time too long or temperature too high
Crust	
Too dark	Too much sugar or milk Underfermentation (young dough) Oven temperature too high Baking time too long Insufficient steam at beginning of baking
Too pale	Too little sugar or milk Overfermentation (old dough) Overproofing Oven temperature too low Baking time too short Too much steam in oven
Too thick	Too little sugar or fat Overfermentation (old dough) Baked too long and/or at too low a temperature Too little steam
Blisters on crust	Too much liquid Improper fermentation Improper shaping of loaves
Flavor	
Flat taste	Too little salt
Poor flavor	Inferior, spoiled, or rancid ingredients Poor bakeshop sanitation Under- or overfermentation

Dough Formulas and Techniques

Bread and Roll Formulas

The basic yeast dough mixing and baking methods discussed earlier in this chapter apply to the following formulas. Therefore, the methods are not repeated in detail for each formula. The basic procedures are indicated, and you should refer to the first part of this chapter if you need to refresh your memory for details.

Makeup techniques for loaves, rolls, and other items are described and illustrated after this recipe section.

Hard Rolls

INGREDIENTS	U.S.	METRIC	PERCENTAGE
Water	1 lb 10 oz	740 g	59 %
Yeast, fresh	1.5 oz	45 g	3.5 %
Bread flour	2 lb 12 oz	1250 g	100 %
Salt	1 oz	30 g	2.25 %
Sugar	1 oz	30 g	2.25 %
Shortening	1 oz	30 g	2.25 %
Egg whites	1 oz	30 g	2.25 %
Yield:	*4 lb 11 oz*	*2155 g*	*171 %*

Per 1 roll: Calories, 90; Protein, 3 g; Fat, 1 g (10% cal.); Cholesterol, 0 mg; Carbohydrates, 17 g; Fiber, 1 g; Sodium, 200 mg.

PROCEDURE

Mixing:
Straight dough method.
10 minutes, 2nd speed (see Note, p. 234).

Fermentation:
About 1 hour at 80°F (27°C).

Scaling and makeup:
Rolls—1 lb (500 g) per dozen.
French-type loaf—18 oz (550 g) per loaf.
See makeup technique after recipe section.
Dock after proofing. Brush with water.

Baking:
425°F (220°C). Steam for first 10 minutes.

Soft Rolls

INGREDIENTS	U.S.	METRIC	PERCENTAGE
Water	1 lb 9 oz	750 g	60 %
Yeast, fresh	1.5 oz	44 g	3.5 %
Bread flour	2 lb 10 oz	1250 g	100 %
Salt	0.8 oz	25 g	2 %
Sugar	4 oz	125 g	9.5 %
Nonfat milk powder	2 oz	60 g	4.75 %
Shortening	2 oz	60 g	4.75 %
Butter or margarine	2 oz	60 g	4.75 %
Yield:	*4 lb 15 oz*	*2374 g*	*189 %*

Per 1 roll: Calories, 120; Protein, 3 g; Fat, 2.5 g (20% cal.); Cholesterol, 0 mg; Carbohydrates, 20 g; Fiber, 0.5 g; Sodium, 190 mg.

PROCEDURE

Mixing:
Straight dough method.
10–12 minutes at 2nd speed (see Note, p. 234).

Fermentation:
1½ hours at 80°F (27°C).

Scaling and makeup:
16–20 oz (450–600 g) per dozen rolls.
See makeup techniques after recipe section.

Baking:
400°F (200°C).

French Bread

INGREDIENTS	U.S.	METRIC	PERCENTAGE
Water	1 lb 12 oz	875 g	58 %
Yeast, fresh	1.5 oz	45 g	3 %
Bread flour	3 lb	1500 g	100 %
Salt	1 oz	30 g	2 %
Yield:	*4 lb 14 oz*	*2450 g*	*163 %*

Per 1 ounce (28.35 g): Calories, 60; Protein, 2 g; Fat, 0.5 g (7% cal.); Cholesterol, 0 mg; Carbohydrates, 13 g; Fiber, 0 g; Sodium, 140 mg.

PROCEDURE

Mixing:

Straight dough method. Dissolve yeast in water before adding flour and salt.

3 minutes at 2nd speed; rest 2 minutes; 3 minutes more at 2nd speed (see Note, p. 234).

Fermentation:

1½ hours at 80°F (27°C).

Punch down.

1 hour at 80°F (27°C).

Scaling and makeup:

French loaves—12 oz (350 g).

Round loaves—18 oz (550 g).

Rolls—16–20 oz (450–600 g) per dozen.

See makeup techniques after recipe section.

Baking:

400°F (200°C). Steam for first 10 minutes.

White Pan Bread

INGREDIENTS	U.S.	METRIC	PERCENTAGE
Water	1 lb 8 oz	750 g	60 %
Yeast, fresh	1.5 oz	45 g	3.75 %
Bread flour	2 lb 8 oz	1250 g	100 %
Salt	1 oz	30 g	2.5 %
Sugar	1.5 oz	45 g	3.75 %
Nonfat milk powder	2 oz	60 g	5 %
Shortening	1.5 oz	45 g	3.75 %
Yield:	*4 lb 7 oz*	*2225 g*	*178 %*

Per 1 ounce (28.35 g): Calories, 70; Protein, 2 g; Fat, 1 g (13% cal.); Cholesterol, 0 mg; Carbohydrates, 13 g; Fiber, 0 g; Sodium, 160 mg.

PROCEDURE

Mixing:

Straight dough method.

10 minutes at 2nd speed (see Note, p. 234).

Fermentation:

1 hour at 80°F (27°C).

Makeup:

Pan loaves. See makeup techniques after recipe section.

Baking:

400°F (200°C).

VARIATION

Whole Wheat Bread

Prepare basic White Pan Bread using

Bread flour	1 lb	500 g	40 %
Whole wheat flour	1 lb 8 oz	750 g	60 %

Rye Bread and Rolls

INGREDIENTS	U.S.	METRIC	PERCENTAGE
Water	1 lb 8 oz	750 g	60 %
Yeast, fresh	1.5 oz	45 g	3.75 %
Rye flour	1 lb	500 g	40 %
Bread flour	1 lb 8 oz	750 g	60 %
Salt	1 oz	30 g	2.5 %
Shortening	1 oz	30 g	2.5 %
Molasses	1 oz	30 g	2.5 %
Caraway seeds	0.5 oz	15 g	1.25 %
Yield:	*4 lb 4 oz*	*2150 g*	*172 %*

Per 1 ounce (28.35 g): Calories, 60; Protein, 2 g; Fat, 1 g (14% cal.); Cholesterol, 0 mg; Carbohydrates, 12 g; Fiber, 2 g; Sodium, 160 mg.

PROCEDURE

Mixing:
Straight dough method.

5–6 minutes at 2nd speed (see Note, p. 234).

Fermentation:
1 hour at 80°F (27°C).

Scaling and makeup:
1 lb (500 g) per pan loaf.

1 lb (500 g) per dozen rolls.

See makeup techniques after recipe section.

Baking:
400°F (200°C). Steam for first 10 minutes.

Focaccia

INGREDIENTS	U.S.	METRIC	PERCENTAGE
Water	1 lb 8 oz	750 g	60 %
Yeast, fresh	1 oz	35 g	2.75 %
Bread flour	2 lb 8 oz	1250 g	100 %
Salt	0.7 oz (3½ tsp)	20 g	1.75 %
Sugar	0.2 oz (1¼ tsp)	6 g	0.5 %
Olive oil	2 oz	60 g	5 %
Yield:	*4 lb 3 oz*	*2121 g*	*170 %*

Per 1 ounce (28.35 g): Calories, 70; Protein, 2 g; Fat, 1 g (13% cal.), Cholesterol, 0 mg; Carbohydrates, 12 g; Fiber, 1 g; Sodium, 115 mg.

PROCEDURE

Mixing:
Straight dough method.

8 minutes at 1st speed (see Note, p. 234).

Fermentation:
1½ hours at 80°F (27°C) or 2 hours at 75°F (24°C).

Makeup:
Oil sheet pans with olive oil. Roll out dough to about ¾ in. (2 cm) thick and place in pans (see **Figure 9.2**). Brush tops generously with olive oil. After proofing, press dimples into the dough at approximately 3-in. (8-cm) intervals.

Baking:
425°F (220°C). Steam for first 10 minutes.

VARIATIONS

Rosemary Focaccia

After pressing in the dimples, sprinkle the top with rosemary (preferably fresh) and coarse salt.

Olive Focaccia

Mix 30% (12 oz/375 g) chopped oil-cured black olives into the dough.

Figure 9.2 Focaccia.

(a) Roll and stretch the dough into a rectangle large enough to fill the pan.

(b) Place the dough in the pan. Top with olive oil.

(c) With the fingertips, poke holes heavily at regular intervals.

(d) Top with the desired topping, such as fresh herbs and coarse salt.

Brioche

INGREDIENTS	U.S.	METRIC	PERCENTAGE
Milk	8 oz	250 g	20 %
Yeast, fresh	2 oz	60 g	5 %
Bread flour	8 oz	250 g	20 %
Eggs	1 lb 4 oz	625 g	50 %
Bread flour	2 lb	1000 g	80 %
Sugar	2 oz	60 g	5 %
Salt	0.5 oz	15 g	1.25 %
Butter, softened	1 lb 8 oz	750 g	60 %
Yield:	*6 lb*	*3010 g*	*241 %*

Per 1 roll: Calories, 160; Protein, 4 g; Fat, 10 g (56% cal.); Cholesterol, 60 mg; Carbohydrates, 14 g; Fiber, 0 g; Sodium, 190 mg.

VARIATION

To make the dough less sticky and less difficult to handle, reduce the butter to 35–50% (14–20 oz/450–625 g). This adjustment also reduces cost. However, the brioche will not be as rich and delicate.

PROCEDURE

Mixing:

Sponge method:

1. Scald milk and cool to lukewarm. Dissolve yeast. Add flour and mix to make a sponge. Let rise until double.
2. Gradually mix in eggs and then dry ingredients (using the paddle attachment) to make a soft dough.
3. Beat in butter, a little at a time, until completely absorbed and dough is smooth. Dough will be very soft and sticky.

Fermentation:

Cover with plastic film and place in retarder overnight.

Makeup:

1½ oz (50 g) per roll.

See makeup techniques after recipe section. Dough is very soft and is easiest to make up when chilled.

Egg-wash after proofing.

Baking:

400°F (200°C).

Sweet Roll Dough

INGREDIENTS	U.S.	METRIC	PERCENTAGE
Milk	1 lb	500 g	40 %
Yeast, fresh	3 oz	100 g	7.5 %
Butter/margarine/ shortening (see Note)	8 oz	250 g	20 %
Sugar	8 oz	250 g	20 %
Salt	0.5 oz	15 g	1.25 %
Eggs	6 oz	175 g	15 %
Bread flour	2 lb	1000 g	80 %
Cake flour	8 oz	250 g	20 %
Yield:	*5 lb 1 oz*	*2540 g*	*203 %*

Per 1 ounce (28.35 g): Calories, 90; Protein, 2 g; Fat, 3 g (31% cal.): Cholesterol, 15 mg; Carbohydrates, 13 g; Fiber, 0.5 g; Sodium, 90 mg.

Note: Any of the fats listed may be used alone or in combination.

PROCEDURE

Mixing:

Modified straight dough method:

1. Scald milk. Cool to lukewarm. Dissolve yeast in milk.
2. Mix fat, sugar, and salt until smooth, using paddle. Beat in eggs.
3. Add liquid and flour. With dough arm, mix 4 minutes at 2nd speed.

Fermentation:

1½ hours at 80°F (27°C).

Makeup:

See makeup techniques after recipe section.

Baking:

375°F (190°C).

VARIATION

Raised Doughnuts

Prepare basic sweet roll dough, but reduce the fat and sugar by half. Mace, nutmeg, or other spices may be added.

Scaling: 1½ oz (50 g) each.

Give full proof.

Frying: 360°F (182°C).

Drain. Roll in cinnamon sugar or 6X sugar when cool.

VIENNOISERIE

Viennoiserie (vee en wahz ree), or Viennese pastry, is the general term given to sweet yeast-raised dough goods, both laminated and non-laminated. Brioche, Danish, and croissants are classic examples of viennoiserie.

Rolled-In Doughs: Danish Pastry and Croissants

Rolled-in or laminated doughs contain many layers of fat sandwiched between layers of dough. These layers create the flakiness you are familiar with in Danish pastry.

Two basic kinds of rolled-in yeast doughs are made in the bakeshop:

- Danish pastry
- Croissants

Rolled-in doughs are mixed only slightly because the rolling-in procedure continues to develop the gluten.

Butter is the preferred fat for flavor and the melt-in-the-mouth quality of rolled-in doughs. Specially formulated shortenings are available when lower cost and greater ease of handling are more important considerations.

Rolling-In Procedure for Danish and Croissant Dough

The rolling-in procedure has two parts.

1. **Enclosing the fat in the dough.**
   In the method illustrated in Figure 9.3, the fat is spotted on two-thirds of the dough and the dough is folded in thirds like a business letter. This results in five layers: three layers of dough and two layers of fat.
2. **Rolling out and folding the dough to increase the number of layers.**
   In these doughs, we use a *simple fold*, or *three-fold*, which means we fold the dough in thirds. Each complete rolling and folding step is called a *turn*. We give the dough three turns, creating over 100 layers of dough and fat.

Figure 9.3 Rolling-in procedure for Danish and croissant dough.

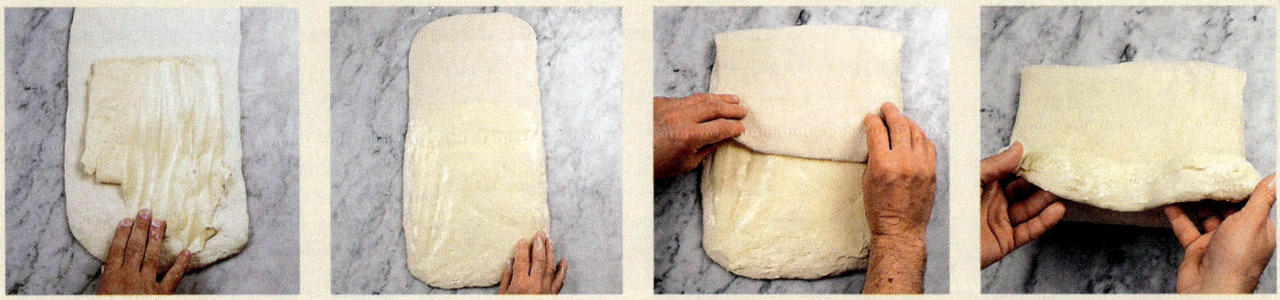

(a, b) Roll the dough into a rectangle about 3 times as long as it is wide and $\frac{1}{2}$ to $\frac{3}{4}$ in. (1 to 2 cm) thick. Smear the butter over two-thirds of the length of the dough, leaving a margin at the edges.

(c) Fold the unbuttered third over the center third.

(d) Fold the remaining third on top. Rest the dough in the retarder (under refrigeration) 20 to 30 minutes to allow the gluten to relax.

(e) Place the dough on the bench at right angles to its position in step (d). Take this step before each rolling-out of the dough so the gluten is stretched in all directions, not just lengthwise. Roll the dough into a rectangle.

(f) Fold again into thirds by first folding the top third over the center. Be sure to brush off excess dusting flour from between the folds.

(g) Fold over the remaining third. You have now completed the first turn or fold. Incorporating the butter doesn't count as a turn. Press one finger in the dough near the end to make one indentation. This indicates "1 turn" to anyone who may have to take up where you left off, or to you if you have several batches going. Refrigerate the dough 20 to 30 minutes to relax the gluten. Repeat the above rolling and folding procedures for a second and third turn, resting the dough between turns. Mark the number of turns in the dough with two or three fingers. After the third turn, rest the dough in the retarder several hours or overnight. Cover it with plastic film to prevent crusting. The dough is then ready for makeup.

In Chapter 13, you will learn an even more complex rolling-in procedure used for puff pastry, which is leavened only by steam, not by yeast. This procedure produces over 1,000 layers!

KEY POINTS TO REVIEW

- What are the 12 steps in yeast dough production?
- What are the steps in the procedure for fermenting yeast doughs?
- What are the steps in the rolling-in procedure for Danish and croissant doughs?

Makeup Techniques

The object of yeast dough makeup techniques is to shape the dough into rolls or loaves that bake properly and have an attractive appearance. When you shape a roll or loaf correctly, you stretch the gluten strands on the surface into a kind of smooth skin. This tight gluten surface holds the item in shape. This is especially important for loaves and rolls that are baked freestanding, not in pans.

Units that are not made up correctly develop irregular shapes and splits and may flatten out on the pan.

Following are a few of the many makeup techniques for yeast doughs.

Hard Rolls and Breads

ROUND ROLLS

1. Scale the dough as indicated in the recipes, usually 1 pound (450 g) per dozen.
2. Round each unit as shown in Figure 9.4.
3. Place rolls 2 inches (5 cm) apart on sheet pans sprinkled with cornmeal.

ROUND LOAVES

1. Flatten the rounded, benched dough into a circle. Fold the four sides over the center, then round again.
2. Place on sheet pans sprinkled with cornmeal.

CLUB ROLLS

1. Make up as shown in Figure 9.5.
2. Place 2 inches (5 cm) apart on sheet pans sprinkled with cornmeal.

Figure 9.4 Rounding small rolls.

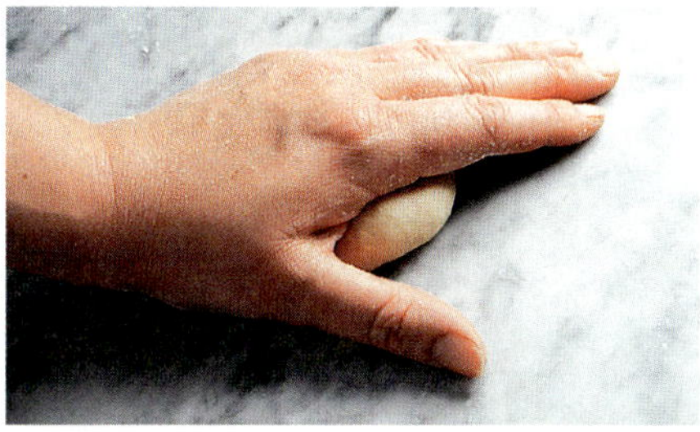

(a) Holding the palm of the hand fairly flat, roll the dough in a tight circle on the workbench. Do not use too much flour for dusting, as the dough must stick to the bench a little for the technique to work.

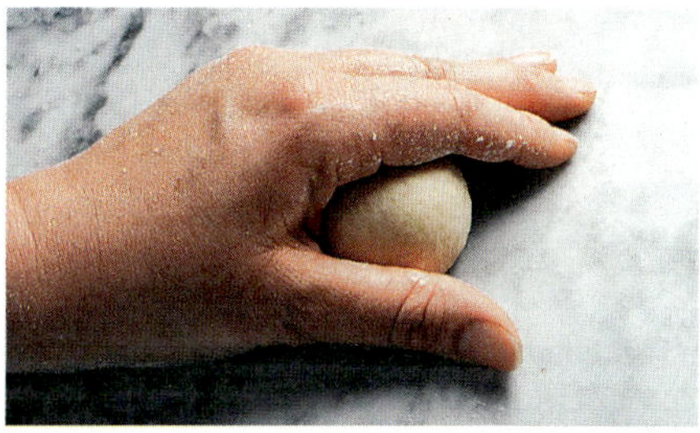

(b) As the ball of dough takes on a round shape, gradually cup your hand.

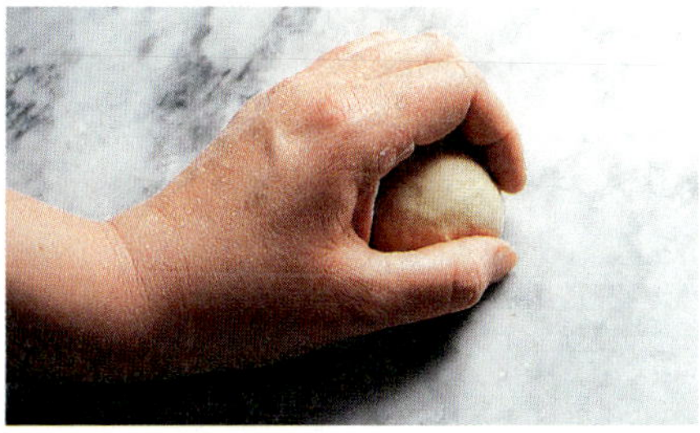

(c) The finished ball of dough should have a smooth surface, except for a slight pucker on the bottom.

Figure 9.5 Making club rolls.

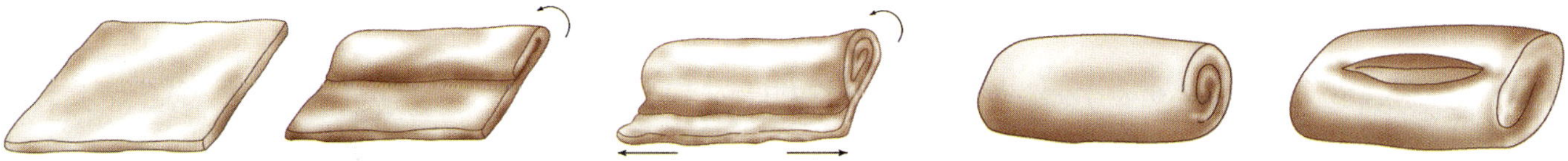

(a) Flatten the piece of dough roughly into a rectangle.

(b) Begin to roll the dough by folding over the back edge of the rectangle. Press the seam firmly with your fingertips.

(c) Continue to roll the dough, always pressing the seam firmly after each turn. As you roll the dough, the front edge will appear to shrink. Stretch the front corners as shown by the arrows to keep the width uniform.

(d) When the roll is finished, seal the seam well so you have a tight roll.

(e) Dock the proofed roll with a single slash to give the baked roll this appearance.

CRESCENT ROLLS

1. Scale dough into 20-ounce (600-g) units.
2. After rounding and benching, flatten the dough and roll it out into a circle 12 inches (30 cm) across.
3. With a pastry wheel, cut the dough circle into 12 equal wedges or triangles. (Alternative method: For large quantities of dough, roll it out into a rectangle and cut like croissant dough.)
4. Roll the triangles into crescents using the same technique as for croissants.

   Note: If using soft roll dough, brush the dough with butter before cutting it into triangles. Do not use any fat.

FRENCH-TYPE LOAVES

1. Scale the dough into units weighing 12 to 18 ounces (350 to 500 g).
2. Make up as shown in Figure 9.6.

Figure 9.6 Making French-type loaves.

(a) Flatten the rounded, relaxed dough with your hands or with a rolling pin.

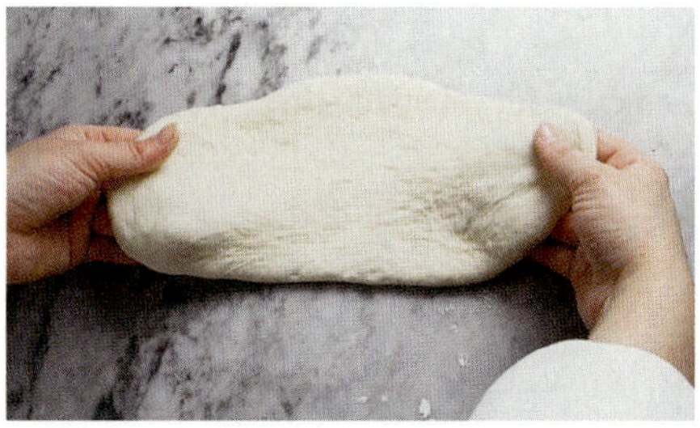

(b) Stretch the oval with the hands to lengthen it.

(c) Roll the dough tightly.

(d) Seal the seam well. If a longer, thinner loaf is required, relax the rolled units again for a few minutes. Flatten them with your palms and stretch the dough lightly to increase its length. Once again, roll tightly and seal the seam. Roll the loaf on the bench under your palms to make it even and to stretch it to the desired shape and length.

(e) Place the dough seam-side down on pans dusted with cornmeal. Proofing the loaves on special trough-shaped pans maintains their shape. Proof. Wash with water. Slash with diagonal cuts or with one lengthwise cut; this can be done before or after proofing.

Soft Roll Doughs

TIED OR KNOTTED ROLLS

1. Scale dough to 16 to 20 ounces (450 to 600 g) per dozen.
2. With the palm of the hand, roll each unit on the workbench into a strip or rope of dough.
3. Tie rolls as shown:

   Single-knot rolls: Figure 9.7

   Double-knot rolls: Figure 9.8

   Braided rolls: Figure 9.9

   Figure-eight rolls: Figure 9.10
4. Place 2 inches (5 cm) apart on greased baking sheets.
5. Egg-wash after proofing.

Figure 9.7 Tying a single-knot roll

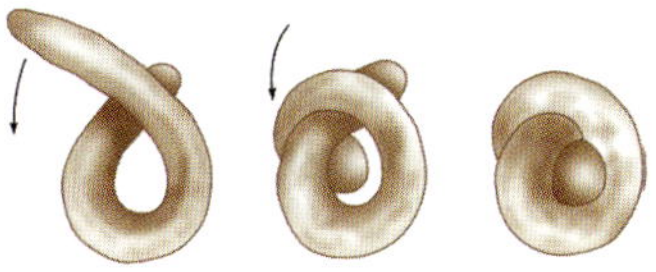

Figure 9.8 Tying a double-knot roll

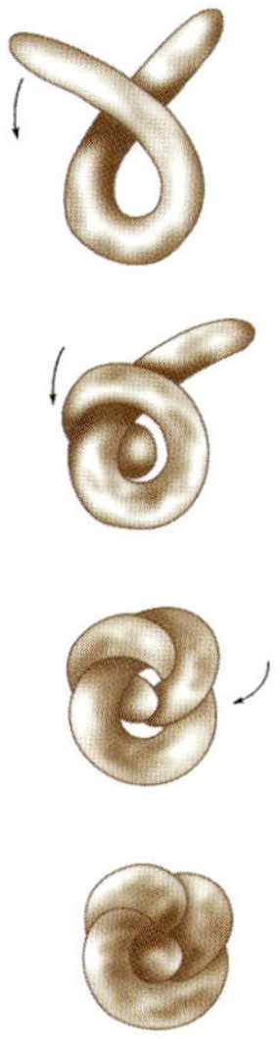

Figure 9.9 Tying a braided roll

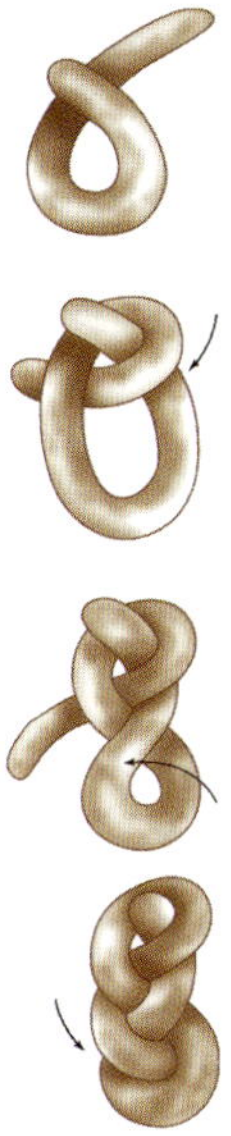

Figure 9.10 Tying a figure-eight roll

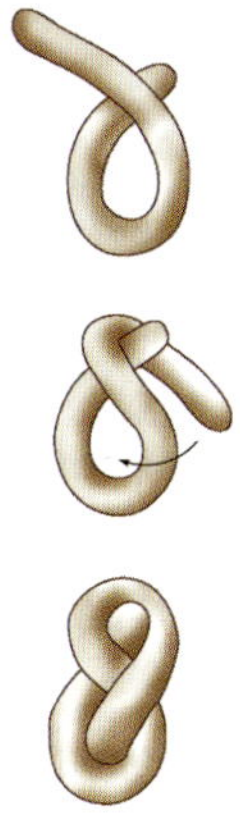

PAN ROLLS

1. Scale dough to 16 to 20 ounces (450 to 600 g) per dozen.
2. Make up as for round hard rolls.
3. Place on greased pans ½ inch (1 cm) apart.

PARKER HOUSE ROLLS

1. Scale dough to 16 to 20 ounces (450 to 600 g) per dozen.
2. Make up as shown in Figure 9.11.
3. Place on greased baking sheet ½ inch (1 cm) apart.

CLOVERLEAF ROLLS

1. Scale dough to 16 to 20 ounces (450 to 600 g) per dozen.
2. Make up and pan as shown in Figure 9.12.

Figure 9.12 Cloverleaf rolls.

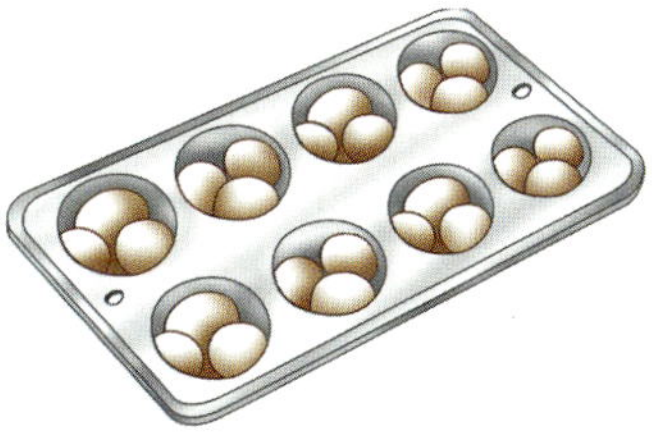

(a) Divide each piece of dough into 3 equal parts. Shape into balls. Place 3 balls in the bottom of each greased muffin tin.

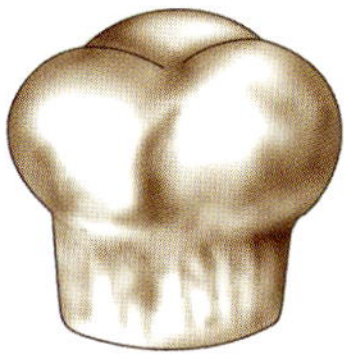

(b) The baked roll has this appearance.

Figure 9.11 Parker House rolls.

(a) Round the scaled piece of dough.

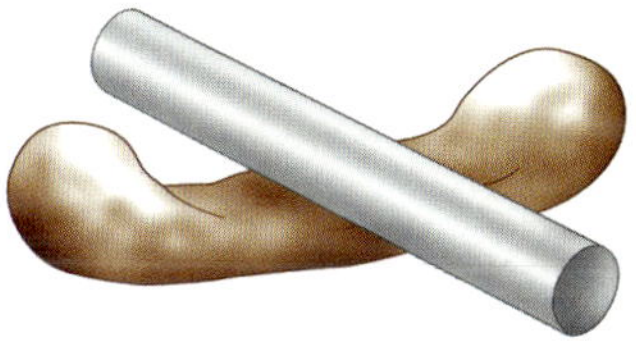

(b) Flatten the center of the dough with a thin rolling pin as shown.

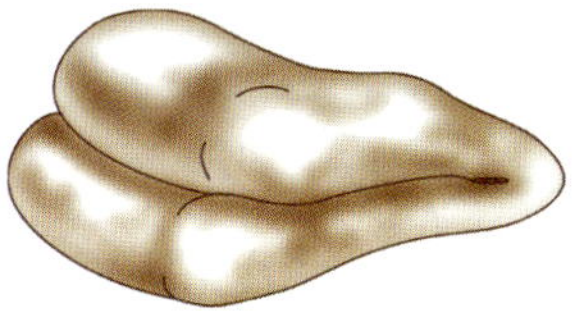

(c) Fold the dough over and press down on the folded edge to make a crease.

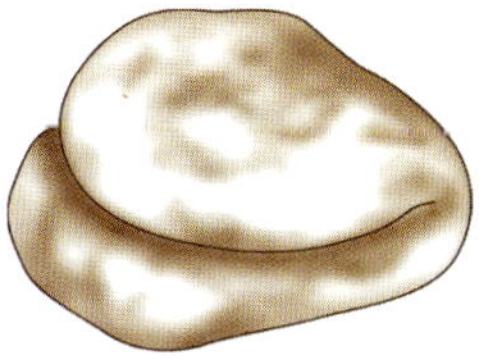

(d) The baked roll has this shape.

BUTTERFLAKE ROLLS

Make up as shown in Figure 9.13.

Figure 9.13 Butterflake rolls.

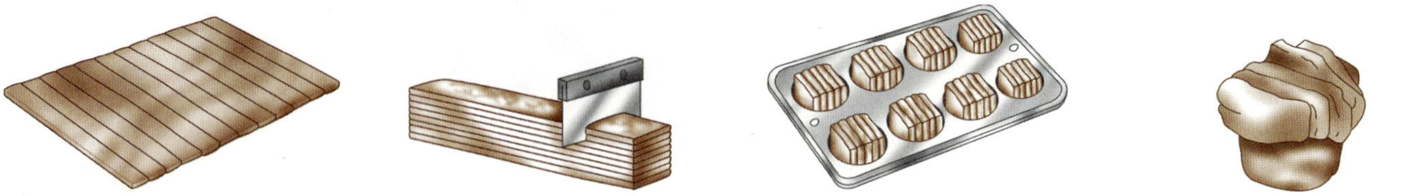

(a) Roll the dough into a thin rectangle. Brush with melted butter. Cut into strips 1 in. (2.5 cm) wide.

(b) Stack 6 strips. Cut into pieces 1½ in. (3.5 cm) long.

(c) Place the pieces on end in greased muffin tins. Proof.

(d) The baked rolls have this appearance.

Pan Loaves

Shaping dough into loaves to be baked in loaf pans is illustrated in Figure 9.14

Figure 9.14 Pan loaves.

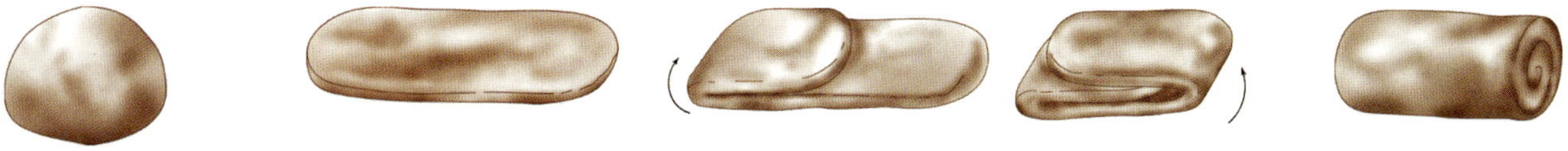

(a) Start with the rounded, benched dough. Flatten it with the palms of the hands.

(b) Stretch it into a long rectangle.

(c, d) Fold into thirds.

(e) Roll the dough into a tight roll of the same length as the pan it is to be baked in. Seal the seam well and place the dough seam side down in the greased pan.

Brioche

Brioche dough may be made into many shapes. The traditional shape is shown in Figure 9.15.

Figure 9.15 Making brioche.

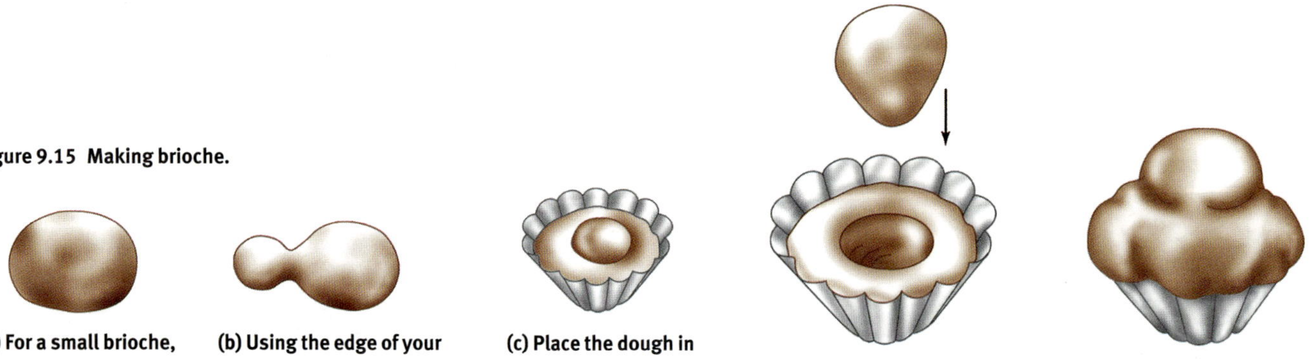

(a) For a small brioche, roll the dough into a round piece.

(b) Using the edge of your hand, pinch off about one-fourth of the dough without detaching it. Roll the dough on the bench so that both parts are round.

(c) Place the dough in the tin, large end first. With your fingertips, press the small ball into the larger one as shown.

(d) For large brioche, separate the two parts of the dough. Place the large ball in the tin and make a hole in the center. Form the smaller ball into a pear shape and fit it into the hole.

(e) A baked large brioche.

Sweet Dough Products

Note: Many sweet dough products may be glazed with clear glaze and/or iced with flat Icing after baking. Flat icing is drizzled over the cooled products without covering them completely.

CINNAMON ROLLS

1. Scale dough into 20-ounce (600-g) units. On a floured board, roll each piece of dough into a rectangle measuring 9 × 12 inches and about ¼ inch thick (23 × 30 × 0.5 cm).
2. Brush with butter and sprinkle with 2 ounces (60 g) cinnamon sugar.
3. Roll up like a jelly roll 12 inches (30 cm) long, as shown in the illustration.
4. Cut into 1-inch (2.5-cm) rolls.
5. Place cut side down in greased muffin tins or on greased sheet pans. One full-size pan, 18 × 26 inches (46 × 66 cm), holds 48 rolls placed 6 by 8.

For variations on the basic cinnamon roll shape, see Figure 9.16.

CINNAMON RAISIN ROLLS

Prepare like cinnamon rolls, but add 2 ounces (60 g) raisins to the filling.

Figure 9.16 The filled dough roll is the starting point for a variety of sweet dough

(a) Roll the dough into a rectangle. Brush with butter and sprinkle with cinnamon sugar, or spread with desired filling.

(b) Roll up like a jelly roll.

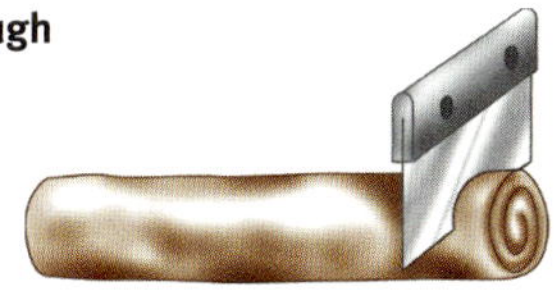

(c) For cinnamon rolls and similar products, cut off pieces 1 in. (2.5 cm) in length.

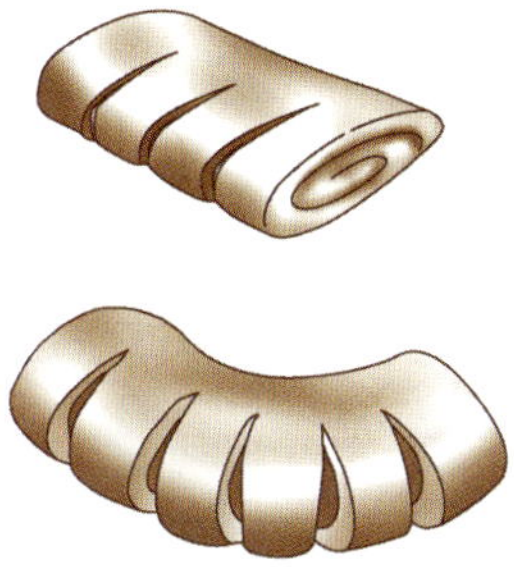

(d) For combs or bear claws, make the roll thinner and cut it into longer pieces. Flatten slightly and cut partway through each piece in 3 to 6 places as shown. Leave straight or bend into a curve to open the cuts.

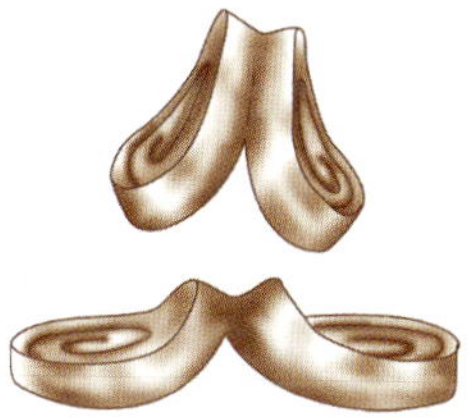

(e) For figure-eight cinnamon rolls, cut the rolls almost through as shown. Open them and lay them flat on the baking sheet.

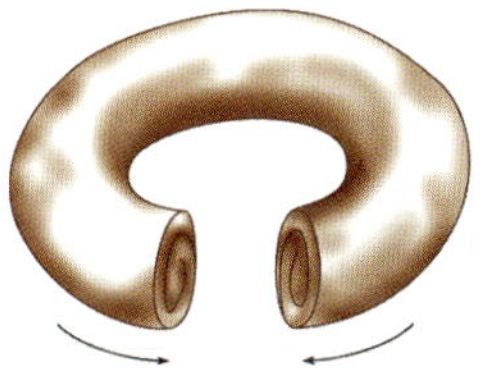

(f) To make a wreath-shaped coffee cake, join the ends of the dough roll to make a circle.

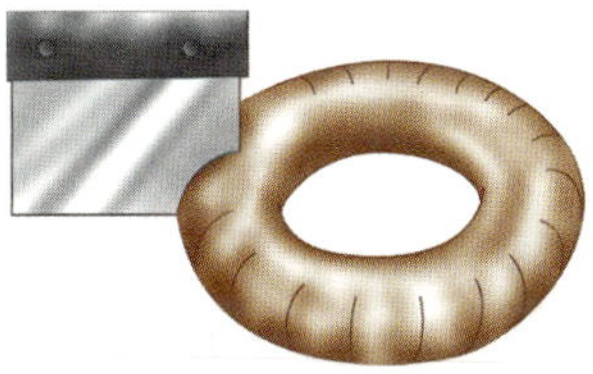

(g) Cut partway through the dough at 1-in. (2.5-cm) intervals as shown.

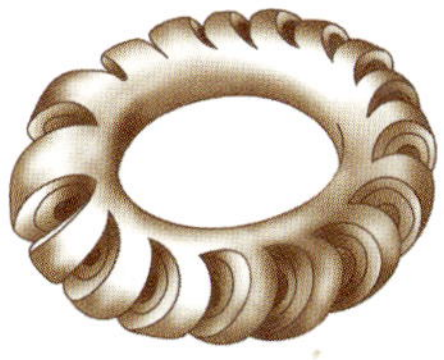

(h) Twist each segment outward to open the cuts.

TERMS FOR REVIEW

lean dough	straight dough method	sponge method	punching
rolled-in or laminated dough	modified straight dough method	fermentation	proofing
		young and old doughs	oven spring

QUESTIONS FOR DISCUSSION

1. What are the three major purposes of mixing yeast doughs?
2. Explain the difference in procedure between the straight dough method and the sponge method. How is the straight dough method sometimes modified for sweet doughs, and why is this necessary?
3. What are the 12 steps in the production of yeast products? Explain each briefly.
4. Judging from what you know about fermentation of doughs, do you think it might be necessary for bakers to modify procedures from winter to summer? How?
5. As you know, butter is very hard when cold and melts easily at warm temperatures. What precautions do you think are necessary when using butter as the rolling-in fat for Danish pastry?

Chapter 10

Blueberry, corn, and bran muffins, page 253.

Quick Breads

After reading this chapter, you should be able to

1. Prepare baking powder biscuits and variations.
2. Prepare muffins, loaf breads, coffee cakes, and corn breads.
3. Prepare popovers.

Quick breads are the perfect solution for operations that want to offer their patrons fresh, homemade bread products but can't justify the labor cost of making yeast breads. Also, quick breads have the advantage of being easily made in almost unlimited varieties, using such ingredients as whole wheat flour, rye flour, cornmeal, bran, oatmeal, and many kinds of fruits, nuts, and spices.

As their name implies, quick breads are quick to make. Because they are leavened by chemical leaveners and steam, not by yeast, no fermentation time is necessary. And because they are usually tender products with little gluten development, mixing them takes just a few minutes.

Although prepared biscuit and muffin mixes are available, the only extra work required to make these products from scratch is the time to scale a few extra ingredients. With a careful and imaginative selection of ingredients and an understanding of basic mixing methods, you can create superior products.

You may already have studied two kinds of quick bread in the breakfast chapter: pancakes and waffles. In this chapter, we present two basic mixing methods and apply them to biscuits, muffins, quick loaf breads and coffee cakes, and corn breads. In addition, we discuss popovers, which are leavened by steam only.

Mixing and Production Methods

Types of Dough

Dough mixtures for quick breads are generally of two types:

1. *Soft doughs* are used for biscuits. These products are rolled out and cut into desired shapes. They are mixed by the biscuit method.
2. *Batters* may be either ***pour batters***, which are liquid enough to pour, or ***drop batters***, which are thicker and drop from a spoon in lumps.

Most quick-bread batters are mixed by the ***muffin method***, except for drop biscuits, which are mixed by the ***biscuit method***, and some rich cakelike muffins and coffee cakes, which are mixed by a cake-mixing method called the *creaming method*. The biscuit and muffin methods are presented in this chapter. The creaming method is presented in Chapter 11, along with other cake methods.

The muffins and loaf breads in this chapter should be thought of as breads rather than as tea cakes. They are lower in fat and sugar than some of the rich, cakelike muffins sometimes seen.

Gluten Development in Quick Breads

Only slight gluten development is desired in most quick breads. Tenderness is the desired quality, in contrast to the chewy quality of yeast breads. In addition, chemical leavening agents do not create the same kind of textures that yeast does and are not strong enough to create a light, tender product if the gluten is too strong.

1. Muffin, loaf bread, and pancake batters are mixed as little as possible, just until the dry ingredients are moistened. This, plus the presence of fat and sugar, keeps gluten development low.

   Overmixing muffins produces not only toughness but also irregular shapes and large, elongated holes inside the product. This latter condition is called ***tunneling***.
2. Biscuit dough is often lightly kneaded, enough to develop some flakiness but not enough to toughen the product.
3. Popovers are the exception among quick breads. They are made with a thin batter and leavened by steam only. Large holes develop inside the product during baking, and the structure must be strong enough to hold without collapsing. Thus, bread flour is used, and the batter is mixed well to develop the gluten. The high percentage of egg in popovers also helps build structure.

The Biscuit Method

Procedure: Biscuit Method

1. Scale all ingredients accurately.
2. Sift the dry ingredients together into a mixing bowl.
3. Cut in the shortening, using the paddle attachment or the pastry knife attachment. If preferred, you may cut in the fat by hand, using a pastry blender or your fingers. Continue until the mixture resembles coarse cornmeal.
4. Combine the liquid ingredients. Biscuits may be prepared in advance up to this point. Portions of each mixture may then be scaled and combined just before baking.
5. Add the liquid to the dry ingredients. Mix just until the ingredients are combined and a soft dough is formed. Do not overmix.
6. Bring the dough to the bench and knead it lightly by pressing it out and folding it in half. Rotate the dough 90 degrees after each fold.
7. Repeat this procedure about 10 to 20 times, or for about 30 seconds. The dough should be soft and slightly elastic but not sticky. Overkneading toughens the biscuits. The dough is now ready for makeup.

Variations on the basic procedure produce different characteristics in the finished product.

1. Using slightly more shortening and cutting it in less—until the pieces are the size of peas—produces a flakier biscuit.
2. Omitting the kneading step produces a tender, crustier biscuit, but one with less volume.

MAKEUP OF BISCUITS

1. Roll the biscuit dough into a sheet about ½ inch (1 cm) thick, being careful to roll it evenly and to a uniform thickness.

   Biscuits approximately double in height during baking.
2. Cut into desired shapes.

   When using round hand cutters, cutting straight down produces the best shape after baking. Do not twist the cutter. Space the cuts closely to minimize scraps.

   Cutting into squares or triangles with a pastry cutter or knife eliminates scraps that would have to be rerolled. Roller cutters also eliminate or reduce scraps. Reworked scraps are tougher.
3. Place the biscuits ½ inch (1 cm) apart on a baking sheet for crisp-crusted biscuits, or touching each other for softer biscuits. Bake as soon as possible.

   If desired, the tops may be brushed with egg wash or milk before baking to aid browning.

THE RUBBED DOUGH METHOD

The method for mixing biscuit doughs, in its simplest form, consists of two essential steps: rubbing or cutting the fat into the dry ingredients, and mixing in the combined wet ingredients. These are the same essential steps as for mixing pie doughs by a method called the *rubbed dough method,* as detailed on page 292. Although the end product is quite different, many pastry chefs consider these methods to be the same and refer to them by the same name.

The Muffin Method

This mixing method is used not only for muffins but also for pancakes, waffles, quick loaf breads, and coffee cakes. Loaf breads and coffee cakes are sometimes higher in fat and sugar than muffins, so they can withstand more mixing without toughening.

The muffin method is not as suitable for formulas high in fat and sugar, unlike the cake-mixing method called the *creaming method*, discussed in Chapter 11. Consequently, quick breads mixed by the muffin method are not as rich and cakelike as many of today's popular muffins, which are closer to cakes than to traditional muffins. Keep this in mind as you practice the muffin method with the recipes in this chapter.

Procedure: Muffin Method

1. Sift together the dry ingredients (see Figure 10.1).
2. Combine all liquid ingredients, including melted fat or oil.
3. Add the liquids to the dry ingredients and mix just until all the flour is moistened. The batter will look lumpy. Do not overmix.
4. Pan and bake immediately. The dry and liquid mixtures may be prepared in advance. Once they are combined, the batter should be baked without delay, or loss of volume may result. When portioning batter into muffin tins, be careful not to stir the mix and toughen it. Scoop the batter from the outside edge for best results.

Figure 10.1 The muffin method.

(a) Sift together the dry ingredients.

(b) Add the combined liquid ingredients to the dry ingredients and mix just until the flour is moistened.

(c) Pan and bake immediately. Scoop the batter from the outside edge to minimize additional mixing.

THE WELL MIXING METHOD

The muffin method is sometimes called the ***well mixing method***. This name comes from the technique, commonly used in European pastry shops, of mixing a dough directly on the workbench rather than in a bowl. In order to keep the liquid ingredients from flowing away, the chef makes a well in the dry ingredients (see Figure 10.2) and pours the liquid ingredients into this well. When you are mixing in a bowl, it is of course not necessary to make a well to confine the liquids. But the habit has stuck, and the name has become attached to this mixing method.

Figure 10.2 Make a well in the mound of flour and add the liquids.

KEY POINTS TO REVIEW

- What are the steps in the biscuit method?
- What are the steps in the muffin method?
- Why must popover batter be mixed more thoroughly than muffin and biscuit doughs?

Summary: Biscuit and Muffin Methods

Biscuit Method

1. Combine dry ingredients and cut in fat.
2. Combine liquid ingredients.
3. Add liquid and dry ingredients and mix just until combined.
4. If required, knead very lightly.

Muffin Method

1. Combine dry ingredients.
2. Combine liquid ingredients, including melted fat.
3. Add liquid to dry ingredients and mix just until combined.

Formulas

Biscuits

INGREDIENTS	U.S.	METRIC	PERCENTAGE
Bread flour	1 lb 4 oz	600 g	50 %
Pastry flour	1 lb 4 oz	600 g	50 %
Salt	0.75 oz	25 g	2 %
Sugar	2 oz	60 g	5 %
Baking powder	2.5 oz	75 g	6 %
Shortening (regular) and/or butter	14 oz	425 g	35 %
Milk	1 lb 10 oz	775 g	65 %
Yield:	*5 lb 5 oz*	*2560 g*	*213 %*

Per 1 biscuit: Calories, 130; Protein, 2 g; Fat, 7 g (48% cal.); Cholesterol, 0 mg; Carbohydrates, 15 g; Fiber 1 g; Sodium, 260 mg.

PROCEDURE

Mixing and makeup:
Biscuit method.

Scaling:
Approximately 1 lb (500 g) per dozen 2-in. (5-cm) biscuits.

Baking:
425°F (220°C), about 15 minutes.

VARIATIONS

Buttermilk Biscuits

Use buttermilk instead of regular milk.

Cheese Biscuits

Add 30% (12 oz/360 g) grated cheddar cheese to dry ingredients.

Currant Biscuits

Add 15% (6 oz/180 g) dried currants to dry ingredients. Increase sugar to 10% (4 oz/125 g). Sprinkle tops with cinnamon sugar before baking.

Herb Biscuits

Add 5% (2 oz/60 g) fresh chopped parsley to the dry ingredients.

Plain Muffins

INGREDIENTS	U.S.	METRIC	PERCENTAGE
Pastry flour	2 lb 8 oz	1200 g	100 %
Sugar	1 lb 4 oz	600 g	50 %
Baking powder	2.5 oz	72 g	6 %
Salt	0.5 oz	15 g	1.25 %
Eggs, beaten	12 oz	360 g	30 %
Milk	1 lb 12 oz	840 g	70 %
Vanilla extract	1 oz	30 g	2.5 %
Melted butter or shortening	1 lb	480 g	40 %
Yield:	*7 lb 8 oz*	*3597 g*	*299 %*

Per 1 muffin: Calories, 170; Protein, 3 g; Fat, 7 g (36% cal.); Cholesterol, 40 mg; Carbohydrates, 25 g; Fiber, 3 g; Sodium, 230 mg.

Muffins, clockwise from top: blueberry, corn, bran

PROCEDURE

Mixing:

Muffin method.

Scaling and panning:

Grease and flour muffin tins, or use paper liners.

Scale batter with a No. 16 scoop, 2 oz (60 g) per unit.

Baking:

400°F (200°C), about 20 minutes.

VARIATIONS

Raisin Spice Muffins

Add 20% raisins (8 oz/250 g), 2½ tsp (12 mL) cinnamon, and 1 tsp (5 mL) nutmeg to the dry ingredients.

Date Nut Muffins

Add 15% (6 oz/185 g) each chopped dates and chopped walnuts to the dry ingredients.

Blueberry Muffins

Gently fold 40% (1 lb/480 g) well-drained blueberries into the finished batter.

Whole Wheat Muffins

Use 70% (1 lb 12 oz/840 g) pastry flour and 30% (12 oz/ 360 g) whole wheat flour. Reduce baking powder to 4% (1½ oz/50 g) and add 0.75% (2 tsp/10 mL) baking soda. Add 10% (4 oz/120 g) molasses to the liquid ingredients.

Corn Muffins

Use 65% (1 lb 10 oz/800 g) pastry flour and 35% (14 oz/ 400 g) yellow cornmeal. (See also Corn Bread formula, p. 254.)

Bran Muffins

Use 30% (12 oz/360 g) bran, 40% (1 lb/480 g) bread flour, and 30% (12 oz/360 g) pastry flour. Add 15% (6 oz/ 180 g) raisins to the dry ingredients. Add 15% (6 oz/180 g) molasses to the liquid ingredients.

Crumb Coffee Cake

Increase fat to 50% (1 lb 4 oz/600 g). Pour into greased, paper-lined sheet pan and spread smooth. Top with 80% (2 lb/1 kg) Streusel Topping. Bake at 360°F (180°C), about 30 minutes.

Corn Bread, Muffins, or Sticks

INGREDIENTS	U.S.			METRIC	PERCENTAGE
Pastry flour	1 lb	4	oz	600 g	50 %
Cornmeal	1 lb	4	oz	600 g	50 %
Sugar		6	oz	175 g	15 %
Baking powder		2	oz	60 g	5 %
Salt		0.75	oz	25 g	2 %
Eggs, beaten		8	oz	250 g	20 %
Milk	2 lb	2	oz	1000 g (1 L)	85 %
Corn syrup		2	oz	60 g	5 %
Melted butter or shortening		12	oz	350 g	30 %
Yield:	*6 lb*	*8*	*oz*	*3120 g*	*262 %*

Per 1 muffin: Calories, 160; Protein, 3 g; Fat, 7 g (39% cal.); Cholesterol, 35 mg; Carbohydrates, 22 g; Fiber, 2 g; Sodium, 290 mg.

PROCEDURE

Mixing:

Muffin method.

Scaling:

60 oz (1700 g) per half-size sheet pan (13 × 18 in./33 × 46 cm).
24 oz (725 g) per 9-in. (23-cm) square pan or per dozen muffins.
10 oz (300 g) per dozen corn sticks.
Grease and flour pans well.

Baking:

400°F (200°C) for corn bread, 25–30 minutes. 425°F (220°C) for muffins or sticks, 15–20 minutes.

TERMS FOR REVIEW

pour batter
drop batter
muffin method
biscuit method
tunneling
well mixing method

QUESTIONS FOR DISCUSSION

1. If you made a batch of muffins that came out of the oven with strange, knobby shapes, what would you expect was the reason?
2. What is the most important difference between the biscuit method and the muffin method?
3. How is the mixing method for popovers different from the mixing method for muffins? What is the leavening agent for popovers?

Chapter 11

Fruit Torte, page 262.

Cakes and Icings

Cakes are the richest and sweetest of all the baked products we have studied so far. From the baker's point of view, producing cakes requires as much precision as producing breads, but for completely opposite reasons. Breads are lean products that require strong gluten development and careful control of yeast action during the long fermentation and proofing periods. Cakes, on the other hand, are high in both fat and sugar. The baker's job is to create a structure that will support these ingredients and yet be as light and delicate as possible. Fortunately, producing cakes in quantity is relatively easy if the baker has good, well-balanced formulas, scales ingredients accurately, and understands basic mixing methods well.

Cakes owe their popularity not only to their richness and sweetness but also to their versatility. They can be presented in many forms, from simple sheet cakes in cafeterias to elaborately decorated works of art for weddings and other important occasions. With only a few basic formulas and a variety of icings, the chef or baker can construct the perfect dessert for any occasion or purpose.

After reading this chapter, you should be able to

1. Demonstrate the five basic cake mixing methods.
2. Describe the characteristics of high-fat cakes and low-fat cakes.
3. Prepare high-fat, or shortened, cakes and low-fat, or foam-type, cakes.
4. Prepare the six basic types of icing.
5. Assemble and ice layer cakes, small cakes, and sheet cakes.

Understanding Cake Making

Basic Mixing Methods

The mixing methods presented in this chapter are basic for most cakes prepared in the modern bakeshop. Each method is used for a particular type of formula.

High-fat or shortened cakes

- Creaming method
- Two-stage or blending method

Low-fat or foam-type cakes

- Foaming or sponge method
- Angel food method
- Chiffon method

We discuss these cake types in detail after you have had a chance to study the actual procedures on pages 259–261.

Creaming Method

The ***creaming method***, also called the *conventional method*, was, for a long time, the standard method for mixing butter cakes. Recently, the development of emulsified or high-ratio shortenings has led to the development of simpler mixing methods for shortened cakes. But the creaming method is still used for many types of butter cakes.

Two-Stage Method

The ***two-stage method***, also called the ***blending method***, was developed for use with modern high-ratio shortenings (see Chapter 8). Although it is simpler than the creaming method, it produces a very smooth batter that bakes up into a fine-grained, moist cake. It is called *two-stage* because the liquids are added in two stages.

Foaming or Sponge Method

All egg-foam cakes are similar in that they contain little or no shortening and depend for most or all of their leavening on the air trapped in beaten eggs.

One mixing method is usually presented as the basic method for all foam cakes. However, because whole-egg foams and egg-yolk foams are handled differently than egg-white foams, we discuss two separate, although similar, methods: the ***foaming method*** and the ***angel food method***. A third method, the ***chiffon method***, is somewhat unusual. It combines an egg-white foam with a high-fat batter made with oil.

Angel Food Method

Angel food cakes are based on egg-white foams and contain no fat.

Chiffon Method

Chiffon cakes and angel food cakes are both based on egg-white foams. But here the similarities in the mixing methods end. In angel food cakes, a dry flour-sugar mixture is folded into the egg whites. In chiffon cakes, a batter containing flour, egg yolks, vegetable oil, and water is folded into the whites.

Whip egg whites for chiffon cakes until they are a little firmer than those for angel food cakes, but not until they are dry. Chiffon cakes contain baking powder, so they do not depend on the egg foam for all their leavening.

Procedure: Creaming Method

1. Scale ingredients accurately. Have all ingredients at room temperature.
2. Place the butter or shortening in the mixing bowl. With the paddle attachment, beat slowly until the fat is smooth and creamy.
3. Add the sugar. Cream the mixture at moderate speed until it is light and fluffy (Figure 11.1).

   Some bakers prefer to add the salt and flavorings with the sugar to ensure uniform distribution.

   If melted chocolate is used, it is added during creaming.
4. Add the eggs, a little at a time. After each addition, beat until the eggs are absorbed before adding more. The mixture should be light and fluffy after the eggs are beaten in.
5. Scrape down the sides of the bowl to ensure even mixing.
6. Add the sifted dry ingredients (including the spices, if they were not added in step 3), alternating with the liquids. This is done as follows:
   - Add one-fourth of the dry ingredients. Mix just until blended in.
   - Add one-third of the liquid. Mix just until blended in.
   - Repeat until all ingredients are used. Scrape down the sides of the bowl occasionally for even mixing.

   The reason for adding dry and liquids alternately is that the batter may not absorb all the liquid unless some of the flour is present. Cocoa, if used, is included with the flour.

Figure 11.1

(a) Cream the butter and sugar until the mixture is light and fluffy.

(b) Beat in the eggs a little at a time.

(c) Add one fourth of the dry ingredients and mix in.

(d) Add one third of the liquid ingredients and mix in. Repeat until all the dry and liquid ingredients are incorporated.

Procedure: Two-Stage Method

1. Scale ingredients accurately. Have all ingredients at room temperature.
2. Sift the flour, baking powder, soda, and salt into the mixing bowl and add the shortening. With the paddle attachment, mix at low speed for 2 minutes. Stop the machine, scrape down the bowl and beater, and mix again for 2 minutes.

   If melted chocolate is used, blend it in during this step.

   If cocoa is used, sift it with the flour in this step or with the sugar in step 3.
3. Sift the remaining dry ingredients into the bowl and add part of the water or milk. Blend at low speed 3 to 5 minutes. Scrape down the sides of the bowl and the beater several times to ensure even mixing.
4. Combine the remaining liquids and lightly beaten eggs. With the mixer running, add this mixture to the batter in three parts. After each part, turn off the machine and scrape down the bowl.

   Continue mixing for a total of 5 minutes in this stage.

   The finished batter is normally quite liquid.

Variation

This variation combines steps 2 and 3 above into one step.

1. Scale ingredients as in the basic method.
2. Sift all dry ingredients into the mixing bowl. Add the shortening and part of the liquid. Mix on low speed 7 to 8 minutes. Scrape down the sides of the bowl and the beater several times.
3. Continue with step 4 in the basic procedure.

Procedure: Foaming or Sponge Method

1. Scale ingredients accurately. Have all ingredients at room temperature.
   If butter is included, it must be melted.
   If liquid and butter are included, heat them together, just until the butter is melted.
2. Combine the eggs and sugar, and warm to about 110°F (43°C). This may be done in one of two ways:
   - Stir the egg-sugar mixture over a hot-water bath.
   - Warm the sugar on a sheet pan in the oven (do not get it too hot) and gradually beat it into the eggs.

   This step is performed because warm foam attains greater volume.
3. With the whip attachment, beat the eggs at high speed until light and thick. This may take 10 to 15 minutes.
   This step is important. One of the most frequent causes of failure in the sponge method is not whipping the eggs and sugar enough. The foam must be very thick. When the beater is lifted from the bowl, the foam should fall slowly from it and make a ribbon that slowly sinks into the batter in the bowl (see Figure 11.2).
4. Fold in the sifted flour, being careful not to deflate the foam. Many bakers do this by hand.
   If other dry ingredients are used, such as cornstarch or baking powder, they are first sifted with the flour.
5. If melted butter or a butter-liquid mixture is being used, fold it in at this point. Be careful not to overmix, or the cake will be tough (because of developed gluten).
6. Immediately pan and bake the batter. Delays cause loss of volume.

Variations

Some formulas contain water or some other liquid, but no butter (so you cannot heat the liquid and butter together, as in the basic procedure). In this case, the liquid is usually added after step 3 and before folding in the flour. Either whip it in in a steady stream or stir it in, as indicated in the recipe.

In some formulas, the egg yolks and whites are separated. Use the yolks and part of the sugar to make the foam in steps 2 and 3. Use the remaining sugar to whip with the whites. Fold the egg-white foam into the batter after step 5.

Figure 11.2

(a) With a wire whip or the whip attachment of a mixer, beat the eggs until they are very thick and light.

(b) Fold in the sifted flour in three or four stages, until all the flour is blended in.

(c) If melted butter is used, fold it in after the flour.

Procedure: Angel Food Method

1. Scale ingredients accurately. Have all ingredients at room temperature. You may warm the egg whites slightly for better volume.
2. Sift the flour with half the sugar. This step helps the flour mix more evenly with the foam.
3. Beat the egg whites, using the whip attachment, until they form soft peaks.
   Add salt and cream of tartar near the beginning of the beating process.
4. Gradually beat in the sugar that was not mixed with the flour. Continue to beat until the egg whites form soft, glossy peaks. Do not overbeat.
5. Fold in the flour-sugar mixture just until it is thoroughly absorbed, but no longer.
6. Pan and bake immediately.

Procedure: Chiffon Method

1. Scale all ingredients accurately, and be sure they are all at room temperature. Use a good-quality, flavorless vegetable oil.
2. Sift the dry ingredients, including part of the sugar, into the mixing bowl.
3. Mixing with the paddle attachment at 2nd speed, gradually add the oil, then the egg yolks, water, and liquid flavorings, all in a slow, steady stream. While adding the liquids, stop the machine several times and scrape down the bowl and the beater. Mix until smooth, but do not overmix.
4. Whip the egg whites until they form soft peaks. Add the cream of tartar and sugar in a stream and whip to firm, moist peaks.
5. Fold the whipped egg whites into the flour–liquid mixture.
6. Immediately deposit batter in ungreased tube pans (like angel food cakes) or in layer pans that have had the bottoms, but not the sides, greased and dusted (like sponge layers).

Prepared Mixes

Many cake mixes are available that contain all ingredients except water and, sometimes, egg. These products also contain emulsifiers to ensure even blending of ingredients. To use them, follow the package instructions exactly.

Most mixes produce cakes with excellent volume, texture, and tenderness. Whether or not they also taste good is a matter of opinion. On the other hand, cakes made from scratch are not necessarily better. They are better only if they are carefully mixed and baked and are prepared using good, tested formulas and high-quality ingredients.

KEY POINTS TO REVIEW

- What are the steps in the creaming method?
- What are the steps in the two-stage method?
- What are the steps in the foaming or sponge method?
- What are the steps in the angel food method?
- What are the steps in the chiffon method?

Cake Formula Types

The proper mixing method for a particular formula depends on the balance of ingredients. A baker can look at the ingredients in a formula and know immediately which mixing method to use.

- If *fat is high*, use the creaming method or the two-stage method.

  The two-stage method may be used if the percentage of sugar is over 100 percent and if the fat is emulsified shortening.

  In other cases, the creaming method is used.

- If *fat is low* and *eggs and sugar are high*, use an egg-foam method.

High-Fat Cakes

The creaming method's major disadvantage is the labor it requires. The two-stage method is quicker, but because the flour is mixed for a long time, two conditions are necessary to prevent the gluten from developing toughness:

1. Increased percentage of sugar (sugar is a tenderizer).
2. Emulsified shortening, which blends thoroughly to prevent toughness.

Cakes made by the two-stage method have good volume and lightness, a fine, velvety texture, and great tenderness. The texture of butter cakes made by the creaming method is coarser, and the tenderness is generally somewhat less.

One factor seems to be neglected when cakes are rated, however—flavor. Shortening contributes no flavor to cakes, only texture. Butter, on the other hand, is highly prized for its flavor. It also influences texture because it melts in the mouth, while shortening does not. Thus, butter cakes are and always will be in demand. Therefore, the creaming method is important for you to know.

Low-Fat Cakes

High-fat cakes depend on air incorporated by the creaming action of the fat and sugar for some of their leavening and much of their texture. Low-fat or no-fat cakes obviously cannot. They must depend on the foaming action of eggs.

Sponge cakes have a springy texture and are tougher than shortened cakes. This makes them valuable for many kinds of desserts that require much handling to assemble. For example, many European-style cakes or tortes are made by cutting sponge cake layers horizontally into thin layers and stacking them with a variety of rich fillings, creams, icings, and fruits.

Fruit torte

Even if a high-ratio cake survived all this without breaking into crumbs, it would probably disintegrate when it absorbed moisture from the fillings. In addition, sponge layers in this kind of cake are usually moistened with a flavored sugar syrup to compensate for their lack of moisture.

The *fruit torte* (illustrated in the photograph) is an example of this type of cake. Genoise layers are split, moistened with dessert syrup, layered and iced with whipped cream, and topped with attractively arranged fruit pieces. The fruit is then coated with glaze (p. 273) to protect it and enhance its appearance.

Sponge sheets for jelly rolls and other rolled cakes are made without shortening, so they do not crack when rolled.

Flour for sponge cakes must be weak to avoid making the cake tough. Cornstarch is often added to cake flour for sponge cakes to weaken the flour further.

Scaling and Panning

Prepare pans before mixing cake batters so cake batters can be baked without delay.

1. For high-fat cakes, the bottoms of layer pans must be greased, preferably with a commercial pan greasing preparation. If this is not available, dust the greased pan with flour and tap out the excess.
2. For sheet cakes, line the pan with greased parchment.
3. For angel food cakes, do not grease the pan. The batter must be able to cling to the sides in order to rise.
4. For sponge cake layers with a small percentage of fat, grease the bottoms but not the sides.

Procedure for Scaling Creaming-Method Batters

These batters are thick and do not pour easily. Scale cakes as follows:

1. Place the prepared cake pan on the left side of a balance scale. Balance the scale by placing another pan on the right side.
2. Set the scale for the desired weight.
3. Add batter to the left pan until the scale balances.
4. Remove the pan from the scale and spread the batter smooth with a spatula.
5. Repeat with remaining pans.
6. Give the pans several sharp raps on the bench to free large trapped air bubbles. Bake immediately.

Procedure for Scaling Two-Stage Batters

These batters are more liquid than creamed batters. They may be scaled like creamed batters or, for greater speed, they may be scaled as follows:

1. Place an empty volume measure on the left side of a balance scale. Balance the scale to zero.
2. Set the scale for the desired weight.
3. Pour batter into the measure until the scale balances.
4. Note the volume of batter in the measure.
5. Pour the measured batter into a prepared pan, quickly scraping out the measure to get all the batter.
6. Scale the remaining cakes with the volume measure, using the volume noted in step 4.
7. Give the pans several sharp raps on the bench to free large trapped air bubbles. Bake immediately.

Procedure for Scaling Foam Cakes

Foam cake batters should be handled as little as possible and baked immediately in order to avoid deflating the beaten eggs. Although they may be scaled like creamed batters, many bakers prefer to eyeball them in order to minimize handling.

1. Have all prepared pans lined up on the bench.
2. Scale the first pan as for creamed batters.
3. Quickly fill remaining pans to the same level as the first pan, judging the level by eye.
4. Spread the batter smooth and bake immediately.

See Table 11.1 for average scaling weights as well as baking temperatures and times.

Table 11.1 Average Cake Scaling Weights, Baking Temperatures, and Times

	Scaling Weight		Baking Temperatures		
Pan Type and Size	U.S.	Metric	U.S.	Metric	Approximate Baking Time in Minutes
High-fat cakes					
Round layers					
6 in. (15 cm)	8–10 oz	230–285 g	375°F	190°C	18
8 in. (20 cm)	14–18 oz	400–510 g	375°F	190°C	25
10 in. (25 cm)	24–28 oz	680–800 g	360F	180°C	35
12 in. (30 cm)	32–40 oz	900–1100 g	360°F	180°C	35
Sheets and square pans					
18 × 26 in. (46 × 66 cm)	7–8 lb	3.2–3.6 kg	360°F	180°C	35
18 × 13 in. (46 × 33 cm)	3½–4 lb	1.6–1.8 kg	360°F	180°C	35
9 × 9 in. (23 × 23 cm)	24 oz	680 g	360°F	180°C	30–35
Loaf (pound cake)					
2¼ × 3½ × 8 in. (6 × 9 × 20 cm)	16–18 oz	450–500 g	350°F	175°C	50–60
2¾ × 4½ × 8½ in. (7 × 11 × 22 cm)	24–27 oz	680–765 g	350°F	175°C	55–65
Cupcakes per dozen	18 oz	510 g	385°F	195°C	18–20
Foam-type cakes					
Round layers					
6 in. (15 cm)	5–6 oz	140–170 g	375°F	190°C	20
8 in. (20 cm)	10 oz	280 g	375°F	190°C	20
10 in. (25 cm)	16 oz	450 g	360°F	180°C	25–30
12 in. (30 cm)	24 oz	700 g	360°F	180°C	25–30
Sheets (for jelly roll or sponge roll)					
18 × 26 in., ½ in. thick (46 × 66 cm, 12 mm thick)	2½ lb	1.2 kg	375°F	190°C	15–20
18 × 26 in., ¼ in. thick (46 × 66 cm, 6 cm thick)	28 oz	800 g	400°F	200°C	7–10
Tube (angel food and chiffon)					
8 in. (20 cm)	12–14 oz	340–400 g	360°F	180°C	30
10 in. (25 cm)	24–32 oz	700–900 g	350°F	175°C	50
Cupcakes per dozen	10 oz	280 g	375°F	190°C	18–20

Note: The weights given are averages. Weights may be increased by 25 percent if thicker layers are desired. Baking times may then need to be increased slightly.

Baking and Cooling

Baking

Cake structure is fragile, so proper baking conditions are essential for high-quality products. The following guidelines will help you avoid cake failures.

1. Preheat the ovens. (To conserve expensive energy, don't preheat longer than necessary.)
2. Make sure ovens and shelves are level.
3. Do not let pans touch each other in the oven. If the pans touch, air circulation is inhibited and the cakes rise unevenly.
4. Bake at the correct temperature.

   Too hot an oven causes the cake to set unevenly or to set before it has fully risen. Crusts will be too dark.

   Too slow an oven causes poor volume and texture because the cake doesn't set fast enough and may fall.
5. Do not open the ovens or disturb the cakes until they have finished rising and are partially browned. Disturbing the cakes before they are set may cause them to fall.
6. If steam in the oven is available, use it for creamed and two-stage batters. These cakes bake with a flatter top if baked with steam because the steam delays the formation of the top crust.
7. Tests for doneness:
   - Shortened cakes shrink away from sides of pan slightly.
   - Cakes are springy. The center of the top springs back when pressed slightly.
   - A cake tester or pick inserted in the center of the cake comes out clean.

Cooling and Removing from Pans

1. Cool layer cakes and sheet cakes 15 minutes in pans and then turn out while slightly warm. They are too fragile to turn out when hot, and they may break.
2. Turn out layer cakes onto racks to finish cooling.
3. To turn out sheet cakes:
   - Sprinkle top lightly with granulated sugar.
   - Set an empty sheet pan on top, bottom side down.
   - Invert both pans.
   - Remove top pan.
   - Peel parchment off cake.
4. Cool angel food cakes upside down in pans. Support the edges of the pan so the top of the cake is off the bench. When cool, loosen the cake from the sides of the pan with a knife or spatula and pull out carefully.

Common Cake Faults and Their Causes

Errors in mixing, scaling, baking, and cooling cakes cause many kinds of defects and failures. For easy reference, these defects and their possible causes are summarized in the troubleshooting guide in Table 11.2.

KEY POINTS TO REVIEW

- What mixing methods are used for high-fat cakes? for low-fat cakes?
- What are the procedures for scaling cake batters?
- How are cakes tested for doneness?
- How are cakes removed from their baking pans?

Altitude Adjustments

At high altitudes, atmospheric pressure is much lower than at sea level. This factor must be taken into account in cake baking. Formulas must be adjusted to suit baking conditions over 2,000 or 3,000 feet (600 or 900 m) above sea level.

Although general guidelines can be given, the exact adjustments required vary for different kinds of cake. Many manufacturers of flour, shortening, and other bakery ingredients supply detailed information and adjusted formulas for any given locality.

In general, the following adjustments must be made above elevations of 2,000 or 3,000 feet (600 or 900 m). See Table 11.3 for more specific adjustments.

LEAVENING

Leavening gases expand more when air pressure is lower, so baking powder and baking soda must be *decreased*.

Creaming and foaming procedures should also be reduced so less air is incorporated.

TOUGHENERS: FLOUR AND EGGS

Cakes require firmer structure at high altitudes. Both eggs and flour must be increased to supply proteins for structure.

TENDERIZERS: SHORTENING AND SUGAR

Shortening and sugar must be decreased so the structure of the cake is firmer.

LIQUIDS

At high altitudes, water boils at a lower temperature and evaporates more easily. Liquids must be *increased* to prevent excess drying both during and after baking. This also helps compensate for the decrease in moisturizers (sugar and fat) and the increase in flour, which absorbs moisture.

BAKING TEMPERATURES

Increase baking temperatures about 25°F (14°C) above 3,500 feet (1050 m).

PAN GREASING

High-fat cakes tend to stick at high altitudes. Grease pans more heavily. Remove baked cakes from pans as soon as possible.

STORING

Wrap or ice cakes as soon as they are cool to prevent drying.

Table 11.2 Common Cake Faults and Their Causes

Fault	Causes
Volume and shape	
Poor volume	Too little flour Too much liquid Too little leavening Oven too hot
Uneven shape	Improper mixing Batter spread unevenly Uneven oven heat Oven racks not level Cake pans warped
Crust	
Too dark	Too much sugar Oven too hot
Too light	Too little sugar Oven not hot enough
Burst or cracked	Too much flour or flour too strong Too little liquid Improper mixing Oven too hot
Soggy	Underbaked Cooling in pans or with not enough ventilation Wrapping before cool
Texture	
Dense or heavy	Too little leavening Too much liquid Too much sugar Too much shortening Oven not hot enough
Coarse or irregular	Too much leavening Too little egg Improper mixing
Crumbly	Too much leavening Too much shortening Too much sugar Wrong kind of flour Improper mixing
Tough	Flour too strong Too much flour Too little sugar or shortening Overmixing
Poor flavor	Poor-quality ingredients Poor storage or sanitation Unbalanced formula

Table 11.3 Approximate Formula Adjustment in Shortened Cakes at High Altitudes

		Percentage Adjustment		
Ingredient	**Increase or Decrease**	**2500 Feet (750 m)**	**5000 Feet (1500 m)**	**7500 Feet (2300 m)**
Baking powder	Decrease	20%	40%	60%
Flour	Increase	—	4%	9%
Eggs	Increase	2.5%	9%	15%
Sugar	Decrease	3%	6%	9%
Fat	Decrease	—	—	9%
Liquid	Increase	9%	15%	22%

To make adjustments, multiply the percentage indicated by the amount of ingredient and add or subtract as indicated.

Example: To adjust 1 lb (16 oz) eggs for 7,500 feet: $0.15 \times 16\ oz = 2.4\ oz$

$16\ oz + 2.4\ oz = 18.4\ oz$

Cake Formulas

Creaming Method

Yellow Butter Cake

Ingredients	**U.S.**	**Metric**	**Percentage**
Butter	1 lb 8 oz	720 g	80 %
Sugar	1 lb 10 oz	780 g	87 %
Salt	0.25 oz (1¼ tsp)	7 g (6 mL)	1 %
Eggs	15 oz	450 g	50 %
Cake flour	1 lb 14 oz	900 g	100 %
Baking powder	1.25 oz	35 g	4 %
Milk	1 lb 14 oz	900 g	100 %
Vanilla	0.5 oz	15 mL	1.5 %
Yield:	*7 lb 14 oz*	*3810 g*	*423 %*

Per 1 ounce (28.35 g): Calories, 90; Protein, 1 g; Fat, 5 g (48% cal.); Cholesterol, 25 mg; Carbohydrates, 11 g; Fiber, 0 g; Sodium, 80 mg.

PROCEDURE

Mixing:

Creaming method.

Scaling and baking:

See **Table 11.1**.

Old-Fashioned Pound Cake

INGREDIENTS	U.S.	METRIC	PERCENTAGE
Butter or butter and shortening combined (see Note)	1 lb	500 g	100 %
Sugar	1 lb	500 g	100 %
Vanilla	2 tsp	10 mL	2 %
Eggs	1 lb	500 g	100 %
Cake flour	1 lb	500 g	100 %
Yield:	*4 lb*	*2000 g*	*402 %*

Per 1 ounce (28.35 g): Calories, 110; Protein, 2 g; Fat, 7 g (51% cal.); Cholesterol, 45 mg; Carbohydrates, 13 g; Fiber, 0 g; Sodium, 70 mg.

Note: If you are using unsalted butter or shortening, add 1.5% (¼ oz /1¼ tsp or 6 mL) salt during the first stage of mixing.

PROCEDURE

Mixing:

Creaming method. Add the eggs and the cake flour alternately to avoid curdling the mixture.

Scaling and baking:

See **Table 11.1**.

VARIATIONS

Mace or grated lemon or orange zest may also be used to flavor pound cake.

Raisin Pound Cake

Add 25% (4 oz/125 g) raisins or dried currants that were soaked in boiling water and drained well.

Chocolate Pound Cake

Add 25% (4 oz/125 g) unsweetened chocolate to the butter and sugar after the creaming stage.

Marble Pound Cake

Fill pans one-third full of the basic yellow batter. Add a layer of Chocolate Pound Cake batter, then finish with the yellow batter. Run a spatula blade through the layers to marble them.

Marble Pound Cake

Two-Stage Method

White Cake

INGREDIENTS	U.S.	METRIC	PERCENTAGE
Cake flour	1 lb 8 oz	700 g	100 %
Baking powder	1.5 oz	45 g	6.25 %
Salt	0.5 oz	15 g	2 %
Emulsified shortening	12 oz	350 g	50 %
Sugar	1 lb 14 oz	875 g	125 %
Skim milk	12 oz	350 g	50 %
Vanilla	2 tsp	10 mL	1.5 %
Almond extract	1 tsp	5 mL	0.75 %
Skim milk	12 oz	350 g	50 %
Egg whites	1 lb	475 g	67 %
Yield:	*6 lb 12 oz*	*3175 g*	*452 %*

Per 1 ounce (28.35 g): Calories, 90; Protein, 1 g; Fat, 3 g (33% cal.); Cholesterol, 0 mg; Carbohydrates, 13 g; Fiber, 0 g; Sodium, 105 mg.

PROCEDURE

Mixing:
Two-stage method.

Scaling and baking:
See **Table 11.1**

VARIATIONS

Use water instead of milk and add 10% (2½ oz/70 g) nonfat dry milk powder to the dry ingredients.

Flavor with lemon extract or emulsion instead of vanilla and almond.

Yellow Cake

Reduce shortening to 45% (11 oz/325 g). Substitute whole eggs for egg whites, using the same total weight (67%). Use 2% vanilla (½ oz/15 g) and omit almond extract.

Devil's Food Cake

INGREDIENTS	U.S.	METRIC	PERCENTAGE
Cake flour	1 lb 8 oz	700 g	100 %
Cocoa	4 oz	125 g	17 %
Salt	0.5 oz	15 g	2 %
Baking powder	0.75 oz	20 g	3 %
Baking soda	0.5 oz	15 g	2 %
Emulsified shortening	14 oz	400 g	58 %
Sugar	2 lb	925 g	133 %
Skim milk	1 lb	475 g	67 %
Vanilla	2 tsp	10 mL	1.5 %
Skim milk	12 oz	350 g	50 %
Eggs	1 lb	475 g	67 %
Yield:	*7 lb 8 oz*	*3500 g*	*500 %*

Per 1 ounce (28.35 g): Calories, 90; Protein, 1 g; Fat, 4 g (39% cal.); Cholesterol, 15 mg; Carbohydrates, 13 g; Fiber, 1 g; Sodium, 105 mg.

PROCEDURE

Mixing:
Two-stage method.

Scaling and baking:
See **Table 11.1**.

Foaming Methods

Sponge Cake (Genoise)

INGREDIENTS	U.S.	METRIC	PERCENTAGE
Eggs	2 lb 4 oz	1050 g	150 %
Sugar	1 lb 8 oz	700 g	100 %
Cake flour	1 lb 8 oz	700 g	100 %
Butter, melted	8 oz	225 g	33 %
Vanilla (or lemon flavor)	0.5 oz	15 mL	2 %
Yield:	*5 lb 12 oz*	*2690 g*	*385 %*

Per 1 ounce (28.35 g): Calories, 90; Protein, 2 g; Fat, 3 g (31% cal.); Cholesterol, 55 mg; Carbohydrates, 13 g; Fiber, 0 g; Sodium, 35 mg.

PROCEDURE

Mixing:
Foaming method.

Scaling and baking:
See **Table 11.1**.

VARIATIONS

Chocolate Genoise

Substitute 4 oz (125 g) cocoa powder for 4 oz (125 g) flour. Use the vanilla, not the lemon flavor.

Sponge Roll or Jelly Roll

Prepare the basic formula, but omit the butter. Add the vanilla to the beaten eggs just before folding in the flour. Spread evenly in parchment-lined pans. When baked and cooled, trim the edges. Cut in half or into quarters. Spread each rectangle with desired filling (jelly, buttercream, etc.) and roll up so the long side of the rectangle becomes the length of the roll. Ice or sprinkle with 6X sugar.

Angel Food Cake

INGREDIENTS	U.S.	METRIC	PERCENTAGE
Egg whites	2 lb	1000 g	267 %
Cream of tartar	0.25 oz (1 tbsp)	8 g (15 mL)	2 %
Salt	1 tsp	5 g (5 mL)	1.5 %
Sugar	1 lb	500 g	133 %
Vanilla	2 tsp	10 mL	2.5 %
Almond extract	1 tsp	5 mL	1.25 %
Sugar	1 lb	500 g	133 %
Cake flour	12 oz	375 g	100 %
Yield:	*4 lb 12 oz*	*2403 g*	*640 %*

Per 1 ounce (28.35 g): Calories, 70; Protein, 2 g; Fat, 0 g (0% cal.); Cholesterol, 0 mg; Carbohydrates, 16 g; Fiber, 0 g; Sodium, 50 mg.

PROCEDURE

Mixing:
Angel food method.

Scaling and baking:
See **Table 11.1**.

VARIATION

Chocolate Angel Food Cake

Substitute 3 oz (90 g) cocoa for 3 oz (90 g) flour.

ICINGS: PRODUCTION AND APPLICATION

Producing and Handling Basic Types

Icings or frostings (the two terms mean the same thing) are sweet coatings for cakes and other baked goods. Icings have three main functions:

1. They improve the keeping qualities of the cake by forming a protective coating around it.
2. They contribute flavor and richness.
3. They improve appearance.

There are six basic kinds of icing:

Fondant	Fudge-type icing
Buttercream	Flat-type icing
Foam-type icing	Royal or decorator's icing

In addition, we consider two other preparations for cakes:

Glazes	Fillings

Use top-quality flavorings for icings so they enhance the cake rather than detract from it. Use moderation when adding flavorings and colors. Flavors should be light and delicate. Colors should be delicate, pastel shades—except chocolate, of course.

Fondant

Fondant is a sugar syrup that is crystallized to a smooth, creamy white mass. It is familiar as the icing for napoleons, èclairs, petits fours, and some cakes. When applied, it sets up into a shiny, nonsticky coating.

Because it is difficult to make in the bakeshop, fondant is almost always purchased already prepared, either in ready-to-use moist form or in a dry form that requires only the addition of water.

Guidelines for Using Fondant

1. Heat fondant over a warm-water bath, stirring constantly, to thin the icing and make it pourable. Do not heat over 100°F (38°C), or it will lose its shine.
2. If the fondant is still too thick, thin it with a little simple sugar syrup or water (simple syrup blends in more easily).
3. Add flavorings and colorings as desired.
4. To make chocolate fondant, stir melted bitter chocolate into warm fondant until the desired color and flavor are reached. Chocolate thickens the fondant, so the icing may require more thinning with sugar syrup.
5. Apply fondant by pouring it over the item or by dipping items into it.

Buttercream

Buttercream icings are light, smooth mixtures of fat and confectioners' sugar. They may also contain eggs to increase their smoothness or lightness. These popular icings are used for many kinds of cake. They are easily flavored and colored to suit a variety of purposes.

We consider three basic kinds of buttercream:

1. *Simple buttercreams* are made by creaming together fat and sugar to the desired consistency and lightness. A small quantity of egg whites may be whipped in.

   Decorator's buttercream is a simple buttercream used for making flowers and other cake decorations. It is creamed only a little because if too much air is beaten in, it would not be able to hold delicate shapes.

2. *Meringue-type buttercreams* are prepared by first beating egg whites and adding a boiling syrup or just sugar. Soft butter is then mixed into the meringue. This is a very light, smooth icing.

3. *French buttercreams* are similar to the meringue type, but the foam is made with egg yolks (and, sometimes, whole eggs) and boiling syrup. This is a very rich, light icing.

Butter, especially sweet, unsalted butter, is the preferred fat for buttercreams because of its flavor and melt-in-the-mouth quality. Icings made with shortening only can be unpleasant because the fat congeals and coats the inside of the mouth and does not melt. However, butter makes a less stable icing because it melts so easily. There are two ways around this problem:

1. Use buttercreams in cool weather only.
2. Blend a small quantity of emulsified shortening with the butter to stabilize it.

Simple Buttercream

YIELD: 4 LB 2 OZ (2075 G)

U.S.	METRIC	INGREDIENTS
1 lb	500 g	Butter
8 oz	250 g	Shortening
2 lb 8 oz	1.25 kg	Confectioners' sugar (10X)
2.5 oz	75 g	Egg whites, pasteurized
1 tsp	5 mL	Lemon juice
1 tbsp	15 mL	Vanilla

Per 1 ounce (28.35 g): Calories, 150; Protein, 0 g; Fat, 10 g (58% cal.); Cholesterol, 15 mg; Carbohydrates, 16 g; Fiber, 0 g; Sodium, 65 mg.

PROCEDURE

1. Cream together the butter, shortening, and sugar until well blended, using the paddle attachment.
2. Add the egg whites, lemon juice, and vanilla. Blend in at medium speed. Then mix at high speed until light and fluffy.

VARIATIONS

Decorator's Buttercream

Use 1 lb 8 oz (750 g) regular shortening, no butter. Omit lemon juice and vanilla. Reduce egg whites to 2 oz (60 g). Blend at low speed until smooth; do not whip.

Cream Cheese Icing

Substitute cream cheese for the butter and shortening. Omit egg whites. If necessary, thin the icing with cream or milk. If desired, flavor with grated lemon or orange zest instead of vanilla.

Meringue-Type Buttercream

YIELD: 5 LB 12 OZ (2900 G)

U.S.	METRIC	INGREDIENTS	PROCEDURE
2 lb 8 fl oz	1 kg 250 mL	Sugar Water	1. Combine the sugar and water in a saucepan. Bring to a boil, stirring to dissolve the sugar. 2. Continue to boil until the syrup reaches a temperature of 240°F (115°C).
1 lb	500 g	Egg whites	3. While the syrup is boiling, beat the egg whites in a clean, grease-free bowl, using the whip attachment, until they form firm, moist peaks. Do not overbeat. 4. As soon as the syrup reaches 240°F (115°C), pour it very slowly into the egg whites while the mixer is running at medium speed.
2 lb 8 oz 2 tsp 1 tbsp	1 kg 250 g 10 mL 15 mL	Butter, soft Emulsified shortening Lemon juice Vanilla	5. Continue to beat until the meringue is cool and forms stiff peaks. (You have now made an Italian meringue. For more information, see Chapter 13.) 6. With the mixer still running at medium speed, begin adding the butter, a little at a time. Add it just as fast as it can be absorbed by the meringue. 7. When all the butter is beaten in, add the shortening in the same way. 8. Beat in the lemon juice and vanilla. 9. Continue whipping until the buttercream is smooth.

Per 1 ounce (28.35 g): Calories, 130; Protein, 1 g; Fat, 10 g (67% cal.); Cholesterol, 20 mg; Carbohydrates, 10 g; Fiber, 0 g; Sodium, 90 mg.

French Buttercream

YIELD: 5 LB 8 OZ (2750 G)

U.S.	METRIC	INGREDIENTS	PROCEDURE
2 lb 8 fl oz	1 kg 250 mL	Sugar Water	1. Combine the sugar and water in a saucepan. Bring to a boil, stirring to dissolve the sugar. 2. Continue to boil until the syrup reaches a temperature of 240°F (115°C).
12 oz	375 g	Egg yolks	3. While the syrup is boiling, beat the yolks with the whip attachment until they are thick and light. 4. As soon as the syrup reaches 240°F (115°C), pour it very slowly into the beaten yolks while the mixer is running at 2nd speed. 5. Continue to beat until the mixture is cool and the yolks are very light and thick.
2 lb 8 oz 1 tbsp	1.25 kg 15 mL	Butter, soft Vanilla	6. With the mixer still running, add the butter, a little at a time. Add it just as fast as it can be absorbed by the mixture. 7. Beat in the vanilla. If the icing is too soft, refrigerate until it is firm enough to spread.

Per 1 ounce (28.35 g): Calories, 150; Protein, 1 g; Fat, 12 g (71% cal.); Cholesterol, 80 mg; Carbohydrates, 10 g; Fiber, 0 g; Sodium, 110 mg.

VARIATIONS

Flavored buttercreams are made by adding the desired flavoring to any of the basic buttercream recipes. In addition to the two variations given below, extracts and emulsions such as lemon, orange, and almond may be used.

Chocolate Buttercream

Add 4–5 oz (125–150 g) sweet chocolate, melted and cooled, to each 1 pound (500 g) buttercream.

Coffee Buttercream

For each 1 pound (500 g) buttercream, add 1½ tbsp (22 mL) instant coffee dissolved in 2 tsp (10 mL) hot water.

Foam-Type Icing

Foam icings, sometimes called *boiled icings*, are simply meringues made with a boiling syrup. Some also contain stabilizing ingredients like gelatin.

Foam-type icings should be applied thickly to cakes and left in peaks and swirls.

These icings are not stable. They should be used the day they are prepared. Italian meringue, discussed in Chapter 13, is the simplest foam-type icing. Follow the recipes on page 312 but add 8 ounces (250 g) corn syrup to the sugar and water for the boiled syrup. The meringue is usually flavored with vanilla.

Flat Icing

Flat icings, also called *water icings*, are simply mixtures of 10X sugar, water, and, sometimes, corn syrup and flavoring. They are used mostly for coffee cakes, Danish pastry, and sweet rolls. Flat icings are warmed to 100°F (38°C) for application and are handled like fondant.

Fudge-Type Icing

Fudge icings are rich cooked icings. Many are made somewhat like candy. Fudge icings are heavy and thick, and they may be flavored with a variety of ingredients. They are used on cupcakes, layer cakes, loaf cakes, and sheet cakes.

Fudge icings are stable and hold up well on cakes and in storage. Stored icings must be covered tightly to prevent drying and crusting.

To use stored fudge icing, warm it in a double boiler until soft enough to spread.

Fudge-type icings do not necessarily contain chocolate. Plain white fudge icings may be flavored with vanilla, almond, maple, coffee, or other desired flavoring.

Royal Icing

Royal icing, also called *decorating* or *decorator's icing*, is similar to flat icings except that it is much thicker and is made with egg whites, which make it hard and brittle when dry. It is used almost exclusively for decorative work.

To prepare royal icing:

1. Place the desired amount of 10X sugar in a mixing bowl. Add a small quantity of cream of tartar (for whiteness)—about ⅛ teaspoon per pound of sugar (1 g per kg).
2. Beat in egg white, a little at a time, until the sugar forms a smooth paste. You will need 2 to 3 ounces egg whites per pound of sugar (125 g per k).
3. Keep unused icing covered with a damp cloth at all times to prevent hardening.

Glazes

Glazes are thin, glossy, transparent coatings that give shine to baked products and help prevent drying.

The simplest glaze is a sugar syrup or diluted corn syrup brushed onto coffee cakes or Danish while the glaze is hot. Syrup glazes may contain gelatin or waxy maize starch. Fruit glazes, the most popular being apricot, are available commercially prepared. They are melted, thinned with a little water, and brushed on while hot.

Fruit glazes may also be made by melting apricot or other preserves and forcing them through a strainer.

One of the most common uses of glazes in cake making is to coat the fruit arranged on the top of fruit tortes (see p. 262).

Ganache is a mixture of heavy cream and melted chocolate. Although it is not transparent like the glazes we have been discussing, it is used like other glazes to give a thin, shiny coating to cakes and other desserts. Making basic ganache is a simple procedure:

1. Heat heavy cream just to the boiling point and remove from the heat.
2. Add chopped chocolate and let stand until the chocolate has melted.
3. Stir until smooth.

Freshly made ganache can be used immediately, or it can be refrigerated and then rewarmed for later use. When it cools, it solidifies and can be used as the base for chocolate truffles.

Chocolate Ganache

YIELD: 1 LB 12 OZ (875 G)

U.S.	METRIC	INGREDIENTS
1 lb	500g	Dark chocolate
12 oz	375 g	Heavy cream

Per 1 ounce (28.35 g): Calories, 130; Protein, 1 g; Fat, 10 g (67% cal.); Cholesterol, 20 mg; Carbohydrates, 10 g; Fiber, 1 g; Sodium, 5 mg.

PROCEDURE

1. Chop the chocolate into small pieces.
2. Bring the cream just to a boil, stirring to prevent scorching. (Use very fresh cream; old cream is more likely to curdle when boiled.)
3. Remove from the heat and add the chocolate. Stir and let stand for a few minutes. Stir again until the chocolate is completely melted and the mixture is smooth.
4. Apply to cakes as a glaze by pouring the ganache over the cake, as for fondant.

VARIATIONS

The proportion of chocolate and cream may be varied. For a firmer product, or if the weather is warm, decrease the cream to as little as half the weight of the chocolate. For a softer ganache, increase the cream to the same weight as the chocolate.

Fillings

Fillings are sometimes used instead of icings between cake layers. Fillings are also used in such products as jelly rolls, Danish, and other pastries.

1. **Fruit fillings.**
   Fruit fillings may be cooked or uncooked.
   Cooked fruit fillings are chopped or purèed fruits or fruit juices thickened with starch or eggs. They are prepared somewhat like pie fillings (see Chapter 13).
   Uncooked fruit fillings include jellies and preserves and dried fruits that have been ground and flavored. Fresh fruits, such as the strawberries in strawberry shortcake, are also used.
   Many ready-to-use fruit fillings are on the market.

2. **Cream fillings.**
   Cream fillings include pastry cream (recipes in Chapter 14) and various pudding-type preparations.
   Desserts with cream fillings should be assembled as close to service time as possible and kept refrigerated to avoid health hazards.

3. **Whipped cream.**
   Whipped cream is used as a dessert topping, filling, and frosting.
   Artificial whipped toppings resemble whipped cream in appearance. They should be used only if your customers actually like them.

Assembling and Icing Cakes

Selection of Icing

The flavor, texture, and color of the icing must be compatible with the cake.

1. **In general, use heavy frostings with heavy cakes and light frostings with light cakes.**
   For example, ice angel food cakes with a simple flat icing, fondant, or a light, fluffy boiled icing.
   High-ratio cakes go well with buttercreams and fudge-type icings.
   Shortened sponge layer cakes (genoise) are often combined with fruits or fruit fillings, light French or meringue-type buttercream, whipped cream, or flavored fondant.

2. **Use the best-quality flavorings, and use them sparingly. The flavor of the frosting should not be stronger than that of the cake.**
   Fudge-type icings may be flavored more strongly, as long as the flavor is of good quality.

3. **Use coloring sparingly. Light, pastel shades are more appetizing than loud colors.**
   Paste colors give the best results. Mix a little color with a small portion of the icing, then use this icing to color the rest.

Small Cakes

1. Cupcakes are iced by dipping the tops in a soft icing. Twist the cakes slightly and pull them out quickly in one smooth motion.
   Cupcakes may also be iced by spreading icing on with a spatula. Practice is necessary to develop speed and efficiency.

2. Petits fours are tiny cakes cut from sheet cakes. Select a cake that doesn't crumble easily. Carefully cut it into desired shapes. Remove all crumbs and place the cakes on a rack over a sheet pan. Ice by pouring fondant or flat icing over them to cover completely.

Procedure for Assembling Layer Cakes

1. Cool cake layers completely before assembling and icing.
2. Trim layers, if necessary.
   - Remove any ragged edges.
   - Slightly rounded tops are easily covered by icing, but excessively large bumps may have to be cut off.
   - If desired, layers may be split horizontally. This makes the cake higher and increases the proportion of filling to cake. See Figure 11.3.
3. Brush all crumbs from cakes. Loose crumbs make the icing process difficult.
4. Place the bottom layer upside down (to give a flat surface for the filling) on a cardboard cake circle of the same diameter. Place the cake in the center of a cake turntable.
   If a cake circle or turntable is not available, place the cake on a serving plate and slip sheets of waxed paper or parchment under the edges of the cake to keep the plate clean.
5. Spread filling on the bottom layer out to the edges. If the filling is different from the icing for the outside of the cake, be careful not to spread the filling over the edges.
   Use the proper amount of filling. If applied too heavily, it will ooze out when the top layer is set in place.
6. Place the top layer on the bottom layer, right side up.
7. Ice the cake:
   - If a thin or light icing is used, pour or spread the icing onto the center of the cake. Then spread it to the edges and down the sides with a spatula.
   - If a heavy icing is used, it may be necessary to spread the sides first, then place a good quantity of icing in the center of the top and push it to the edges with the spatula.

   Pushing the icing rather than pulling or dragging it with the spatula prevents pulling up crumbs and getting them mixed with the icing.
   Use enough icing to cover the entire cake generously, but not excessively, with an even layer.
   Smooth the icing with the spatula or leave it textured or swirled, as desired.
   The finished, iced cake should have a perfectly level top and perfectly straight, even sides.

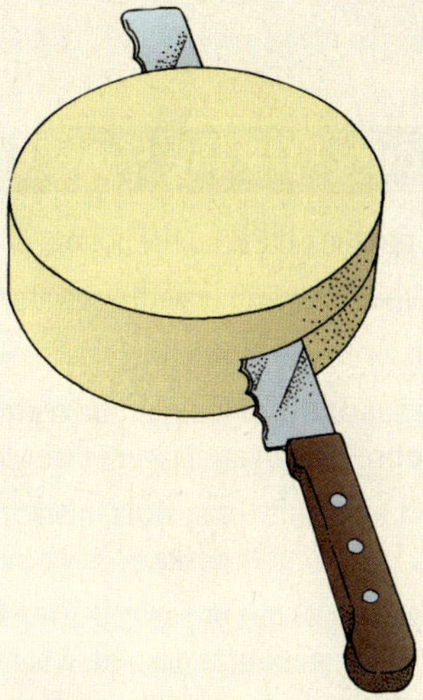

Figure 11.3 Cake layers may be split horizontally, using a long-bladed, serrated knife.

Sheet Cakes

Sheet cakes are ideal for volume service because they require little labor to bake, ice, and decorate, and they keep well as long as they are uncut.

For special occasions, sheet cakes are sometimes decorated as a single unit with a design or picture in colored icing, a "Happy Special Occasion" message, and so on. It is more common, however, to ice them for individual service, as in the following procedure.

Procedure for Icing Sheet Cakes

1. Turn out the cake onto the bottom of another sheet pan or tray, as described on page 264. Cool the cake thoroughly.
2. Trim the edges evenly with a serrated knife.
3. Brush all crumbs from the cake.
4. Place a quantity of icing in the center of the cake. With a spatula, push the icing to the edges. Smooth the top with the spatula, giving the entire cake an even layer of icing.
5. With a long knife or spatula, mark the entire cake off into portions, as in Figure 11.4, by pressing the back of the knife lightly into the icing. Do not cut the cake.
6. Using a paper cone or pastry bag fitted with a star tube, pipe a rosette or swirl of icing onto the center of each marked-off portion, or select another decoration, as desired. Whatever decorations you use, keep them simple, and make them the same for every portion. The finished sheet cake will resemble that in Figure 11.5.
7. Hold for service. Cut as close as possible to service time to keep the cake from drying.

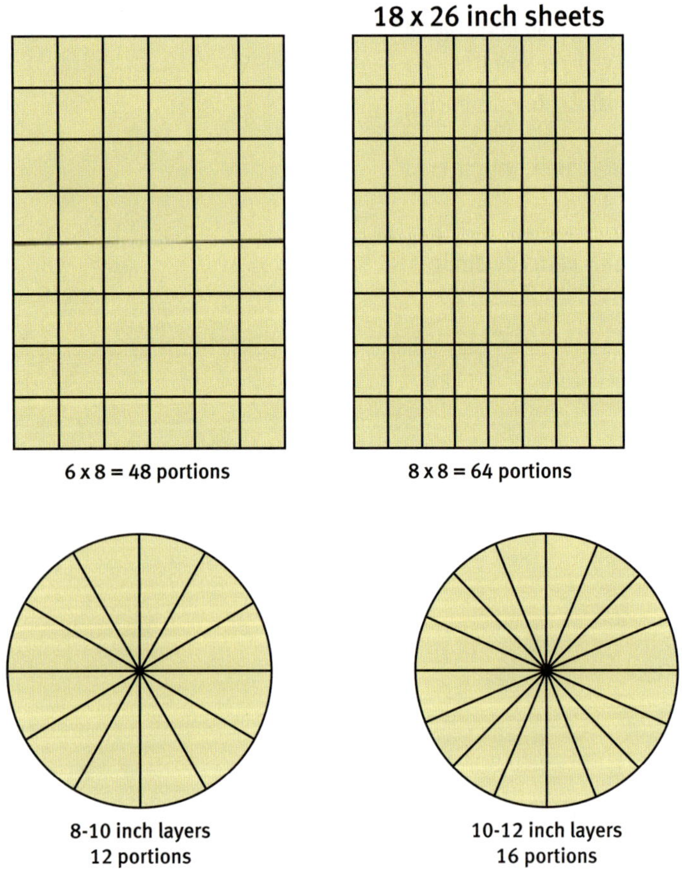

Figure 11.4 Cake-cutting guides for sheet cakes and round layer cakes. For sheets measuring 13 × 18 in. (33 × 46 cm), simply divide the above diagrams for full-sized sheet cakes in half.

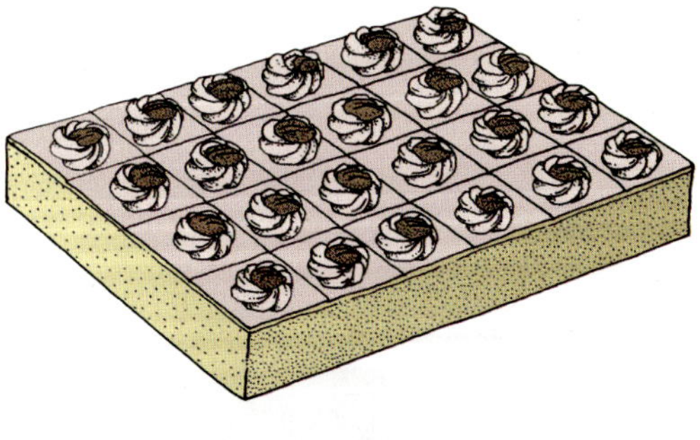

Figure 11.5 A finished sheet cake marked off into portions and decorated so each portion is identical.

KEY POINTS TO REVIEW

- What are the six basic types of icing?
- What are the steps in the procedure for assembling and icing layer cakes?
- What are the steps in the procedure for icing sheet cakes?

TERMS FOR REVIEW

creaming method
two-stage method
blending method
foaming method
angel food method
chiffon method
fondant
buttercream
foam icing
flat icing
fudge icing
royal icing
glaze
ganache

QUESTIONS FOR DISCUSSION

1. Briefly list the steps in each of the four basic cake-mixing methods presented in this chapter.
2. What are the reasons, in the creaming method, for creaming the butter and sugar until the mixture is light and fluffy?
3. In both the creaming method and the two-stage method, scraping down the sides of the bowl is emphasized. Why is this necessary?
4. What might the finished product be like if you tried to mix a low-fat cake by the two-stage method? Explain.
5. Examine the cake formulas below and indicate which mixing method you would use for each.
6. What is the most important rule to consider when using fondant?
7. Compare the keeping qualities of simple buttercreams and meringue-type buttercreams.
8. List the steps in assembling and icing a three-layer cake.

CAKE 1

2 lb		Cake flour	1 kg
1 lb	2 oz	Emulsified shortening	525 g
	1 oz	Salt	30 g
	1.5 oz	Baking powder	45 g
2 lb	8 oz	Fine granulated sugar	1250 g
1 lb		Skim milk	500 g
1 lb	5 oz	Whole eggs	650 g
	10 oz	Skim milk	300 g

CAKE 2

3 lb		Whole eggs	1.5 kg
1 lb		Egg yolks	500 g
2 lb	4 oz	Sugar	1125 g
2 lb		Cake flour	1 kg
	6 oz	Cornstarch	175 g
	6 oz	Melted butter	175 g

CAKE 3

1 lb		Butter	500 g
	8 oz	Shortening	250 g
4 lb		Sugar	2 kg
	1 oz	Vanilla	30 g
1 lb	4 oz	Whole eggs	625 g
3 lb	8 oz	Cake flour	1750 g
	10 oz	Cocoa powder	300 g
	1.5 oz	Baking soda	45 g
3 lb		Buttermilk	1.5 kg
1 lb	8 oz	Water	750 g

Chapter 12

Cookies

The word *cookie* means "small cake," and that's exactly what a cookie is. In fact, some cookies are made from cake batter. Some products, such as certain kinds of brownies, are difficult to classify as cakes or cookies.

Most cookie formulas, however, call for less liquid than cake formulas do. Cookie doughs range from soft to very stiff, unlike the thinner batters for cakes. This difference in moisture content means some differences in mixing methods, although the basic procedures are much like those for cakes.

The most apparent differences between cakes and cookies are in the makeup. Because most cookies are individually formed or shaped, a great deal of hand labor is involved. Learning correct methods and practicing diligently are essential for efficiency.

After reading this chapter, you should be able to

1. List the factors responsible for crispness, softness, chewiness, and spread in cookies.
2. Demonstrate the three basic cookie mixing methods.
3. Prepare the seven basic cookie types: dropped, bagged, rolled, molded, icebox, bar, and sheet.
4. Prepare pans for, bake, and cool cookies.

Cookie Characteristics and Their Causes

Cookies come in an infinite variety of shapes, sizes, flavors, and textures. Characteristics that are desirable in some are not desirable in others. For example, we want some cookies to be crisp and others to be soft. We want some to hold their shape and others to spread during baking. In order to produce the characteristics we want and to correct faults, it is useful to know what causes these characteristics.

Crispness

Cookies are crisp if they are very low in moisture. The following factors contribute to crispness:

1. Low proportion of liquid in the mix. Most crisp cookies are made from a stiff dough.
2. High sugar and fat content.
3. Evaporation of moisture during baking due to high temperatures and/or long baking.
4. Small size or thin shape, so the cookies dry quickly during baking.
5. Proper storage. Crisp cookies can become soft if they absorb moisture.

Softness

Softness is the opposite of crispness, so it has the opposite causes, as follows:

1. High proportion of liquid in mix.
2. Low sugar and fat.
3. Honey, molasses, or corn syrup included in formulas. These sugars are hygroscopic, which means they readily absorb moisture from the air or from their surroundings.
4. Underbaking.
5. Large size or thick shape. The cookies retain moisture.
6. Proper storage. Soft cookies can become stale and dry if not tightly covered or wrapped.

Chewiness

Moisture is necessary for chewiness, but other factors are also required. In other words, all chewy cookies are soft, but not all soft cookies are chewy.

1. High sugar and liquid content, but low fat content.
2. High proportion of eggs.
3. Strong flour, or gluten developed during mixing.

Spread

Spread is desirable in some cookies, while others must hold their shape. Several factors contribute to spread or lack of spread.

1. **Sugar.**
   High sugar content increases spread. Coarse granulated sugar increases spread, whereas fine sugar or confectioners' sugar reduces spread.
2. **Leavening.**
   High baking soda or baking ammonia content encourages spread. So does long creaming, which incorporates air.

3. **Temperature.**
   Low oven temperature increases spread. High temperature decreases spread because the cookie sets up before it has a chance to spread too much.

4. **Liquid.**
   A slack batter—that is, one with a high liquid content—spreads more than a stiff dough.

5. **Flour.**
   Strong flour or activation of gluten decreases spread.

6. **Pan grease.**
   Cookies spread more if baked on a heavily greased pan.

Mixing Methods

Cookie-mixing methods are much like cake-mixing methods. The major difference is that less liquid is usually incorporated, so mixing is somewhat easier.

Less liquid means gluten is less developed by the mixing. Also, a smooth, uniform mix is easier to obtain.

There are three basic cookie mixing methods:

1. One-stage
2. Creaming
3. Sponge

These methods are subject to many variations due to differences in formulas. The general procedures are as follows. Be sure, however, to follow the exact instructions when a formula indicates a variation in the procedure.

One-Stage Method

The *one-stage method* is the counterpart of the blending or two-stage cake-mixing method, discussed in the previous chapter. Cake batters have more liquid, so it must be added in two or more stages in order to blend uniformly. Low-moisture cookies, on the other hand, can be mixed all in one stage.

Creaming Method

The *creaming method* for cookies is nearly identical to the creaming method for cakes. Because cookies require less liquid, it is usually not necessary to add the liquid alternately with the flour. It can be added all at once.

Sponge Method

The *sponge method* for cookies is essentially the same as the egg-foam methods for cakes. The procedure varies considerably, depending on the ingredients. Batches should be kept small because the batter is delicate.

Procedure for One-Stage Method

1. Scale ingredients accurately. Have all ingredients at room temperature.
2. Place all ingredients in mixer. With the paddle attachment, mix at low speed until uniformly blended. Scrape down the sides of the bowl as necessary.

Procedure for Creaming Method

1. Scale ingredients accurately. Have all ingredients at room temperature.
2. Place the fat, sugar, salt, and spices in the mixing bowl. With the paddle attachment, cream these ingredients at low speed.
   For light cookies, cream until the mix is light and fluffy, incorporating more air for leavening.
   For a dense, chewy cookie, cream only slightly.
3. Add the eggs and liquid, if any, and blend in at low speed.
4. Sift in the flour and leavening. Mix until just combined.

Procedure for Sponge Method

1. Scale all ingredients accurately. Have all ingredients at room temperature, or warm the eggs slightly for greater volume, as for sponge cakes.
2. Following the procedure given in the formula used, whip the eggs (whole, yolks, or whites) and the sugar to the proper stage: soft peaks for whites, thick and light for whole eggs or yolks.
3. Fold in the remaining ingredients as specified in the recipe. Be careful not to overmix or to deflate the eggs.

KEY POINTS TO REVIEW

- What are the factors that determine whether a cookie will be crisp, soft, or chewy?
- What are the factors that determine how much a cookie will spread when baked?
- What are the steps in the one-stage method for mixing cookies?
- What are the steps in the creaming method for mixing cookies?
- What are the steps in the sponge method for mixing cookies?

Types and Makeup Methods

We can classify cookie types by makeup method as well as by mixing method. Grouping by the makeup method is perhaps more useful from the point of view of production because mixing methods are relatively simple, whereas makeup procedures vary considerably.

In this section, we present basic procedures for producing seven cookie types:

1. Dropped
2. Bagged
3. Rolled
4. Molded
5. Icebox
6. Bar
7. Sheet

No matter what makeup method you use, follow one important rule: *Make all cookies of uniform size and thickness*. This is essential for even baking. Because baking times are so short, small cookies may burn before large ones are done.

Dropped Cookies

Dropped cookies are made from a soft dough or batter. They are fast and easy to make up. Many sponge or foam-type batters are made up as dropped cookies.

1. Select the proper size scoop for accurate portioning.

   A No. 30 scoop makes a large cookie, about 1 ounce (30 g).

   A No. 40 scoop makes a medium cookie.

   Nos. 50, 60, or smaller scoops make small cookies.

2. Drop the cookies onto the prepared baking sheets. Allow enough space between cookies for spreading.
3. Rich cookies spread by themselves. However, if the formula requires it, flatten the mounds of batter slightly with a weight dipped in sugar.

Bagged Cookies

Bagged cookies, or pressed cookies, are also made from soft doughs. The dough must be soft enough to be forced through a pastry bag but stiff enough to hold its shape.

1. Fit a pastry bag with a tip of the desired size and shape. Fill the bag with the cookie dough.
2. Press out cookies of desired shape and size directly onto prepared cookie sheets.

Rolled Cookies

Rolled cookies, which are cut from a stiff dough, are not often made in commercial food service because they require excessive labor. Also, scraps are always left over after cutting. When rerolled, these scraps make inferior, tough cookies.

1. Chill dough thoroughly.
2. Roll dough to ⅛ inch (3 mm) thick on a floured canvas or floured workbench. Use as little flour as possible for dusting because the flour can toughen the cookies.
3. Cut out cookies with cookie cutters and place on prepared baking sheets. Cut as close together as possible to reduce the quantity of scraps.

Molded Cookies

The first part of the procedure for ***molded cookies*** (steps 1 and 2) is simply a fast and fairly accurate way of dividing the dough into equal portions. Each piece is then molded into the desired shape. This usually consists of simply flattening the pieces out with a weight. For some traditional cookies, special molds are used to flatten the dough and, at the same time, stamp it with a design.

The pieces may also be shaped by hand into crescents, fingers, or other shapes.

1. Roll the dough into long cylinders about 1 inch (2.5 cm) thick, or whatever size is required. (Refrigerate the dough if it is too soft to handle.)
2. With a knife or bench scraper, cut the roll into 1-ounce (30-g) pieces, or whatever size is required.
3. Place the pieces on prepared baking sheets, leaving 2 inches (5 cm) of space between them.
4. Flatten cookies with a weight (such as a can) dipped in granulated sugar after pressing each cookie.

   A fork is sometimes used for flattening the dough, as for peanut butter cookies.
5. Alternative method: After step 2, shape the dough by hand into desired shapes.

Icebox Cookies

The ***icebox method***, or refrigerator method, is ideal for operations that wish to have freshly baked cookies on hand at all times. The rolls of dough may be made up in advance and stored. Cookies can easily be cut and baked as needed.

1. Scale dough into pieces of uniform size, from 1½ pounds (700 g), if you are making small cookies, to 3 pounds (1400 g), for large cookies.
2. Form the dough into cylinders from 1 to 2 inches (2.5 to 5 cm) in diameter, depending on the size cookie desired.

   For accurate portioning, it is important to make all the cylinders of dough the same thickness and length.
3. Wrap the cylinders in parchment or waxed paper, place them on sheet pans, and refrigerate overnight.
4. Unwrap the dough and cut into slices of uniform thickness. The exact thickness required depends on the size of the cookie and how much the dough spreads during baking. The usual range is from ⅛ to ½ inch (3 to 12 mm).

   A slicing machine is recommended for ensuring even thickness. Doughs containing nuts or fruits should be sliced by hand with a knife.
5. Place the slices on prepared baking sheets, allowing 2 inches (5 cm) of space between cookies.

Bar Cookies

Bar cookies are so called because the dough is shaped into long bars, which are baked and then cut. After cutting, they may be baked again, as in the case of biscotti, which means "twice baked." Do not confuse bar cookies with sheet cookies (see below), which are often called *bars* by consumers.

1. Scale the dough into 1¾-pound (800-g) units (1-pound units, or 500-g units, may be used for smaller cookies).
2. Shape the pieces of dough into cylinders the length of the sheet pans. Place three strips on each greased pan, spacing them well apart.
3. Flatten the dough with the fingers into strips about 3 to 4 inches wide and about ¼ inch thick (8 to 10 cm wide, 6 mm thick).

4. If required, brush with egg wash.
5. Bake as directed in the formula.
6. After baking, while cookies are still warm, cut each strip into bars about 1¾ inches (4.5 cm) wide.

Sheet Cookies

Sheet cookies vary so much that it is nearly impossible to give a single procedure for all of them. Some of them are almost like sheet cakes, only denser and richer. They may even be iced like sheet cakes. Others consist of two or three layers added and baked in separate stages. The following procedure is a general guideline only.

1. Spread the cookie mixture into prepared sheet pans. Make sure the thickness is even.
2. If required, add topping, or brush with an egg wash.
3. Bake as directed. Cool.
4. Apply icing or topping, if any.
5. Cut into individual squares or rectangles.

Panning, Baking, and Cooling

Preparing the Pans

1. Use clean, unwarped pans.
2. Lining the sheets with parchment or silicone paper is fast, and it eliminates the necessity of greasing the pans.
3. A heavily greased pan increases the spread of the cookie. A greased and floured pan decreases spread.
4. Some high-fat cookies can be baked on ungreased pans.

Baking

1. Most cookies are baked at a relatively high temperature for a short time.
2. Too low a temperature increases spreading and may produce hard, dry, pale cookies.
3. Too high a temperature decreases spreading and may burn the edges or bottoms.
4. Even one minute of overbaking can burn cookies, so watch them closely. The heat of the pan continues to bake the cookies even after they are removed from the oven.
5. Doneness is indicated by color. The edges and bottoms should just be turning a light golden color.
6. With some rich doughs, burnt bottoms may be a problem. In this case, double-pan the cookies by placing the sheet pan on a second pan of the same size.

Cooling

1. Remove the cookies from the pans while they are still warm, or they may stick.
2. If the cookies are very soft, do not remove them from the pans until they are cool enough and firm enough to handle. Cookies may be soft when hot but become crisp when cool.
3. Do not cool cookies too rapidly or in cold drafts, or they may crack.
4. Cool completely before storing.

KEY POINTS TO REVIEW

- What are the seven makeup methods for making cookies? Describe the procedure for each.
- How are pans prepared for baking cookies?
- When baking cookies, how do you determine when they are done?
- What is the proper way to cool cookies after baking?

Chocolate Chip Cookies

INGREDIENTS	U.S.	METRIC	PERCENTAGE
Butter and/or shortening	10 oz	300 g	50 %
Granulated sugar	8 oz	240 g	40 %
Brown sugar	8 oz	240 g	40 %
Salt	0.25 oz (1½ tsp)	8 g (7 mL)	1.25 %
Eggs	6 oz	175 g	30 %
Vanilla	2 tsp	10 mL	1.5 %
Pastry flour	1 lb 4 oz	600 g	100 %
Baking soda	0.25 oz (1½ tsp)	8 g (7 mL)	1.25 %
Chocolate chips	1 lb 4 oz	600 g	100 %
Chopped walnuts or pecans	8 oz	240 g	40 %
Yield:	*5 lb*	*2421 g*	*404 %*

Per 1 ounce (28.35 g): Calories, 130; Protein, 2 g; Fat, 7 g (47% cal.); Cholesterol, 15 mg; Carbohydrates, 16 g; Fiber, 2 g; Sodium, 85 mg.

PROCEDURE

Mixing:
Creaming method. Blend in chocolate chips and nuts last.

Makeup:
Drop method. Use greased or parchment-lined baking sheets.

Baking:
375°F (190°C), 8–12 minutes, depending on size.

VARIATIONS

Brown Sugar Nut Cookies

Omit granulated sugar and use 100% (1 lb 4 oz/600 g) brown sugar.
Omit chocolate chips and increase nuts to 100% (1 lb 4 oz/600 g).

TOLL HOUSE COOKIES

Chocolate chip cookies, in their many varieties, are the most popular cookies in North America. They owe their origin to the Toll House cookie, said to have been developed in the 1920s or 1930s by Ruth Wakefield, owner of the Toll House Inn in Whitman, Massachusetts. The original Toll House cookies are simple butter cookies with semisweet chocolate morsels mixed into the dough. Today's chocolate chip or chocolate chunk cookies are likely to contain any kind of chocolate plus other ingredients, especially nuts, such as pecans, walnuts, or macadamia nuts.

Oatmeal Raisin Cookies

INGREDIENTS	U.S.	METRIC	PERCENTAGE
Butter and/ or shortening	8 oz	250 g	67 %
Brown sugar	1 lb	500 g	133 %
Salt	1 tsp	5 g (5 mL)	1.5 %
Eggs	4 oz	125 g	33 %
Vanilla	2 tsp	10 mL	3 %
Milk	1 oz	30 g	8 %
Pastry flour	12 oz	375 g	100 %
Baking powder	0.5 oz (1 tbsp)	15 g	4 %
Baking soda	0.25 oz (1½ tsp)	8 g	2 %
Rolled oats (quick cooking)	10 oz	300 g	83 %
Raisins (see Note)	8 oz	250 g	67 %
Yield:	*3 lb 11 oz*	*1858 g*	*501 %*

Per 1 ounce (28.35 g): Calories, 110; Protein, 2 g; Fat, 4 g (31% cal.); Cholesterol, 15 mg; Carbohydrates, 18 g; Fiber, 1 g; Sodium, 135 mg.

Note: If raisins are hard and dry, soak them in hot water 30 minutes, drain, and dry well before adding to cookie dough.

PROCEDURE

Mixing:
Creaming method. Combine oats with other dry ingredients after they are sifted. Mix raisins into dough last.

Makeup:
Drop method. Use greased or parchment-lined baking sheets.

Baking:
375°F (190°C), 10–12 minutes, depending on size.

Sugar Cookies

INGREDIENTS	U.S.			METRIC	PERCENTAGE
Butter and/or shortening	1 lb			500 g	40 %
Sugar	1 lb	4	oz	625 g	50 %
Salt		2	tsp	10 g (10 mL)	0.9 %
Eggs		4	oz	125 g	10 %
Milk		4	oz	125 g	10 %
Vanilla		0.5	oz	15 mL	1.25 %
Cake flour	2 lb	8	oz	1250 g	100 %
Baking powder		1.25	oz	35 g	3 %
Yield:	*5 lb*	*5*	*oz*	*2685 g*	*215 %*

Per 1 ounce (28.35 g): Calories, 120; Protein, 1 g; Fat, 4.5 g (36% cal.); Cholesterol, 15 mg; Carbohydrates, 17 g; Fiber, 0 g; Sodium, 150 mg.

PROCEDURE

Mixing:

Creaming method.

Makeup:

Rolled method. Before cutting the rolled-out dough, wash with milk and sprinkle with sugar. Use greased or parchment-lined baking sheets.

Baking:

375°F (190°C), 8–10 minutes.

VARIATIONS

Lemon rind, extract, or emulsion may be used in place of vanilla.

Rolled Brown Sugar Cookies

Increase butter to 50% (1 lb 4 oz/625 g). Omit granulated sugar and use 60% (1 lb 8 oz/750 g) brown sugar.

Rolled Chocolate Cookies

Substitute 4 oz (125 g) cocoa for 4 oz (125 g) flour.

Shortbread Cookies

INGREDIENTS	U.S.			METRIC	PERCENTAGE
Butter	1 lb	8	oz	750 g	75 %
Sugar	1 lb			500 g	50 %
Salt		0.25	oz (1½ tsp)	8 g (7 mL)	0.75 %
Egg yolks (see Note)		8	oz	250 g	25 %
Flavoring (optional; see Note)					
Pastry flour	2 lb			1000 g	100 %
Yield:	*5 lb*			*2508 g*	*250 %*

Per 1 ounce (28.35 g): Calories, 130; Protein, 2 g; Fat, 8 g (53% cal.); Cholesterol, 55 mg; Carbohydrates, 14 g; Fiber, 2 g; Sodium, 105 mg.

Note: Traditional Scottish shortbread is made with butter, flour, and sugar—no eggs, flavoring, or liquid. Because the dough is crumbly, it is not rolled out but rather pressed into pans or molds and baked, and then cut while still hot. For the recipe given here, you may make the cookies without added flavoring or flavor to taste with vanilla, almond, or lemon.

PROCEDURE

Mixing:

Creaming method.

Makeup:

Rolled method. Roll dough ¼ in. (0.5 cm) thick (this is thicker that most rolled cookies). Use greased or parchment-lined baking sheets.

Baking:

350°F (175°C), about 15 minutes.

Peanut Butter Cookies

INGREDIENTS	U.S.		METRIC	PERCENTAGE
Butter and/or shortening		12 oz	375 g	75 %
Brown sugar		8 oz	250 g	50 %
Granulated sugar		8 oz	250 g	50 %
Salt		1 tsp	5 g (5 mL)	1 %
Peanut butter		12 oz	375 g	75 %
Eggs		4 oz	125 g	25 %
Vanilla extract		2 tsp	10 g	2 %
Pastry flour	1 lb		500 g	100 %
Baking soda		1 tsp	5 g (5 mL)	1 %
Yield:	*3 lb*	*12 oz*	*1895 g*	*379 %*

Per 1 ounce (28.35 g): Calories, 130; Protein, 2 g; Fat, 8 g (53% cal.); Cholesterol, 20 mg; Carbohydrates, 14 g; Fiber, 1 g; Sodium, 135 mg.

PROCEDURE

Mixing:

Creaming method. Cream the peanut butter with the fat and sugar.

Makeup:

Molded method. Use a fork instead of a weight to flatten the cookies. Use greased or parchment-lined baking sheets.

Baking:

375°F (190°C), 8–12 minutes, depending on size.

Brownies

INGREDIENTS	U.S.			METRIC	PERCENTAGE
Unsweetened chocolate	1 lb			450 g	100 %
Butter	1 lb	8	oz	675 g	150 %
Eggs	1 lb	8	oz	675 g	150 %
Sugar	3 lb			1350 g	300 %
Salt		0.25	oz (1½ tsp)	7 g (7 mL)	1.5 %
Vanilla		1	oz	30 mL	6 %
Cake flour	1 lb			450 g	100 %
Chopped walnuts or pecans	1 lb			450 g	100 %
Yield:	*9 lb*	*1*	*oz*	*4087 g*	*907 %*

Per 1 brownie: Calories, 190; Protein, 3 g; Fat, 12 g (54% cal.); Cholesterol, 45 mg; Carbohydrates, 20 g; Fiber, 1 g; Sodium, 95 mg.

PROCEDURE

Mixing:

Sponge method.

1. Melt chocolate and butter together in a double boiler. Stir so that the mixture is smooth. Let it cool to room temperature.
2. Blend the eggs, sugar, and salt until well mixed, but do not whip. Add the vanilla.
3. Blend in the chocolate mixture.
4. Sift the flour and fold it in.
5. Fold in the nuts.

Makeup:

Sheet method. Grease and flour the pans or line them with parchment. Quantity of basic recipe is enough for 1 full sheet pan, 18 × 26. in. (46 × 66 cm), 2 half-size sheet pans, 4 pans measuring 9 × 13 in. (23 × 33 cm), or 6 square pans measuring 9 in. (23 cm) per side.

If desired, batter may be sprinkled with an additional 50% (8 oz/255 g) chopped nuts after panning.

Baking:

325°F (165°C), about 60 minutes. For 2-in. (5-cm) square brownies, cut sheet pan 8 × 12 to yield 96 pieces.

VARIATION

Butterscotch Brownies or Blondies

Omit chocolate. Use brown sugar instead of granulated sugar. Increase flour to 1 lb 6 oz (600 g).

Almond Biscotti

INGREDIENTS	U.S.	METRIC	PERCENTAGE
Eggs	10 oz	300 g	35 %
Sugar	1 lb 2 oz	550 g	65 %
Salt	0.4 oz (2 tsp)	12 g (10 mL)	2 %
Vanilla	0.3 oz (2 tsp)	8 mL	1 %
Grated orange zest	0.1 oz (1¼ tsp)	3 g	0.5 %
Pastry flour	1 lb 12 oz	850 g	100 %
Baking powder	0.7 oz	20 g	2.5 %
Blanched whole almonds	10 oz	300 g	35 %
Yield:	*4 lb 3 oz*	*2047 g*	*241 %*

Per 1 ounce (28.35 g): Calories, 110; Protein, 3 g; Fat, 4.5 g (36% cal.); Cholesterol, 15 mg; Carbohydrates, 15 g; Fiber, 2 g; Sodium, 110 mg.

PROCEDURE

Mixing:

Sponge method.

1. Combine the eggs, sugar, and salt. Stir over hot water to warm the mixture. Whip until thick and light.
2. Fold in the vanilla and orange zest.
3. Sift together the flour and baking powder. Fold in the egg mixture.
4. Mix in the almonds.

Makeup:

Bar method. Shape into logs 2–2½ in. (6 cm) thick. Dust your hands and the workbench with flour. The dough will be soft, sticky, and difficult to handle, but the logs do not have to be perfectly shaped. Egg-wash.

Baking:

325°F (160°C), 30–40 minutes, until light golden.

Finishing:

Let cool slightly. Slice diagonally about ½ in. (12 mm) thick.
Place slices cut side down on sheet pans. Bake at 275°F (135°C) until toasted and golden brown, about 30 minutes.

TERMS FOR REVIEW

one-stage method	dropped cookies	molded cookies	bar cookies
creaming method	bagged cookies	icebox cookies	sheet cookies
sponge method	rolled cookies		

QUESTIONS FOR DISCUSSION

1. What makes cookies crisp, and how can you keep them crisp after they are baked?
2. If you baked some cookies that were unintentionally chewy, how would you correct the problem in the next batch?
3. Describe briefly the difference between the creaming method and the one-stage method.
4. Besides cost control, why are accurate scaling and uniform sizing important when making up cookies?

Chapter 13

Apple Pie with Streusel Topping, page 300.

Pies and Pastries

On the North American frontier, it was not uncommon for the pioneer housewife to bake 21 pies a week—one for every meal. Pies were so important to the settlers that in winter, when fruits were unavailable, cooks would bake pies for dessert out of whatever materials were available, such as potatoes, vinegar, and soda crackers.

Few of us today eat pie at every meal. Nevertheless, pies are still a favorite dessert. Most customers will order and pay a higher price for a piece of chocolate cream pie than for chocolate pudding, even if the pie filling is the same as the pudding and even if they leave the crust uneaten.

In this chapter, we present the preparation of pie crusts and fillings. In addition, we discuss how to make puff pastry, éclair paste, meringues, and fruit desserts.

After reading this chapter, you should be able to

1. Prepare flaky pie dough and mealy pie dough.
2. Prepare crumb crusts and short, or cookie, crusts.
3. Assemble and bake pies.
4. Prepare the following pie fillings: fruit fillings using the cooked juice method, the cooked fruit method, and the old-fashioned method; custard or soft fillings; cream pie fillings; and chiffon fillings.
5. Prepare puff pastry dough and puff dough products.
6. Prepare éclair paste and éclair paste products.
7. Prepare standard meringues and meringue desserts.
8. Prepare fruit desserts.

PIES

Pie Doughs

Before you begin studying this section, it would be a good idea for you to review the section on gluten development in Chapter 8. Pie pastry is a simple product in terms of its ingredients: flour, shortening, water, and salt. Yet success or failure depends on how the shortening and flour are mixed and how the gluten is developed. The key to making pie dough is proper technique, and you will remember the techniques better if you understand why they work.

Ingredients

FLOUR

Pastry flour is the best choice for pie doughs. It has enough gluten to produce the desired structure and flakiness, yet is low enough in gluten to yield a tender product, if handled properly.

If stronger flours are used, the percentage of shortening should be increased to provide more tenderness.

FAT

Regular hydrogenated shortening is the most popular fat for pie crusts because it has the right plastic consistency to produce a flaky crust. It is firm and moldable enough to make an easily worked dough. Emulsified shortening should not be used because it blends too quickly with the flour, making a flaky pastry difficult to achieve.

Butter contributes excellent flavor to pie pastry, but it is not frequently used in volume production for two reasons: It is expensive, and it melts very easily, making the dough difficult to work.

It is desirable, if costs permit, to blend a quantity of butter into the shortening used for pie crusts to improve flavor. The quantity of pie crust dumped in the garbage after customers have eaten out the filling is evidence that many people are not satisfied with the taste of pie crusts made with shortening.

If all butter is used in place of shortening, the percentage of fat in the formula should be increased by about one-fourth. (If 1 pound shortening is called for, use 1 pound 4 ounces butter. If 500 grams shortening are called for, use 625 grams butter.) The liquid should be reduced slightly, as butter contains moisture.

Lard is an excellent shortening for pies because it is firm and plastic. Some people dislike its flavor, however, so it is not widely used in food service.

LIQUID

Water is necessary to develop some gluten in the flour and to give structure and flakiness to the dough. If too much water is used, the crust will become tough because of too much gluten development. If not enough water is used, the crust will fall apart.

Milk makes a rich dough that browns quickly. However, the crust is less crisp, and the production cost is higher.

Whether water or milk is used, it must be added cold (40°F/4°C or colder) to maintain proper dough temperature.

SALT

Salt has some tenderizing and conditioning effect on the gluten. However, its main contribution is to flavor.

Salt must be dissolved in the liquid before being added to the mix to ensure even distribution.

Temperature

Pie dough should be kept cool, about 60°F (15°C), during mixing and makeup for two reasons:

1. Shortening has the best consistency when cool. If it is warm, it blends too quickly with the flour. If it is very cold, it is too firm to be easily workable.
2. Gluten develops more slowly at cool temperatures than at warm temperatures.

Pie Dough Types

There are two basic types of pie dough: flaky and mealy.

The difference between the two is how the fat is blended with the flour. Complete mixing procedures are given later. First, it is important to understand the basic distinction between the two types.

FLAKY PIE DOUGH

For ***flaky pie dough***, the fat is cut or rubbed into the flour until the particles of shortening are about the size of peas or hazelnuts. That is, the flour is not completely blended with the fat, and the fat is left in pieces. (Many bakers distinguish between this crust, which they call *short-flake*, and *long-flake* crusts, in which the fat is left in pieces the size of walnuts and the flour is even less coated with shortening.)

When water is added, the flour absorbs water and develops some gluten. When the dough is rolled out, the lumps of fat and moistened flour are flattened and become flakes of dough separated by layers of fat.

MEALY PIE DOUGH

For ***mealy pie dough***, the fat is blended into the flour more thoroughly, until the mixture looks like coarse cornmeal. Because the flour is more completely coated with fat:

- The crust is very short and tender because less gluten can develop.
- Less water is needed in the mix because the flour won't absorb as much as in flaky dough.
- The baked dough is less likely to absorb moisture from the filling and become soggy.

Mealy dough is used for bottom crusts in baked fruit pies and soft or custard-type pies because it resists sogginess. Flaky doughs are used for top crusts and for prebaked pie shells.

TRIMMINGS

Reworked scraps or trimmings are tougher than freshly made dough. They may be combined with mealy dough and used for bottom crusts only.

Mixing Pie Doughs

Hand mixing is best for small quantities of dough, especially flaky dough, because it gives more control over the mixing. Quantities up to 10 pounds (5 kg) can be mixed almost as quickly by hand as by machine.

For machine mixing, use a pastry knife or paddle attachment and blend at low speed.

The mixing method for pie doughs is called the ***rubbed dough method***. Although the procedure has several steps, the two main steps are characteristic of the method:

1. Rub the fat into the sifted dry ingredients.
2. Carefully mix the combined liquid ingredients into the dry ingredients.

The seven steps in the pie dough recipe that follows explain the rubbed dough method in more detail. Study this procedure well, because most pie doughs and several other basic pastries are mixed with this procedure or a variation. Also, compare this procedure with the biscuit method outlined on page 250. Although biscuit dough is softer and contains leavening, it is mixed with a similar procedure.

Procedures for rolling pie doughs and lining pie pans are discussed in the next section, "Assembly and Baking."

KEY POINTS TO REVIEW

- What are the steps in the rubbed dough method for mixing pie doughs?
- How do you mix pie doughs in order to get flaky dough? mealy dough?
- Flaky dough is best for what kind of pie crusts? Mealy dough is best for what kind of pie crusts?

Flaky Pie Dough / Mealy Pie Dough

INGREDIENTS	FLAKY U.S.	FLAKY METRIC	FLAKY PERCENTAGE	MEALY U.S.	MEALY METRIC	MEALY PERCENTAGE
Pastry flour	2 lb 8 oz	1000 g	100 %	2 lb 8 oz	1000 g	100 %
Shortening	1 lb 12 oz	700 g	70 %	1 lb 10 oz	650 g	65 %
Salt	0.75 oz (4 tsp)	20 g	2 %	0.75 oz (4 tsp)	20 g	2 %
Water	12 oz	300 g	30 %	10 oz	250 g	25 %
Yield:	*5 lb*	*2020 g*	*202 %*	*4 lb 12 oz*	*1920 g*	*192 %*

Per 1 ounce (28.35 g): Calories, 130; Protein, 1 g; Fat, 10 g (65% cal.); Cholesterol, 0 mg; Carbohydrates, 11 g; Fiber, 20 g; Sodium, 105 mg.

PROCEDURE

Mixing:

1. Collect all equipment.
2. Collect and scale ingredients.
3. Dissolve salt in water. Set aside.
4. Place flour and shortening in mixing bowl.
5. Rub or cut shortening into flour to the proper degree:

   For mealy dough—until it resembles coarse cornmeal.

   For flaky dough—until fat particles are the size of peas or hazelnuts.
6. Add salt and water. Mix very gently, just until water is absorbed. Do not overwork the dough.
7. Place the dough in pans, cover with plastic film, and place in refrigerator or retarder for several hours.

Other Pie Crusts

CRUMB CRUSTS

Graham cracker crusts are popular because they have an appealing flavor and are much easier to make than pastry crusts. For variation, vanilla or chocolate wafer crumbs or gingersnap crumbs may be used instead of graham cracker crumbs. Ground nuts may be added for special desserts.

Crumb crusts are used only for unbaked pies, such as cream pies and chiffon pies. Be sure the flavor of the crust is compatible with the filling. Lime chiffon filling in a chocolate crumb crust is not an appealing combination. Some cream fillings are so delicate they would be overwhelmed by a crust that is too flavorful.

Baking the crust makes a firmer, less crumbly crust and increases flavor.

SHORT-DOUGH CRUSTS

Short pastry is actually a kind of cookie dough. It is richer than regular pie pastry and contains butter, sugar, and eggs. Because ***short dough*** is difficult to handle, it is used primarily for small fruit tarts.

KEY POINTS TO REVIEW

- What are the ingredients and procedure for making a graham cracker crust?
- How is mixing a short dough crust different from the rubbed-dough method for mixing pie crust?

Graham Cracker Crust

YIELD: 2 LB (900G) **CRUSTS FOR: FIVE 8-IN. (20-CM) PIES**
FOUR 9-IN. (23-CM) PIES
THREE 10-IN. (25-CM) PIES

U.S.	METRIC	INGREDIENTS
1 lb	450 g	Graham cracker crumbs
8 oz	225 g	Sugar
8 oz	225 g	Butter, melted

Per 1 ounce (28.35 g): Calories, 140; Protein, 1 g: Fat, 7 g (45% cal); Cholesterol, 15 mg; Carbohydrates, 18 g; Fiber, 0 g; Sodium, 140 mg.

PROCEDURE

1. Mix crumbs and sugar in mixing bowl.
2. Add butter and mix until evenly blended and crumbs are all moistened by the melted butter.
3. Scale the mixture into pie pans: 8 oz (225 g) for 9-in. (23-cm) pans; 6 oz (175g) for 8-in. (20-cm) pans.
4. Spread mixture evenly on bottom and sides of pan. Press another pan on top to pack crumbs evenly.
5. Bake at 350°F (175°C) for 10 minutes.
6. Cool thoroughly before filling.

VARIATIONS

Substitute chocolate or vanilla wafer crumbs or gingersnap crumbs for the cracker crumbs.

Short Dough

INGREDIENTS	U.S			METRIC	PERCENTAGE
Butter *or* butter and shortening	1 lb			500 g	67 %
Sugar		6	oz	180 g	25 %
Salt		0.12	oz (¼ tsp)	4 g	0.5 %
Eggs		4.5	oz	140 g	19 %
Pastry flour	1 lb	8	oz	750 g	100 %
Yield	*3 lb*	*2*	*oz*	*1574 g*	*211 %*

Per 1 ounce (28.35 g): Calories, 130; Protein, 2 g; Fat, 8 g (53% cal); Cholesterol, 30 mg; Carbohydrates, 14 g; Fiber, 2 g; Sodium, 100 mg.

PROCEDURE

1. Using the paddle attachment, mix the butter, sugar, and salt at low speed until smooth and evenly blended.
2. Add the eggs and mix just until absorbed.
3. Sift the flour and add it to the mixture. Mix just until evenly blended.
4. Chill several hours before using.

Procedure for Making Small Fruit Tarts

1. Roll out chilled short dough on a floured surface until it is slightly less than ¼ inch (5 mm) thick.
2. With a round cutter about ½ inch (1 cm) larger than the top diameter of your individual tart shells, cut the dough into circles.
3. For each shell, fit a circle of dough into a tin and press it well against the bottom and sides. If you are using fluted tins, make sure the dough is thick enough on the sides so it won't break apart at the ridges.
4. Fit paper liners inside the shells and fill with dried beans to keep the dough from blistering or puffing while baking.
5. Bake at 400°F (200°C) about 15 minutes, or until the shells are fully baked. Remove the paper liners and the beans.
6. Cool the shells completely and remove them from the tins.
7. Fill the shells half full of vanilla pastry cream (see Chapter 14).
8. Arrange well-drained fresh, cooked, or canned fruits over the pastry cream.
9. Brush the top with apricot glaze, melted currant jelly, or other desired glaze (see Chapter 11).
10. Keep refrigerated until service.

Assembly and Baking

Types of Pies

Pies may be classified into two groups based on method of assembling and baking.

1. **Baked pies.**
   Raw pie shells are filled and then baked. ***Fruit pies*** contain fruit fillings and usually have a top crust. ***Soft pies*** are those with custard-type fillings or, in other words, liquid fillings that become firm when their egg content coagulates. They are usually baked as single-crust pies.

2. **Unbaked pies.**
   Baked pie shells are filled with a prepared filling, chilled, and served when the filling is firm enough to slice. ***Cream pies*** are made with pudding or boiled custard-type fillings. ***Chiffon pies*** are made with fillings that are lightened by the addition of beaten egg white.

   Baking a pie or tart shell without a filling is called ***baking blind***.

Procedure for Rolling Pie Dough and Lining Pans

1. **Scale the dough.**

   8 ounces (225 g) for 9-inch (23-cm) bottom crusts
   6 ounces (175 g) for 9-inch (23-cm) top crusts
   6 ounces (175 g) for 8-inch (20-cm) bottom crusts
   5 ounces (150 g) for 8-inch (20-cm) top crusts

   Experienced bakers are able to roll crusts using less dough because less must be trimmed when the dough is rolled to a perfect circle of the exact size needed.
2. **Dust the bench and rolling pin lightly with flour.**
   Too much dusting flour toughens the dough. Use no more than needed to prevent sticking.
3. **Roll out the dough.**
   Flatten the dough lightly and roll it out to a uniform ⅛-inch (3-mm) thickness. Use even strokes and roll from the center outward in all directions. Lift the dough frequently to make sure it is not sticking. The finished dough should form a perfect circle.
4. **Place the dough in a pan.**
   To lift the dough without breaking it, roll it lightly around the rolling pin. Allow the dough to drop into the pan and press it into the corners without stretching it. Stretched dough shrinks during baking. There should be no air bubbles between the dough and the pan.
5. **For single-crust pies, flute the edges, if desired, and trim off excess dough.**
   Some bakers feel that fluted edges add to the appearance of the product. Others feel that fluting takes too much time and produces only a rim of heavy dough that customers leave on their plates.
6. **For two-crust pies:**
   Fill with cold filling, place the second crust on top, and seal the top and bottom crusts together at edges. Flute, if desired, and trim excess dough. Apply desired wash or glaze to top.
7. **Bake as directed in the recipe.**

The Soggy Bottom

A common pie fault is an underbaked bottom crust or a crust that soaks up moisture from the filling. Soggy bottoms can be avoided in several ways.

1. Use mealy dough for bottom crusts. Mealy dough absorbs less liquid than flaky dough.
2. Use high bottom heat, at least at the beginning of baking, to set the crust quickly. Bake the pies at the bottom of the oven.
3. Do not add hot fillings to unbaked crusts.
4. Use dark metal pie tins, which absorb heat. (If you use disposable aluminum pans, choose pans with the bottoms colored black.)

Procedure for Preparing Baked Pies

Note: For pies without a top crust, omit steps 3 through 7.

1. Line the pie pan with pie dough as in the basic procedure (Figure 13.1).
2. Fill with *cooled* filling. See Table 13.1 for scaling instructions. Do not drop filling on the rim of the pie shell; this makes it hard to seal the rim to the top crust. To avoid spilling custard filling, place the empty shell on the rack in the oven and then pour in the filling.
3. Roll out the dough for the top crust.
4. Perforate the top crust to allow steam to escape during baking.
5. Moisten the rim of the bottom crust to help seal it to the top crust.
6. Fit the top crust in place. Seal the edges together firmly and trim excess dough. An easy way to do this is to press the rim with the tines of a fork. Alternatively, the rim may be fluted. An efficient way to trim excess dough is to rotate the pie tin while pressing on the edges with the palms of the hands.
7. Brush the top with the desired wash: milk, cream, eggs and milk, or water. Sprinkle with granulated sugar if desired.
8. Place the pie on the lower level of an oven preheated to 425° to 450°F (220° to 230°C). The high initial heat helps set the bottom crust to avoid soaking. Fruit pies are usually baked at this high heat until done. For custard pies, reduce the heat to 325° to 350°F (165° to 175°C) after 10 minutes to avoid overcooking and curdling the custard. Custard pies include those containing large quantities of egg, such as pumpkin pie and pecan pie.

Table 13.1 Scaling Guidelines for Baked Pies

Pie Size		Weight of Filling	
U.S.	Metric	U.S.	Metric
8 in.	20 cm	26–30 oz	750–850 g
9 in.	23 cm	32–40 oz	900–1150 g
10 in.	25 cm	40–50 oz	1150–1400 g

Note: Weights are guidelines only. Exact weights may vary, depending on the filling and the depth of the pans.

Figure 13.1 Preparing baked pies.

(a) Line the pie pans with the pie dough. **(b) Fill with cooled fillings.** **(c) Fit the top crusts in place.** **(d) Seal the top crust to the rim and trim the dough from the edges.**

Procedure for Preparing Unbaked Pies

1. Line a pie pan with pie dough as in the basic procedure.
2. Dock the crust well with a fork to prevent blistering.
3. Place another pan inside the first one so the dough is between two pans. This is called *double-panning.*
4. Place the pans upside down in an oven preheated at 450°F (230°C). Baking upside down helps keep the dough from shrinking down into the pan.
   Some bakers like to chill the crusts before baking to relax the gluten and help reduce shrinkage.
5. Bake at 450°F (230°C) for 10 to 15 minutes. The top pan may be removed during the last part of baking so the crust can brown.
6. Cool the baked crust completely.
7. Fill with cream or chiffon filling. Fill as close as possible to service time to prevent soaking the crust.
8. Chill the pie until it is set enough to slice.

KEY POINTS TO REVIEW

- What are the steps in the procedure for rolling pie dough and lining pans?
- What are the steps in the procedure for preparing baked pies?
- What are the steps in the procedure for preparing unbaked pies?

Fillings

Starches for Fillings

Many kinds of pie filling, especially fruit fillings and cream fillings, depend on starch for their thick texture.

TYPES

Cornstarch is used for cream pies because it sets up into a firm gel that holds its shape when sliced. Cornstarch may also be used for fruit pies.

Waxy maize and other *modified starches* are best for fruit pies because they are clear when set and make a soft paste rather than a firm gel. Waxy maize should be used for pies that are to be frozen because it is not broken down by freezing.

Flour, tapioca, and other starches are used less frequently. Flour has less thickening power than other starches and makes the product cloudy.

Instant starch or *pregelatinized starch* needs no cooking because it has already been cooked. When used with certain fruit fillings, it eliminates the need to cook the filling before making up the pie. It has no advantage, however, if the filling contains such ingredients as raw fruit or eggs and so must be cooked.

Starches differ in thickening power, so follow the formulas exactly.

COOKING STARCHES

To avoid lumping, starches must be mixed with a cold liquid or sugar before being added to a hot liquid.

Sugar and *strong acids* reduce the thickening power of starch. When possible, all or part of the sugar and strong acids like lemon juice should be added *after the starch has thickened.*

Fruit Fillings

Fruit pie fillings consist of fruits and fruit juices, sugar, spices, and a starch thickener.

FRUITS FOR PIE FILLINGS

Fresh fruits make excellent pies if they are at their seasonal peak. Fresh apples are used extensively for high-quality pies. But the quality of fresh fruits can vary considerably, and fresh fruit pies require a lot of labor.

Frozen fruits are widely used for pies because they are consistent in quality and readily available.

Canned fruits can also be of high quality. Solid pack (with little juice) gives a higher yield of fruit per can than syrup or water pack.

Dried fruits must be rehydrated by soaking and, usually, simmering before they are made into pie fillings.

Fruits must have sufficient acid (tartness) to make flavorful fillings. If they lack natural acid, you may need to add lemon, orange, or pineapple juice to supply the acid.

COOKED JUICE METHOD

The advantage of the ***cooked juice method*** is that only the juice is cooked. The fruit retains better shape and flavor because it is subjected to less heat and handling. This method is used when the fruit requires little or no cooking before filling the pie. Examples: cherry, peach, most frozen or canned fruits. Fresh berries can also be prepared by this method. Some of the berries are cooked or puréed to provide juice. The remaining berries are mixed with the finished gel.

COOKED FRUIT METHOD

The ***cooked fruit method*** is used when the fruit requires cooking or there is not enough liquid for the cooked juice method. Examples: fresh apple, raisin, rhubarb.

Procedure: Cooked Juice Method

1. Drain the juice from the fruit.
2. Measure the juice and, if necessary, add water or other fruit juice to bring it to the desired volume.
3. Bring the juice to a boil.
4. Dissolve the starch in cold water and stir it into the boiling juice. Return the juice to the boil and cook until it is clear and thickened.
5. Add sugar, salt, and flavorings, and stir until dissolved.
6. Pour the thickened juice over the drained fruit and mix gently. Be careful not to break or mash the fruit.
7. Cool.

Procedure: Cooked Fruit Method

1. Bring the fruit and its juice or water to a boil. Some sugar may be added to the fruit to draw out juices.
2. Dissolve the starch in cold water and stir it into the fruit. Return the fruit mixture to a boil and cook until it is clear and thickened. Stir while cooking.
3. Add sugar, salt, flavorings, and other ingredients and stir until dissolved.
4. Cool as quickly as possible.

Variation

Some fruits, such as fresh apples, may be cooked in butter rather than boiled in water for better flavor.

OLD-FASHIONED METHOD

This method is best suited to pies made with fresh apples or peaches. It is not as widely used in food service as the other methods because it is more difficult to control the thickening of the juices.

Procedure: Old-Fashioned Method

1. Mix the starch and spices with the sugar until uniformly blended.
2. Mix the fruit with the sugar mixture.
3. Fill the unbaked pie shell with the fruit.
4. Place lumps of butter on top of the filling.
5. Cover with a top crust or with Streusel and bake.

KEY POINTS TO REVIEW

- What are the steps in the cooked juice method for making fruit pie fillings?
- What are the steps in the cooked fruit method for making fruit pie fillings?
- What are the steps in the old-fashioned method for making fruit pie fillings?

Cooked Juice Method

Apple Pie Filling (Canned Fruit)

YIELD: ABOUT 9½ LB (4.5 KG) FIVE 8-IN. (20-CM) PIES
FOUR 9-IN. (23-CM) PIES
THREE 10-IN. (25-CM) PIES

U.S.	METRIC	INGREDIENTS	PROCEDURE
6 lb 8 oz	3 kg	Canned apples (1 No. 10 can)	1. Drain the apples, reserving the juice.
as needed	as needed	Water	2. Add enough water to the juice to measure 1½ pt (750 mL).
8 fl oz	250 mL	Water, cold	3. Mix the cold water and starch.
3 oz	90g	Cornstarch or modified starch	4. Bring the juice mixture to a boil.
			5. Stir in the starch mixture and return to a boil.
1 lb 4 oz	575 g	Sugar	6. Add the sugar, salt, cinnamon, nutmeg, and butter. Simmer until the sugar is dissolved.
¼ oz (1¼ tsp)	7 g (6 mL)	Salt	7. Pour the syrup over the apples and mix gently. Cool completely.
¼ oz (3½ tsp)	7 g (17 mL)	Cinnamon	8. Fill pie shells. Bake at 425°F (220°C) for 30–40 minutes.
1 tsp	2 g (5 mL)	Nutmeg	
3 oz	90 g	Butter	

Per 1 ounce (28.35 g): Calories, 30; Protein, 0 g; Fat, 0.5 g (14% cal.); Cholesterol, 0 mg; Carbohydrates, 7 g; Fiber, 0 g; Sodium, 25 mg.

VARIATIONS

Dutch Apple Pie Filling

Simmer 8 oz (250 g) raisins in water. Drain and add to Apple Pie Filling.

Cherry Pie Filling

Use 1 No. 10 can sour cherries instead of apples. Increase starch to 4 oz (125 g). Add 1½ fl oz (45 mL) lemon juice in step 6. Increase the sugar to 1 lb 12 oz (800 g). Omit cinnamon and nutmeg. Add almond extract to taste (optional). If desired, color with 2–3 drops red coloring.

Peach Pie Filling

Use 1 No. 10 can sliced peaches, preferably solid or heavy pack, instead of apples. Omit cinnamon and nutmeg.

Pineapple Pie Filling

Use 1 No. 10 can crushed pineapple instead of apples. Increase liquid in step 1 to 1 qt (1 L). Increase starch to 4 oz (125 g). Use 1 lb 8 oz (700 g) sugar and 8 oz (250 g) corn syrup. Omit cinnamon and nutmeg.

Apple Pie with Streusel Topping

Blueberry Pie Filling (Frozen Fruit)

YIELD: ABOUT 7 LB 8 OZ (3375 G) FOUR 8-IN. (20-CM) PIES
THREE 9-IN. (23-CM) PIES

U.S.	METRIC	INGREDIENTS	PROCEDURE
5 lb	2250 g	Frozen unsweetened blueberries	1. Thaw blueberries in original container without opening.
as needed	as needed	Water	2. Drain the berries, reserving juice. Add enough water to the juice to measure 12 oz (250 mL). Stir in the first quantity of sugar.
6 oz	175 g	Sugar	
6 fl oz	190 mL	Water, cold	3. Mix the cold water and cornstarch.
3 oz	90 g	Cornstarch or modified starch	4. Bring the juice mixture to a boil. Stir in the starch. Return to a boil to thicken.
14 oz	412 g	Sugar	5. Stir in the second quantity of sugar and the salt, cinnamon, and lemon juice. Stir over heat until the sugar is dissolved.
¼ oz (1¼ tsp)	8 g (7 mL)	Salt	6. Pour the syrup over the drained blueberries. Mix gently. Cool completely.
⅛ oz (2 tsp)	4 g (10 mL)	Cinnamon	7. Fill pie shells. Bake at 425°F (220°C) about 30 minutes.
1.5 fl oz	45 mL	Lemon juice	

Per 1 ounce (28.35 g): Calories, 30; Protein, 0 g; Fat, 0 g (0% cal.); Cholesterol, 0 mg; Carbohydrates, 8 g; Fiber, 1 g; Sodium, 20 g.

VARIATIONS

Apple Pie Filling

Use 5 lb (2.25 kg) frozen apples instead of blueberries. Reduce second quantity of sugar to 8 oz (225 g). Reduce starch to 1½ oz (45 g). Add ½ tsp (2 mL) nutmeg and 3 oz (87 g) butter in step 5.

Cherry Pie Filling

Use 5 lb (2.25 kg) frozen cherries instead of blueberries. Increase liquid in step 2 to 1 pt (500 mL). Decrease starch to 2½ oz (75 g). Reduce second quantity of sugar to 10 oz (285 g). Omit cinnamon and reduce lemon juice to ¾ fl oz (22 mL).

Fresh Strawberry Pie Filling

YIELD: ABOUT 6 LB (2.75 KG) THREE 8-IN. (20-CM) PIES
TWO 10-IN. (25-CM) PIES

U.S.	METRIC	INGREDIENTS	PROCEDURE
4 lb 8 oz	2050 g	Fresh whole strawberries	1. Hull, wash, and drain the berries. Set aside 3 lb 8 oz (1.6 kg) berries. These may be left whole if small or cut in halves or quarters if large.
8 fl oz	250 mL	Water, cold	2. Mash or purée the remaining 1 lb (450 g) berries. Mix with the water. (If a clear filling is desired, this mixture may be strained.)
14 oz	400 g	Sugar	3. Mix the sugar, starch, and salt. Stir into the cold juice and water mixture until no lumps remain.
2 oz	60 g	Cornstarch or modified starch	4. Bring to a boil, stirring constantly. Cook until thickened.
½ tsp	2 mL	Salt	5. Remove from heat and stir in the lemon juice.
1 fl oz	30 mL	Lemon juice	6. Cool to room temperature, but do not chill.
			7. Stir to eliminate lumps. Fold in the reserved berries.
			8. Fill baked pie shells and chill (do not bake).

Per 1 ounce (28.35 g): Calories, 25; Protein, 0 g; Fat, 0 g (0% cal.); Cholesterol, 0 mg; Carbohydrates, 6 g; Fiber, 0 g; Sodium, 10 mg.

Old-Fashioned Method

Old-Fashioned Apple Pie Filling

YIELD: ABOUT 11 LB (5 KG)
SIX 8-IN. (20-CM) PIES
FIVE 9-IN. (23-CM) PIES
FOUR 10-IN. (25-CM) PIES

U.S.	METRIC	INGREDIENTS	PROCEDURE
9 lb EP	4.1 kg EP	Fresh peeled, sliced apples	1. Select firm, tart apples.
2 fl oz	60 mL	Lemon juice	2. Combine apple slices and lemon juice in a large mixing bowl and toss to coat apples with the juice.
2 lb	900 g	Sugar	3. Mix the sugar, starch, salt, and spices.
3 oz	90 g	Cornstarch	4. Add to the apples and toss gently until well mixed.
¼ oz (1¼ tsp)	7 g (6 mL)	Salt	
¼ oz (3½ tsp)	7 g (17 mL)	Cinnamon	
1 tsp	5 mL	Nutmeg	
3 oz	90 g	Butter	5. Fill pie shells. Dot the filling with butter before setting the top crusts in place. Bake at 400°F (200°C) about 45 minutes.

Per 1 ounce (28.35 g): Calories, 40; Protein, 0 g; Fat, 0.5 g (11% cal.); Cholesterol, 0 mg; Carbohydrates, 9 g; Fiber, 0 g; Sodium, 20 mg.

APPLES FOR PIES

What varieties of apples are best for making pies? Two criteria are important: taste and texture. First, the apples should have a good flavor and a good level of acidity. Apples that are very mild make pies with little flavor. The sugar content, or sweetness, of the apple, is less important, as the sugar in the recipe can be adjusted.

Second, the apples should hold their shape when cooked. Apples that turn to mush, such as McIntosh, are better for applesauce than for pies.

Popular apple varieties that have good taste and texture for use in pie fillings include Granny Smith, Jonathan, Jonagold, Newton Pippin, Rome, Macoun, Pink Lady, Stayman-Winesap, and Golden Delicious.

Custard or Soft Fillings

Custard, pumpkin, pecan, and similar pies are made with an uncooked liquid filling containing eggs. The eggs coagulate when the pie is baked, setting the filling.

The greatest difficulty in cooking soft pies is cooking the crust completely yet not overcooking the filling. Start the pie at the bottom of a hot oven (425° to 450°F/220° to 230°C) for first 10 minutes to set the crust. Then reduce the heat to 325° to 350°F (165° to 175°C) to cook the filling slowly.

To test for doneness:

1. Shake the pie very gently. If it is no longer liquid, it is done. The center will still be slightly soft but will continue cooking in its own heat after the pie is removed from the oven.
2. Insert a thin knife 1 inch (2.5 cm) from the center. It will come out clean if the pie is done.

Custard Pie Filling

YIELD: 8 LB (3.6 KG) FIVE 8-IN. (20-CM) PIES FOUR 9-IN. (23-CM) PIES THREE 10-IN. (25-CM) PIES

U.S.	METRIC	INGREDIENTS	PROCEDURE
2 lb	900 g	Eggs	1. Beat the eggs lightly. Add sugar, salt, and vanilla. Blend until smooth. Do not whip air into the mixture.
1 lb	450 g	Sugar	
1 tsp	5 mL	Salt	
1 fl oz	30 mL	Vanilla	
2½ qt	2.5 L	Milk (see Note)	2. Stir in the milk. Skim off any foam.
1–1½ tsp	5–7 mL	Nutmeg	3. Pour into the unbaked pie shells.
			4. Sprinkle tops with nutmeg.
			5. Bake at 450°F (230°C) for 15 minutes. Reduce heat to 325°F (165°C) and bake until set, about 20–30 minutes more.

Per 1 ounce (28.35 g): Calories, 35; Protein, 2 g; Fat, 1.5 g (33% cal.); Cholesterol, 35 mg; Carbohydrates, 5 g; Fiber, 0 g; Sodium, 35 mg.

Note: For a richer custard, use part milk and part cream.

VARIATION

Coconut Custard Pie Filling

Use 10 oz (275 g) unsweetened, flaked coconut. Sprinkle coconut into pie shells before adding custard mixture. Coconut may be toasted lightly in oven before adding to pies, if desired. Omit nutmeg.

Pecan Pie Filling

YIELD: 2 LB 8 OZ (1640 G) FILLING PLUS 10 OZ (285 G) PECANS TWO 9-IN. (23-CM) PIES

U.S.	METRIC	INGREDIENTS	PROCEDURE
14 oz	400 g	Sugar (see Note)	1. Using the paddle attachment at low speed, blend the sugar, butter, and salt until evenly blended.
4 oz	120 g	Butter	
½ tsp	2 mL	Salt	
14 oz	400 g	Eggs	2. With the machine running, add the eggs, a little at a time, until they are all absorbed.
1 lb 8 oz (about 17 fl oz)	700 g	Dark corn syrup	3. Add the syrup and vanilla. Mix until well blended.
½ fl oz	15 mL	Vanilla	
10 oz	285 g	Pecans	4. To assemble pies, distribute pecans evenly in pie shells. Fill with syrup mixture.
			5. Bake at 450°F (230°C) for 10 minutes. Reduce heat to 325°F (165°C). Bake about 40 minutes more, or until set.

Per 1 ounce (28.35 g): Calories, 120; Protein, 1 g; Fat, 5 g (38% cal.); Cholesterol, 35 mg; Carbohydrates, 17 g; Fiber, 0 g; Sodium, 70 mg.

Note: Brown sugar may be used if darker color and stronger flavor are desired.

Pumpkin Pie Filling

YIELD: ABOUT 4¼ LB (2 KG) TWO 9-IN. (23-CM) PIES

U.S.	METRIC	INGREDIENTS	PROCEDURE
1 lb 10½ oz	750 g	Pumpkin purée, 1 No. 2½ can	1. Place pumpkin purée in the bowl of a mixer fitted with a whip attachment.
1 oz	30 g	Pastry flour	2. Sift together the flour, spices, and salt.
2 tsp	10 mL	Cinnamon	3. Add the flour mixture and sugar to the pumpkin. Mix at 2nd speed until smooth and well blended.
¼ tsp	1 mL	Nutmeg	
¼ tsp	1 mL	Ground ginger	
⅛ tsp	0.5 mL	Ground cloves	
⅝ tsp	3 mL	Salt	
10 oz	290 g	Brown sugar	
10 oz	300 g	Eggs	4. Add the eggs and mix in. Scrape down the sides of the bowl.
2 oz	60 g	Corn syrup or half corn syrup and half molasses	5. Turn the machine to low speed. Gradually pour in the syrup-molasses mixture, then the milk. Mix until evenly blended.
1 pt 4 oz	600 mL	Milk	6. Fill the pie shells. Bake at 450°F (230°C) for 15 minutes. Lower heat to 350°F (175°C) and bake until set, about 30–40 minutes more.

Per 1 ounce (28.35 g): Calories, 30; Protein, 1 g; Fat, 0.5 g (14% cal.); Cholesterol, 10 mg; Carbohydrates, 6 g; Fiber, 0 g; Sodium, 45 mg.

VARIATIONS

Sweet Potato Pie Filling

Substitute canned sweet potatoes, drained and puréed, for the pumpkin.

Squash Pie Filling

Substitute puréed squash for the pumpkin.

Cream Pie Fillings

Cream pie fillings are the same as puddings, which, in turn, are the same as basic pastry creams with added flavorings such as vanilla, chocolate, or coconut. Lemon filling is made by the same method, using water and lemon juice instead of milk.

The one difference between puddings and pie fillings you should note is that *cream pie fillings are made with cornstarch* so slices hold their shape when cut. Puddings may be made with flour, cornstarch, or other starches.

Techniques and recipes for these fillings are included in Chapter 14, along with other basic creams and puddings.

Chiffon Pies

Chiffon fillings are made by adding gelatin to a cream filling or to a thickened fruit and juice mixture and then folding in egg whites and/or whipped cream. The mixture is then poured into baked pie shells and allowed to set.

These preparations are the same as chiffon desserts, bavarians, and some mousses and cold soufflés. To avoid unnecessary repetition, techniques and recipes for these products are included in Chapter 14 with other puddings and creams.

Pastries, Meringues, and Fruit Desserts

In addition to pie dough, two other pastries have great importance in bakeshops and kitchens: *puff pastry*, used for such products as napoleons and turnovers, and *éclair* or *choux paste*, used for éclairs and cream puffs. These products are also used in the hot food kitchen and the pantry in the preparation of a number of hors d'oeuvres, entrées, and side dishes.

Meringues and fruit desserts are also covered in this section. Meringues are not only important as pie toppings but also can be formed, baked until crisp, and used in many of the same ways as pastry shells for desserts.

Puff Pastry

Puff pastry is one of the most remarkable products of the bakeshop. Although it includes no added leavening agent, it can rise to 8 times its original thickness when baked.

Puff pastry is a rolled-in dough, like Danish and croissant dough. This means it is made up of many layers of fat sandwiched between layers of dough. Unlike Danish dough, however, puff pastry contains no yeast. Steam, created when the moisture in the dough layers is heated, is responsible for the spectacular rising power of puff pastry.

Puff pastry or puff dough is one of the most difficult of all bakery products to prepare. Because it consists of over 1,000 layers, many more than Danish dough, the rolling-in procedure requires a great deal of time and care.

As for so many other products, there are nearly as many versions of puff pastry as there are bakers. Both formulas and rolling-in techniques vary. The formula provided here contains no eggs, for example, although some bakers add them.

The folding-in technique used here differs somewhat from that used by European pastry chefs, although it is widely used by American bakers. (See Figure 13.2.)

Butter is the preferred fat for rolling in because of its flavor and melt-in-the-mouth quality. Special puff pastry shortening is also available. This shortening is much easier to work with than butter because it is not as hard when refrigerated and doesn't soften and melt as easily as butter at warm temperatures. It is also less expensive than butter. However, puff pastry shortening can be unpleasant to eat because it tends to congeal and coat the inside of the mouth.

Skill at producing puff pastry requires careful attention to your instructor and diligent practice. Take special note of alternative methods your instructor may present.

Puff Pastry

INGREDIENTS	U.S.	METRIC	PERCENTAGE
Bread flour	1 lb 8 oz	750 g	75 %
Cake flour	8 oz	250 g	25 %
Butter, soft	4 oz	125 g	12.5 %
Salt	0.5 oz	15 g	1.5 %
Water, cold	1 lb 2 oz	562 g	56 %
Butter	2 lb	1000 g	100 %
Bread flour (see Note)	4 oz	125 g	12.5 %
Yield:	*5 lb 10 oz*	*2827 g*	*282 %*

Per 1 ounce (28.35 g): Calories, 120; Protein, 1 g; Fat 9 g (69% cal.); Cholesterol, 25 mg; Carbohydrates, 8 g; Fiber, 0 g; Sodium, 150 mg.

Note: The purpose of the 4 oz (125 g) bread flour is to absorb some of the moisture of the butter. Omit if puff paste shortening is used instead of butter.

PROCEDURE

Mixing:

1. Place the first quantities of flour and butter in a mixing bowl. With a paddle attachment, mix at low speed until well blended.
2. Dissolve the salt in the cold water.
3. Add the salted water to the flour and mix at low speed until a soft dough forms. Do not overmix.
4. Remove the dough from the mixer and let rest in the refrigerator 20 minutes.
5. Cream the last quantities of butter and flour at low speed in the mixer until the mixture is about the same consistency as the dough, neither too hard nor too soft.
6. Roll the butter into the dough following the procedure shown in **Figure 13.2**. Give the dough 4 four-folds or 5 three-folds.

Figure 13.2 Rolling-in procedure for puff pastry.

(a) Dust the bench lightly with flour. Roll dough to a rectangle about 3 times as long as it is wide and about ½ in. (1–1.5 cm) thick. Make the corners as square as possible. Form the butter into a rectangle two-thirds the size of the dough, leaving room around the edges, and place on the dough as shown.

(b) Fold the third without fat over the center third.

(c) Fold the remaining third on top. Fold all ends and corners evenly and squarely. This procedure, enclosing the butter in the dough, does not count as one of the folds. The folding procedure starts with the next step.

(d) Turn the dough 90 degrees on the bench so the length becomes the width. This step must be taken before each rolling-out so the gluten is stretched in all directions, not just lengthwise. Failure to do this results in products that deform or shrink unevenly when they bake. Before rolling, beat the dough lightly as shown so the butter is evenly distributed. Roll the dough into a rectangle. Make sure the corners are square. Roll smoothly and evenly. Do not press down when rolling, or the layers may stick together and the product not rise properly.

(e) Brush excess flour from the top of the dough.

(f) Fold the top edge of the dough to the center. Make sure the corners are square and even. Again brush off excess flour.

(g) Fold the bottom edge to the center.

(h) Fold the dough in half like closing a book. You have now given the dough *1* four-fold. Refrigerate the dough 15 to 20 minutes to relax the gluten. Do not refrigerate it too long, or the butter will become too hard. (If it does, let it soften a few minutes at room temperature before proceeding.)

(i) Give the dough another *3* four-folds, as in steps f to h. After another rest, the dough is ready to be rolled out and made up into the desired products. (Alternative method: Instead of giving the dough *4* four-folds, you may give it *5 three-folds*.)

Blitz Puff Pastry

Blitz puff pastry is much easier and quicker to make than classic puff dough. (*Blitz* is German for "lightning.") It does not rise nearly as high as true puff pastry, so it is not suitable for patty shells and other products where a high, light pastry is desirable. However, it bakes up crisp and flaky and is perfectly suitable for napoleons and similar desserts that are layered with cream fillings.

Blitz puff paste, as you will see, is actually a flaky pie dough that is rolled and folded like regular puff dough.

Blitz Puff Pastry

INGREDIENTS	U.S.	METRIC	PERCENTAGE
Bread flour	1 lb	500 g	50 %
Pastry flour	1 lb	500 g	50 %
Butter, slightly softened	2 lb	1000 g	100 %
Salt	0.5 oz	15 g	1.5 %
Water, cold	1 lb	500 g	50 %
Yield:	*5 lb*	*2515 g*	*250 %*

Per 1 ounce (28.35 g): Calories, 120; Protein, 1 g; Fat 9 g (69% cal.); Cholesterol, 25 mg; Carbohydrates, 8 g; Fiber, 1 g; Sodium, 160 mg.

PROCEDURE

Mixing:

1. Sift the two flours together into a mixing bowl.
2. Cut the butter into the flour as for pie dough, but leave the fat in very large lumps, 1 in. (2.5 cm) across.
3. Dissolve the salt in the water.
4. Add the water to the flour-butter mixture. Mix until the water is absorbed.
5. Let the dough rest for 15 minutes. Refrigerate if the bakeshop is warm.
6. Dust the bench with flour and roll out the dough into a rectangle. Give the dough 3 four-folds.

VARIATION

Reduce the butter to 75% (1 lb 8 oz/750 g).

General Guidelines for Makeup of Puff Dough Products

1. The dough should be cool and firm when it is rolled and cut. If it is too soft, the layers may stick together at the cuts, preventing proper rising.
2. Cut with straight, firm, even cuts. Use a sharp cutting tool.
3. Avoid touching the cut edges with your fingers; this can make the layers stick together.
4. For best rising, place units upside down on baking sheets. Even sharp cutting tools may press the top layers of dough together. Baking upside down puts the stuck-together layers at the bottom.
5. Avoid letting egg wash run down the edges. Egg wash can cause the layers to stick together at the edges.
6. Rest made-up products for 30 minutes in a cool place or in the refrigerator before baking. This relaxes the gluten and reduces shrinkage.
7. Press trimmings together, keeping the layers in the same direction. After being rolled out and given another three-fold, they may be used again, although they will not rise as high.
8. Baking temperatures of 400° to 425°F (200° to 220°C) are best for most puff dough products. Cooler temperatures do not create enough steam in the products to leaven them well. Higher temperatures set the crust too quickly.

Procedure for Making Turnovers

See Figure 13.3.

1. Roll out puff pastry dough to ⅛ inch (3 mm) thick.
2. Cut the dough into 4-inch (10-cm) squares. Wash the edges of each with water.
3. Portion the desired filling into the center of each square.
4. Fold diagonally and press the edges together.
5. Puncture the tops with a knife in two or three places to allow steam to escape. Let rest 30 minutes.
6. Brush the tops with egg wash, if desired, or brush with milk or water and sprinkle with sugar.
7. Bake at 400°F (200°C) until crisp and brown.

Figure 13.3 Makeup of turnovers.

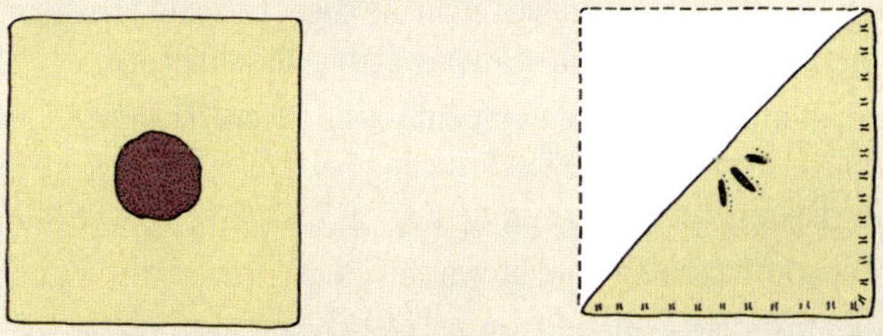

(a) Cut the dough into 4-in. (10-cm) squares. Wash the edges with water and place filling in the center of each square.

(b) Fold over diagonally and press the edges together. Puncture two or three steam holes in top.

Procedure for Making Pinwheels

See Figure 13.4.

1. Roll out puff dough to ⅛ inch (3 mm) thick.
2. Cut the dough into 5-inch (12-cm) squares.
3. Wash the centers with water.
4. Cut diagonally from the corners to about 1 inch (2.5 cm) from the centers.
5. Fold every other corner into the centers and press in place.
6. Bake at 400°F (200°C).
7. Let cool. Spoon desired fruit filling into the centers. Dust lightly with confectioners' sugar. (Pinwheels may also be filled before baking if the filling is thick and not likely to burn.)

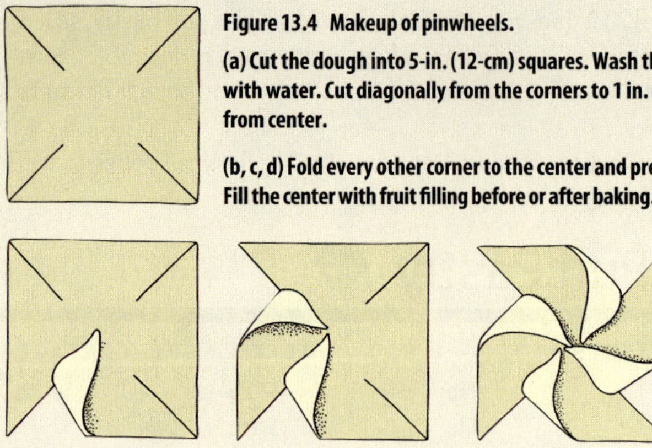

Figure 13.4 Makeup of pinwheels.

(a) Cut the dough into 5-in. (12-cm) squares. Wash the centers with water. Cut diagonally from the corners to 1 in. (2.5 cm) from center.

(b, c, d) Fold every other corner to the center and press down. Fill the center with fruit filling before or after baking.

Procedure for Making Patty Shells

See Figure 13.5.

1. Roll out puff dough to ⅛ inch (3 mm) thick.
2. Roll a second piece of dough to ¼ inch (6 mm) thick.
3. Cut out the same number of circles from each piece of dough with a round 3-inch (7.5-cm) cutter.
4. Using a 2-inch (5-cm) cutter, cut out the centers of the thick circles.
5. Wash the thin circles with water or egg wash and place a ring on top of each. Wash the top carefully with egg wash (do not drip wash down the edges). Let rest 30 minutes.
6. Place a sheet of greased parchment over the tops of the shells to prevent their toppling over while baking.
7. Bake at 400°F (200°C) until brown and crisp.

Figure 13.5 Makeup of patty shells.

(a) Roll 1 sheet of puff dough ⅛ in. (3 mm) thick and another sheet ¼ in. (6 mm) thick. Cut an equal number of 3-in. (7.5-cm) circles from each. Cut out the centers of the thick circles with a 2-in. (5-cm) cutter.

(b) Wash the thin circles with water or egg wash and place the thick circles on top.

Procedure for Making Cream Horns

See Figure 13.6.

1. Roll out puff dough into a sheet ⅛ inch (3 mm) thick and about 15 inches (38 cm) wide.
2. Cut out strips 1¼ inches (3 cm) wide by 15 inches (38 cm) long.
3. Wash the strips with water.
4. With the washed side out, roll the strips diagonally onto cream horn tubes, making a spiral. Overlap the edges by about ⅜ inch (1 cm). If you are using conical tubes, start at the small end.
5. Roll in granulated sugar and lay on baking sheets. The end of the dough strip should be on the bottom so it does not pop up during baking. Let rest 30 minutes.
6. Bake at 400°F (200°C) until brown and crisp.
7. Slip out the tubes while still warm.
8. Just before service, fill the horns from both ends with whipped cream or pastry cream, using a pastry bag with a star tip. Dust with confectioners' sugar.

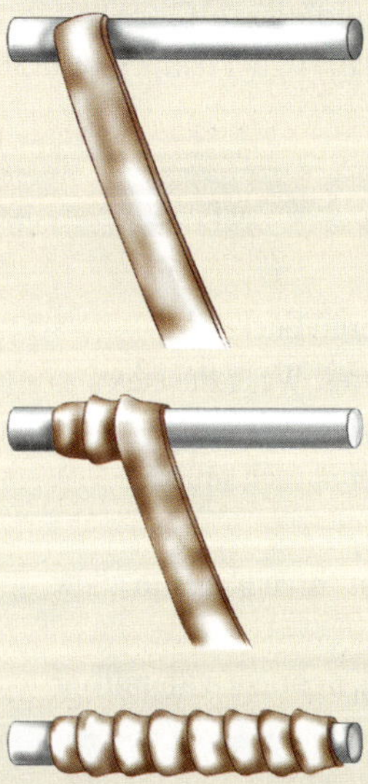

Figure 13.6 Makeup of cream horns.

(a) Roll puff dough to ⅛ in. (3 mm) thick and cut it into strips 1¼ in. (3 cm) wide and 15 in. (38 cm) long. Wash the strips with water and press one end (washed side out) onto one end of a cream horn tube as shown.

(b) Roll the dough strip in a spiral by turning the tube. Overlap the edges by about ⅜ in. (1 cm). Do not stretch the dough.

(c) Roll completely and press the end in place to seal.

Procedure for Making Napoleons

1. Roll puff dough into a very thin sheet about the size of a sheet pan. Blitz puff paste or rerolled trimmings may be used.
2. Place on sheet pan and let rest 30 minutes.
3. Dock with a fork to prevent blistering.
4. Bake at 400°F (200°C) until brown and crisp.
5. Trim the edges of the pastry sheet and cut with a serrated knife into equal strips 4 inches (10 cm) wide. Set the best one aside for the top layer. (If one of the strips breaks, don't be upset. It can be used as the middle layer.)
6. Spread one rectangle with Vanilla Pastry Cream (p. 319) or with a mixture of pastry cream and whipped cream.
7. Top with a second sheet of pastry.
8. Spread with another layer of pastry cream.
9. Place a third pastry rectangle on top, flattest side up.
10. Ice top with fondant (p. 270).
11. To decorate, pipe 4 strips of chocolate fondant lengthwise on the white fondant. Draw a spatula or the back of a knife across the top in opposite directions, 1 inch (2.5 cm) apart, as shown in Figure 13.7.
12. Cut into strips 2 inches (5 cm) wide.

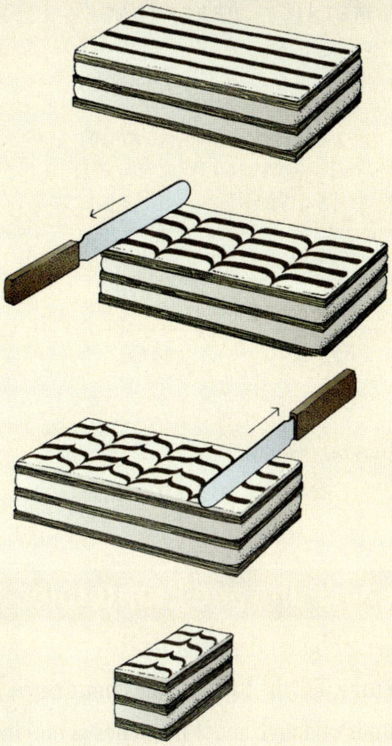

Figure 13.7 Decorating napoleons.

(a) Spread the top of the assembled napoleon with white fondant. With a paper cone, pipe 4 strips of chocolate fondant.

(b) Draw a spatula or the back of a knife across the icing at 2-in. (5-cm) intervals.

(c) Draw the spatula in the opposite direction in the center of these 2-in. (5-cm) intervals as shown.

(d) Cut the napoleon into strips 2 in. (5 cm) wide.

Éclair Paste

Éclairs and cream puffs are made from a dough called ***éclair paste*** or *choux paste*. The French name ***pâte à choux*** (pot a shoo) means "cabbage paste," referring to the fact that cream puffs look like little cabbages.

Unlike puff pastry, éclair paste is extremely easy to make. The dough itself can be prepared in just a few minutes. This is fortunate because for best baking results, the dough should not be prepared ahead of time.

In principle, éclair paste is similar to popover batter, even though one is a thick dough and the other a thin batter. Both products are leavened by steam, which expands the product rapidly and forms large holes in the center. The heat of the oven then coagulates the gluten and egg proteins to set the structure and make a firm product. A strong flour is necessary for sufficient structure.

Éclair paste must be firm enough to hold its shape when piped from a pastry bag. Occasionally, you may find a formula that produces too slack a dough. Correct such a formula by reducing the water or milk slightly.

Proper baking temperatures are important. Start at a high temperature (425° to 475°F/215° to 245°C) for the first 10 minutes to develop steam. Then reduce the heat to 375° to 425°F (190° to 215°C) to finish baking and set the structure. The products must be firm and dry before being removed from the oven. If they are removed too soon or cooled too quickly, they may collapse. Some bakers like to leave them in a turned-off oven with the door ajar. However, if the oven must be heated again for other products, this may not be the best idea, especially in these times of high energy costs. It may be better to bake the products thoroughly, remove them carefully from the oven, and let them cool slowly in a warm place.

Éclair Paste or Pâte à Choux

INGREDIENTS	U.S.	METRIC	PERCENTAGE
Water, milk, or half water and half milk	1 lb	500 g	133 %
Butter or regular shortening	8 oz	250 g	67 %
Salt	1 tsp	5 g (5 mL)	1.5 %
Bread flour	12 oz	375 g	100 %
Eggs	1 lb 4 oz	625 g	167 %
Yield:	*3 lb 8 oz*	*1755 g*	*468 %*

Per 1 ounce (28.35 g): Calories, 70; Protein, 2 g; Fat, 4 g (56% cal.); Cholesterol, 35 mg; Carbohydrates, 5 g; Fiber, 0 g; Sodium, 90 mg.

PROCEDURE

Mixing:

1. Combine liquid, butter, and salt in a heavy saucepan and bring to a boil.
2. Remove pan from heat and add the flour all at once. Stir quickly.
3. Return the pan to moderate heat and stir vigorously until the dough forms a ball and pulls away from the sides of the pan.
4. Transfer the dough to the bowl of a mixer. If you wish to mix by hand, leave it in the saucepan.
5. With the paddle attachment, mix at low speed until the dough has cooled slightly. It should be about 140°F (60°C)—still very warm, but not too hot to touch.
6. At medium speed, beat in the eggs, a little at a time. Add no more than one-fourth of the eggs at once, and wait until each quantity is completely absorbed before adding the next. When all the eggs are absorbed, the paste is ready to use.

Procedure for Making Cream Puffs and Profiteroles

1. Line sheet pans with silicone paper, or butter them lightly.
2. Fit a large pastry bag with a plain tube. Fill the bag with the choux paste.
3. For cream puffs, pipe round mounds of dough about 1½ inches (4 cm) in diameter onto the lined baking sheets (see Figure 13.8).
   For profiteroles, pipe round mounds of dough about ¾ inch (2 cm) in diameter. If you prefer, you may drop the dough from a spoon.
4. Bake at 425°F (215°C) for 10 minutes. Lower the heat to 375°F (190°C) until the puffs are well browned and very crisp.
5. Remove from the oven and cool slowly in a warm place.
6. When cool, cut a slice from the top of each puff. Fill with whipped cream, Vanilla Pastry Cream (p. 319), or desired filling, using a pastry bag with a star tube.
7. Replace the tops and dust with confectioners' sugar.
8. Fill the puffs as close to service as possible. If cream-filled puffs must be held, refrigerate them.
9. Unfilled and uncut puffs, if they are thoroughly dry, may be held in plastic bags in the refrigerator for 1 week. Recrisp in the oven for a few minutes before use.

Figure 13.8 **For cream puffs or profiteroles, pipe choux paste into bulbs of desired size onto greased sheet pans, or onto pans that have been lined with parchment.**

Procedure for Making Éclairs

1. Proceed as for cream puffs, except pipe the dough into strips about ¾ inch (2 cm) wide and 3 to 4 inches (8 to 10 cm) long (see Figure 13.9). Bake as for cream puffs.
2. Fill baked, cooled éclair shells with pastry cream. Two methods may be used:
   - Make a small hole in one end of the shell and fill using a pastry bag or a doughnut-filling pump.
   - Cut a slice lengthwise from the top and fill using a pastry bag.
3. Dip the tops of the éclairs in chocolate fondant (p. 270).
4. For service and holding, see cream puffs procedure.

Variation: Frozen Éclairs or Profiteroles

1. Fill éclairs or profiteroles with ice cream. Keep frozen until service.
2. At service time, top with chocolate syrup.

Figure 13.9 **For éclairs, pipe choux paste into fingers of desired size onto greased sheet pans, or onto pans that have been lined with parchment.**

Procedure for Making French Crullers or French Doughnuts

1. Cut sheets of parchment paper to the same width as your deep fryer.
2. Using a pastry bag with a star tube, pipe choux paste onto the parchment in circles (doughnut shapes) about 2 inches (5 cm) across.
3. Slide the paper with the paste into a deep fryer heated to 375°F (190°C). Remove the paper as the doughnuts release and float free.
4. Fry the doughnuts on both sides until golden brown. French doughnuts must be completely fried, or they may collapse when cooling. Remove and drain on absorbent paper.
5. When cooled, drizzle fondant icing over the tops.

Meringues

Meringues are beaten egg whites sweetened with sugar. Their most frequent use in North America is for pie toppings and cake icings (known as *boiled icing*). They are also used to give volume and lightness to buttercream icings and to such preparations as dessert soufflés.

Another excellent use for meringues is to bake them in a slow oven until crisp. In this form, they can be used in place of cake layers or pastry shells to make light, elegant desserts. Chopped nuts may be folded into meringue before forming and baking to make these desserts more flavorful.

Basic rules for beating egg whites are discussed in your ***Culinary Foundations*** *volume. Please review this section before attempting to make any of the following preparations. We repeat one rule here because it is so important:*

Make sure that all equipment is free of any trace of fat or grease, and that the egg whites have no trace of yolk in them. Even a small trace of fat will prevent the whites from foaming properly.

Soft meringues, used for pie topping, may be made with as little as 1 pound (500 g) sugar per pound (500 g) of egg whites. ***Hard meringues***, baked until crisp, are made with up to twice as much sugar as egg whites.

Basic Meringues

The stiffness to which meringues are beaten may vary, as long as they are not beaten until they are too stiff and dry. For most purposes, they are beaten until they form stiff, or nearly stiff, moist peaks.

1. ***Common meringue*** is made from egg whites at room temperature, beaten with sugar. It is the easiest to make, and it is reasonably stable due to the high percentage of sugar.

2. ***Swiss meringue*** is made from egg whites and sugar warmed over a double boiler while beating. Warming gives this meringue better volume and stability.

3. ***Italian meringue*** is made by beating a hot sugar syrup into the egg whites. This meringue is the most stable of the three because the egg whites are actually cooked by the heat of the syrup. When flavored with vanilla, this meringue is also known as *boiled icing*. It is also used in meringue type buttercream icings.

Meringue

INGREDIENTS	COMMON MERINGUE	SWISS MERINGUE	ITALIAN MERINGUE
Egg whites	1 lb/500 g	1 lb/500 g	1 lb/500 g
Sugar	2 lb/1 kg	2 lb/1 kg	2 lb/1 kg
Water	—	—	8 fl oz/250 mL

Per 1 ounce (28.35 g): Calories, 80; Protein, 1 g; Fat, 0 g (0% cal.); Cholesterol, 0 mg; Carbohydrates, 19 g; Fiber, 0 g; Sodium, 15 mg.

Note: For soft meringues to top pies, use half the amount of sugar.

PROCEDURE

Common Meringue:

1. With the whip attachment, beat the egg whites at high speed until they form soft peaks.
2. Gradually add the sugar with the machine running.
3. Continue to beat until the meringue forms stiff but moist peaks.

Swiss Meringue:

1. Place the egg whites and sugar in a stainless-steel bowl or the top of a double boiler. Beat with a wire whip over hot water until the mixture is warm (about 120°F/50°C).
2. Transfer the mixture to the bowl of a mixing machine and whip at high speed until stiff peaks form.

Italian Meringue:

1. Heat the sugar and water in a saucepan until the sugar dissolves and the mixture boils. Boil until a candy thermometer placed in the mixture registers 240°F (115°C).
2. While the syrup is cooking, beat the egg whites in a mixing machine until they form soft peaks.
3. With the machine running, very slowly beat the hot syrup into the egg whites.
4. Continue beating until the meringue forms firm peaks.

Meringue Desserts

Procedure for Making Pie Topping

1. Make common meringue or Swiss meringue using equal parts sugar and egg whites. Beat until just stiff.
2. Spread a generous amount (2–3 cups/500–700 mL) of meringue on still-warm pies. Mound it slightly, and be sure to attach it to the edge of the crust all around. If this is not done, the meringue may slide around on the finished pie. Leave the meringue in ripples or peaks.
3. Bake at 400°F (200°C) until the surface is attractively browned.
4. Remove from oven and cool.

Procedure for Making Baked Meringue Shells

1. Beat common or Swiss meringue until stiff.
2. Using a pastry bag or a spoon, form the meringue into small nest shapes on a parchment-lined baking sheet.
3. Bake at 200° to 225°F (about 100°C) until crisp but not browned. This will take 1 to 3 hours.
4. Cool the shells and remove from the parchment. Be careful, as they may be fragile.
5. Use in place of pastry shells for fruit tarts, fill with whipped cream and fresh strawberries or raspberries, or fill with a scoop of ice cream and garnish with chocolate or raspberry sauce. Crisp meringues with ice cream make a dessert called *meringue glacée* (glah say).

Procedure for Making Japonaise Meringues

Japonaise (zhah po nez) meringues are used like cake layers. They may be filled and iced with light buttercream, chocolate mousse, whipped cream, or similar light icings and creams.

1. Prepare 1 recipe (1 lb/500 g egg whites plus 2 lb/1 kg sugar) Swiss meringue.
2. Quickly but carefully fold in 1 pound (500 g) finely chopped hazelnuts.
3. With a pastry bag, form circles of the desired diameter and about ½ inch (1.5 cm) thick on parchment-lined sheet pans, as shown in Figure 13.10.
4. Bake as for meringue shells.

Figure 13.10 To make meringue layers, mark a circle on a sheet of parchment and pipe the meringue in a spiral to fill the circle.

Procedure for Making Baked Alaska

1. Pack softened ice cream into a dome-shaped mold of the desired size. Freeze solid.
2. Prepare a layer of sponge cake the same size as the flat side of the mold and about ½ inch (1.5 cm) thick.
3. Unmold the frozen ice cream onto the cake layer so the cake forms a base for the ice cream.
4. With a spatula, cover the entire dessert with a thick layer of meringue. If desired, decorate with more meringue forced from a pastry bag.
5. Bake at 450°F (230°C) until the meringue is golden brown.
6. Serve immediately.

Fruit Desserts

Fruit desserts are included here because many are similar to pies or pie fillings. Special favorites include cobblers, which are much like fruit pies made in large baking pans without a bottom crust; crisps, which are like cobblers, but with brown-sugar streusel topping instead of a pastry crust; and betties, which have alternate layers of rich cake crumbs and fruit. Also, don't overlook fresh fruits for dessert, served plain, lightly sweetened, or with cream.

KEY POINTS TO REVIEW

- What are the steps in the rolling-in procedure for making puff pastry dough?
- What are the steps in mixing éclair paste or pâte à choux?
- What are the three basic types of meringue? Describe how to prepare each.

TERMS FOR REVIEW

flaky pie dough
mealy pie dough
rubbed dough method
crumb crust
short dough
fruit pie
soft pie
cream pie
chiffon pie
baking blind
instant starch
cooked juice method
cooked fruit method
puff pastry
blitz puff pastry
éclair paste
pâte à choux
soft meringue
hard meringue
common meringue
Swiss meringue
Italian meringue
meringue glacée

QUESTIONS FOR DISCUSSION

1. Discuss the factors that affect tenderness, toughness, and flakiness in pie dough. Why should emulsified shortening not be used for pie dough?
2. What kind of crust or crusts would you use for a pumpkin pie? an apple pie? a banana cream pie?
3. What would happen to a flaky pie dough if you mixed it too long before adding the water? after adding the water?
4. How can you prevent shrinkage when baking pie shells?
5. What are the remedies for soggy or undercooked bottom pie crusts?
6. What starch would you use to thicken apple pie filling? chocolate pie filling? lemon pie filling? peach pie filling?
7. Why is lemon juice added to lemon pie filling after the starch has thickened the water? Wouldn't this thin the filling?
8. Why is it important to bake cream puffs and éclairs thoroughly and to cool them slowly?
9. Briefly describe the difference between common, Swiss, and Italian meringues.

Chapter 14

Creams, Custards, Puddings, Frozen Desserts, and Sauces

After reading this chapter, you should be able to

1. Cook sugar syrups to the seven stages of hardness.
2. Prepare crème anglaise, pastry cream, and baked custard.
3. Prepare starch-thickened puddings and baked puddings.
4. Prepare mousses and dessert soufflés.
5. Assemble frozen desserts.
6. Prepare dessert sauces.

A quick glance at this last chapter may give you the impression that you will be overwhelmed with a great many recipes and techniques within a few pages. Among the subjects covered are custard sauces, pastry cream, puddings, custards, mousses, soufflés, ice cream, and dessert sauces.

It's all much simpler than it seems. Once you have learned three basic preparations—vanilla custard sauce, pastry cream, and baked custard—you will have learned most of the rest. Vanilla custard sauce, also called *crème anglaise* or *English cream*, is the basis for ice cream and some dessert sauces. Pastry cream, with a variety of flavorings, is also used for pie fillings and puddings and is the basis for some soufflés. Many baked puddings are baked custard with added starch or fruit ingredients.

There seems little point in giving you recipes for cream pie fillings in the pie section, a recipe for pastry cream filling for napoleons in the puff pastry section, and recipes for boiled puddings in the pudding section, and never telling you they are all basically the same preparation. You are not just learning a collection of unrelated recipes; you are learning to cook and to understand what you are cooking.

Sugar Cooking

Understanding sugar cooking is important in the preparation of desserts and confections because sugar syrups of various strengths are often required (see, for example, Italian Meringue, p. 311–312).

Basic Principles

The principle of sugar cooking is fairly simple. A solution or syrup of sugar and water is boiled to evaporate part of the water. As the water is boiled off, the temperature of the syrup gradually rises. When all the water has evaporated, what you have left is melted sugar. The sugar then begins to caramelize or turn brown and to change flavor. If heating continues, the sugar continues to darken and then burn.

A syrup cooked to a high temperature is harder when it is cooled than a syrup cooked to a lower temperature. For example, a syrup cooked to 240°F (115°C) forms a soft ball when cooled. A syrup cooked to 300°F (150°C) is hard and brittle when cooled.

One part water (by weight) is enough to dissolve and cook 3 to 4 parts sugar. There is no point in adding more water than is necessary because you just have to boil it off.

Simple Syrup

Simple syrup is a solution of equal weights of sugar and water. Combine equal weights of water and granulated sugar in a saucepan, stir, and bring to a boil to dissolve the sugar. Cool the syrup.

Dessert syrup is a flavored simple syrup used to moisten and flavor some cakes (see p. 262). (Many chefs use 2 or 3 parts water to 1 part sugar for a less sweet syrup.) Flavorings may be extracts, such as vanilla, or liquors, such as rum or kirsch. Add flavorings after the syrup has cooled because flavor may be lost if they are added to hot syrup. Syrups may also be flavored by boiling them with lemon or orange rind.

Crystallization

Graininess is a common fault in many candies and desserts. Graininess results when cooked sugar ***crystallizes***, or turns to tiny sugar crystals, rather than staying dissolved in the syrup. If even one sugar crystal comes in contact with a cooked syrup, it can start a chain reaction that turns the whole thing into a mass of sugar crystals.

To avoid crystallization during the first stages of boiling, use one of the following techniques:

1. Wash down the sides of the saucepan with a brush dipped in water. This removes crystals that may seed the whole batch.

2. When first bringing the syrup to a boil, cover the pan and boil for several minutes. Condensed steam will wash down the sides of the pan. Uncover and finish cooking without stirring.

Sometimes an acid such as cream of tartar is added to a syrup before cooking. Acids change some of the sugar to *invert sugar*, which resists crystallizing. Corn syrup is sometimes added for the same reason.

Stages of Sugar Cooking

Testing the temperature with a candy thermometer is the most accurate way to determine the desired doneness of a syrup.

In the old days, syrups were tested by dropping a little bit into a bowl of cold water and checking the hardness of the cooled sugar. The stages of doneness were given names that described their hardness. Table 14.1 lists these stages of sugar cooking.

Table 14.1 **Stages of Doneness in Sugar Cooking**

	Temperature	
Stage	**°F**	**°C**
Thread	230	110
Soft ball	240	115
Firm ball	245	118
Hard ball	250–260	122–127
Small crack	265–270	130–132
Crack	275–280	135–138
Hard crack	290–310	143–155
Caramel	320–340	160–170

Basic Custards and Creams

The three preparations presented in this section are among the most basic and useful preparations in the bakeshop. All three can be classified as custards because they consist of a liquid thickened by the coagulation of eggs.

Crème anglaise (krem awn glezz), or vanilla custard sauce, is a stirred custard. It consists of milk, sugar, and egg yolks (and vanilla) stirred over very low heat until lightly thickened.

Pastry cream contains starch thickeners as well as eggs, resulting in a much thicker and more stable product. It is used as a cake and pastry filling, as a filling for cream pies, and as a pudding. With additional liquid, it is used as a custard sauce.

Baked custard, like vanilla custard sauce, consists of milk, sugar, eggs, and flavoring (usually whole eggs are used for greater thickening power). But, unlike the sauce, it is baked rather than stirred over heat, so it sets and becomes firm. Baked custard is used as a pie filling, as a dessert by itself, and as a basis for many baked puddings.

All of these preparations are subject to a wide range of variation. Because they are based on eggs, it would be helpful for you to review basic egg cooking principles.

Crème Anglaise

The following recipe gives the method for preparing vanilla custard sauce, or crème anglaise. Special care is necessary in preparing this sauce because the eggs can curdle easily if overcooked. The following guidelines will help you succeed.

1. Use clean, sanitized equipment, and follow strict sanitation procedures. Egg mixtures are good breeding grounds for bacteria that cause food poisoning.

2. When combining the egg yolks and sugar, whip the mixture as soon as the sugar is added. Letting sugar and egg yolks stand together without mixing creates lumps that cannot be beaten out. Using a stainless-steel bowl for this step makes the cooking and stirring easier in step 5.

3. Heat the milk to scalding (just below simmering) before combining with the egg yolks. This makes the final cooking much shorter. To avoid scorching, you can set the pan of milk in a pan of boiling water. This takes longer than using direct heat, but the pan can be left unattended for a few minutes while you perform other tasks.

4. *Slowly* beat the hot milk into the beaten eggs and sugar. This raises the temperature of the eggs gradually and helps prevent curdling.

5. Set the bowl containing the egg mixture in a pan of simmering water and stir constantly to prevent curdling.

6. To test for doneness, two methods are available. Keep in mind that this is a very light sauce, so you can't expect a lot of thickening.

Figure 14.1 Crème anglaise coating the back of a spoon.

- Check the temperature with a thermometer. When it reaches 185°F (85°C), the sauce is cooked. Never let the temperature go above 190°F (87°C).
- When the mixture lightly coats the back of a spoon instead of running off like milk, the sauce is cooked (Figure 14.1).

7. *Immediately* cool the sauce by setting the pan or bowl in ice water. Stir occasionally to cool it evenly.
8. If the sauce curdles, it is sometimes possible to save it. Immediately stir in 1 to 2 ounces (30 to 60 mL) cold milk, transfer the sauce to a blender, and blend at high speed.

Crème Anglaise (Vanilla Custard Sauce)

YIELD: ABOUT 2½ PT (1.25 L)

U.S.	METRIC	INGREDIENTS	PROCEDURE
12 8 oz	12 250 g	Egg yolks Sugar	1. Review the guidelines for preparing vanilla custard sauce preceding this recipe. 2. Combine the egg yolks and sugar in a stainless-steel bowl. Whip until thick and light.
1 qt	1 L	Milk	3. Scald the milk in a boiling-water bath or over direct heat. 4. Very gradually pour the scalded milk into the egg yolk mixture while stirring constantly with the whip. 5. Set the bowl over simmering water. Heat it slowly, stirring constantly, until it thickens enough to coat the back of a spoon (or until it reaches 185°F/85°C).
1 tbsp	15 mL	Vanilla	6. Immediately remove the bowl from the heat and set it in a pan of cool water. Stir in the vanilla. Stir the sauce occasionally as it cools.

Per 1 fl oz (29.57 mL): Calories, 60, Protein, 2 g; Fat, 2.5 g (38 % cal.); Cholesterol, 65 mg; Carbohydrates, 7 g; Fiber, 0 g; Sodium, 15 mg.

VARIATIONS

For a richer crème anglaise, substitute heavy cream for up to half the milk. To flavor with a vanilla bean instead of vanilla extract, first split the bean in half lengthwise. Scrape the pulp from inside the bean with a paring knife (**Figure 14.2**). Add the pulp and the split bean to the milk before heating in step 3.

Chocolate Crème Anglaise

Melt 6 oz (175 g) sweetened chocolate. Stir into the crème anglaise while it is still warm (not hot).

Figure 14.2 Vanilla bean technique.

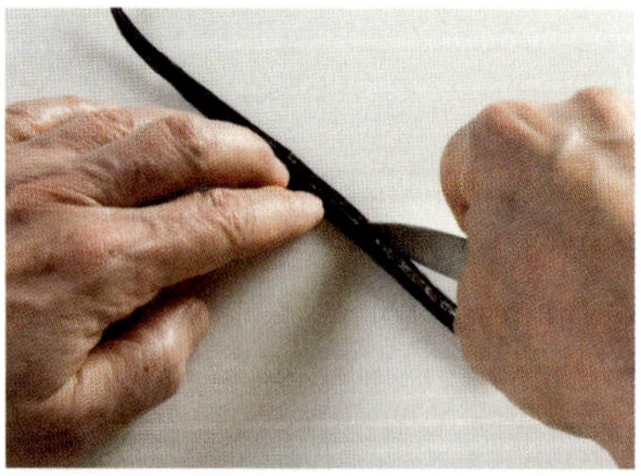

(a) Split the bean in half lengthwise.

(b) Scrape the pulp from inside the bean with a paring knife.

Pastry Cream

Although it requires more ingredients and steps, pastry cream is easier to make than custard because it is less likely to curdle. Pastry cream contains a starch thickening agent that stabilizes the eggs. It can actually be boiled without curdling. In fact, it *must* be brought to a boil, or the starch will not cook completely and the cream will have a raw, starchy taste.

Strict observance of all sanitation rules is essential when preparing pastry cream because of the danger of bacterial contamination. Use clean, sanitized equipment. Do not put your fingers in the cream, and do not taste it except with a clean spoon. Chill the finished cream rapidly in shallow pans. Keep the cream and all cream-filled products refrigerated at all times.

The procedure for preparing pastry cream is given in the following recipe. Note that the basic steps are similar to those for custard sauce. In this case, however, a starch is mixed with the eggs and half the sugar to make a smooth paste. (In some recipes with lower egg content, it is necessary to add a little cold milk to provide enough liquid to make a paste.)

Meanwhile, the milk is scalded with the other half of the sugar (the sugar helps protect the milk from scorching on the bottom of the pan).

The egg mixture is then tempered with some of the hot milk, returned to the kettle, and brought to a boil. Some chefs prefer to add the cold paste gradually to the hot milk, but the tempering procedure given here seems to give better protection against lumping and curdling.

Vanilla Pastry Cream

YIELD: ABOUT 2¼ QT (2.25 L)

U.S.	METRIC	INGREDIENTS	PROCEDURE
8 oz 2 qt	250 g 2 L	Sugar Milk	1. In a heavy saucepan or trunnion kettle, dissolve the sugar in the milk and bring just to a boil.
8 4 5 oz 8 oz	8 4 150 g 250 g	Egg yolks Whole eggs Cornstarch Sugar	2. With a whip, beat the egg yolks and whole eggs in a stainless-steel bowl. 3. Sift the starch and sugar into the eggs. Beat with the whip until perfectly smooth. 4. Temper the egg mixture by slowly beating in the hot milk in a thin stream. 5. Return the mixture to the heat and bring to a boil, stirring constantly.
4 oz 1 fl oz	125 g 30 mL	Butter Vanilla	6. When the mixture comes to a boil and thickens, remove from the heat. 7. Stir in the butter and vanilla. Mix until the butter is melted and completely blended in. 8. Pour into a clean, sanitized hotel pan or other shallow pan. Dust lightly with sugar and cover with waxed paper to keep a crust from forming. Cool and chill as quickly as possible. 9. For filling pastries such as éclairs and napoleons, whip the chilled pastry cream until smooth before using.

Per 1 fl oz (29.57 mL): Calories, 70; Protein, 2 g; Fat, 3 g (38% cal.); Cholesterol, 45 mg; Carbohydrates, 9 g; Fiber, 0 g; Sodium 30 mg.

VARIATIONS

For a lighter pastry cream filling, fold whipped heavy cream into the chilled pastry cream. Quantities may be varied to taste. For every 2 qt (2 L) pastry cream, whip 1–2 cups (250–500 mL) heavy cream.

Chocolate Pastry Cream

Melt together 4 oz (125 g) sweetened chocolate and 4 oz (125 g) unsweetened chocolate. Stir into the hot pastry cream.

Coffee Pastry Cream

Add 4 tbsp (60 mL) instant coffee powder to the milk in step 1.

CREAM PIE FILLINGS

Quantities for four 8-inch (20-cm) pies

Vanilla Cream Pie Filling

This is the same as Vanilla Pastry Cream. Fill prebaked pie shells with cooled but not chilled filling.

Coconut Cream Pie Filling

Add 8 oz (250 g) toasted unsweetened coconut to Vanilla Pastry Cream.

Banana Cream Pie Filling

Using Vanilla Cream Pie Filling, pour half of the filling into the pie shells, cover with sliced bananas, and fill with remaining filling. (Bananas may be dipped in lemon juice to help prevent browning.)

Chocolate Cream Pie Filling I

This is the same as Chocolate Pastry Cream, above.

Chocolate Cream Pie Filling II

In step 1, use only 3½ pt (1.75 L) milk. Add 3 oz (90 g) cocoa to dry ingredients (sugar and cornstarch) in basic Vanilla Pastry Cream recipe. Add 8 fl oz (250 mL) cold milk to the eggs.

Butterscotch Cream Pie Filling

Combine 2 lb (900 g) brown sugar and 10 oz (300 g) butter in a saucepan over low heat. Heat and stir until butter is melted and ingredients are blended. Omit all the sugar from the basic Vanilla Pastry Cream recipe (steps 1 and 3). Increase the starch to 6 oz (175 g). As the mixture is nearing a boil in step 5, gradually stir in the brown sugar mixture. Finish as in basic recipe.

Lemon Pie Filling

Follow the procedure for Vanilla Pastry Cream, but make the following ingredient adjustments:

1. Use water instead of milk.
2. Increase sugar in step 1 to 1 lb (450 g).
3. Increase the cornstarch to 6 oz (175 g).
4. Add the grated zest of 2 lemons to the egg mixture.
5. Add 8 fl oz (250 mL) lemon juice to the finished, hot cream in place of the vanilla.

CREAM PUDDINGS

Vanilla Pudding
Coconut Pudding
Banana Cream Pudding
Chocolate Pudding I and II
Butterscotch Pudding

For each of these puddings, prepare the corresponding pie filling but use only half the cornstarch.

PASTRY CREAM VARIATIONS

Cream pie fillings and puddings are actually pastry cream flavored with various ingredients.

Cornstarch should be used as the thickening agent when the cream is to be used as a pie filling so the cut slices hold their shape. For other uses, either cornstarch or flour may be used. Remember that twice as much flour as cornstarch is required for the same thickening power. Other variations are possible, as you will see in the recipes. Sometimes whipped cream is folded into cold pastry cream to lighten it and make it creamier.

Lemon pie filling is also a variation of pastry cream. It is made with water instead of milk, and it is flavored with lemon juice and grated lemon rind.

Baked Custard

Baked custard is a mixture of eggs, milk, sugar, and flavorings that is baked until the eggs coagulate and the custard is set. A good custard holds a clean, sharp edge when cut.

The following recipe gives the procedure for making baked custard. Note these points in particular:

1. Scald the milk before beating it slowly into the eggs. This reduces cooking time and helps the product cook more evenly.
2. Remove any foam, which would mar the appearance of the finished product.
3. Bake at 325°F (165°C). High temperatures increase the risk of overcooking and curdling.
4. Bake in a water bath so the outside edges are not overcooked before the inside is set.
5. To test for doneness, insert a thin-bladed knife 1 to 2 inches (3–5 cm) from the center. If it comes out clean, the custard is done. The center may not be completely set, but the custard will continue to cook in its own heat after removal from the oven.

KEY POINTS TO REVIEW

- What is the proper procedure to cook a sugar syrup so it doesn't crystallize? How do you tell when a syrup is cooked to the proper stage?
- What is the procedure for cooking crème anglaise?
- What is the procedure for cooking pastry cream?
- What is the procedure for cooking a plain baked custard?

Baked Custard

PORTIONS: 12 PORTION SIZE: 5 OZ (150 G)

U.S.	METRIC	INGREDIENTS	PROCEDURE
1 lb	500 g	Eggs	1. Combine the eggs, sugar, salt, and vanilla in a mixing bowl. Mix until thoroughly blended, but do not whip.
8 oz	250 g	Sugar	
½ tsp	2 mL	Salt	
½ fl oz	15 mL	Vanilla	
2½ pt	1.25 L	Milk	2. Scald the milk in a double boiler or in a saucepan over low heat. 3. Gradually pour the milk into the egg mixture, stirring constantly. 4. Skim off all foam from the surface of the liquid. 5. Arrange custard cups in a shallow baking pan. (Butter the insides of the cups if the custards are to be unmolded.) 6. Carefully pour the custard mixture into the cups. If any bubbles form during this step, skim them off. 7. Set the baking pan on the oven shelf. Pour enough hot water into the pan around the cups so the level of the water is about as high as the level of the custard mixture. 8. Bake at 325°F (165°C) until set, about 45 minutes. 9. Carefully remove from the oven and cool. Store, covered, in refrigerator.

Per serving: Calories, 190; Protein, 8 g; Fat, 7 g (33% cal.); Cholesterol, 175 mg; Carbohydrates, 24 g; Fiber, 0 g; Sodium, 190 mg.

VARIATION

Crème Caramel

Cook 12 oz (375 g) sugar and 2 fl oz (60 mL) water until it caramelizes (see the section on sugar cooking at the beginning of this chapter). Line the bottoms of the custard cups with the hot caramel. (Be sure the cups are clean and dry.) Fill with custard and bake as in basic recipe. When done, cool and refrigerate overnight. Unmold onto a plate for service.

Puddings

It is difficult to give a definition of *pudding* that includes everything called by that name. The term is used for such different dishes as chocolate pudding, blood sausages (blood puddings), and steak-and-kidney pudding. In this chapter, however, we consider only the more popular dessert puddings.

Two kinds of pudding, starch-thickened and baked, are the most frequently prepared in food-service kitchens. These are the types we discuss here. A third type, steamed pudding, is less often served, and then mainly in cold weather, because steamed puddings are usually rather heavy and filling.

Starch-Thickened Puddings

These are also called *boiled puddings* because they are boiled in order to cook the starch that thickens them.

1. **Cornstarch pudding or *blancmange*.**
   Cornstarch pudding consists of milk, sugar, and flavorings and is thickened with cornstarch (or, sometimes, another starch). If enough cornstarch is used, the hot mixture may be poured into molds, chilled, and unmolded for service.

2. **Cream puddings.**
   Cream puddings, as you learned in the previous section, are the same as pastry cream. Puddings are usually made with less starch, however, and may contain any of several flavoring ingredients, such as coconut or chocolate. Butterscotch pudding is given its flavor by using brown sugar instead of white sugar.

   If you look again at the recipe for Vanilla Pastry Cream (p. 319), you will see the only difference between cornstarch puddings and cream puddings is that the latter contain eggs. In fact, cream puddings may be made by stirring hot cornstarch pudding into beaten eggs, then heating the entire mixture to just below the simmer. Care must be taken to avoid curdling the eggs if this method is used.

A basic recipe for cornstarch pudding follows. Recipes for cream puddings are included among the variations following the recipe for Vanilla Pastry Cream.

Blancmange, English Style

PORTIONS: 12 PORTION SIZE: 4 OZ (125 G)

U.S.	METRIC	INGREDIENTS	PROCEDURE
1 qt	1 L	Milk	1. Combine the milk, sugar, and salt in a heavy saucepan and bring to a simmer.
6 oz	190 g	Sugar	
¼ tsp	1 mL	Salt	
4 oz	125 g	Cornstarch	2. Mix the cornstarch and cold milk until perfectly smooth.
8 fl oz	250 mL	Milk, cold	3. Pouring in a thin stream, add about 1 cup (250 mL) hot milk to the cornstarch mixture.
			4. Stir this mixture back into the hot milk.
			5. Stir over low heat until the mixture thickens and comes to a boil.
1½ tsp	7 mL	Almond or vanilla extract	6. Remove from heat and add desired flavoring.
			7. Pour into ½-cup (125-mL) molds. Cool, then chill. Unmold for service.

Per serving: Calories, 150; Protein, 3 g; Fat, 3.5 g (20% cal.); Cholesterol, 15 mg; Carbohydrates, 28 g; Fiber, 0 g; Sodium, 100 mg.

Note: French blancmange is very different from English. The French style is made with almond milk and gelatin.

VARIATIONS

Blancmange or cornstarch pudding may be flavored in any way cream puddings are. See the variations following the Vanilla Pastry Cream recipe (p. 319).

Baked Puddings

Baked puddings are custards that contain additional ingredients, usually in large quantities. Bread pudding, for example, is made by pouring a custard mixture over pieces of bread in a pan and baking it in the oven. Rice pudding, another popular item, is made of cooked rice and custard.

The procedure for making baked puddings is the same as for making baked custard. A water bath may not be necessary if the starch content of the pudding is high.

Soft pie fillings, such as pumpkin, could also be considered baked puddings.

Rice Pudding

PORTIONS: 12 PORTION SIZE: 5 OZ (150 G)

U.S.	METRIC	INGREDIENTS	PROCEDURE
8 oz	225 g	Rice (medium- or long-grain)	1. Wash the rice well. Drain.
1½ qt	1.5 L	Milk	2. Combine the rice, milk, vanilla, and salt in a heavy saucepan. Cover and simmer over very low heat until the rice is tender, about 30 minutes. Stir occasionally to be sure the mixture doesn't scorch on the bottom. Remove from heat when cooked.
1 tsp	5 mL	Vanilla	
¼ tsp	1 mL	Salt	
1	1	Whole egg	3. Combine the egg, yolks, sugar, and cream in a mixing bowl. Mix until evenly combined.
2	2	Egg yolks	4. Ladle some of the hot milk from the cooked rice into this mixture and mix well. Then very slowly stir the egg mixture into the hot rice.
8 oz	250 g	Sugar	
8 fl oz	250 mL	Light cream	
as needed	as needed	Cinnamon	5. Pour into a buttered baking pan, 12 × 20 in. (30 × 50 cm). Sprinkle the top with cinnamon.
			6. Bake in a water bath at 350°F (175°C) for 30–40 minutes, or until set. Serve warm or chilled.

Per serving: Calories, 270; Protein, 7 g; Fat, 9 g (30 % cal.); Cholesterol, 80 mg; Carbohydrates, 40 g; Fiber, 0 g; Sodium, 120 mg.

VARIATION

Raisin Rice Pudding

Add 8 oz (250 g) raisins to the cooked rice and milk mixture.

Bread and Butter Pudding

PORTIONS: 12 PORTION SIZE: 6½ OZ (200 G)

U.S.	METRIC	INGREDIENTS	PROCEDURE
1 lb	500 g	White bread, in thin slices	1. Cut each slice of bread in half. Brush both sides of each piece with melted butter.
4 oz	125 g	Melted butter	2. Arrange the bread overlapping in a buttered baking pan, 12 × 20 in. (30 × 50 cm).
1 lb	500 g	Eggs	3. Mix the eggs, sugar, salt, and vanilla until thoroughly combined.
8 oz	250 g	Sugar	4. Gradually stir in the milk.
½ tsp	2 mL	Salt	
½ fl oz	15 mL	Vanilla	
2½ pt	1.25 L	Milk	
as needed	as needed	Cinnamon	5. Pour the custard mixture over the bread slices in the pan. Let stand, refrigerated, 1 hour or longer, so the bread absorbs the custard mixture.
as needed	as needed	Nutmeg	6. Sprinkle the top lightly with cinnamon and nutmeg.
			7. Set the pan in a larger pan containing about 1 in. (3 cm) hot water.
			8. Place in an oven preheated to 350°F (175°C). Bake about 1 hour, or until set.
			9. Serve warm or cold with whipped cream or light custard sauce, or dusted with confectioners' sugar.

Per serving: Calories, 350; Protein, 11 g; Fat, 16 g (41% cal.); Cholesterol, 190 mg; Carbohydrates, 41 g; Fiber, 1 g; Sodium, 440 mg.

Mousses and Soufflés

All the preparations in this section have one thing in common: They all have a light, fluffy, or puffed texture created by the addition of whipped cream, beaten egg whites, or both.

Although these particular products may be new to you, you should have little trouble learning to prepare them if you have already studied the previous chapter and the first part of this chapter. Once you have learned to prepare crème anglaise, pastry cream, starch-thickened fruit fillings, meringues, and whipped cream and have learned to work with gelatin, all you have to do is combine these products in different ways to make mousses and soufflés.

Let's look at these four items separately to see what they are made of. Afterward, we examine the procedures for assembling them.

Mousses

There are so many varieties of mousse that it is impossible to give a rule for all of them. In general, we define a ***mousse*** as any soft or creamy dessert made light and fluffy by the addition of whipped cream, beaten egg whites, or both. Note that bavarians and chiffons both fit this description. In fact, they are often served as mousses, but with the gelatin reduced or left out so the mousse is softer.

Many kinds of base are used for mousses. The base may be nothing more than melted chocolate or puréed fresh fruit, or it may be more complex, like the bases for chiffons.

Some mousses contain both beaten egg whites and whipped cream. When this is the case, most chefs prefer to fold in the egg whites first, even though they may lose some volume. The reason is that if the cream is added first, there is more danger it will be overbeaten and turn to butter during the folding and mixing procedure.

If egg whites are folded into a *hot* base, they will cook or coagulate, and the mousse will be firmer and more stable. Whipped cream should never be folded into hot mixtures, or it will melt and deflate.

Dessert Soufflés

Soufflés are lightened with beaten egg whites, then baked. Baking causes the soufflé to rise like a cake because the air in the egg foam expands when heated.

To understand the structure of dessert soufflés, we can divide their preparation into four stages:

1. **Base.**
   Many kinds are used for dessert soufflés. Most are heavy, starch-thickened preparations, such as pastry cream or sweetened white sauce.
2. **Egg yolks.**
   When used, these are added to the base.
3. **Egg whites.**
   Whenever possible, egg whites should be whipped with some of the sugar. This makes dessert soufflés more stable than entrée soufflés.
4. **Baking.**
   Review the section on entrée soufflés so you understand the general principles of baking soufflés.

General Procedure for Making Mousses and Soufflés

The following is a general procedure only. It is not a detailed method for one specific dessert, but it will give you a basic understanding that will help you tackle many recipes. These basic steps apply to most mousses and soufflés.

1. Prepare the base.
2. If gelatin is used, soften it in cold liquid and stir it into the hot base until dissolved. Chill until almost set.
3. Fold in the beaten egg whites and/or whipped cream.
4. Chill (mousses) or bake (soufflés).

KEY POINTS TO REVIEW

- What is the difference between a cornstarch pudding and a cream pudding?
- Rice pudding and bread pudding are made the same way as which of the three basic custard preparations discussed in the previous section?
- What are the four basic components of a baked soufflé?

Vanilla Soufflé

PORTIONS: 10 PORTION SIZE: 4½ OZ (125 G)

U.S.	METRIC	INGREDIENTS	PROCEDURE
3 oz	90 g	Flour	1. Work the flour and butter together to form a smooth paste.
3 oz	90 g	Butter	
4 oz	125 g	Sugar	2. Dissolve the sugar in the milk and bring to a boil. Remove from the heat.
1 pt	500 mL	Milk	3. With a wire whip, beat in the flour paste. Beat vigorously to make sure there are no lumps.
			4. Return the mixture to the heat and bring to a boil, beating constantly. Simmer for several minutes, until the mixture is very thick and no starchy taste remains.
			5. Transfer the mixture to a mixing bowl. Cover and let cool 5–10 minutes.
as needed	as needed	Butter	6. While the mixture is cooling, butter the soufflé dishes well and coat with sugar. For 1 recipe, use 1 dish, 10 in. (25 cm) in diameter; 2 dishes, 7 in. (18 cm) in diameter; or 10 single-portion dishes.
as needed	as needed	Sugar	
8	8	Egg yolks	7. Quickly beat the egg yolks and vanilla into the milk mixture.
2 tsp	10 mL	Vanilla	
8–10	8–10	Egg whites	8. Beat the egg whites until they form soft peaks. Add the sugar and beat until the mixture forms firm, moist peaks.
2 oz	60 g	Sugar	9. Fold the egg whites into the soufflé base.
			10. Pour the mixture into the prepared baking dishes and smooth the tops.
			11. Bake at 375°F (190°C). Approximate baking times are 45–50 minutes for a 10-in. (25-cm) dish, 30–40 minutes for a 7-in. (18-cm) dish, and 15 minutes for single-portion dishes.

Per serving: Calories, 270; Protein, 8 g; Fat, 13 g (44% cal.); Cholesterol, 195 mg; Carbohydrates, 29 g; Fiber, 0 g; Sodium, 150 mg.

VARIATIONS

Chocolate Soufflé

Add 3 oz (90 g) melted unsweetened chocolate and 1 oz (30 g) melted sweet chocolate to the base after step 5.

Lemon Soufflé

Instead of vanilla, use the grated zest of 2 lemons for flavoring.

Liqueur Soufflé

Flavor with 2–3 fl oz (60–90 mL) liqueur, such as kirsch or Grand Marnier, added after step 5.

Coffee Soufflé

Flavor with 2 tbsp (30 mL) instant coffee powder, added to the milk in step 2.

Chocolate Mousse

YIELD: ABOUT 2¾ LB (1.25 KG) OR 2½ PT (1.25 L) PORTIONS: 12 PORTION SIZE: 4½ FL OZ (145 ML)

U.S.	METRIC	INGREDIENTS	PROCEDURE
1 lb 4 oz 6 oz	500 g 125 g 180 g	Bittersweet chocolate Butter Egg yolks	1. Melt the chocolate over hot water. 2. Remove from the heat and add the butter. Stir until the butter is melted and completely mixed in. 3. Add the egg yolks, one at a time. Mix in each yolk completely before adding the next.
8 oz 2½ oz	250 g 75 g	Egg whites Sugar	4. Beat the egg whites until they form soft peaks. Add the sugar and beat until the egg whites form stiff but moist peaks. Do not overbeat. 5. Fold the egg whites into the chocolate.
8 fl oz	250 mL	Heavy cream	6. Whip the heavy cream until it forms soft peaks. Fold it into the chocolate mixture. 7. Spoon the mousse into serving dishes, or use a pastry bag fitted with a star tube. 8. Chill the mousse well before serving.

Per serving: Calories, 380; Protein, 6 g; Fat, 29 g (64% cal.); Cholesterol, 220 mg; Carbohydrates, 30 g; Fiber; 2 g; Sodium, 120 mg.

Note: This mixture may also be used as a filling for cakes, pastries, and baked meringues. For another, very different chocolate mousse recipe, see the variation following the recipe for Chocolate Chiffon earlier in this chapter.

Frozen Desserts

The popularity of ice cream needs no explanation. Whether a plain scoop of vanilla ice cream in a dish or an elaborate assemblage of fruits, syrups, toppings, and numerous flavors of ice cream and sherbet, frozen desserts appeal to just about everyone.

Classification

1. **Ice cream.**
   Ice cream is a smooth, frozen mixture of milk, cream, sugar, flavorings, and, sometimes, eggs. ***Philadelphia-style ice cream*** contains no eggs, while ***French-style ice cream*** contains egg yolks. The eggs add richness and help make a smoother product because of the emulsifying properties of the yolks.

   Ice milk is like ice cream, but with a lower butterfat content.

   Frozen yogurt contains yogurt in addition to the normal ingredients for ice cream or ice milk.

2. **Sherbet.**
   Sherbets and ***ices*** are made from fruit juices, water, and sugar. American sherbets usually contain milk or cream and, sometimes, egg whites. The egg whites increase smoothness and volume. Ices, also called ***water ices***, contain only fruit juice, water, sugar, and, sometimes, egg whites. They do not contain milk products. The French word ***sorbet*** (sor bay) is sometimes used for these products. ***Granité*** (grah nee tay) is a coarse, crystalline ice made without egg white.

3. **Still-frozen dessert.**
   Ice cream and sherbet are churn-frozen, meaning they are mixed constantly while being frozen. If they were not churned, they would freeze into solid blocks of ice. The churning keeps the ice crystals small and incorporates air into the ice cream.

   Frozen soufflés and *frozen mousses* are made like chilled mousses and bavarians—that is, whipped cream, beaten egg whites, or both are folded in to give them lightness. This allows them to be still-frozen in an ordinary freezer.

Production and Quality

Until recently, few establishments made their own ice cream because of the labor involved, the equipment required, and the convenience of commercially made products. Also, in some areas, strict health codes made it difficult for all but large producers to make ice cream. Today, more and more restaurants are making their own ice creams and sorbets.

A basic ice cream mix is simply a crème anglaise or custard sauce mixed with 1 or 2 parts heavy cream for every 4 parts milk used in the sauce. This base is flavored as desired with vanilla, melted chocolate, instant coffee, crushed strawberries, and so on. It is then chilled thoroughly and then frozen according to the instructions for the equipment being used.

When the mix has frozen, it is transferred to containers and placed in a deep-freeze at below 0°F (−18°C) to harden. (Soft-frozen or soft-serve ice creams are served directly as they come from the churn freezer without being hardened.)

Whether you make ice cream or buy it, you should be aware of the following quality factors:

1. *Smoothness* is related to the size of the ice crystals in the product. Ice cream should be frozen rapidly and churned well during freezing so large crystals don't have a chance to form.

   Rapid hardening helps keep crystals small. So do eggs and emulsifiers or stabilizers added to the mix.

   Large crystals may form if the ice cream is not stored at a low enough temperature (below 0°F/−18°C).

2. ***Overrun*** is the increase in volume due to the incorporation of air when freezing ice cream. It is expressed as a percentage of the original volume of the mix. For example, if the ice cream doubles in volume, the amount of increase is equal to the original volume and the overrun is 100 percent.

   Some overrun is necessary to give a smooth, light texture. Ice cream with too much overrun is airy and foamy and lacks flavor. It was once thought ice cream should have from 80 to 100 percent overrun and that less would make it heavy and pasty. This may be true for ice creams containing gums and other stabilizers. However, some high-quality manufacturers produce rich (and expensive) ice cream with as little as 20 percent overrun.

3. *Mouthfeel* or *body* depends, in part, on smoothness and overrun as well as on other qualities. Good ice cream melts in the mouth to a smooth, not too heavy liquid. Some ice creams have so many stabilizers they never melt to a liquid. Unfortunately, many people have become so accustomed to these products that an ice cream that actually does melt strikes them as not rich enough.

Storage and Service

1. Store ice creams and sherbets at 0°F (−18°C) or lower. This low temperature helps prevent the formation of large ice crystals.

2. For service, temper frozen desserts at 8° to 15°F (−13° to −9°C) for 24 hours so they are soft enough to serve.

3. When serving, avoid packing the ice cream. The best method is to draw the scoop across the surface of the product so the product rolls into a ball in the scoop.

4. Use standard scoops for portioning ice cream. Normal portions for popular desserts are as follows:

Parfait	3 No. 30 scoops
Banana split	3 No. 30 scoops
À la mode topping for pie or cake	1 No. 20 scoop
Sundae	2 No. 20 scoops
Plain dish of ice cream	1 No. 10, 12, or 16 scoop

5. Measure syrups, toppings, and garnishes for portion control. For syrups, use pumps that dispense measured quantities, or use standard ladles.

Popular Ice Cream Desserts

1. *Parfaits* are made by alternating layers of ice cream and fruit or syrup in a tall, narrow glass. They are usually named after the syrup or topping. For example: a *chocolate parfait* comprises three scoops of vanilla or chocolate ice cream alternating with layers of chocolate syrup and topped with whipped cream and shaved chocolate.

2. *Sundaes* or *coupes* consist of one or two scoops of ice cream or sherbet in a dish or glass and topped with syrups, fruits, toppings, and garnishes. They are quick to prepare, unlimited in variety, and as simple or as elegant as you could wish—served in an ordinary soda fountain glass, a silver cup, or a crystal champagne glass.

   Two sundaes have become classics:

   Peach Melba. Vanilla ice cream topped with a fresh, poached, or canned peach half, napped with sweetened raspberry purée (Melba sauce), and garnished with slivered almonds.

   Pear Belle Hélène. Vanilla ice cream topped with a poached or canned pear half, napped with chocolate sauce, and garnished with toasted sliced almonds.

3. *Bombes* are ice cream molds made by lining a chilled mold with softened ice cream, freezing it hard, and then filling the center with another flavor of ice cream or sherbet and freezing it again. (More than two flavors may be used.) The dessert is unmolded onto a cold platter for service and decorated as desired with whipped cream, fruits, and/or confections.

4. *Meringue glacée*. See discussion of meringues, page 311.

5. *Baked Alaska*. See discussion of meringues, page 312.

6. *Frozen éclairs* and *profiteroles*. See discussion of éclair pastries, page 310.

Dessert Sauces

Most dessert sauces fall into one of three categories.

1. **Custard sauces.**
   Vanilla custard sauce, or crème anglaise, is presented early in this chapter. It is among the most basic preparations in dessert cookery. Chocolate or other flavors may be added to create varieties. See recipe on page 318.

2. **Fruit purées.**
   These are simply purées of fresh or cooked fruits, sweetened with sugar. Other flavorings and spices are sometimes added. Some fruit sauces are thickened with cornstarch or other starch.

   Raspberry sauce and strawberry sauce, two popular items, can be made by simply puréeing frozen sweetened berries or by puréeing fresh berries and adding sugar to taste.

3. **Syrups.**
   This is a broad category that includes such products as chocolate sauce and caramel sauce. An understanding of sugar cooking is necessary to produce many of these sauces.

   The following recipes are popular examples of this category of sauce.

KEY POINTS TO REVIEW

- What are the key temperatures for storing ice cream and for holding it for service?
- How do you control portion size when preparing standard ice cream desserts?
- What are the three main categories of dessert sauce?

Chocolate Sauce

YIELD: 1 QT (1 L)

U.S.	METRIC	INGREDIENTS	PROCEDURE
1 pt 2 lb 6 oz	500 mL 1 kg 190 g	Water Sugar Corn syrup	1. Combine the water, sugar, and corn syrup and bring to a boil, stirring to dissolve the sugar. 2. Boil 1 minute and remove from heat. Let cool 1–2 minutes.
8 oz 2 oz	250 g 60 g	Unsweetened chocolate, melted Butter	3. Melt the chocolate and butter together over low heat. Stir until smooth. 4. Very slowly stir the hot syrup into the chocolate. 5. Place over moderate heat and bring to a boil. Boil 4 minutes. 6. Remove from heat and cool.

Per 1 fl oz (29.57 mL): Calories, 170; Protein, 1 g; Fat, 5 g (24% cal.); Cholesterol, 5 mg; Carbohydrates, 34 g; Fiber, 1 g; Sodium, 25 mg.

Caramel Sauce

YIELD: 1½ QT (1.5 L)

U.S.	METRIC	INGREDIENTS	PROCEDURE
1 lb 4 oz 1½ tsp	500 g 125 g 7 mL	Sugar Water Lemon juice	1. Combine the sugar, water, and lemon juice in a heavy saucepan. Bring to a boil, stirring to dissolve the sugar. 2. When the sugar is dissolved, cover the pan and boil 2 minutes. 3. Uncover and cook to the caramel stage (see pp. 316–317). Toward the end of the cooking time, turn the heat very low to avoid burning the sugar or getting it too dark. It should be a golden color. 4. Remove from heat and cool 5 minutes.
12 fl oz	375 mL	Heavy cream	5. Bring the heavy cream to a boil. Add a few ounces (50–100 mL) of the heavy cream to the caramel. 6. Stir and continue to add the cream slowly. 7. Return to the heat and stir until all the caramel is dissolved. 8. Let cool completely.
8 fl oz	250 mL	Milk	9. Stir the milk into the cooled caramel to thin it.

Per 1 fl oz (29.57 g): Calories, 130; Protein, 1 g; Fat, 6 g (39% cal.); Cholesterol, 20 mg; Carbohydrates, 20 g; Fiber, 0 g; Sodium, 10 mg.

VARIATIONS

Hot Caramel Sauce

Prepare as directed through step 7. Omit the milk.

Clear Caramel Sauce

Substitute 5–6 fl oz (150–175 mL) water for the heavy cream and omit the milk. If the sauce is too thick when cool, add more water.

Clear caramel sauce and caramel sauce with cream

TERMS FOR REVIEW

simple syrup	cream pudding	frozen yogurt	parfait
dessert syrup	baked pudding	sherbet	sundae
crystallize	mousse	ices	coupe
crème anglaise	ice cream	water ices	Peach Melba
pastry cream	Philadelphia-style ice cream	sorbet	Pear Belle Hélène
baked custard	French-style ice cream	granité	bombe
blancmange	ice milk	overrun	

QUESTIONS FOR DISCUSSION

1. How can you avoid unwanted crystallization when cooking sugar syrups?
2. Crème anglaise and pastry cream both contain eggs. Why is it possible to boil pastry cream but not custard sauce?
3. Explain the importance of sanitation in the production of pastry cream. What specific steps should you take to ensure a safe product?
4. Crème anglaise, pastry cream, and baked custard are made with basic techniques that are also used for the following preparations. Identify which of the three techniques is used for each.

   Coconut cream pie
   Baked rice pudding
   Butterscotch pudding
   French vanilla ice cream
   Pumpkin pie
   Custard pie
   Lemon meringue pie

5. Briefly describe the differences between mousses and soufflés.
6. When making dessert soufflés, what is the advantage of beating the egg whites with part of the sugar?

Chapter 15

Paella.

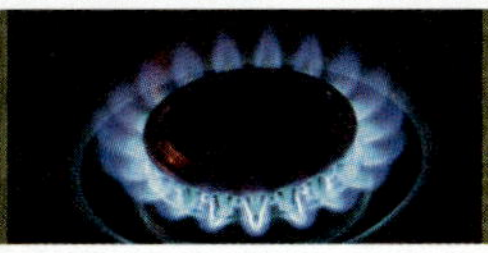

Cuisines Across Cultures

This chapter contains recipes from the following regions of the world:

- Italy
- Germany
- France
- Spain
- Africa
- Middle East
- India
- Southeast Asia
- China
- South America and the Caribbean
- Mexico

The recipes in this chapter, except for Thai Papaya and Mango Salad on page 352 and Beef Fajitas on page 362, are from *International Cuisine* (ISBN 978-0-470-04176-9), © Education Management Corporation

Italy

Orechietti con Carciofi (Orechietti Pasta with Artichokes)

PORTIONS: 4

U.S.	METRIC	INGREDIENTS
4	4	Artichokes
1	1	Lemon
2 oz	60 mL	Olive oil
3 oz	84 g	Pancetta, diced
1 oz	28 g	Onion, minced
2 oz	60 mL	Water or chicken stock
¼ tsp	¼ tsp	Red pepper flakes
16 oz	448 g	Orechietti pasta, dried
to taste	to taste	Salt and pepper
2 tbsp	2 tbsp	Parsley, chopped
4½ oz	126 g	Romano cheese, grated

PROCEDURE

1. Clean the artichokes, leaving on the tender parts of the heart; cut into very thin slices.
2. Squeeze the juice of the lemon over them.
3. Heat olive oil over medium heat and add pancetta. Sauté until crisp; add onions and cook 2 minutes.
4. Add sliced artichokes, water or chicken stock, and red pepper flakes. Cook until the artichokes are tender. Correct seasoning.
5. Cook pasta in boiling salt water; drain.
6. Toss pasta with artichoke sauce, herbs, and cheese. Serve.

Braciole Calabresi (Stuffed Pork Bundles)

PORTIONS: 4

U.S.	METRIC	INGREDIENTS
2	2	Eggs, beaten
2 oz	56 g	Pecorino cheese, thinly sliced or slivered
2	2	Garlic cloves, minced
2 tbsp	10 g	Italian parsley leaves, chopped fine
½ oz	42 g	Italian dried bread crumbs
as needed	as needed	Salt and freshly ground pepper
16 oz	448 g	Pork loin, boned, cleaned of fat and silver skin, cut into 8 pieces
4 oz	120 mL	Olive oil
4 oz	120 mL	Fresh tomato sauce (recipe follows)
4 oz	120 mL	Chicken stock
2 oz	60 mL	Dry red wine
2	2	Fresh rosemary sprigs

PROCEDURE

1. Combine egg, cheese, garlic, and chopped parsley.
2. Slowly drizzle in the seasoned bread crumbs while mixing constantly. Use only enough bread crumbs to bring the mixture to a soft, spreadable paste. Correct seasoning. Be careful with the salt; consider the flavor of the cheese.
3. Tap the pork until the slices are about ⅛ inch (.3 cm) thick and a rectangular shape.
4. Lightly brush the meat with olive oil. Season with salt and pepper.
5. Divided stuffing into 8 portions and spread each piece of pounded pork with stuffing, leaving ¼ inch (.6 cm) space around the edge of each piece.
6. Roll up and tie on each end and once in the middle.
7. Heat remaining oil over medium heat, brown bracioles on all sides. Place in an appropriate-sized ovenproof pan.
8. Combine tomato sauce, stock, red wine, and rosemary; mix well.
9. Pour liquid over the pork, bring to simmer, cover tightly, and cook for about 20 minutes just until tender. (Because the dish is made with loin it does not need to cook for a long period of time. Overcooking will dry and toughen the pork.)
10. When meat is tender, remove and reduce sauce. Serve 1 or 2 pieces, with braising liquid.

Fresh Tomato Sauce

PORTIONS: 4

U.S.	METRIC	INGREDIENTS
1 oz	30 mL	Olive oil
1 oz	28 g	Onions, minced
1	1	Garlic clove, minced
1 oz	28 g	Tomato paste
12 oz	336 g	Tomatoes, peeled, seeded, ¼ inch (.6 cm) dice
to taste	to taste	Salt and white pepper

PROCEDURE

1. Heat oil over medium heat and sauté onion and garlic until onions are translucent, 3 minutes.
2. Add tomato paste and stir well.
3. Add tomatoes; simmer 10 to 15 minutes, until correct consistency is reached. Do not overcook or you will loose the fresh tomato flavor.
4. Correct seasoning.

Germany

Kartoffelsuppe mit Miesmuscheln und Lauch

(Potato Soup with Mussels and Leeks)

PORTIONS: 4

U.S.	METRIC	INGREDIENTS
1½ oz	45 mL	Butter
2 tbsp	2 tbsp	Shallots, minced
6 oz	180 mL	White wine
1 qt	1 qt	Mussels, washed, beards removed
2 oz	60 mL	Cold water
2 oz	56 g	Leek, white and light-green parts, minced
8 oz	224 g	Potato, cooked, peeled, and pureed
to taste	to taste	Salt, white pepper, and cayenne pepper

PROCEDURE

1. In a pan large enough to just hold the mussels, melt the butter over medium-low heat. Add shallot and soften for a minute without browning; add white wine and mussels.
2. Cover and raise the heat to medium-high; cook, shaking the pan from time to time, until the mussels open, 3 to 4 minutes. Do not overcook the mussels or they will become tough.
3. Strain the mussels and cooking liquid into another pan through a cheesecloth-lined strainer.
4. Remove mussels from the shells, set the meat aside, discard the shells, and reserve cooking liquid.
5. Combine cold water and cooking liquid, add leeks, and cook over medium heat, 3 to 4 mlnutes.
6. Add the potato puree to the soup ⅓ at a time, whisking to mix well after each addition. If it is too thick after adding all the potato, thin with a little water.
7. Add mussels, bring back to a boil, remove from heat, and season with salt, pepper, and cayenne.
8. To serve, divide the mussels equally among 4 warm shallow bowls and pour a portion of the soup over.

Schweinelendchen im Schwarzbratmantel

(Pork Tenderloin in a Dark Bread Crust)

PORTIONS: 4

U.S.	METRIC	INGREDIENTS
1 oz	30 mL	Vegetable oil
16 oz	448 g	Pork tenderloin, cleaned
12 oz	12 oz	Lean ground pork
2	2	Eggs
6 oz	180 mL	Heavy cream
to taste	to taste	Salt and pepper
2 oz	56 g	Dark rye bread crumbs, dry
8 oz	240 mL	Pork or beef demi-glace

PROCEDURE

1. Heat the oil over medium high heat, sear the pork tenderloin, and set aside to cool.
2. In a food processor, process ground pork. Add eggs one at time, pulsing to incorporate. Scrape down sides and with machine running, add the cream in a steady stream. Scrape down sides; do not overprocess.
3. Remove mixture to a bowl over an ice bath. Poach or sauté a sample and adjust seasoning; add more cream if mixture is too stiff. Fold in bread crumbs.
4. Lay out a piece of plastic wrap large enough to wrap around the pork tenderloin two or three times. Spread the bread crumb mixture in an even layer just large enough to surround the pork tenderloin. Place the tenderloin in the middle of the bread crumb mixture; surround the tenderloin with the mixture. Wrap plastic around and tie ends so it is watertight. Poach in a 160°F (71.1°C) water bath 30 to 40 minutes or until an internal temperature of 155°F (68°C) is reached. Remove from water bath.
5. Let set 5 to 10 minutes, remove wrap, slice, and serve with demi-glace.

Rotkraut und Spätzle (Braised Red Cabbage and Spaetzle)

PORTIONS: 4

U.S.	METRIC	INGREDIENTS
16 oz	448 g	Red cabbage
1 oz	30 mL	Butter
4 oz	112 g	Onions, ¼ inch (.6 cm) dice
5	5	Juniper berries
4	4	Cloves
½ tbsp	½ tbsp	Granulated sugar
6 oz	168 g	Tart green apples, peeled, cored, ¼ inch (.6 cm) dice
2 oz	60 mL	Red wine vinegar
½ tsp	½ tsp	Salt
1	1	Bay leaf
1 tbsp	1 tbsp	Cornstarch
4 oz	120 mL	Dry red wine
as needed	as needed	Spätzle (recipe follows)

PROCEDURE

1. Trim the coarse outer leaves from the cabbage and discard; quarter the cabbage, remove the hard white core at the point of each quarter and discard, then slice each quarter very thinly.
2. Melt butter over medium high heat; add onions, juniper berries, cloves and sprinkle in the sugar, and cook to dissolve, 2 minutes.
3. Add apples, sauté 5 minutes or until soft and golden.
4. Add cabbage and sauté 5 minutes, until nicely glazed.
5. Add red wine vinegar and bring to a simmer. Add salt and bay leaf; toss to combine, push bay leaf down into the cabbage.
6. Cover and simmer 20 to 25 minutes, until cabbage is crisp-tender.
7. Sprinkle cornstarch over the cabbage and toss well to mix. Add the red wine. Heat to a strong simmer and cook, stirring, 3 to 5 minutes, until liquids are thickened. Remove from heat.
8. Discard bay leaf.
9. Simmer 5 minutes longer, uncovered. Serve with spaetzle.

Spätzle

YIELD: 4 CUPS

U.S.	METRIC	INGREDIENTS
8 oz	224 g	All-purpose flour
⅛ tsp	⅛ tsp	Freshly grated nutmeg
½ tsp	½ tsp	Salt
2	2	Eggs
6 oz	180 mL	Milk
1½ oz	45 mL	Butter, melted
to taste	to taste	Salt and pepper

PROCEDURE

1. Sift together flour, nutmeg, and salt. Make a well in the center.
2. Whisk the eggs with the milk and pour into the well of dry ingredients.
3. Mix with a wooden spoon, then use a mixer or food processor to beat the mixture until it is bubbly and elastic.
4. Pour batter into a spätzle hex or use a colander with medium to large holes. Force the batter through the holes into boiling salted water. Let the dough fall into the slightly bubbling water; cook about 2 to 3 minutes. Generally, the dumplings will float on the surface when sufficiently cooked.
5. Remove from the top with a slotted spoon or skimmer, wash under cold running water to remove excess starch, and let drain.
6. Heat butter over medium heat, add drained spaetzle, and toss to heat, or sautée in butter until golden and crispy. Correct seasoning.

France

Poulet Sauté Marengo (Chicken Sauté Marengo)

PORTIONS: 4

U.S.	METRIC	INGREDIENTS
1 oz	30 mL	Vegetable oil
1 oz	30 mL	Butter
2½ to 3 lb	1.12 kg to 1.34 kg	Chicken, disjointed, (drumstick cut at knuckle, thigh boneless, wing center, wing thick end, breast cut in half)
1 tbsp	1 tbsp	Shallot, minced
1 tbsp	1 tbsp	Garlic, minced
½ oz	15 mL	Tomato paste
6 oz	168 g	Tomato, peeled, seeded ¼ inch (.6 cm) dice
4 oz	120 mL	White wine
12 oz	360 mL	Espagnole, demi-glaze or jus lié
4 oz	112 g	Button mushrooms, washed and trimmed
as needed	as needed	Salt and pepper
Garnish:		
4	4	Crayfish tails or 4 large shrimp
1 oz	30 mL	Stock
4	4	Eggs
1 tbsp	1 tbsp	Parsley, chopped
4	4	Bread slices, cut into heart shapes
2 oz	60 mL	Butter

PROCEDURE

1. Heat oil and butter over medium high heat and brown the chicken pieces on all sides. Remove chicken from the pan; drain and reserve the fat.
2. In the same pan, return 2 tablespoons (1 ounce, 30 mL) reserved fat; add the shallot and garlic; cook 2 minutes or until soft.
3. Add tomato paste, cook 1 to 2 minutes. Add chopped tomato; cook gently, stirring 3 to 4 minutes.
4. Add wine and reduce by half. Add espagnole sauce, return chicken pieces, add mushrooms, and bring to a simmer. Cover and cook slowly 25 to 30 minutes or until the chicken is tender. Remove pieces as they cook.
5. To prepare the garnish, simmer the crayfish tails or shrimp in the stock until just cooked, 2 to 3 minutes; drain and keep warm.
6. Heat the reserved fat and French fry the eggs (cook egg in fat at 160 degrees, very slowly until the whites are creamy and the yolk is hot but still liquid.)
7. Heat the remaining butter and fry the heart-shaped bread slices.
8. Arrange the chicken on a platter, spoon the sauce over.
9. Dip the point of each crouton in the sauce, then into the chopped parsley, and arrange around the edge with the crayfish tails. Place a fried egg on each crouton and serve at once.

Le Blanc de Poisson Belle Mouginoise (Fillet of Fish Mouginoise)

PORTIONS: 4

U.S.	METRIC	INGREDIENTS
2 (5 × 6 in)	2 (12.5 cm × 15 cm)	Firm red tomatoes, peeled
1 each	1 each	English seedless cucumber, unpeeled
4 each	4 each	Very large mushrooms, white as possible, more if large are not available
4 (5 oz)	4 (140 g)	Skinless and boneless fish fillet, ½ inch (1.2 cm) thick (sea bass, red snapper, ling, turbot, orange roughie, or any firm white fish)
to taste	to taste	Salt and pepper
enough to grease pan	enough to grease pan	Butter
3 tbsp	3 tbsp	Shallots, minced
1½ oz	45 mL	Vermouth
3 oz	90 mL	White wine
1 oz	30 mL	Chicken or fish stock, jelled
4 oz	120 mL	Heavy cream
2 oz	60 mL	Butter
2 tbsp	2 tbsp	Chives, minced

PROCEDURE

1. Finely slice (⅛ inch, .3 cm) tomatoes, cucumbers, and mushrooms.
2. Arrange the vegetables in 3 separate neat rows along the length of the fish fillets, with slices overlapping: mushrooms overlapped by tomatoes and cucumbers overlapping the tomatoes. Season with salt and pepper.
3. Butter a pan large enough to hold the fish. Spread the shallots on the bottom of the pan and the place the fish on top.
4. Add the vermouth and wine, place in a preheated 400°F (205°C) oven, and cook 4 to 6 minutes or until fish is just cooked; do not overcook.
5. Remove the fish from the cooking liquid; set aside and keep moist and warm.
6. Add fish stock and cream; reduce liquids to sauce consistency (coats the back of a spoon), 1 to 2 minutes. Whisking vigorously, add the butter, then the chives. Correct seasoning and remove from heat.
7. Sauce the base of each plate. With a pastry, brush the vegetables with a little melted butter to give them sheen.
8. Place fish on the sauced plate and serve hot.

Note: Roger Verges' Moulin de Mougins restaurant is the inspiration for this recipe.

Spain

Croquetas de Jamón (Serrano Ham Fritters)

YIELD: 15 FRITTERS

U.S.	METRIC	INGREDIENTS
2 oz	56 g	Butter
1 oz	28 g	Spanish onion, ¼ inch (.6 cm) diced
6 oz	168 g	All-purpose flour
16 oz	480 mL	Milk
3 oz	84 g	Jamón serrano (Spanish cured ham), finely chopped
to taste	to taste	Salt
pinch	pinch	Nutmeg
1	1	Large egg, beaten with teaspoon of water
1 oz	28 g	Dry bread crumbs
16 oz	480 mL	Olive oil, for frying

PROCEDURE

1. Heat butter over medium heat; add onion and sauté until translucent, 3 minutes.
2. Add 1 cup (4½ ounces, 126 g) flour and mix well. Cook to a blond roux, about 5 minutes.
3. Add milk gradually, stirring continuously; cook 3 to 4 minutes, until a thick béchamel.
4. Add ham, salt, and nutmeg; cook 2 minutes. The mixture should be thick enough to mold by hand. Test for correct consistency by carefully picking up a tablespoon-size bit and balling it with your hands. It should not be very sticky. If mixture sticks to your hands, return to heat and cook 2 more minutes; recheck.
5. Spread mixture out on a half sheet pan and cool to room temperature.
6. Form the mixture into small cylinders the size of a wine cork, using about a tablespoon of mixture for each.
7. Roll each fritter in remaining flour, the egg, and breadcrumbs.
8. Refrigerate for 30 minutes before frying.
9. Heat oil to 375°F (190°C).
10. Deep-fry fritters in small batches. Fry until golden color, about 1 minute; turn as needed.
11. Transfer to absorbent towels to drain. Repeat with all fritters and serve hot.

Bacalad al Ajo Arriero (Bacalao Hash)

PORTIONS: 4

U.S.	METRIC	INGREDIENTS
3 oz	84 g	Salt cod, soaked, cooked, drained
1 oz	30 mL	Olive oil
2 oz	56 g	Onion, ¼ inch (.6 cm) dice
2	2	Garlic cloves, minced
1 oz	28 g	Green bell pepper, ¼ inch (.6 cm) dice
2 oz	2 oz	Piquillo peppers (from can or jar) or pimientos, or Red bell pepper, julienne cut
6 oz	168 g	Boiling potatoes (Yukon gold), peeled, boiled, drained, ¼ inch (.6 cm) dice
¼ tsp	¼ tsp	Sweet (not smoked) paprika
1 oz	30 mL	Tomato sauce
¼ tsp	¼ tsp	White wine or sherry vinegar
to taste	to taste	Coarse salt and freshly ground black pepper
1 tbsp	1 tbsp	Flat-leaf parsley, minced
for serving	for serving	Sliced crusty baguette

PROCEDURE

1. Flake salt cod finely, discard bones, skin, and any tough bits.
2. Heat olive over medium-low heat. Add onion and sauté until translucent, 3 minutes. Add garlic; cook 2 minutes.
3. Add green pepper and cook until pepper and onions are very soft, 5–6 minutes. Do not brown.
4. If pan looks dry add a little more oil, stir in cod, piquillo peppers, and potatoes; mix well, cover, and cook 5 minutes. Stir only 2–3 times.
5. Add paprika and stir for a few seconds. Add tomato sauce and wine, reduce heat to very low, re-cover, and simmer 7–8 minutes. Hash should still be moist; if not, add a little water and simmer 1 or 2 minutes.
6. Let hash cool to warm or room temperature; the flavor will develop as it cools.
7. Stir in parsley, adjust seasoning, and serve on or with bread.

Note: Cooked with care, desalted reconstituted bacalao is moist, plump, and falling apart in big, luxurious flakes. Depending on the grade of the fish and the salting method used, bacalao can take anywhere from 24 hours to 2 days to desalt properly. To desalt, cover with 2 inches of cold water and refrigerate, changing water every 4–5 hours if possible. Taste a small piece and if it is still too salty, soak longer, changing water as needed. It can also be cooked in milk instead of water to draw out some of the salt. It is important to cook salt cod very gently or it will become tough and rubbery; never boil it. The fish is cooked when it flakes easily with the point of a knife. There are small bones that need to be removed.

Gambas al Ajillo (Sizzling Garlic Shrimp)

PORTIONS: 4

U.S.	METRIC	INGREDIENTS
16 z	448 g	Large shrimp (26 to 30 ct), in shell
to taste	to taste	Coarse salt
8 oz	240 mL	Olive oil
5	5	Garlic cloves, finely chopped
½	½	Small dry red chile (arbol), crumbled
2 tbsp	2 tbsp	Flat-leaf parsley, minced
for serving	for serving	Bread

PROCEDURE

1. Pat shrimp dry and sprinkle with salt.
2. Combine olive oil and garlic over medium-low heat until oil is hot and garlic begins to sizzle gently. Cook until garlic is very fragrant but not colored, 2--3 minutes; reduce heat if necessary.
3. Add chile and stir for 30 seconds.
4. Add shrimp; cook, stirring, until shrimp are just cooked, about 3 minutes.
5. Season with salt to taste, stir in parsley, and cook 15 seconds.
6. Serve with bread.

Paella Valenciana

PORTIONS: 4

U.S.	METRIC	INGREDIENTS
10 oz	280 g	Skinless, boneless chicken thighs, 1½ inch (3.75 cm) chunks
16 oz	448 g	Rabbit, bone-in, cut into small pieces
1½ tsp	1½ tsp	Smoked sweet Spanish paprika
to taste	to taste	Salt and fresh black pepper
6	6	Garlic cloves, minced or crushed with a garlic press
32 oz	960 mL	Chicken stock
pinch	pinch	Saffron, pulverized in a mortar
2½ oz	75 mL	Olive oil
6 oz	168 g	Spanish chorizo, 1½ inch (3.75 cm) pieces
2 oz	56 g	Green beans (Italian flat beans), trimmed, 1½ inch (3.75 cm) lengths
3 oz	84 g	Cooked butter beans or baby lima beans
6 oz	168 g	Frozen artichoke hearts, thawed, patted dry
3 oz	90 mL	Tomato, cut in half and grated on box grater, skin discarded
pinch	pinch	Cayenne
14 oz	392 g	Short- to medium-grain rice
12 large	12 large	Snails (optional)
3 oz	84 g	Red bell pepper, roasted, peeled, julienned

PROCEDURE

1. Preheat oven to 425°F (218°C).
2. Combine chicken, rabbit, ½ teaspoon paprika, salt, pepper, and half the garlic; toss well and set aside for 15 minutes.
3. Bring chicken stock to a simmer. Add the saffron and continue to keep hot.
4. Using only one burner, place 4 tablespoons (2 ounces, 60 mL) olive oil in a 14-inch (53.6 cm) paella pan over medium heat until oil begins to smoke.
5. Add chicken and rabbit; brown, 6 to 7 minutes.
6. Add chorizo; cook 2 minutes.
7. Add green beans, butter beans, and artichokes; toss until vegetables begin to take on color, 5 minutes. Move all items to the edge of pan.
8. Add remaining oil to center of paella pan, add remaining garlic, and cook until fragrant, about 30 seconds.
9. Add tomatoes to center of the pan, reduce heat to low, and cook, stirring, until tomato is thickened and reduced, 5 to 6 minutes.
10. Toss tomato mixture with meat and vegetables, add remaining paprika and cayenne; stir to combine.
11. Add rice to pan and stir to coat. Add hot stock.
12. Place pan over two burners, stir in snails if using, and shake pan to distribute rice evenly. Cook over medium low heat until the cooking liquid is almost level with the rice, 6–8 minutes; rice will still be soupy. Move and rotate pan so the liquid cooks evenly. If liquid is absorbed too fast and the rice seems raw, add a little more stock.
13. Transfer paella pan to oven and bake until the rice is tender but still al dente, about 15 minutes. Check and sprinkle with more stock if necessary.
14. Remove paella from the oven, cover with aluminum foil, and let stand 5 minutes. Uncover and let stand 10 minutes; flavors will develop as it rests.
15. Garnish with roasted peppers and serve.

Note: According to Valencian traditionalists, this is the only legitimate paella. This dish evolved from a range of simpler rices prepared by laborers in the Levantine rice paddies and *huertas* (vegetable plots) with whatever could be hunted and gathered.

Paella is not a pilaf or risotto; the rice is never washed or the barley stirred. It should have a crispy, caramelized, toasted bottom (called socarrat).

Africa

Tagine of Chicken, Preserved Lemon, and Olives

PORTIONS: 4

U.S.	METRIC	INGREDIENTS	PROCEDURE
1 tbsp	1 tbsp	Garlic, minced	1. Combine the garlic, olive oil, and black pepper. Rub the chicken with the mixture and let set 2 hours.
½ oz	15 mL	Olive oil	
½ tsp	½ tsp	Black pepper	
1 2½ lb	1 1.12 kg	Chicken, cut into 8 pieces	
1 oz	30 mL	Olive oil	2. Heat oil over medium heat and brown chicken on all sides, 8 to 10 minutes.
¼ tsp	¼ tsp	Black pepper	3. Add spices; cook 1 minute. Add onions and sauté over medium-high heat, 2 to 3 minutes.
¼ tsp	¼ tsp	Ginger, ground	4. Add stock and bring to a boil, reduce to a simmer, and cover, leaving lid ajar to allow steam to escape. Simmer 20 to 30 minutes or until chicken is tender.
pinch	pinch	Saffron	5. Add olive and preserved lemons; cook 5 minutes. Remove chicken and reduce to sauce consistency, stirring. Correct seasoning.
1 tsp	1 tsp	Cumin, ground	6. Serve covered with sauce on couscous.
1 stick	1 stick	Cinnamon	
1 tsp	1 tsp	Coriander, ground	
5 oz	140 g	Onions, ¼ inch (.6 cm) dice	
16 oz	480 mL	Chicken stock	
5 oz	140 g	Green olives, pitted	
3 oz	84 g	Preserved lemons, quartered strips (rinse lemons as needed under running water, removing and discarding pulp)	
to taste	to taste	Salt and pepper	
as needed	as needed	Couscous (see p. 367 of **Culinary Foundations**)	

Akara (Black-Eyed Pea Fritters) Western Africa

PORTIONS: 4

U.S.	METRIC	INGREDIENTS	PROCEDURE
8 oz	224 g	Dried cowpeas (black-eyed peas)	1. Clean, pick over, and wash black-eyed peas. Soak, covered, in hot water 30 minutes. Drain and remove the skins by rubbing them between your hands. Rinse and drain well in a colander.
2 oz	56 g	Onions, ⅛ inch (.3 cm) dice	2. Crush or process the peas to a thick paste. Add enough water to form a smooth, thick batter that will cling to a spoon. Add remaining ingredients except oil; mix well and let stand 30 minutes.
½ tsp	½ tsp	Salt	3. Heat 2 inches (5 cm) oil over medium heat to 325°F (162°C).
1 oz	28 g	Green bell pepper, ⅛ inch (.3 cm) dice	4. Drop batter by the tablespoonful into the hot oil. Fry until golden, 2 to 3 minutes per side. Drain on paper towels. Serve hot with African hot sauce.
1 oz	28 g	Red bell pepper, ⅛ inch (.3 cm) dice	
1 tbsp	1tbsp	Jalapeño, minced	
½ tsp	½ tsp	Ginger, grated	
as needed	as needed	Peanut oil, for frying	
as needed	as needed	African Hot Sauce (see recipe on page 341)	

Harissa

YIELD: 8 OUNCES

U.S.	METRIC	INGREDIENTS
2 oz	2 oz	Chile peppers, dried mixture of anchos, New Mexican, and guajillos
2 oz	2 oz	Cumin seeds
1 tsp	1 tsp	Paprika
4 oz	112 g	Onions, ¼ inch (.6 cm) dice
3 tbsp	3 tbsp	Flat-leaf parsley, chopped
8 oz	240 mL	Olive oil
to taste	to taste	Fresh lemon juice
to taste	to taste	Salt

PROCEDURE

1. Combine chile peppers, cumin seeds, and paprika over low heat, stirring constantly; toast 5 to 7 minutes. Cool.
2. Using a mortar and pestle, pulverize to a fine consistency.
3. Combine all ingredients and blend well.
4. Correct seasoning with lemon juice and salt

Mchuzi wa Biringani (Eggplant Curry) Eastern Africa

PORTIONS: 4

U.S.	METRIC	INGREDIENTS
16 oz	448 g	Eggplant, unpeeled, 1 inch (2.4 cm) cubes
2 oz	60 mL	Peanut oil
4 oz	112 g	Onions, ¼ inch (.6 cm) dice
2 tsp	2 tsp	Garam masala (see recipe on page 347) or curry powder
1 tsp	1 tsp	Ginger, grated
1 tbsp	1 tbsp	Garlic, minced
1	1	Green chile (serrano), seeded, minced
6 oz	168 g	Tomato, peeled, seeded, ½ inch dice
to taste	to taste	Salt, pepper, and cayenne pepper

PROCEDURE

1. Toss eggplant with a little salt; rub well and set aside 1 hour. Rinse and squeeze out as much liquid as possible from the eggplant cubes; pat dry with paper towels.
2. Heat oil over medium-high heat and sauté onions until soft, 3 minutes. Add garam masala, ginger, garlic and green chile. Cook, stirring continuously, 3 minutes.
3. Add eggplant; stir-fry until it begins to brown.
4. Add tomatoes and simmer until sauce is thickened and eggplant is tender.
5. Adjust seasoning.

Grilled Tilapia

PORTIONS: 4

U.S.	METRIC	INGREDIENTS
4 5-oz	4 112–140 g	Boneless, skinless tilapia fillets
4 oz	120 mL	Vegetable oil
4 oz	112 g	Onions, ¼ inch (.6 cm) dice
4 oz	112 g	Green bell pepper, ¼ inch (.6 cm) dice
½ oz	15 mL	Fresh lemon juice
2 tsp	10 mL	White vinegar
1 tsp	1 tsp	Cayenne
½ tsp	½ tsp	Salt
		African hot sauce (recipe follows)

PROCEDURE

1. Combine all the ingredients except the tilapia. Mix well, add the fish fillets and marinate for 30 minute to 1 hour.
2. Remove from marinade, grill, broil or sauté.
3. Serve with African hot sauce.

Note: Tilapia are native to the lakes and rivers of Africa, where it is called *ngege*. Outside of Africa, tilapia is called St. Peter's fish.

African Hot Sauce

PORTIONS: 4

U.S.	METRIC	INGREDIENTS
6	6	Chile peppers; dried mixture of anchos, New Mexican, and guajillos, or any hot red peppers
4 oz	112 g	Green bell pepper, stemmed, seeded, chopped
1	1	Garlic clove, chopped
2 oz	56 g	Onions, chopped
6 oz	168 g	Tomato paste
1 oz	30 mL	Water
½ tsp	½ tsp	Granulated sugar
½ tsp	½ tsp	Salt

PROCEDURE

1. Remove stems and seeds from peppers. Combine all ingredients in a food processor, or process to a paste using a mortar and pestle.
2. Simmer over medium heat 1 hour. Cool and serve.

Middle East

Tabbouleh (Cracked Wheat and Herb Salad)

PORTIONS: 4

U.S.	METRIC	INGREDIENTS
3.5 oz	98 g	Bulgur wheat, fine
10 oz	300 mL	Cold water
2.25 oz	63 g	Flat-leaf parsley, coarsely chopped
2 oz	48 g	Green onions, coarsely chopped
1 oz	28 g	Mint, coarsely chopped
1.5 oz	45 mL	Olive oil
¾ oz	23 mL	Fresh lemon juice
1 tsp	5 g	Salt
½ tsp	3 g	Black pepper, freshly ground
3 oz	84 g	Tomato, peeled, seeded ¼ inch (.6 cm) dice
4	4	Romaine leaves
2 oz	60 mL	Fresh lemon juice
½ tsp	½ tsp	Salt

PROCEDURE

1. Cover bulgur with cold water; soak 30 minutes. Drain through a fine sieve, pressing with back of a spoon to extract moisture. Spread out on a lined pan to dry further.
2. Wash parsley, shake off excess, and remove thick stalks. Wrap in cheesecloth and refrigerate for 30 minutes to dry and crisp.
3. Combine dry bulgur and green onions; squeeze mixture so bulgur absorbs onion flavor.
4. Chop parsley, measure, and add to bulgur with mint.
5. Combine olive oil, 1½ tablespoons (¾ ounce, 23 mL) lemon juice, 1 teaspoon (5 g) salt, and black pepper; add to bulgur and toss well.
6. Gently stir in tomato; cover and chill 1 hour or more.
7. Serve with romaine. Combine remaining lemon juice and salt to serve on the side, to be added according to individual taste.

Qahwah (Arabic Coffee)

YIELD: 8 OUNCES

U.S.	METRIC	INGREDIENTS
1	1	Cardamom pods
8 oz	240 mL	Water
½ oz	14 g	Dark roast ground coffee beans

PROCEDURE

1. Bruise cardamom pods.
2. Combine all ingredients and bring to boil.
3. Serve in Arabic coffee cups, half filled.

Traditionally a little silver urn of rose water or orange blossom water accompanies the coffee, so a few drops may be added to individual taste. Sugar is not generally served.

Note: Cardamom has a very strong flavor, and too much of it can cause a soapy taste.

Khobz (Whole Wheat Flat Bread)

YIELD: 6 ROUNDS

U.S.	METRIC	INGREDIENTS
6 oz	168 g	Whole wheat flour
½ tsp	3 g	Salt
½ cup	½ cup	Tepid water
as needed	as needed	Oil

PROCEDURE

1. Combine flour and salt.
2. Add water and work to a soft dough.
3. Knead for 10 minutes. Dough will feel slightly sticky at first but will become smooth as it is kneaded.
4. Cover and rest for at least 2 hours.
5. Divide dough into 6 even-sized balls the size of a large egg; roll out to 6-inch (15 cm) diameter rounds. Dough should be shaped without flour; dust lightly with white flour if needed.
6. Cover and rest rounds 20 minutes.
7. Heat a heavy frying pan or flat griddle. Cooking surface is hot enough when a little water sprinkled on bounces off the surface. Rub surface with a little oil.
8. Put in a round of dough and cook for about 1 minute, pressing top lightly with a folded cloth to encourage even bubbling of dough. When browned on the first side, turn and cook 1 minute or until bread looks cooked.
9. As breads are cooked, wrap in a cloth to keep soft and warm. Rub cooking surface occasionally with oil.

Note: Whole wheat: Whole grains that have been milled to a finer texture rather than leaving the grain intact become whole wheat. Whole wheat contains all the components of the grain, so whole wheat foods are also whole grain. Whole wheat bread and rye bread are typical examples of products made with whole wheat.

Falafel (Dried Bean Croquettes)

YIELD: ABOUT 35 CROQUETTES

U.S.	METRIC	INGREDIENTS
6 oz	168 g	Fava beans (broad beans), dried and shelled, soaked overnight and drained
6 oz	168 g	Garbanzo beans (chickpeas), dried, soaked overnight, and drained
2 oz	56 g	Onion, ¼ inch (.6 cm) dice
2	2	Garlic cloves
1 oz	28 g	Flat-leaf parsley, finely chopped
2 tbsp	6 g	Cilantro leaves, finely chopped
⅛ tsp	⅛ tsp	Hot chile pepper, ground
1 tsp	4 g	Coriander, ground
½ tsp	2 g	Cumin, ground
1 tsp	4 g	Baking soda
to taste	to taste	Salt and freshly ground black pepper
		Oil for deep-frying
as needed	as needed	Taratour bi tahini (recipe follows)
as needed	as needed	Khoubiz (Arabic flat bread; see recipe on page 344)

PROCEDURE

1. Combine fava beans, chickpeas, onion, and garlic and grind twice in food grinder using a fine die, or process in food processor to form a coarse paste.
2. Combine with remaining ingredients except oil and tahini. Knead well and let rest for 30 minutes. Correct seasoning.
3. Shape a tablespoon of the mixture at a time into balls, then flatten into thick patties 1½ inches (4 cm) in diameter. Let rest 30 minutes at room temperature.
4. Deep-fry in two inches of oil at 375°F (190°C), 6 to 8 at a time; cook 4 to 5 minutes, turning to brown evenly. Falafel should be toasty brown and crunchy on the outside. Remove and drain on a paper towel.
5. Serve hot as an appetizer with taratour bi tahini or in split khoubiz with the same sauce and salad vegetables.

Note: Favas have a wonderful flavor, but if you can't find them, dried white beans, such as cannellini or navy, can be substituted.

Taratour bi Tahini

YIELD: ABOUT 1½ CUPS

U.S.	METRIC	INGREDIENTS
2	2	Garlic cloves, crushed with ½ teaspoon salt
4 oz	120 mL	Tahini
2–4 oz	60–120 mL	Cold water
4 oz	120 mL	Fresh lemon juice
to taste	to taste	Salt

PROCEDURE

1. Using a food processor, combine garlic and tahini until smooth.
2. Beat in a little water and lemon juice alternately. The water thickens the mixture; lemon juice thins it.
3. Add all the lemon juice and enough water to give a thin or thick consistency, depending on the use. Correct seasoning; flavor should be tart.

Khubz Khoubiz (Arabic Flat Bread)

YIELD: 10 6-INCH KHUBZ

U.S.	METRIC	INGREDIENTS
4 oz	120 mL	Warm water
2 tsp	8 g	Active dry yeast
16 oz	448 g	Bread flour
1 tsp	5 g	Salt
8 oz	240 mL	Warm milk
as needed	as needed	Olive oil

PROCEDURE

1. Set a pizza stone on the bottom rack of a preheated 500°F (260°C) oven.
2. Combine warm water and yeast; let stand until foamy, about 10 minutes.
3. In a mixer, food processor, or by hand, combine flour and salt.
4. Add yeast mixture and then the warm milk; work to form dough.
5. On a lightly floured surface, knead one minute. Form the dough into a ball.
6. Lightly oil a bowl with olive oil. Transfer the dough to the bowl and turn to coat; cover and let rise in a warm place until doubled in bulk, about 1 hour.
7. Lightly dust a work surface with flour. Punch down dough and cut in half. Cut each half into 5 pieces, roll them into balls, then flatten into 6-inch rounds; cover. Let rise until puffy, 25 minutes.
8. Rub stone with oil and then slide dough rounds a few at a time onto it. Bake for 4 to 5 minutes until it puffs up like a balloon. To brown, turn quickly and leave for one minute. Remove bread and wrap in a cloth to keep warm and soft.

Note: To cook in a sauté pan, preheat pan on highest heat with lid on. When heated, oil the base of the pan quickly and slide in the dough. Cover and cook 3 minutes, remove lid, turn bread over, re-cover, and cook 2 minutes.

Baba Ghannouj Moutabal (Eggplant Dip)

PORTIONS: 4

U.S.	METRIC	INGREDIENTS
12 oz	336 g	Eggplant
2 oz	60 mL	Fresh lemon juice
2 oz	60 mL	Tahini
2	2	Garlic cloves
2 tsp	10 g	Salt
½ oz	15 mL	Olive oil
½ oz	14 g	Flat-leaf parsley, chopped fine
as needed	as needed	Khoubiz (Arabic flat bread; see recipe above)

PROCEDURE

1. Grill eggplant or roast in a hot oven, turning often; cook until soft.
2. Peel off skin while hot and remove stem and end if still firm.
3. Chop flesh and pound to a puree in a mortar with pestle, or puree in a blender or food processor.
4. Blend in ¾ of the lemon juice and gradually add the tahini.
5. Crush garlic to a paste with 1 teaspoon salt and add to eggplant. Beat well; adjust flavor with more lemon juice and salt.
6. Beat in olive oil and parsley. Do not puree the parsley.
7. Serve with khoubiz as an appetizer.

Muhammara (Red Pepper and Walnut Dip)

PORTIONS: 4

U.S.	METRIC	INGREDIENTS
1 lb	448 g	Red bell peppers
2 oz	56 g	Walnuts, coarsely ground
2 tbsp	2 tbsp	Bread crumbs or sesame cracker crumbs
½ oz	15 mL	Pomegranate molasses
½ oz	15 mL	Fresh lemon juice
½ tsp, plus more for dusting	½ tsp, plus more for dusting	Cumin, ground
½ tsp	½ tsp	Aleppo pepper, or ¼ teaspoon crushed red pepper or red chile paste
to taste	to taste	Salt and pepper
½ oz	15 mL	Olive oil

PROCEDURE

1. Roast bell peppers over gas flame or under broiler, turning until blackened and blistered. Wrap with film or place in a bag to steam 10 minutes to loosen the skin. Let cool slightly; remove skin, membranes, stems, and seeds. Allow to drain.
2. Combine walnuts and bread crumbs in a food processor and process until finely ground.
3. Add bell peppers, pomegranate molasses, lemon juice, cumin, and aleppo or crushed red pepper; blend until creamy. Adjust seasoning with salt, pepper, and aleppo or crushed peppers.
4. Chill at least two hours.
5. Serve with a dusting of ground cumin and a drizzle of olive oil.

Fattoush (Toasted Bread Salad)

PORTIONS: 4

U.S.	METRIC	INGREDIENTS
1 6-inch	1 6-inch	Khoubiz, toasted golden brown, ½ inch (1.2 cm) dice
6 oz	168 g	Romaine, shredded or broken into small pieces
4 oz	112 g	Cucumber, peeled, ½ inch (1.2 cm) dice
6 oz	168 g	Tomato, peeled, seeded, ½ inch (1.2 cm) dice
1 oz	28 g	Green onion, chopped
½ oz	14 g	Flat-leaf parsley, chopped
3 tbsp	3 tbsp	Fresh mint, chopped
3 oz	84 g	Green bell pepper, ½ inch (1.2 cm) dice
as needed	as needed	Salad dressing (recipe follows)

PROCEDURE

1. Combine all ingredients and toss with salad dressing.

Salad Dressing

U.S.	METRIC	INGREDIENTS
1	1	Garlic clove
1 tsp	1 tsp	Salt
4 oz	120 mL	Fresh lemon juice
4 oz	120 mL	Olive oil
to taste	to taste	Black pepper

PROCEDURE

1. Mash garlic with salt and stir in remaining ingredients.

Garithes Saganaki (Baked Shrimp)

PORTIONS: 4

U.S.	METRIC	INGREDIENTS
1 lb	448 g	16–20 count uncooked shrimp, peeled and deveined
1 oz	30 mL	Fresh lemon juice
2 oz	60 mL	Olive oil
4 oz	112 g	Onions, ¼ inch (.6 cm) dice
1 oz	28 g	Pepperoncini, minced
2	2	Garlic cloves, minced
2 oz	56 g	Green onion, minced
6 oz	240 mL	Tomatoes, peeled, seeded, ¼ inch (.6 cm) dice
2 oz	60 mL	Dry white wine
½ oz	14 g	Parsley, chopped
½ tsp	½ tsp	Oregano
to taste	to taste	Salt and pepper
2 oz	56 g	Feta cheese, crumbled

PROCEDURE

1. Sprinkle the cleaned shrimp with lemon juice and let stand until sauce is ready.
2. Heat oil over medium heat and sauté onions until transparent, 2 to 3 minutes. Add pepperoncini and garlic and cook 2 minutes; add green onion and cook 1 minute.
3. Add tomato to onion mixture and cook 5 minutes. Add shrimp, white wine, and half the parsley and oregano; cook 2 minutes. Correct seasoning.
4. Spoon half the tomato sauce into 4 individual oven dishes or 1 large dish. Add shrimp and spoon remaining sauce over shrimp; top with crumbled cheese.
5. Bake in a 450°F (232°C) oven for 6 to 7 minutes or until shrimp are firm (160°F, 71.1°C) and the feta is melted and lightly browned. Do not overcook or the shrimp will be tough.
6. Sprinkle with remaining parsley and serve with crusty bread.

Sis Kebap (Skewered Lamb and Vegetables)

PORTIONS: 4

U.S.	METRIC	INGREDIENTS
20 oz	560 g	Lamb meat, boneless from leg, 1¼ inch (3.18 cm) cubes
1 oz	30 mL	Fresh lemon juice
2 oz	60 mL	Olive oil
3 oz	84 g	Onion, thinly sliced
to taste	to taste	Black pepper, freshly ground
1	1	Bay leaf, crumbled
½ tsp	½ tsp	Thyme, dried
8	8	Wooden skewers, soaked in water 1 hour
Garnish		
8	8	Pearl onions, peeled and parboiled in salted water
8 cubes	8 cubes	Red bell pepper, cored, seeded, white membrane removed, cut in 1¼ inch (3.18 cm) cubes
8 cubes	8 cubes	Green bell pepper, cored, seeded, white membrane removed, cut in 1¼ inch (3.18 cm) cubes

PROCEDURE

1. Combine lamb cubes, lemon juice, olive oil, onions, black pepper, bay leaf, and thyme. Do not add salt, it draws out the meat juices. Mix well and marinate at room temperature 1 hour or refrigerate 2 to 3 hours.
2. Blanch bell peppers in boiling salted water for 30 seconds; let cool.
3. To assemble skewers, remove meat from marinade and thread onto 8 skewers, alternating cubes of meat with onions and peppers.
4. Grill over medium high heat, turning frequently and brushing with marinade when required. After searing meat, move to lower heat to avoid burning vegetables.
5. Serve hot on a bed of Beyaz Pilav, colored with turmeric.

India

Garam Masala (Ground Spice Mixture)

PORTIONS: 4

U.S.	METRIC	INGREDIENTS
½	½	Whole nutmeg
3 tbsp	3 tbsp	Cardamom seeds
2 tbsp	2 tbsp	Whole cloves
2 tbsp	2 tbsp	Whole cumin
1 tbsp	1 tbsp	Whole coriander
2 tbsp	2 tbsp	Whole black peppercorns
3 in	3 in	Cinnamon stick
4	4	Bay leaf

PROCEDURE

1. Dry-roast all ingredients separately in a heated heavy skillet over medium heat until the spices emit a toasty aroma. Let cool.
2. Combine all ingredients except nutmeg in a clean spice grinder and grind them into a very fine powder or use a mortar and pestle. Finely grate nutmeg.
3. Store in a tightly closed jar until needed.

Podina Chatni (Green Chutney)

PORTIONS: 4

U.S.	METRIC	INGREDIENTS
2 oz	56 g	Mint leaves, picked
⅓ oz	8 g	Cilantro leaves
1	1	Green chile (jalapeño), seeded
2 oz	56 g	Green onions, 1 inch (2.4 cm) lengths
2 oz	60 mL	Jalapeño, seeded, minced
to taste	to taste	Lemon juice
1 tsp	1 tsp	Garam masala (see recipe above)
2 tsp	2 tsp	Granulated sugar
1 teaspoon	1 tsp	Salt
2 oz	60 mL	Water

PROCEDURE

1. Place all ingredients in a food processor and purée, or pound in mortar and pestle a little at a time, until ground to a paste. If too dry, add a little oil and/or water. Chill.

Tamarind Sauce

PORTIONS: 4

U.S.	METRIC	INGREDIENTS
3½ oz	105 g	Tamarind paste
5 oz	150 g	Palm sugar
16 oz	480 mL	Water
to taste	to taste	Cayenne pepper
to taste	to taste	Salt

PROCEDURE

1. Combine tamarind, sugar, and water; bring to a boil, reduce to a simmer, and cook to a jamlike consistency.
2. Add salt and cayenne to taste.

Note: Frequently used in Indian cuisine, dark brown, crumbly palm sugar—also known as jaggery or *gur*—is made from the reduced sap of either the sugar palm or the palmyra palm. Substitute brown sugar only as a last resort.

Basmati Chaaval (Plain Basmati Rice)

PORTIONS: 4 TO 6

U.S.	METRIC	INGREDIENTS
15 oz	450 g	Long-grain rice
1 tsp	1 tsp	Salt
½ oz	15 mL	Butter
19 oz	570 mL	Water

PROCEDURE

1. Wash rice in several changes of water. Drain.
2. Soak rice in 5 cups (40 ounces, 1.2 L) water 30 minutes. Drain thoroughly.
3. Combine rice, salt, butter, and water. Bring to boil. Cover with a tight-fitting lid, turn heat to low, and cook for 20 minutes.
4. Lift lid, mix gently but quickly with a fork, and cover again.
5. Cook additional 5 to 10 minutes or until rice is tender.

Kheere ka Raita (Yogurt with Cucumber and Mint)

PORTIONS: 4

U.S.	METRIC	INGREDIENTS
12 oz	360 mL	Plain yogurt
4 oz	120 mL	Cucumber, peeled, coarsely grated
1½ tbsp	1½ tbsp	Fresh mint, chopped
½ tsp	½ tsp	Cumin seeds, roasted and ground
¼ tsp	¼ tsp	Cayenne pepper
to taste	to taste	Salt and freshly ground black pepper

PROCEDURE

1. Whisk yogurt until smooth and creamy.
2. Combine all ingredients and correct seasoning.

Pork Vindaloo

PORTIONS: 4

U.S.	METRIC	INGREDIENTS	PROCEDURE
Marinade			1. Combine all ingredients except pork and mix well. Add pork, and marinate 1 hour.
1½ oz	120 mL	Malt vinegar	
1½ tsp	1½ tsp	Black peppercorns, crushed	
1½ tsp	1½ tsp	Brown sugar or jaggery	
8	8	Cardamom seeds, green	
8	8	Cloves	
3	3	Green chiles, seeded	
to taste	to taste	Salt	
1½ lb	1½ lb	Boneless pork shoulder, 1 inch (2.4 cm) cubes	
Vindaloo Spice Mixture			2. Using a mortar and pestle or blender, make a paste with the garlic, ginger, spices, and vinegar.
4	4	Garlic cloves, chopped	
½ oz	½ oz	Ginger, peeled, chopped	
2	2	Red chiles, seeded	
½ tsp	½ tsp	Mustard seed	
½ tsp	½ tsp	Fenugreek seed	
1 tsp	1 tsp	Cumin seeds	
2 tsp	2 tsp	Coriander seeds	
½ tsp	½ tsp	Turmeric	
½ tsp	½ tsp	Cinnamon, ground	
1 oz	30 mL	Malt vinegar	
1½ oz	45 mL	Oil	3. Heat the oil over medium heat, add onions, and cook until golden brown, 6 to 8 minutes.
6 oz	168 g	Onions, ¼ inch (.6 cm) dice	4. Add spice paste and cook over medium low heat, 10 minutes, or until the oil separates from the paste. Add up to 2 tablespoons (1 ounce, 30 mL) water, if necessary. 5. Remove pork cubes from marinade and add to pan. Cook 5 minutes over medium-high heat, stirring constantly. Add marinade. 6. Add 1 cup (8 ounces, 240 mL) warm water. Bring to simmer, cover, and lower heat. Cook 45 minutes or until pork is tender. Stir to prevent sticking.

Note: Pork Vindaloo is the benchmark of Goan food. Goa is a tiny state on the west coast of India, famous for its distinctive cuisine.

Naan

PORTIONS: 4

U.S.	METRIC	INGREDIENTS
1 oz	30 mL	Milk, 110°F (43°C)
1 tsp	1 tsp	Granulated sugar
1 tsp	1 tsp	Dry yeast
8 oz	224 g	All-purpose flour
½ tsp	½ tsp	Baking powder
¼ tsp	¼ tsp	Salt
2 oz	60 mL	Yogurt
2 oz	60 mL	Milk
1	1	Egg yolk
2 oz	60 mL	Ghee

PROCEDURE

1. Combine the milk and sugar; stir to dissolve. Sprinkle yeast over and let stand until the yeast begins to froth, about 10 minutes.
2. Sift together flour, baking powder, and salt.
3. In another container, mix together the yogurt, milk, egg yolk, and ghee.
4. Make a well in the center of the flour and add the liquid mixtures; work to form dough.
5. On a floured surface, knead the dough until it is smooth and elastic, 15 minutes.
6. Shape into a ball, cover, and let stand in warm area 1 hour.
7. Set a heavy baking tray (sheet pan) on the bottom rack of a preheated 500°F (260°C) oven. Preheat broiler.
8. Divide dough into 6 equal pieces and shape into balls. Flatten a piece of dough with your palm, dust with flour, and roll the dough from the center outward into a tear-shaped naan, about 8 inches (19.2 cm) long and 4 inches (9.6 cm) at its widest.
9. Remove the hot baking tray from the oven and slap the naan on to it. Immediately return the tray to the oven for 3 minutes; the naan should puff up.
10. Place the baking tray and naan under the broiler, about 3 to 4 inches (7.2–9.6 cm) away from the heat, for about 30 seconds or until the top of the naan browns slightly.
11. Wrap naan and serve hot.

Chana Dal (Yellow Dal)

PORTIONS: 4

U.S.	METRIC	INGREDIENTS
9 oz	250 g	Chana dal (Indian yellow split peas)
40 oz	1 L	Water
1	1	Dried red chile, soaked and seeded
3	3	Ginger, unpeeled, sliced ¼ inch (.6 cm) thin
¼ tsp	¼ tsp	Turmeric, ground
¼ tsp	¼ tsp	Garam masala (p. 347)
to taste	to taste	Salt
1½ oz	45 mL	Ghee
1 tsp	1 tsp	Cumin seeds
2	2	Garlic cloves, chopped
½ tsp	½ tsp	Red chile powder

PROCEDURE

1. Pick over dal to remove small stones and discolored seeds. Put in a bowl of water, soak 15 minutes, and remove any that float. Wash well and drain thoroughly.
2. Combine dal and water, bring to a boil, and remove any surface scum.
3. Add red chile, ginger, and turmeric. Cover, leaving lid slightly ajar, and simmer gently 45 to 50 minutes or until the dal is tender. Stir every 5 minutes to prevent sticking. Remove ginger slices and chile. Add garam masala and salt; stir to mix.
4. Heat the ghee over medium heat. When hot, add cumin seeds; 10 seconds later add garlic. Cook until garlic is slightly brown. Add chile powder, stir to mix, and immediately add contents of pan to the dal. Stir to mix.

Note: Chana dal is perhaps the "meatiest" tasting, with the slight sweetness of all the dals. Yellow split peas may be substituted; however, they are not the same.

Southeast Asia

Satay Ayam (Chicken Satay)

PORTIONS: 4

U.S.	METRIC	INGREDIENTS
1 lb	448 g	Chicken thigh meat, boneless, skinless
1 stalk	1 stalk	Lemongrass, finely minced
2	2	Garlic cloves, minced
½ tsp	½ tsp	Turmeric, ground
½ tsp	½ tsp	Fennel, ground
½ tsp	½ tsp	Cumin, ground
1 oz	30 mL	Vegetable oil
to taste	to taste	Salt
		12-inch bamboo skewers, soaked in water for 1 hour

PROCEDURE

1. Slice chicken across the grain into thin slices ¼ inch (.6 cm) wide by 3 to 4 inches (7.2 to 9.6 cm) long.
2. Combine lemongrass, garlic, turmeric, fennel, cumin, and oil to a paste. Add chicken, mix well, and let stand 2 hours.
3. Remove from marinate and thread on to skewers. Season with salt before cooking.
4. Grill or broil, basting occasionally with oil.
5. Serve hot or warm with peanut sauce and cucumber salad.

Sambal Kacang (Bumbu Sate) Peanut Sauce

YIELD: 1 CUP (8 OZ, 240 ML)

U.S.	METRIC	INGREDIENTS
2 tsp	2 tsp	Coriander seed, toasted
1 tsp	1 tsp	Fennel seed, toasted
1 tsp	1 tsp	Cumin seed, toasted
6	6	Dry red chiles, seeded and soaked
½ tsp	½ tsp	Shrimp paste
5	5	Shallots, sliced thin
2	2	Garlic clove, sliced thin
½ oz	15 mL	Vegetable oil
2½ oz	75 g	Peanuts, roasted, roughly ground (crunchy peanut butter)
6 oz	180 mL	Coconut milk
1 tbsp	1 tbsp	Tamarind paste, dissolved in 4 tablespoons (2 ounces, 60 mL) water
1 tsp	1 tsp	Palm sugar
to taste	to taste	Salt and pepper

PROCEDURE

1. Grind the dry spices in a spice grinder or mortar and pestle.
2. Pound or process the chiles, shrimp paste, shallots, and garlic into a paste.
3. Over low heat, sauté the paste lightly until fragrant in oil, 1 minute. Add the dry spices and cook 1 minute. Be careful not to burn the paste after adding the dry spices.
4. Add the peanuts, coconut milk, tamarind, and sugar. Simmer about 10 minutes, adding water if the sauce thickens too fast.
5. Adjust seasoning and serve warm.

Thai Papaya and Mango Salad

PORTIONS: 12 PORTION SIZE: 4 OZ (125 G)

U.S.	METRIC	INGREDIENTS	PROCEDURE
6 fl oz	180 mL	Lime juice	1. Mix the lime juice, fish sauce, chiles, scallions, and sugar. Stir until the sugar is dissolved.
1 fl oz	30 mL	Nam pla (Thai fish sauce) or nuoc nam (Vietnamese fish sauce)	
2	2	Serrano chiles, seeded, chopped fine	
2	2	Scallions, chopped fine	
1 oz	30 g	Brown sugar or raw sugar	
1½ lb	750 g	Mango, medium dice	2. Mix the mango and papaya.
1½ lb	750 g	Papaya, medium dice	3. Arrange 1 oz (30 g) cabbage on each salad plate.
12 oz	360 g	Napa cabbage, shredded	4. Top with a mound of the fruit mixture.
4 tbsp	60 mL	Chopped peanuts	5. Drizzle each portion with 4 tsp (20 mL) dressing.
			6. Sprinkle each portion with 1 tsp (5 mL) chopped peanuts.

Per serving: Calories, 100; Protein, 2 g; Fat, 1.5 g (13% cal.); Cholesterol, 0 mg; Carbohydrates, 21 g; Fiber, 3 g; Sodium, 240 mg.

Thai Papaya and Mango Salad

Dua Chua (Pickled Carrot and Daikon Salad)

PORTIONS: 4

U.S.	METRIC	INGREDIENTS
8 oz	224 g	Carrots, julienned
8 oz	224 g	Daikon, julienned
1 tsp	1 tsp	Salt
4 oz	120 mL	Water
5½ oz	165 mL	Rice wine vinegar
2 oz	56 g	Granulated sugar
½ tsp	½ tsp	Vietnamese fish sauce (*nuoc mam*)
1 tbsp	1 tbsp	Cilantro leaves, shredded
1 tbsp	1 tbsp	Mint leaves, shredded
1 tbsp	1 tbsp	Basil leaves, shredded

PROCEDURE

1. Combine carrots, daikon, and salt; toss to coat. Place in a colander to drain for 30 minutes. Rinse and squeeze dry.
2. Combine water, vinegar, sugar, and fish sauce, bring to a boil, and cool to room temperature.
3. Add vegetables to cool vinegar mixture and let marinate 1 hour.
4. Just before serving, toss with herbs.

Pho Bo (Vietnamese Beef and Noodle Soup)

YIELD: 3 TO 4 QUARTS

U.S.	METRIC	INGREDIENTS
1 lb	448 g	Oxtail, cut 3 inch (7.2 cm) pieces
1 lb	448 g	Beef bones
64 oz	1.92 L	Beef stock
½ oz	15 mL	Vegetable oil
2	2	Onions, cut in ¼ inch (.6 cm) slices
8 oz	224 g	Daikon, chopped
1½ oz	42 g	Ginger, peeled, sliced
3	3	Green onions, crushed
3	3	Garlic cloves
1	1	Cinnamon stick, 2 inch (4.8 cm)
1 piece	1 piece	Star anise
1 tsp	1 tsp	Black pepper
Garnish		
4 oz	112 g	Dried rice sticks (*bahn pho*), soaked in hot water for 30 minutes, drained
8 oz	224 g	Flank steak, cut very thin
4 oz	112 g	Bean sprouts
4 oz	112 g	Red onions, thinly sliced
1	1	Green chili pepper (jalapeño), sliced thinly
2 oz	56 g	Green onions, ½ inch pieces
1 oz	28 g	Cilantro leaves, fresh
1 oz	28 g	Mint leaves, fresh
1 oz	28 g	Basil leaves, fresh
1 oz	30 mL	Vietnamese fish sauce (*nuoc mam*)
8	8	Lime wedges

PROCEDURE

1. Rinse the oxtail and beef bones. Cover with cold stock and additional water if necessary, bring to a slow boil. Reduce heat and simmer, skim as necessary for the first 30 minutes.
2. Heat oil and add sliced onions; cook, stirring until the onions are browned. Remove and drain the fat.
3. After the stock has stopped foaming add the browned onions, daikon, ginger, green onions, garlic, cinnamon, star anise and black pepper. Simmer and continue to skim for 2 hours. Strain the stock using two layers of cheese cloth. Remove oxtail and shred the meat; serve with the soup.
4. Blanch the bean sprouts in boiling water for 3 seconds. Drain, rinse with cold water and drain.
5. Arrange the sliced beef on a platter. Garnish with red onions, sliced chilies, lime wedges, mint leaves, and basil.
6. At serving time, cook rice sticks in boiling water to heat. Drain.
7. Divide rice sticks equally among 4 serving bowls.
8. Season hot beef stock with fish sauce and black pepper.
9. Each person adds cooked beef, raw flank steak and red onions to their noodles; ladle hot stock over the meat, stirring to cook the meat.
10. Add green chili, bean sprouts, cilantro, mint, basil, and lime to taste.

China

Pungent and Hot Soup (Hot and Sour Soup)

PORTIONS: 4

U.S.	METRIC	INGREDIENTS
Seasoning		
1 tsp	1 tsp	Tapioca powder or cornstarch
1½ tsp	1½ tsp	Soy sauce
¼ tsp	¼ tsp	Sugar
3 oz	84 g	Pork, lean boneless, julienned ⅛ × ⅛ × 2 inches (.3 × .3 × 5 cm)
Hot and Sour Mixture		
1½ tsp	7 mL	Sesame oil
½ oz	15 mL	Soy sauce
½ tsp	½ tsp	White pepper
½ oz	15 mL	Black or rice vinegar
½ tsp	½ tsp	Sugar
3 cups	3 cups	Chicken stock
3	3	Medium dried black mushrooms, soaked in hot water 5 minutes, or until soft, rinsed thoroughly, tough ends trimmed; cut into ⅛ × ⅛ × 2 inch (.3 × .3 × 5 cm) pieces
¼ oz	4 g	Dried black cloud ears, soaked in hot water 20 minutes, cut into ⅙ × ⅙ × 2 inch (.3 × .3 × 5 cm) pieces
3 oz	84 g	Bamboo shoots, ⅛ × ⅛ × 2 inches (.3 × .3 × 5 cm)
1½ tsp	1½ tsp	Tapioca powder or cornstarch
½ oz	15 mL	Water
6 oz	168 g	Soft bean curd, ⅛ × ⅛ × 2 inches (.3 × .3 × 5 cm)
1	1	Egg, lightly beaten
1 tbsp	1 tbsp	Green onion, minced
2 tbsp	2 tbsp	Cilantro leaves and short stems, 2 inches (5 cm)

PROCEDURE

1. Mix seasoning ingredients and combine with julienne pork; mix well.
2. Combine hot and sour mixture ingredients.
3. Bring chicken stock to a boil; add mushrooms, bamboo shoots, and pork shreds. Bring back to a boil; reduce heat to medium. Stir to separate pork shreds and cook for 5 minutes.
4. Reduce heat to low. Mix 1½ tablespoons tapioca powder with the water and add gradually to soup, stirring constantly until thickened. Add bean curd.
5. Add hot and sour mixture to soup. Stir, correct seasoning.
6. Return to a boil, using a ladle float the eggs in very thin petals. Immediately remove from heat. Allow soup to set for 15 seconds. Garnish with green onion and cilantro.

Note: Different versions of this soup are found in northern, eastern, central, and even southern China. This northern version has the lightest color.

Chinese black mushrooms are the dried mushrooms sold in Asian grocery stores. The name is a bit of a misnomer, since Chinese black mushrooms can be light brown, dark brown, and even gray. They are frequently speckled.

Red-Cooked Duck

PORTIONS: 4

U.S.	METRIC	INGREDIENTS
3½ lb	1.5 kg	Young duck, cut in quarters
1 oz	30 mL	Vegetable oil
1	1	Garlic clove, flattened
2	2	Green onions, ¼ inch (.6 cm) lengths
1	1	Star anise
2 tsp	2 tsp	Tapioca powder or cornstarch
½ oz	15 mL	Water
1 tsp	1 tsp	Sesame oil
to taste	to taste	Salt
Marinade		
2 tsp	2 tsp	Ginger juice
1 oz	30 mL	Dry sherry
1 oz	30 mL	Dark soy sauce
½ tsp	½ tsp	Salt
Braising Mixture		
16 oz	480 mL	Chicken stock
½ oz	15 mL	Oyster sauce
½ oz	14 g	Rock sugar or granulated sugar
1	1	Thai bird chile (small red)

PROCEDURE

1. Remove excess loose fat from duck, then flatten the duck. Rinse and pat dry. Prick the skin.
2. Combine marinade ingredients, mix well, and rub evenly on the skin and cavity. Let marinate at room temperature for at least 1 hour, turning occasionally.
3. Drain duck, reserving excess marinade. Set wok over high heat; when hot, add 2 (1 ounce, 30 mL) tablespoons oil. Swish oil around and then place duck in wok. Turn heat to medium and brown the duck slowly and evenly on all sides.
4. Mix together the braising mixture and bring to boil over high heat, then add the duck. Return to a boil; add reserved marinade, garlic, green onion, and star anise. Cover and reduce to a simmer; cook 1 to 1½ hours or until a chopstick pierces through the thigh easily. Remove duck and chile; degrease the sauce.
5. Return braising liquid to a boil, add duck to reheat, remove, drain, cut into serving pieces, and place on serving platter.
6. Mix tapioca powder with the water and add to the liquid in the wok, stirring constantly until thickened. Correct seasoning, then glaze sauce with sesame oil. Pour over duck. Serve hot or cold.

Note: Cold Red-Cooked Duck is outstanding, should be served garnished with cilantro.

Sichuan Spicy Fired Beef Shreds

PORTIONS: 4

U.S.	METRIC	INGREDIENTS
16 oz	448 g	Flank steak, ⅛ × ⅛ × 1½ inch (.3 × .3 × 3.6 cm) shreds
4½ oz	135 mL	Vegetable oil
2	2	Garlic cloves, flattened
3	3	Dried hot chiles, seeds removed
4 oz	112 g	Celery, ⅛ × ⅛ × 1½ inch (.3 × .3 × 3.6 cm) shreds
2 oz	56 g	Carrot, peeled, ⅛ × ⅛ × 1½ inch (.3 × .3 × 3.6 cm) shreds
3	3	Fresh hot chiles, ⅛ × ⅛ × 1½ inch (.3 × .3 × 3.6 cm) shreds
to taste	to taste	Salt
1 tbsp	1 tbsp	Sesame oil
Marinade		
2 oz	60 mL	Dark soy sauce
		Juice of 3 slices gingerroot
½ oz	15 mL	Dry sherry
2 tsp	10 g	Granulated sugar

PROCEDURE

1. Mix marinade ingredients, add the meat, and toss. Let sit at room temperature for at least 30 minutes. Turn the meat occasionally.
2. Set wok over high heat; when very hot add ½ cup (4 ounces, 120 mL) oil. Flavor the oil with the garlic; remove the garlic when it turns brown.
3. Add meat; stir-fry 1 to 2 minutes, or until strips separate. Turn heat to medium low; continue to stir-fry until strips turn brown, 1 to 2 minutes; remove from wok.
4. Rinse wok and wipe dry. Set on medium high heat; when hot, add sesame oil. Flavor oil with dried chile until brown. Add celery, carrots, and fresh chiles, stirring 30 seconds to 1 minute; season with salt.
5. Return meat and mix with vegetables. Glaze the meat with sesame oil and serve with rice.

Tea Leaf Eggs

PORTIONS: 4

U.S.	METRIC	INGREDIENTS
4	4	Large eggs
Tea Leaf Mixture		
24 oz	720 mL	Water
½ oz	15 mL	Dark soy sauce
1	1	Star anise, whole
2 tsp	2 tsp	Salt
2 tbsp	2 tbsp	Green tea leaves
½ oz	15 mL	Rock sugar

PROCEDURE

1. Combine eggs and enough cold water to cover. Bring to a boil and cook 10 minutes.
2. Remove eggs and immerse in ice water until cool.
3. Using a tablespoon, tap the shells gently to make fine cracks.
4. Combine tea-leaf ingredients and bring to a boil. Add the cracked eggs and bring back to a boil. Turn heat to low and simmer for 30 minutes.
5. Remove pan from heat and let eggs cool to room temperature.
6. Shell the eggs and serve cold.

Korea

Kimchi (Traditional Napa Cabbage)

YIELD: 1 GALLON

U.S.	METRIC	INGREDIENTS
8½ oz	238 g	Salt
64 oz	1.92 L	Water
2	2	Napa cabbage heads, cut into 2 inch (5 cm) wedges
1	1	Garlic head, cloves separated and peeled
2	2	Ginger root, 1 inch (2.4 cm) pieces
2 oz	60 ml	Fish sauce or Korean salted shrimp
1 bunch	1 bunch	Green onion, 1 inch (2.4 cm) pieces
4 oz	112 g	Korean ground chile
1 tsp	1 tsp	Granulated sugar

PROCEDURE

1. Dissolve 1 cup (8 ounces, 224 g) salt in water. Soak cabbage in salt water 3 to 4 hours.
2. Combine garlic, ginger, and fish sauce and process until almost smooth.
3. Combine green onions, garlic mixture, chile, 1 tablespoon (½ ounce, 14 g) salt, and sugar.
4. Drain cabbage and rinse thoroughly. Drain well in colander, squeezing as much water from the leaves as possible.
5. Spread green onion/chile mixture between cabbage leaves, making sure to fill each leaf adequately.
6. When all the cabbage has been stuffed, wrap a few of the larger leaves tightly around the rest of the cabbage, making tight bundles.
7. Divide cabbage among four 1-quart (960 mL) jars or one 1-gallon (1.28 L) jar, pressing down firmly to remove any air bubbles.
8. Let stand 2 to 3 days in the refrigerator to ferment.

Kalbi-Kui (Barbecue Beef Ribs)

PORTIONS: 4

U.S.	METRIC	INGREDIENTS
4 oz	120 mL	Soy sauce
1 oz	28 g	Granulated sugar
¼ tsp	¼ tsp	Dry mustard
¼ tsp	¼ tsp	Black pepper, freshly ground
1 tsp	1 tsp	Sesame seeds
1 oz	30 mL	Rice vinegar
1 oz	30 mL	Sesame oil
1 tsp	1 tsp	Ginger, minced
4	4	Garlic cloves, minced
1 oz	28 g	Green onions, chopped
2½ lb	1.12 kg	Korean-style short ribs (beef chuck flanken), cut ⅓ to ½ inch (.83 cm to 1.2 cm) thick across the bones, about 8 to 10 pieces

PROCEDURE

1. Combine all ingredients except short ribs; whisk well.
2. Trim the excess fat from the ribs. Score the meat deeply every ½ inch (1.2 cm), almost to the bone.
3. Add short ribs to the marinade and coat evenly, turning the meat so the scored side is face-down in the marinade. Cover and let stand at least 3 hours, or refrigerate overnight, if possible.
4. Broil over charcoal, grill, or cook under a broiler. Look for outside to become crisp.

South America and the Caribbean

Ceviche Mixto (Shellfish Ceviche)

PORTIONS: 4

U.S.	METRIC	INGREDIENTS
Marinade		
2 oz	60 mL	Fresh lemon juice
2 oz	60 mL	Fresh lime juice
4 oz	120 mL	Fresh orange juice
4 oz	120 mL	Fish or chicken stock
½ oz	14 mL	Olive oil
½ tsp	3 g	Sugar
½ tsp	3 g	Salt
¼ tsp	2 g	Black pepper, freshly ground
to taste	to taste	Hot pepper sauce

PROCEDURE

1. Combine all ingredients and mix well.

U.S.	METRIC	INGREDIENTS
32 oz	938 mL	Water
1	1	Green onion, white part and 1 inch green, sliced
12 oz	340 g	Shrimp (16–20 count), peeled and deveined
6 oz	168 g	Scallops, rinsed
2 oz	60 mL	Dry white wine
12 oz	340 g	Mussels, scrubbed and debearded
12	12	Baby clams

2. Bring water and green onion to boil; let simmer 5 minutes. Add shrimp, remove from heat, and let stand 1 minute or until shrimp are just cooked. Remove from hot water (reserving the cooking liquid) and cool shrimp so they do not become rubbery.
3. Return cooking liquid to boil, add scallops, remove from heat, and let stand for 3 minutes, depending on size. Cut a scallop in half to see if it is cooked through (it should be milky white in the center). Drain and rinse under cold running water.
4. Bring wine, mussels, and clams to a boil over high heat. Cover and let cook until the shells are open, 3 to 5 minutes. Discard any clams or mussels that do not open. Remove clams and mussels from shells and discard shells. Cool shellfish.
5. Combine cooked shellfish with marinade and refrigerate for at least 2 hours.
6. Before serving, check seasoning for salt, sugar, and hot pepper sauce.

U.S.	METRIC	INGREDIENTS
Garnishes		
3 oz	84 g	Tomato, peeled, seeded, ¼ inch (.6 cm) dice
2 oz	56 g	Green bell pepper, seeded, ⅛ inch (.3 cm) dice
2 oz	56 g	White onion, ⅛ inch (.3 cm) dice, rinsed with hot water, and drained
2 tbsp	6 g	Cilantro, leaves only, minced
2 tbsp	6 g	Parsley, minced

7. Divide seafood equally between four serving containers. Garnish each in the center with 1 teaspoon each chopped tomato, bell pepper, onion, cilantro, and parsley.
8. Serve with the side dishes.
   - Popcorn
   - Tostado (corn nuts)

Jamaican Jerk Chicken

PORTIONS: 4

U.S.	METRIC	INGREDIENTS
2 oz	60 mL	Fresh lime juice
2 oz	60 mL	Water
3½ lb	3½ lb	Whole chicken, cut into eighths
2	2	Garlic cloves, minced
Jerk Marinade		
2 tsp	2 tsp	Jamaican pimiento, ground
½ tsp	½ tsp	Nutmeg, grated
½ tsp	½ tsp	Mace, ground
1 tsp	1 tsp	Salt
1 tsp	1 tsp	Sugar
2 tsp	2 tsp	Dried thyme
1 tsp	1 tsp	Black pepper
4 oz	112 g	Green onions, chopped
4 oz	112 g	Yellow onion, chopped
1	1	Whole Scotch bonnet
1 oz	30 mL	Vegetable oil

PROCEDURE

1. Preheat grill.
2. Combine lime juice and water and use to rinse chicken. Pat dry and rub with garlic.
3. Combine remaining ingredients in a blender, mortar, or food processor. Process ingredients to almost smooth and pour over chicken; marinate in refrigerator for at least 2 hours.
4. Remove chicken from marinade.
5. Grill, turning often, until fully cooked. Cut chicken into 8 to 12 pieces.

Chimichurri Sauce

PORTIONS: 4–6

U.S.	METRIC	INGREDIENTS
4 oz	120 mL	Olive oil
2 oz	60 mL	Lemon juice, fresh
2 oz	60 mL	Sherry or red wine vinegar
2 oz	56 g	Onion; finely minced
1 tbsp	6 g	Garlic, finely minced
1 oz	28 g	Flat-leaf parsley; chopped
1 tbsp	3 g	Fresh oregano leaves, chopped
½ tsp	½ tsp	Dried red chile pepper
1½ tsp	1½ tsp	Salt
1 tsp	1 tsp	Black pepper, freshly ground

PROCEDURE

1. Combine all ingredients; rest for at least 2 hours. This is best if prepared overnight. The parsley may be added just before serving to preserve the color.

Mexico

Mole Verde con Hierbas (Pork Herbed Green Mole)

PORTIONS: 4

U.S.	METRIC	INGREDIENTS
24 oz	672 g	Pork stew meat, 1½ inch (3.8 cm) cube
½ tsp	1 g	Black peppercorns, bruised
4 oz	112 g	White onion, cut 1½ inch (3.8 cm) cube
10	10	Garlic cloves, peeled and split lengthwise
8	8	Cloves, whole, or ¼ teaspoon ground
1 tsp	2 g	Cumin seeds
2	2	Jalapeño chiles, seeds removed
16 oz	448 g	Tomatillos, husks removed
2	2	Thyme sprigs, fresh
2	2	Marjoram sprigs, fresh
8 oz	224 g	Masa, either fresh or reconstituted by mixing 6 tablespoons masa harina to a smooth paste with 1 cup water
1 oz	28 g	Italian parsley, chopped
1 oz	28 g	Cilantro leaves, chopped
½ oz	14 g	Epazote, fresh or ⅛ cup dried, crumbled
½ oz	14 g	Hoja santa leaves, fresh, or 3 dried leaves (Also called hierba santa or root beer plant, it has a distinctive anise flavor that's hard to duplicate.)
14 oz	392 g	White beans, cooked
to taste	to taste	Salt and pepper

PROCEDURE

1. Combine pork stew meat, peppercorns, ½ cup white onions, and 5 garlic cloves, cover by 1 inch with cold water. Bring to a boil, cover, and reduce to simmer. Cook until just tender, 30–45 minutes. Remove meat and strain stock, reserve.
2. Grind the cloves and cumin seeds with a spice grinder or a mortar and pestle.
3. In a blender combine ground spices, jalapeño, tomatillos, thyme, marjoram, remaining garlic cloves and onions and ½ cup stock from the cooked pork. Blend until smooth.
4. Combine reserved pork stock and tomatillo mixture; simmer, uncovered, 3 minutes.
5. Whisk masa into pork and tomatillo liquid; whisking constantly, return to simmer.
6. Cook, uncovered, over low heat 10 minutes, whisking occasionally. If lumps form, pass through a medium-mesh sieve and return to heat. Mixture should thicken to the consistency of whipping cream; if necessary, reduce to correct consistency or thin with more stock.
7. Combine parsley, cilantro, *epazote*, and *hoja santa* in a blender or food processor. If necessary, add a few tablespoons of liquid; process to a smooth puree.
8. Add beans, cooked pork, and pureed herbs to the *masa*-thickened sauce and let return to a simmer. Correct seasoning and serve.

Note: Green mole is most commonly found in the states of Puebla, Tlaxcala, and Oaxaca, where it is one of *los siete moles*—the seven famous moles, each with a distinctive color, flavor, and aroma. Unlike the other moles, which nearly always contain nuts and seeds, this recipe gets its characteristic flavor and bright green color from fresh herbs. If you prefer chicken, it may be substituted for pork in this recipe.

Corn Tortillas

YIELD: 1 POUND

U.S.	METRIC	INGREDIENTS
10 oz	280 g	Prepared masa harina
21 oz	588 mL	Warm water, approximately
1 tsp	1 tsp	Salt

PROCEDURE

1. Dissolve the salt in the warm water. To the masa harina, add the water all at once (this keeps lumps from forming) and mix quickly, just until the ingredients are combined.
2. Let rest 5 minutes. Masa will dry out quickly, so keep covered with plastic wrap or a damp cloth.
3. Pinch off golf ball sized pieces and roll into balls.
4. Flatten the balls and roll out to ⅛ inch (.3 cm) thick or use a tortilla press. If using a tortilla press, line both sides with plastic.
5. Gently place the tortilla on a hot skillet or griddle. It should make a soft sizzling sound. Cook for 30–40 seconds or until the tortilla starts to bubble on top. Turn tortilla over and cook an additional 20–30 seconds.
6. Remove the tortilla from pan and keep warm.
7. To reheat, bake covered in a 350°F (176°C) oven for 10–12 minutes.

Pavo con Salsa de Achiote a la Yucataneca

(Yucatán-Style Steamed Turkey in Achiote Sauce)

PORTIONS: 4

U.S.	METRIC	INGREDIENTS
4 oz	112 g	Achiote paste (recipe follows)
18 oz	504 mL	Seville or sour orange juice
2 oz	46 mL	Honey
¼ oz	6 grams	Cumin seeds, toasted and ground
1 tsp	1 g	Oregano, dried
47 oz	1.33 kg	Turkey breast, bone in, skin on
2 oz	46 g	Butter, softened, or lard
3	3	Banana leaves or enough fresh corn husks to line the roasting pan and cover the turkey
1 oz	28 mL	Vegetable oil
12 oz	336 mL	Beer
8 oz	113 g	Pickled red onion, thinly sliced (recipe follows)
8 oz	224 g	Avocado, sliced
8	8	Corn tortillas, 8 inches (20 cm), warmed
		Pico de Gallo (recipe follows)
		Salsa de Jitomate Cocida (recipe follows)

PROCEDURE

1. Combine achiote paste, juice, honey, cumin, and oregano.
2. Lift the turkey skin and rub softened butter over meat.
3. Spread the achiote mixture evenly over turkey; let marinate at room temperature for 45 minutes or under refrigeration 3–4 hours.
4. Line a pan with half the banana leaves or corn husks. Place the turkey on a rack on top of the banana leaves and cover with excess marinade.
5. Add beer to pan, cover turkey with remaining banana leaves or cornhusks.
6. Wrap pan with foil or use an airtight lid.
7. Steam until turkey reaches an internal temperature of 165°F (74°C). Steaming may be done in a preheated 350°F (176°C) oven. Check liquid level and add more beer or water if necessary. (Some Mexican cooks place a coin at the bottom of the steamer; when the coin begins to rattle, they add more water.)
8. When cooked, remove from pan and let cool. Shred as for tacos, combining meat with any sauce left in steamer. Turkey can also be placed on a platter, whole or in pieces, with any remaining sauce poured over it.
9. Serve turkey with pickled onion, avocado, tortillas, salsa (Pico de Gallo) and Salsa de Jitomate Cocida (cooked tomato sauce).

Achiote Paste

YIELD: ¼ CUP

U.S.	METRIC	INGREDIENTS
4 tbsp	4 tbsp	Achiote seeds
15	15	Peppercorns
1 tbsp	1 tbsp	Oregano
1 tbsp	1 tbsp	Cumin seeds
2	2	Whole cloves
1 tbsp	1 tbsp	Coriander seeds
6	6	Garlic cloves
4 tbsp	4 tbsp	White wine vinegar

PROCEDURE

1. Grind all but the garlic and vinegar in a coffee grinder. Crush the garlic in a mortar; gradually add the vinegar. Add the ground spices to the crushed garlic and mix well.

Pico de Gallo

PORTIONS: 4

U.S.	METRIC	INGREDIENTS
½ oz	0.015 L	Olive oil
4 oz	113 g	Yellow onion, ¼ inch (.6 cm) dice
1	1	Serrano pepper, minced
1	1	Garlic clove, minced
1½ tbsp	1½ tbsp	Cilantro, minced
6 oz	170 g	Tomatoes, peeled, seeded, ¼ inch (.6 cm) dice
½ oz	0.015 L	Fresh lime juice
to taste	to taste	Salt and black pepper

PROCEDURE

1. Heat oil over medium heat. Add onions, serrano pepper, garlic, and cilantro. Toss and remove from heat. Let cool.
2. Combine onion mixture with tomatoes and lime juice and correct seasoning.
3. Serve warm or at room temperature.

Pickled Red Onions

PORTIONS: 4

U.S.	METRIC	INGREDIENTS
16 oz	448 g	Red onions, ¼ inch slices
1 tbsp	2 g	Kosher salt
1 tbsp	2 g	Oregano
1 tsp	1 g	Cumin seed
10 oz	280 mL	Vinegar
1¾ oz	49 g	Granulated sugar
1 tsp	2 g	Black pepper

PROCEDURE

1. Separate the onion rings, toss with the salt until coated, and let stand 30 minutes.
2. Rinse the onions under cold water, drain very well, and pat dry with paper towels.
3. Combine well the oregano, cumin seeds, vinegar, sugar, and black pepper; pour over the rings in the bowl; toss to coat well. Chill for at least 2 hours before serving.

Frijoles Refritos (Well-Fried Beans)

PORTIONS: 4

U.S.	METRIC	INGREDIENTS
1½ oz	42 g	Pork lard or vegetable oil
1 oz	28 g	White onion, ¼ inch (.6 cm) dice
9 oz	252 g	Black, pink, or pinot beans, cooked, with cooking liquid
to taste	to taste	Salt and pepper

PROCEDURE

1. In a heavy pan, heat the lard or oil over medium-high heat.
2. Sauté the onions until brown, 3–4 minutes.
3. Increase heat to high and add half the beans and all the cooking liquid; mash well.
4. Gradually add the remaining beans and mash to a coarse puree.
5. Cook additional 10–12 minutes or until the beans begin to dry out and sizzle at the edges.

Salsa de Jitomate Cocida (Cooked Tomato Sauce)

YIELD: 1½ CUPS

U.S.	METRIC	INGREDIENTS
1	1	Poblano chile, charred, peeled, seeded, and ¼ inch (.6 cm) dice (see step 1)
8 oz	224 g	Tomatoes, charred, seeded, and chopped (see step 1)
½ oz	14 mL	Vegetable oil
3 oz	84 g	Red onion, ¼ inch (.6 cm) dice
2	2	Garlic cloves, minced
1 tsp	3 g	Oregano, fresh, or ½ teaspoon dried
1 tsp	3 g	Basil, fresh, or ½ teaspoon dried
4 oz	112 g	Tomato sauce
1 tsp	5 g	Fresh lime juice
to taste	to taste	Salt and pepper

PROCEDURE

1. Char poblano and tomatoes, turning frequently, until lightly charred on all sides, 3 to 5 minutes for chiles, 6 to 8 minutes for tomatoes (flesh should be soft).
2. Heat oil over medium heat and sauté onion and garlic until translucent, about 5 minutes.
3. Puree charred tomato and poblano.
4. Combine all ingredients except lime juice and salt and pepper, and cook over medium heat until slightly thickened and flavors are blended, about 5 minutes.
5. Add lime juice and correct seasoning.

Mexican Hot Chocolate

PORTIONS: 4

U.S.	METRIC	INGREDIENTS
32 oz	896 mL	Milk
16 oz	448 g	Mexican chocolate or dark bitter chocolate
2	2	Vanilla beans, split lengthwise

PROCEDURE

1. Warm milk and chocolate.
2. Scrape seeds from the vanilla bean and add the seeds and beans to milk.
3. Stir with a *molinillo* or whisk until the chocolate is melted and the mixture begins to boil. Remove the vanilla beans. Remove from the heat and froth the chocolate with the *molinillo* or the whisk. Serve immediately in ample mugs.

Note: Mexican chocolate is a grainy chocolate disk flavored with sugar, cinnamon, almonds, and vanilla. It is used to prepare hot chocolate and mole sauces. For 1 ounce Mexican chocolate, substitute 1 ounce semisweet chocolate, ½ teaspoon ground cinnamon, and 1 drop almond extract.

Beef Fajitas

PORTIONS: 12 PORTION SIZE: 4 OZ (150 G), PLUS GARNISH

U.S.	METRIC	INGREDIENTS
3 fl oz	90 mL	Vegetable oil
6 fl oz	180 mL	Lime juice
4 tsp	20 mL	Ground cumin
4 tsp	20 mL	Chili powder
4	4	Garlic cloves, chopped fine
4 tsp	20 mL	Salt
2 tsp	10 mL	Pepper
4 lb	1.9 kg	Beef skirt steak or flank steak, trimmed of fat

PROCEDURE

1. To make a marinade, mix together the oil, lime juice, cumin, chili powder, garlic, salt, and pepper.
2. Place the meat in a nonreactive container with the marinade, turning the meat so it is coated on all sides. Refrigerate 2–4 hours.
3. Remove the meat from the marinade. Grill the meat on both sides on a grill or under a broiler until it is lightly charred and rare to medium done, as desired.

U.S.	METRIC	INGREDIENTS
1 fl oz	30 mL	Vegetable oil
1 lb 8 oz	700 g	Bell peppers, assorted colors, cut into strips
1 lb 8 oz	700 g	Onion, in thick slices

4. While the beef is grilling, heat the oil in a large sauté pan over high heat.
5. Add the peppers and sauté briefly, keeping them slightly crisp.
6. Remove the peppers from the pan, and then sauté the onions in the same way.
7. When the beef is done, remove it from the grill and let it rest 5 minutes.
8. Slice the meat across the grain into thin slices.

U.S.	METRIC	INGREDIENTS
24, or as desired	24, or as desired	Flour tortillas, steamed to soften
as desired	as desired	Garnishes: Guacamole or sliced avocado; Sour cream; Shredded lettuce; Diced tomato; Salsa Cruda

9. Serve the meat strips and vegetables on a hot plate or sizzle platter. Serve the tortillas and the garnishes on the side in separate containers. Diners make their own soft tacos by rolling meat, vegetables, and choice of condiments in tortillas.

Per serving: Calories, 740; Protein, 44 g; Fat, 22 g (27% cal.); Cholesterol, 60 mg; Carbohydrates, 88 g; Fiber, 6 g; Sodium, 830 mg.

Tamales de Espinaca con Queso (Spinach and Cheese Tamales)

YIELD: ABOUT 12, DEPENDING ON SIZE OF CORN HUSKS

U.S.	METRIC	INGREDIENTS	PROCEDURE
Basic Tamales			
12	12	Dried corn husks	1. Place corn husks in warm water to cover and soak 2 hours. Remove, drain, and pat dry.
8 oz	224 g	Lard or vegetable shortening	2. Beat the lard by hand or in mixer until soft and light.
6 oz	176 mL	Chicken stock or water	3. Gradually add stock to the masa harina and knead until the dough is no longer sticky. Add salt and baking powder.
18 oz	504 g	Masa harina or fresh masa (1½ pounds)	4. Move masa harina mixture to mixer and beat lard into the dough, a little at a time, until the dough is light and fluffy. Test for lightness by pinching off a small piece and dropping into a glass of cold water. It should float when ready; if not, continue to beat and test again. The lighter the dough, the better; it results in moist and fluffy tamales. It is impossible to overmix this dough.
2 tsp	10 g	Salt	
1 tsp	4 g	Baking powder	
Spinach and Cheese Filling			
¾ oz	21 mL	Vegetable oil	5. Heat oil and sauté onions until translucent. Add tomatoes and cook until almost dry.
2 oz	56 g	Onion, ¼ inch (.6 cm) dice	6. Add spinach and wilt.
3 oz	84 g	Tomato, peeled, seeded, ¼ inch (.6 cm) dice	7. Let cool and mix well with cheese.
8 oz	224 g	Fresh spinach, or 8 ounces frozen chopped	8. Adjust seasoning.
4 oz	112 g	Adobera, Asadero, or Monterey Jack cheese, shredded	9. Combine spinach and cheese filling with Basic Tamales (masa harina mixture); mix well and check seasoning again.
to taste	to taste	Salt and pepper	

To Make Tamales

10. Place an unbroken corn husk on a work surface in front of you with the small tapering end of the husk facing you.
11. Using a spatula or masa spreader, spread approximately ¼ cup of dough onto the husk, leaving a border of at least 1½ inches of husk at the tapered end.
12. Fold the two long sides of the corn husk in over the corn mixture.
13. Fold the tapered end up, leaving the top open.
14. Secure the tamale by tying with a strip of husk or a string.
15. Line the steamer with husks. Stand the tamales up in a row around the edge of the steamer.
16. Cover and steam, checking water level frequently and replenishing with boiling water as needed, until tamales easily come free from husks, about 1 hour for tamales made with fresh masa or 1¼ to 1½ hours if made with masa harina mixture.

Chapter 16

Duck Confit with Walnut Mesclun Salad, page 48.

Food Presentation and Garnish

This chapter builds on what you learned in Chapter 15 of *Culinary Foundations*. The focus of this book so far has been the preparation of food but as you know, presenting food to diners in an appealing and attractive manner is a critical part of your work as a cook.

The first section of this chapter discusses hot platter garnishes. Then, we explore cold food presentation and buffet service, ranging from how a buffet is arranged to how to present cold platters, and finishing up with a section of the preparation and holding of hot foods.

Food must look good as well as taste good in order for our customers to enjoy their meal.

After reading this chapter, you should be able to

1. Garnish a banquet platter with attractive and appropriate vegetable accompaniments.
2. Plan and arrange attractive food platters for buffets.

Modern Hot Platter Garnish

In classical cuisine, food was nearly always brought to the dining room on large platters and then served, rather than being plated in the kitchen, as is most often done today.

Although this practice is not nearly as common as it was a few decades ago, it is still sometimes used for banquet service, and nothing stimulates appetites as much as a succulent roast on a silver platter, sumptuously adorned with a colorful variety of vegetable garnishes.

The classical garnitures most often adapted to modern platter presentation are those called *bouquetière*, *jardinière*, and *printanière*. At one time, these were specific vegetable assortments cut in prescribed ways. Today the terms are taken in a more general way indicating colorful assortments of fresh vegetables.

Platter garnish need not be elaborate or difficult to prepare. A simple assortment of colorful vegetables, carefully cut and properly cooked to retain color and texture, is appropriate to the most elegant presentation. Stuffed vegetables, such as tomato halves filled with peas, are a little fancier, but still easy to prepare. Borders of duchesse potatoes are also popular.

Many of the rules of proper plating apply to platter arrangement as well—for example, those that call for neatness, balance of color and shape, unity, and preserving the individuality of the items. Following are a few more guidelines that apply to hot platter presentation and garnish.

1. **Vegetables should be in easily served units.**
   In other words, don't heap green peas or mashed potatoes on one corner of the platter. More suitable are vegetables such as cauliflower, broccoli, boiled tomatoes, asparagus spears, whole green beans, mushroom caps, or anything that comes in large or easy-to-handle pieces. Small vegetables such as peas can be easily served if they are used to fill artichoke bottoms, tomato halves, or tartlet shells.

2. **Have the correct number of portions of each item.**
   Vegetables like Brussels sprouts and tournéed carrots are easily portioned in the dining room if they are arranged in little portion-size piles.

3. **Arrange the garnishes around the platter to get the best effect from the different colors and shapes.**
   The meat, poultry, or fish is usually placed in the center of the platter, or in a row or rows, and the garnishes arranged around it.

4. **Avoid being too elaborate.**
   While it is sometimes desirable to make ornate platters, simplicity is usually preferable to an overworked appearance. Let the attractiveness of the food speak for itself. The garnish should never dominate or hide the meat, which is the center of attention.

5. **Serve extra sauce or gravy in a sauceboat.**
   If it is appropriate, dress or nap the meat or fish items with some of the sauce, but don't drown the entire platter with it.

6. **Serve hot foods hot, on a hot platter.**
   Don't spend so much time arranging the food that it's cold by the time it reaches the dining room.

KEY POINTS TO REVIEW

- What is meant by *balance* when applied to plate arrangements? What elements should be balanced?
- What are some examples of different plating styles?
- What guidelines should be observed when plating food or planning plate arrangements?

Cold Food Presentation and Buffet Service

The buffet is a popular and profitable form of food presentation found in nearly every kind of food-service operation. There are at least three reasons for this popularity:

1. **Visual appeal.**
   An attractive presentation of foods has the effect of lavishness and ample quantity, and careful arrangement and garnish suggest quality as well.
2. **Efficiency.**
   The buffet allows the restaurant to serve a large number of people in a short time with relatively few service personnel.
3. **Adaptability.**
   Buffet service is adaptable to nearly every kind of food (except items that must be cooked to order, like broiled and deep-fried foods) and to all price ranges, occasions, restaurant styles, and local food customs.

Buffet Arrangement and Appearance

The buffet's visual appeal is, perhaps, its greatest attraction for the customer. Eye appeal of food is always important, but perhaps nowhere more important than on a buffet, because the appearance sells the food. A buffet is not just food service—it is food display.

Lavishness and Abundance

Above all else, a buffet should look lavish and plentiful. The appearance of an abundance of food beautifully laid out is exciting and stimulating to the appetite. There are many ways to create this look.

1. **Color.**
   A variety of colors is as vital on a buffet as it is on a single plate. Plan menus and garnish so you have enough color on the table.
2. **Height.**
   Flat foods on flat trays on flat tables are uninteresting to the eye.
   A centerpiece is an important feature, giving height and focus to the buffet. Ice carvings, tallow sculptures, and floral or fruit displays are some possibilities. These should be placed on a separate table behind the food table.
   Centerpieces on individual platters also add height. Large food items such as large cheeses and whole roasts being carved at the table are also effective. Multilevel tables, when available, are used to good effect.
3. **Full platters and bowls.**
   Replenish items as they become depleted. A nearly empty bowl isn't as appetizing as a full one.
   Arrange platters so they still have interest even when portions have been removed (more on this later).
4. **Proper spacing.**
   While you shouldn't crowd the items, don't spread them so far apart that the table looks half empty.

Simplicity

This sounds like a contradiction to the lavishness principle, but it's not. You need to strike a good balance between the two. Lavishness is not the same as clutter.

1. **Overdesigned, overdecorated food scares people away from eating it.**
   How many times have you heard someone say, "Oh, it's so pretty I don't want to touch it"? Even if they don't say it, they may think it.

Too much design detracts from the food. Sometimes food is so overdecorated that it no longer looks like food. This completely defeats the purpose. The customer should at least be able to identify the food for what it is.

2. **Excessive garnish is quickly destroyed as customers take portions.**

Orderliness

A buffet should look like it was planned, not like it just happened. Customers prefer food presentations that look carefully done, not just thrown together.

1. Simple arrangements are much easier to keep neat and orderly than complicated designs.
2. Colors and shapes should look lively and varied, but make sure they go together and do not clash.
3. Keep the style consistent. If it's formal, then everything should be formal. If it's casual or rustic, then every part of the presentation should be casual or rustic. If it's a Mexican fiesta, don't include German sauerbraten just because your specialty happens to be sauerbraten.

   This is true not only of the food but of the dishes and serving pieces, too. Don't use ornate silver serving pieces for a country theme, for example.

Menu and Serving Sequence

Practical reasons as well as visual appeal determine the order in which foods are arranged on the buffet. As far as possible, it is good to have items in the proper menu order (for example, appetizers first, main course afterward, desserts last) if only to avoid confusing the customers, who might otherwise wonder what the food is and how much they should take. But there are many reasons for changing the order. The following should be taken into account when arranging a buffet.

1. Hot foods are best served last. If served first, hot foods get cool while the guests make other selections from the cold foods. Also, it is more effective, visually, to place the decorative cold platters first and the less attractive chafing dishes last.
2. The more expensive foods are usually placed after the less expensive items. This gives you some control of food cost, as the guests' plates will be nearly full of other attractive foods by the time they get to the costly items.
3. Sauces and dressings should be placed next to the items with which they are to be served. Otherwise, the customer might not match them with the right foods.
4. A separate dessert table is often a good idea. This approach allows guests to make a separate trip for dessert without interfering with the main serving line. It is also possible, if the menu is large, to have a separate appetizer table.
5. Plates, of course, must be the first items on the table. Silverware, napkins, and other items not needed until the guest sits down to eat should be at the end of the buffet table or set in place on the dining tables.

The Cocktail Buffet

One kind of buffet doesn't conform to this menu order pattern. The cocktail buffet displays appetizers intended to accompany drinks and other refreshments at receptions, cocktail parties, and cocktail hours preceding banquets and dinners. There is no serving line—or, looking at it a different way, there is a separate line for each item.

1. Only appetizer-type foods are served: tasty, well-seasoned foods in small portions.
2. Stacks of small plates are placed beside each item rather than at the beginning of the table.

3. The table or tables must be easy to get to from all parts of the room and must not block traffic. Do not place them next to the entry because guests gather around them, blocking movement into and out of the room.

Cold Platter Presentation

The cold platter is the mainstay of the buffet and offers the most opportunity for visual artistry. It also can be one of the most demanding forms of food presentation, particularly in the case of show platters, which require great precision, patience, and artistic sense.

Cold platters can range from a simple tray of cold cuts to elaborate constructions of pâtés, meats, poultry, or fish decorated with aspic, truffles, and vegetable flowers. In this chapter, we have space only for a discussion of general guidelines you can apply both to formal buffet platters and to simple cold food arrangements. To learn more detailed, complex techniques, you must depend on your instructors, more advanced courses, and on-the-job experience. But this section should help you take the foods available in whatever kitchen you find yourself working and produce an attractive, appetizing buffet.

Basic Principles of Platter Presentation

1. The three elements of a buffet platter:
   - Centerpiece or ***grosse pièce*** (gross pyess). This may be an uncut portion of the main food item, such as a pâté or a cold roast, decorated and displayed whole. It may be a separate but related item, such as a molded salmon mousse on a platter of poached slices of salmon in aspic. It may be something as simple as a bowl or ***ravier*** (rahv yay; an oval relish dish) of sauce or condiment. Or it may be strictly for decoration, such as a butter sculpture or a squash vase filled with vegetable flowers. Whether or not the grosse pièce is intended to be eaten, it should be made of edible materials.
   - The slices or serving portions of the main food item, arranged artistically.
   - The garnish, arranged artistically, in proportion to the cut slices.
2. The food should be easy to handle and serve, so one portion can be removed without ruining the arrangement.
3. A simple design is best. Simple arrangements are easier to serve, more appetizing than overworked food, and more likely to remain attractive when they are half demolished by the guests.

   Simple arrangements may be the hardest to produce. Everything must be perfect because less decoration is available to divide the attention.
4. Attractive platter presentations may be made on silver or other metals, mirrors, china, plastic, wood, or many other materials, as long as they are presentable and suitable for use with food. Metal platters that might cause discoloration or metallic flavors are often covered with a thin layer of aspic before the food is placed on them.
5. Once a piece of food has touched the tray, do not remove it. Shiny silver or mirror trays are easily smudged, and you'll have to wash the tray and start over again. This shows the importance of good planning.

   Following this rule also helps eliminate overhandling of food, which is a bad sanitary practice.
6. Think of the platter as part of the whole buffet. It must look attractive and appropriate not only by itself but among the other presentations on the table. The arrangement should always be planned from the same angle from which it will be seen on the buffet.

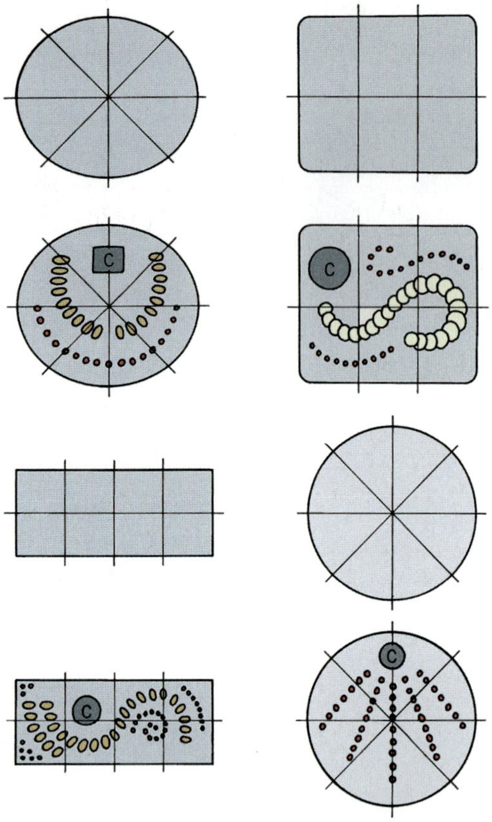

Figure 16.1 Begin your planning sketch of a buffet platter by dividing the tray into six or eight sections. This helps you lay out a balanced, symmetrical design. The examples shown here indicate the placement of the main items (usually slices of foods), the centerpiece (labeled c), and the garnish (shown as tiny circles).

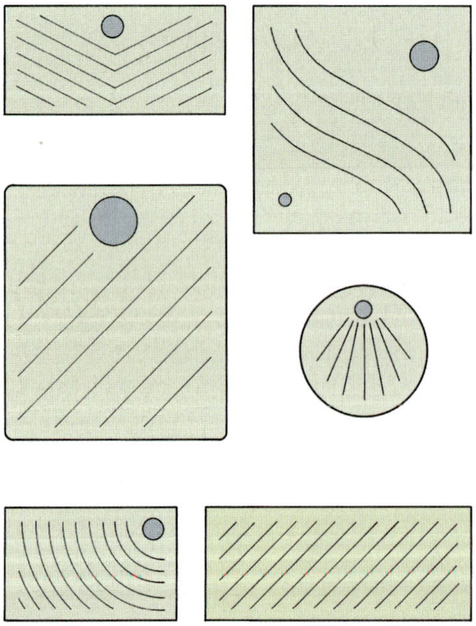

Figure 16.2 Arranging rows of foods in curves or angled lines gives movement to the design.

Designing the Platter

1. **Plan ahead.**
   Making a sketch is a good idea. Otherwise, you might have half the food on the platter and suddenly realize you have to start over because everything doesn't fit the way you had hoped. The result is wasted time and excessive handling of food. One way to start a sketch is to divide the platter into six or eight equal parts, as in Figure 16.1. This helps you avoid lopsided or crooked arrangements by giving you equally spaced markers as guides. It is relatively easy, then, to sketch in a balanced, symmetrical layout, as the examples show.

2. **Plan for movement in your design.**
   This doesn't mean you should mount the food on little wheels. It means that a good design makes the eye move across the platter, following the lines you have set up.

   Most food for platters consists of single small portions arranged in rows or lines. The trick is to put movement into those lines by curving or angling them, as shown in Figure 16.2. In general, curves and angles are said to have movement. Square corners do not.

3. **Give the design a focal point.**
   This is the function of the centerpiece, which emphasizes and strengthens the design by giving it direction and height. This may be done directly, by having the lines point at it, or more subtly, by having the lines angle toward it or sweep around it in graceful curves. Again, see Figures 16.1 and 16.2.

   Note that the centerpiece isn't always in the center, in spite of its name. Because of its height, it should be at the back or toward the side so it doesn't hide the food. Remember, you are designing the platter from the customer's point of view.

   It's not necessary for every platter on the buffet to have a centerpiece. Some of them should, however, or the buffet will lack height and be less interesting to the eye.

4. **Keep items in proportion.**
   The main items on the platter—the slices of meat, pâté, or whatever—should *look* like the main items. The centerpiece should not be so large or so tall that it totally dominates the platter. The garnish should enhance, not overwhelm, the main item in size, height, or quantity. The number of portions of garnish should be in proportion to the amount of the main item.

   The size of the platter should be in proportion to the amount of food. Don't select one that is so small as to become crowded or so large as to look almost empty even before the first guest has arrived.

   Keep enough space between items or between rows so the platter doesn't look jumbled or confused.

   Figure 16.1 indicates placement of garnish as well as of the main item. Note how the arrangement of garnish reflects or accents the pattern established by the sliced foods.

5. **Let the guest see the best side of everything.**
   Angle overlapping slices and wedge-shaped pieces toward the customer. Make sure the best side of each slice is face up.

Cheese Platters

Cheese trays are popular on both luncheon buffets as a main course item and on dinner buffets as a dessert item. Cheeses are presented much differently than the other cold buffet foods we have been talking about.

First, whole cheeses or cheeses in large pieces are generally more attractive than an arrangement of slices. This also helps the guest identify the varieties. Be sure to supply several knives so guests can cut their own portions.

Second, an assortment of fresh fruit is often included on a cheese tray. This adds a great deal to the appearance of a cheese presentation, and the flavors go well with cheese. The photograph on this page shows an example of a cheese and fruit presentation.

One type of cheese and fruit presentation for buffet service.

A Note on Sanitation

Cold food for buffets presents a special sanitation problem. This is because the food spends a great deal of time out of refrigeration while it is being assembled and decorated and again while it sits on the buffet. For this reason, it is particularly important to follow all the rules of safe food handling. Keep foods refrigerated whenever they are not being worked on. Also, keep them chilled until the last minute before they are brought out for service.

For a buffet service that lasts a long time, it is a good idea to arrange each course or item on a number of small platters rather than on one big one. The replacements can then be refrigerated until needed.

Hot Foods for Buffets

Everything you have learned about the preparation and holding of hot foods in quantity applies to hot foods for buffets. Hot items are nearly always served from chafing dishes, which may be ornate silver affairs or simple steam table pans kept warm over hot water. These foods cannot be elaborately decorated and garnished the way cold foods can. On the other hand, the bright, fresh, juicy appearance and good aroma of properly cooked hot food is generally sufficient to arouse appetites.

Hot foods for chafing dishes should be easily portioned (such as vegetables served with a kitchen spoon) or already portioned in the pan (braised pork chops, sliced baked ham, and poached fish fillets, for example). Items less suitable for buffets are those that must be cooked to order and served immediately, such as most broiled and deep-fried foods.

Whole roasts are popular items at buffets, carved to order by a member of the kitchen staff. Especially attractive are large roasts such as hams, turkeys, and large cuts of beef such as steamship round.

As previously noted, hot foods are best placed at the end of the buffet so they do not cool on the guests' plates before they are seated and so the decorated cold foods can steal the show.

KEY POINTS TO REVIEW

- What guidelines should be observed when arranging hot foods on platters?
- When planning a buffet, how do you create the impression of lavishness? What guidelines help you achieve simplicity and orderliness?
- In general, in what order should items be arranged on a buffet?
- What guidelines should be observed when planning a cold buffet platter?

TERMS FOR REVIEW

classical garnish

grosse pièce

ravier

QUESTIONS FOR DISCUSSION

1. What is meant by plating food for the convenience of the customer, and how does this affect other rules of plating?
2. What is the difference between a cocktail buffet and a luncheon or dinner buffet?
3. Customers like to see a lot of food on a buffet. Is it correct to say, then, that the best way to please customers is to put out as much food as possible? Explain your answer.
4. When you are preparing a cold buffet platter, why is it a good idea to plan ahead by making a sketch? What would you include in the sketch? What do the terms *movement* and *focal point* mean in platter design?

Chapter 17

Traditional Falafel in Pita, page 385

Sandwiches

The sandwich is a favorite and convenient lunchtime food. It is quickly made and served, and it is adaptable to so many variations that it satisfies nearly every taste and nutrition requirement.

Sandwiches have long been the domain of the pantry department, along with salads and other cold preparations. However, when you consider that the most popular sandwich today is the hamburger, you realize that sandwich preparation is as much the responsibility of the short-order cook as it is of the pantry cook.

Preparing hot and cold sandwiches to order is one of the fundamental skills required in modern food service. In this chapter, we start by looking at the fundamentals of sandwich making, the basic ingredients, and basic sandwich types. We then look at the setup of the sandwich station and methods for efficient production.

After reading this chapter, you should be able to

1. Select, store, and serve fresh, good-quality breads for sandwiches.
2. Use sandwich spreads correctly.
3. Identify the most popular types of sandwich filling.
4. Set up an efficient sandwich station.
5. Prepare the major types of sandwiches to order.
6. Prepare sandwiches in quantity.

Breads

One of the functions of the bread in a sandwich is to provide an edible casing for the food inside. Ideally, though, the bread should do more than this. Good-quality breads provide variety, texture, flavor, and eye appeal to sandwiches, as well as bulk and nutrients.

Types

Pullman or sandwich loaves of white bread are most frequently used for simple sandwiches. These are long, rectangular loaves that provide square slices of specified thickness, from $\frac{3}{8}$ to $\frac{5}{8}$ inch (10 to 16 mm) thick.

Commercial sandwich bread should be of fine rather than coarse texture and firm enough to accommodate spreads well. Supermarket white bread is unsuitable because it is too soft for spreading and for holding most fillings, and it becomes pasty in the mouth.

Because of its neutral flavor, white bread is suitable for the largest variety of fillings.

Other kinds of breads add variety and interest, provided they harmonize with the filling. The following are some possibilities:

- Rolls, including hard and soft rolls, hamburger and hot dog rolls, long rolls for submarine sandwiches
- French or Italian bread and rolls, including sourdough and ciabatta, split horizontally
- Whole wheat
- Cracked wheat
- Rye and pumpernickel
- Pita bread
- Raisin bread
- Cinnamon bread
- Fruit and nut breads
- Focaccia

Storage

Fresh bread is essential for top-quality sandwiches. Stale or dry bread is undesirable. The following measures can be taken to ensure freshness.

1. Daily delivery, or delivery as frequent as possible, depending on your location. Bread stales rapidly, and day-old bread has lost much of its freshness.
2. Keep bread tightly wrapped in moistureproof wrapping until it is used. This prevents drying and guards against absorption of odors.

Breads made of various flours: top row: multigrain, white pan loaf, marble rye, whole wheat, and olive loaf. Bottom row: raisin swirl, pumpernickel, and Jewish rye.

Breads in various shapes: Top row: Pullman loaf, baguette, home-style, bâtard, sub roll, and hearth. Middle row: Cuban, kaiser, hot dog, New England hot dog, hamburger roll, ciabatta, and steak roll. Bottom row: naan, flour tortillas, whole wheat wrap, and pita.

3. French bread and other hard-crusted breads should not be wrapped, or the crusts will soften. These breads stale rapidly and should be used the day they are baked.
4. Store at room temperature, away from ovens or hot equipment. Do not refrigerate, because refrigerated bread becomes stale faster.
5. If bread must be kept more than one day, it may be frozen. Thaw frozen bread without unwrapping.
6. Day-old bread may be used for toasting without loss of quality.

Spreads

Purposes of Spreads

1. To protect the bread from soaking up moisture from the filling.
2. To add flavor.
3. To add moisture or mouthfeel.

Butter

Butter should be soft enough to spread easily without tearing the bread. It may be softened by whipping in a mixer or by simply letting it stand at room temperature for half an hour.

Whipping gives the butter greater volume, and this cuts food cost. However, whipped butter does not keep as well because the incorporated air speeds the development of rancidity.

Some operators whip a small amount of water or milk into the butter. This increases both spreadability and volume. However, it adds nothing to the quality of the sandwich and increases the likelihood of soaking the bread.

Margarine is sometimes used instead of butter, if food costs require it or if customers request it.

Flavored butters, may be used with appropriate fillings.

Mayonnaise

Mayonnaise is often preferred to butter as a spread because it contributes more flavor. However, it does not protect the bread from moisture as well as butter does.

Because of the danger of food-borne disease, sandwiches made with mayonnaise should be served immediately or refrigerated at once and kept refrigerated until served.

Other Spreads

Although butter and mayonnaise are the most widely used spreads, almost any food of a spreadable consistency can be used to add flavor interest to sandwiches. Be aware, however, that most of these do not protect the bread from soaking up moisture from the filling. Moist spreads are best if applied just before serving.

Fillings

The filling is the heart of the sandwich. As we have already said, nearly any kind of food may be served between two slices of bread. The following are possible fillings that may be used separately or in combination.

Meats and Poultry

Most meats for sandwiches are precooked, though some are cooked to order. Sliced meats dry out and lose flavor, so avoid slicing farther ahead than necessary, and keep sliced meats covered or wrapped.

Leftovers may be used, but only if they are of good quality and have been properly handled and stored to avoid contamination.

Thin slices are more tender, and sandwiches made with them are easier to eat. Also, many thin slices make a thicker sandwich than one or two thick slices of the same total weight.

1. **Beef**
   - Sliced roast beef, hot or cold
   - Hamburger patties
   - Small steaks
   - Corned beef
   - Pastrami
   - Tongue, fresh or smoked
2. **Pork products**
   - Roast pork
   - Barbecued pork
   - Ham, all kinds
   - Bacon
   - Canadian bacon
3. **Poultry**
   - Turkey breast
   - Chicken breast
4. **Sausage products**
   - Salami
   - Frankfurters
   - Bologna
   - Liverwurst
   - Luncheon meats
   - Grilled sausages

Cheese

Like meats, cheese dries out rapidly when unwrapped and sliced. When slicing is done ahead, the slices should remain covered until service time. See Chapter 19 for a summary of cheese varieties.

The most popular sandwich cheeses are:

- Cheddar types
- Swiss types
- Process cheese
- Provolone
- Cream cheese, mascarpone
- Cheese spreads

Fish and Shellfish

Most seafood fillings for sandwiches are highly perishable and should be kept well chilled at all times.

Some popular seafood fillings are:

- Tuna
- Sardines
- Smoked salmon and lox
- Shrimp
- Anchovies
- Fried fish portions
- Grilled or pan-fried fish fillets

Bound Salads

The most popular salads for sandwich fillings are tuna salad, egg salad, chicken or turkey salad, and ham salad.

Vegetable Items

Lettuce, tomato, and onion are indispensable in sandwich production. In addition, nearly any vegetable used in salads may also be included in sandwiches. Grilled vegetables are popular not only in vegetarian sandwiches but also as part of the filling in meat sandwiches.

Miscellaneous

- Peanut butter
- Jelly
- Egg
- Fruits, fresh or dried
- Nuts (such as sliced almonds)

Types of Sandwiches

Cold Sandwiches

Figure 17.1 **Cutting a club or multidecker sandwich.**

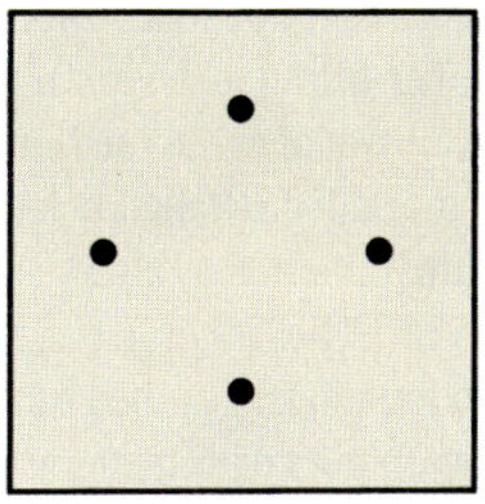

(a) Place four picks in the sandwich in the locations shown by the dots in the illustrations.

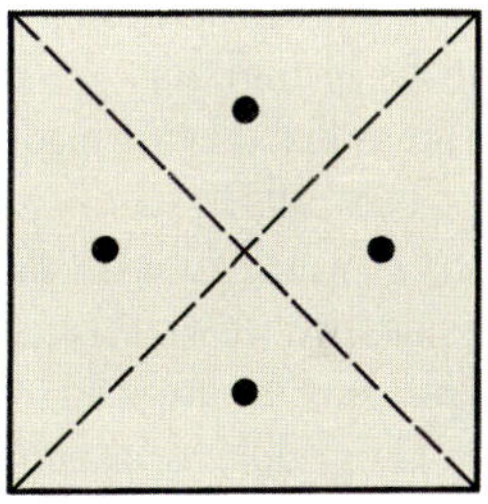

(b) Cut the sandwiches into quarters from corner to corner. Plate the sandwich with the points up.

1. ***Simple cold sandwiches*** are those made with two slices of bread or two halves of a roll, a spread, and a filling. They are called *simple* because they are made with just two slices of bread, not because they are necessarily simple in construction. Simple cold sandwiches range from a single slice of cheese or meat between two slices of buttered bread to complex constructions like the submarine sandwich (also called a *hero sandwich* or *grinder*), a long Italian roll filled with salami, ham, capocollo, mortadella or bologna, provolone cheese, peppers, onions, olives, tomatoes, and more.

   Most popular sandwiches fall into this category.

2. ***Multidecker sandwiches*** are made with more than two slices of bread (or rolls split into more than two pieces) and with several ingredients in the filling.

   The ***club sandwich*** is a popular multidecker sandwich made with three slices of toast and filled with sliced chicken or turkey breast, mayonnaise, lettuce, tomato, and bacon. It is cut into four triangles, as shown in Figure 17.1.

3. ***Open-faced sandwiches*** are made with a single slice of bread, like large canapés, which is what they are. Also as in canapés, the filling or topping should be attractively arranged and garnished. Canapé ingredients and method are discussed in Chapter 18.

4. ***Tea sandwiches*** are small, fancy sandwiches generally made from light, delicate ingredients and bread trimmed of crust. They are often cut into fancy shapes. Fillings and spreads can be the same as those for canapés.

5. ***Wraps*** are sandwiches in which the fillings are wrapped, like a Mexican burrito, in a large flour tortilla or similar flatbread. They may be served whole or cut in half if large.

Hot Sandwiches

1. ***Simple hot sandwiches*** consist of hot fillings, usually meats but sometimes fish, grilled vegetables, or other hot items, between two slices of bread or two halves of a roll. They may also contain items that are not hot, such as a slice of tomato or raw onion on a hamburger.

   Hamburgers and hot dogs and all their variations are the most popular hot sandwiches.

2. ***Open-faced hot sandwiches*** are made by placing buttered or unbuttered bread on a serving plate, covering it with hot meat or other filling, and topping with a sauce, gravy, cheese, or other topping. Some versions are browned under the broiler before serving. This type of sandwich is eaten with a knife and fork.

3. ***Grilled sandwiches***, also called *toasted sandwiches*, are simple sandwiches buttered on the outside and browned on the griddle, in a hot oven, or in a panini grill (see sidebar, p. 378). Sandwiches containing cheese are popular for grilling.

4. ***Deep-fried sandwiches*** are made by dipping sandwiches in beaten egg and, sometimes, in bread crumbs, and then deep-frying. This type of sandwich is often cooked on a griddle or in a hot oven instead, as deep-frying makes it greasy.

5. If wraps are classified as cold sandwiches, then hot burritos, quesadillas, and filled enchiladas could be considered hot sandwiches. ***Pizzas*** could be considered open-faced hot sandwiches, and we can define them as thin sheets of lean bread dough baked with a topping. In fact, one could classify any food made with a dough product filled or topped with another food product as a sandwich. Dough products, whether breads, puff pastry, tortillas, or egg roll skins, make useful and versatile bases or cases for foods, whether or not the result resembles something we might think of as a sandwich. Several of these items (enchiladas, quesadillas, and egg rolls) are considered in

Panini grill

other chapters of this book. Pizzas are included in this chapter for convenience. The recipe on page 388 gives the basic procedure for baking pizzas. For other flavors, vary the toppings as desired, using the same technique for baking.

PANINI

The basic meaning of the Italian word *panino* (plural: *panini*) is "roll," as in bread roll or dinner roll—literally, "little bread." By extension, *panini* are sandwiches made of small rolls plus fillings. The filling for a typical panino is a slice or two of cured meat, such as salami, mortadella (Italian bologna), or prosciutto. Cheese may also be used, as well as a variety of other items, such as sliced tomato and canned tuna. In summary, Italian panini are most often small, simple, cold sandwiches.

Outside of Italy, *panino* has come to mean something quite different. It is usually a hot grilled sandwich, often with a fairly substantial filling. What distinguishes panini from other grilled sandwiches is that they are made on a special griddle called a *panini grill* or *panini press*, which grills the sandwich on both sides at once while compressing or squeezing the bread and filling together. The griddle surfaces may be smooth or grooved. Grooved griddles toast grill marks onto the bread for the typical panino look.

Grilled panini often contain cheese as one of the filling ingredients. The melted cheese as well as the crisp toasted crusts are part of the attraction of this type of sandwich.

If a sandwich press is not available, you can create a similar kind of sandwich by toasting it on a standard flat griddle or grooved griddle, putting a grill brick on the sandwich to compress it, and turning it over when heated halfway through to toast both sides.

For pressed sandwiches, avoid making the fillings too thick. Unlike for grilled sandwiches, it is not always necessary to butter or oil the outside surfaces of the bread. The moisture and fat in the filling may be enough to moisten the bread as it grills. Adding more sometimes makes the sandwich too greasy.

KEY POINTS TO REVIEW

- What kinds of spread are used for sandwiches? What is their purpose?
- What categories of ingredients are used for sandwich fillings? List as many examples of each category as possible.
- What are the major kinds of hot and cold sandwiches?

Making Sandwiches

The preparation of sandwiches requires a great deal of handwork. Many individual motions may be required, especially if the sandwiches are multideckers or have several ingredients. Whether you are making sandwiches in quantity or to order, your goal must be to reduce your motions to make the production as efficient and quick as possible.

Setting Up the Station for Prepared-to-Order Sandwiches

A station setup depends on the menu and on the available equipment and space, so there is no single correct way to set up.

Any setup involves two elements: ingredients and equipment.

INGREDIENTS

This phase of the setup has two parts:

1. **Prepare ingredients.**
   Mix fillings, prepare spreads, slice sandwich meats and cheeses, separate lettuce leaves, slice tomatoes, prepare garnishes, and so on. In other words, have everything ready ahead of time, so nothing is left to do but assemble the ingredients.

2. **Arrange or store ingredients for maximum efficiency.**
   To reduce your movements to a minimum, the ideal setup has everything you need within easy reach of both hands. Depending on the kitchen layout, this may not be possible, especially if the sandwich menu is large. But try to get as close to it as possible.

   Arrange ingredients so you can use both hands. For example, while the left hand reaches for the bread, the right hand reaches for the butter spreader. Then, while the right hand puts the spreader back, the left reaches for the sliced ham. The right hand, on its way back from the butter, picks up a slice of cheese and so on. On a busy sandwich station, every second counts.

Two other considerations are important while we're talking about ingredients:

1. **Sanitation.**
   Because cold sandwiches are subjected to a lot of handling and are not cooked, it is especially important that ingredients be properly refrigerated and protected at all times. A refrigerated table—sort of a cold version of a steam table—is usually used. Refrigerated drawers or under-the-counter reach-ins are used for less frequently needed items.

   Wash hands carefully and thoroughly before beginning work. In addition, be aware of local sanitation requirements. In some places, laws require that workers wear gloves when handling ready-to-eat foods.

2. **Portion control.**
   Sliced items are portioned by the count and by weight. If portioning is by the count, you must take care, during pre-prep, to slice to the proper thickness. If done by weight, each portion can be placed on squares of waxed paper and stacked in a container.

EQUIPMENT

The equipment needed for a sandwich station depends, of course, on the menu and the size of the operation.

1. *Storage equipment* for ingredients includes refrigeration equipment for cold ingredients and a steam table for hot ingredients, such as roasted meats.
2. *Hand tools* are basic requirements for sandwich making and are often the only tools necessary. These include spreaders, spatulas, and knives, including a serrated knife and a sharp chef's knife for cutting the finished sandwich. A cutting board, of course, is also required. A power slicer may be necessary for any slicing not done ahead.
3. *Portion control equipment* includes scoops for fillings and a portion scale for other ingredients.
4. *Cooking equipment* is necessary for most hot sandwiches. Griddles, grills, broilers, and deep fryers are all used for cooking sandwich ingredients to order. Microwave ovens are sometimes used to heat ingredients or finished sandwiches.

Setting Up and Preparing Sandwiches in Quantity

Once the ingredients are prepared and the hand tools assembled, all that's needed for a complete sandwich station is a large table.

Assembly-line production is the most efficient method because it simplifies movements.

Procedure for Making Simple Cold Sandwiches in Quantity

1. Prepare and assemble all ingredients.
2. Assemble necessary equipment, including wrapping materials.
3. Arrange bread slices in rows on the tabletop.
4. Spread each slice with butter or whatever spread is required.
5. Place fillings evenly and neatly on alternate slices, leaving the other slices plain. Fillings should not hang over the edges of the bread. If the filling is spreadable, spread it evenly to the edges. See Figure 17.2 for spreading technique.
6. Top the filled slices with the plain buttered slices.
7. Stack two or three sandwiches and cut with a sharp knife.
8. To hold, do one of the following:
   - Wrap separately in plastic, waxed paper, or sandwich bags.
   - Place in storage pans, cover tightly with plastic wrap, and cover with clean, damp towels. The towels must not touch the sandwiches; their purpose is to provide a moisture barrier to help prevent drying.
9. Refrigerate immediately and hold until served.

Figure 17.2 Spread sandwiches efficiently with three quick strokes as shown.

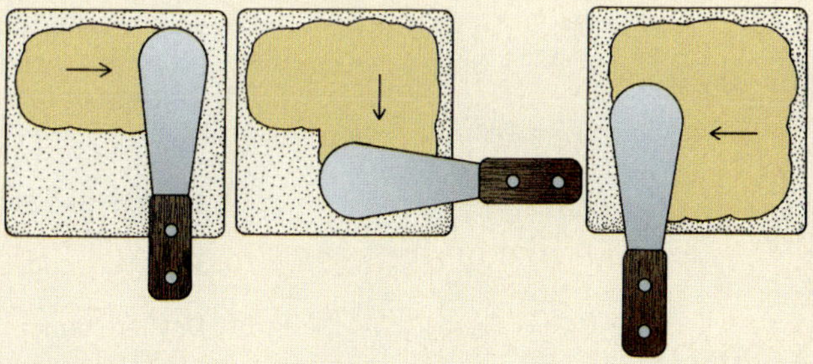

Service

With a few exceptions, such as hamburgers and hot dogs, sandwiches are cut before serving. Cutting serves two purposes: It makes the sandwich easier to handle and eat, and it makes possible a more attractive presentation.

The first purpose is usually accomplished by simply cutting the sandwich in half or, if it is very large or thick, into thirds or quarters.

The second purpose can be served by displaying the cut edges rather than the crust edges to the outside. If the sandwich was neatly made of good ingredients and tastefully garnished, it will be appetizing and attractive. Little purpose is served by cutting and arranging the sandwich in complicated ways.

Hamburgers and other uncut sandwiches may be presented open-face to display the attractive ingredients. For example, a hamburger version often called a *California burger* is presented with the meat on the bottom half of the bun and, alongside, a lettuce leaf and a slice of tomato on the top half of the bun.

Hot sandwiches prepared to order offer the same challenges for creative and attractive presentation as other hot foods, as discussed in Chapter 16. The most important factors in the presentation are using good, fresh ingredients and preparing them with care, using proper techniques for cooking meats, poultry, fish, vegetables, and any other components of the sandwich.

Cold Sandwich Combinations

The following suggestions are only a few of the many sandwiches that can be made from the ingredients listed in the first part of this chapter.

1. Roast beef on rye bread spread with a mixture of softened cream cheese and horseradish.
2. Beef tongue, lettuce, and tomato on onion roll; mayonnaise.
3. Bologna, provolone cheese, tomatoes, and chopped pimiento on hard roll; mayonnaise.
4. Liverwurst, onion slices, and sour pickles on pumpernickel; mayonnaise or butter.
5. Corned beef or ham, Swiss cheese, mustard, and dill pickle slices on rye; mayonnaise or butter.
6. Corned beef, coleslaw (well drained), and Swiss cheese on rye; mayonnaise or butter.
7. Ham, salami, tomato slice, Russian dressing, and lettuce on rye toast.
8. Chicken or turkey, ham, Swiss cheese, and lettuce on white or whole wheat toast; mayonnaise.
9. Chicken and cucumber slices on whole wheat; mayonnaise.
10. Turkey, bacon, Swiss cheese, and lettuce on white or whole wheat toast; mayonnaise.
11. Deviled ham, pineapple slice, and lettuce on white toast.
12. Tuna salad, lettuce, tomato, and shredded cheddar cheese on white toast.
13. Sardines and onion slices on dark rye spread with cream cheese; served open-face.

KEY POINTS TO REVIEW

- How is a typical sandwich station set up and organized? What equipment is used?
- What are the steps in the procedure for making simple cold sandwiches in quantity?

California Burger

YIELD: 1 SANDWICH

U.S.	METRIC	INGREDIENTS
1	1	Hamburger patty, 4 oz (125 g)
1	1	Hamburger roll
as needed	as needed	Butter
2 tsp	10 mL	Mayonnaise
1	1	Lettuce leaf
1	1	Thin slice of onion (optional)
1	1	Tomato slice

PROCEDURE

1. Cook the hamburger patty on a griddle or grill to desired doneness.
2. While the meat is cooking, prepare the roll. Butter the bottom half very lightly. Spread the top half with mayonnaise.
3. Place the halves of the roll side by side on a serving plate.
4. On the top half, place the lettuce leaf, the onion slice (if used), and the tomato slice.
5. When the hamburger patty is cooked, place it on the bottom half of the roll. Serve immediately, open faced.

Per serving: Calories, 480; Protein, 24 g; Fat, 32 g (61% cal.); Cholesterol, 85 mg; Carbohydrates, 23 g; Fiber, 2 g; Sodium, 370 mg.

VARIATIONS

California Cheeseburger

Prepare as in the basic recipe, except place a slice of cheddar or American cheese on the hamburger patty 1 minute before it is done. Cook until the cheese melts.

Cheeseburger (Plain)

Omit mayonnaise, lettuce, onion, and tomato, but add the slice of cheese as in California Cheeseburger.

Cheeseburger with Bacon

Prepare like a cheeseburger, but place 2 half-strips of cooked bacon on the cheese.

California Cheeseburger Deluxe

Prepare like a California Cheeseburger, but place 2 half-strips of bacon on the cheese.

California Burger

Submarine Sandwich

YIELD: 1 SANDWICH

U.S.	METRIC	INGREDIENTS
1	1	Submarine roll
2 tbsp	30 mL	Mayonnaise
1 oz	30 g	Salami, cut in thin slices
1 oz	30 g	Ham, cut in thin slices
1 oz	30 g	Bologna, cut in thin slices
1 oz	30 g	Provolone cheese, cut in thin slices
2	2	Tomato slices
2	2	Onion slices, very thin
3	3	Green bell pepper rings

PROCEDURE

1. Split the roll horizontally, but leave it hinged on one side.
2. Spread the roll with mayonnaise.
3. Arrange the meats and cheese in the sandwich in layers. If the slices of meat are too wide to fit, fold them in half.
4. Arrange the tomato, onion, and pepper slices on top of the meats and cheese.
5. Close the sandwich. Leave it whole or cut it in half for service.
6. Serve the sandwich with mustard and olives or pickles on the side.

Per serving: Calories, 770; Protein, 28 g; Fat, 51 g (60% cal.); Cholesterol, 85 mg; Carbohydrates, 50 g; Fiber, 5 g; Sodium, 1650 mg.

Club Sandwich

YIELD: 1 SANDWICH

U.S.	METRIC	INGREDIENTS
3 slices	3 slices	White bread, toasted
as needed	as needed	Mayonnaise
2 leaves	2 leaves	Lettuce
2 slices	2 slices	Tomato, about ¼ in. (0.5 cm) thick
3 strips	3 strips	Bacon, cooked crisp
2 oz	60 g	Sliced turkey or chicken breast

Per serving: Calories, 580; Protein, 32 g; Fat, 25 g (40% cal.); Cholesterol, 75 mg; Carbohydrates, 53 g; Fiber, 3 g; Sodium, 910 mg.

PROCEDURE

1. Place the toast slices on a clean work surface. Spread the tops with mayonnaise.
2. On the first slice, place 1 lettuce leaf, then 2 slices of tomato, then 3 strips of bacon.
3. Place the second slice of toast on top, spread side down.
4. Spread the top with mayonnaise.
5. On top of this, place the turkey or chicken, then the other lettuce leaf.
6. Top with the third slice of toast, spread side down.
7. Place frilled picks on all 4 sides of the sandwich, as shown in **Figure 17.1**.
8. Cut the sandwich from corner to corner into 4 triangles. Each triangle will have a pick through the center to hold it together.
9. Place on a plate with the points up. The center of the plate may be filled with potato chips, French fries, or other garnish or accompaniment.

VARIATION

Bacon, Lettuce, and Tomato Sandwich (BLT)

Using only 2 slices of toast, prepare the basic recipe through step 3.

Omit remaining ingredients. Cut sandwich in half diagonally for service.

Club Sandwich

Reuben Sandwich

YIELD: 1 SANDWICH

U.S.	METRIC	INGREDIENTS
2 slices	2 slices	Dark rye bread
4 tsp	20 mL	Russian or Thousand Island dressing
2 oz	60 g	Corned beef, sliced very thin
1 oz	30 g	Sauerkraut, well drained
1 oz	30 g	Swiss cheese (1 or 2 slices)
as needed	as needed	Butter

Per serving: Calories, 590; Protein, 25 g; Fat, 39 g (59% cal.); Cholesterol, 105 mg; Carbohydrates, 35 g; Fiber, 4 g; Sodium, 1580 mg.

PROCEDURE

1. Place the slices of bread on a clean work surface.
2. Spread each slice with about 2 tsp (10 mL) dressing.
3. On one of the slices, place the corned beef, then the sauerkraut, then the cheese.
4. Place the second slice of bread on top, spread side down.
5. Butter the top of the sandwich and place buttered side down on a preheated griddle. Immediately butter the other side of the sandwich, which is now on top. (This method is less messy than buttering both sides before placing it on the griddle.)
6. Griddle the sandwich, turning once, until browned on both sides and hot through.
7. Cut the sandwich into halves and serve immediately.

Grilled Cheese Sandwich

YIELD: 1 SANDWICH

U.S.	METRIC	INGREDIENTS
1 slice (1 oz)	1 slice (30 g)	Cheddar or American cheese cut to the size of the bread
2 slices	2 slices	White bread
as needed	as needed	Butter

Per serving: Calories, 360; Protein, 13 g; Fat, 20 g (49% cal.); Cholesterol, 55 mg; Carbohydrates, 34 g; Fiber, 1 g; Sodium, 580 mg.

PROCEDURE

1. Place the slice of cheese between the slices of bread.
2. Butter the outsides of the sandwich and place on a griddle preheated to 350°–375°F (175°–190°C).
3. Cook until golden brown on one side. Turn over and cook until the second side is golden brown and the cheese starts to melt.
4. Remove the sandwich from the griddle. Cut in half diagonally and serve immediately.

VARIATIONS

Grilled Ham and Swiss Sandwich

Make the sandwich with a ½-oz (15-g) slice of Swiss cheese and a 1-oz (30-g) slice of ham. Griddle as in basic recipe.

Croque Monsieur

Make like the Grilled Ham and Swiss Sandwich, above, except use 1 oz (30 g) Gruyère cheese and 1½ oz ham, sliced thin. As a variation, a croque monsieur may also be coated in mornay sauce and heated in an oven until lightly browned.

Grilled Cheese and Bacon Sandwich

Make the sandwich with 1 oz (30 g) cheddar or American cheese and 2 strips of crisp cooked bacon. Griddle as in the basic recipe.

Turkey BLT Wrap

YIELD: 1 SANDWICH

U.S.	METRIC	INGREDIENTS
1	1	Flour tortilla, 10 in. (25 cm) in diameter
½ oz	15 g	Mayonnaise
½–1 oz	15–30 g	Lettuce leaves
3	3	Tomato slices, thin
1 oz	30 g	Cooked bacon, crumbled
2 oz	60 g	Turkey breast, sliced thin

Per serving: Calories, 810; Protein, 32 g; Fat, 35 g (52% cal.); Cholesterol, 75 mg; Carbohydrates, 42 g; Fiber, 3 g; Sodium, 920 g.

PROCEDURE

1. Spread the tortilla with the mayonnaise, leaving a ½-in. (15-mm) border around the outside unspread. (For a richer, moister sandwich, double the quantity of mayonnaise.)
2. Arrange the lettuce leaves in the center of the tortilla, leaving a border of about 2 in. (5 cm) uncovered.
3. Arrange the tomato, bacon, and turkey on top of the lettuce.
4. To roll the wrap, first fold the uncovered rim of the tortilla on opposite edges of the circle toward the center. This closes the ends of the roll to hold in the filling. Then roll the tortilla tightly. The mayonnaise on the edge of the tortilla helps seal it closed.
5. Serve whole or cut in half on the diagonal.

Figure 17.3 Making a wrap sandwich.

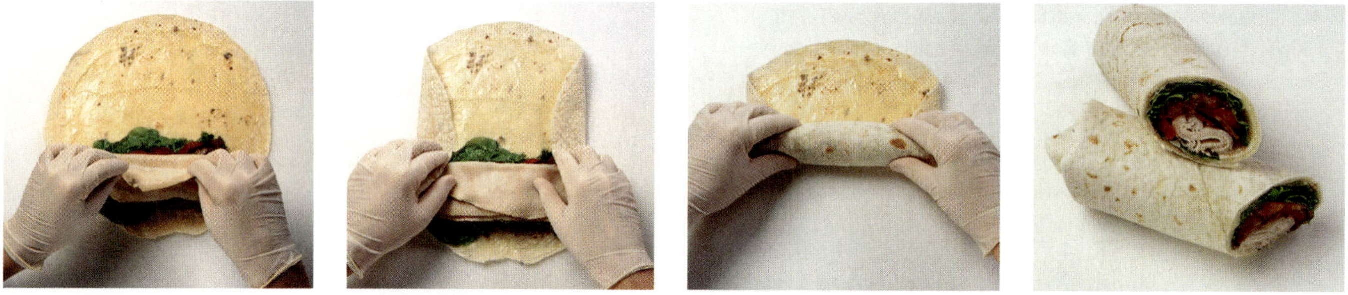

(a) Spread the tortilla with the desired spread. Arrange the fillings toward one edge.

(b) Fold over the sides of the tortilla so the ends of the wrap will be closed.

(c) Roll up.

(d) The finished, cut Turkey BLT Wrap.

Vegetarian Wrap with Mixed Beans

YIELD: 1 SANDWICH

U.S.	METRIC	INGREDIENTS
1	1	Flour tortilla, 10 in. (25 cm) in diameter
as needed	as needed	Olive oil
½–1 oz	15–30 g	Lettuce leaves
3 oz	90 g	Mixed Bean Salad
1½ oz	45 g	Cooked rice, white or brown, cold
½ oz	15 g	Green bell pepper, diced

Per serving: Calories, 510; Protein, 13 g; Fat, 21 g (38% cal.); Cholesterol, 0 mg; Carbohydrates, 65 g; Fiber, 6 g; Sodium, 360 mg.

PROCEDURE

1. Lay the tortilla flat on the workbench. Brush it very lightly with olive oil.
2. Arrange the lettuce leaves in the center of the tortilla, leaving a border of about 2 in. (5 cm) uncovered.
3. Place the bean salad in a sieve to drain excess vinaigrette, reserving the vinaigrette. Mix the bean salad and the rice. If the mixture is dry, add enough of the dressing back to the mixture so it is just sufficiently moistened.
4. Mix in the diced pepper.
5. Place the bean mixture on the tortilla in an oblong mound. Roll and wrap the tortilla tightly around the filling as in the recipe for Turkey BLT Wrap in Figure 17.3 above.

Falafel and Roasted Vegetables in Pita

YIELD: 1 SANDWICH

U.S.	METRIC	INGREDIENTS
1	1	Pita
1 fl oz	30 mL	Tahini Yogurt Dressing (below)
2 oz	60 g	Falafel, 1-oz (30-g) balls, hot
2 oz	60 g	Roasted Summer Vegetables, hot

Per serving: Calories, 350; Protein, 12 g; Fat, 11 g (28% cal.); Cholesterol, 20 mg; Carbohydrates, 53 g; Fiber, 5 g; Sodium, 660 mg.

PROCEDURE

1. The sandwich may be made by splitting open the pita to make a pocket or by wrapping the whole pita around the filling. If you are splitting open the pita, spread the inside with 1 tbsp (15 mL) dressing.
2. Fill with the falafel and vegetables.
3. Drizzle the remaining dressing over the filling.
4. Serve immediately.

VARIATION

Traditional Falafel in Pita

Omit the roasted vegetables. Use two 2-oz (60-g) falafel patties or four 1-oz (30-g) balls. Fill the pita with the falafel, ½ oz (15 g) shredded lettuce, ½–1 oz (15–30 g) diced tomato, and the tahini yogurt dressing.

Traditional Falafel in Pita

Tahini Yogurt Dressing

YIELD: 10 FL OZ (300 ML)

U.S.	METRIC	INGREDIENTS
8 oz	240 g	Plain yogurt
1 oz	30 g	Tahini (sesame paste)
1 fl oz	30 mL	Lemon juice

Per 1 fl oz (29.57 mL): Calories, 30; Protein, 1 g; Fat, 2 g (60% cal.); Cholesterol, 5 mg; Carbohydrates, 2 g; Fiber, 0 g; Sodium, 10 mg.

PROCEDURE

1. Mix all ingredients together.
2. Refrigerate until needed.

Grilled Vegetable Sandwich with Goat Cheese and Sun-Dried Tomatoes

YIELD: 8 SANDWICHES

U.S.	METRIC	INGREDIENTS
8 oz	250 g	Zucchini, trimmed
8 oz	250 g	Eggplant, trimmed
8 oz	250 g	Bell peppers, any color
8 oz	250 g	Onion, large
as needed	as needed	Olive oil
as needed	as needed	Salt
as needed	as needed	Balsamic vinegar

PROCEDURE

1. Cut the zucchini lengthwise into slices about ¼ in. (6 mm) thick.
2. If the eggplant is large, with a thick skin, peel it. Cut large eggplant crosswise into slices ¼ in. (6 mm) thick. Cut small eggplants lengthwise to make larger slices.
3. Core and seed the peppers. Cut into quarters lengthwise.
4. Cut the onion crosswise into slices about ⅓ in. (8 mm) thick. Hold the rings of each slice together with a bamboo skewer.
5. Brush the vegetables with oil and sprinkle them with salt.
6. Grill the vegetables over medium heat, turning as necessary, until they are tender and lightly grill-marked. Cooking times will vary for different vegetables. Regulate the heat or the distance from the flame so the vegetables cook without browning too much.
7. Remove from the grill and brush with a little balsamic vinegar.

U.S.	METRIC	INGREDIENTS
(see step 8)	(see step 8)	Focaccia
4–6 oz	125–180 g	Sun-dried tomatoes, packed in oil, drained, cut julienne
8 oz	250 g	Fresh, soft goat cheese, sliced

8. Cut the focaccia into 3½ × 5-in. (9 × 13-cm) rectangles. If the focaccia is thick, split the rectangles in half horizontally. If it is thin, use 2 rectangles per portion.
9. Arrange the grilled vegetables on half of the rectangles.
10. Arrange the tomatoes on top of the vegetables.
11. Top with the goat cheese and the rest of the bread rectangles.
12. For service, serve whole or cut in half at an angle.

Per serving: Calories, 180; Protein, 8 g; Fat, 10 g (47% cal.); Cholesterol, 15 mg; Carbohydrates, 17 g; Fiber, 3 g; Sodium, 640 mg.

Grilled Portobello and Boursin Sandwich

YIELD: 1 SANDWICH

U.S.	METRIC	INGREDIENTS
1 tbsp	15 mL	Olive oil
1½ tsp	7 mL	Balsamic vinegar
¼ tsp	1 mL	Prepared mustard, French or Dijon style
pinch	pinch	Salt
1	1	Portobello mushroom cap, large
1 oz	30 g	Boursin or other soft, creamy cheese
1	1	Whole-grain roll or bun, split in half
6–8	6–8	Arugula leaves, torn

Per serving: Calories, 390; Protein, 7 g; Fat, 28 g (64% cal.); Cholesterol, 35 mg; Carbohydrates, 28 g; Fiber, 4 g; Sodium, 560 mg.

PROCEDURE

1. With a wire whip, mix the oil, vinegar, mustard, and salt to make a vinaigrette.
2. Brush the mushroom cap with about two-thirds of the vinaigrette. Reserve the rest of the vinaigrette for step 6.
3. Place the mushroom cap on a grill or broiler grid, stem side down. Grill until about half cooked.
4. Turn the mushroom over so the bottom of the cap faces up. Top with the cheese.
5. Grill until the mushroom is tender and the cheese is partly melted.
6. Toss the arugula with the rest of the vinaigrette.
7. Place the mushroom cap, cheese side up, on the bottom half of the roll.
8. Top with the arugula and the top of the bun.

VARIATION

Grilled Portobello and Tomato Sandwich

Omit the cheese. Spread the bread with mayonnaise and top with the grilled mushroom, 2 tomato slices, and the arugula.

Pizza Margherita

YIELD: ONE 12-INCH (30-CM) PIZZA

U.S.	METRIC	INGREDIENTS	PROCEDURE
12 oz	360 g	Fresh, ripe plum tomatoes or canned Italian-style plum tomatoes	1. If using fresh tomatoes, peel, seed, and chop them. If using canned, chop and drain them.
1 tbsp	15 mL	Olive oil	2. Combine the tomatoes and oil in a saucepan. Cook uncovered over moderate heat until the tomatoes are no longer watery.
to taste	to taste	Salt	3. Add salt to taste.
			4. Cool.
12 oz	360 g	French Bread dough (p. 239), fermented	5. Flatten the dough and roll it out into a circle. Drape the dough over the backs of the hands and carefully stretch the circle to a diameter of 12 in. (30 cm). Leave the dough thicker around the rim than in the center.
6	6	Fresh basil leaves, torn in half	6. Flour a peel so the dough does not stick. Lay the circle of dough on it.
4 oz	120 g	Fresh mozzarella cheese, preferably Italian buffalo-milk mozzarella, sliced	7. Spread the tomatoes over the dough, leaving the rim uncovered.
1 tbsp	15 mL	Parmesan cheese (optional)	8. Distribute the basil and the mozzarella cheese over the pizza.
1½ tbsp	22 mL	Olive oil	9. If using the parmesan, sprinkle it over the pizza.
			10. Drizzle with olive oil.
			11. Slide directly onto the hearth of a deck oven preheated to 500°F (260°C). Bake until the dough is browned and the cheese is melted.
			12. Using the peel, remove from the oven and serve immediately.

Per pizza: Calories, 1450; Protein, 49 g; Fat, 63 g (39% cal.); Cholesterol, 90 mg; Carbohydrates, 170 g; Fiber, 9 g; Sodium, 1880 mg.

VARIATION

Pizza Marinara

Omit the mozzarella cheese and the basil. Increase the tomatoes to 2 lb (900 g). Increase the first quantity of olive oil to 1½ tbsp (22 mL). In step 2, cook the tomatoes with 3 cloves garlic, sliced thin, and ½ tsp (2 mL) fresh chopped oregano or ¼ tsp (1 mL) dried oregano.

Pizza Margherita before baking.

Pizza Margherita after baking.

ASSOCIAZIONE VERACE PIZZA NAPOLETANA

Naples, Italy, takes pride in being the birthplace of pizza. Today the Associazione Verace Pizza Napoletana sets down the rules by which its members must abide if they wish to claim they serve authentic Neapolitan pizza. The rules state the dough must contain only flour, water, salt, and natural yeast and it must be made by hand or in an approved mixer. The pizza must be shaped by hand and baked on the hearth of a wood-burning oven. Toppings are limited to a list of approved ingredients.

Two pizzas—Margherita, topped with tomatoes, basil, and buffalo mozzarella, and Marinara, topped with tomatoes, garlic, oregano, and olive oil—are considered the original and true Neapolitan pizzas.

Pizza has grown beyond its origins to become an international favorite. In North America, most of the pizzas served make no claim to being authentically Italian and instead sport toppings such as barbecued chicken, beef with peppers and taco seasonings, and smoked salmon with artichokes, in addition to old favorites like sausage and pepperoni.

TERMS FOR REVIEW

pullman loaf
simple sandwich (hot or cold)
multidecker sandwich
club sandwich
open-faced sandwich (hot or cold)
tea sandwich
wrap
grilled sandwich
deep-fried sandwich
pizza
panino

QUESTIONS FOR DISCUSSION

1. If you cannot get daily bread delivery, what are some measures you can take to ensure the bread in the sandwiches you serve is always fresh?
2. What precautions must you take when using mayonnaise as a sandwich spread?
3. Briefly describe the setup of a short-order sandwich station.
4. How does a setup for preparing sandwiches in quantity differ from a short-order sandwich setup?
5. Why are most sandwiches cut before serving?

Chapter 18

Assorted Canapés, page 395.

Hors d'Oeuvres

In addition to salads and salad dressings, the pantry or garde manger department is generally responsible for the small food items known as *appetizers* or *hors d'oeuvres*. The function of these foods is to enliven the appetite before dinner, often to the accompaniment of drinks, so they are generally small in size and spicy or piquant in flavor.

There is some confusion as to the distinction, if any, between the terms *appetizer* and *hors d'oeuvre*. In general, the first course of a multicourse meal is called an ***appetizer***, and the finger foods served at receptions and with cocktails are called ***hors d'oeuvres***. In some regions, however, the terms are used interchangeably.

This chapter deals not with first courses but primarily with the kinds of food usually encountered away from the dinner table—foods that are the special domain of the pantry chef. They include finger foods such as canapés and relishes, indispensable accompaniments to receptions and parties.

After reading this chapter, you should be able to

1. Name and describe the two principal methods of serving hors d'oeuvres at a reception.
2. Prepare canapés.
3. Prepare hors d'oeuvre cocktails and relishes.
4. Prepare dips.
5. Prepare a variety of other hors d'oeuvres, including antipasti, bruschette, and tapas.
6. Name and describe the three types of sturgeon caviar, and name and describe three other kinds of caviar.

Serving Hors d'Oeuvres

This chapter focuses on foods not served as part of a normal lunch or dinner menu. These foods are usually small items that may be served at a formal reception preceding a meal, as part of a separate event not connected with a meal, or simply as accompaniments to beverages at an informal gathering.

The two most common ways of serving hors d'oeuvres are butler-style and buffet-style.

In ***butler-style service***, the hors d'oeuvre selections are offered to guests by service staff carrying small trays as they pass among the assembled group. Several points should be kept in mind when planning this style of service:

- Each item should be small enough to be eaten in one or two bites.
- Each item should be easily handled by the guest. Canapés or other foods that can be picked up without soiling the fingers are ideal. For foods with a moist or oily surface, offer picks that guests can use to handle the food without touching it. Cocktail napkins should always be offered. Foods requiring a plate are better served on a cocktail buffet.
- Strive for simple, attractive arrangements on the tray. The foods should look appetizing even when only a few items are left. Trays that no longer look appealing should be brought back to the kitchen or pantry area to be refreshed and refilled.
- Ideally, each tray should hold only one food selection. For simple items, two or three selections can be presented on a single tray, but avoid making the tray too complex or overloaded.
- Avoid presenting hot and cold items on the same tray. Cold items are easiest to serve. Hot items should be brought back to the kitchen or pantry area as soon as they are no longer warm.
- For items to be offered with dips, a small bowl of the dip can be presented on the same tray as the individual hors d'oeuvres.

In ***buffet-style service***, hors d'oeuvres are arranged attractively on one or more tables, and guests help themselves. Small plates can be offered on buffet tables, so it is not necessary to confine the food selections to finger foods. Cold hors d'oeuvres are usually presented arranged on trays, which can be easily replaced when they are depleted. Canapés and similar items are best arranged in neat rows, circles, or other arrangements. Raw vegetables may be piled in neat stacks, with bowls of dips placed among them. Hot items should be offered in chafing dishes, which keep them hot.

Buffet presentation is discussed in more detail in Chapter 16.

Finally, hors d'oeuvres are also served informally as accompaniments to beverages. This category is often known as *bar food* and may be served one item at a time, as ordered by the customer, or presented on a buffet. The classic bar food is the popular Spanish-style tapas, discussed on page 401.

Canapés

Canapés may be defined as bite-size open-faced sandwiches.

Canapés are perhaps the most traditional and also the most modern of hors d'oeuvres. This is no doubt because they are so varied and so versatile. Because they consist of tiny portions of food presented on bases of bread, toast, or pastry, they are perfect finger food, easily handled and easily eaten. Nearly any food that can be served in a small portion can be served as a canapé topping. The variety of possible combinations is nearly unlimited.

Most canapés consist of three parts: base, spread, and garnish.

Base

Canapé bases may be made from several items. The following are suggestions:

- Bread cutouts
- Toast cutouts
- Crackers
- Melba toasts
- Tiny unsweetened pastry shells (short dough, phyllo dough, or other pastry)
- Profiteroles (miniature unsweetened cream puff shells, p. 310)
- Toasted pita wedges
- Tortilla chips or cups
- Tiny biscuits, split in half if necessary
- Polenta cutouts
- Miniature pancakes

Many of these items, such as crackers and Melba toasts, can be purchased ready-made, but bread and toast cutouts are the most widely used and offer the lowest food cost, though they require more labor.

Untoasted bread for canapés should be firm enough to allow the finished product to be handled easily. It may be cut thick and flattened slightly with a rolling pin to make firmer. Toast is, of course, firmer, and it gives a pleasing texture and crispness to canapés.

"OUTSIDE THE WORK"

The French expression *hors d'oeuvre* literally translates as "outside the work," meaning "apart from the main meal or main part of the meal." In French, the term is not spelled or pronounced with an *s* at the end to make it plural, so you will often see the plural form spelled the same as the singular. The term has been thoroughly adopted into English, however, and in English-language dictionaries, the plural is spelled and pronounced with a final *s*.

Procedure for Preparing Canapés from Toast

Method 1

1. You may use ready-sliced bread (after trimming the crusts), but it is usually most efficient to use long, unsliced pullman loaves. Cut the crusts from all sides (save for bread crumbs). Cut the bread horizontally into slices ¼ inch (6 mm) thick, as shown in Figure 18.1.
2. Toast the slices in the oven or in a large toaster.
3. Let the toasts cool.
4. Cover with a thin, even layer of the chosen spread and cut into desired shapes with a knife (see Figure 18.2). Make the cuts neat and uniform.

   Alternatively, cut the toasts into desired shapes with small cutters and reserve the trim for bread crumbs. Spread each cutout with desired topping. (This method is more time-consuming, but it may be used with round or odd-shaped cutters if you want to save food cost by not losing spread on unused trimmings.)
5. Garnish the cutouts as desired.

Method 2

1. Cut bread slices as in step 1 above.
2. Cut into desired shapes. Brush both sides of each cutout with melted butter and arrange on sheet pans. Place in a hot oven (450°F/230°C) until golden brown and very crisp, 6 to 8 minutes.
3. Let the bases cool.
4. Assemble the canapés.

This method is more costly but gives a crisper base that holds up better with a moist spread.

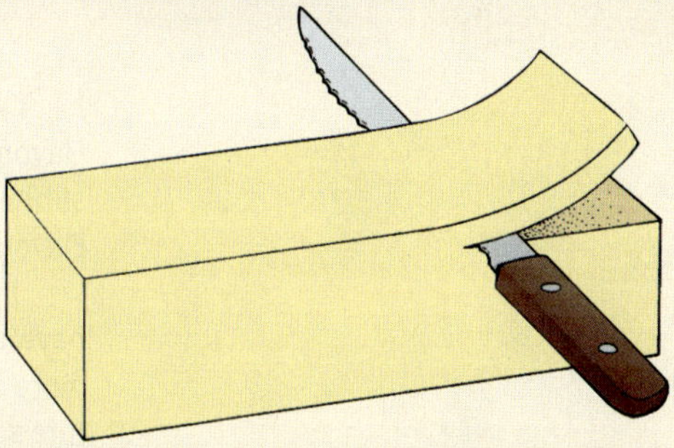

Figure 18.1 For canapés, trim the crusts from a pullman loaf. With a serrated knife, cut the loaf horizontally into thin slices.

Figure 18.2 Bread slices for canapés can be cut into several basic shapes with no waste.

Spread

Canapé spreads may be as simple as butter or softened cream cheese, but it is better to use a more highly flavored spread because sharp or spicy flavors are better for stimulating the appetite.

The spread should be thick enough to cling well to the base and so the garnish sticks to it without falling off.

Spreads may be divided into three basic categories, as follows.

FLAVORED BUTTERS

Most flavored butters are made simply by blending the flavoring ingredients with the softened butter until completely mixed. Solid ingredients should be puréed or chopped very fine so the butter can be spread smoothly.

Proportions of flavoring ingredients to butter can be varied widely, according to taste. For example, to make anchovy butter, you could double the quantity of anchovies to get a stronger flavor, or you could decrease it to get a milder flavor. Because of this variability, and because the basic procedure is so simple, you should be able to make many flavored butters without individual recipes. Popular and versatile flavors for butter spreads include

Lemon	Caviar	Shrimp
Parsley	Mustard	Olive
Tarragon	Horseradish	Shallot or scallion
Chive	Pimiento	Curry
Anchovy	Blue cheese	Caper

FLAVORED CREAM CHEESE

Flavored cream cheese spreads are made like flavored butters, except cream cheese is substituted for the butter. Alternatively, use a mixture of cream cheese and butter, well blended. Flavor variations are the same as those listed above for butter.

In addition, cream cheese is often blended with sharper, more flavorful cheeses that have been mashed or grated. Adding cream cheese to firmer cheese helps make the latter more spreadable. A liquid such as milk, cream, or port wine may be added to make the mixture softer. Such cheese spreads are often flavored with spices and herbs such as paprika, caraway seeds, dry mustard, parsley, or tarragon.

MEAT OR FISH SALAD SPREADS

You can use many cold meat or fish mixtures, such as cooked salads, to make canapé spreads. Popular examples include tuna salad, salmon salad, shrimp salad, chicken salad, deviled ham, and liver pâté.

To convert a salad recipe to a spread recipe, you may need to make one or more of the following modifications:

1. Chop the solid ingredients very fine, or grind or purée them, so the mixture is spreadable and not chunky.

2. Do not add the liquid ingredients and mayonnaise all at once. Add them a little at a time, just until the mixture reaches a thick, spreadable consistency.

3. Check the seasonings carefully. You may want to increase the seasonings to make the spread more stimulating to the appetite.

Garnish

The garnish of a canapé is any food item or combination of items placed on top of the spread. It may be a major part of the canapé, such as a slice of ham or cheese, or it may be a small tidbit selected for color, design, texture, or flavor accent, such as a pimiento cutout, a slice of

Guidelines for Assembling Canapés

1. **Good mise en place is essential.**
   Preparing thousands of canapés for large functions can be tedious work, so it is essential that all bases, spreads, and garnishes be prepared ahead of time in order that final assembly may go quickly and smoothly.
2. **Assemble as close as possible to serving time.**
   Bases quickly become soggy, and spreads and garnishes dry out easily. As trays are completed, they may be covered lightly with plastic and held for a short time under refrigeration. Be sure to observe all rules for safe food handling and storage.
3. **Select harmonious flavor combinations in spreads and garnish.**
   For example, caviar and chutney or anchovy and ham are not appealing combinations, but these combinations are:

   Mustard butter and ham
   Lemon butter and caviar
   Pimiento cream cheese and sardine
   Horseradish butter and smoked salmon or smoked tongue
   Tuna salad and capers
   Anchovy butter, hard-cooked egg slice, and olive
4. **Be sure that at least one of the ingredients is spicy or pronounced in flavor.**
   A bland canapé has little value as an appetizer.
5. **Use high-quality ingredients.**
   Canapés can be a good way to utilize leftovers, but only if the leftovers have been carefully handled and stored to retain freshness.
6. **Keep it simple.**
   Simple, neat arrangements are more attractive than elaborate, overworked designs. Besides, you don't have time to get too fancy. Be sure the canapés hold together and do not fall apart in the customers' hands.
7. **Arrange the canapés carefully and attractively on trays.**
   Much of the attraction of canapés is eye appeal, and the customer never sees just one at a time, but a full tray. Each tray should carry an assortment of flavors and textures, so there is something for every taste.
   Figure 18.3 shows a tray of simple, attractive canapés.

Figure 18.3 Assorted canapés, from left: gravlax with mustard cream cheese; chicken liver pâté with mustard butter and black olive; caviar, red onion, and sour cream in red potato; herbed Boursin cheese with almonds; beef tenderloin with horseradish cream cheese and capers.

radish, a caper, or a dab of caviar. Even the spread can be used as a garnish. For example, you may make a canapé with a mustard butter spread and a slice of ham, then decorate the ham with a border or design of mustard butter piped on with a paper cone.

Here are some of the many food items that may be used alone or in combination to decorate canapés:

VEGETABLES, PICKLES, AND RELISHES

- Radish slices
- Olives
- Pickles
- Capers
- Pimiento
- Pickled onions
- Chutney
- Asparagus tips
- Cucumber slices
- Cherry tomato slices or halves
- Watercress leaves
- Marinated mushrooms
- Parsley

KEY POINTS TO REVIEW

- What are the two styles of hors d'oeuvre service? Describe each.
- What are canapés? What are the three components of canapés?
- What are the guidelines for assembling canapés?

FISH

Smoked oysters and clams	Herring	Salmon or tuna flakes
Smoked salmon	Shrimp	Crab meat
Smoked trout	Rolled anchovy fillets	Lobster chunks or slices
	Caviar	Sardines

MEATS

Ham	Smoked tongue
Salami	Roast beef
Chicken or turkey breast	

OTHER

Cheese
Hard-cooked egg slices

Cocktails

The term ***cocktail*** is used not only for alcoholic beverages and vegetable and fruit juices but also for a group of appetizers made of seafood or fruit, usually with a tart or tangy sauce. Such cocktails are always served well chilled, often on a bed of crushed ice.

Oysters and clams on the half-shell are popular seafood cocktails, as are shrimp, crabmeat, lobster, and firm, flaked white fish with an appropriate sauce.

Fresh oysters and clams on the half-shell should be opened just before they are served (see pp. 69–71) and arranged on flat plates, preferably on a bed of ice. Provide cocktail sauce in a small cup in the center or at the side of the plate. Lemon wedges should also be provided.

Cocktails of shrimp and other cooked seafood are generally served in a stemmed glass or in a small, cup-shaped bowl, which may be nestled in a bed of ice. The cocktail sauce may be put in the glass first and the seafood then arranged on top, partially immersed. Or the cocktail sauce may be added to the seafood as a topping. A third alternative is to serve the sauce separately in a small cup, as for raw oysters. Garnish the dish attractively with lettuce or other salad greens and with lemon wedges.

Fruit cups served as cocktails should be pleasantly tart and not too sweet. Many fruit salads may be served as cocktails. Adding fresh lemon or lime juice to fruit mixtures or serving with a garnish of lemon or lime wedges provides the necessary tartness. A simple wedge of melon with lime is a refreshing cocktail.

A few drops of a flavored liqueur can also be used to perk up the flavor of a fruit cocktail.

Relishes

The term ***relish*** covers two categories of foods: raw vegetables and pickled items.

Raw Vegetables

Raw vegetables are also known as ***crudités*** (croo dee tays; *cru* in French means "raw").

Any vegetable that can be eaten raw may be cut into sticks or other attractive, bite-size shapes and served as a relish. Most popular are celery, carrots, and radishes. Other good choices are green and red peppers, zucchini, cucumbers, scallions, cauliflower and broccoli florets, peeled broccoli stems, peeled kohlrabi, cherry tomatoes, and Belgian endive leaves. Crudités are often served with an appropriate dip (see the next section).

Raw vegetables must be served crisp and well chilled, just as in salads. Use the freshest, most attractive vegetables possible. If they are a little wilted, they can be recrisped by holding them for a short time in ice water. Serving vegetables embedded in crushed ice will maintain their crispness.

An imaginative pantry chef can make an attractive, colorful bouquet of raw vegetables.

Pickled Items

A wide variety of items such as dilled cucumber pickles, gherkins, olives, watermelon pickles, pickled peppers, spiced beets, and other preserved vegetables and fruits are served as relishes. These items are rarely made in-house but are purchased already prepared. Like raw vegetables, they should be served chilled.

Dips

Savory ***dips*** are popular accompaniments to potato chips, crackers, and raw vegetables.

Proper consistency is important for any dip you prepare. It must not be so thick it cannot be scooped up without breaking the chip or cracker, but it must be thick enough to stick to the items used as dippers. Proper consistency means thickness *at serving temperature*. Most dips become thicker when held in the refrigerator.

Many mixtures used as spreads (see section on canapés) can also be used as dips. Thin or soften them by adding a little mayonnaise, cream, or other appropriate liquid.

The recipes here are examples of typical dips. Many other sauces and salad dressings can be used as dips. Salsas and aïoli are two popular examples.

Blue Cheese Dip

YIELD: 1 QT (1 L)

U.S.	METRIC	INGREDIENTS
12 oz	375 g	Cream cheese
5 fl oz	150 mL	Milk
6 oz	175 g	Mayonnaise
1 fl oz	30 mL	Lemon juice
1 oz	30 g	Onion, minced
½ tsp	2 mL	Hot red pepper sauce
½ tsp	2 mL	Worcestershire sauce
10 oz	300 g	Blue cheese, crumbled

Per 1 fl oz (29.57 mL): Calories, 110; Protein, 3 g; Fat, 11 g (86% cal.); Cholesterol, 20 mg; Carbohydrates, 1 g; Fiber, 0 g; Sodium, 190 mg.

PROCEDURE

1. In a mixer with the paddle attachment, beat the cream cheese at low speed until soft and smooth.
2. With the machine running, slowly beat in the milk.
3. Add the rest of the ingredients and blend in well.
4. Taste and adjust seasonings. Chill.

VARIATION

Cheddar Cheese Dip

Substitute grated sharp cheddar cheese for the blue cheese. If desired, add chopped chives.

Garlic Cheese Dip

Add mashed garlic to taste to Cheddar Cheese Dip.

Bacon Cheese Dip

Add crumbled crisp bacon to Cheddar Cheese Dip.

Cheese and Chile Dip

Flavor Cheddar Cheese Dip with canned green chiles, chopped.

Romesco

YIELD: 1 PT (500 ML)

U.S.	METRIC	INGREDIENTS	PROCEDURE
1 oz	30 g	White bread	1. Sauté the bread in the olive oil until golden.
½ fl oz	15 mL	Olive oil	2. Toast the almonds in an oven at 350°F (175°C) about 15 minutes or in a skillet over moderately low heat until light golden, not dark brown. Remove the almonds from the pan as soon as they are golden so they do not brown further.
3 oz	90 g	Blanched almonds	
2 tsp	10 mL	Garlic, chopped	3. Combine the bread, almonds, and garlic in a food processor. Grind until fine.
10 oz	300 g	Tomatoes, peeled	4. Add the tomatoes, paprika, and cayenne. Process to a paste.
2 tsp	10 mL	Spanish paprika	5. With the machine running, gradually add the vinegar and then the oil in a slow stream.
⅛ tsp	0.5 mL	Cayenne	6. Adjust the seasonings with salt and pepper. Add more vinegar if required. The sauce should not be too acidic but should have a definite sharpness.
1½ fl oz	45 mL	Red wine vinegar	
3–4 fl oz	90–120 mL	Olive oil	
to taste	to taste	Salt	
to taste	to taste	Pepper	

Per 1 fl oz (29.57 mL): Calories, 100; Protein, 2 g; Fat, 9 g (80% cal.); Cholesterol, 0 mg; Carbohydrates, 3 g; Fiber, 1 g; Sodium, 15 mg.

Hummus (Chickpea Dip)

YIELD: 1 QT (1 L)

U.S.	METRIC	INGREDIENTS	PROCEDURE
1 lb	500 g	Cooked or canned chickpeas, drained	1. Purée the chickpeas with the tahini, garlic, lemon juice, and olive oil.
8 oz	250 g	Tahini (sesame paste)	2. If necessary, thin the purée with a little water or additional lemon juice, depending on the taste.
¼ oz	8 g	Garlic, crushed	3. Season with salt to taste and with cayenne.
4 fl oz	125 mL	Lemon juice	4. Chill at least 1 hour to allow the flavors time to blend.
1 fl oz	30 mL	Olive oil	
to taste	to taste	Salt	
pinch	pinch	Cayenne	
1–2 fl oz	30–50 mL	Olive oil	5. Spoon the hummus into serving bowls. Drizzle additional olive oil over each bowl before serving.

Per 1 fl oz (29.57 mL): Calories, 80; Protein, 3 g; Fat, 6 g (63% cal.); Cholesterol, 0 mg; Carbohydrates, 5 g; Fiber, 2 g; Sodium, 0 mg.

Hummus

VARIATION

Babaganouj

Substitute eggplant purée for the chickpeas. Make the eggplant purée as follows: Toast whole eggplants under a broiler, over a gas burner, or directly on a flattop range until the skin is charred and the eggplant is soft. Peel off the charred skin under running water and cut off the tops. Remove large clumps of seeds, if desired. Let stand in a china cap or sieve to let excess moisture drain, then purée the pulp. Reduce the lemon juice to 2–3 fl oz (60–90 mL) and the tahini to 4 oz (125 g). Double the olive oil.

Guacamole

YIELD: APPROXIMATELY 1 QT (1 L)

U.S.	METRIC	INGREDIENTS
4	4	Ripe avocados, medium size
2 oz	60 g	Onion, grated
1	1	Small, hot green chile such as jalapeño, minced
1 fl oz	30 mL	Lime or lemon juice
1 fl oz	30 mL	Olive oil
to taste	to taste	Salt
12 oz	375 g	Fresh tomato (optional)

Per 1 fl oz (29.57 mL): Calories, 45; Protein, 1 g; Fat, 4 g (75% cal.); Cholesterol, 0 mg; Carbohydrates, 2 g; Fiber, 2 g; Sodium, 0 mg.

Note: If fresh chiles are not available, use canned chiles or a few dashes of hot red pepper sauce.

PROCEDURE

1. Pit and peel the avocados. Mash the pulp coarsely. The purée should be slightly lumpy rather than smooth.
2. Mix in the onion, minced chile, lime or lemon juice, olive oil, and salt to taste.
3. If desired, peel, seed, and dice the tomato and mix it into the avocado.
4. Cover tightly with plastic wrap placed on the surface of the guacamole. This is to protect it from air, which will darken it. For the same reason, guacamole should not be made too long before serving time. Chill the guacamole until ready to serve.

VARIATION

Sour Cream Avocado Dip

Use 1 oz (30 g) onion. Omit the olive oil and tomato. Mash the avocado to a smooth purée. Add ½–¾ pt (250–375 mL) sour cream.

Guacamole

Parmesan Dip

YIELD: 1 PT (480 ML)

U.S.	METRIC	INGREDIENTS
1 pt	480 mL	Mayonnaise
3½ oz	105 g	Parmesan cheese, grated
4½ tsp	22 mL	White vinegar
4 tsp	20 mL	Sugar
4 tsp	20 mL	Dijon mustard
1 tsp	5 mL	Garlic powder
1½ tsp	7 mL	Paprika
3 tbsp	45 mL	Water

Per 1 fl oz (29.57 mL): Calories, 240; Protein, 3 g; Fat, 24 g (92% cal.); Cholesterol, 15 mg; Carbohydrates, 2 g; Fiber, 0 g; Sodium, 280 mg.

PROCEDURE

1. Combine the mayonnaise, cheese, vinegar, sugar, mustard, garlic powder, and paprika in a bowl. Mix thoroughly.
2. Stir in a little water to thin to desired consistency.

Miscellaneous Hors d'Oeuvres

A great variety of other foods, both hot and cold, can be served as hors d'oeuvres. If they are to be served away from the dinner table, it is best if they can be eaten with the fingers or speared with a pick. At a reception at which many hors d'oeuvres are served, it is all right if a few of them must be eaten with forks from small plates, but finger food is much easier for the guests, who are likely to be standing and holding a wineglass or cocktail glass while eating.

Of course, there are thousands of hors d'oeuvre recipes, including many adapted from the cuisines of other lands. Those included here are a sampling of some popular types.

Many of the recipes given elsewhere in this book can be adapted as hors d'oeuvre recipes. In most cases, unit size or portion size should be decreased. For example, meatballs should be made small enough to be eaten in one or two bites. Among the items most readily adapted are the following:

- Barbecued Spareribs
- Shish Kebab
- Deep-Fried Chicken (using wing sections)
- Baked Clams Oreganata
- Oysters and Clams Casino
- Broiled Shrimp, Scampi Style
- Broiled Scallops
- Fried Breaded Scallops, Shrimp, Oysters, or Clams
- Steamed Mussels (served on the half-shell, with a sauce)
- Cod Cakes or other fish cakes
- Fish Tartares
- Seviche
- Vegetable Fritters
- Many salads
- Quiche
- Cheese Wafers and Straws
- Sushi
- Gravlax
- Smoked Salmon
- Smoked Trout
- Smoked Duck
- Pâtés, Terrines, and Galantines
- Ham Mousse
- Foie Gras Mousse and Terrine

In addition to the categories of hors d'oeuvres introduced so far, the following additional terms merit brief explanation.

Antipasto

Italian cuisine is particularly rich in hors d'oeuvres, or *antipasti*, as they are called (singular form: ***antipasto***). Many books give a recipe for a mixed salad called *antipasto*. This is misleading, however, because the Italian term does not refer to a specific recipe but to any typically Italian hors d'oeuvre, hot or cold.

Many Italian-style restaurants offer a cold antipasto plate or platter comprising an assortment of flavorful tidbits. Typical components include the following:

- Cured meats, such as salami, prosciutto, bologna, and boiled ham.
- Seafood items, especially canned or preserved items such as sardines, anchovies, and tuna.
- Cheeses, such as provolone and mozzarella.
- Hard-cooked eggs and stuffed eggs.
- Relishes, such as raw carrots, celery, fennel, radishes, cauliflower, and tomatoes, and cooked or pickled items, such as olives, artichoke hearts, small hot peppers, and onions.
- Mushrooms and other vegetables prepared à la grecque.
- Cooked dried beans and other firm vegetables in a piquant vinaigrette.

Bruschetta

In recent years, one of the most popular hors d'oeuvres is the Roman garlic bread called ***bruschetta*** (broo sket ta; plural: *bruschette*, pronounced broo sket teh). Bruschetta, in its most basic form, is a slice of Italian bread that is toasted, rubbed with crushed garlic, and drizzled with olive oil. When made with good bread and extra-virgin olive oil, this simple hors d'oeuvre is fine on its own. But it is no doubt the variety of toppings that can be served on this garlic-bread base that accounts for its popularity.

Perhaps the best-known topping is a seasoned mixture of diced fresh tomatoes and olive oil, but this is far from the only possibility. Meats, cheeses, cooked dried beans, and raw and cooked vegetables are all appropriate. In fact, the bruschetta is a type of antipasto, and many of the items listed in the preceding section may also be served as bruschetta topping. Several variations are included among the recipes in this chapter.

Bruschette are similar to canapés in that they are toast with topping. However, they are larger and heartier than typical canapés and can be served as the appetizer course of a dinner.

Tapas

Another type of hors d'oeuvre that has become increasingly popular is the Spanish *tapa*. The variety of tapas is so great that it is difficult to give a definition, except to say that a tapa is a small food item intended to be eaten with wine or other drinks, usually in taverns and bars. The Spanish term literally means "lid," and the original tapa is thought to be a small bit of food, perhaps a slice of cured ham, placed on top of a glass of sherry.

As varied as they are, tapas have a few points in common. They are served in small portions and are intended to be eaten immediately and quickly. In most cases, they are served on small plates. Many can be eaten by hand, but many others, especially those served in a sauce, are eaten with a fork. Often they are the same kinds of foods that can be served as first courses of a dinner, but presented in smaller portions.

SPANISH TAPAS TRADITIONS

Normal lunchtime in Spain is two or three o'clock, while dinner usually isn't eaten before ten o'clock at night. What better way to spend some of those long hours after work and before dinner than to meet friends at a local tavern and enjoy a glass or two of sherry? People go to tapas bars not so much to eat but to talk and to enjoy each other's company. But of course lunch was hours earlier, and dinner will be hours later, so having a few bites to eat with your wine is almost a necessity.

Out of these traditional dining habits grew the sociable custom of tapas, which has spread around the world.

Caviar

Caviar is the salted roe, or eggs, of the sturgeon. In the United States and Canada, any product labeled simply *caviar* must come from sturgeon. Roe from any other fish must be labeled as such (for example, *whitefish* caviar).

The most important caviar-producing countries have traditionally been Russia and Iran, both of which border the Caspian Sea, where the sturgeon are harvested. Sturgeon live in other waters as well, including North American waters. Production of North American caviar has been growing in recent years, in part because of difficulties obtaining caviar from the Caspian.

To categorize it further, caviar is given the name of the species of sturgeon it is taken from. The beluga is the largest and scarcest sturgeon, and it yields the largest and most expensive eggs. Next in size are osetra and sevruga.

Although the larger eggs are generally more expensive, size or price alone does not necessarily indicate quality. All three types of caviar vary considerably in quality. The only sure way to determine the quality of a particular tin or jar of caviar is to taste it.

Good-quality caviar is made up of shiny, whole eggs, with few, if any, broken. It should not have a strong, fishy smell, and it should not look watery or oily.

Caviar made with a relatively low proportion of salt is labeled *malassol*, which means "little salt." Malassol caviar is considered to be of better quality than the more highly salted varieties. However, for those who must restrict their salt intake, there is no such thing as low-sodium caviar. Even malassol is salty.

Caviar is either fresh or pasteurized. Fresh caviar in an unopened tin will keep for a few weeks, as long as it is kept cold. Once opened, it begins to deteriorate quickly and should be eaten the same day, if possible. Pasteurized caviar is of lower quality because it has been heat-treated. Unopened, it will keep much longer than fresh caviar, but once opened, it too should be eaten as quickly as possible, or within a few days.

Sturgeon caviar

Salmon caviar

Tobiko

OTHER CAVIARS

Roe from other fish, including trout, salmon, whitefish, and lumpfish, is also salted to make caviar. Once again, quality varies considerably, ranging from good to nearly inedible. Those of better quality are useful alternatives to expensive sturgeon caviar. Three popular types are *salmon caviar*, large red eggs, often paired with smoked salmon or other salmon products in appetizer dishes; *bleak roe*, tiny, mild-tasting, orange eggs from a fish native to the Baltic; and *tobiko*, tiny orange eggs from Japanese flying fish, introduced to the West in Japanese sushi restaurants.

SERVING CAVIAR

The best caviar should be served ice-cold and as simply as possible. The traditional caviar accompaniments of chopped onion, lemon, chopped egg, and sour cream may be all right for inexpensive roes, but they overwhelm the delicate flavor of top-quality beluga, osetra, and sevruga. Spoons for eating caviar should be made of bone, porcelain, mother of pearl, or even plastic, but not metal, which reacts with the caviar to give it an unpleasant taste.

For more elaborate presentations, caviars a notch or two below the best quality are more economical choices. Foods served with caviar should be fairly mild or delicate. Such items as mild smoked salmon, oysters, and potatoes are often used.

Amuse Bouche

An ***amuse bouche*** (ah mews boosh) is a tiny appetizer or hors d'oeuvre offered, compliments of the chef and usually in more expensive restaurants, to guests seated at their tables, either before or after they have ordered from the menu. It is an opportunity to showcase an aspect of the chef's cooking style and talent and to welcome the guests.

Nearly anything that can be served in a tiny portion can be served as an amuse bouche, including salads, soups (in espresso cups), canapés, and little portions of meat, fish, or vegetable with a few drops of sauce and a garnish. Usually chefs don't use a separate category of recipe for these items but borrow something from one of their regular menus, preferably not a dish on the menu that evening, and give it a different presentation, garnish, or sauce.

KEY POINTS TO REVIEW

- What are hors d'oeuvre cocktails? What are relishes?
- What is the proper consistency for dips?
- What do the following terms mean: antipasto; bruschetta; tapas? Give examples of each.
- What does the term *caviar*, when used by itself, mean? What are the three types of sturgeon caviar? Give the names and descriptions of three other types of caviar.

Prosciutto and Melon Balls

YIELD: AS DESIRED

U.S.	METRIC	INGREDIENTS
as needed	as needed	Melon (cantaloupe, honeydew, crenshaw, etc.)
to taste	to taste	Lime juice
as needed	as needed	Prosciutto ham

Per serving: Calories 20; Protein, 2 g; Fat, 1 g (43% cal.); Cholesterol, 5 mg; Carbohydrates, 1 g; Fiber, 0 g; Sodium, 175 mg.

One serving equals ½ ounce (15 g) melon with ¼ ounce (7 g) prosciutto.

PROCEDURE

1. Using a ball cutter, cut the melon into small balls.
2. Sprinkle the melon balls with lime juice and let stand 10 minutes.
3. Using a slicing machine, cut the ham into paper-thin slices. Cut large slices in half crosswise.
4. Shortly before serving, wrap each melon ball in a slice of ham and fasten with a pick.

VARIATION

Other fruits may be substituted for the melon, such as pineapple sticks or chunks, fresh figs (whole, halved, or quartered), and fresh pear or peach slices. Pears and peaches must be coated with lime or lemon juice to prevent darkening.

Spinach Boreks

YIELD: 50 PIECES

U.S.	METRIC	INGREDIENTS	PROCEDURE
2 lb	900 g	Spinach	1. Trim, wash, and steam or boil the spinach just until it is thoroughly wilted. 2. Drain, cool under cold running water, and squeeze dry. Chop fine.
4 oz	100 g	Butter	3. Heat the butter in a sauté pan. Sauté the onions and scallions over low heat until soft.
4 oz	100 g	Onions, chopped fine	4. Remove from the heat and add the spinach and dill. Mix to coat the spinach lightly with butter.
1 oz	30 g	Scallions, chopped fine	5. Mix in the cheese.
1 oz	30 g	Fresh dill weed, chopped	6. Season to taste with salt and pepper.
1 lb	450 g	Feta cheese, crumbled	
to taste	to taste	Salt	
to taste	to taste	Pepper	
25 sheets	25 sheets	Phyllo dough (about 1 lb/450 g)	7. Thaw the phyllo if it is frozen. Unwrap and unfold the stack of sheets and cut them in half lengthwise. Keep them covered to prevent drying.
8 oz approximately	225 g approximately	Melted butter	8. Taking one sheet at a time, brush each lightly with melted butter. Fold the sheet in half lengthwise and butter it again. 9. Put a small mound (about ½–⅔ oz/15–20 g) of the spinach mixture toward the bottom of the strip and a little to one side, as shown in **Figure 18.4**. 10. Fold into triangular packets as indicated in the illustration. 11. Arrange the triangles on baking sheets with the loose ends of the phyllo on the bottom. Brush the tops with melted butter. 12. Bake at 375°F (190°C) until golden brown and crisp, 20–25 minutes. 13. Serve warm.

Per 1 piece: Calories, 110; Protein, 2 g; Fat, 8 g (69% cal.); Cholesterol, 25 mg; Carbohydrates, 6 g; Fiber, 1 g; Sodium, 210 mg.

VARIATION

Many other fillings can be baked wrapped in phyllo, as long as they are not too juicy. The following are some suggestions:

Diced ham, cheddar cheese, and prepared mustard

Gruyère cheese, blue cheese, walnuts

Feta and cream cheese (2 parts feta to 1 part cream cheese) mixed together, plus 1 egg yolk per 12 oz (350 g) cheese

Sautéed mushrooms and onions, crumbled bacon, parsley, parmesan cheese

Diced cooked chicken, mozzarella cheese, sun-dried tomatoes, basil

Crabmeat, sautéed shellfish, cream cheese, hot pepper sauce

Ratatouille

Figure 18.4 Folding phyllo dough triangles.

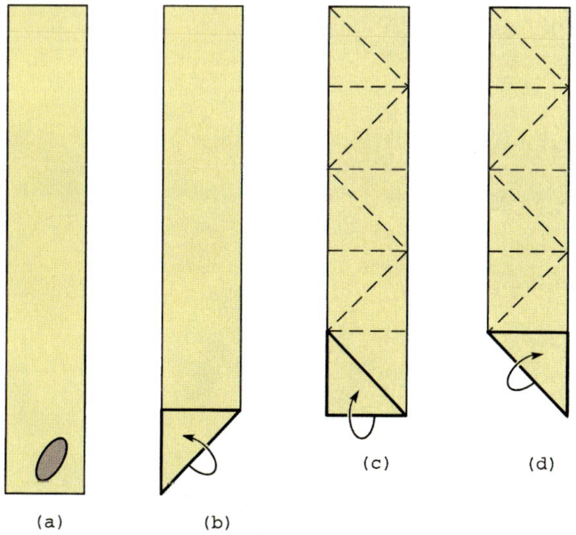

(a) Place the filling at the bottom of the strip of buttered phyllo dough and a little to one side.
(b) Fold the bottom corner over at a 45-degree angle to form a triangle.
(c, d) Continue folding the triangle as shown in the diagram.

Rumaki

U.S.	METRIC	INGREDIENTS
15	15	Chicken livers
8 fl oz	250 mL	Soy sauce
1 clove	1 clove	Garlic, cut in half
3 slices	3 slices	Fresh ginger root
15 (approx.)	15 (approx.)	Water chestnuts
30 strips	30 strips	Bacon

Per 1 piece: Calories, 62; Protein, 2 g; Fat, 5 g (79% cal.); Cholesterol, 25 mg; Carbohydrates, 1 g; Fiber, 0 g; Sodium, 390 mg.

PROCEDURE

1. Trim the chicken livers and cut them into quarters.
2. Marinate the livers overnight with the soy sauce, garlic, and ginger.
3. Cut each water chestnut into 3–5 pieces to make the same number as liver pieces.
4. Cut each slice of bacon in half.
5. Wrap each liver piece together with a water chestnut piece in a piece of bacon and secure with a pick.
6. Bake at 400°F (200°C) until the bacon is cooked, about 15 minutes. Brush with the marinade 2 or 3 times during baking.

Chicken Satay

YIELD: ABOUT 24 PIECES, 1 OZ (30 G) EACH

U.S.	METRIC	INGREDIENTS
		Marinade:
1 stalk	1 stalk	Lemongrass
1 tbsp	15 mL	Peanut butter
1½ oz	45 g	Shallots, chopped fine
1½ tsp	7 mL	Brown sugar
1 tsp	5 mL	Salt
½ tsp	2 mL	Ground cumin
¼ tsp	1 mL	Ground coriander
¼ tsp	1 mL	Cinnamon
¼ tsp	1 mL	Turmeric
1 tbsp	15 mL	Oil
1½ lb	720 g	Chicken breasts, boneless, skinless, trimmed of all fat
1 pt, or as needed	500 mL, or as needed	Indonesian Peanut Sauce

Per 1 piece: Calories, 110; Protein, 9 g; Fat, 7 g (55% cal.); Cholesterol, 17.5 mg; Carbohydrates, 4 g; Fiber, 1 g; Sodium, 240 mg.

PROCEDURE

1. Trim and discard the lower end of the lemongrass. Cut the tender bottom portion of the stalk into paper-thin slices. Discard the top.
2. Mix the lemongrass, peanut butter, shallots, sugar, salt, spices, and oil into a coarse paste. If necessary, add a few drops of water.
3. Cut the chicken breast lengthwise into thin strips. You should have about 24 pieces.
4. Mix the chicken with the marinade so all pieces are coated. Refrigerate 3 hours.
5. While the chicken is marinating, soak bamboo skewers in water at least 3 hours to keep them from burning during grilling.
6. Thread each chicken strip onto a skewer, leaving the top half of the skewer empty so it can be used as a handle.
7. Grill the chicken skewers about 2 minutes on each side, or until done.
8. Serve with the sauce for dipping.

Chicken Satay

CHICKEN SATAY

Satay, or saté, is a snack food, often sold by street vendors, popular throughout Southeast Asia. Although it originated in Indonesia, where there are many dozens of versions, it can also be found in Malaysia, Singapore, Thailand, the Philippines, and neighboring countries. Satay consists of cubes or strips of meat or poultry that are marinated, threaded on skewers, and grilled. It is usually served with some kind of spicy sauce.

The marinade for the satay included here is inspired by the famous satays of Singapore.

Beef Teriyaki Skewers

YIELD: ABOUT 50 PIECES

U.S.	METRIC	INGREDIENTS
		Marinade:
1½ fl oz	45 mL	Sake
3 fl oz	90 mL	Mirin (sweet Japanese rice wine)
3½ fl oz	105 mL	Soy sauce
1 tbsp	15 mL	Sugar
1 lb 8 oz	720 g	Beef tenderloin, or other tender beef cut, trimmed of all fat and silverskin

Per 1 piece: Calories, 20; Protein, 2 g; Fat, 1 g (52% cal.); Cholesterol, 5 mg; Carbohydrates, 0 g; Fiber, 0 g; Sodium, 20 mg.

PROCEDURE

1. Combine the sake, mirin, soy sauce, and sugar in a saucepan. Bring to a boil to dissolve the sugar.
2. Cool thoroughly, then chill.
3. Cut the beef into ¾-in. (2-cm) cubes.
4. Mix the beef with the marinade so all of it is coated. Refrigerate 3–4 hours.
5. Impale each cube of meat on the end of a bamboo skewer.
6. Grill or broil the meat to the desired doneness. Serve immediately.

VARIATION

For more authentic Japanese teriyaki, do not marinate the beef (see sidebar on p. 36). Instead, when the meat is about half cooked, begin basting frequently with the marinade to give it a light glaze.

Dates Stuffed with Gorgonzola

YIELD: 40 PIECES

U.S.	METRIC	INGREDIENTS
40	40	Medjool or other large dates
4 oz	120 g	Gorgonzola cheese

Per 1 piece: Calories, 80; Protein, 1 g; Fat, 1 g (10% cal.); Cholesterol, 0 mg; Carbohydrates, 19 g; Fiber, 2 g; Sodium, 54 mg.

PROCEDURE

1. With the point of a paring knife, slit each date lengthwise and carefully remove the pit.
2. Divide the cheese into as many small portions as you have dates. (Don't worry if the cheese crumbles; you just need enough to fit in each date, about ⅒ oz/3 g per date, whether it's a whole piece or small crumbles.)
3. Carefully stuff the dates with the cheese, being careful to keep the dates intact. Squeeze the slits closed as you fill the dates.
4. Place the dates on a sheet pan, cut side up. Bake at 350°F (175°C) until the dates are very warm but not hot.
5. Serve warm. Present with picks so diners can spear a date rather than pick it up with the fingers. Alternatively, spear each date with a pick before serving.

VARIATIONS

Dates Stuffed with Manchego Cheese

Substitute Spanish Manchego cheese for the gorgonzola.

Date Rumaki

Prepare Dates Stuffed with Manchego Cheese, but do not bake them. Wrap each date in a half-strip of bacon and secure with a pick. Bake at 400°F (200°C), turning once or twice, until the bacon is cooked, about 15 minutes. Serve warm.

Smoked Trout Rollups

YIELD: 24 PIECES

U.S.	METRIC	INGREDIENTS	PROCEDURE
10 oz	300 g	Smoked trout fillets (p. 198), skinless	1. Carefully examine the trout fillets and remove all bones.
2 oz	30 g	Cream cheese	2. Shred the trout, breaking up all lumps.
3 tbsp	15 mL	Mayonnaise	3. In a bowl, mix the cream cheese and mayonnaise until softened and smooth.
1 oz	30 g	Shallot, chopped fine	4. Add the trout and shallot. Mix well.
2 fl oz	75 mL	Mayonnaise	5. Mix the mayonnaise and mustard.
1 tsp	7 mL	Dijon-style mustard	6. Lay 1 crêpe on a work surface, good side down.
6	6	Crêpes (p. 407), 6 in. (15 cm) in diameter	7. Drop 2 tsp (10 mL) of the mayonnaise mixture on the crêpe and spread it over the crêpe to cover it completely in a thin layer.
5	5	Cornichons (see Note)	8. Portion 1½ oz (45 g) of the trout mixture and spread it in a wide band across the center of the crêpe.
			9. Roll up the crêpe, pressing gently (to avoid tearing the crêpe) but firmly to make a tight roll.
			10. Repeat with the remaining crêpes.
			11. Slice the cornichons on the diagonal into thin slices.
			12. Trim the ends off the crêpe rolls, then cut the rolls crosswise into fourths.
			13. Push the point of a cocktail pick through a cornichon slice and stick the pick into the center of a rollup. Repeat with the remaining rollups.

Per 1 piece: Calories, 80; Protein, 3 g; Fat, 5 g (65% cal.); Cholesterol, 30 mg; Carbohydrates, 3 g; Fiber, 0 g; Sodium, 150 mg.

Note: Cornichons are tiny, sour cucumber pickles packed in vinegar, usually flavored with tarragon.

VARIATION

Smoked Trout Purses

Instead of making rollups, cut a circle from the center of a crêpe using a 4-in. (10-cm) cutter. Place about 2 tsp (10–12 g) of the trout mixture in the center of the circle. (Omit the mustard mixture.) Gather the edges of the circle over the top of the trout and tie with a length of chive. (You will need 30–36 crêpes for the quantity of trout in the basic recipe.)

Cucumber Cups with Dilled Shrimp Salad

YIELD: 24 PIECES

U.S.	METRIC	INGREDIENTS	PROCEDURE
2, or as needed (see step 2)	2, or as needed (see step 2)	Long, slender English, cucumbers about 6 oz (180 g) each	1. Channel the cucumbers.
as needed	as needed	Salt	2. Trim off the ends of the cucumbers, then cut the cucumbers into slices ¾ in. (1 cm) thick. (You need enough cucumbers to make 24 slices. Use an additional cucumber if necessary.)
12 oz	360 g	Dilled Shrimp Salad	3. With a parisienne scoop, hollow out each slice to make a shallow cup.
24 tiny sprigs	24 tiny sprigs	Fresh dill	4. Sprinkle the hollowed side of each slice lightly with salt, then turn upside down on a sheet pan lined with paper towels to drain. Refrigerate 1 hour.
			5. Turn the cucumber slices hollow side up. Fill each with ½ oz (15 g) shrimp salad.
			6. Decorate the top of each with a tiny sprig of dill.
			7. Refrigerate until service time.

Per 1 piece: Calories, 30; Protein, 2 g; Fat, 2.5 g (75% cal.); Cholesterol, 15 mg; Carbohydrates, 0 g; Fiber, 0 g; Sodium, 40 mg.

Crêpes

YIELD: ABOUT 50 CRÊPES

U.S.	METRIC	INGREDIENTS
8 oz	250 g	Bread flour
8 oz	250 g	Cake flour
½ oz	15 g	Salt
12 oz	375 g	Eggs, lightly beaten
1 qt	1 L	Milk
5 fl oz	150 mL	Oil or clarified butter
as needed	as needed	Oil for seasoning pan
as needed	as needed	Clarified butter for frying

PROCEDURE

1. Sift the flours and salt into a bowl.
2. Add the eggs and just enough of the milk to make a soft paste with the flour. Mix until smooth and lump-free.
3. Gradually mix in the rest of the milk and the oil. The batter should be about the consistency of heavy cream. If it is too thick, mix in a little water. If it has lumps, pour it through a strainer.
4. Let the batter rest 2 hours before frying.
5. Rub a 6- or 7-in. (15–18-cm) crêpe pan or skillet with oil (**Figure 18.5**). Heat the pan over moderately high heat until it is very hot.
6. Brush the pan lightly with clarified butter and pour off any excess.
7. Remove the pan from the heat and pour in 3–4 tablespoons (45–60 mL) of the batter. Very quickly tilt the pan to cover the bottom with a thin layer. Immediately dump out any excess batter, as the crêpe must be very thin.
8. Return to the heat for 1–1½ minutes, until the bottom is lightly browned. Flip over and brown the second side. The second side will brown in only a few spots and will not be as attractive as the first. The first side should always be the visible side when the crêpe is served.
9. Slide the crêpe onto a plate. Repeat with the remaining batter. Butter the pan lightly when necessary.
10. Cover the finished crêpes and refrigerate until needed.

Per 1 crêpe: Calories, 100; Protein, 3 g; Fat, 6 g (53% cal.); Cholesterol, 40 mg; Carbohydrates, 9 g; Fiber, 0 g; Sodium, 135 mg.

VARIATION

Dessert Crêpes

Sift 2 oz (60 g) sugar with the flour and salt.

Figure 18.5 Preparing crêpes.

(a) Brush the hot pan lightly with clarified butter.

(b) Ladle in 3–4 tablespoons (45–60 mL) of the batter. Very quickly tilt the pan to cover the bottom with a thin layer. Immediately dump out any excess batter.

(c) Cook until the crêpe is lightly browned on the bottom.

(d) Flip the crêpe over.

(e) Brown the other side.

Spiced Shrimp with Smoked Paprika

YIELD: 26–30 PIECES

U.S.	METRIC	INGREDIENTS
1 lb	480 g	Peeled, deveined shrimp, size 26-30
3 tbsp	15 mL	Lemon juice
1½ tsp	7 mL	Olive oil
½ tsp	2 mL	Peppercorns, crushed
1 clove	1 clove	Garlic, crushed
1 oz	30 g	Onion, sliced
1	1	Bay leaf
¼ tsp	1 mL	Cayenne
1 tbsp	15 mL	Salt
as needed	as needed	Water

PROCEDURE

1. Combine the shrimp, lemon juice, oil, peppercorns, garlic, onion, bay leaf, cayenne, and salt in a stainless-steel saucepan. Add just enough water to cover the shrimp.
2. Bring to a boil, then reduce to a slow simmer. Cook 2–4 minutes, or until just cooked through.
3. Remove the pan from the heat and set in an ice bath to cool quickly. Refrigerate.

U.S.	METRIC	INGREDIENTS
1 fl oz	30 mL	Olive oil
1 tbsp	15 mL	Lemon juice
1 tbsp	15 mL	Smoked paprika

4. Mix the olive oil, lemon juice, and paprika in a bowl large enough to hold the shrimp.
5. Drain the shrimp and dry on clean towels.
6. Add the shrimp to the bowl with the olive oil mixture. Toss until all the shrimp are well coated with the mixture.
7. Arrange the shrimp on a platter and serve with cocktail picks. Alternatively, place on round toast cutouts and serve as canapés.

Per 1 piece: Calories, 30; Protein, 4 g; Fat, 1.5 g (46% cal.); Cholesterol, 30 mg; Carbohydrates, 0 g; Fiber, 0 g; Sodium, 55 mg.

Mushrooms Stuffed with Tapenade

YIELD: 50 PIECES

U.S.	METRIC	INGREDIENTS
8 oz	250 g	Pitted Mediterranean or Greek black olives
1 oz	30 g	Capers, drained
1 oz	30 g	Anchovies, drained
1 oz	30 g	Tuna, drained
1 tsp	5 mL	Dijon-style mustard
2½ fl oz	75 mL	Olive oil
1 tsp	5 mL	Lemon juice
2 tbsp	30 mL	Chopped parsley
pinch	pinch	Dried thyme
to taste	to taste	Salt
to taste	to taste	Pepper

PROCEDURE

1. In a blender or food processor, purée the olives, capers, anchovies, tuna, mustard, oil, lemon juice, and herbs. Season to taste.
2. Chill the mixture several hours to let the flavors blend.

U.S.	METRIC	INGREDIENTS
50	50	Small to medium fresh white mushrooms
as needed	as needed	Pimiento

3. Remove the stems from the mushrooms and clean the caps.
4. Fill each cap with a small spoonful of the tapenade.
5. Garnish the top of each with a dot of pimiento.

Per 1 piece: Calories, 30; Protein, 1 g; Fat, 25 g (74% cal.); Cholesterol, 0 mg; Carbohydrates, 1 g; Fiber, 0 g; Sodium, 110 mg.

Deviled Eggs

YIELD: 50 PIECES

U.S.	METRIC	INGREDIENTS
25	25	Hard-cooked eggs
½ pt	250 mL	Mayonnaise
1 fl oz	30 mL	Lemon juice or vinegar
1 tsp	5 mL	Dry mustard
1 tsp	5 mL	Worcestershire sauce
to taste	to taste	Salt
to taste	to taste	White pepper
to taste	to taste	Cayenne
as needed	as needed	Assorted garnish, such as:
		Chopped parsley
		Tiny dill sprigs
		Capers
		Diced pimiento
		Sliced stuffed olives
		Paprika
		Red or black caviar

Per 1 piece: Calories, 70; Protein, 3 g; Fat, 7 g (84% cal.); Cholesterol, 110 mg; Carbohydrates, 0 g; Fiber, 0 g; Sodium, 45 mg.

PROCEDURE

1. Halve the eggs lengthwise and remove the yolks.
2. Mash the yolks or force them through a sieve.
3. Add the remaining ingredients (except the garnish) and mix to a smooth paste.
4. Using a pastry bag with a star tip, fill the egg white halves.
5. Using a variety of garnishes, decorate the top of each egg.

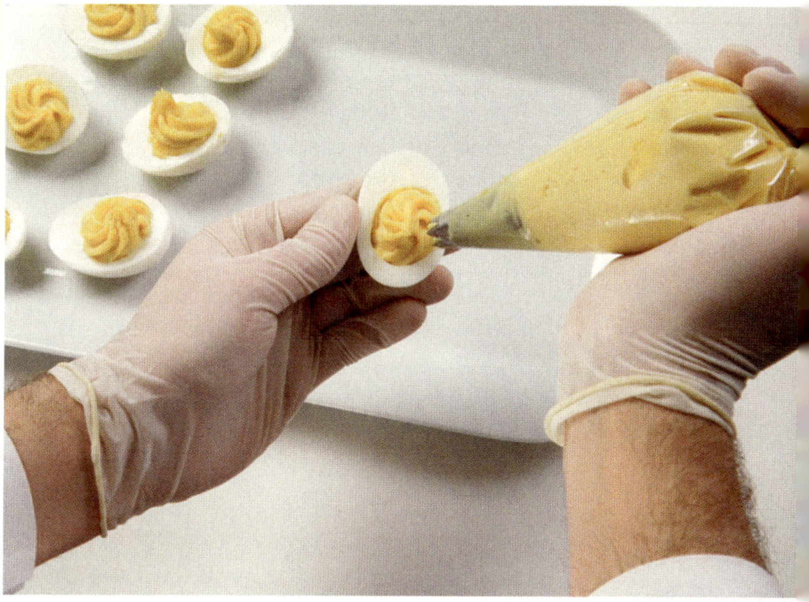

Filling deviled eggs with a pastry bag

VARIATION

Vary the flavor of stuffed eggs by adding any of the following ingredients to the egg yolk mixture in the basic recipe.

Anchovy: 2–3 oz (60–90 g) anchovy paste.

Curry: 2 tbsp (30 mL) curry powder, heated very gently with a little oil and cooled.

Blue cheese: 6 oz (175 g) mashed blue cheese.

Parmesan: 3 oz (90 g) grated parmesan cheese.

Tarragon: Use tarragon vinegar in the filling and add 2 tsp (10 mL) dried tarragon.

Tuna: 6 oz (175 g) well-mashed, drained tuna.

Miniature Gougère Puffs

YIELD: ABOUT 160 PIECES

U.S.	METRIC	INGREDIENTS
2½ lb	1.1 kg	Éclair Paste (p. 310)
8 oz	225 g	Gruyère cheese, grated
as needed	as needed	Egg wash

Per 1 piece: Calories, 25; Protein, 1 g; Fat, 1.5 g (63% cal.); Cholesterol, 15 mg; Carbohydrates, 1 g; Fiber, 0 g; Sodium, 25 mg.

PROCEDURE

1. Mix the éclair paste and the cheese.
2. Using a pastry bag with a small, plain tip, pipe small mounds of about 1 tbsp (15 mL) each onto sheet pans lined with parchment. See page 310 for guidelines on making tiny cream puff shells or profiteroles, which is essentially what these are.
3. Bake at 400°F (200°C) until puffed and brown, 20–30 minutes.
4. Make a little slit in the side of each to allow steam to escape. Put the puffs in a warm oven until they are dry.
5. Serve warm or at room temperature.

Egg Rolls or Spring Rolls

YIELD: 16 PIECES

U.S.	METRIC	INGREDIENTS
1 oz	30 mL	Oil
6 oz	175 g	Cooked meat or poultry, cut fine julienne
6 oz	175 g	Chinese cabbage, shredded
3	3	Scallions, shredded
6 oz	175 g	Bean sprouts
5	5	Dried black mushrooms (stems discarded), soaked in boiling water, cut julienne
2 oz	60 g	Bamboo shoots, cut julienne
1½ oz	45 g	Raw shrimp, chopped
2 tsp	10 mL	Soy sauce
1 tsp	5 mL	Sherry or Shaoxing wine
3 fl oz	100 mL	Chicken stock
1½ tsp	7 mL	Cornstarch
1 tbsp	15 mL	Water, cold

PROCEDURE

1. Heat the oil in a wok or sauté pan. Stir-fry the meat, cabbage, scallions, bean sprouts, black mushrooms, bamboo shoots, and shrimp.
2. Add the soy sauce, sherry, and stock. Continue to stir and cook for another 1–2 minutes.
3. Mix the cornstarch with the cold water. Stir into the vegetable mixture and cook until reduced and thickened.
4. Remove from the heat and adjust the seasonings. Cool thoroughly.

U.S.	METRIC	INGREDIENTS
16	16	Egg roll skins or spring roll skins
as needed	as needed	Egg, beaten

5. Lay an egg roll skin on the worktable with one of the corners toward you. Spoon about 1½ oz (45 g) filling onto the lower half of the skin in a sort of sausage shape. (See **Figure 18.6**.)
6. Fold the lower corner of the skin (the corner pointing at you) over the filling so it is covered. Then start to roll it up like a cylinder, giving it just a half turn.
7. Brush the left and right corners with a little beaten egg. Fold one corner over the filling, then the other, pressing down to seal. At this point, it should look like an open envelope.
8. Brush the top corner with beaten egg. Roll into a firm, compact cylinder. Seal the top corner well.
9. Repeat with the remaining skins and filling.
10. Deep-fry the egg rolls until the skins are crisp and brown. (*Note:* Egg roll skins are heavier than spring roll skins. They must be thoroughly fried or they will be doughy.) Drain and serve at once, with a little hot mustard or bottled duck sauce for dipping.

Per 1 roll: Calories, 180; Protein, 8 g; Fat, 8 g (38% cal.); Cholesterol, 25 mg; Carbohydrates, 21 g; Fiber, 1 g; Sodium, 240 mg.

Figure 18.6 Rolling egg rolls.

(a) Lay an egg roll skin on the bench with one corner toward you. Place the filling as shown.

(b) Fold the lower corner of the skin over the filling and roll it up about one-third of the way.

(c) Brush the left and right corners of the skin with beaten egg.

(d) Fold the corners over the filling so the skin resembles an open envelope.

(e) Brush the top edge with egg and roll up tightly.

(f) When completely rolled, egg rolls are ready to be cooked.

Bruschetta (Basic)

YIELD: 24 PIECES

U.S.	METRIC	INGREDIENTS
24 slices	24 slices	Italian or French bread, 3–4 in. (8–10 cm) wide and ½ in. (6 mm) thick
4–6	4–6	Garlic cloves, cut in half
8–12 fl oz	240–360 mL	Extra-virgin olive oil
to taste	to taste	Salt
to taste	to taste	Pepper

Per 1 piece: Calories, 140; Protein, 2 g; Fat, 10 g (65% cal.); Cholesterol, 0 mg; Carbohydrates, 10 g; Fiber, 1 g; Sodium, 115 mg.

PROCEDURE

1. Toast the bread on a grill or under a broiler until golden brown.
2. While the bread is still hot, rub one side of each slice with a cut clove of garlic.
3. Brush or drizzle olive oil generously over each slice. The toast should be partly soaked with the oil.
4. Add salt and pepper to taste.
5. Serve warm.

Bruschette, clockwise from left: Bruschetta with White Beans and Prosciutto, Bruschetta with Parmesan Cheese, Bruschetta with Tomato and Basil

VARIATIONS

Bruschetta with Tomato and Basil

Toast the bread and rub with garlic as in the basic recipe. Cut 2 lb (1 kg) ripe plum tomatoes in half and remove the seeds. Cut into medium dice. Tear 16 fresh basil leaves into small pieces and mix with the tomatoes. Top the toasts with the tomatoes. Drizzle with olive oil and add salt and pepper to taste.

Bruschetta with Parmesan Cheese

Toast the bread and rub with garlic as in the basic recipe. Using a vegetable peeler, cut cheese, preferably a good-quality Parmigiano-Reggiano, into thin shavings. While the toast is still hot, top each piece with about ¼ oz (7 g) cheese and drizzle with olive oil. Sprinkle with black pepper.

Bruschetta with White Beans and Prosciutto

Toast the bread and rub with garlic as in the basic recipe. Mix 1 lb 4 oz (600 g) cooked or canned and drained white kidney beans, 2 oz (60 g) red onion cut in small dice, 6 oz (180 g) prosciutto, sliced thin and chopped, and 4 fl oz (120 mL) olive oil. Add salt and pepper to taste. Top toasts with this mixture.

Spicy Meat Empanadas

YIELD: 24 PIECES

U.S.	METRIC	INGREDIENTS	PROCEDURE
8 oz	240 g	Bread flour	1. Sift the two flours together into a mixing bowl.
4 oz	120 g	Cake flour	2. Add the lard or shortening and blend it thoroughly with the flour.
1½ oz	45 g	Lard or vegetable shortening	3. Dissolve the salt in the water and add it to the flour mixture. Mix to make a moderately stiff dough. Knead the dough for a few minutes, until smooth.
¾ tsp	3 mL	Salt	4. Let the dough rest 30 minutes.
6 fl oz	180 mL	Warm water	5. Divide the dough into 24 equal parts by rolling it into a long cylinder and cutting it into equal segments.
			6. Roll each piece into a ball. Cover and let rest 15–30 minutes.
18 oz	480 g	Picadillo (p. 181)	7. For each empanada, flatten a ball of dough and roll out into a circle 4 in. (10 cm) in diameter.
			8. Brush the rim of the circle lightly with water.
			9. Place about ¾ oz. (20 g) picadillo on one side of the circle. Fold the other side over it to make a turnover. Press the dough around the filling to force out air. Seal the edge well by crimping with the tines of a fork.
			10. Deep-fry at 375°F (190°C) until golden brown.
			11. Serve immediately. If desired, accompany with guacamole or salsa cruda.

Per 1 piece: Calories, 130; Protein, 6 g; Fat, 6 g (43% cal.); Cholesterol, 15 mg; Carbohydrates, 12 g; Fiber, 1 g; Sodium, 140 mg.

VARIATION

Empanadas with Roasted Poblanos and Cheese

Roast and peel poblano peppers. Dice the poblanos. In place of the picadillo, fill the empanadas with poblanos and grated Monterey jack or mild cheddar cheese.

Cauliflower Pakoras

YIELD: 30–40 PIECES

U.S.	METRIC	INGREDIENTS	PROCEDURE
8 oz	240 g	Chickpea flour	1. Sift together into a bowl the chickpea flour, pepper, cayenne, cumin, turmeric, baking powder, and salt.
¼ tsp	1 mL	Black pepper	2. Gradually stir in the water until the mixture forms a thick batter about the consistency of ketchup. You may not need all the water.
¼ tsp	1 mL	Cayenne	
½ tsp	2 mL	Ground cumin	
¼ tsp	1 mL	Turmeric	
½ tsp	2 mL	Baking powder	
½ tsp	2 mL	Salt	
12 fl oz	360 mL	Water	
1½ lb	720 g	Cauliflower, trimmed	3. Divide the cauliflower into florets no bigger than 1 in. (2.5 cm) across.
			4. Dip the florets into the batter and deep-fry at 360°F (180°F) until lightly browned and tender.

Per 1 piece: Calories, 50; Protein, 2 g; Fat, 3 g (49% cal.); Cholesterol, 0 mg; Carbohydrates, 5 g; Fiber, 1 g; Sodium, 45 mg.

VARIATIONS

Other vegetables, such as peppers, onion rings, potatoes (thin slices), broccoli, eggplant, and okra, may be substituted for the cauliflower.

Cauliflower Pakoras

TERMS FOR REVIEW

appetizer	canapé	dip	caviar
hors d'oeuvre	cocktail	antipasto	amuse bouche
butler-style service	relish	bruschetta	
buffet-style service	crudité	tapa	

QUESTIONS FOR DISCUSSION

1. What is butler-style service? Describe at least five guidelines to keep in mind when planning butler-style service of hors d'oeuvres.
2. How can you avoid soggy canapé bases?
3. In order to use a ham salad recipe to make a ham spread, you may need to change the recipe slightly. What are three modifications you may need to make?
4. What is the difference between a fruit salad and a fruit cocktail?
5. What is the proper consistency or thickness for a dip?
6. List six or more items that might appear on a cold antipasto platter.
7. Describe how to prepare the simplest type of bruschetta.
8. Describe the best way to serve the best-quality caviar.

Chapter 19

Various Goat Cheeses, page 425.

Dairy and Beverages

Milk is one our most versatile foods, not only as a beverage but even more importantly as a cooking and baking ingredient and as a raw material for the production of a wide array of other foods, including cream, butter, and hundreds of kinds of cheese.

This chapter identifies and describes the many dairy products used regularly in the kitchen and gives guidelines for handling, storing, and cooking with them. The last section of the chapter describes the many types of cheese produced in North America and Europe and gives examples of each type.

The chapter concludes with a discussion of coffee and tea beverages, including guidelines for their production.

After reading this chapter, you should be able to

1. Describe the major milk, cream, and butter products.
2. Explain why milk curdles and why it scorches, and identify the steps to take to prevent curdling and scorching.
3. Whip cream.
4. Describe the most important kinds of cheese used in the kitchen.
5. Store and serve cheese properly.
6. Cook with cheese.
7. Prepare coffee and tea.

Dairy Products

Milk and Cream

Categories and Definitions

When we talk about milk and cream used in food service, we are nearly always talking about milk from cows. Milk from other animals, including goats, sheep, and water buffalo, is used to make some cheeses, but most of the liquid milk we see, except for a small amount of goat milk, is milk from dairy cows.

Milk is used as a beverage and also in cooking. Similarly, other milk products, including cream, butter, and cheese, are eaten as purchased and also used in cooking.

PASTEURIZATION

Liquid milk, directly as it comes from the cow and before anything is done to it, is called *raw milk*. Because raw milk may contain disease-causing bacteria or other organisms, it is almost always ***pasteurized*** before being sold or before being processed into other products. Pasteurized milk has been heated to 161°F (72°C) and held at this temperature for 15 seconds to kill disease-causing organisms, and then quickly chilled. By law, all Grade A liquid milk and cream must be pasteurized. (Grades B and C are used in food processing and industrial uses and are rarely seen in food service or in the retail market.)

Even after pasteurizing, milk and cream are highly perishable products. Some cream products are ***ultra-pasteurized*** to extend their shelf life. By heating the product to a much higher temperature (275°F/135°C) for 4 seconds, this process kills not only disease-causing bacteria but nearly all organisms that cause spoilage. Ultra-pasteurized products must still be refrigerated both before and after opening.

Ultra-High-Temperature (UHT) pasteurization involves even higher temperatures. The resulting product is packed into sterile cartons. If the cartons are unopened, the milk will keep at room temperature for up to 10 months. Once opened, the milk must be refrigerated like regular pasteurized milk. UHT milk has a somewhat cooked taste and is better suited to cooking than for drinking as a beverage.

FRESH MILK PRODUCTS

Whole milk is fresh milk as it comes from the cow, with nothing removed and nothing (except vitamin D) added. It contains about 3.5 percent fat (known as ***milk fat*** or ***butterfat***), 8.5 percent nonfat milk solids, and 88 percent water.

Skim or ***nonfat milk*** has had most or all of the fat removed. Its fat content is 0.5 percent or less.

Low-fat milk has a fat content of 0.5 to 2 percent. Its fat content is usually indicated, usually 1 percent or 2 percent.

Fortified nonfat or low-fat milk has had substances added to increase its nutritional value, usually vitamins A and D and extra nonfat milk solids.

Flavored milks, such as *chocolate milk*, have had flavoring ingredients added. A label such as *chocolate milk drink* or *chocolate-flavored drink* indicates the product does not meet the standards for regular milk. Read ingredient labels.

Except, of course, for nonfat milk, natural liquid milk contains fat, which, because it is lighter than water, will gradually separate and float to the top in the form of cream. ***Homogenized milk*** has been processed so the cream doesn't separate. This is done by forcing the milk through very tiny holes, which breaks the fat into particles so small they stay distributed in the milk. Nearly all liquid milk on the market has been homogenized.

FRESH CREAM PRODUCTS

Whipping cream has a fat content of 30 to 40 percent. Within this category, you may find light whipping cream (30 to 35 percent) and heavy whipping cream (36 to 40 percent). Whipping cream labeled *ultra-pasteurized* keeps longer than regular pasteurized cream. Pure ultra-pasteurized cream does not whip as well as regular pasteurized cream, so additives such as vegetable gums are added to it to make it more whippable.

Light cream, also called *table cream* or *coffee cream*, contains 18 to 30 percent fat, usually about 18 percent.

Half-and-half has a fat content of 10 to 18 percent, too low to be called *cream*.

FERMENTED MILK AND CREAM PRODUCTS

Sour cream has been cultured or fermented by added lactic acid bacteria, which makes it thick and slightly tangy in flavor. It has about 18 percent fat.

Crème fraîche (kremm fresh) is a slightly aged, cultured heavy cream. It is widely used for sauce making in Europe because of its pleasant, slightly tangy flavor and its ability to blend easily into sauces. Unlike regular heavy cream, it usually doesn't require tempering and can be added directly to hot sauces. It is available commercially but is expensive. A close approximation can be made by warming 1 quart (1 L) heavy cream to about 100°F (38°C), adding 1½ ounces (50 mL) buttermilk, and letting the mixture stand in a warm place until slightly thickened, 6 to 24 hours.

Buttermilk is fresh, liquid milk, usually skim milk, which has been cultured or soured by bacteria. It is usually called *cultured buttermilk* to distinguish it from the original buttermilk, which was the liquid left after butter making. Buttermilk is used in recipes calling for sour milk.

Yogurt is milk (whole or low-fat) cultured by special bacteria. It has a custardlike consistency. Most yogurt has additional milk solids added, and some of it is flavored and sweetened.

MILK PRODUCTS WITH WATER REMOVED

Evaporated milk is milk, either whole or skim, with about 60 percent of the water removed. It is then sterilized and canned. Evaporated milk has a somewhat cooked flavor.

Condensed milk is whole milk that has had about 60 percent of the water removed and is heavily sweetened with sugar. It is available canned and in bulk.

Dried whole milk is whole milk that has been dried to a powder. *Nonfat dry milk* is skim milk that has been dried in the same way. Both are available in regular form and in instant form, which dissolves in water more easily.

Artificial Dairy Products

A wide variety of imitation cream and dessert topping products are made from various fats and chemicals, which are listed on the label. They are used in some institutions because they keep longer and are generally less expensive than dairy products. Some people feel they are acceptable, but many find their flavors objectionable.

Problems in Cooking Milk and Cream Products

CURDLING

Curdling is a process by which milk proteins solidify and separate from the whey. Curdling is usually caused by acids, tannins, salt, and heat. The mild acids in many vegetables and the tannins in potatoes are often enough to curdle milk.

Starches partially stabilize milk and cream. This is why it is possible to make soups and sauces with both milk or cream and acid ingredients. Avoid combining milk or cream with strong acids unless a starch is present.

Reducing temperatures and cooking times also helps. Curdling is more likely at high heat or with prolonged cooking.

Salt lightly, unless the milk has been stabilized by starch.

When adding milk or cream to a hot liquid, heat it first in a separate pot, or temper it by stirring a little of the hot liquid into it first.

Reconstituted dry milk is more likely to curdle than fresh milk.

SCORCHING

Scorching occurs when milk that is being heated coagulates on the bottom of the pan due to high heat. This deposit is likely to burn if cooking continues.

Figure 19.1 Whipping cream.

(a) The cream has begun to thicken.

(b) The cream has reached the soft-peak stage. Stop at this stage if the cream is to be folded into a batter or other mixture.

(c) The cream has reached the firm-peak stage. Whipping beyond this stage causes the cream to break or separate.

To avoid scorching, heat milk in a double boiler, steamer, or steam-jacketed kettle rather than over direct heat.

SKIN FORMATION

The formation of scum or skin on top of heated milk or milk sauces is caused by coagulation of proteins in contact with air. Prevent it by covering the utensil or by coating the surface with a layer of melted fat.

Whipping Cream

Cream with a fat content of 30 percent or more can be whipped into a foam (see Figure 19.1). One quart or liter of cream produces up to 2 quarts or liters of whipped cream.

For the best results, observe the following guidelines:

1. Have cream and all equipment well chilled.
2. Do not sweeten until the cream is whipped. Sugar decreases stability and makes the cream harder to whip. Use powdered sugar instead of granulated sugar for best stability.
3. Do not overwhip. Stop beating when the cream forms stiff peaks. If it is whipped longer, it first becomes granular and then turns into butter and whey.
4. Cream to be folded into other ingredients should be underbeaten because the action of folding it in whips it more and may overwhip it.

Butter

Butter Characteristics and Grades

Fresh ***butter*** in the United States and Canada consists of about 80 percent milk fat. The remainder is milk solids and water.

In Europe, butter often has a higher fat content, usually around 82 percent. Some manufacturers in North America have begun processing and selling European-style butters with this higher fat content. They are intended to replicate the qualities of European butters in cooking and baking.

In the United States, butter is graded according to USDA standards for flavor, body, color, and salt content, although grading is not mandatory. Grades are AA, A, B, and C. Most operations use grades AA and A because the lower grades may have off flavors.

Most butter on the market is lightly salted. A maximum of 2 percent salt is permitted. ***Unsalted butter*** is more perishable but has a fresher, sweeter taste.

Because of its flavor, butter is the preferred cooking fat for most purposes. It has no equal in sauce making and is used as a sauce itself, as discussed in Chapter 8.

Clarified butter is used as a cooking fat more often than whole butter because the milk solids in whole butter burn easily.

The smoke point of butterfat is only 300° to 350°F (150° to 175°C), so another product, such as vegetable oil, should be used when high cooking temperatures are required.

Storing

Have you ever been served butter that tasted like onions? Butter absorbs odors and flavors easily, so it should be kept well wrapped and away from foods that might transfer odors to it in the refrigerator.

Best storage temperature is 35°F (2°C).

EUROPEAN BUTTERS

As explained in the text, typical European butters have a higher fat content and lower moisture content than American butters.

A second difference is in the type of cream used. Most North American butters are made from fresh cream and are called *sweet cream butter*. By contrast, many European butters are made from slightly cultured cream, somewhat like crème fraîche (p. 419). This gives the butter a more complex, richer flavor.

Margarine

Margarine is a manufactured product meant to resemble butter in taste, texture, and appearance. It is made from vegetable and animal fats, plus flavoring ingredients, emulsifiers, coloring agents, preservatives, and added vitamins. Like butter, it is about 80 percent fat. Diet and low-fat margarines have less fat and a much higher water content, so they can't be used in cooking like butter or regular margarine.

Flavors of different brands should be evaluated carefully because they vary considerably. Margarine should have a reasonably clean, fresh flavor, although you should not expect even the best to taste like high-grade butter.

Margarines that include an emulsifier called *lecithin* foam and brown like butter when heated. Those without lecithin do not. In all other respects, margarine is handled and stored like butter.

KEY POINTS TO REVIEW

- What are three types of pasteurization? Describe them.
- What are the major milk, cream, and butter products?
- What is curdling? How can it be prevented? How can scorching of milk products be prevented during cooking?
- What guidelines should be observed when whipping cream?

Cheese

Composition

Cheese is a food produced by separating milk solids from whey by curdling or coagulation. This curdling is brought about by introducing selected bacteria or an enzyme called *rennet* into the milk (see sidebar). The resulting curds are drained, processed, and cured or aged in a variety of ways. The liquid that drains from the curds is called *whey*.

Processing techniques are so numerous that from a single basic ingredient (milk from cows, sheep, or goats) it is possible to produce hundreds of kinds of cheese, from cottage cheese to parmesan, from cheddar to Swiss, from blue to Limburger. Variables that produce these differences include the type of milk used, the method of curdling and the temperatures during curdling, the method of cutting and draining the curd, the way the curds are heated, pressed, or handled, and all the conditions of ripening or curing.

Ripening is the process that converts freshly made curds into distinctive, flavorful cheeses. Ripening is brought about by certain bacteria or molds that are introduced during manufacture. Much of a cheese's final character is determined by its ripening agent and the way it acts on the cheese.

Cheeses can be classified by the way in which they are ripened.

Bacteria ripened from inside, such as cheddar, Swiss, Gouda, and parmesan. This category includes most hard-ripened and hard grating cheeses. These ripen uniformly throughout the interior.

Washed-rind cheeses, such as Limburger and Liederkranz. These are so called because the surface of each cheese is periodically washed with a salt brine solution during the first stages of aging and ripening. Washed-rind cheeses usually have an orange or reddish rind that is thinner than the mold rind of mold-ripened cheeses. They usually become softer as they ripen. Many washed-rind cheeses have a pungent aroma when ripe.

RENNET AND VEGETARIAN DIETS

The most commonly used curdling agent in cheese production is rennet, as the text explains. Most traditional cheeses are made with rennet extracted from the stomach lining of calves. As a result, vegetarians usually avoid such cheeses. However, rennet derived from a plant base is also available. Cheeses made with a vegetable-based rennet can be included in the diets of lacto-vegetarians. In addition, some cheeses are made without rennet but with other curdling agents, such as citric acid or other mild acid.

Top row: Morbier, cheddar, and fontina.
Bottom row: Tilsit, baby Gouda, and Emmentaler.

Washed-rind cheeses, clockwise from left: Époisses, Livarot, Limburger, and Reblochon.

Blue-veined cheeses, clockwise from left: Stilton, Cabrales, Roquefort, and Bleu d'Auvergne.

Top row: Brie, Explorateur, Taleggio.
Bottom row: Camembert, Edel de Cleron.

Unripened cheeses. Back row: queso blanco, ricotta, fresh mozzarella.
Front row: string cheese, cream cheese, fresh chèvre, and Boursin.

Blue-veined cheeses, such as Roquefort and Stilton. These contain mold cultures that spread through the interior of the cheese.

Mold-rind cheeses, such as Brie, Camembert, and St. André. These have a mold crust or rind that is white and velvety when the cheese is young but that may darken or become mottled with orange or brown as the cheese ages.

Unripened cheeses, such as cottage, cream, and baker's cheese.

The three major components of cheese are water, fat, and protein. The water content of cheese ranges from about 80 percent for a fresh, soft cheese like cottage cheese to about 30 percent for a very hard, aged cheese like parmesan.

The fat content of cheese, when it is listed on a label, generally refers to the percentage of solids. In other words, if a cheddar cheese has a 50 percent fat content, this means the cheese would be 50 percent fat if all the moisture were removed. In fact, the cheese may have a moisture content of about 40 percent, and its actual fat content may be about 30 percent of the total.

Double-crème (at least 60 percent fat) and ***triple-crème*** (at least 75 percent fat, dry weight) are very rich cheeses. Most of these styles of cheese originated in France, but they have become popular and are now made in many countries. Most of them fall into the unripened, soft-ripened, or blue-veined categories, discussed on the next page.

Varieties

Hundreds, possibly even thousands, of cheeses are produced in North America and Europe. The following is a representative sampling of most of the types of cheese commonly available. See also the accompanying photographs.

UNRIPENED CHEESES

These are soft, white, freshly made cheeses.

Cottage cheese is a moist, loose-curd cheese that may or may not have cream added. *Baker's cheese* or *pot cheese* is similar but drier. Baker's cheese is used in cheesecakes and pastry.

Ricotta cheese is sometimes called *Italian cottage cheese*, but it is smoother, moister, and sweeter than cottage cheese. Traditional ricotta is made from whey, but most ricotta in the North American market is made from fresh milk.

Cream cheese is a smooth, mild cheese with a high fat content. It is extensively used in making sandwiches, canapés, and hors d'oeuvres and in baking.

Neufchâtel is similar to cream cheese, but it has less fat. An Italian cream cheese called *mascarpone* is very soft and rich, and it looks almost like whipped cream. It has a slightly tangy taste that goes well with fruits as a dessert.

Mozzarella is a soft, mild cheese made from whole milk or part skim milk. It has a stringy texture that comes from being pulled and stretched during production. It is widely used in pizzas and Italian-style dishes. The freshly made mozzarella one finds in Italian neighborhoods is moister and more tender than the packaged varieties.

Mozzarella di bufala, made from the milk of water buffaloes, is imported from Italy and is available in some areas at a somewhat high price. It is much softer and more delicate in texture than regular mozzarella, and it has a slightly acidic flavor that is refreshing.

Feta is a crumbly, curdy cheese that originated in Greece and other Balkan countries. Instead of being aged or cured, it is pickled in brine. This, plus the fact that it is generally made from goat's or sheep's milk, gives it a distinctive and salty flavor.

Buffalo mozzarella

Feta

SEMISOFT CHEESES

Bel Paese and *fontina* from Italy, *Port Salut* from France, and American *muenster* and *brick* cheeses are the best known of a large group of cheeses that range from bland and buttery when young to more earthy and full-flavored when older. They are often used as dessert cheeses and as hors d'oeuvres.

France produces many washed-rind soft cheeses with orange rinds and with flavors that range from mild to pungent. Among the better-known ones are *Pont l'Évêque* and *Livarot* from Normandy and *Munster* from Alsace. (These cheeses might also be categorized as soft-ripened cheeses, below, although they may not become as soft and runny as the washed-rind cheeses discussed in the next section.)

Port Salut

SOFT-RIPENED CHEESES

These cheeses ripen from the outside toward the center. When very young, they are firm and cakey and have little flavor. As they mature, they gradually become softer and, when fully ripe, may be actually runny. The ripening starts just inside the rind and spreads to the center.

Soft-ripened cheeses include two categories: mold-ripened and washed-rind or bacteria-ripened.

Brie and *Camembert* from France are ripened by mold. They are made in flat, round shapes and are covered with a crust that varies in color from white to straw. When ripe, these cheeses are creamy and flavorful, but they develop a sharp odor of ammonia when overripe.

Many rich double- and triple-crème cheeses fall into this category, including *Explorateur*, *Brillat-Savarin*, *St. André*, *Boursault*, and *Boursin* (which may be flavored with pepper or with garlic and herbs). *Chaource* is similar in texture and appearance to a double-crème cheese but is actually closer in composition to Brie, having a fat content of 45 to 50 percent.

Liederkranz, made in the United States, and its Belgian cousin, *Limburger*, are ripened by bacteria rather than mold, but they also become softer as they age. They are widely misunderstood because of their aroma. Actually, when not overripe, these cheeses are not nearly as strong as most people expect, and they have a pleasant, smooth texture.

Brie

Cheddar

Époisses from Burgundy, France, is one of the great soft-ripened washed-rind cheeses. Small cheeses are packed individually in round wooden boxes. They are so soft when ripe that they are left in their boxes and served with a spoon.

HARD CHEESES

These are cured cheeses with a firm texture and varying degrees of mildness or sharpness, depending on their age.

Cheddar is an English invention, but American versions are so popular in the United States that it is often thought of as a distinctly American cheese. It ranges in flavor from mild to sharp and in color from light yellow to orange. Cheddar is eaten as is and is also widely used in cooking. *Colby* and *Monterey jack* are similar to very mild cheddars. Monterey jack is usually sold when quite young. In this case, it is more like American muenster and belongs in the semisoft category.

Clockwise from top: Emmentaler, gorgonzola, provolone, Gruyère, Gouda, Locatelli Romano, Pont l'Évêque, baby Gouda; Lower center: Livarot.

Swiss-type cheeses are also popular. They are produced in many countries, but the original Swiss cheese from Switzerland, *Emmentaler*, is perhaps the most flavorful. These are very firm, slightly rubbery cheeses with a nutty taste. Their large holes are caused by gases formed during ripening. *Gruyère* is another Swiss-type cheese from either Switzerland or France. It has smaller holes and a sharper, earthier flavor. Gruyère is important in cooking, and both it and Emmentaler are widely used for sauces, soufflés, fondue, and gratinéed items. Other cheeses related to Swiss are *Comté* from France, *Appenzeller* and *Raclette* from Switzerland, and *Jarlsberg* from Norway.

Edam and *Gouda* are the familiar round Dutch cheeses with the yellow and red wax rinds. Hard in texture, with a mellow, nutlike flavor, they are often seen on buffet platters and among dessert cheeses.

Provolone is an Italian cheese that resembles mozzarella when very young, but it becomes sharper as it ages. It is also available smoked.

BLUE-VEINED CHEESES

These cheeses owe their flavor and appearance to the blue or green mold that mottles their interiors. The most famous of the blue cheeses is *Roquefort*, made in France from sheep's milk and cured in limestone caves near the town of Roquefort. *Stilton*, from England, is a mellower, firmer blue cheese that the English call "Roquefort with a college education." Italy's *gorgonzola* is a soft, creamy cheese with an unmistakable pungency. Spanish *Cabrales* is a mellow but intensely flavorful blue cheese. Blue cheeses made in Denmark and in the United States are also widely used.

Jarlsberg

Less widely known but worth seeking out are a number of special blues, including *Bleu de Bresse*, *Fourme d'Ambert*, and *Pipo Crem'* from France, *Saga* from Denmark, and *Bavarian Blue* and *Blue Castello* from Germany. The last four of these are double- or triple-crèmes.

Edam

Blue Stilton

Gorgonzola

GOAT CHEESES

Cheeses made from goat's milk are produced in dozens of varieties in France, where this type of cheese, called ***chèvre*** (shev r', or shev), is very popular. It has also become well known in the United States, which now has many producers. With a few exceptions, most goat cheeses are small, ranging in size from tiny buttons to logs, cakes, cones, and pyramids weighing up to 5 or 6 ounces (140 to 170 g).

Chèvre

Fresh, unaged chèvres are the most popular and the mildest in flavor. Their paste is very white, with a soft but interestingly dry texture. They have a distinctive peppery, slightly acidic taste. The most widely available fresh French chèvre is probably the cylindrical *Montrachet*, either plain or with a coating of edible ash. Other fresh goat cheeses, both domestic and imported, may be available in different localities, and many have no name other than *chèvre*.

As goat cheese ages it becomes firmer, and the peppery, acidic flavor becomes stronger. Cheeses two or three months old can be quite powerful, while the youngest might taste almost like the unaged ones. Some names of chèvres are *Boucheron, Banon* (wrapped in chestnut leaves), *Pyramide, Crottin de Chavignol, Chabis*, and *Rocamadour*. *Saint-Marcellin* is made of part goat's milk and part cow's milk. Shaped into small disks, it softens rather than hardens as it ripens.

Goat cheeses, top row: Bucheron, Humboldt Fog, and Valençay; Bottom row: Banon and button chèvres.

HARD GRATING CHEESES

The hard grating cheeses, typified by Italian *parmesan*, are called *grana* cheeses, referring to their grainy textures. The best of all granas is called *Parmigiano-Reggiano*. It is the true parmesan, aged at least two years, and it is very expensive. It is imitated widely around the world, and the imitations vary from bad to very good. Another Italian grana is *Romano*. Italian Romanos are made with sheep's milk, but American versions are usually made with cow's milk. Romano is stronger and saltier than parmesan.

These cheeses are often sold already grated. This is a convenience for commercial kitchens, of course, but, unfortunately, pre-grated cheese has much less flavor than freshly grated cheese. A merchant was once arrested for selling what he claimed was grated parmesan cheese but was actually grated umbrella handles. A large share of pre-grated cheese sold today resembles grated umbrella handles in flavor.

Hard cheeses, clockwise from top left: Parmigiano-Reggiano, Caerphilly, dry jack, Pecorino Romano, and aged Gouda.

PROCESS CHEESES

Up to now, we have been talking about so-called natural cheeses, made by curdling milk and ripening the curds. ***Process cheese***, by contrast, is manufactured by grinding one or more natural cheeses, heating and blending them with emulsifiers and other ingredients, and pouring the mixture into molds to solidify. Process cheese is a uniform product that does not age or ripen like natural cheese. Thus, it keeps very well. It is usually mild in flavor and gummy in texture.

Because of its melting quality and low price, it is often used in cooking. However, it is not as good a value as its price implies. Because it is relatively flavorless, you have to use much more of it to get the same flavor as from a smaller quantity of sharp cheddar.

In addition to its price and keeping qualities, the chief advantages of process cheese are that it melts easily and that its blandness appeals to many people who don't like more flavorful cheese.

American cheese usually refers to process cheese, although some people use this name for cheddar. In the United States, most process cheeses are made from cheddar, while European process cheeses more often contain Swiss-type cheeses. Among them is a process cheese called *Gruyère*, which bears little resemblance to true *Gruyère*.

Process cheese food and *process cheese spread* contain a lower percentage of cheese and more moisture than a product labeled simply *process cheese*. *Cold pack* or *club cheese*, on the other hand, is not heated and pasteurized like process cheese but is simply ground and mixed with flavorings and seasonings to a spreadable consistency. Some brands are fairly flavorful.

NORTH AMERICAN ARTISAN CHEESES

Many of the fine cheeses from France, Italy, and other European countries, including many of those listed above, are handmade in small batches. By contrast, until recently, nearly all the cheese produced in North America was made by large industrial concerns.

In recent years, the production of small-batch artisan cheeses in North America has skyrocketed. This development has been stimulated, no doubt, by the adoption of the European practice of offering a cheese course after dinner in fine dining establishments. Increased interest in specialty cheeses has created a new market for these products. North American chefs have made their cheese menus into showcases for fine local cheeses.

The American Cheese Society offers the following definitions of limited-production cheeses:

> ***Specialty cheese*** is cheese of limited production, with particular attention to natural flavor and texture profiles. Specialty cheeses may be made from all types of milk and may include flavorings.
>
> ***Artisan*** or ***artisanal cheese*** is cheese produced primarily by hand, in small batches, with particular attention to the tradition of the cheese-maker's art and using as little mechanization as possible.
>
> ***Farmstead cheese*** is cheese made with milk from a farmer's own herd or flock on the farm where the animals are raised. No milk from an outside source may be used.

European cheeses are the product of hundreds of years of tradition and include nearly every type of cheese imaginable, so it is natural that North American producers looked to European cheeses as models. At the same time, the best producers have also tried to develop distinctive products that set new standards of quality. Today, cheese producers all across Canada and the United States produce cheeses that compare in quality with the best from Europe.

It is impossible in a short space to list all the fine artisan and farmstead cheeses in North America. The following are just small random samples of the hundreds of varieties from many regions.

Fresh unripened cheeses

- Mozzarella Company Mascarpone, Texas
- Shepherd's Way Ricotta (sheep's milk), Minnesota
- Silani Sweet Cheese Ricotta, Ontario

Soft washed-rind cheeses

- Harvest Moon, Colorado
- Cowgirl Creamery Red Hawk, California
- Le Douanier, Québec
- Colo Rouge, Colorado

Mold-rind soft-ripened

- Blythedale Farm Brie and Camembert, Vermont
- Groupe Fromage Côté Triple Crème, Quebec
- Bittersweet Plantation Fleur-de-Teche Triple Cream, Louisiana
- Sweet Grass Dairy, Georgia

Hard cheeses

- Roth Kase Gruyère, Wisconsin
- Gort's Gouda, British Columbia
- Sylvan Star Gouda, Alberta
- Mona (sheep and cow's milk blend), Wisconsin
- BelGioioso Romano, Wisconsin
- Carr Valley Canaria, Wisconsin
- McCadam Cheddar, New York

Blue cheeses

- Rogue River Blue, Oregon
- Dragon's Breath, Nova Scotia
- Firefly Farms Mountain Top Blue, Maryland
- Point Reyes Blue, California
- Hubbardston Blue, Massachusetts

Goat cheeses, fresh and aged

- Vermont Butter and Cheese Company, Chèvre, Vermont
- Humboldt Fog, California
- Fromagerie Bergeron Patte Blanche, Québec
- Capriole Pipers Pyramid, Indiana

Storage and Service

STORING

Keeping qualities of cheese vary considerably. In general, *the firmer and more aged the cheese, the longer it will keep*. Cottage cheese must be used within a week, while a whole, uncut parmesan may keep a year or more.

Soft-ripened cheeses like Brie, Camembert, and Liederkranz deteriorate rapidly once they reach maturity. They are difficult cheeses to purchase because in their whole lifespan there may be only one week when they are neither underripe nor overripe.

Other ripened cheeses are not as fussy, as long as you store them under refrigeration and well wrapped to prevent drying. Cut cheeses dry especially quickly, so they must be wrapped in plastic at all times.

SERVING

Serve cheese at room temperature. This is the single most important rule of cheese service. Only at room temperature will the full flavors develop. (This does not apply to unripened cheese like cottage cheese.)

Cut cheese just before service to prevent drying. Better yet, set out whole cheeses and large pieces when possible so portions can be cut to order by the customer or service personnel.

Cooking with Cheese

Three varieties of cheese account for the majority of cheese used in cooking. *Cheddar* is the most frequently used in North American dishes, especially in sauces, as a casserole ingredient, and as a melted or gratinéed topping. *Swiss-type* cheeses are used more often in European-style dishes. Emmentaler and Gruyère are essential ingredients in fondue, Mornay sauce, gratinéed dishes, soufflés, and quiches. *Parmesan-type* cheeses are used in grated form for toppings and for seasoning and flavoring purposes.

Guidelines for Cooking with Cheese

1. Use low temperatures. Cheese contains a high proportion of protein, which toughens and becomes stringy when heated too much. Sauces containing cheese should not be boiled.
2. Use short cooking times, for the same reasons. Cheese should be added to a sauce at the end of cooking. Stirring it into the hot sauce *off the heat* is usually enough to melt it.
3. Grate cheese for faster and more uniform melting.
4. Aged cheeses melt and blend into foods more easily than young cheeses.
5. Aged cheeses add more flavor to foods than young, mild cheeses, so you need less of it.

KEY POINTS TO REVIEW

- What are five categories of cheese based on type of ripening? Give examples of each category.
- How should cheese be stored and served?
- What guidelines should be observed when cooking with cheese?

Welsh Rabbit

PORTIONS: 25 PORTION SIZE: 4 OZ (125 G)

U.S.	METRIC	INGREDIENTS
3 tbsp	45 mL	Worcestershire sauce
2 tsp	10 mL	Dry mustard
pinch	pinch	Cayenne
2½ cups	625 mL	Beer or ale
5 lb	2.5 kg	Sharp cheddar cheese, grated

PROCEDURE

1. Mix the Worcestershire sauce and spices in a heavy saucepan.
2. Add the beer or ale. Heat almost to a simmer.
3. Set the pan over very low heat. Add the grated cheese, a little at a time. Stir constantly. Continue to stir over low heat until the mixture is smooth and thick.
4. Remove from heat. The mixture may be kept warm in a steam table or bain-marie, but it is better if served immediately.

U.S.	METRIC	INGREDIENTS
25 slices	25 slices	White bread

5. Toast the bread.
6. For each portion, place a slice of hot toast on a plate. Ladle 4 fl oz (125 mL) cheese mixture over the toast. Serve.

Per serving: Calories, 470; Protein, 26 g; Fat, 31 g (60% cal.); Cholesterol, 95 mg; Carbohydrates, 19 g; Fiber, 1 g; Sodium, 750 mg.

Note: This dish is sometimes called Welsh Rarebit, although Rabbit is the original name.

Cheese Wafers

YIELD: ABOUT 150 WAFERS

U.S.	METRIC	INGREDIENTS
1 lb	500 g	Sharp cheddar cheese, grated
8 oz	250 g	Butter, softened
12 oz	375 g	Bread flour
½ tsp	2 mL	Salt
¼ tsp	1 mL	White pepper

PROCEDURE

1. Combine all ingredients in the bowl of a mixer. Mix at low speed with the paddle attachment until the mixture forms a dough.
2. Remove from the mixer and knead lightly on a floured board until the dough holds together well.
3. Divide the dough into 4 or 5 pieces. Roll each piece into a cylinder 1 in. (2.5 cm) in diameter. Wrap in waxed paper or plastic film and chill.
4. Slice the dough into thin rounds a little less than ¼ in. (0.5 cm) thick. Place on greased baking sheets.
5. Bake at 450°F (230°C) about 10 minutes, or until crisp and lightly browned.
6. Serve hot or cold as an hors d'oeuvre or as a soup accompaniment.

Per 1 wafer: Calories, 30; Protein, 1 g; Fat, 2.5 g (65% cal.); Cholesterol, 5 mg; Carbohydrates, 2 g; Fiber, 0 g; Sodium, 40 mg.

VARIATIONS

Cheese Straws

Roll out the dough like pie dough, slightly less than ¼ in. (0.5 cm) thick. Cut into strips, ¼ × 3 in. (0.5 × 7.5 cm). Bake as in basic recipe.

Swiss Fondue

PORTIONS: 4 PORTION SIZE: 8 OZ (250 G)

U.S.	METRIC	INGREDIENTS
1	1	Garlic clove
1 pt	500 mL	Dry white wine
1 lb	500 g	Swiss Emmentaler cheese, or half Emmentaler and half Gruyère, grated
1 tsp	5 mL	Cornstarch
3 tbsp	45 mL	Kirsch (see Note)
to taste	to taste	Salt
to taste	to taste	White pepper
to taste	to taste	Nutmeg
2	2	Small loaves French bread, cut into bite-size pieces

PROCEDURE

1. Cut the garlic clove in half. Rub the inside of a 1½-qt (1.5-L) fondue pot or casserole with the garlic.
2. Add the wine to the pot and set over moderate heat. Heat the wine until it is hot but not simmering. Do not boil.
3. Add the cheese to the wine, about one-fourth at a time. Stir well between each addition.
4. Dissolve the cornstarch in the kirsch. Stir into the cheese mixture. Stir over very low heat until smooth and slightly thickened.
5. Season to taste with salt, white pepper, and just a trace of nutmeg.
6. Set the casserole over a chafing dish heating element for service. Serve the bread cubes in baskets. To eat fondue, the diner spears a cube of bread on a special fondue fork and swirls it in the cheese mixture, which is kept hot over the heating element.

Per serving: Calories, 870; Protein, 43 g; Fat, 35 g (36% cal.); Cholesterol, 105 mg; Carbohydrates, 70 g; Fiber, 3 g; Sodium, 1000 mg.

Note: Kirsch is a white (that is, clear) alcoholic beverage distilled from cherries. While it is traditional in Swiss fondue, it may be omitted if unavailable. In this case, dissolve the cornstarch in cold water, or mix it with the grated cheese.

COFFEE AND TEA

Coffee

Many people judge a restaurant by its coffee. Regardless of the quality of the food, one of the things they are most likely to remember about an establishment is whether the coffee is good or bad.

Whether or not that seems fair to you, it is at least a clear signal that you ought to learn to make coffee properly. Coffee making is a simple procedure. All you do is pass hot water through ground coffee. The care with which you perform this operation, paying attention to all the details, makes the difference between a rich, aromatic, satisfying beverage and a bitter, unpleasant liquid.

Varieties, Roasts, and Blends

Coffee beans are harvested as berries from a tropical shrub. Two species of coffee account for nearly all the beans grown worldwide: *Arabica* coffees are delicate plants, difficult to grow. Nevertheless, they supply 65 to 75 percent of the world's coffee. Most of the finest coffees are from arabica beans. *Robusta* coffee plants are hardier and easier to grow. Most ordinary supermarket coffee is made from robusta beans, but robusta can also yield beans of very high quality.

Each coffee berry contains two seeds. The harvested berries are fermented and hulled, yielding green or gray-green coffee beans. The green beans are roasted to develop their flavor. The degree of roasting—light, medium, dark—affects the flavor. Most Americans drink medium roast, sometimes called *city roast*, while darker roasts, sometimes called *Viennese roast* (medium dark) and *French roast* (very dark), are popular in Europe and increasingly popular in North America. The darkest roast, *espresso roast*, is nearly black and is brewed using a special process discussed below.

Coffee roast varieties, left to right: city roast, medium dark roast, French roast.

Coffee is grown in many tropical countries, and each producing area is known for certain quality and flavor characteristics. Excellent coffees are grown in Colombia, Brazil, Venezuela, Mexico, Jamaica, Hawaii, Indonesia, and nations in Africa and the Middle East.

Most ground coffees are blends of several varieties. Blending enables the processor to combine desirable quantities from a number of beans to produce a well-balanced beverage.

Coffee may be purchased in whole bean or ground form. Whole beans stay fresh longer, but unopened vacuum packs of ground coffee keep well for a week or two and, for many establishments, are the easiest and most economical way to buy coffee. Ground coffee, once opened, should be kept in airtight containers and used within a few days. Better yet, buy ground coffee in premeasured packs suitable for your brewing equipment. Whole beans keep several weeks once opened and months in the freezer. The best practice, though, is to have frequent small deliveries so you always have the freshest coffee on hand.

Brewing procedures for fresh coffee are discussed in the procedures below.

In addition to the standard cup of regular hot coffee, the following coffee drinks are sometimes served.

1. ***Instant coffee*** is a powdered, soluble extract from coffee beans. To simplify somewhat, instant coffee is made by brewing regular coffee and drying it. In the process, the coffee loses a portion of its flavor and aroma. Most coffee lovers agree that it does not taste as good as freshly brewed coffee. Instant coffee is rarely used in food service.

2. ***Decaffeinated coffee***. Caffeine is a chemical stimulant that occurs naturally in coffee, tea, and chocolate. Decaffeinated coffee is coffee from which the caffeine has been

Basic Principles of Coffee Making

Coffee is made by extracting flavors from ground coffee beans by dissolving them in hot water. The essence of making good coffee is to extract enough of these solids to make a flavorful beverage, but not to brew so long as to extract those solids that make the coffee bitter.

With this principle in mind, study the following guidelines for making good coffee. The list is long, and every item is important.

1. **Use fresh coffee.**
   Once it is ground, coffee loses flavor and aroma rapidly. To maintain freshness, store coffee, tightly sealed, in a cool, dry place. Even with the best storage, however, you should not use coffee more than a week old. Vacuum-packed coffee keeps longer, but it too deteriorates as soon as it is opened. If you can't grind your own coffee daily (some restaurants do), at least you can arrange for frequent delivery.

2. **Use the right grind and the right brewing time.**
   A coarse grind requires more time for extraction than a fine grind. You must use the grind that is suited to your equipment.

Grind	*Extraction Time*
Fine or vacuum	2 to 4 minutes
Drip or urn	4 to 6 minutes
Regular (percolator)	6 to 8 minutes

3. **Use the right proportions.**
   Always measure. Recommended proportions are 1 pound of coffee and 1¾ to 2½ gallons of water (500 g coffee and 7.5 to 10.5 L water), depending on the strength desired.

   To make weaker coffee, add more hot water after removing the used grounds. Using more water while actually making the coffee extends the brewing time, resulting in overextraction and bitterness. In fact, many experts feel that passing no more than 2 gallons of water through 1 pound of ground coffee (8 L to 500 g) and then diluting to taste is the surest way to avoid bitterness.

   Coffee strength is a matter of customer preference and varies from region to region. For example, people in New York generally prefer stronger coffee than people in Chicago. In some areas, the preferred ratio is 1 pound (500 g) coffee to 3 gallons (12 L) water.

4. **Use fresh water.**
   Fresh, cold water brought to a boil contains dissolved air. Water that has been kept hot for a long time does not, so it tastes flat, and it makes flat-tasting coffee.

   Tap water is usually best to use. Special filtration systems are available for tap water that has off flavors or is heavily chlorinated. Do not use chemically softened water.

5. **Use water at the right brewing temperature: 195° to 200°F (90° to 93°C).**
   Water that is too hot extracts bitter solids. Water that is too cold does not extract enough flavor and yields coffee that is too cool for serving.

6. **Use a good brewing procedure.**
   Most operations use either urns, for large volume, or automatic drip makers, which make one pot at a time, as shown in the photograph. These machines can make excellent coffee because water passes through the grounds only once.

   Percolator-type coffee makers should not be used. They boil the coffee as it is being brewed and pass it through the grounds repeatedly.

7. **Use clean equipment.**
   Urns and coffee makers must be cleaned every day. Coffee leaves oily deposits that quickly turn rancid or bitter and can ruin the next batch of coffee.

8. **Use good filters.**
   Good filters are the only way to ensure sparkling, clear coffee. Most operations use paper filters, which are discarded after use. If cloth filters are used, they must be perfectly clean and free from odors.

9. **Use proper holding procedures.**
   Proper holding temperature is 185° to 190°F (85° to 88°C). Higher temperatures decompose the coffee quickly. Lower temperatures mean the customer gets cold coffee.

   Coffee made in carafe-type coffee makers is usually kept warm over electric burners.

   Do not hold brewed coffee over heat longer than 30 minutes. After this time, loss of quality is considerable. If it must be held longer, transfer it as soon as it is brewed to preheated Thermos containers. Plan production so coffee is always fresh. Discard old coffee.

Decanter-type automatic drip coffee maker
Courtesy of Cecilware.

Procedure for Making Coffee in an Urn

1. Be familiar with your equipment. Models differ in details.
2. Check to make sure the urn holds sufficient fresh water at the proper temperatures for brewing.
3. Fit the filter securely in place.
4. Spread a measured amount of coffee evenly in the filter. An even bed is necessary for uniform extraction.
5. Pass the correct amount of water through the ground coffee. If the urn is manual, pour the water slowly in a circular motion. If it is automatic, all you need to do is make sure the nozzle is in place.
6. Keep the top covered during brewing to retain heat.
7. Remove the filter with the used grounds as soon as brewing is complete. Leaving the grounds in the urn results in overextraction and bitterness.
8. Mix the coffee. Because the coffee at the bottom is stronger, you must draw out some of it—about 1 gallon (4 L) per pound (500 g) of coffee—and pour it back into the top of the urn.
9. Hold at 185° to 190°F (85° to 88°C) for up to 1 hour.
10. Clean the urn thoroughly after use.

    Using special urn brushes, clean the inside of the urn as well as inside spigots and glass gauges. Rinse and fill with several gallons of fresh water if the urn is to stand for a time. Empty and rinse with hot water before next use.

    Twice a week, clean thoroughly with urn cleaning compound, following manufacturer's instructions.

Twin urn
Courtesy of Cecilware.

An espresso maker
Courtesy of Cecilware.

removed. Most decaffeination processes use chemical solvents, although the Swiss water process uses water only. Decaffeinated coffee is often specially requested by some customers. In the past, most restaurants offered decaffeinated coffee only in the instant form. Now, however, nearly all restaurants serve freshly brewed decaffeinated coffee.

3. ***Espresso*** or ***expresso*** is a strong, dark coffee made from beans roasted until they are almost black and ground to a powder. Espresso is served in small cups as an after-dinner beverage. In addition, several popular coffee drinks are made with brewed espresso, as discussed in the next section.

4. ***Iced coffee*** is made from double-strength brewed coffee to compensate for dilution by melting ice.

ESPRESSO DRINKS

Espresso and espresso drinks have grown in popularity in recent years, and specialty coffee shops have sprung up seemingly on almost every street corner.

Espresso is a concentrated coffee beverage brewed in special machines (see photo) from dark-roast, finely ground beans. For each drink, the ground coffee is packed into a small metal filter, which is then firmly attached to the machine. Water is forced through the grounds under high steam pressure, making a small cup of strong beverage topped with a layer of rich foam called the *crema*. A shot of espresso is about 2 fluid ounces (55 mL), and it is usually served in a tiny cup or as a double shot in a standard coffee cup.

In addition, the following drinks are made with brewed espresso:

Cappuccino (cap oo chee no): equal parts espresso and frothy steamed milk.

Latte (lah tay): short for *caffe latte*, or "coffee milk." One part espresso to two (or more) parts steamed milk, without the layer of foam found on cappuccino. The French ***café au lait*** (cah fay oh lay; meaning "coffee with milk") is basically the same as a latte, but it may be made with strong regular dark roast coffee rather than espresso.

Macchiato (mah kee ah toe): espresso topped with a little frothed milk.

Americano: espresso diluted with hot water.

Breve (bray vay): espresso with steamed half-and-half.

Mocha (moh kah): espresso mixed with hot chocolate or cocoa, topped with whipped cream.

Specialty coffee shops also sell a great variety of flavored espresso coffee drinks, hot and cold, using flavored syrups such as caramel, vanilla, and mint.

Tea

Tea is one of the world's most popular beverages, and it is widely drunk even in coffee-drinking countries. In many regions, tea is a much more popular beverage in the home than in the restaurant. Part of the difference may be due to mishandling in the restaurant and indifference on the part of restaurateurs.

Food-service professionals would do well to pay more attention to tea. First of all, it is much less expensive than coffee to serve. One pound (500 g) of tea yields 200 servings, as compared with 40 servings from 1 pound (500 g) of coffee. Moreover, tea is one of the simplest of beverages to serve and does not require the equipment or the labor of coffee service.

Varieties

All the world's varieties of tea are produced from one species of evergreen shrub. Most of the differences among varieties are the results of growing conditions and modifications in processing techniques.

As in the case of coffee, different regions produce teas of different quality and flavor characteristics. Most of the tea consumed in North America is imported from India and Sri Lanka (Ceylon).

Variations in processing produce three categories of tea. *Black tea* is fermented by allowing the freshly harvested leaves to oxidize in a damp place. *Green tea* is dried without fermenting. *Oolong tea* is partially fermented to a greenish-brown color. Specialty teas and flavored teas are also available.

Black teas are graded by leaf size according to a rather complicated system. This is important to remember because most people think of orange pekoe as a variety of tea, whereas it is actually a specific leaf size of any black variety.

After grading, teas are blended to ensure consistency and uniformity. A blend may contain as many as 30 individual teas.

Many excellent blends are available from numerous purveyors. A smart food-service operator would do well to shop around rather than serve the same mediocre blend the competition serves.

Tea varieties, from left to right: black tea, green tea, oolong tea.

HERBAL TEAS AND SPECIALTY TEA DRINKS

Herbal teas are beverages that are brewed like tea but that are made with herbs, spices, dried fruits, and other plant ingredients in place of tea leaves, or sometimes in addition to tea leaves. In other words, most herbal tea contains no actual tea. Hundreds of flavors and blends are available, far too many to list, and most purveyors have their own proprietary blends. Mint and chamomile are among the most popular herb teas.

Chai (rhymes with pie) is a spiced milk and tea blend that originated in India and has become popular in the West. *Chai* is the word for "tea" in several languages. The mixed beverage called *chai* is made of black tea, milk, spices such as cardamom, cinnamon, ginger, and black peppercorns, and sugar or another sweetener. In the West, chai is generally made from commercial mixes.

Packaging and Market Forms

Tea is packaged in bulk as loose tea and in tea bags of various sizes. Standard cup-size bags are packaged 200 to the pound (500 g), while the pot-size bag (that is, individual service pot) is packaged at 150 to 175 per pound (500 g). This is important for you to know if you are purchasing tea because the larger bags will not be as economical if the service in your establishment is by the cup.

Larger tea bags that contain 1 or 2 oz (30 to 60 g) of tea are available for brewing larger quantities, especially for iced tea.

Instant tea is a soluble extraction made by brewing a very strong tea, using lesser grades, and drying the liquid to obtain a powder. This product is used primarily for iced tea because the processing results in the loss of much of the flavor and aroma essential to a good hot tea.

Preparing Tea

In most restaurants, it seems, when one orders tea, one receives a cold cup, a tea bag in a little package, and a pot of warm water that has been standing in an urn for hours. This is absolutely the worst possible way to serve tea, with the possible exception of brewing a large quantity and keeping it warm all day. No wonder most people don't order tea.

Here is the right way:

Procedure for Making Hot Tea

1. Use proper proportions of tea and water. One teaspoon (5 mL) loose tea or one single-service tea bag makes a 6-oz (175-mL) cup.
2. Rinse the teapot with hot water to warm it. Use china, glass, or stainless steel. Other metals may give an off flavor.
3. Bring fresh, cold water to a boil. Water that has been kept warm for a time makes flat-tasting tea.
4. Place the loose tea or tea bag in the pot and pour the water directly over it.
5. Let the tea steep 3 to 5 minutes. Then remove the tea bag or strain off the tea from the loose leaves.

   Establishments specializing in tea service present the customer with the pot of tea and a pot of hot water so they can dilute the tea to taste.
6. Serve immediately. Tea does not hold well.

Procedure for Making Iced Tea

The following method makes 1 gallon (4 L). The tea is brewed stronger to allow for melting ice.

1. Place 2 ounces (60 g) tea in a pot.
2. Bring 1 quart (1 L) water to a boil and pour over the tea.
3. Steep 5 minutes. Remove tea bags, or strain out loose leaves.
4. Add 3 quarts (3 L) cold tap water.
5. Hold at room temperature up to 4 hours. Refrigeration may make the tea cloudy.
6. Serve over ice.

KEY POINTS TO REVIEW

- What nine guidelines should be observed when making coffee?
- What is the procedure for making coffee in an urn?
- What is espresso? What popular drinks are made from espresso?
- What is the procedure for making hot tea? Iced tea?

TERMS FOR REVIEW

pasteurized
ultra-pasteurized
Ultra-High-Temperature (UHT) pasteurization
whole milk
milk fat
butterfat
skim (nonfat) milk
low-fat milk
flavored milk
homogenized milk
whipping cream
light cream
half-and-half
sour cream
crème fraîche
buttermilk
yogurt
evaporated milk
condensed milk
dried whole milk
nonfat dry milk
curdling
scorching
butter
unsalted butter
clarified butter
margarine
ripening
double-crème cheese
triple-crème cheese
chèvre
process cheese
specialty cheese
artisan(al) cheese
farmstead cheese
instant coffee
decaffeinated coffee
espresso/expresso
iced coffee
cappuccino
latte
café au lait
macchiato
Americano
breve
mocha
herbal tea
chai

QUESTIONS FOR DISCUSSION

1. What is curdling, and how can you prevent it when cooking with milk?
2. What is washed-rind cheese? Describe the typical appearance of washed-rind cheese, and compare it to mold-rind cheese.
3. Why does cheese combine more smoothly with a sauce at low heat than at high heat?
4. Why is using the proper grind important in making coffee?
5. Describe the procedure for making coffee in an urn.
6. Describe the proper method for making tea.

Chapter 20

Making Pâté en Croûte, page 443.

Pâtés, Terrines, and Other Cold Foods

The techniques and procedures presented in this chapter belong to the culinary department known as ***garde manger*** (gard mawn zhay), a term whose basic meaning is "larder" or "food storage place." This area, because of its cooler temperature, was traditionally used for the preparation of cold foods. Thus, the work carried out in the storage area, or garde manger, became known by the same name.

The art of garde manger includes the techniques of cold food decoration, cold platter design and presentation, and the design and planning of buffets. Garde manger is an intricate and complex discipline that is the subject of whole books and of extended courses of study.

This book is primarily concerned with à la carte cooking. Buffet service is beyond its scope. Nevertheless, à la carte restaurants have inherited from classical garde manger a number of special food preparations that can be served in single portions as well as on butler platters. Pâtés, terrines, galantines, and mousses are not only ideal for buffets, they are also popular in many restaurants. This chapter serves as an introduction to these preparations.

After reading this chapter, you should be able to

1. Prepare livers for use in forcemeats.
2. Prepare basic meat and poultry forcemeats.
3. Prepare pâtés and terrines using basic forcemeats.
4. Prepare galantines.
5. Prepare mousseline forcemeats and make terrines based on them.
6. Prepare specialty terrines and other molded dishes based on aspics and mousses.
7. Handle raw foie gras and prepare foie gras terrines.
8. Prepare baked liver terrines.
9. Prepare rillettes.

The Handling and Service of Cold Dishes

Because the dishes featured in this chapter are served cold, factors relating to their handling and service require special consideration. These have to do with sanitation and presentation.

Sanitation and Storage

Hot foods that have been handled in a sanitary manner and that are served at or above a temperature that kills microorganisms can usually be considered safe and sanitary to eat. Cold foods, on the other hand, present special problems because they are stored and handled after cooking. During this time, they may be exposed to disease-causing organisms. Because these foods are not subjected to further cooking, the organisms will not be destroyed.

For this reason, it is particularly important to follow all the rules of safe food handling. Make sure tools, containers, and work surfaces are clean and sanitary. Keep ingredients refrigerated when they are not being worked on, and keep the finished product refrigerated until service time.

The length of time terrines and other cold foods can be stored in the refrigerator depends on the ingredients, the type of item, and the method of preparation. Uncut meat terrines sealed with a layer of fat (see p. 445) may keep as long as several weeks (although the quality may start to decline after a week or so), while seafood and vegetable terrines may keep no more than two or three days, or even less. Pâtés en croûte (see p. 442) do not keep as well as terrines because the pastry loses its freshness. Aspics should be kept covered or wrapped to prevent them from drying out.

Presentation

Attractive plating or presentation of foods is, of course, always important, but it could be argued that it is even more important for cold foods than for hot foods. Foods presented hot and steaming, directly from the sauté pan or carving board, have an immediate appeal to the nose as well as the eye, but cold foods must rely more completely on visual impact to make their first impression.

Furthermore, because the urgency in getting the plate from the kitchen to the dining room before the food cools down is absent, the cook has more time to arrange cold foods on the plate. This does not mean, however, that the most elaborate or intricate presentation is the best. "Keep it simple" is a good rule of thumb. Food is not made more appetizing by excessive handling.

Arrangements should be kept neat, but this does not mean they must always be symmetrical or regular. As in the case of salads, a deliberate casualness in the arrangement can be appetizing when it suggests the dish has been freshly assembled with minimum handling and rushed to the table.

In the case of pâtés and terrines, careful handling is essential to the presentation. Slice these items carefully and plate each slice with the best side up. To make neat slices, use a sharp, thin-bladed slicing knife. Before each slice, wipe off any residue from the previous slice and dip the blade in hot water. Slice the pâté with a gentle sawing motion, using the full length of the blade. Don't force the knife straight down or make little jagged cuts; this will make the cut surface uneven rather than smooth.

If the cut end of the pâté has discolored somewhat from exposure to air, plate the first slice with this side down. In contrast to pâtés for buffet presentation, slices of pâté for à la carte service are often garnished with greens or other colorful items, which enliven the sometimes drab appearance of a plain meat pâté. In addition, greens and other vegetable garnish provide a pleasant flavor contrast to the somewhat rich, processed flavor of the pâté or terrine.

Tart or piquant garnishes and accompaniments, as well as tart sauces such as vinaigrette and mayonnaise variations, help counter the richness of pâtés, which are often rather fatty. This is why sour pickles and mustard are classic accompaniments for these foods.

Consideration must be given to the serving temperature of cold foods such as aspics, pâtés, and terrines. A common error is to serve these items too cold. At refrigerator temperature, their flavors are masked. Furthermore, their textures are too firm; the fat in pâtés and the gelatin in aspics are firmly congealed. A little warmer temperature is necessary to enable them to melt pleasantly in the mouth.

To bring them to suitable serving temperature, remove individual portions from refrigeration and let stand at room temperature about 5 or 10 minutes, but no longer. Remember the sanitation guidelines discussed earlier. This period is long enough to let them warm slightly but not long enough to give microorganisms time to start multiplying. Keep in mind, too, that this short period of tempering applies only to those portions to be served right away. Whole pâtés from which portions were cut, for example, should be returned immediately to refrigeration.

Special Forcemeat Dishes

This section is concerned with classic meat and poultry dishes called *pâtés*, terrines, and galantines. Some terrines are based on vegetables and other items rather than meats, but these are the subject of a later section. The main ingredients of the items discussed here are a forcemeat and, usually but not always, a garnish.

A ***forcemeat*** may be defined as a mixture of seasoned, ground meats used as a stuffing or filling. The name comes from the French word *farce*, which means "stuffing."

The ***garnish*** in a pâté or terrine is not just a decoration but a major ingredient that adds body, flavor, and nutritional value as well as appearance. Garnish usually consists of meats or other foods cut in dice, strips, or other shapes, or left whole if they are small. Classic pâté garnishes include:

- Ham
- Veal
- Chicken, duck, or turkey breast
- Chicken, duck, or goose livers
- Foie gras
- Game
- Fresh pork fatback
- Tongue
- Pistachios
- Truffles

Types of Forcemeat

The following are the three basic types of forcemeat:

1. **Straight forcemeat (including country-style forcemeat).**
   This is a mixture of seasoned ground meats. As such, it is basically a form of sausage meat, except the grind is generally, but not always, finer. Consequently, many of the guidelines for making and handling sausage meat, discussed in Chapter 7, apply here as well. It may be helpful to read or to review pages 200–205 in conjunction with this discussion. Straight forcemeats are the basis of most traditional pâtés and terrines and are the major focus of this chapter.

   A *country-style forcemeat* is made the same way, except the grind is coarser. Most country-style forcemeats are made from pork and pork fat and contain some liver.

2. **Gratin forcemeat.**
   This type of forcemeat differs from a straight forcemeat in that a portion of the meat is seared, and thus partially cooked, and cooled before it is ground. Because the partial cooking eliminates some of the binding power of the meat protein, gratin forcemeats usually contain a starch binder called a *panada* (also called *panade*). This type of forcemeat is not used as often as straight or mousseline forcemeats and is not covered in this book.

3. **Mousseline forcemeat.**
   This type of forcemeat consists of white meat (usually poultry or veal) or seafood processed to a purée and combined with heavy cream and egg. See page 448 for a discussion.

Straight Forcemeats

A basic straight forcemeat consists of the following:

50 to 65 percent lean meat

35 to 50 percent fat

Seasonings

The many variations on this basic formula depend on the ingredients used and how they are combined.

MEAT

Pork is the basic ingredient, but many other meats can be included in addition to or instead of pork, including veal, chicken, turkey, ham, duck, rabbit, and game of all kinds.

LIVER

Chicken, goose, duck, or pork liver is often included in forcemeats. Liver gives flavor and also acts as a binder.

FAT

The classic proportion in forcemeats is equal parts fat and meat. Many forcemeats, however, contain less than 50 percent fat, especially in recent years, as people have become more attentive to nutrition and dietary considerations. Nevertheless, a certain amount of fat is necessary for both moisture and flavor. A pâté with too little fat tastes dry. Hard fat, such as pork fatback, gives best results. Heavy cream is sometimes used to add fat as well as liquid to a forcemeat.

Note that this discussion of fat content refers only to the solid fat specifically added as a measured ingredient. There is, of course, some fat in the lean meat as well.

OTHER INGREDIENTS

Eggs or egg whites may be added as a binder. Flour or other starches may be added for the same purpose. Extra binders are not absolutely necessary in a forcemeat made purely of meat and fat because the meat proteins are sufficient to bind the product when cooked. On the other hand, when brandy, cream, and other liquids are added to the forcemeat, extra binders may be needed or at least beneficial.

THE GRIND

Forcemeat may be ground coarse, medium, or fine. Country-style pâté, or ***pâté de campagne*** (cawm pah nyuh), is characterized by a coarse texture. Galantines, on the other hand, are usually made from finely ground forcemeats.

PREPARING STRAIGHT FORCEMEATS

Many, if not most, pâté and terrine forcemeats contain some liver. Chicken livers or other poultry livers, both economical and widely available, are the most often used. For best results, livers should be soaked in milk and then cleaned according to the procedure below. Pork liver and other larger livers can be cut into pieces and prepared in the same way.

The following recipe can be used with many garnishes to make a great variety of pâtés, terrines, and galantines. It can also be changed according to any of the variations listed by using different meats. Once the basic technique is understood, any kind of pâté can be produced.

The recipe should be viewed as a basic procedure that can be varied in ways other than those indicated following the recipe, just as sausage meat can be varied. The varieties and quantities of spices can be changed. In addition, the fineness of the grind can be varied to make pâtés of varying textures.

The proportion of fat can be increased or reduced, but remember that making the forcemeat too lean will reduce its eating quality. Although at first glance the recipe looks as if it calls for 50 percent fat, this is not the case, as the liver should be included as part of the meat. The proportion of fat is 44 percent. Taking the first column of ingredient quantities as an example, using 1 lb lean pork, 12 oz fat, and 4 oz liver lowers the proportion of fat to 38 percent (not counting, of course, the smaller amount of fat within the meats). Using 12 oz lean pork, 1 lb fat, and 4 oz liver raises the fat proportion to 50 percent.

Procedure for Preparing Poultry Livers for Forcemeats

1. Rinse the livers in cold water, drain, then soak 24 hours in enough milk to cover.
2. Drain and rinse thoroughly in cold water. Drain again.
3. Remove all fat and connective tissue. At this point, the livers are ready to be used whole as garnish for pâtés and terrines. If they are to be added to forcemeats, continue with steps 4 and 5.
4. Blend in a blender until liquid.
5. Strain through a chinois or fine strainer to remove all traces of connective tissue.

Basic Pork Forcemeat

YIELD: 2 LB (900 G)

U.S.	METRIC	INGREDIENTS	PROCEDURE
14 oz	400 g	Lean pork	1. Before beginning, make sure all equipment and all ingredients are well chilled. Forcemeats must be kept cold at all times to prevent the fat from softening or melting.
14 oz	400 g	Pork fat	2. Cut the meat and fat into small dice.
		Marinade:	3. Sweat the minced shallots in the butter until soft. Add half of the white wine and reduce by half. Cool completely.
1½ oz	45 g	Shallots, minced	4. Combine the meat and fat with the shallots, the rest of the wine, the bay leaves, brandy, salt, spice mixture, and pepper. Toss to mix well. Cover and refrigerate overnight.
½ oz	15 g	Butter	5. Remove the bay leaves. Grind the meat and fat twice through the fine blade of a meat grinder.
2 fl oz	60 mL	White wine	
2	2	Bay leaves	
1 fl oz	30 mL	Brandy	
2½ tsp	12 mL	Salt	
½ tsp	2 mL	Pâté spice or quatre épices (see Note)	
¼ tsp	1 mL	White pepper	
4 oz	100 g	Chicken livers, soaked, cleaned, and puréed (see above)	6. Combine the ground meats and liver purée.
2	2	Eggs (see step 7)	7. Beat the eggs lightly and mix in thoroughly. (*Note:* The eggs are optional and are omitted in many pâtés.)
			8. Make a quenelle (a small ball of forcemeat) and poach it in simmering water. Cool. Taste and correct the seasonings in the forcemeat.
			9. Keep the forcemeat chilled until ready for use.

Per 1 ounce (28.35 g): Calories, 150; Protein, 3 g; Fat, 14 g (89% cal.); Cholesterol, 54 mg; Carbohydrates, 0 g; Fiber, 0 g; Sodium, 200 mg.

Note: Pâté spice may be purchased in various blends, or you may make your own blend to taste. Pâté spice usually contains black and white pepper, cloves, nutmeg, ginger, cayenne, bay leaf, thyme, and marjoram. Grind very fine and sift through a sieve. For quatre épices, see page 207.

VARIATIONS

Omit the pork, fat, livers, and eggs in the basic recipe. Substitute the following ingredients and quantities. Vary seasonings to taste.

Veal Forcemeat

9 oz	250 g	Lean pork
9 oz	250 g	Lean veal
14 oz	400 g	Fresh pork fat
3	3	Eggs

Chicken Forcemeat I

9 oz	250 g	Lean pork
9 oz	250 g	Chicken meat
14 oz	400 g	Fresh pork fat
3	3	Eggs

Chicken Forcemeat II

1 lb 2 oz	500 g	Chicken meat
14 oz	400 g	Fresh pork fat
3	3	Eggs

Duck, Pheasant, or Game Forcemeat

7 oz	200 g	Lean pork, or a mixture of pork and veal
7 oz	200 g	Duck, pheasant, or game meat
14 oz	400 g	Fresh pork fat
4 oz	100 g	Livers, soaked, cleaned, and puréed
1	1	Egg

Terrines and Pâtés

Terrines and pâtés are baked forcemeats, often but not always containing one or more types of garnish. Strictly speaking, the difference between the two lies in how they are baked. By definition, a **terrine** is baked in an earthenware dish. The dish itself is also called a *terrine*, a word derived from the French *terre*, meaning "earth." Today, other materials besides earthenware, such as glass or metal, may be used for terrines. Terrines may be presented in their baking dish, or they may be unmolded.

Pâtés include products baked in a crust, although chefs disagree about the correct usage of the terms (see sidebar). In this book, we use the term **pâté** to indicate products baked with a crust and *terrine* for products baked without a crust. Popular usage of the terms, however, is much looser.

It should be noted that many kinds of products are called *terrines* because they are prepared in terrine molds. The terrines discussed in this section are based on the straight forcemeats we have just considered. Other kinds of terrines are discussed in a later section.

Pâtés and Pastry

Many experts argue that a pâté is, by definition, baked in a crust. The word pâté (with an accent on the *e*) is derived from the word *pâte* (without the accent), meaning "pastry." Others insist the root meaning of *pâte* is "paste," so it can apply to any kind of paste, including meat pastes. This agrees with modern usage, in which the word *pâté* is used for products with or without a crust, and even for spreadable meat pastes.

To avoid confusion, perhaps the best advice is to use the term **pâté en croûte** if you want to specify a pâté with a crust.

PREPARING PÂTÉS

The essential difference between a pâté and a terrine, as we are using the terms, is the crust. Although a heavy pastry crust may not be suitable for all kinds of terrine mixtures, the typical baked forcemeat-type terrine under consideration here can usually be made with or without a crust.

This section concentrates on the specific procedures for making the pastry and finishing the assembled pâté. Making the meat filling is the same as for terrines and is not repeated here. To make a pâté en croûte, apply the following procedure to the Veal and Ham Terrine and to any of the variations following the basic recipe (see p. 446).

Pastries used to enclose pâtés are of various types, but the most commonly used are similar to pie pastries, but sturdier. A recipe for this type of **pâte à pâté**, or pâté pastry, is included here. Its advantage over many other types of pâté pastry is that it is relatively good to eat. Some authorities argue about whether the dough around a pâté is meant to be eaten. But because customers are not necessarily aware of this argument, it is best to use a pastry that is reasonably pleasant to eat.

Traditional English pâtés, or raised meat pies, use a hot-water pastry that can be modeled like clay and is sturdy when baked. Pastries used for display—that is, for show platters not intended to be eaten—are also made to be sturdy and easy to handle. These pastries are not considered here.

One type of procedure for assembling a pâté follows the pastry recipe (Figure 20.1).

Pâté Pastry (Pâte à Pâté)

YIELD: 1 LB 12 OZ (900 G)

U.S.	METRIC	INGREDIENTS	PROCEDURE
1 lb	500 g	Flour	1. Place the flour in a large mixing bowl. Add the butter and lard. Rub them in until no lumps of fat remain.
4 oz	125 g	Butter	
3½ oz	100 g	Lard	
1	1	Eggs	2. Beat the eggs with the water and salt until the salt is dissolved.
3 fl oz	100 mL	Water, cold	3. Add the liquid to the flour mixture. Mix gently until it is completely absorbed.
1¼ tsp	7 mL	Salt	4. Gather the dough into a ball. On a work surface, knead the dough a few minutes, or until it is smooth.
			5. Place the dough in a pan and cover with plastic film. Refrigerate until needed, or at least 4 hours.

Per 1 ounce (28.35 g): Calories, 120; Protein, 2 g; Fat, 7 g (53% cal.); Cholesterol, 20 mg; Carbohydrates, 20 g; Fiber, 0 g; Sodium, 140 mg.

Figure 20.1 Making a pâté en croûte.

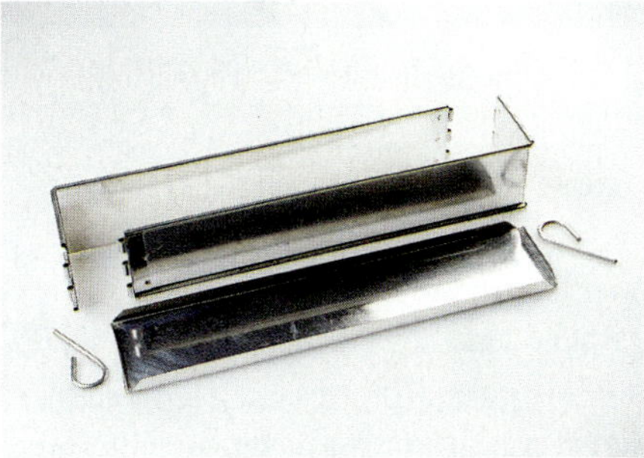

(a) Collapsible molds are used to make pâtés en croûte because they can be removed from the mold without damaging it. Assemble the mold and grease the inside well.

(b) Lightly roll the pastry into a rectangle, keeping it thick.

(c) Work the dough into a boat shape. Dust heavily with flour and fold the dough lengthwise to make a pocket.

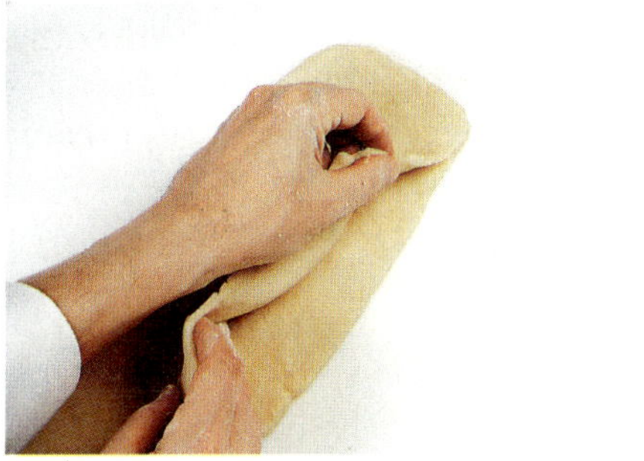

(d) Roll the double thickness of dough into a rectangle the size of the mold. Open the pocket.

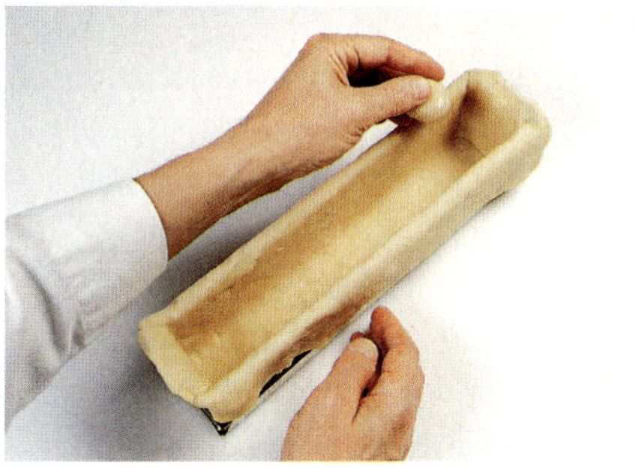

(e) Fit the dough into the mold. Carefully work it to fit snugly. A ball of dough dipped in flour helps fit the dough into the corners without tearing it.

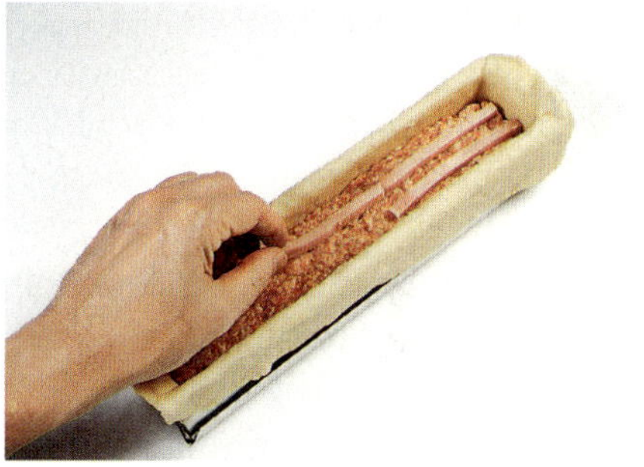

(f) Partially fill the mold with forcemeat and arrange the garnish according to the instructions in the specific recipe.

(g) Finish filling the mold, mounding the forcemeat slightly.

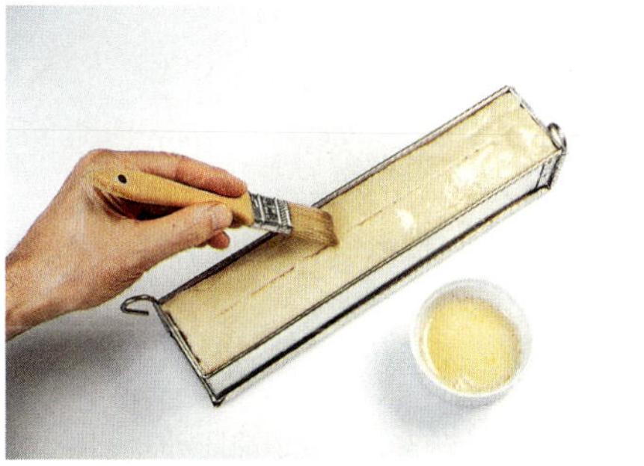

(h) Fold the ends and then sides of the dough over the top of the forcemeat, trimming the dough so it meets in the middle. Egg-wash the dough.

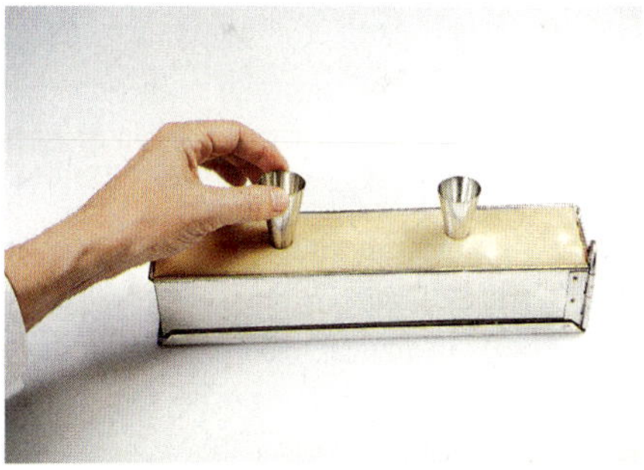

(i) Roll out and cut the top pastry and fit it in place, making sure it is sealed well to the dough below it. Egg-wash. Make holes in the top and fit pastry tubes in them to serve as chimneys to allow the escape of steam and to prevent melted fat from bubbling over the top crust as the pâté bakes.

(j) After the pâté has baked and cooled, pour liquid aspic through the chimneys to fill the spaces left when the forcemeat shrank during baking.

Procedure for Lining and Filling Pâté Molds and Finishing Pâtés

1. Prepare the pastry in advance so it has plenty of time to rest. Remove it from refrigeration long enough ahead of time to allow it to warm up slightly.
2. Prepare the molds by greasing them well on the inside. The directions here pertain to standard rectangular pâté molds. These usually are hinged and collapsible so it is easy to remove the pâté without damaging it. If you are using bottomless molds, then also grease the sheet pans on which they are to set. For molds of other shapes, modify the pastry-molding procedure as necessary to fit the shape.
3. For best results, mold the pastry so it is of even thickness, has no seams, and fits the mold perfectly. First, work the pastry with the hands for a few seconds to make it pliable. Then shape it into a rectangle and roll it slightly with a rolling pin to flatten it, keeping it quite thick.
4. Make an indentation down the center of the dough with the fingers. Gradually make the dough into a sort of boat shape. Dust the inside of the dough shape well with flour (to keep the two layers of dough from sticking together) and fold the dough along the indentation to make a pocket.
5. Gently roll out the dough to make a rectangle the size of the mold. Be careful not to roll the dough too thin, which would make it fragile. Open up the pocket.
6. Fit the opened pocket into the mold. Carefully mold the pastry to the shape of the mold by pushing the dough with your fingers. Make sure there are no air bubbles between the dough and mold. A ball of dough dipped in flour is useful for pushing the dough into the corners of the mold without tearing it.
7. If the pâté is to be made without a top crust, leave a rim of dough about ¼ inch (5 mm) above the top of the mold. Crimp this rim to make a decorative border. If there is to be a top crust, leave a rim of half the width of the mold and let it hang over the sides. (For an alternative method, see step 10.)
8. The mold is now ready to fill. For display pieces, it is common practice to line the inside of the dough with thin sheets of fatback. For pâtés to be eaten, however, it is more appetizing to omit the fat lining. Fill the mold with the desired forcemeat and garnish as for terrines (see p. 445). Mound the filling slightly so the top crust, if used, will have an attractive domed shape. The dough should hold this shape even as the forcemeat shrinks and settles during baking.

   If the pâté is not to have a top crust, it is now ready for baking. Skip to step 12. Baking without a top crust is easier and allows you to make an attractive aspic glaze with decorations for the top.
9. Fold the rim of the dough from the sides of the mold over the top of the filling. If using a top crust:
   - Roll out a sheet of dough.
   - Lay the sheet of dough on top of the mold, trim it to size, and remove it.
   - Brush the edges of dough from the sides of the mold with egg wash.
   - Return the pastry top to the mold and fit it in place, gently sealing it to the egg-washed dough.
10. As an alternative method for fitting the top crust:
    - Leave a ¼-inch (5-mm) rim of dough, as in step 7.
    - Brush the inside of this rim with egg wash.
    - Roll out and cut a top crust slightly larger than the top of the mold. Place it on top of the filled mold.
    - Crimp or pinch the two layers of pastry together with the fingers to seal.
11. Decorate the top crust with pastry cutouts, if desired. Seal the cutouts to the crust with egg wash. Make one or two vent holes in the top crust to allow steam to escape. Fit pastry tubes into these holes to form chimneys in order to keep juices from running over the top crust and spoiling its appearance.
12. To bake:
    - Preheat an oven to 400°F (200°C). Place the pâté on a sheet pan (if you are using a bottomless mold, it will, of course, already be on a sheet pan) and put it in the oven.
    - After 10 minutes, reduce the heat to 350°F (175°C). The higher initial temperature helps brown the pastry. Bake at this lower temperature until the internal temperature reaches 160° to 165°F (72°C).
    - For an average rectangular mold, the baking time will be 1 to 2 hours. Small molds that make 1 to 4 portions will take 45 minutes or less.
    - For very large molds, use a baking temperature of 325°F (160°C) so they cook evenly. Extend the baking time accordingly.
13. Remove the pâté from the oven. Let the pâté cool to room temperature in its mold. For a pâté made without a top crust, first let it cool until it is warm. Then let it finish cooling with a weight on top in order to give the pâté a firmer texture. The weight should be large enough to cover the meat but small enough so it doesn't touch the pastry rim. This can be accomplished by cutting a board to the proper size, laying it in place on the pâté, and placing weights on the board. (Obviously, this cannot be done if there is a top crust.) Refrigerate.
14. When the pâté is cold, prepare an aspic jelly. Melt the aspic and flavor it, if desired, with a little sherry, port, or Madeira. Fill the pâté with the aspic.
    - If the pâté has a pastry top, pour the aspic through the vent hole or holes, using a funnel, until the pâté is completely full.
    - If the pâté has no top crust, fill it with enough aspic to completely cover the top of the meat.
    - Refrigerate until the aspic is set.
15. Remove the pâté carefully from the mold.
16. Pâtés without a top crust may now be decorated and reglazed with aspic if desired. Decorate as desired by dipping the decorations in liquid aspic and setting them in place. Chill briefly, then apply a little more aspic to glaze the top.
17. For storage, handling, and presentation, see page 438.

PREPARING FORCEMEAT TERRINES

Terrines, like pâtés, may be baked in molds of various shapes and sizes. Traditional oval molds, for example, have long been popular. For ease of portion control, however, rectangular molds are the most appropriate.

A terrine may be lined with thin sheets of fatback, although this is optional. The layer of fat does not contribute significantly, as is widely believed, to keeping the meat moist during baking; after all, the terrine mold itself is more moistureproof than the layer of fat. Although such a fat lining is traditional, today's diners are more likely to find a rim of fat unappetizing. Of course, the fat layer can be removed before serving. Alternatively, a sheet of caul fat, which is much thinner than fatback, can be used to line the mold.

Procedure for Preparing Forcemeat Terrines

1. Prepare the desired forcemeat (see p. 441).
2. Prepare the selected garnish. Meat garnishes are usually cut into strips, which are laid lengthwise in the mold.
3. Marinate the garnish as desired. This step is optional but adds to the flavor.
4. Prepare the mold. Do not use a hinged or collapsible mold, which cannot be placed in a water bath. If desired, line the mold with thin sheets of fatback (sliced on a slicing machine) or with a sheet of caul fat, letting the excess hang over the sides. Make the sheets of fat sufficiently large so the amount of fat hanging over the sides can be folded over to cover the top completely. If the mold is not lined with fat, grease it well.
5. Place a layer of forcemeat in the bottom of the mold. If no garnish is used, simply fill the mold. Spread the forcemeat evenly and rap the mold sharply on the workbench to dislodge any air bubbles.
6. Arrange a layer of garnish on top of the forcemeat.
7. Continue adding forcemeat and garnish until they are all used. End with a layer of forcemeat on top. Two or three layers of garnish are usually sufficient.
8. If a fat lining has been used, fold the excess fat over the top of the forcemeat to cover it.
9. Cover the top with a sheet of aluminum foil. Cut a few holes in the foil to allow steam to escape.
10. Place the mold in a water bath for baking. Make sure the bath is deep enough to allow the hot water to come halfway up the sides of the mold. Bake at 350°F (175°C) until the internal temperature registers 165°F (74°C).
11. Remove the terrine from the water bath and place it on a rack to cool. When it has cooled somewhat but is still warm, finish cooling it with a weight, as explained in the procedure for making pâtés. It should not be weighted when it is still hot because it is too fragile and may split or fracture, and the weight may force out too much juice. If a looser texture is desired, cool the terrine without weighting it.
12. When the terrine is completely cool, cover and refrigerate it.
13. The terrine may be sealed with a layer of fat or aspic. These protect the terrine from air and help preserve it.
    - To add a layer of fat, melt lard (or rendered duck fat or other fat appropriate to the terrine), then let stand until cool but still liquid. The terrine should be cool, about 50°F (10°C). Pour in enough fat to cover the meat completely. Let stand until the fat has congealed, then cover and refrigerate. The purpose of this fat is only to extend the keeping quality of the terrine. It should be removed before serving.
    - Add aspic to a terrine in the same way as adding a layer of fat; see also the procedure for adding aspic to a pâté, page 444. Unlike melted fat, aspic extends the storage life of a terrine only a few days because the aspic itself dries out. On the other hand, aspic contributes to both flavor and appearance. If desired, apply decorations to the top of the terrine and add another layer of aspic to glaze.

Veal and Ham Terrine

YIELD: APPROXIMATELY 2 LB (1 KG)

U.S.	METRIC	INGREDIENTS	PROCEDURE
2 lb	1 kg	Veal Forcemeat (p. 441)	1. Prepare the forcemeat according to the recipe on page 441. Refrigerate it until very cold.
		Garnish:	
4 oz	125 g	Veal, lean, trimmed	2. Cut the veal, ham, and fatback for the garnish into strips about ¼ in. (6 mm) thick. Mix with the brandy and marinate in the refrigerator 1 hour or longer.
4 oz	125 g	Smoked ham	
1 oz	30 g	Fresh pork fatback	
2 fl oz	60 mL	Brandy	
as needed	as needed	Fresh pork fatback or caul fat for lining molds (optional)	3. Have ready a 2-qt (2-L) rectangular terrine mold.

4. If using fatback to line the mold, have the fat very cold. Cut it on a slicer into broad, thin slices less than ⅛ in. (3 mm) thick. Line the mold with the slices, overlapping them by about ¼ in. (5 mm). Let the tops of the slices hang over the edges.

   If using caul fat, line the mold with a large sheet of caul, letting the edges hang over the side of the mold.

   If not using caul or fat, grease the mold well.
5. Fill the terrine with alternating layers of forcemeat and garnish, beginning and ending with forcemeat and laying the strips of garnish lengthwise in the terrine. Press the meat firmly into the terrine so there are no air bubbles.
6. If using sheets of fat or caul to line the mold, fold the overhanging fat over the top of the forcemeat to cover.
7. Cover with foil.
8. Set the terrine in a hot-water bath. Bake at 350°F (175°C) until the internal temperature is 165°F (74°C).
9. Remove from the oven and cool until just warm. Weight and continue to cool, following the basic procedure on page 444. Finish, if desired, with a layer of melted fat or aspic, as described in the basic procedure.

Per 1 ounce (28.35 g): Calories, 170; Protein, 5 g; Fat, 15 g (83% cal.); Cholesterol, 50 mg; Carbohydrates, 0 g; Fiber, 0 g; Sodium, 250 mg.

VARIATIONS

Veal and Ham Terrine with Foie Gras

Prepare as in the basic recipe, but place a layer of sliced, cooked foie gras down the center of the terrine. Use slices of foie gras terrine (p. 455) or canned foie gras pâté. A row of sliced truffles may be placed on top of the foie gras layer.

Veal and Tongue Terrine

Use cooked, cured beef tongue in place of the ham.

Rabbit Terrine

Bone out a rabbit, keeping the loin meat in 2 long strips. Make a rabbit forcemeat by following the veal forcemeat recipe but substituting meat from the rabbit legs for all or part of the veal. Soak, clean, and liquefy the rabbit liver according to the procedure on page 441. Add it to the forcemeat. Omit the garnish from the basic recipe, instead using the rabbit loins marinated in the brandy. Fold the thin end of each loin back on itself so it is of uniform thickness. When filling the terrine, put half the forcemeat into the mold, lay the loins end to end down the center of the terrine, then fill with the remaining forcemeat.

Optional step: Make a stock with the rabbit bones. Reduce the stock to a glaze, cool, and mix with the forcemeat.

Optional step: Add a small quantity of nuts, such as skinned pistachios, to the forcemeat.

Country Terrine

Use pork forcemeat, keeping the grind rather coarse. Chop the garnish coarsely and mix with the forcemeat.

Game Terrine

Prepare as in the basic recipe, using Game Forcemeat (p. 441) and strips of game meat instead of the veal and ham for garnish. Optional: Add a small quantity of green peppercorns, rinsed and drained, to the forcemeat.

Duck Terrine

Bone out a duck. Use the leg meat, any trimmings, and the liver for making Duck Forcemeat (p. 441). Flavor the forcemeat lightly with grated orange zest, using the zest of ½ orange for each 2 lb (1 kg) forcemeat. If desired, flavor the forcemeat with duck stock reduced to a glaze and cooled. Use the breast meat for garnish, omitting the veal and ham from the basic recipe but keeping the fatback. Cut the breast meat into strips and marinate in the brandy with the fatback strips.

Galantines

A *galantine* is a ground meat mixture—that is, a forcemeat—wrapped in the skin of the product it is made from, such as chicken or duck. A galantine is almost always poached although, in some instances, it is roasted.

A galantine is made by rolling up a forcemeat in a large piece of skin, giving it a cylindrical or sausage shape that yields round slices. Consequently, the name *galantine* is also given to forcemeats or other mixtures (such as mousselines) that are rolled into a sausage shape in a piece of parchment, plastic film, or other material.

A finished galantine is often displayed whole, decorated and glazed with aspic, with a few slices removed to show a cross section. For à la carte service, slices of galantine are served the same way as slices of pâté and terrine.

The following is a representative galantine recipe. The procedure is illustrated in Figure 20.2.

Figure 20.2 Making a chicken galantine.

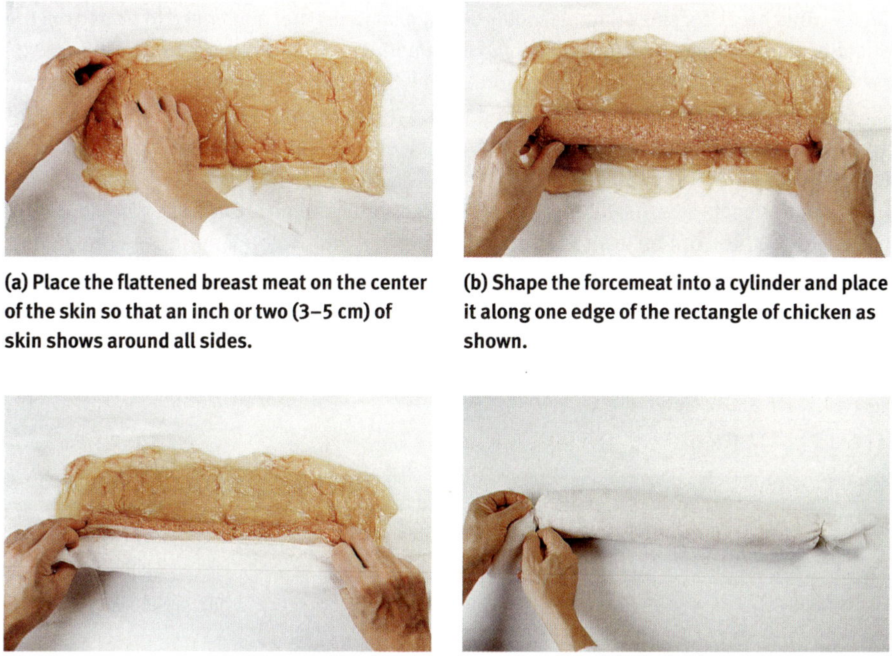

(a) Place the flattened breast meat on the center of the skin so that an inch or two (3–5 cm) of skin shows around all sides.

(b) Shape the forcemeat into a cylinder and place it along one edge of the rectangle of chicken as shown.

(c) With the aid of the cheesecloth, roll up the forcemeat in the chicken skin. Do not roll the cheesecloth into the chicken.

(d) Tie the ends of the cheesecloth securely. Proceed as indicated in the recipe.

KEY POINTS TO REVIEW

- What are the three basic types of forcemeat? Describe them. What are their primary ingredients?
- What are the steps in the procedure for preparing poultry livers for use in forcemeats?
- What are the steps in the procedure for preparing forcemeat terrines?
- What are the steps in the procedure for making a pâté en croûte, beginning with lining the mold?
- What is a galantine? How is it made?

Terrines Based on Mousselines

The body of most fish terrines, as well as some vegetable terrines and other specialty items, consists of a mousseline forcemeat. These are made like traditional terrines, except a mousseline forcemeat takes the place of the straight forcemeat.

A ***mousseline forcemeat*** consists of raw, puréed fish, poultry, or meat combined with heavy cream and, usually but not always, eggs or egg whites. Because they contain no starch or binder, and because of the large quantity of cream they contain, mousselines are the most delicate of forcemeats. The procedure for making a mousseline forcemeat is detailed in the basic recipe below.

Ingredient proportions in mousseline forcemeat depend on the qualities of the meat or fish being used. The albumin content of the egg white makes the mousseline firm when it is cooked. If the meat or fish you are using has a high albumin content, however, you may be able to reduce the quantity of egg white. In some cases, you may not need any egg. Similarly, the amount of cream depends on the firmness of the fish and on the intended use of the forcemeat. If it is to be the base of a terrine that will be sliced, too much cream will make it too delicate. On the other hand, for small timbale molds and similar items that don't need to be as firm, the quantity of cream can be increased beyond the amount indicated in the recipe below.

As for straight forcemeats, it is important to keep the ingredients cold at all times.

The procedure for assembling and cooking a mousseline terrine is the same as for making a regular forcemeat terrine (see p. 445), except the internal temperature, when done, is slightly lower, 158° to 160°F (70°C).

Cooked vegetables, fish fillets, and other appropriate items are used as garnish. Two or more mousselines can be layered in the mold to make multicolored terrines. Alternatively, a mousseline forcemeat can be spread on the bottom and sides of the mold, which is then filled with a different mousseline plus garnish and topped with a layer of the first mousseline.

Basic Mousseline Forcemeat

YIELD: APPROXIMATELY 1 LB 12 OZ (875 G)

U.S.	METRIC	INGREDIENTS
1 lb	500 g	Chicken meat, lean veal, fish, or shellfish (see Note)
2 oz	60 g	Egg whites
12 fl oz	375 mL	Heavy cream (quantity variable)
1 tsp or to taste	5 mL or to taste	Salt
to taste	to taste	White pepper
small pinch	small pinch	Cayenne
to taste	to taste	Nutmeg

PROCEDURE

1. Have all ingredients and equipment very cold. In addition, have ready a bowl set in an ice bath for step 7. It is important to keep all ingredients cold throughout the production process.
2. Purée the meat or fish in a food processor.
3. Add the egg whites and process until they are well blended in and the mixture is smooth.
4. With the machine running, slowly pour in the cream through the feed tube. The mixture should be light, fluffy, and firm enough to hold a shape. If it starts to become softer than this while the cream is being added, stop adding cream.
5. Season. The amount of salt needed depends on the meat or fish and the intended use. For example, freshwater fish may need more salt than ocean fish.
6. Keep the mixture cold while preparing a poach test to check seasonings. Wrap a small quantity of the mousseline tightly in plastic wrap and poach in simmering water. Taste and adjust seasonings.
7. Force the mixture through a fine sieve into a bowl set in ice, in order to remove any bits of sinew, skin, or bone. This step is sometimes omitted, but it much improves the texture.

Per 1 ounce (28.35 g): Calories, 70; Protein, 5 g; Fat, 6 g (73% cal.); Cholesterol, 35 mg; Carbohydrates, 0 g; Fiber, 0 g; Sodium, 120 mg.

Note: Use lean, skinless chicken meat, lean veal, fillets from lean, white fish, or shellfish such as scallops, shrimp, or lobster.

VARIATION

Herbed Mousseline

Add a mixture of chopped fresh herbs to the sieved mousseline mixture.

Terrine of Vegetables with Chicken Mousseline

YIELD: 2 LB (1 KG)

U.S.	METRIC	INGREDIENTS	PROCEDURE
1 lb 8 oz	750 g	Chicken Mousseline Forcemeat (p. 448)	1. Mix the chicken mousseline with the chopped herbs and the glace de volaille, if used.
2 tbsp	7 g	Chopped parsley	
1 tsp	1 g	Chopped fresh tarragon	
½ oz	15 g	Glace de volaille, melted (optional)	
2 oz	60 g	Zucchini, small, trimmed	2. Cut the zucchini into strips ¼–½ in. (1 cm) wide. Blanch 2 minutes in salted water, drain, and chill.
2 oz	60 g	Red bell pepper, cored and seeded	3. Char and peel the red pepper. Cut it into strips.
2 oz	60 g	Carrots, trimmed and peeled	4. Cut the carrots into strips like the zucchini. Blanch 3 minutes, drain, and chill.
2 oz	60 g	Green beans, trimmed	5. Blanch the green beans 1–2 minutes, depending on their tenderness.
2 oz	60 g	Shiitake mushroom caps	6. Cut the mushroom caps in half. Blanch 30 seconds, drain, cool, and pat dry to remove extra moisture.

7. Butter well the bottom and sides of a 1½-qt (1.5-L) terrine mold.
8. Spread one-third of the mousseline on the bottom of the mold, being sure to eliminate air bubbles.
9. Arrange the carrot strips and beans lengthwise in the mold, pushing them partway into the mousseline. Keep the vegetables at least ¼ in. (5 mm) from the sides of the mold (see **Figure 20.3**).
10. Spread a thin layer of mousseline over the vegetables. Arrange the mushroom caps down the center of the mold, then cover with another thin layer of mousseline. About one-third of the mousseline should be left.
11. Arrange the pepper and zucchini strips lengthwise in the mold, adding a little more mousseline as necessary.
12. Top with the remaining mousseline, again spreading it carefully to avoid air bubbles. Rap the terrine sharply on the workbench to eliminate any remaining air bubbles. Smooth the top of the mousseline with a spatula.
13. Cover tightly with foil. Set in a hot-water bath and bake in an oven heated to 325°F (165°C) until set firm, about 1 hour and 15 minutes.
14. Cool thoroughly, then chill well in the refrigerator.
15. Unmold. Slice carefully with a knife dipped in hot water. Serve garnished with a few salad greens and an appropriate cold sauce.

Per 1 ounce (28.35 g): Calories, 60; Protein, 4 g; Fat, 5 g (67% cal.); Cholesterol, 25 mg; Carbohydrates, 1 g; Fiber, 0 g; Sodium, 90 mg.

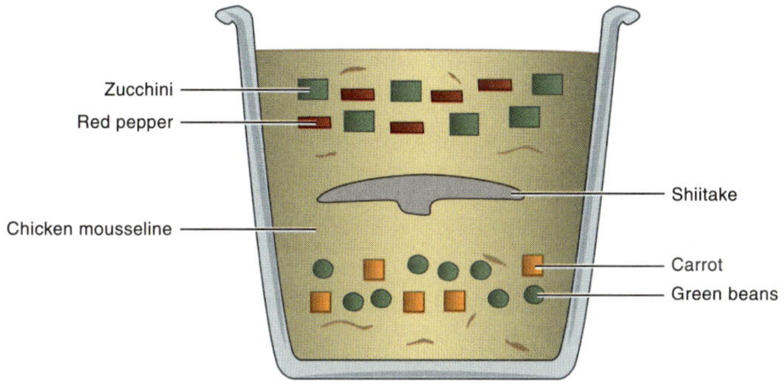

Figure 20.3 Cross-section diagram of Terrine of Vegetables with Chicken Mousseline

VARIATIONS

Instead of the vegetables indicated, select your choice of seasonal vegetables.

For a more luxurious terrine, include thin slices of truffle with the garnish, or omit the parsley and add minced truffle to the mousseline.

Seafood Terrine with Vegetables

Use a fish or shellfish mousseline instead of the chicken mousseline. Reduce the number and quantity of vegetables. Add to the garnish some strips of smoked salmon.

Terrines and Other Molds with Gelatin

All the terrines we have discussed so far are traditional cooked terrines—that is, the raw forcemeat is cooked in the mold. There are many kinds of uncooked terrines as well. These are not cooked after assembly but rather chilled until set. Any ingredients that require cooking are cooked before assembly. The terrines we discuss in this section rely on gelatin for their structure.

Preparing these items in terrine molds allows them to be cut into slices for serving, just as traditional forcemeat terrines are. They can also be made in molds of any other shape, including portion-size molds, which can simply be unmolded and garnished for serving. Cooked terrines, on the other hand, are best made in regularly shaped, symmetrical molds so they cook uniformly.

Most molds bound with gelatin fall into two general categories: those based on aspics and those based on mousses.

Aspic Molds

Aspic-based terrines are simply glorified gelatin molds—that is, they consist of solid ingredients held together by gelatin in the form of aspic jelly.

The proportion of aspic to solids can vary greatly. At one extreme, there may be just enough aspic to hold the solid ingredients together, so the aspic jelly itself is almost not evident. On the other hand, the aspic may predominate, with solid ingredients suspended in it at intervals. For this latter type to succeed, the aspic jelly must be of excellent quality, with good flavor, a firm but not rubbery texture, and sparkling clarity.

The majority of aspic terrines fall between these extremes.

The following procedure is applicable to the production of most aspic terrines and other aspic molds:

1. Either line the mold with aspic, or pour a layer of aspic into the bottom of the mold. Chill until firm.
2. Arrange a layer of garnish in the mold.
3. Add just enough aspic jelly to cover the solid garnish. Chill until firm.
4. Repeat steps 2 and 3 until the mold is full.
5. For best storage, leave the aspic in the mold, covered tightly with plastic film, until service time.

Terrines made by this method depend on a crystal-clear aspic jelly for their appearance and are often very elegant. Another approach is simply to combine the jelly with a mixture of ingredients and fill the terrine with this mixture. A clarified aspic may not be necessary for this method. Terrines made this way range from coarse, peasant-style dishes to more elaborate constructions.

Headcheese and a number of other commercially made luncheon-meat loaves are examples of this type of terrine.

Mousses

A savory cold ***mousse***, as used for the base of a terrine, is a preparation of puréed meat, poultry, fish, vegetable, or other food, bound with gelatin and usually lightened with the addition of partially whipped heavy cream. (It is true that the terms *mousse* and *mousseline* are often used more or less interchangeably, but we use them here in two distinct senses in order to avoid confusion.)

The gelatin used to bind or set the mousse may be added in the form of an aspic jelly or as powdered gelatin softened and dissolved in another liquid ingredient.

Because mousses, like aspics, are not cooked after assembly but merely chilled, they are often prepared not only in terrines but in decorative, irregularly shaped molds. The production of mousses is relatively simple. The procedure consists of four main steps:

1. Purée the main ingredient.
2. Add the aspic jelly or dissolved gelatin.
3. Fold in the lightly whipped cream and season to taste.
4. Pour into the prepared mold.

Molds are usually lined with aspic jelly and decorated. As with other kinds of terrine, garnish, if any, is either mixed with the mousse or arranged in the mold as the mousse is added.

Although this method is really little more than mixing together the ingredients in a given order, two precautions must be taken:

1. **Carry out the entire procedure, including the pouring of the mixture into the mold, quickly and in one continuous process.**
   If you stop partway through the procedure, the gelatin is likely to set, and you will have a lumpy, poorly mixed product.
2. **Do not overwhip the cream.**
   Whip it only until it forms soft mounds. When cream is overwhipped, it breaks and becomes grainy. This same effect can be caused by the extra beating the cream gets when it is being folded into the mousse mixture. A mousse made with overwhipped cream tastes dry and grainy, not smooth and creamy.

Mousses can also be made without gelatin or other binders. A soft mousse is simply a puréed or ground food with the addition of lightly whipped cream. Although these soft mousses are too soft to be used in terrines, they can be spooned into neat, oval quenelle shapes onto salad plates, garnished attractively, and served as first courses.

Tricolor Vegetable Terrine

YIELD: APPROXIMATELY 1 LB 12 OZ (800 G)

U.S.	METRIC	INGREDIENTS
1 lb	450 g	Spinach
¼ oz	7 g	Shallot, minced
¼ oz	7 g	Butter
1 tsp	5 mL	Gelatin powder
1 fl oz	30 mL	Chicken stock, vegetable stock, or water, cold
to taste	to taste	Salt
2 fl oz	60 mL	Heavy cream

PROCEDURE

1. Have ready a 1-qt (1-L) terrine mold. For ease of unmolding, line with plastic film.
2. Trim the stems from the spinach and wash it well in several changes of water. Cook in boiling, salted water until done, about 2 minutes, and drain. Rinse under cold water to cool. Drain. Squeeze dry.
3. Chop the spinach into fine pieces by hand or in a food processor.
4. Sweat the shallots in butter until soft. Add the spinach and cook slowly until quite dry. Cool thoroughly, but do not chill.
5. Soften the gelatin in the stock, then heat until it is dissolved. Cool and stir into the spinach. Add salt to taste.
6. Quickly whip the cream until it forms soft peaks. Immediately fold it into the spinach mixture. Pour it into the mold and smooth with a spatula. Chill until set.

U.S.	METRIC	INGREDIENTS
5 oz	150 g	Cauliflower, trimmed
2 oz	60 g	White turnips, peeled
1 tsp	5 mL	Gelatin powder
1 fl oz	30 mL	Chicken stock, vegetable stock, or water, cold
to taste	to taste	Salt
2 fl oz	60 mL	Heavy cream

7. Steam the cauliflower and turnips until they are tender. Purée in a food processor. For the smoothest texture, force the purée through a sieve. Mix the vegetables together. Heat slowly in a large sauté pan to dry the purée slightly. Cool thoroughly, but do not chill.
8. Repeat steps 5 and 6 to make the white mousse. Pour it into the mold on top of the green mousse. Chill.

U.S.	METRIC	INGREDIENTS
7 oz	200 g	Carrots, trimmed and peeled
1 tsp	5 mL	Gelatin powder
1 fl oz	30 mL	Chicken stock, vegetable stock, or water, cold
to taste	to taste	Salt
2 fl oz	60 mL	Heavy cream

9. Trim, cook, and purée the carrots in the same way, and dry the purée as above. Repeat steps 5 and 6 to make the orange mousse, and add it to the terrine (see **Figure 20.4**). Chill until set firm.
10. Unmold the terrine and slice to serve. Garnish as desired and serve with an appropriate cold sauce.

Per 1 ounce (28.35 g): Calories, 30; Protein, 1 g; Fat, 3 g (65% cal.); Cholesterol, 10 mg; Carbohydrates, 2 g; Fiber, 1 g; Sodium, 20 mg.

VARIATIONS

Other vegetable purées may be substituted for those in the basic recipe.

For a low-fat version, omit the gelatin powder, stock, and heavy cream. In place of the stock and cream, use an equal quantity of a strong aspic. Mix the aspic with the vegetable purées.

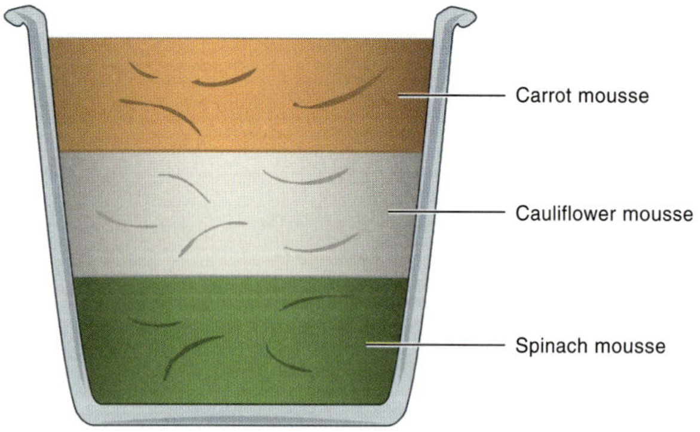

Figure 20.4 Cross-section diagram of Tricolor Vegetable Terrine.

Foie Gras, Liver Terrines, and Rillettes

The chapter concludes with three traditional terrines that require somewhat different techniques from those already discussed. It should be noted that, although these items are especially high in fat and cholesterol, they are as popular as they have ever been, even in these times of diet consciousness.

Foie Gras Terrines

The most prized and, perhaps, the most famous ingredient for pâtés and terrines in classical cuisine is *foie gras* (fwah grah). This French term means "fat liver." Foie gras is the fatted liver of specially fed varieties of ducks and geese. Until recently, only canned or processed foie gras products were available in the United States. Now, however, the breed of duck that is raised to produce foie gras (called the *mullard* or *moulard*, a cross between the muscovy and White Pekin ducks) is grown on American farms. Consequently, fresh, raw duck foie gras is now sold in this country. Its availability has created a great deal of enthusiasm among American cooks in spite of its high price.

The special feeding of the ducks makes their livers very large, more than 1 lb (500 g) as a rule, with a high fat content. A good-quality fresh foie gras is a pale yellowish-tan color with a smooth, velvety texture, almost like butter. The liver has two lobes, one large and one small.

It is important to be aware that foie gras consists mostly of fat. Indeed, the rich flavor of the fat is the whole reason foie gras is so highly prized. Any fat that cooks out during preparation is carefully saved and used for another purpose. Those who must avoid fats, especially animal fats, should probably steer clear of this delicacy. For the rest of us, the high price of foie gras helps protect our health by making overindulgence unlikely.

There are usually two grades of domestic duck foie gras. The A grade is larger, usually 1¼ lb (600 g) or more, with relatively few blemishes and blood spots. The B grade is smaller and has more blood spots and veins. (There is also a C grade, but it is not used in food service.)

PREPARING FOIE GRAS FOR COOKING

No matter how a raw foie gras is to be prepared, it should first be rinsed in cold water and examined closely for green spots. These are caused by bile; they must be cut or scraped away because the bile has a strong, bitter taste. Also, if there are any bits of external fat, remove them.

Next, the liver should be soaked. (This step is not required, but it does improve the product.) Place it in lightly salted ice-cold water or milk to cover. Let stand for up to 2 hours, no longer. Remove from the salted liquid and rinse in fresh, cold water.

For cold preparations such as terrines and mousses, the liver should first be deveined. To devein the foie gras, first let it come to room temperature. Its fat content makes the cold liver too brittle to devein without excessive breakage, which would result in more cooking loss. When the liver is at room temperature, even the heat of the hands melts the fat, so it is important to handle the liver lightly and to work quickly.

Begin by separating the two lobes and laying them, smooth side down, on a clean work surface (Figure 20.5). Carefully trim off any bloody spots. Grasping a lobe with your thumbs at the sides and fingers underneath in the center, very lightly bend the lobe lengthwise. The top, rough surface should open up slightly, revealing a heavy vein that runs lengthwise through the liver. (If it does not open up, help it along with a shallow incision with the point of a paring knife.) Carefully pull out this vein, along with any other heavy veins that are attached, all the while being careful to keep the liver as intact as possible. Repeat with the other lobe. The foie gras is now ready to be made into a terrine.

No matter how a foie gras is cooked, it is essential to avoid even the slightest overcooking. The liver is delicate, and the fat cooks out very quickly. Even a few seconds too long in a sauté pan can reduce a slice of foie gras to a few specks of connective tissue floating in a puddle of very expensive grease.

Figure 20.5 Deveining foie gras.

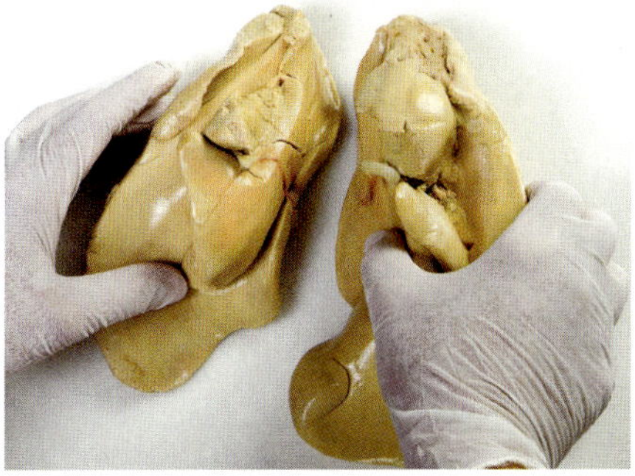

(a) Slowly and gently pull the two lobes apart.

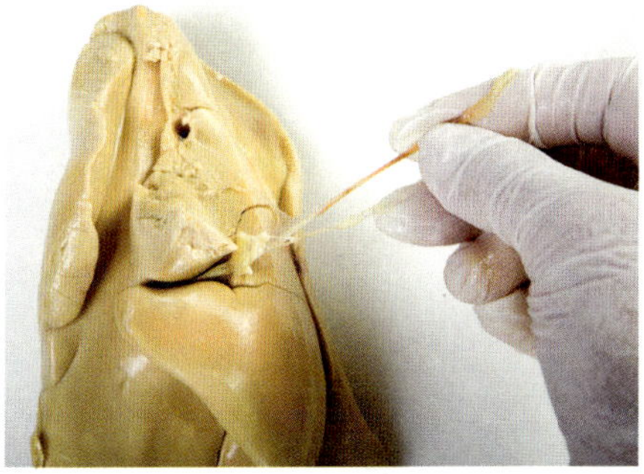

(b) Remove any visible membrane and surface blemishes from each lobe.

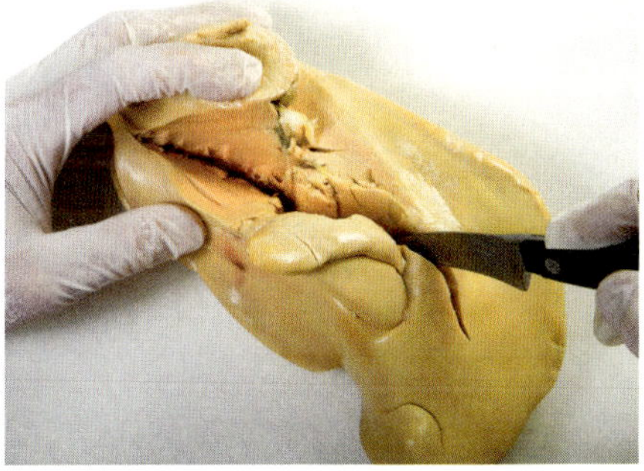

(c) Starting at the narrow, top end of each lobe, slit open the lobe about halfway to the other end and about halfway into its depth.

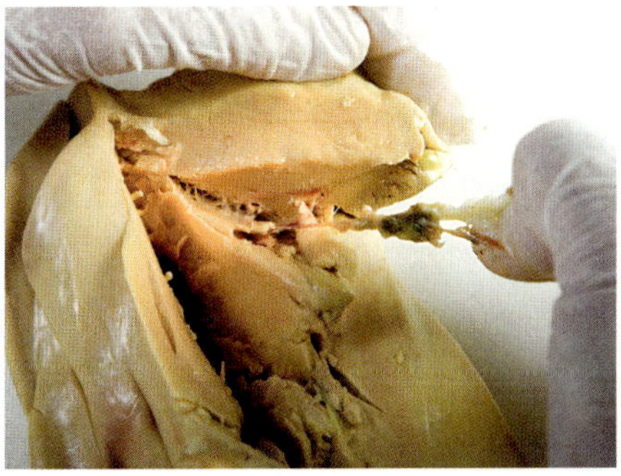

(d) Grasp the thick, top part of the vein network and pull gently while holding back the meat of the liver with the other hand.

Liver Terrines

Liver terrines, often called *liver pâtés*, are popular, inexpensive appetizers—except, of course, for those made with foie gras. The classic liver terrine is a mixture of liquefied livers—that is, cleaned, soaked, blended, and strained according to the procedure on page 441—with eggs and seasonings, baked in a terrine until set.

This kind of liver terrine generally contains flour as a stabilizer. Because the liver forcemeat is liquid, the flour improves the texture of the cooked product by helping bind the moisture. Heavy cream is also included in most recipes as a source of fat. Other sources of fat sometimes used in addition to or in place of the cream are ground pork fat, ground bacon, marrow, and rendered foie gras fat left over from making terrines.

Another type of liver terrine consists of a basic pork forcemeat with a liver content high enough for the flavor of the liver to predominate. To make this type of terrine, make the forcemeat on page 441, but use 6 times the quantity of liver. The forcemeat will be quite soft. Follow the basic procedure for making forcemeat terrines (see p. 445), using whole, trimmed chicken livers marinated in brandy as the garnish.

A quick and simple substitute for these more elaborate terrines might be considered a type of rillettes (see the next section), as it consists of a seasoned mixture of cooked meat (liver, in this case) and fat. This is the type of chicken liver pâté found on delicatessen and coffee shop menus. To make this type of pâté, sauté some chicken livers, mash or purée them, and mix the purée with about one-eighth its weight in rendered chicken fat, pork fat, soft butter, or other fat, or else with one-fourth its weight in cream cheese. Season as desired, with salt, pepper, herbs, brandy or sherry, and/or sautéed minced onion.

Rillettes

In France's Loire Valley, the first thing customers are likely to be served in a typical neighborhood restaurant, whether they order it or not, is a crock of rillettes and some country bread to spread it on. Variations on this unpretentious dish have become widely popular and are served even in elegant North American restaurants.

Rillettes (ree yet) is a dish made of pork cooked slowly until it is very tender, then shredded, mixed with its own fat, seasoned, and packed into crocks or terrines.

Variations of the classic dish can be made by using other meats in addition to or instead of pork. Items rich in fat, such as duck and goose, are especially appropriate. Rillettes of lean meats, such as chicken, turkey, and rabbit, can be made, but some pork fat or other fat must be added to them when they are cooking.

Some chefs even serve rillettes made from fish, such as salmon or cod. The basic procedure is the same, except the cooking time is, of course, much shorter. The cooked fish is shredded, mixed with just enough butter or other fat to give it a pleasant texture, and seasoned well.

A typical recipe for classic pork rillettes is on page 456. Follow the same basic procedure to make duck rillettes and other variations. A recipe for rillettes made with fish is on page 457.

KEY POINTS TO REVIEW

- What are the basic ingredients in a mousseline forcemeat? How is the forcemeat made?
- What is a mousse? How is it made?
- What is foie gras? How is it prepared for cooking?
- What are rillettes? How are they prepared?
- How is a baked liver terrine made?

Terrine of Foie Gras

YIELD: VARIABLE, DEPENDING ON SIZE OF LIVER

U.S.	METRIC	INGREDIENTS
1	1	Fresh, A-grade duck foie gras, about 1½ lb (700 g)
1 tsp	5 mL	Salt
¼ tsp	1 mL	White pepper
½–1 fl oz	15–30 mL	Choice of wine or liquor: port, Madeira, Sauternes, cognac, or Armagnac

Per 1 ounce (28.35 g): Calories, 50; Protein, 6 g; Fat, 2 g (32% cal.); Cholesterol, 165 mg; Carbohydrates, 1 g; Fiber, 0 g; Sodium, 160 mg.

PROCEDURE

1. Soak, rinse, and devein the foie gras as described on page 453.
2. Place the liver in a bowl and season with salt and white pepper. Add the selected wine or liquor, using the smaller quantity for cognac or Armagnac; if using a sweet wine, use up to but not more than the larger quantity indicated. Turn the liver gently so that all sides are moistened.
3. Cover and refrigerate. Marinate 24 hours.
4. Remove the livers from refrigeration 1–2 hours before cooking time, and let them come to room temperature. This is essential for the proper cooking of the terrine.
5. Pack the large lobe (or the pieces of the large lobe, if it broke during deveining) into the selected terrine, smooth side down. Top with the small lobe, smooth side up. Press the liver in firmly to eliminate air spaces. Cover with foil.
6. Place several folded kitchen towels on the bottom of a roasting pan or other pan used as a hot-water bath. (This helps insulate the terrine from strong bottom heat.) Place the terrine in the pan and add warm, not hot, water to come halfway up the sides of the terrine.
7. Place the terrine in an oven preheated to 200°–215°F (100°C). Bake until the proper doneness, as determined by an instant-read thermometer (see the following paragraph). This will take from 45 minutes to a little over 1 hour.

   The terrine is done when the thermometer reads 113°–130°F (45°–54°C). At the lower end of this range, the cooled terrine will be rather pink in the center, with a soft, creamy texture. At the higher end, the terrine will be firmer and less pink, but more fat will have cooked out, resulting in a lower yield. The right degree of doneness is a matter of personal preference.
8. Remove the terrine from the hot-water bath and set on a rack to cool. After about 10 minutes, weight it with a board that just fits inside the top of the terrine, or with another terrine, and several pounds of weights. When the terrine is almost cool but the fat is still liquid, pour off all the melted fat and juices. Separate and discard the juices. Reserve the fat. Put the weights back on the terrine and continue to cool.
9. When the terrine is cold, unmold it and remove and discard any bits of blood or juice on the bottom of the foie gras. Clean out the mold and put the foie gras back in it. Heat the reserved fat just until melted and pour it over the terrine. Refrigerate until cold, then cover tightly and refrigerate 3–5 days so the flavors can develop.
10. To unmold, dip the terrine in warm water for a few seconds, then invert on a platter or cutting board. Slice with a sharp knife dipped in hot water before each slice. Serve with a little chopped aspic and toasted brioche, or with salad greens and a mild vinaigrette made with walnut oil.

Rillettes of Pork

YIELD: APPROXIMATELY 1 LB (500 G)

U.S.	METRIC	INGREDIENTS
2 lb	1 kg	Pork butt or shoulder, with fat but without skin and bones
1	1	Onion, small
2	2	Cloves
2	2	Bay leaves
pinch	pinch	Dried thyme
2 fl oz	60 mL	Water
1½ tsp	2 mL	Salt

Per 1 ounce (28.35 g): Calories, 110; Protein, 9 g; Fat, 8 g (67% cal.); Cholesterol, 35 mg; Carbohydrates, 2 g; Fiber, 0 g; Sodium, 240 mg.

PROCEDURE

1. Cut the meat, with all the fat, into large dice.
2. Cut off 1–2 oz (30–60 g) of the fat and render it slowly in a large, heavy pot. Add the meat and brown it lightly and gently over moderate heat.
3. Stick the onion with the cloves. Add the onion and the remaining ingredients. Cover and cook slowly in a low oven or on the range over very low heat, until the meat is very tender. This will take several hours. Check periodically to see if the meat has become dry. If it has, add 1–2 oz (30–60 mL) water.
4. Remove the bay leaves, onion, and cloves. Place the contents of the pot in a colander set over a large bowl. Press firmly on the meat and collect the fat and drippings in the bowl. Separate the fat and juices and reserve them separately.
5. Pound the meat with a large pestle or mallet, then shred it with two forks until the meat is a mass of fibers and no lumps. Alternatively, place the meat in the bowl of a mixer and mix with the paddle attachment at lowest speed until the meat is thoroughly shredded.
6. Add as much of the rendered fat as desired and mix it with the shredded meat. Taste and adjust the seasonings. It should be well seasoned because it is to be served cold. If the mixture seems dry, add some of the reserved juices to achieve the desired consistency. The mixture should be thick but spreadable, neither too dry nor too soft.
7. Pack into crocks or terrines and smooth the top. If the rillettes are to be kept for more than 1–2 days, seal the surface from the air by covering with a layer of melted fat. Refrigerate overnight or longer. Remove the layer of fat before serving.
8. Serve with crusty bread and sour pickles.

VARIATIONS

Rillettes of Duck, Goose, Rabbit, Turkey, or Chicken

Substitute any of the above meats for all or part of the pork. Lean meats should be cooked with additional pork fat to supply enough rendered fat to blend with the shredded meat.

Rillettes of Salmon, Haddock, or Finnan Haddie

YIELD: 1 LB 4 OZ (600 G)

U.S.	METRIC	INGREDIENTS	PROCEDURE
1 lb	500 g	Salmon, haddock, or finnan haddie, skinless and boneless	1. Combine the fish and wine in a saucepan or sauté pan. Poach the fish gently just until it is done. Because there is not enough wine to cover the fish, turn the fish over occasionally during cooking so it cooks evenly. 2. Drain the fish and cool completely.
8 fl oz	250 mL	White wine	
4 oz	125 g	Butter, unsalted	3. Break the fish into small pieces, then mash with a fork until there are no lumps. 4. Soften the butter, then mix it with the fish until uniformly blended. Season to taste with lemon juice, salt, white pepper, and hot pepper sauce. 5. Pack the mixture into small ramekins or crocks for individual service. Chill.
2 tsp	10 mL	Lemon juice	
to taste	to taste	Salt	
to taste	to taste	White pepper	
to taste	to taste	Hot pepper sauce	
as desired	as desired	Caviar, for garnish	6. Top each portion with a small spoonful of caviar just before serving. Use salmon caviar for salmon rillettes, or any desired caviar for haddock or finnan haddie rillettes. 7. For service, place the ramekin on a small plate lined with a folded napkin or a doily. Arrange slices of toast or bread on the underliner around the ramekin, or serve the toast on the side.

Per 1 ounce (28.35 g): Calories, 70; Protein, 59 g; Fat, 6 g (72% cal.); Cholesterol, 25 mg; Carbohydrates, 0 g; Fiber, 0 g; Sodium, 55 mg.

TERMS FOR REVIEW

garde manger
forcemeat
garnish (pâté)
pâté de campagne
terrine
pâté
pâte à pâté
pâté en croûte
galantine
mousseline forcemeat
mousse
foie gras
rillettes

QUESTIONS FOR DISCUSSION

1. Explain how to slice a meat terrine.
2. Why are mustards and vinaigrettes often served with pâtés and terrines?
3. What are the basic ingredients in a typical pork forcemeat?
4. How are raw livers prepared for use in forcemeats?
5. What is the purpose of pouring a layer of melted fat over a terrine after baking?
6. What is the difference between the terms *mousseline* and *mousse*, as used in this chapter?
7. What are the four basic steps in the production of a molded mousse? Why is it important to perform these steps quickly?
8. Why is it important not to overcook foie gras?

Chapter 21

Noodle Bowl with Stir-Fried Vegetables, Tofu, and Peanuts, page 468.

Cooking for Vegetarian Diets

After reading this chapter, you should be able to

1. Describe the main types of vegetarian diets.
2. Describe complementary proteins and describe how to include them in the diet.
3. List three nutrients other than proteins that nonvegetarians get mostly from animal products, and describe how vegetarians can include these nutrients in their diet.
4. Name and describe five food types derived from soybeans.
5. Explain why refined sugar may not be permitted in a vegan diet.
6. List seven guidelines for building a vegetarian menu.

Vegetarian diners are an important and growing segment of the dining public. In the United States, for example, it is estimated that about 15 million people consider themselves vegetarians. Young people in particular embrace many forms of vegetarianism. In college dining rooms, the proportion of clients choosing vegetarian options may be as high as 40 percent. Clearly, food service cannot afford to ignore this segment.

It is important that cooks and chefs who want to please their customers know something about the needs of vegetarian diners. Beyond the financial benefits of serving foods that appeal to the widest range of customers, chefs find other benefits as well. Vegetarians are often more knowledgeable and enthusiastic about their dining choices because they have thought more about them. Accomplished cooks often say that meeting the challenge of cooking for knowledgeable diners is one of the most satisfying aspects of their jobs and that vegetarian menus give them new opportunities for creativity.

In addition to people who have a strong commitment to vegetarianism, many others eat meat on other occasions but choose vegetarian items simply because the choices are so appealing in a particular dining facility. Chefs who create satisfying, innovative choices for vegetarians often find that creating a good vegetarian menu selection is one of their best professional decisions.

Understanding Vegetarian Diets

Preparing food for anyone who follows a restricted diet requires understanding the nature and limitations of that diet. Vegetarian diets present challenges because there are several types of vegetarianism.

Types of Vegetarian Diet

A *vegetarian* diet is one consisting entirely or mostly of foods derived from plants. Most committed vegetarians fall into one of the categories listed below.

The *vegan* diet is the most restrictive form of vegetarianism. Vegans eat plant products only. All animal products, including dairy products and eggs, are off limits. Even foods that might sound safe are off limits to the strictest vegans. Examples of such foods include honey, because it comes from bees, and cane sugar, which may be refined with the use of animal products (more on this subject on p. 465). When preparing a vegetarian menu, the chef should keep in mind that a menu appropriate to a vegan diet has the broadest appeal because it can be eaten by all categories of vegetarians.

Lacto-vegetarians eat dairy products in addition to plant products but will not eat other animal products.

Ovo-vegetarians eat eggs in addition to plant products.

Lacto-ovo-vegetarians eat dairy and egg products as well as plant products.

Pesco-vegetarians eat fish and plant products but not meat or poultry. They may or may not eat dairy and egg products.

Vegetarianism may be based on strong ethical or moral beliefs or on health concerns. Naturally, the chef who cares for his or her customers is eager to respect these beliefs and concerns. Vegetarians may have chosen their diet based on deeply held ethical or religious beliefs and may be dedicated to following their diet rigorously.

In addition, many people choose vegetarianism for health reasons. Vegetarian diets are usually low in fat and cholesterol and in addition are free of the hormones and drugs often used in the raising of meat animals. Environmental concerns also lead some people to vegetarianism. Producing plant foods requires fewer natural resources than raising meat animals. Economic factors are yet another consideration in that vegetables and grains are, on average, much less expensive than meat, poultry, and seafood. Finally, some people are occasional vegetarians simply because they enjoy the food.

Nutritional Considerations

Because vegetarians eliminate major categories of food from their diet, nutrients otherwise obtained from animal products are lost and must be obtained from other foods. Note that although dairy products, meats, fish, and eggs do not form the largest portions of the pyramid, they form an important part. When those foods are eliminated, the pyramid must be rebuilt, as in Figure 21.1, in order to ensure adequate nutrition.

PROTEIN

The major nutritional concern of a vegetarian diet is getting enough protein. Dairy products, eggs, and fish supply adequate amounts of good-quality protein, but vegans must plan their diet carefully in order to get adequate protein. Some plant products, such as grains, nuts, and dried beans, contain proteins. Note that in the standard Food Guide Pyramid, dried beans and nuts are included in the meat group. However, with the important exception of soybeans and soy products such as tofu, most of these protein foods, *when eaten alone*, are not adequate for human nutrition.

AMINO ACIDS

These 9 compounds are called *essential amino acids*:

Histidine	Phenylalanine
Isoleucine	Threonine
Leucine	Tryptophan
Lysine	Valine
Methionine	

These 11 amino acids can be made by the body and so are called *nonessential amino acids*. It is not necessary to include them in the diet.

Aniline	Glutamine
Arginine	Glycine
Asparagine	Proline
Aspartic acid	Serine
Cysteine	Tyrosine
Glutamic acid	

When the body manufactures proteins, it puts together a chain of amino acids using those it has available, like a factory assembling an appliance out of parts. If it finds that one of the parts—in this case, amino acids—is missing, it takes apart the partial protein it has already assembled and sends the parts back to the supply room—the bloodstream.

This means that if one amino acid is in short supply, it limits the usefulness of those that are plentiful. An amino acid that is in short supply, thus limiting the usefulness of the others, is called a *limiting amino acid*.

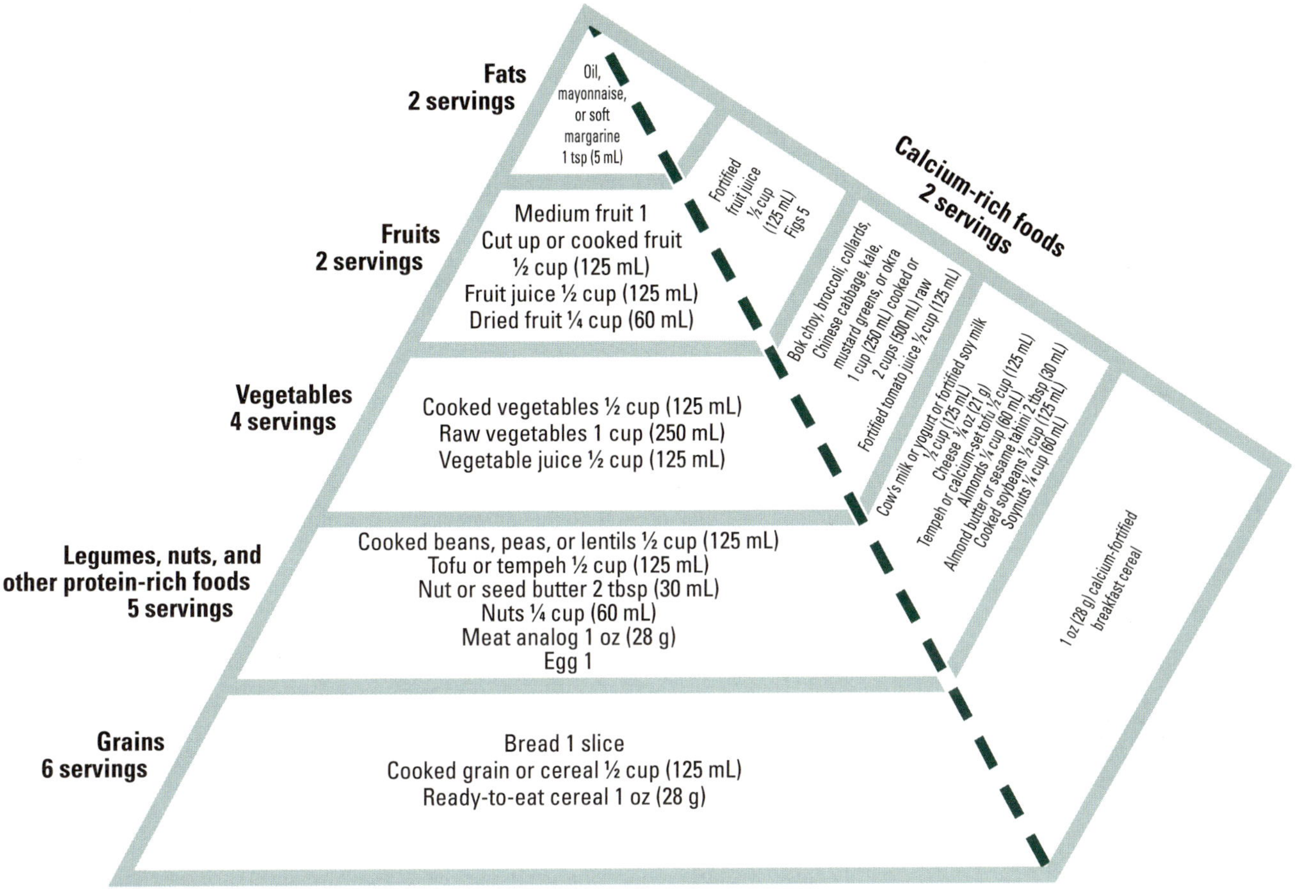

Figure 21.1 Vegetarian food guide pyramid. Reprinted from *Journal of the American Dietetic Program*, Volume 103, Messina, Virginia, Melina, Vesanto, and Mangels, Ann Reed, "A new food guide for North American vegetarians," pages 771–775, Copyright 2003, with permission from American Dietetic Association.

Proteins are long chains of smaller compounds called ***amino acids***. There are, in all, 20 amino acids that, when joined in various combinations, make up over 100,000 proteins in the human body. Eleven of these amino acids can be made in the body, so it is not necessary to include them in the diet. All remaining nine amino acids must be included in the diet in order for the body to make all the proteins it needs. These nine are called ***essential amino acids***.

Any food protein that contains all nine essential amino acids is called a ***complete protein***. Proteins found in meat, poultry, seafood, milk and milk products, and eggs are complete proteins.

Some plant foods, especially dried legumes, grains, nuts, and seeds, contain ***incomplete proteins***. This means that one or more of the essential amino acids is either missing or is not present in high enough concentration. Soybeans, quinoa, and amaranth are unusual among grains and legumes in that they contain complete proteins.

The key to getting enough protein in a plants-only diet is to eat, in the course of each day, a balance of these foods, so that amino acids missing from one of these foods is supplied by another one of them. Such proteins are called ***complementary proteins***. For example, kidney beans are high in the amino acids isoleucine and lysine, but low in some of the others. Millet is low in lysine but high in the amino acids that kidney beans are missing. So if both kidney beans and millet are eaten during the day, all the essential amino acids are included in the diet.

INCLUDING COMPLEMENTARY PROTEINS IN THE DIET

Contrary to what you might think after reading the preceding discussion, you do not have to be a biochemist to prepare vegetarian menus. A basic understanding of what foods go together to supply complete proteins is the best place to start and will carry you a long way.

The following pairings of food categories are the most useful complementary proteins for planning vegetarian diets:

Dried legumes plus grains

Dried legumes plus seeds and nuts

Grains plus milk products

The first two of these pairings are important in vegan diets. The third pairing can be included in the diet of lacto-vegetarians.

Examining the cultures and cuisines of other lands, we see these complementary protein groupings have long been a part of the staple diet of peoples with limited supplies of meat. Think, for example, of the beans and corn tortillas (dried legumes plus grains) of Mexico and the rice and dal (also grains plus dried legumes) of India. People who have long relied on these foods have found tasty and varied ways to prepare them. Studying traditional vegetarian cuisines is a useful way to learn how to include these items in your own menus.

KEY POINTS TO REVIEW

- What are the main types of vegetarian diet? What kinds of food can be eaten in each of these diets?
- What are complete proteins? What are complementary proteins? How can complementary proteins be included in the diet?
- In addition to protein, what other nutrients are of special concern to people who follow a vegetarian diet? How can these nutrients be included in the diet in healthy quantities?

OTHER NUTRIENTS

In addition to protein, other nutrients normally found in animal products must be supplied in other ways in vegetarian diets.

Vitamin B_{12}. This vitamin is found only in animal foods, including milk and eggs. Vegans must obtain it from grain foods, such as breakfast cereals, that have been fortified with this vitamin, or else take vitamin supplements. Vegetarians who eat sufficient dairy products and eggs usually can get enough vitamin B_{12}.

Vitamin D. This vitamin is found in vitamin D-fortified milk, and it is created in the skin on exposure to sunlight. A vegan or other vegetarian who doesn't get enough exposure to sunlight can get this nutrient from vitamin-fortified cereals or some soy beverages.

Calcium. Dairy products are rich in calcium, but vegans and other vegetarians who don't consume dairy products must get calcium from other sources, including green leafy vegetables and dried legumes. Calcium supplements or calcium-fortified beverages may be necessary in the vegan diet.

Menus for Vegetarian Diets

To a meat-eater, the idea of a vegetarian diet might seem monotonous or boring, but the reality can be the opposite. A typical meat-based diet often features the same few meats—beef, pork, chicken, and occasionally fish—over and over, accompanied by the same few simple vegetable side dishes and potatoes. By contrast, a diet in which vegetables are the focus and not a routine side dish can feature dozens of fresh vegetables, a great variety of grains and legumes, and, for at least some vegetarians, dairy products and possibly eggs to round out the selection.

The appeal of vegetarian menus can be seen in many fine restaurants that feature tasting menus. At such restaurants, the dinner menu each evening may offer a multi-course vegetarian menu in addition to the meat and seafood options. It is common for a pair of diners, even nonvegetarians, to order one vegetarian menu and one nonvegetarian menu so they can sample all the chef's creations.

Ingredients

Because animal protein is omitted from vegetarian diets, some important ingredients get more attention than they do in meat diets. Several categories of plant food take on the role of main courses.

DRIED LEGUMES

Dried beans, peas, and lentils are some of the most important sources of protein for vegans and other vegetarians.

One legume not mentioned earlier is the peanut, which is not a nut but a legume with an unusual growing habit. As the plants grow, the branches bearing the pods bend to the ground so the pods develop underground. Although peanuts are used in the kitchen like other nuts, nutritionally they are similar to other legumes. Keep this in mind when planning complementary proteins.

Dried soybeans are high in protein, but they are rarely cooked and served like other dried beans. They are very hard and take hours of cooking if whole, and when cooked they do not appeal to most tastes. Furthermore, their protein is not as usable as the protein in products derived from soybeans, such as soy milk and tofu. These are so important that they are discussed separately below.

GRAINS

Grains are sources of complementary protein when eaten with legumes or dairy products. Of the grains described, rice is no doubt the most important worldwide. Many vegans and other vegetarians use brown rice instead of white rice to take advantage of its vitamin and fiber content. Wheat and corn are also important protein foods. In the form of bread, noodles, and tortillas, these grains are especially versatile.

Don't overlook the other grains. Products such as farro, barley, millet, and triticale add variety to the menu. Quinoa and amaranth are especially valuable for vegan diets because they contain complete protein.

NUTS AND SEEDS

Nuts and seeds are rich in protein, so almonds, cashews, hazelnuts, pecans, walnuts, pistachios, pumpkin seeds, sesame seeds, and sunflower seeds are useful in vegetarian diets. They are high in fat, however, and can't be relied on as heavily as other vegetable proteins.

Nut butters, such as cashew butter and almond butter, are simply nuts or seeds that have been roasted and ground to a paste. They are a flavorful and attractive way to include these foods in a diet. Sesame butter, or tahini, is especially prominent in Mediterranean diets and used in many recipes. See, for example, the recipe for hummus on page 398, which uses legumes (chickpeas) and seeds (tahini) to supply complementary protein.

SOY PRODUCTS

Borrowed from Asian cuisines, soy derivatives such as tofu have long been familiar in the West and are important sources of protein for many people.

Soy milk is made by soaking dried soybeans, draining them, grinding them, combining them with water, boiling, and then straining the resulting milky liquid.

Plain soy milk can be used in cooking and as a beverage. Many brands of flavored and sometimes sweetened soy beverages are also available, and these can also be used in coffee beverages and in desserts.

Tofu, or ***bean curd***, is made by curdling soy milk, just as cheese is made by curdling dairy milk. The result is a soft, white cake with a mild, faintly beany flavor that is adaptable to many sauces and accompaniments.

Tofu is available in several varieties, described here. Most types are available packed in water in sealed plastic packages. It keeps well as long as it is unopened, but it should be used within a day or two of opening.

Japanese silken tofu is the softest type. Unlike other tofu varieties, the curd of silken tofu is not pressed to remove moisture. Silken tofu has the most delicate texture and also the mildest flavor. In Japan it is regularly eaten cold with a light dipping sauce, or it is diced and added as a garnish to miso soup.

Japanese cotton tofu is firmer than the silken variety and can stand up to more vigorous handling. It is often deep-fried or added to stir-fried dishes.

Chinese firm tofu is the firmest of these three tofu types and is the coarsest in texture. It can be fried, stir-fried, grilled, baked in casseroles, simmered in stews, and put on skewers.

Silken tofu

Firm tofu

When tofu is to be marinated, fried, or stewed, removing excess moisture first helps the tofu absorb the added flavors more readily. Place the cakes of tofu on several layers of paper towel or on a perforated sheet pan, cover with several more layers of paper towel, place a weighted tray or sheet pan on top, and let stand about 15 minutes.

To make tofu even firmer and less likely to break apart when cooked, press it as above and then deep-fry until it has a light golden color. Or drop it into simmering water and simmer 5 minutes. Precooking coagulates the proteins, making them firmer.

Tempeh is a fermented soybean product that originated in Indonesia. In addition to the original version made with only soybeans, it is also made from soy plus grains, including barley, millet, and rice. Tempeh is sold in cakes and has a dense, meaty texture. It can be sliced or diced and braised, sautéed, stir-fried, baked, and added to casseroles.

Miso, also called ***bean paste***, is a paste made of fermented soybeans, sometimes with the addition of wheat, rice, or barley, depending on the variety. There are several types of miso ranging from light, sweet, and mild to dark, salty, and robust. The lightest, called *white miso* (*shiromiso* in Japanese), is yellow, with a sweet flavor and soft, moist texture. It is often used in soups and in dressings or sauces for vegetables. Other light miso types may be darker yellow and saltier. *Red miso* (*akamiso*) is brown or reddish brown, salty, and fuller in flavor. It may be smooth or chunky. Red miso is used in soups and in cooked dishes rather than in uncooked dressings. The thickest, darkest, strongest-tasting miso is *hatcho miso*. It is dark brown and thick enough to cut, almost like fudge. It is used in soups and cooked dishes.

Textured vegetable protein (TVP) is made from defatted soy flour, processed and dried to give it a spongelike texture. It is available unflavored or flavored to resemble various meats. To prepare TVP, mix with water, let stand until softened, and then add to recipes as you would meat. Because it doesn't taste exactly like real meat, it is best used in highly flavored or seasoned dishes such as chili. TVP is high in protein and fiber and free of cholesterol. It is useful on some menus for its nutritional value, but some vegetarians avoid it because they are not interested in highly processed foods that pretend to be meat.

DAIRY AND EGGS

For lacto-ovo vegetarians, milk products and eggs are valuable sources of protein, vitamin D, calcium, and other nutrients. Cheeses and eggs, however, are high in fat and cholesterol, so it is a good idea not to rely on them for one's sole source of protein.

Dairy products and eggs are discussed in later chapters.

Modifying Recipes

You have probably noticed by now that many of the recipes in this book are labeled with a small icon, shown at left, indicating they are vegetarian. These include recipes for lacto-ovo vegetarians as well as vegans. The presence of any egg or dairy product indicates that the recipe cannot be used on a vegan menu, although it is suitable for other vegetarians. Before using any of these recipes on vegetarian menus, please note the discussion of sugar below.

Other recipes, in this book and elsewhere, can be modified for vegetarian diets. Always read the list of ingredients to make sure they are all permitted. If any of the ingredients is a packaged or manufactured food, read the list of ingredients on the package as well. Remember:

- No animal product of any kind may be used as an ingredient in a recipe intended for vegans.
- Dairy products (such as milk, cream, butter, and cheese) and eggs may be included as ingredients in recipes for lacto-ovo vegetarians, and thus they may be labeled as vegetarian. However, they will not be eaten by vegans.
- Service staff must be adequately trained to accurately answer patrons' questions about the menu.

Sometimes a soup, salad, or side dish recipe consists primarily of plant products but contains one or more animal products, such as a stock. The following methods can be used to modify existing recipes to adapt them for vegetarian menus:

1. Remove meat, poultry, and fish stocks from recipes and substitute an equal quantity of water or vegetable stock.
2. Omit sauces based on meat, poultry, or fish stocks, and, for vegans, omit sauces using dairy products or eggs. Substitute another suitable sauce. Vinaigrettes, salsas, vegetable coulis, and flavored oils are often good sauces for vegetarian dishes.
3. For vegans, substitute oil for butter. Substitute soy milk or other soy products for dairy products.

SUGAR IN VEGETARIAN RECIPES

Refined white sugar and most brown sugar are processed either from sugar cane or sugar beets. Refineries that process sugar from cane often use charcoal made from animal bones as a filter. Sugar made from beets, however, is not made with bone char. Vegans and many other vegetarians often avoid all refined sugar because of the difficulty of determining the sugar's origin. For home use, they may use unbleached sugar or beet sugar, but away from home it is easier just to avoid sugar altogether.

Some of the recipes in this book labeled as vegetarian have sugar as an ingredient. *If you use any of these recipes on a vegetarian menu, make sure to use sugar from a purely vegetarian source, such as beet sugar or unbleached sugar.*

Other recipes in this book may appear to be vegetarian but are not labeled as such. For example, the recipe for Cocktail Sauce contains only plant products, and sugar is not listed as an ingredient. However, two of the ingredients, ketchup and chili sauce, contain sugar. Because there is no way to tell the source of the sugar, the recipe can't easily be adapted to a vegetarian menu. In this book, no recipe is labeled as vegetarian if one of the ingredients is a manufactured product that may contain sugar or other impermissible ingredient.

Center of the Plate

In the world of food service, the expression *center of the plate* is often used to describe the meat, poultry, fish, or other principal item that is the focus of the main course. For vegetarian menus, we need to rethink the concept of center of the plate somewhat.

One of the problems in developing vegetarian menu choices is constructing a plate that is satisfying as a main course. Appetizers or first courses are less of a problem. Vegetarians and nonvegetarians alike enjoy soups, salads, and vegetable dishes as first courses. Similarly, a succession of four to six small courses in a tasting menu can be pleasing and satisfying. A main course, on the other hand, must usually feel like a complete meal in its own right, and a selection of steamed vegetables on a plate usually will not satisfy.

Begin by thinking about the categories of foods we rely on for complementary proteins: legumes, grains, seeds and nuts, and dairy products, and, if appropriate, soy products like tofu. Dishes made with these ingredients tend to be more substantial than simple vegetables and thus are often suitable for main courses, especially when combined with vegetables and perhaps a sauce or condiment.

Complex dishes—dishes that have had something done to them beyond simple boiling or steaming—are appealing vegetarian main courses. For example, a baked squash stuffed with a well-seasoned grain and vegetable mixture holds its own in the center of the plate. Regional cuisines give us other examples, such as a bean-filled enchilada served with rice and a spicy tomato sauce.

Some preparations work as main courses whether or not they are made with meat. Examples are listed below. These types of dishes can be prepared many ways using only plant products, with or without the use of dairy products or eggs.

Stews

Curries

Chili

Stir-fries served with rice or noodles

Risotto

Pasta

Pizza

Pot pies, or foods served inside dough or pastry

Casseroles

Gratins

The ingredient information and prep and cooking procedures in other chapters in this book, especially in the chapters on vegetables; potatoes; legumes, grains, pastas, and other starches; and salads, give you tools you can use to build creative and satisfying vegetarian menus. Many of the recipes in those chapters can be used by vegetarians without modification. In addition, examples of other vegetarian items are in this chapter.

Guidelines for Building a Vegetarian Menu

1. Offer dishes containing no ingredients of animal origin, to appeal to vegans, and offer dishes containing dairy products and eggs for vegetarians who eat those foods.
2. Select a variety of legumes, grains, and seeds, and use them in combinations that provide complementary proteins.
3. Complementary proteins don't need to be on the same plate. For example, you could offer a grain salad as a first course and a vegetable stew with beans as a main course.
4. Use a wide variety of vegetables.
5. Offer dishes made with tofu and other soybean derivatives.
6. To limit fat and cholesterol, consider using low-fat milk products, and use eggs sparingly.
7. Offer foods containing nutrients, such as vitamin B_{12}, that are of special concern to vegetarians (see p. 462).
8. Read the ingredient labels of all packaged food products to make sure they contain no ingredients of animal origin.

KEY POINTS TO REVIEW

- What foods are important sources of protein for vegetarians?
- What foods commonly used in vegetarian diets are derived from soybeans?
- What problems does sugar pose for vegan diets?
- What are some ways nonvegetarian recipes can be modified to fit vegetarian diets?
- What guidelines should be followed when building a vegetarian menu?

Yellow Split Pea and Vegetable Curry with Spiced Rice and Cucumber Raita

PORTIONS: 12 PORTION SIZE: 3½ OZ (100 G) RICE, 6 OZ (180 G) VEGETABLE CURRY, 2 OZ (60 ML) RAITA

U.S.	METRIC	INGREDIENTS	PROCEDURE
		Spiced rice:	1. Wash the rice in several changes of cold water. Drain. Add cold water to cover by 1–2 in. (3–5 cm) and soak 1 hour or longer.
1 lb	500 g	Long-grain brown rice, preferably basmati	2. Heat the oil in a heavy saucepan.
2 fl oz	60 mL	Vegetable oil	3. Add the onion, garlic, and ginger. Sauté until the onion is lightly browned.
4 oz	125 g	Onion, chopped	4. Add the spices.
1 tsp	5 mL	Finely chopped garlic	5. Drain the rice and add it to the pan. Stir to coat the grains with oil.
1 tsp	5 mL	Finely chopped fresh ginger root	6. Add the water or stock and the salt. Bring to a boil.
¼ tsp	1 mL	Ground cardamom	7. Cover and simmer over low heat about 40 minutes, or until the rice is tender. Check after about 30 minutes to make sure the liquid hasn't all been absorbed before the rice is done. If it has, add a little more hot water.
¼ tsp	1 mL	Cinnamon	
⅛ tsp	0.5 mL	Ground cumin	
⅛ tsp	0.5 mL	Ground cloves	
⅛ tsp	0.5 mL	Nutmeg	
⅛ tsp	0.5 mL	Cayenne	
1 qt	1 L	Water or vegetable stock, hot	
2 tsp	10 mL	Salt	
8 oz	250 g	Yellow split peas	8. Pick over the peas to remove stones and other foreign matter. Rinse and drain the peas.
1 qt	1 L	Water	9. Simmer the peas in the water until they are very tender and falling apart. Do not drain.
2 fl oz	60 mL	Vegetable oil	10. Heat the oil in a heavy saucepot.
8 oz	250 g	Onion, medium dice	11. Add the onion and garlic. Sauté until lightly browned.
2 tsp	10 mL	Finely chopped garlic	12. Stir in the curry powder and salt.
2 tbsp	30 mL	Curry powder	13. Add the carrots, parsnips, and eggplant. Sauté 2–3 minutes over medium heat.
2 tsp	10 mL	Salt	14. Add the cauliflower. Sauté another minute.
8 oz	250 g	Carrots, thickly sliced	15. Add the cooked peas. Simmer 15–20 minutes, or until the vegetables are nearly tender.
6 oz	180 g	Parsnips, large dice	16. Add more water if the mixture becomes too thick. The peas should have the consistency of a sauce.
6 oz	180 g	Eggplant, peeled, large dice	17. Add the broccoli and continue to simmer until all the vegetables are tender. Taste and add more salt if necessary.
8 oz	250 g	Cauliflower, broken into small florets	18. Stir in the yogurt and lemon or lime juice.
8 oz	250 g	Broccoli, broken into small florets	
8 fl oz	250 mL	Plain yogurt	
2 fl oz	60 mL	Lemon juice or lime juice	
1½ pt	750 mL	Cucumber Raita	19. For each portion, spoon rice to cover about two-thirds of a plate, leaving space at one side. Make a well in the center. Spoon a portion of the vegetable curry into the center of the rice.
as needed	as needed	Cilantro leaves	20. To the side of the rice, spoon a portion of the raita.
as needed	as needed	Paprika	21. Top the curry with a few cilantro leaves.
			22. Sprinkle a dash of paprika onto the center of the raita.

Per serving (excluding Raita): Calories, 370; Protein, 12 g; Fat, 13 g (30% cal.); Cholesterol, 5 mg; Carbohydrates, 55 g; Fiber, 6 g; Sodium, 1030 mg.

Per serving (Raita only): Calories, 30; Protein, 2 g; Fat, 2 g (53% cal.); Cholesterol, 0 mg; Carbohydrates, 2 g; Fiber, 0 g; Sodium, 210 mg.

VARIATION

Vegan Vegetable and Split Pea Curry

Omit the yogurt. Increase the lemon juice or lime juice to taste.

Noodle Bowl with Stir-Fried Vegetables, Tofu, and Peanuts

PORTIONS: 12 PORTION SIZE: 4 OZ (125 G) NOODLES, 6 OZ (180 G) VEGETABLES

U.S.	METRIC	INGREDIENTS	PROCEDURE
2 fl oz	60 mL	Vegetable oil	1. Heat the oil in a large sauté pan or wok over high heat. 2. Add the scallions, garlic, and ginger. Stir-fry 1 minute. 3. Add the carrots, peppers, and mushrooms. Continue to stir-fry another minute. 4. Add the bok choy and bean sprouts. Stir-fry until the vegetables are wilted but still crisp. 5. Add the snow peas and continue to cook about 30 seconds. 6. Add the tofu and peanuts. Toss the mixture to blend, and cook until the tofu is hot.
4	4	Scallions, chopped	
2	2	Garlic cloves, chopped	
1 tsp	5 mL	Finely chopped ginger root	
6 oz	180 g	Carrots, cut julienne	
6 oz	180 g	Red bell peppers, cut bâtonnet	
8 oz	250 g	Shiitake mushroom caps, cut bâtonnet	
1 lb	500 g	Bok choy, cut into 1-in. (2.5-cm) pieces	
4 oz	125 g	Mung bean sprouts	
8 oz	250 g	Snow peas, trimmed	
1 lb 4 oz	625 g	Firm tofu, pressed (pp. 463–464), cut in ½-in. (1-cm) dice	
6 oz	180 g	Roasted peanuts, shelled, skinless	
3 fl oz	90 mL	Soy sauce	7. Pour in the soy sauce, hoisin sauce, stock or water, and oil. Toss to mix.
2 fl oz	60 mL	Hoisin sauce	
4 fl oz	125 mL	Vegetable stock or water	
1 tbsp	15 mL	Sesame oil or chili oil	
3 lb	1.5 kg	Cooked Chinese wheat noodles or egg noodles, hot	8. Put the noodles into individual serving bowls and top with the vegetable mixture with its liquid.

Per serving: Calories, 400; Protein, 19 g; Fat, 18 g (39% cal.); Cholesterol, 0 mg; Carbohydrates, 45 g; Fiber, 6 g; Sodium, 830 mg.

Noodle Bowl with Stir-Fried Vegetables, Tofu, and Peanuts

Zucchini and Eggplant Lasagne

PORTIONS: 12 PORTION SIZE: 8 OZ (250 G)

U.S.	METRIC	INGREDIENTS
1½ lb	750 g	Eggplant
1½ lb	750 g	Zucchini
as needed	as needed	Salt
as needed	as needed	Olive oil

PROCEDURE

1. Trim and peel the eggplant.
2. Trim the stem ends of the zucchini.
3. Cut the eggplant and the zucchini lengthwise into slices about ⅓ in. (8 mm) thick.
4. Salt the slices lightly on both sides and let stand 15 minutes.
5. Pat dry. Brush both sides of each slice lightly with oil.
6. Arrange the eggplant and zucchini on separate sheet pans.
7. Bake the eggplant in an oven at 425°F (210°C) until the bottoms are brown. Turn over and bake another 15 minutes.
8. At the same time, bake the zucchini until softened but still somewhat crisp, 5–10 minutes.
9. Remove the vegetables from the oven and let cool. These slices will serve as noodles for the lasagna.

U.S.	METRIC	INGREDIENTS
2 oz	375 g	Ricotta cheese
1 oz	30 g	Parmesan cheese, grated
1	1	Egg, beaten
2 tbsp	30 mL	Chopped parsley
to taste	to taste	Salt
to taste	to taste	Pepper

10. Mix the ricotta, parmesan, egg, parsley, salt, and pepper.

U.S.	METRIC	INGREDIENTS
1½ qt	1.5 L	Tomato Sauce for Pasta, made without sugar
1 lb	500 g	Mozzarella cheese, sliced
2 tbsp	30 mL	Fresh basil, cut chiffonade
2 oz	60 g	Parmesan cheese, grated

11. Ladle a little tomato sauce into a half-hotel pan, 10 × 12 in. (25 × 30 cm). Spread it across the bottom.
12. Lay the eggplant slices in a single layer over the sauce.
13. Add the ricotta mixture, carefully spreading it in an even layer over the eggplant.
14. Add the zucchini in a single layer.
15. Cover with half the remaining sauce.
16. Arrange the mozzarella slices over the top. Sprinkle the mozzarella with a little of the basil.
17. Cover with the remaining sauce.
18. Sprinkle with the second quantity of parmesan cheese.
19. Bake at 375°F (190°C) until hot and bubbling.

Per serving: Calories, 410; Protein, 15 g; Fat, 34 g (73% cal.); Cholesterol, 65 mg; Carbohydrates, 14 g; Fiber, 4 g; Sodium, 1030 mg.

Pinto Bean Enchiladas

PORTIONS: 12 PORTION SIZE: 2 ENCHILADAS

U.S.	METRIC	INGREDIENTS
as needed	as needed	Vegetable oil
24	24	Corn tortillas
2 qt	2 L	Ancho Sauce (made with water) or Salsa Roja
2 lb 4 oz	1.1 kg	Vegetarian Pinto Beans, warmed
2 lb	1 kg	Monterey jack cheese, grated

PROCEDURE

1. Heat a thin layer of oil in a sauté pan over moderate heat.
2. One at a time, dip the tortillas in the hot oil and fry them a few seconds, first on one side, then the other, just until they are soft. The purpose is to soften them, so do not fry until crisp. Drain and lay them on a work surface or in a pan.
3. Pour 1–2 cups (250–500 mL) sauce in a shallow pan.
4. One at a time, dip the tortillas in the sauce to coat both sides and let the excess drip off. Lay the sauced tortilla on the work surface. Place 1½ oz (45 g) beans and ½ oz (15 g) grated cheese in the center of the tortilla and roll up.
5. Add more sauce to the pan as it gets used up. You will need about 1 qt (1 L) of the sauce for dipping.
6. Arrange the rolled tortillas against each other in a baking pan, putting the loose ends on the bottom. Alternatively, place them in individual gratin dishes, allowing 2 per portion.
7. Pour the remaining sauce over the tortillas, making sure to cover the ends so they don't dry out.
8. Top with the remaining cheese.
9. Bake at 375°F (190°C) until heated through, about 20 minutes.

U.S.	METRIC	INGREDIENTS
3 lb	1.5 kg	Arroz Verde or Arroz à la Mexicana, made with water instead of stock
as desired	as desired	Guacamole (p. 399)
as desired	as desired	Salsa Cruda
as desired	as desired	Sour cream

10. Serve 2 enchiladas per portion with 4 oz (125 g) rice.
11. Serve with guacamole, salsa, and sour cream as desired.

Per serving: Calories, 830; Protein, 35 g; Fat, 41 g (43% cal.); Cholesterol, 70 mg; Carbohydrates, 89 g; Fiber, 17 g; Sodium, 1040 mg.

Pinto Bean Enchiladas

ENCHILADAS

The Spanish word *enchilar* means "to put chile on something." The word *enchilada* is short for *tortilla enchilada*, meaning a tortilla covered with chile sauce. In the non-Spanish-speaking world, an enchilada is a corn tortilla rolled around a filling. Strictly speaking, however, the tortilla must first be coated with chile sauce before being rolled. A plain, dry tortilla with a filling is more accurately called a *soft taco*.

There are two basic methods for making enchiladas. In both methods, part of the procedure is to soften the tortilla enough so it can be rolled without breaking.

Fry the tortilla just enough to soften it, then dip in sauce, fill, and roll up.

Or coat the tortilla in chile sauce, then fry briefly, fill, and roll up.

Once the tortilla is filled, it can be served immediately. For North American tastes, however, it is usually baked with additional sauce and sometimes cheese toppings.

Three-Bean Chili with Tostaditas

YIELD: 6 LB PORTIONS: 12 PORTION SIZE: 8 OZ (250 G)

U.S.	METRIC	INGREDIENTS	PROCEDURE
8 oz	250 g	Black turtle beans	1. Sort, wash, and drain the black turtle beans. Soak them overnight in cold water. 2. Drain the beans. Place them in a heavy saucepot and add enough water to cover them by 1 in. (2.5 cm). 3. Bring to a boil, reduce heat to a simmer, and simmer until the beans are just tender. 4. Keep an eye on the beans and add a little more water whenever necessary to keep the beans covered with water.
8 oz	250 g	White kidney beans	5. Repeat steps 1–4 for the white beans. It is necessary to cook the beans separately because they may have different cooking times.
1	1	Bay leaf	
8 oz	250 g	Red kidney beans or pinto beans	6. Repeat steps 1–4 for the red kidney or pinto beans.
1	1	Bay leaf	
2 fl oz	60 mL	Vegetable oil	7. Heat the vegetable oil in a sauté pan over moderate heat.
2 tbsp	30 mL	Cumin seed	8. Add the cumin and cook in the oil until aromatic.
6 oz	180 g	Onion, medium dice	9. Add the onion, garlic, and spices. Sauté until the onion is lightly browned.
1 oz	30 g	Garlic, chopped fine	10. Add the tomatoes and salt. Simmer 15 minutes.
¼ cup	60 mL	Chili powder	11. Combine all three pots of beans in one large pot and add the spice and tomato mixture. Simmer until the beans are very tender. As before, add water if the stew becomes too dry.
1½ tsp	7 mL	Chipotle chili powder	12. Taste for seasonings and add more salt if necessary.
1 tbsp	15 mL	Paprika	
2 tbsp	30 mL	Dried oregano	
2 lb	1 kg	Tomatoes, canned, chopped, with their juice	
1 tsp	5 mL	Salt	
24	24	Tortillas	13. To make the tostaditas, cut the tortillas into quarters, and then cut each quarter into 2 wedges. 14. Deep-fry the tortillas until they are crisp. Drain well. 15. To serve, ladle the chili into bowls. 16. Set the bowls on large dinner plates as underliners. Arrange the tostaditas around the bowls on the plates. 17. Place 1 tbsp (15 mL) salsa on top of each portion of chili.
6 fl oz	180 mL	Salsa Cruda	

Per serving: Calories, 400; Protein, 17 g; Fat, 10 g (22% cal.); Cholesterol, 0 mg; Carbohydrates, 65 g; Fiber, 16 g; Sodium, 580 mg.

Three-Bean Chili with Tostaditas

Red Rice, Spinach with Tofu Dressing, and Eggplant Dengaku

PORTIONS: 10 PORTION SIZE: APPROXIMATELY 5 OZ (150 G) RICE, 3 OZ (90 G) SPINACH, 3 OZ (90 G) EGGPLANT

U.S.	METRIC	INGREDIENTS	PROCEDURE
¾ cup	180 mL	Azuki beans	1. Wash and drain the beans.
4½ cups	1.1 L	Water	2. Place the beans and the water in a saucepan and bring to a boil. Simmer 10 minutes, or until the beans are just soft enough to be crushed between the fingers but not completely cooked.
4 cups	1 L	Glutinous rice	3. Drain, reserving the cooking water. Cool both the beans and the water to room temperature. Refrigerate the beans.
			4. Wash the rice in several changes of cold water. Drain.
			5. Add the red bean cooking water to the rice and soak overnight.
			6. The next day, drain the rice and mix it with the beans.
			7. Cover the rack of a steamer with several layers of cheesecloth.
			8. Place the rice and bean mixture on top of the cheesecloth in a layer no more than 1½ in. (4 cm) thick.
			9. Steam until the rice and beans are tender, about 40 minutes.
10 oz	280 g	Firm Japanese-style tofu	10. Simmer the tofu in water 2 minutes. Drain.
2 tbsp	30 mL	Sesame seeds	11. Wrap the tofu in cheesecloth or in a clean towel and weight with a dinner plate 30–60 minutes to remove excess moisture.
2 tsp	10 mL	Soy sauce	12. Lightly toast the sesame seeds in a dry skillet, and then grind them coarsely in a mortar or spice mill.
1 tsp	5 mL	Mirin (Japanese sweet rice wine)	13. Rub the tofu through a fine sieve.
1 tbsp	15 mL	Sugar	14. Mix the puréed tofu with the sesame seeds, soy sauce, mirin, and sugar.
1 lb 12 oz	850 g	Spinach, fresh, cooked and lightly squeezed	15. Chop the pressed spinach into large pieces, and then mix with the tofu dressing.
to taste	to taste	Salt	16. Add salt to taste.
6 oz	180 g	White miso	17. In a stainless-steel bowl, combine the miso and egg yolk and stir until smooth.
1	1	Egg yolk	18. Stir in the sake, mirin, sugar, and dashi.
1 tbsp	15 mL	Sake (Japanese rice wine)	19. Set the bowl in a pan of simmering water and stir until thick.
1 tbsp	15 mL	Mirin (sweet Japanese rice wine)	20. Cool.
1 tbsp	15 mL	Sugar	21. Trim the ends off the eggplant. Cut crosswise into rounds 1 in. (2.5 cm) thick.
2 fl oz	60 mL	Vegetarian dashi	22. Brush the cut sides of the eggplant slices with oil.
2 lb	900 g	Eggplant	23. Grill, broil, or pan-fry the eggplant until tender.
			24. Spread a layer of the miso mixture on top of each of the rounds.
			25. Pass under the broiler or salamander just until the miso topping is lightly colored.
as needed	as needed	Gomashio (see Note)	26. Serve each of the three items in separate bowls, one of each per diner. Sprinkle the top of the red rice with a little goma-shio as garnish.

Per serving: Calories, 430; Protein, 16 g; Fat, 4.5 g (9% cal.); Cholesterol, 20 mg; Carbohydrates, 81 g; Fiber, 10 g; Sodium, 770 mg.

Note: Gomashio, or sesame salt, is a mixture of toasted black sesame seeds and coarse salt. If it is not available, toast sesame seeds and mix with a little kosher salt.

Red Rice, Spinach with Tofu Dressing, and Eggplant Dengaku

Vietnamese Vegetable Pancakes

PORTIONS: 6 PORTION SIZE: 1 PANCAKE

U.S.	METRIC	INGREDIENTS	PROCEDURE
		Dipping sauce:	1. Combine the dipping sauce ingredients and stir until the sugar is dissolved.
4 fl oz	125 mL	Soy sauce	2. Set aside.
1 tsp	5 mL	Finely chopped garlic	
2 tsp	10 mL	Sugar	
½ tsp	2 mL	Black pepper	
1 tbsp	15 mL	Chopped fresh red chile	
2 tbsp	30 mL	Chopped peanuts	
1 tbsp	15 mL	Lime juice	
½ cup	120 mL	Rice flour	3. Whip together the rice flour, eggs, water, and salt to make a thin batter. Let stand 10 minutes
3	3	Eggs, beaten	4. Strain to remove any lumps.
9 fl oz	270 mL	Water	
⅛ tsp	0.5 mL	Salt	
4 oz	125 g	Shiitake mushroom caps, cut bâtonnet	5. Sauté the mushrooms in hot oil until tender. Cool.
1 tbsp	15 mL	Vegetable oil	
2 fl oz	60 mL	Vegetable oil	6. In a well-seasoned 10-in. (25-cm) sauté pan or, preferably, a nonstick pan, heat 2 tsp (10 mL) oil until very hot.
6 oz	180 g	Snow peas, trimmed	7. Add about 2½ fl oz (75 mL) of the batter and swirl it around to cover the bottom of the pan.
6 oz	180 g	Bean sprouts	8. Add one-sixth of the mushrooms and snow peas. Cover and cook 1 minute.
2 oz	60 g	Scallions, sliced thin	9. Remove the lid and add one-sixth of the bean sprouts and scallions.
			10. Cook uncovered until the pancake is crisp.
			11. Slide the pancake onto a dinner plate.
			12. Repeat with the remaining batter and vegetables.
			13. Serve with dipping sauce.

Per serving: Calories, 400; Protein, 17 g; Fat, 10 g (22% cal.); Cholesterol, 0 mg; Carbohydrates, 65 g; Fiber, 16 g; Sodium, 580 mg.

Vietnamese Vegetable Pancake

Winter Vegetable Gratin with Feta Cheese and Bulgur Pilaf

PORTIONS: 10 PORTION SIZE: 6½ OZ (185 G) VEGETABLES, 3 OZ (90 G) PILAF

U.S.	METRIC	INGREDIENTS
10 oz	300 g	Turnips, peeled
10 oz	300 g	Parsnips, peeled
10 oz	300 g	Carrots, peeled
10 oz	300 g	Cauliflower, trimmed
6 oz	180 g	Brussels sprouts, trimmed
4 oz	125 g	Pearl onions, peeled
3 oz	90 g	Olive oil or melted butter
1 tsp	5 mL	Salt
½ tsp	2 mL	Pepper
1 tsp	5 mL	Dried thyme
1 tsp	5 mL	Dried oregano

PROCEDURE

1. Cut the turnips, parsnips, and carrots into 1½-in. (4-cm) pieces.
2. Break or cut the cauliflower into small florets.
3. Cut the Brussels sprouts in half lengthwise.
4. In a large bowl, toss the vegetables, including the onions, with the oil, salt, pepper, and herbs to coat them.
5. Transfer to a half-hotel pan, 10 × 12 in. (25 × 30 cm), or a gratin dish of the same capacity. (Alternatively, bake in single-serving gratin dishes.)
6. Bake at 400°F (200°C) until the vegetables are lightly browned and tender. Stir them occasionally during cooking so they brown evenly.

U.S.	METRIC	INGREDIENTS
12 oz	375 g	Feta cheese, crumbled
4 oz	125 g	Olive oil or melted butter
8 oz	250 g	Fresh bread crumbs
30 oz (1 recipe)	900 g (1 recipe)	Bulgur Pilaf with Lemon, made with vegetable stock

7. Remove the pan from the oven and sprinkle the feta cheese over the vegetables.
8. Mix the oil or butter with the crumbs until they are evenly mixed.
9. Sprinkle the crumbs over the vegetables in an even layer.
10. Return to the oven and bake until the top is browned. If necessary, place under a broiler or salamander to finish browning.
11. Serve with bulgur pilaf.

Per serving: Calories, 490; Protein, 12 g; Fat, 31 g (55% cal.); Cholesterol, 35 mg; Carbohydrates, 44 g; Fiber, 9 g; Sodium, 830 mg.

Winter Vegetable Gratin with Feta Cheese and Bulgur Pilaf

Falafel

YIELD: ABOUT 2 LB 4 OZ (1.1 KG)

U.S.	METRIC	INGREDIENTS
2 lb	1 kg	Chickpeas, cooked or canned, drained
1 oz	30 g	Garlic, chopped fine
4 oz	125 g	Scallion, chopped fine
3 tbsp	45 mL	Chopped parsley
2 tsp	10 mL	Ground cumin
2 tsp	10 mL	Ground coriander
¼ tsp	1 mL	Cayenne
2 tsp	10 mL	Salt
1 tsp	5 mL	Black pepper
1 oz	30 g	Tahini (sesame paste)
2	2	Eggs, beaten
2 oz	60 g	Soft bread crumbs

Per serving: Calories, 70; Protein, 3 g; Fat, 3 g (36% cal.); Cholesterol, 10 mg; Carbohydrates, 9 g; Fiber, 2 g; Sodium, 150 mg.

PROCEDURE

1. Process the chickpeas in a food processor until well chopped but not completely puréed.
2. Add the remaining ingredients and mix well.
3. To make large falafel, use a No. 20 scoop to portion the mix. Roll each portion into a ball and then flatten into a thick patty. Handle the portions quickly and lightly. If they are handled too much, a loose crust may form during frying that will flake off after draining.
4. To make small, appetizer-size falafel, use a No. 40 or 50 scoop to portion the mix, and roll into balls.
5. Deep-fry at 375°F (190°C) until browned and crisp.

TERMS FOR REVIEW

vegetarian
vegan
lacto-vegetarian
ovo-vegetarian
lacto-ovo-vegetarian
pesco-vegetarian
limiting amino acid
amino acid
essential amino acid
complete protein
incomplete protein
complementary protein
soy milk
tofu
bean curd
tempeh
miso
bean paste
textured vegetable protein (TVP)

QUESTIONS FOR DISCUSSION

1. Explain how complementary proteins enable vegans to get enough protein in their diet without eating animal products.
2. What vitamin is most difficult for vegans to get in their diet? Why is this so? What are alternative sources for this vitamin?
3. Considering them as sources of protein, what makes soybeans, amaranth, and quinoa unique among foods from plants?
4. Name and describe the three main types of tofu.
5. What is TVP? Describe how to prepare it for use in recipes.
6. Explain why some refined sugars are not suitable for use in vegetarian recipes. Which sugars are unsuitable, and which sugars can be used?

Subject Index

Note: Please see Recipe Index that follows for specific recipes.

A

Active dry yeast, 226
Aging meat, 124–126
À la meunière, 92
À la nage, 103
Americano, 433
Amino acids, 460, 461
Amuse bouche, 402
Anadromous fish, 58
Angel food method (cakes), 258, 260, 269
Antelope, 151
Antipasto, 400
Appetizers, 391
Arctic char, 59
Artisan cheeses, 426–427

B

Bagged cookies, 282
Baked Alaska, 313
Baked custard, 317, 320
Baked puddings, 322
Bakers' percentages, 215
Baker's scale, 215
Bakeshop production, 213–228
  baking process, 218
  eggs, 225
  fats, 221–222
  flours, meals, and starches, 219–221
  formulas and measurement, 214–217
  leavening agents, 226–227
  liquids, 224–225
  mixing and gluten development, 217–218
  principles of baking, 214
  salt, flavorings, and spices, 227–228
  staling, 219
  sugars, 222–224
Baking:
  bread and yeast products, 235–236
  cakes, 264, 265
  cookies, 284
  fish and shellfish, 84–89
  meat, 156–166
  poultry and game birds, 16–25
Baking ammonia, 227
Baking blind, 296
Baking powder, 227
Baking soda, 226–227
Bar cookies, 283–284, 288
Barding, 122, 141, 157
Basic grind, for sausages, 203–204
Basting, 16, 157
Bean curd, 463
Bean paste, 464
Beef:
  aging, 125
  cooking methods, 140, 141
  cuts, 128–129, 131–132
  fabricating, 135–136
  grades, 125
Biscuit method, 250–252
Bison, 151
Bivalves, 68
Black sea bass, 59
Blancmange, 321
Blanquette, 183
Blending method (cakes), 258
Blitz puff pastry, 307
Bluefish, 59
Boar, 150–151
Boiled icing, 311
Bombes, 327
Bones, in meat, 127, 131
Bound salads, 376
Brains, 147, 148
Braising:
  fish and shellfish, 84–85
  meat, 182–191
  poultry and game birds, 42–48
  sausages, 206
Bread:
  baking, 235–236
  brioche, 246
  faults and their causes, 236–237
  formulas, 238–241
  hard rolls and bread, 238, 243–244
  makeup techniques, 243–247
  mixing and production, 232–235
  pan loaves, 246
  quick, 249–254
  for sandwiches, 374
  soft rolls, 238, 245–246
  storage, 236, 374, 375
  types, 232
Bread flour, 220
Breve, 433
Brine cures, 196
Brioche, 246
Broiling:
  fish and shellfish, 86–91
  meat, 166–169
  poultry and game birds, 26–30
  sausages, 206
Brown sugar, 223
Bruschetta, 401
Buffalo, 151
Buffet-style service, 366–369, 371, 392
Butchers, 131
Butler-style service, 392
Butter, 420
Buttercream, 270–272
Buttermilk, 419

C

Café au lait, 432
Cage-free foods, 2
Cake, 257–277
  altitude adjustments, 265, 266
  angel food method, 258, 260, 269
  assembling, 274–276
  baking and cooling, 264, 265
  chiffon method, 258, 261
  creaming method, 258, 259, 266–267
  cutting, 276
  faults and their causes, 264–265
  fillings, 274
  foaming (sponge) method, 258, 260, 269
  high-fat, 261
  icings for, 270–276
  low-fat, 262
  mixing methods, 258–261
  scaling and panning, 262–263
  two-stage method, 258, 259, 268
Cake flour, 220
Calamari, 73
Canapés, 392–396
Capons, 4, 5
Cappuccino, 432
Carbohydrates, 122
Carcasses, meat, 126
Caribou, 151
Carpaccio, fish, 115
Carryover cooking, 144
Casings (sausages), 201–202
Catadromous fish, 58
Catfish, 64
Caul, 149
Caviar, 401–402
Cephalopods, 68, 73
Certified pork, 200
Ceviche (seviche), 115
Chai, 433
Charcuterie, 193
Charcutier, 193
Cheese, 421–429
  on buffets, 370–371
  composition, 421–422
  cooking with, 427
  in sandwiches, 376
  storage and service, 427
  varieties, 423–427
Chemical leaveners, 226–227
Chèvre, 425
Chicken, 2–5
  cooking methods for, *see under* Poultry
  cutting, 10–13
  doneness, 8
  legs, boning and stuffing, 24
  trussing, 9
Chiffon desserts and pies, 296, 304
Chiffon method (cakes), 258, 261
Chilean sea bass, 59
Chitterlings, 149
Clams, 69–70
Clarified butter, 420
Classical garnish, 366
Club sandwiches, 377
Coagulation, 122
Cockles, 70
Cocktails, 396
Cocktail buffets, 368–369
Cod, 60
Coffee, 430–433
Cold smoking, 196
Collagen, 123
Collagen casings (sausages), 202
Common meringue, 311
Complementary proteins, 461–462
Complete proteins, 461
Condensed, 419
Confectioners' sugars, 223
Confit, 48
Connective tissue, 123–124, 140–141
Cooked fruit method (pies), 298, 299
Cooked juice method (pies), 298, 299
Cookies, 279–288
  characteristics, 280–281
  mixing methods, 281
  panning, baking and cooling, 284
  types and makeup methods, 282–284
Coral, 74
Cornish hens, 4, 5
Corn syrup, 223
Coupes, 327
Court bouillon, 101
Crabs, 78–80
Crayfish, 80
Cream(s), 418–420
  crème anglaise, 317–318
  pastry, 317–320
Cream horns, 308
Creaming method, 227
  cakes, 258, 259, 266–267
  cookies, 281, 285–286
  quick breads, 250, 251
Cream pies, 296, 304
Cream puddings, 321
Cream puffs, 310
Crème anglaise, 317–318
Crème fraîche, 419
Crêpes, 407
Crêpinette, 149
Croissants, 242–243
Crudités, 396
Crumb pie crusts, 294, 295
Crustaceans, 68, 74–80
Cryovac®, 125
Crystallization, 316
Cuisines across cultures, *See* International cuisines
Cuisson, 102
Curdling, 419
Cured sausage, 199–200
Curing foods, 194–197
Custard, 317–320
Custard pies, 303–304
Custard sauces, 327
Cuttlefish, 73

D

Dairy products, 418–429, 460, 464
  butter, 420–421
  cheese, 421–429
  milk and cream, 418–420
Danish pastry, 242–243
Dark meat, 2–3
Decaffeinated coffee, 430, 432
Decorator's (decorating) icing, 273
Deep-fried sandwiches, 377
Deep-frying:
  fish and shellfish, 96–110
  poultry and game birds, 31–37
Deglazing, 160, 170
Desserts, *see specific types of desserts*
Dessert sauces, 327–328
Dessert syrup, 316
Dips, 397–399
Double-acting baking powders, 227
Double-crème cheese, 422
Doughnuts, 311
Dover sole, 59
Dressing, for poultry, 21, 49–50
Dressing fish, 56
Dried whole milk, 419
Drop batters, 250
Dropped cookies, 282, 285
Dry aging, 126
Dry cures, 195–196
Duck, 5–7

E

Éclairs, 310
Éclair paste, 309–311
Eel, 65
Eggs:
  for baking, 225
  in vegetarian diet, 460
Egg rolls, 411
Elastin, 124
Elk, 151
Emu, 7
Emulsified (emulsion) grind, for sausages, 203, 205
Emulsified shortening, 222
Emulsions, 228
English sole, 59
En papillote, 110
Escargots, 81
Escolar, 60
Espresso (expresso), 432–433
Essential amino acids, 460
Étuver, 110
Evaporated milk, 419
Extracts, 228

F

Fabricated cuts, 127–133
Fabricating meat, 131
Farmstead cheese, 426
Fat fish, 54, 55
Feet (meat), 149
Fermentation, 226, 234
Fish and shellfish, 53–80
  baking, 84–85
  broiling and grilling, 86–91
  cephalopods, 73
  composition and structure, 54
  cooking methods, 54–55
  crustaceans, 74–80
  cutting and filleting, 55–58
  deep-frying, 96–100
  doneness, 54
  fin fish, 53–67
  freshness, 66
  handling and storage, 66–67
  inspection, 66–67
  market forms, 55
  mixed cooking techniques, 110–114
  mollusks, 68–72

poaching and simmering, 101–109
in sandwiches, 376
sautéing and pan-frying, 92–95
served raw, 115–119
shellfish, 53, 68–80
steaming, 110–114
Flaking (fin fish), 54
Flaky pie dough, 293, 294
Flatfish, 58–59
Flat icings, 272
Flavored milks, 418
Flounder, 58
Flours:
for baking, 219–221
and gluten, 217
Foaming method, 227, 258, 260, 269
Foam-type icings, 272
Foie gras terrines, 453
Fondant, 270
Food safety, *see* Sanitation
Forcemeat, 439–446
Foresaddles, meat, 127
Fortified milk, 418
Free-range chickens, 2
French crullers or doughnuts, 311
French-style ice creams, 325
Fresh sausage, 199
Freshwater fish, 64–65
Fresh yeast, 226
Fricassée, 43, 183
Frogs' legs, 81
Frosting, *see* Icing
Frozen desserts, 325–327
Frozen yogurt, 325
Fruit desserts, 295, 313
Fruit pies, 298–302
Fruit purées, 327
Fruit tarts, 295
Fudge-type icings, 272–273

G
Galantines, 447
Game, 149–152
Game birds, 6–7
braising, 42–48
broiling, 26–30
dressings and stuffings for, 49–50
pan gravy for, 19
roasting and baking, 16–25
sautéing, pan-frying, deep-frying, 31–37
simmering and poaching, 38–41
Ganache, 273
Garde manger, 437–457
foie gras terrines, 453
forcemeat, 439–446
galantines, 447
liver terrines, 454
pâtés, 442–444
presentation, 438–439
rillettes, 454
sanitation and storage, 438
terrines, 440, 445–455
Garnish, 366
Gelatin, 450–452
Glazes, for cakes, 273
Glazing fish, 103
Glucose syrup, 223
Gluten, 217–218, 250
Goat cheese, 425
Goose, 5, 6
Graham cracker pie crusts, 294, 295
Grains, in vegetarian diet, 463
Granité, 325
Granulated sugar, 223
Gras-double, 149
Gratin forcemeat, 439
Gravy, 158
Green meat, 124, 125
Griddling, 170–177
Grilled sandwiches, 377
Grilling:
fish and shellfish, 86–91
meat, 166–169
poultry and game birds, 26–30
sausages, 206
Grind, for sausages, 203–205
Grosse pièce, 369
Grouper, 60
Guineas, 5, 6

H
Haddock, 60
Half-and-half, 419
Halibut, 59
Hard meringues, 311
Hard rolls and breads, 237, 238, 243–244
Hare, 151–152
Heart, 148
Herbs, 195
Herbal teas, 433
Herring, 60
Hindsaddles, meat, 127
Homogenized milk, 418
Honey, 224
Hors d'oeuvres, 391–414
adapted from other recipes, 400
canapés, 392–396
cocktails, 396
dips, 397–399
relishes, 396–397
serving, 392
Hot smoking, 196

I
Ices, 325
Icebox cookies, 283
Ice cream, 325–327
Iced coffee, 432
Ice milk, 325
Icing, 270–276, 311
buttercream, 270–272
flat, 272
foam-type, 272
fondant, 270
fudge-type, 272–273
royal, 273
selecting, 274
Incomplete proteins, 461
Instant coffee, 430
Instant dry yeast, 226
Instant starch, 298
International cuisines, 331–361
Africa, 339–341
China, 353–355
France, 335–336
Germany, 333–335
India, 347–350
Italy, 332–333
Korea, 355
Mexico, 358–361
Middle East, 341–346
South America and Caribbean, 356–357
Southeast Asia, 351–352
Spain, 336–338
Intestines (meat), 149
Irradiation, 134–135
Italian meringue, 311, 312

J
Jack, 60
Jamaican Jerk, 30
Japonaise meringues, 313
John Dory, 61
Jus, 158

K
Kidneys, 146–147

L
Lacto-ovo-vegetarians, 460
Lacto-vegetarians, 460
Lamb:
aging, 125
cooking methods, 140, 141
cuts, 130, 132
fabricating, 136–137
grades, 125
Laminated doughs, 232
Langostes, 76
Langoustines/langostinos, 77
Lard, 222
Larding, 139, 141
Latte, 432
Lean doughs, 232
Lean fish, 54–55
Leavening agents, 226–227
Legumes, in vegetarian diet, 463
Light cream, 419
Light meat, 2–3
Limiting amino acids, 460
Liver, 146
Liver terrines, 454
Lobsters, 74–76
Low-fat milk, 418

M
Macciato, 433
Mackerel, 61
Magret, 6
Mahi-mahi, 61
Malt syrup, 224
Marbling, 122
Margarine, 222, 421
Marinating, 150
Matignon, 25
Maturity, poultry, 2
Mayonnaise, 375
Mealy pie dough, 293, 294
Meat, 121–153
aging, 124–126
bone structure, 127, 131
braising, 182–191
broiling, grilling, pan-broiling, 166–169
composition, 122
cooking methods, 139–142
cuts, 126–133
doneness, 143–145
fabricating, 135–139
game and specialty, 149–152
inspection and grading, 124
roasting and baking, 156–166
in sandwiches, 376
in sausage, 200
sautéing, pan-frying, griddling, 170–177
selecting, 134–135
simmering, 177–182
specifications, 134–135
storage, 152–153
structure, 123–124
variety meats, 146–149
Meringues, 311–313
Meringue glacée, 312
Meringue shells, 312
Milk, 418–420
Mirepoix, 157
Miso, in vegetarian diet, 464
Mocha, 433
Modified straight dough method, 233
Molasses, 223
Molded cookies, 283, 287
Mollusks, 68–72
Monkfish, 61
Moose, 151
Moulard, 6
Mousses, 323, 325, 450–451
Mousseline-based terrines, 448–449
Mousseline forcemeat, 439
Muffin method, 250–254
Multidecker sandwiches, 377
Mussels, 70–72

N
Napoleons, 309
Natural casings (sausages), 201–202
Nitrites and nitrates, 194–195
Nitrosamines, 194
Nonessential amino acids, 460
Nonfat dry milk, 419
Nonfat milk, 418
Nuts, 463
Nutrition, 460–462

O
Ocean perch, 61
Octopus, 73
Oils, 222
Old doughs, 234
One-stage method (cookies), 281
Ono, 64
Open-faced sandwiches, 377
Orange roughy, 61
Organic, 2
Ostrich, 7
Oven spring, 235
Overrun (ice cream), 326
Ovo-vegetarians, 460
Oxtails, 148
Oysters, 68–69

P
Pan-broiling, 168
Pan-frying:
fish and shellfish, 92–95
meat, 170–177
poultry and game birds, 31–37
sausages, 206
Pan gravy, 19, 158
Panini, 378
Pan jus, 160
Pan loaves, 246
Parfaits, 327
Partridges, 7
Pasteurized milk, 418
Pastry, 305–311
Danish, 242–243
éclair paste, 309–311
pâté, 440
puff, 305–309
Pastry creams, 317–320
Pastry flour, 220
Pâtés, 438–439, 442–444
Pâté à choux, 310
Pâté à pâté, 440
Pâté de campagne, 440
Pâté en croûte, 443
Patty shells, 308
Paupiettes, 107
Peach Melba, 327
Pear Belle Hélène, 327
Perch, 65
Pesco-vegetarians, 460
Pheasant, 7
Philadelphia-style ice creams, 325
Pies, 296–297
assembly and baking, 296–297
doughs, 292–295
fillings, 298–304
Pie crusts, 292–295
Pie dough, 292–294
Pie filling, 298–304
chiffon, 304
cream, 304, 319
custard or soft, 303–304
fruit, 298–302
Pigeon, 5
Pike, 65
Pinwheels, 308
Pizzas, 377
Poaching:
fish and shellfish, 101–109
poultry and game birds, 38–41
Poêlés, 17
Pompano, 62
Porgy, 62
Pork:
aging, 125
cooking methods, 140, 141
cuts, 130, 133
doneness, 143
fabricating, 137, 139
grades, 125
yield grades, 124
Portion-controlled cuts, 127
Pot roasts, 182
Poultry, 1–13. *See also specific kinds of poultry*
braising, 42–48
broiling and grilling, 26–30
classifications and market forms, 4–7
composition and structure, 2–3
doneness, 8
dressings and stuffings for, 21, 49–50
handling and storage, 8
inspection and grading, 3–4
pan gravy for, 19
roasting and baking, 16–25
in sandwiches, 376
sautéing, pan-frying, deep-frying, 31–37
simmering and poaching, 38–41
trussing, 9
Pour batters, 250
Poussin, 4
Prague Powders, 195
Prawns, 77
Presentation, 366–371
Primal cuts, 127–133
Process cheeses, 425–426
Profiteroles, 310
Progressive grinding (sausages), 203
Proofing (yeast doughs), 235
Proteins, 122, 460–462
Puddings, 321–322
Puff pastry, 222, 305–309
Pullman loaves, 374
Punching (dough), 234

Q
Quail, 7
Quarters, meat, 127
Quatre épices, 201
Quick breads, 249–254
formulas, 252–254
mixing and production methods, 250–252

R
Rabbit, 151
Ratites, 7
Ravier, 369
Red mullet, 62
Red snapper, 62
Regular shortening, 221
Relishes, 396–397
Rich doughs, 232, 233, 235
Rillettes, 454
Ripening (cheese), 421
Roasts, tying, 138
Roasting:
meat, 156–166
poultry and game birds, 8, 16–25
Rock Cornish game hens, 4, 5
Rock lobsters, 76–77

Rock shrimp, 77
Rolls, 232, 236, 238, 240, 243–246
Rolled cookies, 282, 286
Rolled-in dough products, 232
Round fish, 59–64
Royal icing, 273
Rubbed dough method, 251, 293
Rye flour, 220

S
Safety, *see* Sanitation
Salads, bound, 376
Salmon, 62
Saltwater fish, 58–64
Sandwiches, 373–389
  breads for, 374–375
  fillings, 375–376
  production, 378–380
  spreads for, 375
  types, 377–378
Sanitation:
  for cold foods, 371
  garde manger, 438
  and pastry cream, 318
  in sandwich making, 378
Sardine, 62
Sauce(s):
  dessert, 327–328
  for fish, 103
Sausages, 199–210
  casings, 201–202
  categories, 199–200
  cooking, 205–206
  curing, 194–197
  equipment for, 202–203
  grind for, 203–205
  ingredients, 200–201
  smoking, 196–199, 205
Sautéing:
  fish and shellfish, 92–95
  meat, 170–177
  poultry and game birds, 31–37
  sausages, 206
Scallops, 72
Scampi, 77
Scorching (milk products), 419–420
Seafood, 81. *See also* Fish and shellfish
Searing meat, 156, 157
Seeds, in vegetarian diet, 463
Seviche (ceviche), 115
Shad, 63
Shallow poaching (fish), 101, 102
Shark, 63
Sheet cookies, 284, 287
Shellfish, *see* Fish and shellfish
Sherbets, 325
Short-dough pie crusts, 294, 295
Shortening, 217, 221–222
Shrimp, 77–78
Sides, meat, 127
Silverskin, 135
Simmering:
  fish and shellfish, 101–109
  meat, 177–182
  poultry and game birds, 38–41
  sausages, 206
Simple sandwiches, 377–379
Simple syrup, 316
Single-acting baking powders, 227
Skate, 63
Skim milk, 418
Smoked sausages, 200, 205
Smoke-roasting, 156
Smoking foods, 196–199
Snails, 81
Sodium nitrate, 194
Sodium nitrite, 194
Soft meringues, 311
Soft pies, 296, 303–304
Soft rolls, 238, 245–246
Sole, 59
Sorbet, 325
Soufflés, 323, 324
Sour cream, 419
Sous vide cooking, 177
Soy milk, 463
Specialty cheeses, 426
Specialty meats, 149–152
Spices, 195, 228
Sponge method:
  cakes, 258, 260, 269
  cookies, 281, 287, 288
  yeast products, 233
Squabs, 6
Squid, 73
Staling, 219
Starches, instant, 298
Steaming fish and shellfish, 110–114
Stewing, 177, 183
Stir-frying, 170, 171
Storage:
  breads, 236, 374, 375
  butter, 420
  cheese, 427
  fin fish, 66–67
  frozen desserts, 326
  garde manger, 438
  meat, 152–153
  poultry, 8
  shellfish, 69, 70, 72, 76–80
Straight dough method, 233
Striped bass, 63
Strong flours, 217
Stuffing, for poultry, 21, 49–50
Submersion method (fish), 101
Sucrose, 223
Sugar(s):
  cooking, 316–317
  in vegetarian diets, 465
Sundaes, 327
Suprême (chicken), 11
Surimi, 81
Sushi, 115, 117
Sweetbreads, 147, 148
Sweet dough products, 232, 233, 247
Swiss meringue, 311, 312
Swiss steak, 182
Swordfish, 63
Syrups, 316, 327

T
Tandoori chicken, 29
Tapas, 401
Tartare, fish, 115
TCM (tinted curing mix), 195
Tea, 433–434
Tea sandwiches, 377
Tempeh, 464
Tempura, 100
Teriyaki, 36
Terrines, 438, 439, 442, 445–455
  based on mousselines, 448–449
  foie gras, 453, 455
  forcemeat, 445–446
  liver, 454
  uncooked, 450–452
Textured vegetable protein (TVP), 464
Tilapia, 65
Tilefish, 63
Tinted curing mix (TCM), 195
Tofu, 463–464
Toll House cookies, 285
Tomally, 74
Tongue, 148
Triggerfish, 64
Tripe, 149
Triple-crème cheese, 422
Trout, 65
Truite au bleu, 101
Trussing poultry, 9
Tuna, 64
Tunneling, 250
Turbot, 59
Turkey, 2–3, 5, 6
  carving, 21
  cooking methods for, *see under* Poultry
  doneness, 8
  quantity service, 21
Turnovers, 307
TVP (textured vegetable protein), 464
Two-stage method (cakes), 258, 259, 268

U
Ultra-high-temperature (UHT) pasteurization, 418
Univalves, 68
Unsalted butter, 420

V
Vanilla custard sauce, 317–318
Variety meats, 146–149
Veal:
  aging, 125
  cooking methods, 140, 141
  cuts, 129, 133
  doneness, 143
  fabricating, 138
  grades, 125
Vegan diet, 460
Vegetables, in sandwiches, 376
Vegetarian diets, 421, 459–475
  menus for, 462–466
  nutrition, 460–462
  types, 460
Venison, 150
Viennoiserie, 242

W
Wahoo, 64
Water, 122
Water ices, 325
Weakfish, 64
Weak flours, 217
Wet aging, 125
Whipping cream, 418–420
Whitefish, 65
White Pekin duck, 6
White wheat flour, 219–220
Whiting, 64
Whole milk, 418
Whole wheat flour, 220
Wild duck, 7
Wraps, 377

Y
Yeast, 226
Yeast dough products, 231–247
  bread and roll formulas, 238–241
  Danish pastry and croissants, 242–243
  makeup techniques, 243–247
  mixing methods, 232–233
  steps in production of, 233–237
  types, 232
Yield grading, 124
Yogurt, 325, 419
Young doughs, 234

Z
Zander, 65

Recipe Index

A

Achiote Paste, 359
African Hot Sauce, 341
Akara (Black-Eyed Pea Fritters), 339
Almond Biscotti, 288
Angel Food Cake, 269
Apple Pie Filling, 300–302
  Canned Fruit, 300
  Dutch, 300
  Frozen Fruit, 301
  Old Fashioned, 302
Arabic Coffee, 342
Arroz con Pollo (Spanish Rice with Chicken), 47
Artichokes, Orechietti Pasta with, 332
Avocado:
  Guacamole, 399
  Sour Cream Avocado Dip, 399

B

Babaganouj, 398
Baba Ghannouj (Eggplant Dip), 344
Bacalad al Ajo Arriero, 337
Bacalao Hash, 337
Bacon:
  BLT (Bacon, Lettuce, and Tomato Sandwich), 382
  Date Rumaki, 405
  Dip, Bacon Cheese, 397
  Grilled Cheese and Bacon Sandwich, 383
Baked Chicken, 17
  Herbed, 17
  Parmesan, 17
  Rosemary, 17
Baked Cod Fillets Portugaise, 85
Baked Custard, 320
Baked Meatballs, 165
Baked Shrimp, 346
Banana Cream Pie Filling, 319
Banana Cream Pudding, 319
Barbecue Beef Ribs, 355
Barbecued Spareribs, 164
Barbecue-Style Grilled Chicken, Spicy, 29
Barciole Calabresi (Stuffed Pork Bundles), 332
Basic Bread Dressing, 50
Basic Mousseline Forcemeat, 448
Basic Pork Forcemeat, 441
Basmati Chaaval (Plain Basmati Rice), 348
Beans. *See also specific kinds of beans*
  Chile with, 188
  Croquettes, Dried Bean, 343
  Three-Bean Chili with Tostaditas, 471
  Well-Fried, 360
Beef:
  Boeuf Bourguignon, 187
  Braised, Jardinière, 185
  Broiled Strip Loin Steak Maître d'Hôtel, 168
  Burgers, 381
  Calf's Liver Lyonnaise, 176
  Chile con Carne, 188
  Chile with Beans, 188
  Home-Style All-Beef Meatloaf, 165
  Hungarian Goulash, 190
  New England Boiled Dinner, 179
  Pot Pie, 187
  Pot Roast, 185
  Ribs, Barbecue, 355
  Roast, with Gravy, 159
  Roast Rib-Eye Roll, 159
  Roast Rib of, au Jus, 159
  Roast Sirloin, 159
  Roast Strip Loin, 159
  Roast Top Round, 159
  Salisbury Steak, 165
  Sausage, 208
  Short Ribs, Braised, 186
  Short Ribs, Texas, 188
  Short Ribs Sous Vide, with Bordelaise Sauce, 182
  Shreds, Sichuan Spicy Fired, 354
  Skewers, Teriyaki, 405
  Soup, Vietnamese Noodle and, 352
  "Steaks," Grilled Chopped, with Marjoram, 169
  Stew, 187
  Stew, with Red Wine, 187
  Stroganoff, 175
  Swiss Steak, 186
  Swiss Steaks in Red Wine Sauce, 186
  Swiss Steaks in Tomato Sauce, 186
  Swiss Steaks with Sour Cream, 186
  Texas Red, 188
Bell Pepper(s):
  Crab Cakes with Roasted Pepper Rémoulade, 94
Biscotti, Almond, 288
Biscuits, 252
  Buttermilk, 252
  Cheese, 252
  Currant, 252
  Herb, 252
Black-Eyed Pea Fritters, 339
Le Blanc de Poisson Belle Mouginoise (Fillet of Fish Mouginoise), 336
Blancmange, English Style, 321
Blanquette of Veal, 180
Blitz Puff Pastry, 307
Blondies (Butterscotch Brownies), 287
Blueberry Muffins, 253
Blueberry Pie Filling (Frozen Fruit), 301
Blue Cheese Dip, 397
Boar, Smoke-Roasted Shoulder of, 163
Boeuf Bourguignon, 187
Boiled Dinner, New England, 179
"Boiled" Shellfish (Lobster, Crab, Shrimp), 105
Boudin Blanc (White Sausage), 210
Braised Beef Jardinière, 185
Braised Lamb Shanks, 186
Braised Lamb Shoulder, 185
Braised Oxtails, 186
Braised Red Cabbage and Spaetzle, 334
Braised Short Ribs, 186
Bran Muffins, 253
Bratwurst, Fresh, 209
Bread:
  Biscuits, 252
  Brioche, 241
  Bruschetta, 412
  Doughnuts, Raised, 241
  Flat, Whole Wheat, 342
  Focaccia, 240
  French, 239
  Hard Rolls, 238
  Muffins, 253
  Naan, 350
  Rye Bread and Rolls, 240
  Soft Rolls, 238
  Sweet Roll Dough, 241
  White Pan, 239
  Whole Wheat, 239
Bread and Butter Pudding, 322
Breaded Pork Cutlets, 172
Breaded Veal Cutlets, 172
Brioche, 241
Broiled Chicken, 27
  Deviled (Poulet à la Diable), 27
  Quantity Method, 27
Broiled Fish:
  Fillets or Steaks, with Garlic Butter, 90
  Steaks, Maître d'Hôtel, 87
Broiled Lamb Chops, 168
Broiled Rock Cornish Game Hen, 27
Broiled Scallops, 90
Broiled Shrimp, Scampi Style, 90
Broiled Strip Loin Steak Maître d'Hôtel, 168
Broiled Tarragon Chicken, 27
Brownies, 287
Brown Lamb Stew, 187
Brown Sugar Cookies, Rolled, 286
Brown Sugar Nut Cookies, 285
Brown Veal:
  Stew, 187
  with White Wine, 187
Bruschetta, 412
  with Parmesan Cheese, 412
  with Tomato and Basil, 412
  with White Beans and Prosciutto, 412
Bulgur Pilaf, Winter Vegetable Gratin with Feta Cheese and, 474
Bumbu Sate (Peanut Sauce), 351
Burgers:
  Beef, 381
  California, 381
Buttercream, 271–272
  Chocolate, 272
  Coffee, 272
  Decorator's, 271
  French, 272
  Meringue-Type, 271
  Simple, 271
Buttermilk Biscuits, 252
Butterscotch:
  Brownies (Blondies), 287
  Cream Pie Filling, 319
  Pudding, 319

C

Cabbage:
  Braised Red, and Spaetzle, 334
  Traditional Napa, 355
Cake:
  Angel Food, 269
  Chocolate Angel Food, 269
  Chocolate Genoise, 269
  Devil's Food, 268
  Jelly Roll, 269
  Pound, Chocolate, 267
  Pound, Marble, 267
  Pound, Old-Fashioned, 267
  Pound, Raisin, 267
  Sponge, (Genoise), 269
  Sponge or Jelly Roll, 269
  White, 268
  Yellow, 268
  Yellow Butter, 266
Calamari, Deep-Fried, with Spicy Tomato Sauce and Aïoli, 99
Calf's Liver Lyonnaise, 176
California Burger, 381
California Cheeseburger, 381
California Cheeseburger Deluxe, 381
Capon, Roast, 20
  with Cream Gravy, 20
Caramel:
  Crème, 320
  Sauce, 328
  Sauce, Clear, 328
  Sauce, Hot, 328
Carnitas, 181
Catfish, Pan-Fried with Shrimp Etouffée, 95
Cauliflower Pakoras, 414
Ceviche Mixto (Shellfish Ceviche), 356
Chana Dal (Yellow Dal), 350
Cheddar Cheese Dip, 397
Cheese. *See also specific kinds of cheese*
  Biscuits, 252
  Dip, Bacon Cheese, 397
  Dip, Cheese and Chile, 397
  Dip, Garlic Cheese, 397
  Empanadas with Roasted Poblanos and, 413
  Sandwich, Grilled Cheese, 383
  Sandwich, Grilled Cheese and Bacon, 383
  Straws, 428
  Swiss Fondue, 429
  Tamales, Spinach, 361
  Wafers, 428
  Welsh Rabbit, 428
Cheeseburgers, 381
Cherry Pie Filling:
  Canned Fruit, 300
  Frozen Fruit, 301
Chicken:
  Arroz con Pollo, 47
  Baked, 17
  Baked, Herbed, 17
  Baked, Parmesan, 17
  Baked, Rosemary, 17
  Bercy, 44
  Boudin Blanc (White Sausage), 210
  Breasts, Parmesan, 37
  Broiled, 27
  Broiled, Deviled, 27
  Broiled, Quantity Method, 27
  Broiled, Tarragon, 27
  Chasseur, 44
  Coq au Vin, 46
  Deep-Fried, 34
  Forcemeat I, 441
  Forcemeat II, 441
  Fricassée, 43
  Fricassée à l'Indienne, 43
  Fricassée with Tarragon, 43
  Fried, Country-Style, 32
  Fried, Maryland, 34
  Fried Breast Strips, 34
  Grilled, Marinated in Yogurt and Spices, 29
  Grilled, Oriental Style, 29
  Grilled, Southwestern, 29
  Grilled, Spicy Barbecue-Style, 29
  Grilled, with Garlic and Ginger, 29
  Hongroise, 44
  Jamaican Jerk, 357
  Jerk, 30
  Legs, Stuffed, with Pecan Butter, 23
  Mousseline, Terrine of Vegetables with, 449
  Paillard, with Grilled Vegetables, 28
  Pan-Fried, 32
  Paprika, 45
  Poached Breast, Florentine, 39
  Poached Breast, Princesse, 39
  Poêlé, 25
  Portugaise, 44
  Pot Pie, 40
  Poulet à la Diable, 27
  Rillettes of, 456
  Roast (large), 20
  Roast, Herbed, 18
  Roast, with Cream Gravy, 18, 20
  Roast, with Gravy, 18
  Roast, with Natural Gravy, 18
  Satay, 351, 404
  Sautéed Boneless Breast of, with Mushroom Sauce, 33
  Smoked, 199
  Spanish Rice with, 47
  Tagine of Preserved Lemon, Olives, and, 339
  Teriyaki, 36
Chicken Liver:
  Rumaki, 404
Chicken Satay, 351
Chicken Sauté Marengo, 335
Chickpea(s):
  Dip, 398
  Falafel, 475
Chile, 188
  with Beans, 188
  con Carne, 188
  Game, 188
Chile peppers:
  Harissa, 340
Chili, Three-Bean, with Tostaditas, 471
Chimichurri Sauce, 357
Chirashizushi (Scatter Sushi), 116
Chocolate:
  Angel Food Cake, 269
  Buttercream, 272

Cookies, Rolled, 286
Cream Pie Filling, 319
Ganache, 273
Genoise, 269
Mousse, 325
Pastry Cream, 319
Pound Cake, 267
Pudding I, 319
Pudding II, 319
Sauce, 328
Soufflé, 324
Chocolate Chip Cookies, 285
Chutney, Green, 347
Clams:
Casino, 91
Fried, 96
Zuppa di Frutti di Mare, 109
Zuppa di Vongole, 109
Clear Caramel Sauce, 328
Club Sandwich, 382
Coconut:
Cream Pie Filling, 319
Custard Pie Filling, 303
Pudding, 319
Cod:
Baked Fillets Portugaise, 85
Cakes, 98
Coffee:
Arabic, 342
Buttercream, 272
Pastry Cream, 319
Soufflé, 324
Coffee Cake, Crumb, 253
Common Meringue, 312
Cooked Tomato Sauce, 360
Cookies:
Brown Sugar Nut, 285
Chocolate Chip, 285
Oatmeal Raisin, 285
Peanut Butter, 287
Rolled Brown Sugar, 286
Rolled Chocolate, 286
Shortbread, 286
Sugar, 286
Coq au Vin, 46
Cornbread Dressing, 50
Corned Beef:
New England Boiled Dinner, 179
Cornish Hen, Broiled, 27
Cornish Hen, Grilled Spiced, 28
Corn Muffins, 253
Corn Tortillas, 358
Country-Style Fried Chicken, 32
Country Terrine, 446
Court Bouillon, 104
Couscous, Grilled Spiced Squab with Fig Compote and, 28
Crab(s):
"Boiled," 105
Cakes, with Roasted Pepper Rémoulade, 94
Soft-Shell, Sautéed, 93
Cracked Wheat and Herb Salad, 341
Cream Cheese Icing, 271
Cream Gravy:
Roast Capon or Turkey with, 20
Roast Chicken with, 18, 20
Crème Anglaise (Vanilla Custard Sauce), 318
Crème Caramel, 320
Crêpes, 407
Crêpinettes, 207
Crispy Duck, 41
Croque Monsieur, 383
Croquetas de Jamón (Serrano Ham Fritters), 336
Crumb Coffee Cake, 253
Cucumber(s):
Cups, with Dilled Shrimp Salad, 406
Roll (Kappa-Maki), 116
Currant Biscuits, 252
Curry:
Eggplant, 340
Vegan Vegetable and Split Pea, 467
Yellow Split Pea and Vegetable, with Spiced Rice and Cucumber Raita, 467
Custard:
Baked, 320
Coconut Custard Pie Filling, 303
Crème Anglaise (Vanilla Custard Sauce), 318
Pie Filling, 303

D

Date(s):
Rumaki, 405
Stuffed with Gorgonzola, 405
Stuffed with Manchego Cheese, 405
Decorator's Buttercream, 271
Deep-Fried Calamari with Spicy Tomato Sauce and Aïoli, 99
Deep-Fried Chicken, 34
Desserts. *See also* Cake; Cookies; Pastry; Pie crusts; Pie Filling; Pudding
Baked Custard, 320
Blancmange, English Style, 321
Blitz Puff Pastry, 307
Chocolate Mousse, 325
Chocolate Soufflé, 324
Coffee Soufflé, 324
Crème Caramel, 320
Éclair Paste or Pâte à Choux, 310
Italian Meringue, 312
Lemon Soufflé, 324
Liqueur Soufflé, 324
Meringue, 312
Puff Pastry, 305
Swiss Meringue, 312
Vanilla Soufflé, 324
Dessert Crêpes, 407
Deviled Chicken, Broiled, 27
Deviled Eggs, 409
Devil's Food Cake, 268
Dip:
Bacon Cheese, 397
Blue Cheese, 397
Cheddar Cheese, 397
Cheese and Chile, 397
Garlic Cheese, 397
Guacamole, 399
Hummus (Chickpea), 398
Parmesan, 399
Red Pepper and Walnut, 345
Romesco, 398
Sour Cream Avocado, 399
Dough, Sweet Roll, 241
Doughnuts, Raised, 241
Dressing, 50
Basic Bread, 50
Chestnut, 50
Cornbread, 50
Giblet, 50
Mushroom, 50
Sausage, 50
Tahini Yogurt, 385
Dried Bean Croquettes, 343
Dua Chua (Pickled Carrot and Daikon Salad), 352
Duck:
Breast of, Tangerine-Marinated, 35
Confit, 48
Crispy, 41
Forcemeat, 441
Red-Cooked, 354
Rillettes of, 456
Roast Duckling à l'Orange, 22
Roast Duckling Bohemian Style, 22
Sausage, 209
Smoked, 199
Tea-Smoked, 41
Terrine, 446
Dutch Apple Pie Filling, 300

E

Éclair Paste or Pâte à Choux, 310
Eggs. *See also* Soufflés
Deviled, 409
Tea Leaf, 355
Eggplant:
Babaganouj, 398
Curry, 340
Dengaku, Red Rice, Spinach with Tofu Dressing, and, 472
Dip, 344
Lasagne, Zucchini and, 469
Eggplant Curry, 340
Egg Rolls, 410–411
Empanadas, 413
Enchiladas, Pinto Bean, 470

F

Falafel, 343, 385, 475
Fattoush (Toasted Bread Salad), 345
Fig Compote, Grilled Spiced Squab with Couscous and, 28
Fillet(s) of Fish:
Broiled, with Garlic Butter, 90
Doré, 93
Fried Breaded, 96
Mouginoise, 336
Sole Meunière, 93
Finger Sushi (Nigirizushi), 116
Finnan Haddie, Rillettes of, 457
Fish. *See also specific types of fish*
Broiled Fillets or Steaks, with Garlic Butter, 90
Broiled Steaks, Maître d'Hôtel, 87
and Chips, 97
Court Bouillon with White Wine, 104
Fillets of, Doré, 93
Fisherman's Platter, 97
Fried Breaded Fillets, 96
Glazed Poached, 107
Gravlax, 197
Grilled Tilapia, 340
Mouginoise, Fillet of, 336
Ordinary Court Bouillon for, 104
Poached, Bonne Femme, 107
Poached, Dugléré, 107
Poached, Florentine, 107
Poached, Mornay, 107
Poached, Steaks, 105
Poached, Whole, 105
Sauté Amandine, 93
Sauté Grenobloise, 93
Sushi, 116
Zuppa di Pesce, 109
Fisherman's Platter, 97
Flaky Pie Dough, 294
Flat Bread, Whole Wheat, 342
Focaccia, 240
Olive, 240
Rosemary, 240
Foie Gras:
Terrine of, 455
Veal and Ham Terrine with, 446
Fondue, Swiss, 429
Forcemeat, 441. *See also* Terrine
Duck, 441
Game, 441
Mousseline, 448
Pheasant, 441
Pork, Basic, 441
Veal, 441
French Bread, 239
French Buttercream, 272
French Garlic Sausage, 208
Fresh Bratwurst, 209
Fresh Strawberry Pie Filling, 301
Fresh Tomato Sauce, 333
Fricassée:
Chicken, 43
Chicken, à l'Indienne, 43
Chicken, with Tarragon, 43
Pork, 43
of Turkey Wings, 43
Veal, 43
Fried Breaded Fish Fillets, 96
Fried Breaded Scallops, 96
Fried Breaded Shrimp, 96
Fried Chicken, 32, 34
Fried Chicken Maryland, 34
Fried Oysters or Clams, 96
Frijoles Refritos (Well-Fried Beans), 360
Fritters:
Black-Eyed Pea, 339
Serrano Ham, 336
Fruit:
-Glazed Ham, 164
Pie Filling, 300–302

G

Gambas al Ajillo (Sizzling Garlic Shrimp), 337
Game. *See also specific types of game*
Chile, 188
Forcemeat, 441
Terrine, 446
Ganache, Chocolate, 273
Garam Masala (Ground Spice Mixture), 347
Garithes Saganaki (Baked Shrimp), 346
Garlic Dip, Cheese, 397
Genoise (Sponge Cake), 269
Chocolate, 269
Giblet Dressing, 50
Giblet Gravy, Roast Turkey with, 20
Glazed Ham with Cider Sauce, 164
Glazed Poached Fish, 107
Goose:
Rillettes of, 456
Roast, 22
Gorgonzola, Dates Stuffed with, 405
Gougère Puffs, Miniature, 409
Graham Cracker Crust, 295
Gratin, Winter Vegetable, with Feta Cheese and Bulgur Pilaf, 474
Gravlax, 197
Gravy:
Cream, Roast Chicken with, 18, 20
Giblet, Roast Turkey with, 20
Natural, Roast Chicken with, 18
Roast Beef, 160
Green Chutney, 347
Grilled Chicken:
Barbecue-Style, Spicy, 29
with Garlic and Ginger, 29
Marinated in Yogurt and Spices, 29
Oriental Style, 29
Southwestern, 29
Grilled Chopped Beef "Steaks" with Marjoram, 169
Grilled Chopped Lamb "Steaks" with Rosemary and Pine Nuts, 169
Grilled Mahi-Mahi with Fruit Salsa, 89
Grilled Sandwich:
Cheese, 383
Cheese and Bacon, 383
Ham and Swiss, 383
Portobello and Boursin, 387
Portobello and Tomato, 387
Vegetable, with Goat Cheese and Sun-Dried Tomatoes, 386
Grilled Spiced Cornish Hen, 28
Grilled Spiced Squab with Couscous and Fig Compote, 28
Grilled Tilapia, 340
Grilled Tuna with Balsamic Vinaigrette and Sweet-Sour Baby Onions, 88
Ground Spice Mixture, 347
Guacamole, 399

H

Haddock, Rillettes of, 457
Ham:
with Brown Cider Sauce, 164
Fruit-Glazed, 164
Glazed, with Cider Sauce, 164
Prosciutto and Melon Balls, 402
Sandwich, Grilled Ham and Swiss, 383
Serrano Ham Fritters, 336
Terrine, Veal and, 446
Terrine, Veal and, with Foie Gras, 446
Hard Rolls, 238
Harissa, 340
Hash, Bacalao, 337
Herb Biscuits, 252
Herbed Lamb Sausage, 209
Herbed Mousseline, 448
Home-Style All-Beef Meatloaf, 165
Home-Style Meatloaf, 165
Hors d'oeuvres. *See also* Dip
Beef Teriyaki Skewers, 405
Bruschetta, 412
Bruschetta with Parmesan Cheese, 412
Bruschetta with Tomato and Basil, 412
Bruschetta with White Beans and Prosciutto, 412
Cauliflower Pakoras, 414
Chicken Satay, 404
Crêpes, 407
Cucumber Cups with Dilled Shrimp Salad, 406
Date Rumaki, 405
Dates Stuffed with Gorgonzola, 405
Dates Stuffed with Manchego Cheese, 405
Dessert Crêpes, 407
Deviled Eggs, 409
Dips, 397–399
Egg Rolls, 410–411
Empanadas with Roasted Poblanos and Cheese, 413
Miniature Gougère Puffs, 409
Mushrooms Stuffed with Tapenade, 408
Prosciutto and Melon Balls, 402
Rumaki, 404
Smoked Trout Purses, 406
Spiced Shrimp with Smoked Paprika, 408
Spicy Meat Empanadas, 413
Spinach Boreks, 403
Spring Rolls, 410–411
Hot and Sour Soup, 353
Hot Caramel Sauce, 328
Hot Chocolate, Mexican, 361
Hot Italian Sausage, 208
Hot Sauce, African, 341
Hummus (Chickpea Dip), 398
Hungarian Goulash (Veal, Beef, or Pork), 190

I

Icing:
Chocolate Ganache, 273
Coffee Buttercream, 272
Cream Cheese, 271
Decorator's Buttercream, 271
French Buttercream, 272
Meringue-Type Buttercream, 271
Simple Buttercream, 271
Irish Lamb Stew, 180
Italian Meringue, 312

Italian Sausage, 208
Italian-Style Meatloaf, 165

J
Jamaican Jerk Chicken, 357
Jelly Roll, 269
Jerk Chicken, 30
Jerk Spice Mixture, 30
Jus Lié, 160

K
Kalbi-Kui (Barbecue Beef Ribs), 355
Kappa-Maki (Cucumber Roll), 116
Kartoffelsuppe mit Miesmuscheln und Lauch (Potato Soup with Mussels and Leeks), 333
Kheere ka Raita (Yogurt with Cucumber and Mint), 348
Khobz (Whole Wheat Flat Bread), 342
Khubz/Khoubiz (Arabic Flat Bread), 344
Kimchi (Traditional Napa Cabbage), 355

L
Lamb:
- Chops, Broiled, 168
- Navarin of, 187
- Rack of, aux Primeurs (with Spring Vegetables), 162
- Rack of, Persillé, 162
- Rack of, Roast, 162
- Sausage, 209
- Sausage, Herbed, 209
- Shanks, Braised, 186
- Shoulder, Braised, 185
- Skewered, Vegetables and, 346
- "Steaks," Grilled Chopped, with Rosemary and Pine Nuts, 169
- Stew, Brown Lamb, 187
- Stew, Irish, 180

Lasagne, Zucchini and Eggplant, 469
Leeks, Potato Soup with Mussels and, 333
Lemon:
- Pie Filling, 319
- Soufflé, 324

Liqueur Soufflé, 324
Lobster, "Boiled," 105

M
Mackerel, en Papillote, 113
Mahi-Mahi, Grilled, with Fruit Salsa, 89
Manchego Cheese, Dates Stuffed with, 405
Marble Pound Cake, 267
Mchuzi wa Biringani (Eggplant Curry), 340
Mealy Pie Dough, 294
Meat, *see specific meats*
Meatballs, Baked, 165
Meat Empanadas, Spicy, 413
Meatloaf, 165
Melon Balls, Prosciutto and, 402
Meringue, 312
- Common, 312
- Italian, 312
- Swiss, 312

Meringue-Type Buttercream, 271
Mexican Hot Chocolate, 361
Mild Italian Sausage, 208
Miniature Gougère Puffs, 409
Mole Verde con Hierbas (Pork Herbed Green Mole), 358
Moules Marinière (Steamed Mussels), 112
Mousse, Chocolate, 325
Mousseline:
- Chicken, Terrine of Vegetables with, 449
- Forcemeat, Basic, 448
- Herbed, 448

Moutabal (Eggplant Dip), 344
Muffins, 253
- Blueberry, 253
- Bran, 253
- Corn, 253
- Date Nut, 253
- Plain, 253
- Raisin Spice, 253
- Whole Wheat, 253

Muhammara (Red Pepper and Walnut Dip), 345
Mushroom(s):
- Dressing, 50
- Portobello and Boursin Sandwich, Grilled, 387
- Portobello and Tomato Sandwich, Grilled, 387
- Sauce, Sautéed Boneless Breast of Chicken with, 33
- Stuffed with Tapenade, 408

Mussels:
- in Cream, 112
- Potato Soup with Leeks and, 333
- Steamed, 112
- Steamed (without wine), 112
- Zuppa di Cozze, 109
- Zuppa di Frutti di Mare, 109

N
Naan, 350
Natural Gravy, Roast Chicken with, 18
Navarin of Lamb (Brown Lamb Stew), 187
New England Boiled Dinner, 179
Nigirizushi (Finger Sushi), 116
Noodle Bowl with Stir-Fried Vegetables, Tofu, and Peanuts, 468
Noodle Soup, Vietnamese Beef and, 352
Nut(s):
- Brown Sugar Nut Cookies, 285
- Chestnut Dressing, 50
- Date Nut Muffins, 253
- Noodle Bowl with Stir-Fried Vegetables, Tofu, and Peanuts, 468
- Peanut Sauce, 351
- Pecan Pie Filling, 303
- Red Pepper and Walnut Dip, 345

O
Oatmeal Raisin Cookies, 285
Oerchietti con Carciofi (Orechietti Pasta with Artichokes), 332
Old-Fashioned Apple Pie Filling, 302
Old-Fashioned Pound Cake, 267
Olive Focaccia, 240
Onions, Pickled Red, 360
Ordinary Court Bouillon for Fish, 104
Orechietti Pasta with Artichokes, 332
Oriental Style Grilled Chicken, 29
Osso Buco, 189
Oxtails, Braised, 186
Oysters:
- Casino, 91
- Fried, 96

P
Paella Valenciana, 338
Pancakes, Vietnamese Vegetable, 473
Pan-Fried Catfish with Shrimp Etouffée, 95
Pan-Fried Chicken, 32
Paprika Chicken, 45
Parmesan Dip, 399
Pasta:
- Lasagne, Zucchini and Eggplant, 469
- Noodle Bowl with Stir-Fried Vegetables, Tofu, and Peanuts, 468
- Orechietti, with Artichokes, 332

Pastry:
- Blitz Puff, 307
- Pâté (Pâté à Pâté), 442
- Puff, 305

Pastry Cream, 319
- Chocolate, 319
- Coffee, 319
- Vanilla, 319

Pâté:
- à Choux, 310
- Pastry (Pâté à Pâté), 442

Pavo con Salsa de Achiote a al Yucataneca (Yucatán-Style Turkey in Achiote Sauce), 359
Pea(s), *see* Split Pea(s)
Peach Pie Filling, 300
Peanut Butter Cookies, 287
Peanut Sauce, 351
Pecan Pie Filling, 303
Persillade, 162
Pheasant Forcemeat, 441
Pho Bo (Vietnamese Beef and Noodle Soup), 352
Picadillo, 181
Pickled Carrot and Daikon Salad, 352
Pickled Red Onions, 360
Pico de Gallo, 359
Pie crusts, 294, 295
- Flaky Dough, 294
- Graham Cracker, 295
- Mealy Dough, 294
- Short Dough, 295

Pie Filling:
- Apple, Dutch, 300
- Banana Cream, 319
- Blueberry (Frozen Fruit), 301
- Butterscotch Cream, 319
- Cherry (Canned Fruit), 300
- Cherry (Frozen Fruit), 301
- Chocolate Cream I, 319
- Chocolate Cream II, 319
- Coconut Cream, 319
- Coconut Custard, 303
- Custard, 303
- Lemon, 319
- Peach, 300
- Pecan, 303
- Pineapple, 300
- Pumpkin, 304
- Squash, 304
- Strawberry, Fresh, 301
- Sweet Potato, 304
- Vanilla Cream, 319

Pilaf, Bulgur, Winter Vegetable Gratin with Feta Cheese and, 474
Pineapple Pie Filling, 300
Pinto Bean Enchiladas, 470
Pita:
- Falafel and Roasted Vegetables in, 385
- Traditional Falafel in, 385

Pizza Margherita, 388
Pizza Marinara, 388
Plain Basmati Rice, 348
Plain Muffins, 253
Poached Chicken Breast Florentine, 39
Poached Chicken Breast Princesse, 39
Poached Fillets of Sole in White Wine Sauce (Vin Blanc), 106
Poached Fish, 105, 107
- Dugléré, 107
- Florentine, 107
- Mornay, 107
- Steaks, 105
- Whole, 105

Poblanos, Empanadas with Cheese and, 413
Podina Chatni (Green Chutney), 347
Pork. *See also* Ham; Sausage
- Barbecued Spareribs, 164
- Bratwurst, Fresh, 209
- Chops, Charcutière, 174
- Chops, Piquante, 174
- Chops, Robert, 174
- Country Terrine, 446
- Cutlets, Breaded, 172
- Forcemeat, Basic, 441
- Fricassée, 43
- Herbed Green Mole, 358
- Hungarian Goulash, 190
- Loin, Roast, with Sage and Apples, 161
- Picadillo, 181
- Picadillo, Shortcut, 181
- Rillettes of, 456
- Shoulder, Smoke-Roasted, 163
- Shredded (Carnitas), 181
- Stuffed Pork Bundles, 332
- Tenderloin, in a Dark Bread Crust, 334
- Vindaloo, 349

Portobello Sandwich, Grilled:
- Boursin and, 387
- Tomato and, 387

Potato Soup with Mussels and Leeks, 333
Pot Pie:
- Beef, 187
- Chicken or Turkey, 40

Poulet à la Diable, 27
Poulet Sauté Marengo (Chicken Sauté Marengo), 335
Pound Cake, 267
- Chocolate, 267
- Marble, 267
- Old-Fashioned, 267
- Raisin, 267

Prosciutto and Melon Balls, 402
Pudding:
- Banana Cream, 319
- Blancmange, English Style, 321
- Bread and Butter, 322
- Butterscotch, 319
- Chocolate I, 319
- Chocolate II, 319
- Coconut, 319
- Raisin Rice, 322
- Rice, 322
- Vanilla, 319

Puff Pastry, 305
- Blitz, 307

Pumpkin Pie Filling, 304
Pungent and Hot Soup, 353

Q
Qahwah (Arabic Coffee), 342
Quatre Épices, 207

R
Rabbit:
- with Mustard, 190
- Rillettes of, 456
- Roast Loin of, with Risotto, 166
- Terrine, 446

Rack of Lamb:
- aux Primeurs (with Spring Vegetables), 162
- Persillé, 162

Raised Doughnuts, 241
Raisin:
- Pound Cake, 267
- Raisin Spice Muffins, 253
- Rice Pudding, 322

Red-Cooked Duck, 354
Red Pepper and Walnut Dip, 345
Red Rice, Spinach with Tofu Dressing, and Eggplant Dengaku, 472
Reuben Sandwich, 382
Rice:
- Arroz con Pollo (Spanish Rice with Chicken), 47
- Plain Basmati, 348
- Pudding, 322
- Pudding, Raisin, 322
- Red, Spinach with Tofu Dressing, and Eggplant Dengaku, 472
- Spanish, with Chicken, 47
- Sushi, 116

Rillettes, 456, 457
- of Pork, 456
- of Salmon, Haddock, or Finnan Haddie, 457

Risotto, Roast Loin of Rabbit with, 166
Roast Beef Gravy, 160
Roast Beef with Gravy, 159
Roast Capon, 20
Roast Chicken, 18, 20
- with Cream Gravy, 20
- with Gravy, 18
- large, 20
- with Natural Gravy, 18

Roast Duckling à l'Orange, 22
Roast Duckling Bohemian Style, 22
Roasted Pepper Rémoulade, Crab Cakes with, 94
Roast Goose, 22
Roast Herbed Chicken, 18
Roast Loin of Pork with Sage and Apples, 161
Roast Loin of Rabbit with Risotto, 166
Roast Loin or Rack of Veal with Sage and Apples, 161
Roast Rack of Lamb, 162
Roast Rib-Eye Roll, 159
Roast Rib of Beef au Jus, 159
Roast Sirloin, 159
Roast Strip Loin, 159
Roast Top Round, 159
Roast Turkey:
- with Cream Gravy, 20
- with Giblet Gravy, 20

Rock Cornish Game Hen, Broiled, 27
Rolls:
- Hard, 238
- Rye, 240
- Soft, 238
- Sweet Roll Dough, 241

Rolled Brown Sugar Cookies, 286
Rolled Chocolate Cookies, 286
Romesco, 398
Rosemary Focaccia, 240
Rotkraut und Spätzle (Braised Red Cabbage and Spaetzle), 334
Rumaki, 404
Rye Bread and Rolls, 240

S
Salad:
- Pickled Carrot and Daikon, 352
- Toasted Bread, 345

Salisbury Steak, 165
Salmon:
- à la Nage, 108
- Cakes, 98
- Gravlax, 197
- Rillettes of, 457
- Smoked, 198
- Tartare, 118
- Tartare of Sea Bass and, 118

Salsa de Jitomate Cocida (Cooked Tomato Sauce), 360
Saltimbocca alla Romana, 191
Sambal Kacang (Peanut Sauce), 351
Sandwich(es):
- Bacon, Lettuce, and Tomato, 382
- California Burger, 381
- California Cheeseburger, 381
- California Cheeseburger Deluxe, 381
- Cheeseburger, Plain, 381
- Cheeseburger, with Bacon, 381
- Club, 382
- Croque Monsieur, 383
- Falafel and Roasted Vegetables in Pita, 385

Grilled Cheese, 383
Grilled Cheese and Bacon, 383
Grilled Ham and Swiss, 383
Grilled Portobello and Boursin, 387
Grilled Portobello and Tomato, 387
Grilled Vegetable, with Goat Cheese and Sun-Dried Tomatoes, 386
Reuben, 382
Submarine, 381
Traditional Falafel in Pita, 385
Turkey BLT Wrap, 384
Vegetarian Wrap with Mixed Beans, 384
Satay Ayam (Chicken Satay), 351
Sauce:
African Hot Sauce, 341
Caramel, 328
Caramel, Clear, 328
Caramel, Hot, 328
Chimichurri, 357
Chocolate, 328
Crème Anglaise (Vanilla Custard), 318
Jus Lié, 160
Mushroom, Sautéed Boneless Breast of Chicken with, 33
Peanut, 351
Tamarind, 347
Tomato, Cooked, 360
Tomato, Fresh, 333
Vanilla Custard (Crème Anglaise), 318
Sausage:
Beef, 208
Boudin Blanc (White Sausage), 210
Crêpinettes, 207
Dressing, 50
Duck, 209
French Garlic, 208
Hot Italian, 208
Lamb, 209
Lamb, Herbed, 209
Mild Italian, 208
Pork, 207
Spicy Garlic, 208
Toulouse, 207
Veal, 208
Venison, 208
Sautéed Boneless Breast of Chicken with Mushroom Sauce, 33
Sautéed Scallops with Tomato, Garlic, and Parsley, 94
Sautéed Shrimp, 94
Sautéed Soft-Shell Crabs, 93
Sautéed Veal Sweetbreads with Shiitake Mushrooms and Port Wine Sauce, 177
Scallop(s):
à la Nage, 108
Broiled, 90
Fried Breaded, 96
Sautéed, with Tomato, Garlic, and Parsley, 94
Seviche, 119
Scatter Sushi (Chirashizushi), 116
Schnitzel à la Holstein, 172
Schweinelendchen im Schwarzbratmantel (Port Tenderloin in a Dark Bread Crust), 334
Sea Bass:
Sous Vide, with Asian Sweet-and-Sour Sauce, 114
Tartare of Salmon and, 118
Seafood. *See also* Fish; Shellfish
à la Nage, 107
Curry, 114
Mousseline, Sole Poupiettes with, 107
Newburg, 114
Terrine, with Vegetables, 449
Zuppa di Pesce, 109
Serrano Ham Fritters, 336
Seviche, Scallop, 119
Shellfish. *See also specific shellfish*
"Boiled," 105
Ceviche, 356
Zuppa di Frutti di Mare, 109
Zuppa di Pesce, 109
Shortbread Cookies, 286
Shortcut Picadillo, 181
Short Dough, 295
Shredded Pork (Carnitas), 181
Shrimp:
à la Nage, 108
Baked, 346
"Boiled," 105
Brochettes, 90
Broiled, Scampi Style, 90
Etouffée, Pan-Fried Catfish with, 95
Fried Breaded, 96
Sautéed, 94
Sizzling Garlic, 337
Spiced, with Smoked Paprika, 408
Tempura, 100
Zuppa di Frutti di Mare, 109
Sichuan Spicy Fired Beef Shreds, 354
Simple Buttercream, 271
Sis Kebap (Skewered Lamb and Vegetables), 346
Sizzling Garlic Shrimp, 337
Skewered Lamb and Vegetables, 346
Smoked Chicken, 199
Smoked Duck, 199
Smoked Salmon, 198
Smoked Trout, 198
Smoked Trout Purses, 406
Smoked Turkey, 199
Smoke-Roasted Pork Shoulder, 163
Smoke-Roasted Shoulder of Boar, 163
Soft Rolls, 238
Soft-Shell Crabs, Sautéed, 93
Sole:
Fillets of, Meunière, 93
Poupiettes, with Seafood Mousseline, 107
Vin Blanc (Poached Fillets of Sole in White Wine Sauce), 106
Soufflés, 324
Coffee, 324
Lemon, 324
Liqueur, 324
Vanilla, 324
Soup:
Potato, with Mussels and Leeks, 333
Pungent and Hot, 353
Vietnamese Beef and Noodle, 352
Sour Cream Avocado Dip, 399
Southwestern Grilled Chicken, 29
Spaetzle:
Braised Red Cabbage and, 334
Spanish Rice with Chicken, 47
Spareribs, Barbecued, 164
Spätzle, 335
Spiced Shrimp with Smoked Paprika, 408
Spice mixtures:
Ground Spice, 347
Jerk, 30
Quatre Épices, 207
Quatre Épices II, 207
Spice Rub, 163
Spicy Barbecue-Style Grilled Chicken, 29
Spicy Garlic Sausage, 208
Spicy Meat Empanadas, 413
Spinach:
Boreks, 403
Tamales, Cheese and, 361
with Tofu Dressing, Red Rice, Eggplant Dengaku and, 472
Split Pea(s):
Curry, Vegan Vegetable and, 467
Yellow, and Vegetable Curry with Spiced Rice and Cucumber Raita, 467
Sponge Cake (Genoise), 269
Chocolate Genoise, 269
Sponge or Jelly Roll, 269
Sponge Roll, 269
Spring Rolls, 410–411
Spring Vegetables, Rack of Lamb aux Primeurs, 162
Squab, Grilled Spiced, with Couscous and Fig Compote, 28
Squash Pie Filling, 304
Squid:
Deep-Fried Calamari with Spicy Tomato Sauce and Aïoli, 99
Zuppa di Frutti di Mare, 109
Steamed Mussels (without wine), 112
Stew:
Beef, 187
Beef, with Red Wine, 187
Lamb, Brown, 187
Lamb, Irish, 180
Veal, Brown, 187
Stir-Fry Vegetables, Noodle Bowl with Tofu, Peanuts and, 468
Strawberry Pie Filling, Fresh, 301
Stuffed Chicken Legs with Pecan Butter, 23
Stuffed Pork Bundles, 332
Submarine Sandwich, 381
Sugar Cookies, 286
Sushi, 116
Sushi Rice, 116
Sweet Potato Pie Filling, 304
Sweet Roll Dough, 241
Swiss Fondue, 429
Swiss Meringue, 312
Swiss Steak, 186
in Red Wine Sauce, 186
with Sour Cream, 186
in Tomato Sauce, 186

T

Tabbouleh (Cracked Wheat and Herb Salad), 341
Tagine of Chicken, Preserved Lemon, and Olives, 339
Tahini:
Taratour bi, 343
Yogurt Dressing, 385
Tamales de Espinaca con Queso (Spinach and Cheese Tamales), 361
Tamarind Sauce, 347
Tangerine-Marinated Breast of Duck, 35
Tapenade, Mushrooms Stuffed with, 408
Taratour bi Tahini, 343
Tarragon Chicken, Broiled, 27
Tartare of Salmon and Sea Bass, 118
Tea Leaf Eggs, 355
Tea-Smoked Duck, 41
Tekka-Maki (Tuna Roll), 116
Tempura, Shrimp and Vegetable, 100
Terrine:
Country, 446
Duck, 446
of Foie Gras, 455
Game, 446
Rabbit, 446
Seafood, with Vegetables, 449
Tricolor Vegetable, 452
Veal and Ham, 446
Veal and Ham, with Foie Gras, 446
Veal and Tongue, 446
of Vegetables, with Chicken Mousseline, 449
Texas Red, 188
Texas Short Ribs, 188
Three-Bean Chili with Tostaditas, 471
Tilapia, Grilled, 340
Toasted Bread Salad, 345
Tofu, Noodle Bowl with Stir-Fried Vegetables, Peanuts and, 468
Tomato Sauce:
Cooked, 360
Fresh, 333
Tongue and Veal Terrine, 446
Tortillas, Corn, 358
Toulouse Sausage, 207
Traditional Falafel in Pita, 385
Traditional Napa Cabbage, 355
Tricolor Vegetable Terrine, 452
Trout:
Meunière, 93
Smoked, 198
Smoked, Purses, 406
Tuna:
Cakes, 98
Carpaccio, 115
Grilled, with Balsamic Vinaigrette and Sweet-Sour Baby Onions, 88
Roll (Tekka-Maki), 116
Tartare, 118
Turkey:
BLT Wrap, 384
Pot Pie, 40
Rillettes of, 456
Roast, with Cream Gravy, 20
Roast, with Giblet Gravy, 20
Smoked, 199
Wings, Fricassée of, 43
Yucatán-Style, in Achiote Sauce, 359

V

Vanilla Cream Pie Filling, 319
Vanilla Custard Sauce (Crème Anglaise), 318
Vanilla Pastry Cream, 319
Vanilla Pudding, 319
Vanilla Soufflé, 324
Veal:
Blanquette of, 180
Brown, with White Wine, 187
Brown Veal Stew, 187
Chops, 174
Cordon Bleu, 172
Cutlet, Sauté Gruyère, 172
Cutlet, Viennese-Style (Wiener Schnitzel), 172
Cutlets, Breaded, 172
Forcemeat, 441
Fricassée, 43
Hungarian Goulash, 190
Osso Buco, 189
Parmigiana, 172
Roast Loin or Rack of, with Sage and Apples, 161
Saltimbocca alla Romana, 191
Sausage, 208
Scaloppine, à la Crème, 173
Scaloppine, alla Marsalla, 173
Scaloppine, with Lemon, 173
Scaloppine, with Mushrooms and Cream, 173
Scaloppine, with Sherry, 173
Schnitzel à la Holstein, 172
Sweetbreads, Sautéed, with Shiitake Mushrooms and Port Wine Sauce, 177
Terrine, Ham and, 446
Terrine, Ham and, with Foie Gras, 446
Terrine, Tongue and, 446
Wiener Schnitzel, 172
Vegan Vegetable and Split Pea Curry, 467
Vegetable(s). *See also specific vegetables*
Pancakes, Vietnamese, 473
Seafood Terrine with, 449
Tempura, 100
Terrine, Tricolor, 452
Terrine of, with Chicken Mousseline, 449
Vegan Vegetable and Split Pea Curry, 467
Winter, Gratin with Feta Cheese and Bulgur Pilaf, 474
Yellow Split Pea and Vegetable Curry with Spiced Rice and Cucumber Raita, 467
Vegetarian Wrap with Mixed Beans, 384
Venison Sausage, 208
Vietnamese Beef and Noodle Soup, 352
Vietnamese Vegetable Pancakes, 473

W

Well-Fried Beans, 360
Welsh Rabbit, 428
White Cake, 268
White Pan Bread, 239
White Sausage (Boudin Blanc), 210
Whole Wheat Bread, 239
Whole Wheat Flat Bread, 342
Whole Wheat Muffins, 253
Wiener Schnitzel, 172
Winter Vegetable Gratin, with Feta Cheese and Bulgur Pilaf, 474
Wrap:
Turkey BLT, 384
Vegetarian, with Mixed Beans, 384

Y

Yellow Butter Cake, 266
Yellow Cake, 268
Yellow Dal, 350
Yellow Split Pea Curry, Vegetable and, with Spiced Rice and Cucumber Raita, 467
Yogurt with Cucumber and Mint, 348
Yucatán-Style Turkey in Achiote Sauce, 359

Z

Zucchini Lasagne, Eggplant and, 469
Zuppa:
di Cozze, 109
di Frutti di Mare, 109
di Pesce, 109
di Vongole, 109
Zuppas, 109